11-S Francescone 2004-0

S0-BFA-628

READING
LITERATURE

Purple Level
YELLOW LEVEL
Blue Level
Orange Level

READING
LITERATURE

The McDougal, Littell English Program

American Literature

McDougal, Littell & Company
Evanston, Illinois

New York   Dallas   Sacramento   Columbia, SC

Authors

Staff of McDougal, Littell & Company
Marilyn Sherman

Consultants

Ronald L. Gearring, Teacher, Evanston Township High School, Evanston, Illinois

Gary Lindsay, Teacher, John F. Kennedy Senior High School, Cedar Rapids, Iowa

Robert A. Moss, Chairman, English Department, Langley High School, McLean, Virginia

Karen Ostermiller, Chairman, English Department, Ramona High School, Riverside, California

Mary Payne, Chairman, English Department, T. C. Williams Senior High School, Alexandria, Virginia

Nancy Trombley, Teacher, Lakeland High School, Milford, Michigan

John Warmington, Chairman, English Department, Medford Senior High School, Medford, Oregon

Jan Whittlesey, Teacher, Beaverton High School, Beaverton, Oregon

Frontispiece: *Estate*, 1963, ROBERT RAUSCHENBERG. Philadelphia Museum of Art, gift of the Friends of the Philadelphia Museum of Art.

Acknowledgments

Richard Armour: for "Money" by Richard Armour, from *Light Armour* (McGraw-Hill). Atheneum Publishers, Inc.: For *The Miracle Worker* by William Gibson; copyright © 1956, 1957 William Gibson; copyright © 1959, 1960 Tamarack Productions, Ltd. and Georges Klein and Leo Garel as trustees under three separate deeds of trust.

(continued on page 746)

98 / 9 8 7 6 5 4

ISBN: 0-8123-7177-1

CONTENTS

Responding to Literature: Introductory Essay

CHAPTER ONE
The Colonial Period *(1600–1750)*

CHAPTER FOUR
Techniques Writers Use

CHAPTER FIVE
The Early National Period
(1800–1855)

CHAPTER SIX
The Late Nineteenth Century
(1855–1900)

The Civil War

Native American

The Frontier

CHAPTER SEVEN
Twentieth Century Fiction   351

CHAPTER EIGHT
Twentieth Century Nonfiction   423

Autobiographies and Biographies

Speeches

Essays

CHAPTER NINE

Twentieth Century Poetry   *497*

Reading Literature: More About Poetry   *530*

Focus on LANGSTON HUGHES   *538*

■ *Chapter 9 Review*   *580*

CHAPTER TEN
Twentieth Century Drama

Handbook for Reading and Writing

Responding to Literature

As a reader, you come to a work of literature with experiences, ideas, and feelings. Because your background is unique—because you are unique—you make sense of the writer's work in your own special way.

Reading is an active process. As you read, you might find yourself questioning or remembering events from your own life. You might imagine yourself in a similar situation or stop to reread puzzling lines or paragraphs.

When you finish reading, you understand a work in your own way. Then you are ready to share your ideas with other readers.

STRATEGIES FOR EFFECTIVE RESPONSE

BEFORE READING

1. Think about what you already know.
Read the title of the selection and look at the art. Recall your past experiences with the kind of literature you are about to read. Jot your ideas in your Reader's Journal.

2. Set a purpose for reading.
Read the SETTING A PURPOSE direction, and think about what you will be looking for. Write a question or two in your own words. Think about personal experiences that relate to the literature.

DURING READING

3. Be an active reader.
Pause often and ask yourself questions such as: What am I thinking about? What has happened so far? What is about to happen? In your Reader's Journal jot predictions, questions, personal associations, reactions, and quotations. Make connections with other works of literature. Remember to remain aware of your purpose for reading.

AFTER READING

4. Respond in writing.
When you finish reading, spend a few quiet minutes answering this question in your Reader's Journal: What am I thinking and feeling about what I have just read? Then go on to complete the lesson in the book.

Ætatis suæ 21. Aº. 1616.

Matoaks als Rebecka daughter to the mighty Prince
Powhatan Emperour of Attanoughkomouck als virginia
converted and baptized in the Christian faith, and
Wife to the worll Mr Tho: Rolff.

CHAPTER ONE

The Colonial Period (1600–1750)

OPTIONS FOR RESPONDING

Activity Ideas

As you read:

- Note items that you think should be part of "A Teenage Code," modeled on Edwards' "A Puritan Code," and later write the code with a group of classmates.
- On a map of the United States, locate the places associated with the selections.
- Note everyday activities such as planting, weaving, and cooking; and later invent a tool to be used in one of the activities, using only natural materials (for example, rocks, bark, water).
- List words associated with the Puritans, and later play a game modeled on "Jeopardy" or "Pictionary."

After you read:

- With a partner, present a skit in which you explain the meaning of Thanksgiving to a recent immigrant.
- On a chart, compare the travel time between England and New England by colonial ship, by a modern ship, by commercial aircraft, and by the Concorde.
- Negotiate an agreement between rival individuals or groups.
- Work with a group to rank ten basic items, such as water, rope, matches, and a knife, according to their importance for survival.
- Send for tourist information on Plymouth, Massachusetts; Mystic, Connecticut; and Colonial Williamsburg, Virginia.

Pocahontas, 18th century (?) painting after a 1616 engraving, artist unknown. National Portrait Gallery, Smithsonian Institution, gift of Andrew Mellon. Washington, D.C.

All literature reflects the people who create it and the land they live in. To truly enjoy American literature, a reader must know something about the people and history of the United States. The best place to begin is with the Native Americans and English colonists.

Native Americans

The ancestors of Native Americans began arriving on the continent at least 10,000 years ago. It was not until the late 1400's and early 1500's that Europeans began to arrive. By this time, there were more than seven hundred Indian tribes living in North America. These tribes had a wide variety of languages, religions, social customs, and governments. Each tribe also had its own folklore and mythology, which were passed on orally to each new generation.

English Colonists

In 1607, a group of English settlers landed in the New World. At Jamestown, Virginia, they founded the first permanent English colony in America. These first settlers were largely unprepared for the harsh realities of

1600	1620	1640	1660	1680

Literature

1624 John Smith records history of Jamestown colony in *The General History of Virginia*

1630 William Bradford begins writing his history *Of Plymouth Plantation*

1640 *The Massachusetts Bay Psalm Book* is first book printed in colonies

1644 Roger Williams publishes *The Bloudy Tenent of Persecution*

1650 Anne Bradstreet publishes her first volume of poetry

History

1607 English establish first permanent colony at Jamestown

1620 Pilgrims land at Plymouth

1621 Pilgrims and Indians celebrate first Thanksgiving Day

1630 Puritans found Massachusetts Bay Colony

1636 Harvard University founded

1636 Roger Williams founds Rhode Island Colony

1675–1676 War between Wampanoags and Massachusetts Bay colonists the new land. By the end of the first winter, starvation, disease, and attacks by Indians had claimed the lives of half the colonists.

Conditions at Jamestown improved when Captain John Smith took over leadership of the colony. Smith saw to it that crops were planted and houses were built. He began to trade with the Indians for food and tried to establish peaceful relations with them. For a time, the two groups lived together comfortably and provided each other with needed help and a variety of goods. Eventually, however, new conflicts arose.

The Puritans

A group of settlers who were later called the Pilgrims arrived in Plymouth, Massachusetts, in 1620. Like the Jamestown settlers, they faced starvation, disease, and problems with the Indians. But unlike the settlers at James-

town, the Pilgrims were bound together by a common religious faith: Puritanism.

The Puritans wanted to "purify" the Church of England, which they thought was too similar to the Roman Catholic Church. Their own religion was organized around three main beliefs. They felt that the Bible was the sole source of God's law. They also felt that people were basically sinful. Finally, they felt that God decides in advance who will be "saved" and who will not.

After Plymouth, the Puritans established the Massachusetts Bay Colony and settlements in Connecticut and Virginia. They organized their governments around their religion. The Puritans valued education highly. They also valued art and literature, and produced a number of important writers and poets.

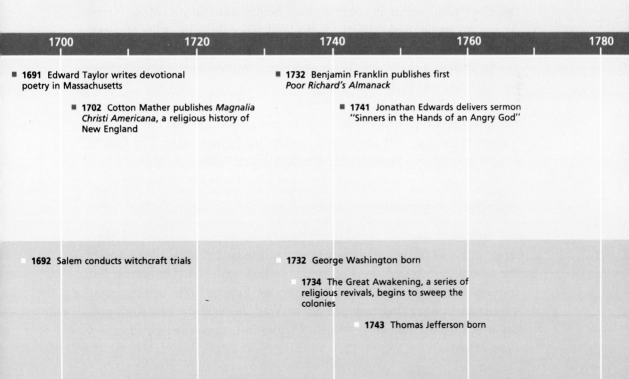

| 1700 | 1720 | 1740 | 1760 | 1780 |

■ **1691** Edward Taylor writes devotional poetry in Massachusetts

■ **1702** Cotton Mather publishes *Magnalia Christi Americana*, a religious history of New England

■ **1732** Benjamin Franklin publishes first *Poor Richard's Almanack*

■ **1741** Jonathan Edwards delivers sermon "Sinners in the Hands of an Angry God"

1692 Salem conducts witchcraft trials

1732 George Washington born

1734 The Great Awakening, a series of religious revivals, begins to sweep the colonies

1743 Thomas Jefferson born

Reading Literature

The Colonial Period

During the colonial period several literary traditions flourished in North America. One was the Native American tradition, which was rich and well established. Another was the tradition of the English colonists who settled along the east coast.

Native American Literature

Each Native American group had a rich body of **oral literature**—literature that was passed to the next generation by word of mouth. This literature served to entertain, to teach, and to reinforce tribal customs and traditions. It was presented in the form of myths, folk tales, and songs.

The literatures of the different North American tribes varied a great deal. However, one theme was common to all of them. That theme was the close relationship between human beings and nature. Most Native Americans had a deep respect for the land. They thought of the elements of nature, such as land, sky, and water, as ancestors and relatives. This can be seen in a line from the second poem in this unit: "O our Mother the Earth, O our Father the Sky."

Native American literature during the colonial period also reflects the growing struggle between Indians and settlers. When the colonists wanted more land, they often tried to drive the Indians away. The Indians fought back in what was destined to be a losing battle for them.

Colonial Literature

Some colonists recorded their thoughts in journals or diaries. Others wrote histories of their experiences in the new land. Captain John Smith, for example, recorded the history of the first settlers at Jamestown. He published them in *The General History of Virginia*. His writings were important in attracting new settlers to Virginia. William Bradford, governor of Plymouth Colony, wrote a Pilgrim history entitled *Of Plymouth Plantation*.

The importance of Puritanism in colonial America can be seen in the literature of the period. The first book printed in the colonies was *The Massachusetts Bay Psalm Book,* a Puritan translation of the psalms.

Cotton Mather, an influential Puritan minister, published a large number of sermons and other religious writings. According to some historians, Mather's influence helped lead to the Salem witchcraft trials.

Jonathan Edwards was another influential Puritan minister. His sermons and writings sparked The Great Awakening in 1734. This was a religious revival in which people were urged to recommit themselves to God. Edwards's most famous sermon, "Sinners in the Hands of an Angry God," was delivered in 1741.

The New England Primer, a Puritan schoolbook, also reflects the colonists' concern with religion and morality. In the book, the child reader is taught how to be a good person and a responsible member of the community. Important Puritan beliefs, such as the sinful nature of people, are reflected in lines such as the following: "In Adam's fall, we sinned all."

Opposition to Puritan rule is also reflected in colonial literature. Roger Williams believed that government had no right to interfere in religion. He also defended the rights of the Indians to their land. Because of his beliefs, the Puritans planned to send Williams back to England. Instead, Williams escaped and founded Rhode Island Colony in 1636. In his writings, Williams argued for the separation of church and state. He also urged an end to religious persecution.

Not all Puritan literature was harsh, however. Both Anne Bradstreet and Edward Taylor wrote poems of simple devotion and love. Taylor's poems focused on religion. Bradstreet's centered on her life and family.

The Importance of Colonial Literature

The colonial period produced few works that could be considered great literature. Nevertheless, the literature of this era is of great value, especially from an historical perspective. It gives us a record of our nation's beginnings. The literature of colonial America shows people in relationship to God and to their surroundings. Most important, it helps us understand what the first settlers had to endure in order to build a better life for future generations.

Comprehension Skills

Inferences and Conclusions

Reading is an active process. Good readers do more than simply read the words and sentences on the page. As they read, they think about the ideas, look for relationships, make inferences, and draw conclusions.

Making Inferences

An **inference** is a logical guess based on specific facts. As you read, you can use reasoning to discover ideas or facts that the writer did not state. By thinking about the evidence or clues that are given, you can better understand what the writer is trying to communicate.

Read the following lines from the opening of "A Puritan Code." Use the information that is provided to guess, or infer, this Puritan writer's view of his relationship with God.

> Being sensible that I am unable to do anything without God's help, I do humbly entreat him by his grace to enable me to keep these resolutions, so far as they are agreeable to his will.

From the information given, you can infer that the writer has a deep belief and trust in God. He also believes that God determines his fate.

Drawing Conclusions

A **conclusion** is based on several inferences. By drawing conclusions, you can often learn more from a selection than is actually stated. To draw a conclusion, carefully consider all the evidence that has been presented. Then decide what the evidence means when taken as a whole.

Read the following lines from a speech by Powhatan, a great Native American chief. Based on the information given, draw a conclusion about the situation that exists between the colonists and the Indians.

> Why will you take by force what you may obtain by love? Why will you destroy us who supply you with food? What can you get by

war? . . . We are unarmed, and willing to give you what you ask, if you come in a friendly manner. . . .

The information indicates that a tense situation exists. The colonists have been attacking the Indians, who feel this treatment is unjust.

Direct and Indirect Description

Sometimes a writer will state an idea directly. For example, he or she might write, "Captain Smith fought bravely." However, the writer often chooses to let the reader infer the same idea from the details provided. Such a description would be indirect. Suppose, for example, you read that Captain Smith fought two hundred enemies single-handedly. You could draw your own conclusion about his bravery.

Whenever you read, be alert for indirect descriptions of character, setting, and action. Examine every detail closely. Then use your skills of making inferences and drawing conclusions.

Exercises: Making Inferences and Drawing Conclusions

A. Read the following lines from a poem. Based on the information given, make a logical guess, or inference, about what is being described.

> Along the entire length and breadth
> of the earth, our grandmother,
> extended the green reflection
> of her covering

B. Read the following lines from a journal. What conclusion can you draw about the relationship between this group of settlers and Squanto? How does it compare with the impression created by Powhatan's speech?

> After these things [Massasoit] returned to his place, called Sowams, some 40 miles from this place. Squanto continued with them [the colonists] and was their interpreter and was a special instrument sent of God for their good beyond their expectation. He directed them how to set their corn, where to take fish, and to procure other commodities, and was also their pilot to bring them to unknown places for their profit, ...

$\mathcal{V}$ocabulary Skills

How Language Grows

The English you use today has a long history. The original source for English was a prehistoric language called Indo-European. It was used across the European continent in ancient times. English, along with German, French, and Spanish, developed from this source.

The early English language developed in Great Britain as invaders brought their languages to the island. These invaders were Anglo-Saxon tribes from Germany in the fifth and sixth centuries. Their dialects formed the base of early English. Later, many words from Latin, Greek, German, and French were mixed with English as other invaders and settlers moved in. In that way, English went through different stages, finally developing into "modern" English in the sixteenth century. Since the sixteenth century thousands of words have been added to English. In addition, spellings and usages have changed.

The English language is living and growing. Even today, new words are constantly added, and old words change to take on new meaning.

How Words Entered the Language

Borrowed Words. Throughout its history, English has gained words by borrowing them from other languages. Early American settlers, for example, borrowed words from Native American tribes. These words include *toboggan, hammock,* and *squaw.* Here are a few other words that have been supplied by other languages:

Dutch—brake, yacht, gruff, landscape
Latin—candle, acquire, terror, visual
Greek—lyric, myth, skeleton, drama, geography
French—precious, difficult, gentle, perfume
Italian—piano, solo, opera, balcony

Compounds and Blends. New words have also been added to English by combining existing words. A **compound word** such as *lunchbox* combines two entire words. A **blend** unites parts of two words to make a new one. *Smog,* for example, is a blend of *smoke* and *fog.*

Echoic Words. Echoic words are created to imitate a sound. Echoic words include *thump, boom, katydid, chickadee,* and *jingle.*

Technical Terms. Sometimes technical jargon, or terms from a specialized field, becomes widely used. Some words that were once the specialized jargon of television include *video, close-up,* and *prime time.*

Clipped Words. Clipped words are new words that are created by shortening existing words. The word *prof,* for example, was clipped from *professor.* The word *dorm* came from *dormitory.*

Words from Names. Other words entered English from the names of people or places. The word *hamburger,* for example, comes from the name of Hamburg, Germany.

Exercises: Recognizing the Sources of English Words

A. Decide whether each word below was made by clipping, blending, compounding, borrowing, or imitating a sound. Use a dictionary, if necessary. Then tell the meaning of each word.

1. stonecutter	5. mosaic	9. humble	13. tab
2. matador	6. lab	10. motorcade	14. squawk
3. sideline	7. huff	11. photo	15. margarine
4. wide-eyed	8. frizzle	12. tick-tock	16. premed

B. An English word came from each of the following names. For each name, write the word that developed from it. Also write the word's meaning.

1. Sylvester Graham (1794–1851), dietary reformer
2. H. Shrapnell (1761–1842), British general
3. Frankfurt, a city in Germany
4. John Montagu, fourth Earl of Sandwich (1718–1792)
5. A. J. Sax (1814–1894), Belgian inventor

This Newly Created World

WINNEBAGO INDIAN

Pleasant it looked,
this newly created world.
Along the entire length and breadth
of the earth, our grandmother,
extended the green reflection
of her covering
and the escaping odors
were pleasant to inhale.

Developing Comprehension Skills

1. What time period in earth's history is the poet referring to?

2. Who is the grandmother? Why do you think the poet uses this name?

3. What is the "green reflection of her covering"?

4. What feeling do you think inspired the poet to write this poem? Find at least two lines that prove your point.

5. What can you guess about the writer of this poem? What is the writer's outlook on life?

6. Do you think that people today have the respect for nature that is shown in this poem? Explain your answer.

Reading Literature

1. **Understanding Oral Literature.** For centuries, some literature has been passed from one generation to the next by word-of-mouth. This is called **oral literature**. Oral literature has many purposes. One purpose is to provide entertainment. Oral literature is also a way to pass along religious beliefs, rituals, customs, and even tribal history to

River Bluffs, 1,320 Miles Above St. Louis, 1832, GEORGE CATLIN. National Museum of American Art, Smithsonian Institution, Gift of Mrs. Joseph Harrison, Jr. Washington, D.C.

young people. In your opinion, what is the purpose of "This Newly Created World"?

2. **Recognizing Personification. Personification** is a technique that a writer uses to give human qualities to an object or idea. The use of personification helps the writer express a mood, and helps the reader to "see" an idea. Find the personification in this poem. How does it help you appreciate the poem more?

3. **Appreciating Mood.** The feeling that the poet creates for the reader is called the **mood.** One way a poet creates mood is by carefully selecting the words in the poem. What feel- ing do you get when you read this poem? What words help create this mood?

4. **Being Aware of Translation.** It is important to realize that some Native American literature has been translated from another language. The translator must try to keep the idea of the writing the same. In a poem, the translator must also try to preserve the rhythm and flow of the words. Do you think the translator of "This Newly Created World" accomplished these things? Does the poem read smoothly and gently as its mood indicates it should? Explain your answer.

Song of the Sky Loom

TEWA INDIAN

SETTING A PURPOSE | *The Tewa Indians offer gifts of love and honor to their gods. What do these Native Americans request in return?*

O our Mother the Earth, O our Father the Sky,
Your children are we, and with tired backs
We bring you the gifts you love.
Then weave for us a garment of brightness;
May the warp be the white light of morning,
May the weft be the red light of evening,
May the fringes be the falling rain,
May the border be the standing rainbow.
Thus weave for us a garment of brightness,
That we may walk fittingly where birds sing,
That we may walk fittingly where grass is green,
O our Mother the Earth, O our Father the Sky.

Navajo sand painting rug, early 20th century.
Handspun wool. Denver Art Museum, Colorado. (1950.185)

Developing Comprehension Skills

1. This poem sounds like a prayer. For whom is this prayer intended?

2. Who is speaking this prayer?

3. The Earth and Sky are referred to as parents. Do you think this is appropriate? Why?

4. What are the Tewas asking in return for their devotion?

Reading Literature

1. **Recognizing Extended Metaphor.** A **metaphor** is a direct comparison between two unlike things. The comparison does not use the words *like* or *as*. Metaphors make unfamiliar or difficult ideas easier to understand. An **extended metaphor** is a comparison which is developed throughout an entire verse, poem, or paragraph.

   A comparison is made in "Song of the Sky Loom" between a woven garment and a happy life. What are some of the aspects of a happy life for the Tewas? To what part of the garment is each thing compared? Do you think these are good comparisons? Why or why not?

2. **Appreciating Imagery.** Descriptive words and phrases that appeal to the senses are called **imagery**. Images may appeal to sight, hearing, taste, smell, or touch. Find several examples of sensory images in this poem. Explain which of the five senses each image appeals to.

3. **Understanding Repetition.** When words or lines are repeated at regular intervals, the writer or speaker is using **repetition**. Repetition may be used to create a particular sound pattern or rhythm. Find two examples of repetition in this poem. Explain what each example adds to the poem.

I Went To Kill the Deer

Although they killed animals for food, Native Americans had great respect for the creatures and their place in nature. How does the hunter in this poem feel about the deer eluding him?

TAOS PUEBLO INDIAN

I went to kill the deer
Deep in the forest where
The heart of the mountain beats
For all who live there.
An eagle saw me coming and
Flew down to the home of the deer
And told him that
A hunter came to kill.
The deer went with the eagle
Into the heart of the mountain
Safe from me who did not hear
The heart of the mountain beating.

Developing Comprehension Skills

1. Why does the speaker go into the forest?

2. What does the speaker mean by "The heart of the mountain beats / For all who live there"? What is the heart of the mountain? Who can hear it? Who cannot?

3. How does the deer escape?

4. Do you think this hunter has the same attitude as a modern hunter? Explain.

Reading Literature

1. **Appreciating Personification.** As in the first two poems you read, "I Went To Kill the Deer," contains examples of personification. In this poem, the mountain is personified. What human qualities are given to the mountain? How could it protect the deer, even though a mountain is not a living thing?

2. **Understanding a Narrative Poem.** A poem that tells a story is called a **narrative poem**. Many times, the story makes an important point or teaches a lesson. In this poem, the speaker tells the story of a hunter who goes to the mountains to hunt deer. He is unsuccessful. Why do you think the Taos Indians tell this story? What does the poem say about humans and their relationship with nature?

I Have Killed the Deer

SETTING A PURPOSE | *The natural cycle of life was a very important idea to early Native Americans. How do humans fit into this cycle of birth, life, and death?*

TAOS PUEBLO INDIAN

I have killed the deer.
I have crushed the grasshopper
And the plants he feeds upon.
I have cut through the heart
Of trees growing old and straight.
I have taken fish from water
And birds from the sky.
In my life I have needed death
So that my life can be.
When I die I must give life
To what has nourished me.
The earth receives my body
And gives it to the plants
And to the caterpillars
To the birds
And to the coyotes
Each in its own turn so that
The circle of life is never broken.

Deer Rattle—Deer Dancer, 1981, FRANK LaPENA. Private collection.

Developing Comprehension Skills

1. Why has the speaker killed the deer, grasshopper, plants, and trees?

2. The speaker knows that eventually he too will die. What will happen to his body then?

3. How does the speaker feel about the fact that he will not live forever? Is he angry or sad, or does he accept it? How do you know?

4. Do you think the speaker has a good outlook on life and death? Explain your answer.

Reading Literature

1. **Identifying the Speaker.** The poet and the speaker of a poem are not necessarily the same person. The **speaker** may be a character created by the poet to express a certain kind of idea. In this poem, do you think the speaker and the poet are the same? Could the speaker be presenting the ideas of a whole group of people? Give reasons to support your answer.

2. **Teaching Beliefs.** One of the purposes of the Native American oral tradition was to teach religious beliefs. What idea about life and death is presented in "I Have Killed the Deer"? According to this poem, how do humans fit into nature's plan? Are humans more important than animals? Support your answer with evidence from the poem.

3. **Appreciating a Writer's Style.** A writer's **style** is the way he or she uses words to express ideas. Look carefully at the language in this poem. Although the ideas are important, the words and style are simple and beautiful. What does the style of this poem tell you about the writer?

4. **Reading Poetry.** Poems are written in lines. However, the end of a line often does not signal the end of a sentence or thought. To appreciate a poem, you must look at both the lines and the sentences.

    What is the main idea or image in each line of "I Went To Kill the Deer"? Why do you think the poet broke the lines in this way? Now look at the poem as a whole. How does the punctuation help you understand where complete thoughts end? Examine "I Have Killed the Deer" in the same way. Is the structure similar or different?

Developing Vocabulary Skills

Recognizing Terms from Specialized Fields. Some words are used in a particular field and later become familiar to the general public. This is one way that American English grows. For Example, "Song of the Sky Loom" includes the words *warp* and *weft*. These are specialized words in the field of weaving.

Look at the following words. Use a dictionary to find the field each one is from. Write the meaning of the word as it is used in the field. If the word also has a more commonly used meaning, write that, too.

doldrums	monopoly	light year
interface	debit	blitz
network	catalyst	quasar

Developing Writing Skills

1. **Understanding History Through Literature.** So far in this chapter, you have read several samples of Native American literature. Think about the ideas presented in each poem. Think also about the purpose of each one.

From these selections, do you think that you have developed any new ideas about Native Americans? Write a short composition in which you explain what you have discovered about Native Americans' religion, their attitudes toward the earth, and their way of life.

2. **Writing a Story with a Lesson.** Native American literature often appeared in the form of a brief, entertaining story. The story usually taught a lesson about something that was very important to the writer. Imagine that you have been asked to write a brief story that would teach others about something very important to you. In one or two paragraphs, or a poem, write a brief story similar to those of the Native Americans.

Pre-Writing. List several beliefs or customs that are very important to you. Consider, for example, beliefs about honesty, friendship, courage, love, and dealings with others. Choose one to illustrate in a brief story. Think of the lesson to be taught, characters, and a situation that will allow the characters to discover the lesson.

Writing. Write your story in paragraph form or as a poem. If you write a poem, look at the poems in this chapter for a guide.

Revising. Read your story aloud. Ask yourself these questions as you revise:

Is my story complete? Does it make sense?
Does my story teach a lesson? Is the lesson obvious?
Have I spelled each word correctly?
Have I capitalized and punctuated correctly?

Developing Skills in Study and Research

Understanding the Classification of Books. Your library contains books on almost any subject. **Fiction books** are stories about imaginary characters and events. They are arranged alphabetically by the author's last name on a separate section of shelves. **Nonfiction books** deal with real people and events. For example, books about Native Americans in early American history are nonfiction. Nonfiction books are arranged on their shelves by subject.

Many libraries use the Dewey Decimal System. This system groups nonfiction books into numbered categories (see Guidelines for Study and Research at the back of this book). Books on Native Americans are located between 900 and 999. This category also contains biographies, travel books, and geography books.

Locate the history shelves in your library. Look at the books with classification numbers in the 900's. Find three books that deal with Native Americans or American Indians. Write down the location of the books and the information on the spine of each book. Save this information in your notebook.

The Algonquian Confederacy Speech, 1609

SETTING A PURPOSE

One popular image of early Native Americans is that of a hostile people. What does the following message to English settlers show about Powhatan, an early American Indian leader?

POWHATAN

Why will you take by force what you may obtain by love? Why will you destroy us who supply you with food? What can you get by war? . . . We are unarmed, and willing to give you what you ask, if you come in a friendly manner. . . .

I am not so simple as not to know it is better to eat good meat, sleep comfortably, live quietly with my women and children, laugh and be merry with the English, and being their friend, trade for their copper and hatchets, than to run away from them. . . .

Take away your guns and swords, the cause of all our jealousy, or you may die in the same manner.

Developing Comprehension Skills

1. What is the purpose of Powhatan's speech? What is he asking for?

2. The reader does not know the relationship between the Algonquians and the settlers at the time of this speech. After reading the speech, can you infer, or guess, what the relationship might be?

3. Why is it important for Powhatan to live in peace with the English settlers? Explain your answer.

4. Despite the peaceful nature of the speech, what warning does Powhatan give in his last sentence?

5. Considering the problems between Native Americans and new settlers throughout American history, does this speech surprise you? Why or why not?

Reading Literature

1. **Understanding the Purpose of a Speech.** A speech can be an effective way to *entertain*, *inform*, or *persuade*. What do you think was the purpose of Powhatan's speech? Do you think he accomplished this purpose?

2. **Recognizing a Rhetorical Question.** A **rhetorical question** is one that does not require an answer. It is a question intended to make the audience think about something. What rhetorical questions does Powhatan ask? What do each of these questions ask the audience to think about? Do you think it is more effective to ask a rhetorical question or to tell people to think about something?

3. **Appreciating Contrast.** When a writer uses **contrast**, he or she shows the differences between two things or ideas. The use of contrast is sometimes an effective way for a writer to make a point. Powhatan uses contrasts in his appeal to the English. He begins by contrasting methods the English might use to get what they want. What contrasting methods could the English use? Which would make more sense according to Powhatan? What other contrasts does Powhatan use to make his point? Are the contrasts effective? Explain your answer.

Pocahontas

JOHN SMITH

SETTING A PURPOSE | *Captain John Smith was an adventurer and an early leader of Jamestown, the first English colony in the New World. What indicates that Smith may have made up this "true" tale about his rescue by Pocahontas?*

Captain John Smith was attacked by 200 savages. Two of them he slew, still defending himself with the aid of a savage, his guide, whom he bound to his arm with his garters. Yet he was shot in his leg, and had many arrows that stuck in his clothes, but no great hurt, till at last they took him prisoner.

When this news came to Jamestown, much was their sorrow for his loss. Few expected what ensued.

Six or seven weeks those barbarians kept him prisoner. Many strange triumphs and conjurations they made of him. Yet he so demeaned himself among them, as he not only diverted them from surprising the fort, but procured his own liberty. He also got himself and his company such estimation among them that those savages admired him more than their own [brothers.]

Their order in holding him captive was thus. Drawing themselves all in file, the King had all their swords carried before him. Captain Smith was led after him by three great savages, holding him fast by each arm, and on each side went six in file with their arrows ready. . . . They conducted Smith to a long house, where thirty or forty tall fellows did guard him. Before long more bread and venison was brought him than would have served twenty men. I think his stomach at that time was not very good. What he left they put in baskets and tied over his head. About midnight, they set the meat again before him. The next morning they brought him as much more, and they did eat all the old, and reserved the new as they had done the other. This made him think they would fatten him to eat him. Yet in this desperate estate, to defend him from the cold, one Indian brought him his gown, in payment for some beads and toys Smith had given him at his first arrival in Virginia.

At last they brought him to Werowocomoco, where was Powhatan, their emperor. Here more than two hundred of those grim courtiers stood wondering at him as [if] he had been a monster, till Powhatan and his train had put themselves in their greatest braveries. Before a fire upon a seat like a bedstead he sat covered with a great robe made of raccoon skins, and all the tails hanging by. On either hand did sit a young wench of sixteen or eighteen years, and along on each side the house two rows of men. And behind them as many women, with all their heads and shoulders painted red, many of their heads

Ould Virginia, 1627, ROBERT VAUGHAN. Etching from the book, *Generall Historie of Virginia* by John Smith. The Newberry Library, Chicago.

bedecked with the white down of birds but everyone with something, and a great chain of white beads about their necks.

At his entrance before the king all the people gave a great shout. The queen of Appomattoc was appointed to bring him water to wash his hands, and another brought him a bunch of feathers instead of a towel to dry them. Having feasted him after their best barbarous manner they could, a long consultation was held. But the conclusion was: two great stones were brought before Powhatan, then as many as could laid hands on him, dragged him to them, and thereon laid his head. And being ready with their clubs to beat out his brains, Pocahontas, the king's dearest daughter, when no entreaty could prevail, got his head in her arms and laid her own upon his to save him from death. Whereat the emperor was contented he should live to make him hatchets and her bells, beads, and copper; for they thought him as capable of all occupations as themselves.

Developing Comprehension Skills

1. Who wrote this story? Who is the main character and the hero?

2. How long is Smith held prisoner? Who is the chief of the Indian tribe that captures him?

3. How is Smith saved?

4. How does John Smith seem to feel about himself and his accomplishments? Give examples from the story to support your answer.

5. How is Powhatan described by Smith? Does Smith's description of Powhatan seem to match the image you developed when you read the Algonquian Confederacy Speech?

6. Why might a tale like this one have been popular in England in 1624? Do you think it would encourage or discourage settlement in the New World?

Reading Literature

1. **Understanding History Through Literature.** Literature serves many purposes. One is to record history. Nonfiction selections such as journal entries or autobiographies provide a personal look at many famous events in American history.

   John Smith's adventure with Powhatan and Pocahontas is an example of personal literature that has historical value. There is some question about the truthfulness of Smith's report of this incident. However, the reader does get to see how Native Americans were often described by the colonists at that time. Why would personal literature such as journals and autobiographies sometimes be inaccurate? Despite this, what can you learn from such literature?

2. **Appreciating Description.** In his journal, John Smith describes Chief Powhatan and his people in great detail. Reread the description of Powhatan. What vivid sight details help you to picture the chief, his followers, and their surroundings? Why would such descriptions be especially important to the Europeans who read his account?

3. **Understanding Point of View.** When the writer of a nonfiction selection is also a character, the story is usually written in first-person point of view. The words *I* and *me* are used to identify the writer. However, Smith writes this account of his "true" adventure using the third-person point of view. The words *he* and *him* are used to refer to himself. Why do you think Smith wrote the tale of Pocahontas in this way? What did this method allow him to do? What did he expect from his readers?

4. **Evaluating Personal Literature.** Smith writes an exciting tale about his adventures in Powhatan's village. Do you think some of the details are exaggerated? Which ones? Consider the number of braves required to capture Smith, the length of time he was held prisoner, and the number of guards needed to prevent his escape. Also think about the reaction of the colonists to the news of his capture. Why might Smith have deliberately exaggerated details in this incident?

Developing Vocabulary Skills

Identifying Borrowed Words. The main way that the English language has grown is by borrowing words from other languages. Many English words were borrowed from Latin, Greek, French, German, Dutch, and other languages. For example, English borrowed *kindergarten* from German and *tuck* and *spot* from Dutch. Quite a few words in modern English came from North American Indian languages. One such word is *raccoon*, which is used by John Smith in "Pocahontas."

You can use a dictionary to find the origin of a word. You will find a word's history in brackets at the beginning or end of its dictionary entry. Here is an example of a word that originally came from Latin:

bo·nus (bō′nəs) *n., pl.* **bo′nus·es** [L., good] anything given or paid in addition to what is due or expected, as an incentive, reward, etc.

Use a dictionary to find out which of the following words were borrowed from North American Indian languages. Most will be labeled either *Algonq.* or *Am Ind.* What do these words have in common?

opossum	skunk	chipmunk
legend	waltz	uniform
persimmon	hickory	woodchuck
moose	wampum	idol
squash	challenge	muskeg

Developing Writing Skills

1. **Comparing Literary Works.** John Smith creates a wild, savage picture of the American Indian. This image is very different from the impression created in the poems, prayers, and speeches presented earlier in the chapter. Write a paragraph contrasting, or showing the differences between, these two points of view.

   Pre-Writing. List the positive qualities of the American Indian found in the Native American selections. Then, list the negative qualities suggested by John Smith in his story of Pocahontas. Pair similar ideas. Then look for passages from the literature that support these ideas.

   Writing. Write an opening sentence that mentions the contrasting views of Native Americans in early American literature. This statement of the main idea is sometimes called a **thesis statement**. Develop your paragraph by contrasting at least three positive and negative qualities from your list.

   Revising. Read your paragraph carefully. Does the paragraph begin with a good thesis statement telling the purpose of the paragraph? Have enough positive and negative qualities been contrasted in the balance of the paragraph? Is each point supported by several examples?

2. **Telling a Tale.** John Smith was an early American adventurer. His tales and reports were often the only information Europeans had about the New World. Imagine that you are an explorer and adventurer of the near future. You may be exploring another world or an unexplored region on earth. Write a brief report describing what you have seen. Remember, you have the opportunity to be a hero much as John Smith was. Will this fact make a difference as to what you tell the people back home?

Developing Skills in Study and Research

Using the Card Catalog. When looking for a book in the library, you should first consult the card catalog. Each book in the library is listed in this file at least three times—by *author, title,* and *subject.* Each card gives the author, title, publisher, number of pages, and other important information. The card for a nonfiction book also includes the call number. Each card also tells whether the book has illustrations or maps. A card may also describe the book or list related books. (See the Handbook for Reading and Writing at the back of this book for additional information.)

Use the card catalog to find the following information:

a book about John Smith, Powhatan, or Pocahontas

a book about early Native Americans

a book about colonial Americans, the Pilgrims, or Jamestown

Write down the author, title, publisher, number of pages, and call number for each book.

Developing Skills in Critical Thinking

Evaluating Statements of Fact. John Smith wrote his story as though it really happened. Yet some historians doubt the truth of the story. They doubt the story because they evaluated, or examined, certain statements and found problems with them.

Statements of fact may be checked in the following ways:

1. through observation
2. by referring to a reference source or authority
3. by seeing whether the statement contradicts other known facts

Check some of John Smith's information on your own. Look up information about Pocahontas, Powhatan, and Smith himself. Does anything you find contradict the story that Smith tells? Also review the Algonquian Confederacy Speech. Look at the date of the speech and the date of Smith's story which was written in 1624. Do you see any problems, or contradictions, in what you learn from the two selections?

From
Of Plymouth Plantation

WILLIAM BRADFORD

A small group of Pilgrims led by William Bradford founded Plymouth Colony in 1620. What does Bradford's journal reveal about the hardships, fears, and surprises experienced by these early pioneers?

Safe Arrival at Cape Cod

Being thus arrived in a good harbor, and brought safe to land, they fell upon their knees and blessed the God of Heaven who had brought them over the vast and furious ocean, and delivered them from all the perils and miseries thereof, again to set their feet on the firm and stable earth, their proper element. . . .

But here I cannot but stay and make a pause, and stand half amazed at this poor people's present condition. So I think will the reader, too, when he well considers the same. Being thus passed the vast ocean, and a sea of troubles before in their preparation, they had now no friends to welcome them nor inns to entertain or refresh their weatherbeaten bodies. [There were] no houses or much less towns to repair to, to seek for succour. In truth, the savage barbarians, when they met with them were readier to fill their sides full of arrows than otherwise. And for the season it was winter, and they that know the winters of that country know them to be sharp and violent, and subject to cruel and fierce storms, dangerous to travel to known places, much more to search an unknown coast.

Besides, what could they see but a hideous and desolate wilderness, full of wild beasts and wild men? And what multitudes there might be of them they knew not. For summer being done, all things stand upon them with a weatherbeaten face, and the whole country, full of woods and thickets, represented a wild and savage hue. If they looked behind them, there was the mighty ocean which they had passed and was now as a main bar and gulf to separate them from all the civil parts of the world. . . .

Compact with the Indians

All this while [during January and February, 1621] the Indians came skulking about them, and would sometimes show themselves aloof off, but when any approached near them, they would run away. Once they stole away their tools where they had been at work and were gone to dinner. But about the 16th of March, a certain Indian came boldly amongst them and spoke to them in broken English, which they could well understand but marveled at it. At length they understood by discourse with him, that he was not of these parts, but belonged to the eastern parts where

Prayer, 1919–24, THOMAS HART BENTON. The Nelson-Atkins Museum of Art, bequest of Thomas Hart Benton. Kansas City, Missouri.

some English ships came to fish, with whom he was acquainted and could name sundry of them by their names, amongst whom he had got his language. He became profitable to them in acquainting them with many things concerning the state of the country in the east parts where he lived, which was afterwards profitable unto them. [He told] also of the people here, of their names, number and strength, of their situation and distance from this place, and who was chief amongst them. His name was Samoset. He told them also of another Indian whose name was Squanto, a native of this place, who had been in England and could speak better English than himself.

Being, after some time of entertainment and gifts dismissed, a while after he came again, and five more with him, and they brought again all the tools that were stolen away before, and made way for the coming of their great Sachem[1] called Massasoit. Who, about four or five days after, came with the chief of his friends and other attendance, with the aforesaid Squanto. With whom, after friendly entertainment and some gifts given him, they made a peace with him (which hath now continued this 24 years) in these terms:

1. That neither he [Massasoit] nor any of his should injure or do hurt to any of their people.
2. That if any of his did hurt to any of theirs, he should send the offender, that they might punish him.
3. That if anything were taken away from [them], he should cause it to be restored; and they should do the like.
4. If any did unjustly war against him, they would aid him; if any did war against them, he should aid them.
5. He should send to his neighbors confederates to certify them of this, that they might not wrong them, but might be likewise comprised in the conditions of peace.
6. That when their men came to them, they should leave their bows and arrows behind them.

---

1. **Sachem**, the chief among some North American Indian tribes.

After these things [Massasoit] returned to his place called Sowams some 40 miles from this place. Squanto continued with them and was their interpreter and was a special instrument sent of God for their good beyond their expectation. He directed them how to set their corn, where to take fish, and to procure other commodities, and was also their pilot to bring them to unknown places for their profit, . . .

The First Thanksgiving

They began now to gather in the small harvest they had, and to fit up their houses and dwellings against winter, being all well recovered in health and strength and had all things in good plenty. For as some were thus employed in affairs abroad, others were exercised in fishing, about cod and bass and other fish, of which they took good store, of which every family had their portion. All the summer there was no want; and now began to come in store of fowl, as winter approached, of which this place did abound. And besides waterfowl there was great store of wild turkeys, of which they took many, besides venison, etc. Besides they had about a peck a meal a week to a person, or now since harvest, Indian corn to that proportion. Which made many afterwards write so largely of their plenty here to their friends in England, which were not feigned but true reports.

Developing Comprehension Skills

1. What was the season when the Pilgrims arrived in the New World?

2. How did the Indian Samoset learn English?

3. What problems did the Pilgrims and Indians solve in their peace treaty?

4. Do you think the treaty between the two groups of people was fair? Did both sides receive equal benefits?

5. Why was the first Thanksgiving so meaningful to the Pilgrims?

6. The settlers wrote letters telling of the wonderful harvest and good hunting in the New World. What effect might these have had on those who had not seen the New World?

Reading Literature

1. **Recognizing a Journal.** A **journal** is a writer's record of personal experiences and adventures. Some journals also include the writer's comments and feelings. Bradford does not often express his feelings. However, you can guess, or infer, many of his feelings from the way he describes events. How, for example, does Bradford feel about the Pilgrims' arrival in the New World? What adjectives describe his feelings?

2. **Understanding History Through Journals.** Many early settlers kept journals because they were the simplest way to record important events. Reading a journal is therefore an interesting way to learn about history and the attitudes of the people at that time.

   What do you think is the most interesting historical information Bradford provides in his journal? Are you surprised by any of Bradford's information?

3. **Distinguishing Between Objective and Subjective Writing.** When writing is **objective**, an author describes or explains something without passing judgment. When writing is **subjective**, the author often presents only one side of a story. He or she may give opinions and try to persuade the reader.

   Contrast Bradford's account of his meetings with the Indians with John Smith's story. Which is written in more objective language? Which is written in subjective language?

Developing Vocabulary Skills

Recognizing Compound Words. New words are often added to English by joining two existing words. The new words formed in that way are called **compounds**. For example, the word *houseboat* was made from the words *house* and *boat*. Some compound words are written with hyphens, as in *left-handed*.

Skim *Of Plymouth Plantation* to find at least three compound words. Write them on your paper, and explain how their meanings combine the meanings of two words.

Developing Writing Skills

1. **Writing a Summary.** A **summary** shortens a selection without losing its basic meaning. A summary is useful for studying and remembering great amounts of information.

   Look again at the treaty developed between the Indians and the settlers. Write a summary of the treaty.

   Pre-Writing. Read the treaty again carefully. Write down the important ideas. State these ideas in your own words.

   Writing. Write the important ideas in each point of the treaty. Drop any unnecessary details, examples, or repetitions.

Revising. Check your summary to see that it includes each important idea in the original treaty. Has all unnecessary information been dropped? Does your summary give all necessary information in a way that the reader can use without looking first at the original?

2. **Writing a Journal.** Early explorers and adventurers were not the only people to keep journals. Writers have long kept journals to use as sources of ideas as well as records of personal experiences. Begin a journal of your own. Use a spiral notebook to record your ideas, thoughts, feelings, impressions, and experiences. Refer to your journal when you need ideas for writing.

Developing Skills in Study and Research

Finding Information in a Book. This literature book, like many other books, contains a wealth of information. The two most helpful parts of a book are the table of contents and the index.

The **table of contents** is a summary, or outline, of the contents of the book. These contents are arranged in the order in which they appear in the book. Refer to the table of contents in this book. How many chapters are in this book? How are the selections grouped? What special features are included in each chapter?

The **index** is an alphabetical list of subjects covered in the book. Each entry is followed by page numbers that tell you where specific information can be found. Use the Index of Titles and Authors to locate the page that provides information about Abigail Adams or about Martin Luther King, Jr. Check the Index of Skills to find the pages that provide information on the SQ3R study method.

Developing Skills in Speaking and Listening

Participating in a Group Discussion. Group discussion skills are among the most valuable speaking skills you can learn. They are used to explore ideas, solve problems, and reach agreements. The Indians and settlers, for example, used group discussion to come to an agreement on terms of treaties.

Divide the class into groups of five or six students. Choose one of the following topics to discuss, or choose a topic of your own.

a. Discuss and agree on the skills a student should have to graduate from high school.

b. Discuss and agree on a classroom contract between teacher and students. Consider the rights and responsibilities of the teacher as well as the students.

Follow these steps to complete your discussion.

1. Choose a chairperson. This person will lead the discussion and make sure that everyone has a chance to speak.

2. Choose a secretary to take notes on suggestions made by the speakers.

3. Decide on the purpose. Make sure that each member of the group understands the purpose of the discussion.

4. During the discussion, make certain that each participant has a chance to present an opinion or offer a suggestion. After a suggestion is made, any group member may make a comment on it.

5. Try to reach consensus, or agreement, on as many points as possible.

6. At the end of the discussion the chairperson or the secretary should provide a summary of all the points agreed upon.

Psalm 23

SETTING A PURPOSE | *The* Bay Psalm Book *was the first book published in the American colonies. It was written by Puritan ministers in 1640. How did it change traditional verses from the* King James Bible?

The Lord is my shepherd, I shall not want.

He maketh me to lie down in green pastures: he leadeth me beside the still waters.

He restoreth my soul; he leadeth me in the paths of righteousness, for his name's sake.

Yea though I walk through the valley of the shadow of death, I will fear no evil: for thou art with me, thy rod and thy staff they comfort me.

Thou preparest a table before me, in the presence of mine enemies: thou anointest my head with oil, my cup runneth over.

Surely goodness and mercy shall follow me all the days of my life: and I will dwell in the house of the Lord for ever.

—*King James Bible*

The Lord to me a shepherd is,
    want therefore shall not I.
He in the folds of tender grass,
    doth cause me down to lie:
To waters calm me gently leads
    Restore my soul doth he:
he doth in paths of righteousness:
    for his name's sake lead me.
Yea though in valley of death's shade
    I walk, none ill I'll fear:
because thou art with me, thy rod,
    and staff my comfort are.
For me a table thou hast spread,
    in presence of my foes:
thou dost anoint my head with oil:
    my cup it overflows.
Goodness & mercy surely shall
    all my days follow me:
and in the Lord's house I shall dwell
    so long as days shall be.

—*Bay Psalm Book*

Newport embroidery sampler, 1733, KATHERINE HOLDEN. The Rhode Island Historical Society, Providence.

4. How does the speaker of Psalm 23 feel about the Lord? What leads you to this conclusion?

5. Which version of Psalm 23 do you enjoy more? The *King James Bible* version or the *Bay Psalm Book* version? Why?

Reading Literature

1. **Recognizing a Psalm.** A psalm is a sacred song, or hymn, used as a prayer. Many popular psalms were collected in the Old Testament Book of Psalms. These have been enjoyed by people for hundreds of years. In what ways does Psalm 23 resemble a song? Why might these qualities make Psalm 23 a favorite prayer?

2. **Understanding History Through Literature.** Although the Bible was first printed as a book in the 1400's, its poems, songs, hymns, riddles, essays, and proverbs have existed as oral literature for thousands of years. What can you learn about the people who used Psalm 23 in the prayer? Why do you think this psalm continued to be meaningful to English colonists in the 1600's?

3. **Appreciating Religious and Poetic Language.** Many of the words in Psalm 23 seem unusual to speakers of modern English. The words *doth* and *dost*, for example, are forms of the word *do*. Such words are archaic. **Archaic words** are ancient words that are used today only in poetry or religious rituals. Can you find other examples of unusual or archaic words in Psalm 23? What do they add to the mood or feeling of the psalm?

Developing Comprehension Skills

1. To what is the Lord compared in the first line of both versions of Psalm 23?

2. What is different in the sentence order of the *Bay Psalm* version? Do you think this is an improvement? Why or why not?

3. Read the last line of Psalm 23. What does the speaker hope to achieve through faith?

Developing Vocabulary Skills

Understanding Echoic Words. Some words in the English language were formed to imitate a sound. These words are said to have **echoic** origins. *Crinkle, buzz, shoo,* and *moo,* for example, came into English as echoic words. Write down six words that you think are echoic in origin. Check their origins in a dictionary. Keep trying until you have six echoic words.

Developing Writing Skills

1. **Analyzing Historical Writing.** Journals and religious literature have served as important historical records of the Colonial Period in American history. Think about the selections you have read in this chapter. Then write a paragraph explaining at least three things that were important to the colonists.

2. **Rewriting for a Different Audience.** The King James version of Psalms was rewritten by Richard Mather. He did this so that his congregation would have a verse that would be easier to sing and understand. The earlier version was thought to be more difficult.

   Similarly, the language William Bradford used in his journal may seem confusing to modern readers. Study this portion of Bradford's journal. In it, he describes the Puritan search for a place to settle.

   They set forth the 15th of November; and when they had marched about the space of a mile by the seaside, they espied five or six persons with a dog coming towards them, who were savages; but they fled from them and ran up into the woods, and the English followed them, partly to see if they could speak with them, and partly to discover if there might not be more of them lying in ambush. But the Indians seeing themselves thus followed, they again forsook the woods and ran away on the sands as hard as they could, so

as they could not come near them but followed them by the track of their feet sundry miles and saw that they had come the same way.

Rewrite this journal entry in language that would be easy for a modern audience to understand.

Pre-Writing. Read the journal entry carefully. Break down long sentences to discover main ideas and thoughts.

Writing. Write your version of this journal entry. Use your own words to capture the feeling and the message of the original verse. Simplify the language by using shorter sentences. Place the words in an order familiar to you. Use the words that a modern audience will understand. Your version may be shorter than the original.

Revising. As you read your version of Bradford's journal entry, ask yourself these questions:

Is the information in the rewritten entry similar to that in the original?

Does my version capture the same mood, or feeling, of the original?

Are my sentences shorter than those in the original?

Is the new word order easier for modern readers to understand?

Developing Skills in Speaking and Listening

Comparing Versions of Literature. Read each version of Psalm 23 aloud. Listen for the differences in rhythm, sound, and meaning. Which version is easier to understand? Which version is more pleasing to listen to?

Desiderata

MAX EHRMANN

SETTING A PURPOSE | *"Desiderata" is often printed with the note that it was found in a Baltimore church in 1692. Actually, Max Ehrmann, an Indiana poet, wrote it in 1927. What does "Desiderata" say about people, their fears, and their hopes?*

Memory, 1870, ELIHU VEDDER. Los Angeles County Museum of Art, Mr. and Mrs. William Preston Harrison Collection.

Go placidly amid the noise and Haste, and remember what peace there may be in silence. As far as possible without surrender be on good terms with all persons. Speak your truth quietly and clearly; and listen to others, even the dull and ignorant; they too have their story. Avoid loud and aggressive persons, they are vexatious to the spirit. If you compare yourself with others, you may become vain and bitter; for always there will be greater and lesser persons than yourself. Enjoy your achievements as well as your plans. Keep interested in your own career, however humble; it is a real possession in the changing fortunes of time. Exercise caution in your business affairs; for the world is full of trickery. But let this not blind you to what virtue there is; many persons strive for high ideals; and everywhere life is full of heroism. Be yourself. Especially, do not feign affection. Neither be cynical about love; for in the face of all aridity and disenchantment it is perennial as the grass. Take kindly the counsel of the years, gracefully surrendering the things of youth. Nurture strength of spirit to shield you in sudden misfortune. But do not distress yourself with imaginings. Many fears are born of fatigue and loneliness. Beyond a wholesome discipline, be gentle with yourself. You are a child of the universe, no less than the trees and the stars; you have a right to be here. And whether or not it is clear to you, no doubt the universe is unfolding as it should. There-fore be at peace with God, whatever you conceive Him to be, and whatever your labors and aspirations, in the noisy confusion of life keep peace with your soul. With all its sham, drudgery and broken dreams, it is still a beautiful world. Be cheerful. Strive to be happy.

Developing Comprehension Skills

1. What sort of person might have written "Desiderata"?

2. What error often occurs with this work?

3. What advice does the writer give about comparing yourself with others?

4. According to "Desiderata," one important quality that each person must try to develop is a sense of modesty. How does the writer say one should try to achieve this goal?

5. "Desiderata" is the Latin word meaning "things needed or wanted." Find two more traits that the author believes are necessary for a happy life. Point out specific lines that instruct people in these traits.

6. Which advice given in "Desiderata" do you think is most important for a happy, contented life? Is there any advice that you would add to "Desiderata"? Explain your answer.

Reading Literature

1. **Recognizing Simile.** A **simile** is a comparison between two unlike things. A simile uses the words *like* or *as*. "Neither be cynical about love . . . it is perennial as the grass." This simile compares the ability of love to survive to the grass that returns each spring. Do you think this is a good comparison? Why or why not?

2. **Understanding Opposites.** A writer often emphasizes an idea by discussing it along with its opposite idea. The writer of "Desiderata" speaks of being placid, or calm, amid the haste of everyday life. The writer also recommends the peace that comes with silence in a noisy world. How does the use of these opposites help the writer to emphasize the important qualities in life? Find at least two other examples of the writer's use of opposites.

3. **Analyzing Style.** This selection was once incorrectly thought to be written during Puritan times. Usually, the language in a piece of writing provides clues about when it was written. Is there anything in the language of this piece that may have added to the confusion about its date? What words and phrases might sound unfamiliar to contemporary readers?

A Puritan Code

JONATHAN EDWARDS

SETTING A PURPOSE | *Jonathan Edwards was a Puritan minister known for his fiery sermons. How does his code for living compare with the one in "Desiderata"?*

Being sensible that I am unable to do anything without God's help, I do humbly entreat him by his grace to enable me to keep these resolutions so far as they are agreeable to his will,

REMEMBER TO READ OVER THESE RESOLUTIONS ONCE A WEEK.

Resolved, never to lose one moment of *time*; but improve it in the most profitable way I possibly can.

Resolved, to live with all my might while I do live.

Resolved, never to do anything which I should be afraid to do if it were the last hour of my life.

Resolved, never to do anything out of revenge.

Resolved, never to suffer the least motions of anger to irrational beings.

Resolved, never to speak evil of any person except some particular good call for it.

Resolved, never to do anything which if I should see in another, I should count a just occasion to despise him for or to think any way the more meanly of him.

Resolved, never to speak anything that is ridiculous or matter of laughter on the Lord's day.

Whenever I hear anything spoken in conversation of any person, if I think it would be praiseworthy in me, resolved to endeavor to imitate it.

Resolved, after afflictions, to inquire what I am the better for them; what good I *have got*, and what I *might* have got by them.

Reverend Jonathan Edwards,, 1750–55, JOSEPH BADGER. Yale University Art Gallery, Bequest of Eugene Phelps Edwards. New Haven, Connecticut.

Developing Comprehension Skills

1. What does the introduction to "A Puritan Code" tell you about Jonathan Edwards?

2. How would Edwards feel about playing games or just relaxing? Which resolution led you to your conclusion?

3. According to Edwards, how can a person judge whether or not to "do something"?

4. When does Edwards say it is acceptable to "speak evil" of a person? Do you agree?

5. After reading this code, do you think Edwards felt that people were generally good, or generally weak? Explain.

6. Do you think Edwards's code is a good one to live by? Is it practical? Which resolutions

would be the most difficult for you to follow? What would you add to the code?

Reading Literature

1. **Appreciating Tone.** **Tone** is the writer's attitude toward his or her subject. You can determine a writer's tone by carefully examining the word choice, style of writing, and content. Look at the Puritan code carefully. What can you infer, or guess, about the writer's attitude toward himself and the people he is speaking to? Use specific evidence from the code to support your opinion.

2. **Determining a Writer's Purpose.** Resolutions are decisions that a person makes about how to act in the future. They are usually written by someone as a personal guideline. Do you think that Edwards was thinking only of himself when he wrote the code? Can you think of another purpose Edwards may have had for writing it? Explain your answer.

3. **Comparing Styles.** Both "Desiderata" and "A Puritan Code" give advice about how to live. Which one do you find most pleasing and helpful? Did the writers' tone and way of writing affect your decision?

Developing Vocabulary Skills

Identifying Words That Come from Names. Some words in English evolved from the names of people or places. An example in "Desiderata" is the word *cynical.* It came from the name of a school of ancient Greek philosophers, the Cynics. Another example is *jovial,* which comes from the name of the Roman god, Jove.

Look up the following words in a dictionary. Their origins will be listed in brackets at the beginning or end of the dictionary entry. Determine the name that is the origin of the word. Then write the definition of the word.

1. herculean
2. filbert
3. volt
4. March
5. knickers
6. madeleine
7. mesmerize
8. zeppelin
9. chauvinist
10. tuxedo

Developing Writing Skills

1. **Contrasting an Author's Works.** Jonathan Edwards is well known for his sermon "Sinners in the Hands of an Angry God." Edwards warns his fellow Puritans to reject evil and live a good, moral life. In this passage, he writes about God's attitude toward sinners.

> The God that holds you over the pit of Hell, much as one holds a spider, or some loathsome insect, over the fire, abhors you, and is dreadfully provoked; his wrath towards you burns like fire; he looks upon you as worthy of nothing else, but to be cast into the fire.

Write a paragraph contrasting Edwards's ideas in this passage with the ideas shown in "A Puritan Code." When you contrast two works, you are describing differences. As you contrast the two selections, consider Edwards's tone. Think also about the way he talks about people and God in each selection.

2. **Writing Resolutions.** Jonathan Edwards wrote resolutions intended to improve a person's life. Write six resolutions of your own. These resolutions should be statements of action that you plan to take. They may also direct other people to a happy, contented life in our modern world.

Pre-Writing. Think about the things that you consider important in your life. Are education, health, and friendship important to you? Choose six points that you feel are most important. Think about a statement, or resolution that tells what you plan to do to achieve each goal.

Writing. Begin each of your resolutions with the word *Resolved*, just as Jonathan Edwards began his. Remember, your resolutions will also be a guide for others. Each should be clear and easy to understand.

Revising. Read each of your resolutions carefully. Does each make a strong statement about some action you intend to take? Does each deal with a subject that you consider to be very important to your life? Is each easy to understand?

Developing Skills in Study and Research

Using the Encyclopedia. An encyclopedia is a collection of articles arranged alphabetically in volumes. Guide letters on the spine of each volume help you to locate the book you need.

Locate an encyclopedia in your library. Begin your research by looking for information under several headings. For example, to locate information about John Smith's adventures, you might look under these headings:

Smith, John   Jamestown
Pocahontas   Indians—American
Powhatan

Now list several headings that you might look for to find information about Colonial Life in America, the Puritans, the Plymouth Colony, or Native Americans.

To My Dear and Loving Husband

ANNE BRADSTREET

SETTING A PURPOSE

Anne Bradstreet was an educated Puritan woman. She was also the first well-known poet in the New World. Read to see what her poem, published in 1678, reveals about her attitude toward her husband and her life.

If ever two were one, then surely we.
If ever man were lov'd by wife, then thee;
If ever wife was happy in a man,
Compare with me, ye women, if you can.
I prize thy love more than whole mines of gold
Or all the riches that the East doth hold.
My love is such that rivers cannot quench,
Nor ought but love from thee, give recompense.
Thy love is such I can no way repay,
The heavens reward thee manifold, I pray.
Then while we live, in love let's so persevere
That when we live no more, we may live ever.

Developing Comprehension Skills

1. How does Anne Bradstreet feel about her husband and her marriage?

2. What does she pray for concerning her husband?

3. What does Bradstreet mean when she says "That when we live no more, we may live ever"?

4. Bradstreet wrote many poems about family relationships, personal tragedy, and religious faith. To which category do you think this poem belongs?

5. Do you think this poem says something positive about the benefits of marriage? Explain your answer.

Reading Literature

1. **Recognizing Poetry.** Poetry is writing that appeals to the senses and the imagination. It expresses ideas in a tighter, more compact way than prose. Poets combine the sounds and meanings of words to help the reader understand these ideas.

Poems are often highly emotional. They express people's feelings of happiness, despair, hope, and, as in this poem, love. What words in this poem help you sense Anne Bradstreet's love for her husband and for life?

2. **Recognizing Hyperbole. Hyperbole** is a great exaggeration a writer uses to make a point or create a certain effect. An example of hyperbole from this poem is, "I prize thy love more than whole mines of gold." Why is this exaggeration a good way for Bradstreet to show how deeply she feels? Find one more hyperbole in this poem. Explain how it helps the poet make her point more effectively.

3. **Recognizing the Couplet.** The repetition of syllable sounds at the ends of words is called **rhyme**. When two lines occur next to each other and have the same end rhyme, they are called a **couplet**. For example, the end words of the first two lines, *we* and *thee*, rhyme. Locate the other couplets in this poem. What effect do these couplets have on the way the poem sounds?

Anne Bradstreet, 1944. St. Botolph's Church, bequeathed by Annie Clarke. Boston, Lincolnshire, England.

Boast Not, Proud English

ROGER WILLIAMS

SETTING A PURPOSE | *Roger Williams was an early American clergyman. He had strong ideas about personal and religious freedom. What was he trying to teach his fellow English settlers in this message?*

Boast not, proud English, of thy birth and blood:
  Thy brother Indian is by birth as good.
Of one blood God made him, and thee, and all.
  As wise, as fair, as strong, as personal.
By nature, wrath's his portion, thine, no more
  Till Grace his soul and thine in Christ restore.
Make sure thy second birth, or thou shalt see
  Heaven ope to Indians wild, but shut to thee.

Developing Comprehension Skills

1. Of what are the English settlers extremely proud?

2. According to Williams, what traits do the Native American Indians share with the colonists? What accounts for these similarities?

3. Williams speaks of "wrath," or anger, as part of Indian nature. Why do you think it is no longer part of the colonists' nature? In what way will both colonists and Indians be united?

4. What do you think most English settlers thought of Williams's plea? Do you think he chose good arguments to prove why the colonists should accept the Indians? Explain your answer.

Reading Literature

1. **Identifying the Author's Purpose.** Like other forms of literature, a poem may have many purposes. It may be intended to entertain, to teach, or to persuade. What purpose

A Sioux Chief, about 1898, JOSEPH TURNER KEILEY. The Metropolitan Museum of Art, the Alfred Stieglitz Collection, 1933 (33.43.174). New York

did Williams have in writing "Boast Not, Proud English"? What personal belief, or moral value, was he trying to teach the settlers?

2. **Appreciating Organization.** When a writer wishes to persuade an audience to accept an idea, he or she must present several good arguments or reasons. Usually, the strongest point is saved for the final statement. Williams presents his last argument in the form of a warning. Do you think this warning

would persuade the Puritans to accept the Native Americans as equals? Consider what you have learned about the Puritans throughout this chapter.

Developing Vocabulary Skills

1. **Identifying Blends and Clipped Words.** You know that compound words are made by joining two words together. With **blends**, two words are also combined. However, in the process, some letters are dropped, as

when *breakfast* and *lunch* were combined to form the blend *brunch*.

Clipped words are words that come into use when an existing word is shortened. Examples of clipped words are *hi-fi* from *high-fidelity*, *fed* from federal, and *bus* from *autobus*.

Tell whether the words below are clipped words or blends. Then explain the word or words from which each was made. Use a dictionary to help you.

a. gel	f. splatter
b. chortle	g. bookmobile
c. fan	h. steno
d. squiggle	i. retro
e. rep	j. happenstance

2. **Reviewing How Words Develop.** Tell how the words listed below were formed. They may be echoic words, words made from names, compounds, clipped words, blends, or borrowed words. Explain the origin of each word. You will need to use a dictionary.

a. guillotine	i. heartbeat
b. el	j. denim
c. chili	k. photo
d. kazoo	l. stagflation
e. groundhog	m. slimsy
f. backspin	n. barbecue
g. explore	o. whiff
h. coo	p. prop

Developing Writing Skills

1. **Contrasting Puritan Poetry.** The poems of Anne Bradstreet and Roger Williams differ in a number of ways. Write a paragraph in which you compare Bradstreet's "To My Dear and Loving Husband" and Williams's "Boast Not, Proud English." Look for both similarities and differences. Consider the purpose each author had in writing the poem. Also think about the tone, the mood, and the point of view.

2. **Writing To Persuade.** Successful persuasive writing is built on sound opinions supported by facts. Write a paragraph in which you attempt to persuade others to accept your point of view.

Pre-Writing. Think about a subject you feel strongly about. It may be an item in the news, a rule by which you live your life, or something you feel needs to be changed. Write your opinion on the subject. Then think of several reasons that support this opinion. These reasons may be further supported by facts, statistics, or other types of information. Arrange your reasons in order from least to most important.

Writing. Begin your persuasive paragraph with a sentence stating your belief. Then, develop your paragraph with the information from your pre-writing notes. Save the most convincing opinion until last. Use transitional words such as *first, next*, and *most important* to connect your ideas.

Revising. Work in an editing group with two or three other people. Read and comment on each other's rough drafts. As you read, ask yourself these questions:

Is an opinion clearly stated in the first sentence?

Is each reason convincing? Is each developed by facts?

Is the most convincing opinion presented last?

Are more or better reasons needed?

Is each reason presented clearly?

When your paper is returned, make any necessary corrections.

Developing Skills in Study and Research

Using Specialized References. In addition to general encyclopedias, the reference area of your library contains many specialized reference works. These references can provide detailed information on many topics. The following specialized references are just a few that contain information about the Colonial Period in America.

Encyclopedia of American Facts and Dates
Encyclopedia of American History
The Indian Heritage of America
Documents of American History, 7th ed.
Oxford Companion to American History
American Heritage Book of Indians

Check the reference shelves in your library. Are any of the references listed above in your library? Did you find other specialized references dealing with American History?

Developing Skills in Critical Thinking

Understanding Generalizations. From the selections you have read in this chapter, you may be tempted to make a generalization about the early colonists. A **generalization** is a broad statement based on several specific facts. Sometimes a generalization is made without enough facts to back it up. Think about this statement based on the selections in this chapter.

Early American colonists had no respect for Native Americans.

This is an **unfair generalization**. It is true that some colonists had no respect for Native Americans. But others treated Native Americans as equals and learned from their wisdom. Find examples of both attitudes in the selections you have read.

A good way to keep from making unfair generalizations is to avoid using **absolute words**. Words such as *all, everyone, nobody,* and *never* should be replaced with qualifiers. **Qualifiers,** such as *some, many, few,* and *sometimes,* limit the statement being made.

Chapter 1 *Review*

Using Your Skills in Reading Literature

Read the following excerpt from a journal written in 1622. Then answer the following questions. What does the journal tell you about living conditions in the colonial period? How does the literature help you to understand the Puritan colonists?

> This summer they built a fort with good timber—a handsome building and a good defense made with a flat roof and battlement. . . where they kept constant watch, especially in time of danger. It served them also as a meeting house and was fitted accordingly for that use. It was a big undertaking for them at this period of weakness and want; but the dangerous times necessitated it. The continual rumors about the Indians here, especially the Narragansetts, and also the news of the great massacre in Virginia, made all hands willing to complete it.
>
> Now the welcome time of harvest approached, in which all had their hungry bellies filled. But it amounted to but little compared with a full year's supply . . . .

Using Your Comprehension Skills

Read the following passage from Benjamin Franklin's autobiography in Chapter Three. It tells of a period when Ben was an apprentice to his older brother, James, a newspaper editor.

> Being still a boy and suspecting that my brother would object to printing anything of mine in his paper if he knew it to be mine, I contrived to disguise my hand. Writing an anonymous paper, I put it at night under the door of the printing house. It was found in the morning and communicated to his writing friends when they called in as usual. They read it, commented on it in my hearing, and I had the exquisite pleasure of finding it met with their approval.

Based on this passage, draw an inference about the attitude of James Franklin toward his younger brother Ben. Draw another inference about Ben Franklin's character. Finally, based on the information given, draw a conclusion about the quality of Ben's writing.

Using Your Vocabulary Skills

Read the following sentences from Chapters Three and Five. Decide if the underlined words began as borrowed words, echoic words, or single words that were joined into compounds. Look up the definitions of the words in a dictionary.

1. We hold these truths to be self-evident: . . .
2. A common murderer, a highwayman, or a housebreaker, has as good a pretense as he.
3. I assembled a number of my playfellows.
4. Her situation is remote from all the wrangling world.
5. It is merely a cricket which has made a single chirp.
6. Meanwhile the hellish tattoo of the heart increased.
7. To prove this, let facts be submitted to a candid world.
8. . . . suddenly there came a tapping.

Using Your Writing Skills

Choose one of the writing assignments below.

1. Choose one poem and one nonfiction piece from this chapter. Compare or contrast these examples of colonial literature. For example, you might write about purpose, mood, and author's attitudes.
2. Think of a situation that one of these people experienced: Pocahontas, Powhatan, or Squanto. Imagine yourself to be that historical figure. Then write a journal entry describing the situation and expressing your thoughts and feelings.

Using Your Skills in Critical Thinking

In some colonial writing, information is presented as fact when actually it is only partly true. Which facts from the journal on the preceding page do you think need to be checked for accuracy?

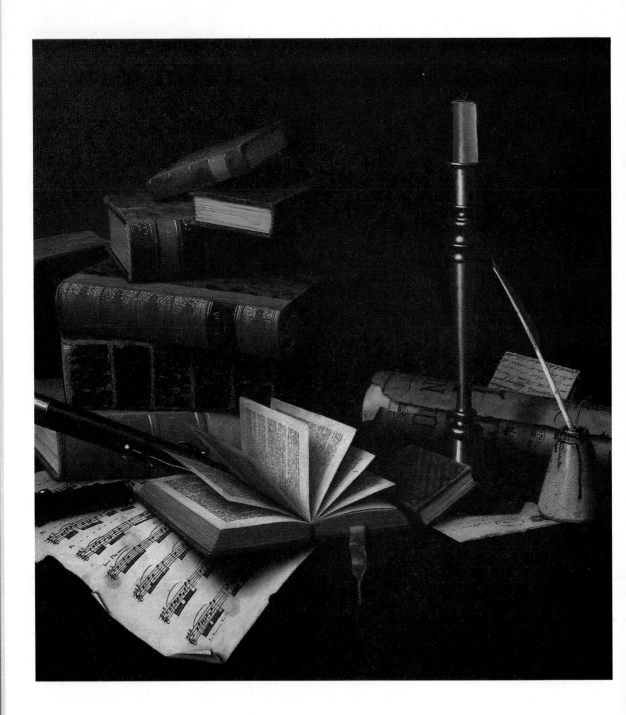

CHAPTER TWO

How Writers Write

Music and Literature (detail), 1878, WILLIAM HARNETT.
Oil on canvas, 24" × 32⅛". Albright-Knox Art Gallery, gift of Seymour H. Knox, 1941. Buffalo, New York.

Understanding the Process of Writing

Picture your favorite meal spread out in front of you. It looks wonderful. Its tempting aromas draw you eagerly to the table. Its taste, bite after luscious bite, makes you wish for more.

You can certainly enjoy the flavor and appearance of food without knowing how it is prepared. However, trying to prepare that same meal yourself might make you appreciate how skilled a good cook must be.

A well written story, poem, or essay is every bit as much of a feast as a wonderful meal. You can enjoy a piece of writing without knowing how it was created. However, you appreciate it even more when you understand the talent and skill that go into all written work.

In this chapter, you will learn how great American writers write. In Chapter 4, you will learn about some of the techniques writers use. As you learn these skills, you will enjoy the selections you read even more. You will also be able to apply these processes and techniques to your own writing.

Most writers complete the same three basic stages whenever they write. These stages, taken together, are called the **process of writing.**

pre-writing—the planning stage
writing
revising—the rewriting and reworking stage

Pre-Writing

Pre-writing is a time of thinking, reading, and planning. For many, it is the most important stage in the writing process. Pre-writing includes:

1. Choose and limit a topic. Very few writers say that they get bursts of inspiration for their writing. Most find their ideas through the simple acts of reading, observing, daydreaming, discussing, and just plain thinking. "The problem is to teach ourselves to think," said Christopher Morley, "and the writing will take care of itself."

To find a subject, think about areas that interest you. What would you like to learn more about? What is important to you? What have you observed that you reacted to strongly? Answers to these questions can lead to good topics for writing.

Most writers agree that the best subject for writing is one that you care about and know well. Nineteenth-century poet Henry Wadsworth Longfellow had this advice for writers:

> O thou sculptor, painter, poet!
> Take this lesson to thy heart;
> That is best which lieth nearest;
> Shape from that thy work of art.

Many writers record their observations and opinions in a journal or notebook. Later these notes become a rich source for ideas to use in writing. Novelist Frank Bonham gives this advice:

> Keep notes—notes about everything that interests you. . . . I make observations on a great many things—the weather, what acquaintances look like, their mannerisms, how a battleship cruises up the harbor, how discouragement feels, how joy makes the blood sing.

Practice these different ways of finding ideas. Once you have a topic for your writing, limit it. Make sure that you narrow the topic so that it is appropriate for the length and type of writing you are planning.

2. Decide on your purpose.   Your purpose is your reason for writing. Do you want to entertain readers with light-hearted humor? Do you want to inform them about an important issue? Do you want to persuade them to share one of your beliefs? For each of these different purposes, you would write differently. Your purpose guides you in what and how to write.

Edgar Allan Poe developed theories of the short story that influenced many writers who followed. He stressed the need for a single guiding purpose in writing a short story. This single effect, he said, should shape every sentence:

> In the whole composition there should be no word written of which the tendency, direct or indirect, is not to the one pre-established design.

Keep your purpose firmly in mind as you plan and write.

3. Know your audience.   Decide who will read your writing. Is your audience children or adults? Will your readers be well informed on the topic or not? Once you know your readers, decide how you can best reach them. Choose details and descriptions that they will enjoy. Select the style of writing and level of language that is best for them.

Each writer approaches the idea of audience differently. John Updike always has the same audience in mind:

> When I write, I aim in my mind not toward New York but toward a vague spot to the east of Kansas. I think of the books on library shelves, without their jackets, years old, and a countryish teen-aged boy finding them, and having them speak to him.

Saul Bellow trusts that he is writing for someone like himself:

> I have in mind another human being who will understand me. I count on this.

Finally, some writers decide what is right for their audience by what pleases them. As Ralph Waldo Emerson said, "He that writes to himself writes to an eternal public."

4. Gather supporting information. Collect information on your topic by thinking, reading, observing, and discussing with others. Begin by jotting down details that you think are important and that suit your purpose and your audience. List questions that a reader would want answered. Then try to find the answers to these questions.

For a description or a story, list details that will bring an experience to life for your readers. Use your imagination, your memory, and your powers of observation. For informative writing, you will need to do research in the library. You may also interview experts on the topic. Biographer William Manchester gathers a great deal of factual material before he begins to write:

> I go into very extensive research, particularly when I'm dealing with a very important figure. I read everything he has published and try to read everything of significance that has been published about him.

As you gather information, take careful notes. Without these, you may not remember what you learn.

5. Organize your ideas. At first, this stage is like weeding a garden. You look through your notes and weed out what is not needed. The remaining ideas should relate to your purpose. If you discover that you do not have enough material, go back and do more research and thinking.

Once you have a list of ideas, decide how they can be organized most effectively. In stories, events are usually arranged in the order in which they occurred. In descriptions, details are often told in the order they are noticed, or in an order that visually links the details. In a persuasive piece of writing, reasons may be arranged in order of their importance.

Writers frequently use outlines to help them organize their ideas or information. Novelist Joseph Heller, for example, finds that an outline keeps his material under tight control:

> When I don't use an outline, . . . a chapter that should have been six pages would grow to forty or fifty pages. . . . I'm convinced that I save time and work by outlining as thoroughly as I can.

Instead of using formal outlines, some authors work from sketchy notes or plans in their heads. Each writer uses the organizing tool that is most effective for him or her.

Writing

After a thorough planning session, you are ready to write the first draft. Often, writers find that this is the most difficult stage of the writing process. Poet James Russell Lowell expressed the challenge of beginning to write:

> In creating, the only hard thing's to begin; A grass blade's no easier to make than an oak; If you've once found the way, you've achieved the grand stroke.

The important thing is to apply pen to paper and start writing. Write quickly. Get the ideas from your notes into paragraph form. Follow your outline, but don't feel bound by it if new ideas occur to you. Author Rachel Carson explains this process:

> The discipline of a writer is to learn to be still and listen to what his subject has to tell him.

In your first draft, don't worry about grammar, spelling, and punctuation. These can be checked later. Fiction writer Frank O'Connor explains his approach to the first draft:

> I don't give a hoot what the writing's like. I write any sort of rubbish which will cover the main outlines of the story; then I can begin to see it.

Remember that what you write is never carved in stone. It can always be changed, reorganized, trimmed, or developed. After you write your first draft, it is time to take a close look at what you have written.

O Captain! dearest Captain! wake up [yet]
& hear the bells;
Wake up & see the [shining sun], & see the
flags a-flying; [splendid sun]
For you it is the Cities [about] — for you the
shores are crowded;
For you the red-rose garlands, and [electric] eyes
of women;
O Captain! O my father! my arm I [push/place]
around you;
It is some Dream that on the deck
you [slumber pale] cold & dead.

A handwritten draft of the second stanza of "O Captain! My Captain!" The poem, written by Walt Whitman, was intended to honor the memory of Abraham Lincoln. The Bettmann Archive, New York.

Revising

Your first draft is only a start. From there, you revise or rewrite. You thoughtfully examine your writing, looking for ways to improve it.

Even the most famous writers revise their work. Most find revising very important.

> It's part of a constant attempt on my part to make the finished version smooth, to make it seem effortless. A story I've been working on—'The Train on Track Six,' it's called—was rewritten fifteen complete times.
> —James Thurber

During the revising process, you must step back and be objective about your own work. As you review your work, ask yourself these questions:

1. Is my writing interesting? Will it keep my readers involved?.
2. Did I stick to my topic? Have I included any unrelated details?
3. Did I include enough information to develop my topic fully? Should any details be added?

4. Are my ideas arranged logically? Is my writing clear and easy to understand? Do the ideas flow smoothly?
5. Have I chosen the most exact, precise words I can?
6. Have I accomplished my purpose?

Revising is your chance to polish your writing. As you revise, most writers advise that you cut out anything that is not absolutely necessary. Keep this poem by Joel Chandler Harris in mind:

> Life is short—a fleeting vapor—
> Don't you fill the whole blamed paper
> With a tale which, at a pinch,
> Could be cornered in an inch!
> Boil her down until she simmers,
> Polish her until she glimmers.

During the revising process, two techniques that writers find valuable are reading their work aloud and seeking the opinion of others. Novelist Paul Horgan stresses that reading aloud can help a writer to spot weaknesses. "The ear must always be satisfied by what the pen has silently written. Always read aloud," he noted. "The ear will often correct what the eye misses."

Another good technique for revising is to set the writing aside for a while before trying to judge and improve it. This helps to give a fresh perspective. Author Truman Capote used this technique:

> When the . . . draft is finished, I put the manuscript away for a while, a week, a month, sometimes longer. When I take it out again, I read it as coldly as possible, then read it aloud to a friend or two, and decide what changes I want to make and whether or not I want to publish it.

Proofreading. Proofreading is mainly a chance to correct errors in grammar, capitalization, punctuation, and spelling. Take care to eliminate these kinds of errors that disturb the sense of your writing. To make needed corrections, you may refer to a dictionary and a grammar and usage book. Mark each correction on your draft.

Preparing the Final Copy. Your final copy is the finished product that your readers will see. Recopy your final draft carefully and neatly. Make all the changes that you have marked. As a last check, proofread your writing one final time.

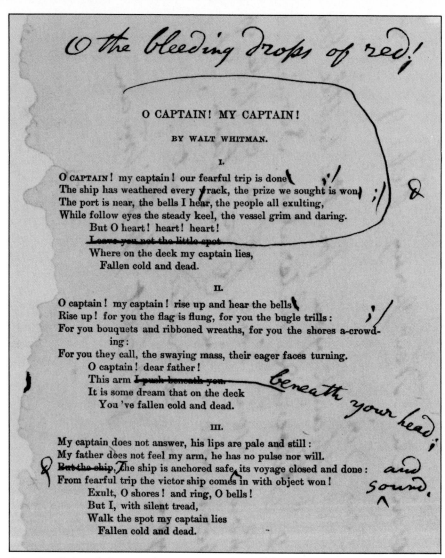

O the bleeding drops of red!

O CAPTAIN! MY CAPTAIN!

BY WALT WHITMAN.

I.

O CAPTAIN! my captain! our fearful trip is done
The ship has weathered every rack, the prize we sought is won
The port is near, the bells I hear, the people all exulting,
While follow eyes the steady keel, the vessel grim and daring.
    But O heart! heart! heart!
    ~~Leave you not the little spot~~
      Where on the deck my captain lies,
        Fallen cold and dead.

II.

O captain! my captain! rise up and hear the bells
Rise up! for you the flag is flung, for you the bugle trills:
For you bouquets and ribboned wreaths, for you the shores a-crowd-
    ing:
For you they call, the swaying mass, their eager faces turning.
    O captain! dear father!
    This arm ~~I push beneath you~~ *beneath your head,*
    It is some dream that on the deck
      You 've fallen cold and dead.

III.

My captain does not answer, his lips are pale and still:
My father does not feel my arm, he has no pulse nor will.
~~But the ship,~~ The ship is anchored safe, its voyage closed and done: *and sound,*
From fearful trip the victor ship comes in with object won!
    Exult, O shores! and ring, O bells!
    But I, with silent tread,
    Walk the spot my captain lies
      Fallen cold and dead.

An early printing of "O Captain! My Captain!" Poet Walt Whitman continued to revise his works even after they were published. Compare this version with the draft on page 52. Then compare it to the version that is currently printed. Library of Congress, Washington, D.C.

Practicing the Process of Writing

Every time you write, use the ideas from this chapter. Refer also to the guidelines for The Process of Writing that are provided at the back of this text.

Write as often as you can. "The main necessity for the beginner is to write regularly, steadily, and not be put off," advised best-selling novelist Irving Wallace. As you write, your skills will grow and blossom.

Chapter 2 *Review*

Understanding the Process of Writing

Below are statements by seven writers about their writing habits. About which stage in the process of writing—pre-writing, writing, or revising—is each one speaking?

1. The 'right' way means setting the words down as zestfully as possible, even if you must make changes later.

   —Frank Bonham

2. I try to be as ruthless as possible. I ask myself of each sentence, 'Is it clear? Is it true? Does it feel good?' And if it's not, then I rewrite it.

   —William Manchester

3. Usually we read about five hundred volumes for each of our books . . . . We read them at approximately the same time, discuss them, and take notes.

   —Will Durant

4. My next thought concerned the choice of an impression, or effect, to be conveyed: and here I may as well observe that, throughout the construction, I kept steadily in view the design.

   —Edgar Allan Poe

5. I do not worry or even think about spelling, grammar, paragraphing, or punctuation (except periods) at this point. . . . In the early throes of an idea there is for me only grammar of the mind, which is a flow of thought, as natural and precise as the flow of a river to the sea.

   —Mary O'Neill

6. When I have got a lot of it down, the policeman has got to come in and say, 'Now look here, you've got to give this some sort of unity and coherence and emphasis,' the old grammatical rules—and then the hard work begins.

   —William Faulkner

7. I always rewrite each day up to the point where I stopped. When it is all finished, naturally you go over it. You get another chance to correct and rewrite when someone else types it, and you see it clean in type. The last chance is in the proofs. You're grateful for these different chances.

   —Ernest Hemingway

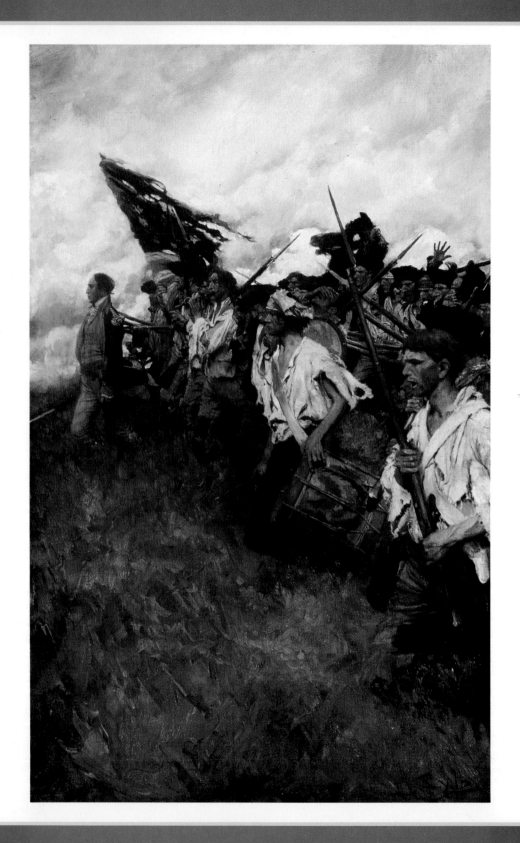

CHAPTER THREE

The Revolutionary Period (1750–1800)

Activity Ideas

As you read:
- Note the advice given by the writers that still applies today.
- Think of people today who are most like the writers in this chapter.
- In a reading log, record quotations and your responses.

After you read:
- Clip newspaper articles on revolutions happening today.
- Create a collage titled "What Is an American Today?".
- Write a "Declaration of Independence for Teens."
- Plan a meaningful Fourth of July celebration for your community, and design a flyer to advertise the celebration.
- Hold an election in which you choose a school principal from among the writers in this chapter.
- List the virtues that you admire (use Franklin's list as a starting point), and then rate yourself each day in how well you put the virtues into practice.

The Nation Makers, 1903, HOWARD PYLE. Brandywine River Museum, purchased through a grant from the Mabel Pew Myrin Trust. Chadds Ford, Pennsylvania.

The Age of Reason

The eighteenth century is often called the Age of Reason, or the Enlightenment. During this century, European writers and thinkers emphasized the role of reason. They believed that the universe was a well-ordered place, able to be understood by the use of reason. These thinkers felt that people could use their reason to produce scientific advances, better government, and an ideal society.

Reason also was emphasized by American writers and thinkers of the eighteenth century.

Many of these writers and thinkers were also the political and social leaders of the era. Such people included Patrick Henry, Thomas Paine, Benjamin Franklin, and Thomas Jefferson.

The Birth of a New Nation

British policy toward the American colonies changed during the 1760's. After the French and Indian War ended in 1763, heavy taxes were imposed on the colonies to help pay England's debts. The Stamp Act, passed

1750	1755	1760	1765	1770

Literature

- 1754 Jonathan Edwards publishes book of religious essays
- 1765 Patrick Henry delivers speech against Stamp Act
- 1771 Benjamin Franklin begins *The Autobiography*
- 1774 Abigail Adams begins her letters to John Adams

History

- 1754 French and Indian War begins
- 1765 British pass Stamp Act
- 1767 British pass the Townshend Acts
- 1770 British kill colonists in Boston Massacre
- 1773 Colonists protest in Boston Tea Party
- 1774 First Continental Congress assembles in Philadelphia

in 1765, was one of the first such taxes. To protest the tax, the American colonists organized a boycott of British goods. The boycott worked, resulting in the repeal of the Stamp Act.

Soon, however, new taxes were imposed in the form of the Townshend Acts. Once again, the colonists banded together to boycott British goods. The Townshend Acts eventually were repealed, although the tax on tea was kept. This tax was protested in the famous Boston Tea Party of 1773.

The basic conflict between the colonists and the mother country was one of representation. The colonists were not represented in Parliament. Therefore, they believed, Parliament had no right to pass laws affecting them. Parliament, on the other hand, claimed the right to pass laws affecting the colonies "in all cases whatsoever."

Opposition to Britain's colonial policies led to the First Continental Congress in 1774. The Congress declared a boycott of British goods until Parliament repealed laws that the colonists considered unfair. The Second Continental Congress, held during 1775 and 1776, resulted in the Declaration of Independence, which was signed on July 4, 1776. But even before the Declaration had been signed, fighting had broken out between British soldiers and colonists.

The signing of the Declaration of Independence meant that a new nation had been formed. It also meant that the new country was at war with England. The Revolutionary War would be fought until 1781, when the British surrendered at Yorktown. Then the United States Constitution, approved in 1788, was written to guarantee the liberty that had finally been won.

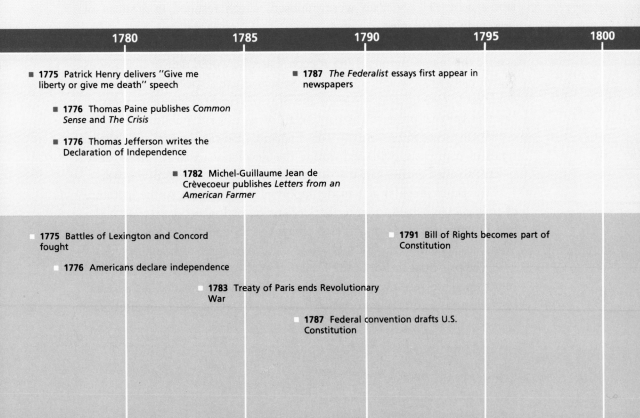

| 1780 | 1785 | 1790 | 1795 | 1800 |

■ **1775** Patrick Henry delivers "Give me liberty or give me death" speech

■ **1787** *The Federalist* essays first appear in newspapers

■ **1776** Thomas Paine publishes *Common Sense* and *The Crisis*

■ **1776** Thomas Jefferson writes the Declaration of Independence

■ **1782** Michel-Guillaume Jean de Crèvecoeur publishes *Letters from an American Farmer*

□ **1775** Battles of Lexington and Concord fought

□ **1791** Bill of Rights becomes part of Constitution

□ **1776** Americans declare independence

□ **1783** Treaty of Paris ends Revolutionary War

□ **1787** Federal convention drafts U.S. Constitution

Reading Literature

The Revolutionary Period

The revolutionary period was an extremely political era. Not surprisingly, most of the literature of this era was also highly political. Writers produced pamphlets, speeches, and letters that argued for political or social reform. Both the Declaration of Independence and the United States Constitution were written during this period. Even much of the poetry written during the era was of a political nature. Literature that was not political in nature was often very practical. Such literature included letters, almanacs, and travel books.

The Literature of Politics

The French and Indian War finally ended in 1763. King George III and Parliament decided to force the American colonists to help pay England's debts. Heavy taxes were imposed, which resulted in a storm of protest in the colonies.

Patrick Henry, an early opponent of British rule in America, argued against the Stamp Act in a 1765 speech. Later he would deliver his famous "Give me liberty or give me death" speech. In this speech he urged the colonists to take up arms to defeat the British. Thomas Paine also opposed Britain's colonial policies. His pamphlet *Common Sense,* published in 1776, urged Americans to break away from England. Paine also wrote *The Crisis,* a series of pamphlets published during the Revolutionary War. These pamphlets provided encouragement during the most difficult days of the war.

Benjamin Franklin also made important contributions to the literature of politics. He helped to write the Declaration of Independence. He had a role in writing the Treaty of Paris, which put an end to the Revolutionary War. The United States Constitution also contains some of Franklin's ideas.

The principal author of the Declaration of Independence was Thomas Jefferson. The Declaration is noted for its literary value as well as its great political and historical importance. In the Declaration, Jefferson used *nat-*

ural laws—the laws of nature that God designed—to justify America's separation from Britain. Jefferson's draft of the Declaration of Independence was approved with relatively few changes. As Richard Lee of Virginia remarked, "The Thing in its nature is so good that no cookery can spoil the dish for the palates of freemen."

Only two other documents of the era rank in importance with the Declaration of Independence: the United States Constitution and the Bill of Rights. The Constitution was the work of a convention of state delegates. The Bill of Rights, which became part of the Constitution in 1791, spells out the basic rights and freedoms of all citizens.

Although the Constitution was written in 1787, it was not approved until 1788. Many patriots, including Patrick Henry and Mercy Otis Warren, opposed the Constitution. Alexander Hamilton, James Madison, and John Jay argued in favor of the Constitution in *The Federalist* essays. These were a series of letters originally published in a New York newspaper.

Other Kinds of Literature

Although most of the literature of the revolutionary era was political, other kinds of literature also were produced. Benjamin Franklin continued to publish *Poor Richard's Almanack* until 1758. The wise and witty sayings in the *Almanack* helped to make it a best seller. In 1771 Franklin began his masterpiece, *The Autobiography,* finished in 1790.

Letters also were an important means of communication. In 1782, the French immigrant Jean de Crèvecoeur published *Letters from an American Farmer.* These letters give an account of the immigrant experience in America, and discuss what it means to be an American. The letters Abigail Adams wrote to her husband, John Adams, give us valuable information about life in the young nation. They also contain many of Abigail's opinions on the political issues of the day.

Other forms of literature from the revolutionary period include poetry, histories, and travel books. The leading poet of the era was Philip Freneau. Although many of his poems deal with patriotic topics, he also wrote about nature. Phillis Wheatley, a female slave, was another noted poet. The first professional author was novelist Charles Brockden Brown, who began his career during this era.

Comprehension Skills

Subjective Writing

Writers sometimes present only the facts about a subject. This is called **objective** writing. At other times, writers mix their own views, or opinions, with these facts. As a reader, you must be able to distinguish between fact and opinion and recognize slanted, or **subjective,** writing. That way, you can develop your own opinions.

Distinguishing Between Fact and Opinion

A **fact** is a statement that can be proved to be true by observation or by checking a source such as an encyclopedia. An **opinion** is a statement that cannot be proved to be true. It is simply the belief of one or more persons. An opinion is often signaled by **judgment words,** such as *good, weak, beautiful,* and *terrible.* Opinions may or may not be based on facts.

Writers sometimes mix opinions with facts, as in the following passage. Can you tell which statements are facts and which is an opinion?

> British policy toward the American colonies changed during the 1760's. After the French and Indian War ended in 1763, heavy taxes were imposed on the colonies to help pay England's debts. These taxes were unfair.

Recognizing Slanted Writing

Slanted writing presents facts so that they favor a writer's point of view. Language that carries a strong emotional appeal is used to lead the reader to a certain conclusion. One type of slanted writing is called stacking. **Stacking** presents only one side of a question. Campaign speeches, for example, often list only a candidate's strengths. Be sure you get all the facts. Only then can you have an informed opinion.

Writers also may slant their writing by choosing words with strong connotations. **Connotations** are the feelings or ideas suggested by a word. Connotations can be positive or negative. Both of the following sentences concern the same idea, but one is positive, the other negative.

Thomas Paine was an enthusiastic patriot who stirred emotions with his persuasive writing.

Thomas Paine was a rabble-rouser who worked people up with his over-emotional scribblings.

Exercises: Identifying Objective and Subjective Writing

A. Decide which sentences are facts and which are opinions. Explain how each fact can be proved to be true.

1. Benjamin Franklin's autobiography is a masterpiece.

2. Patrick Henry delivered his "Give me liberty or give me death" speech in 1775.

3. The Boston Massacre was one of the most shameful acts in history.

4. "I could point out to you a family whose grandfather was English, whose wife was Dutch, whose son married a French woman, and whose present four sons now have four wives from different nations."

5. Abigail Adams was the wife of one President and the mother of another.

6. Jefferson was the most important political leader of the revolutionary era.

7. The Congress declared a boycott of British goods until Parliament repealed laws that the colonists considered unfair.

B. The following sentences contain words with strong connotations. Identify these words in each sentence. Then tell whether the feelings or ideas suggested by these words are positive or negative.

1. "He has plundered our seas, ravaged our coasts, burnt our towns, and destroyed the lives of our people."

2. George Washington was a brilliant general and a distinguished President.

3. ". . . I cannot see on what grounds the king of Britain can look up to heaven for help against us: a common murderer, a highwayman or a house-breaker has as good a pretense as he . . . ."

4. The brave men and woman who fought in the Revolutionary War helped to ensure liberty for future generations of Americans.

5. "And, for the support of this declaration, with a firm reliance on the protection of Divine Providence, we mutually pledge to each other our lives, our fortunes, and our sacred honor."

Vocabulary Skills

Levels of Language

Imagine the following conversation:

Speaker 1. The impetuous young man in that vehicle has a tendency to exceed the speed limit.

Speaker 2. Isn't that driver dangerous?

Speaker 3. Sure he is! Why don't somebody toss that loony in the slammer pronto?

All three speakers are commenting on the same event. Each one, however, is using a different type, or **level,** of language.

Standard English

Standard English is language that all speakers and writers accept. There are two types of standard English: **formal English** and **informal English.** Both types use correct grammar, punctuation, and spelling.

Formal English. This level of language is made up of long, complicated words and sentences and has a serious tone. It is used for professional documents, official statements, academic reports, formal speeches, serious literature, and other similar purposes.

Informal English. This level of language is marked by shorter words and sentences. It also uses a more casual or personal approach. Informal English uses contractions, clipped words, and informal expressions.

Choosing the Right Level of Language

The situation and the audience will tell you which level of language to use. If you are speaking or writing for a serious or dignified occasion, formal English would be more appropriate. When the situation is casual and the audience is more general, informal English can be used.

Nonstandard English

Nonstandard English is language that is not acceptable in most situations. It is often garbled by slang or errors in grammar.

Slang. Slang is highly informal language. It is made up of words and phrases that often have meaning only to a specific group. Although some slang eventually becomes standard, most quickly disappears.

"Gobbledygook." The special terms and phrases used by people in the same line of work are called **jargon.** To people outside that field, jargon may not be understandable. When jargon unnecessarily confuses a piece of writing, it is called gobbledygook. This should always be avoided.

Errors. Errors in grammar, usage, and mechanics also make language nonstandard. These are a few examples:

Incorrect	Correct
He *don't* know the time.	He *doesn't* know the time.
That there TV is *broke.*	*That* TV is *broken.*
Her and me is singing.	*She and I are* singing.

Exercise: Recognizing Levels of Language

Rewrite the following nonstandard sentences to make them standard informal English. You will have to correct errors and eliminate slang and jargon.

1. Get off my back about that there job.

2. The heat is on not to play no jazzy music.

3. Tom ain't eating his grub.

4. Him and me is up the creek.

5. Persons wishing to submit a claim on the policy for the purposes of receiving reimbursement for those items listed in said policy shall submit an itemized accounting of the items and the circumstances of the loss.

6. The financial assets in your checking account have fallen below the minimum acceptable balance.

From
What Is an American?

SETTING A PURPOSE | *Jean de Crèvecoeur was a Frenchman who came to the colonies as a young man. What was his opinion of this New World and its people?*

JEAN de CRÈVECOEUR

What then is the American, this new man? He is either a European, or the descendant of a European. I could point out to you a family whose grandfather was English, whose wife was Dutch, whose son married a French woman, and whose present four sons now have four wives from different nations.

He is an American, who left behind him all his ancient prejudices and manners. Here individuals of all nations are melted into a new race of men, whose labors and heritage will one day cause great changes in the world. Americans are the western pilgrims, who are carrying along with them that great mass of arts, sciences, vigor, and industry.

The Americans were once scattered all over Europe. Here they are part of one of the finest systems which has ever appeared.

The American ought therefore to love this country much better than that where either he or his forefathers were born. Here his industry will be quickly rewarded. Children, who before demanded of him a morsel of bread, are now fat and frolicsome. They gladly help their father to clear those fields where crops will rise. No cruel prince, rich abbot, or mighty lord will claim part of their riches.

Pat Lyon at the Forge, 1826–27, JOHN NEAGLE.
Museum of Fine Arts, Boston, Herman and Zoe Oliver Sherman Fund, 1975.

The American is a new man, who acts upon new principles. He must therefore entertain new ideas and form new opinions. From idleness, dependence, poverty, and useless labor, he has passed to toils for which he will be amply rewarded. This is an American.

Developing Comprehension Skills

1. According to de Crèvecoeur, why should an American love his new country better than his old country?

2. Reread the first paragraph about the family with four sons. Each son has a wife from a different nation. What point is the author making with this example?

3. De Crèvecoeur thinks that everyone in America will be "melted into a new race." What does he mean?

4. Does de Crèvecoeur believe that the new Americans will have a good chance for success? Find at least two statements from the essay that support your answer.

5. De Crèvecoeur says that new Americans have left behind their old prejudices and manners. Do you think that this really happened? Explain your answer.

Reading Literature

1. **Identifying the Essay.** One type of nonfiction is the essay. An **essay** may inform, entertain, or persuade.

   "What Is an American?" was written to tell Europeans about a new breed of people, the Americans. Each paragraph of the essay adds to the definition of an American. For example, the first paragraph defines an American as a European or a descendent of a European. What other parts of the definition are added in the remaining paragraphs? What effect do you think these descriptions might have had on European attitudes toward Americans?

2. **Using Contrasts.** De Crèvecoeur uses a number of contrasts to highlight his defini-

tion of an American. He points out the differences between this "new breed" and other people. For example, he says that an American is a strange mixture of blood that can be found in no other country. He also contrasts the quality of life in America with that in other countries. What other contrasts does de Crèvecoeur use to define Americans? Why do you think he chose this technique to develop his subject?

Developing Vocabulary Skills

Recognizing Standard and Nonstandard English. There are different levels of English. The level of English that is suitable at any time and in any place is called **standard English**. It follows the traditional rules of grammar and usage. In contrast, **nonstandard English** does not follow all rules of grammar, usage, and mechanics. It sometimes includes slang and unnecessary jargon.

Rewrite the following nonstandard sentences in standard English. Then look carefully at "What Is an American?" Find de Crèvecoeur's versions of the same ideas.

1. Americans is kind of a melting pot.

2. What are these here folks that call themselves Americans?

3. These dudes have got to think about cool new ideas and new opinions.

4. Americans left a bad scene behind them.

5. The American ought to dig this country more better than where his old man was born at.

Developing Writing Skills

1. **Analyzing an Opinion.** In his essay of 1782, de Crèvecoeur wrote that Americans are part

of the finest system that ever appeared. He supported this opinion with facts. Write a paragraph that summarizes de Crèvecoeur's opinion and supporting information.

2. **Writing a Definition.** De Crèvecoeur's essay defines an American of the eighteenth century. Write a brief essay entitled "What Is a Modern American?" Describe an American of the twentieth century, just as de Crèvecoeur described the Americans he knew more than two hundred years ago.

Pre-Writing. Work with others in a group. Each member of the group should list several qualities and traits that describe the Americans of today. When you have all finished, compare lists. Do any of these traits appear on several lists? Decide on at least three traits you feel are most important.

Writing. Begin with a topic sentence that gives a general definition of a modern American. Develop your topic sentence with statements about the traits you have identified. You may wish to use examples to help explain these traits. You may also include traits you did not include in your list.

Revising. As you revise, check to see if your topic sentence clearly states the purpose of the essay. Then, make sure each sentence develops your topic sentence. When you are satisfied with the content, check your essay for correct spelling, grammar, and punctuation. Make a clean, final copy if necessary.

Developing Skills in Study and Research

Using the SQ3R Study Method. An organized method of study will help you remember more of what you read. One such method is called SQ3R. It consists of five steps: **Survey**, **Question**, **Read**, **Recite**, and **Review**.

Survey. Look over the entire selection to get a general idea of what it is about. Read the titles and subtitles. Notice the illustrations. Read the introduction and summary.

Question. List questions that you should be able to answer when you finish reading. Use any study questions provided at the end of the selection. Write additional questions by turning chapter titles and headings into questions. Pictures, tables, maps, or graphs can also be used to form questions.

Read. Read the selection to find answers to your questions. Look for the main ideas and supporting details. Pay careful attention to definitions, topic sentences, and chapter headings.

Recite. After reading, recite the answers to your questions. Write your answers in note form.

Review. Try to answer each of your original questions without notes. This will help you recall the information later on.

Use the first two steps of SQ3R as you prepare to read Benjamin Franklin's autobiography, pages 70–74.

Focus on

BENJAMIN FRANKLIN
1706–1790

Benjamin Franklin, 1785–90, CHARLES WILLSON PEALE. The Pennsylvania Academy of the Fine Arts, Joseph and Sarah Harrison Collection. Philadelphia.

One career was not enough for Benjamin Franklin. He had five.

The many-talented Franklin was a printer, an author, a statesman, a philosopher, and a scientist. "God helps them that help themselves," Franklin wrote. From his beginnings as a poor boy in a large family, Franklin worked his way to success, wealth, and fame.

Franklin's most famous writing was *The Autobiography*, which clearly illustrated what made him a remarkable man.

Franklin was also well known for his *Poor Richard's Almanack* (page 77). Its witty sayings expressed homey, practical wisdom. The *Almanack* became enormously popular, and its advice influenced the American character. The *Almanack* also demonstrated a sense of humor that is distinctly American.

Besides being a writer, Franklin also played a starring role in the political drama of the Revolutionary Period. For fourteen years, Franklin served in the Pennsylvania Assembly. Then, as a loyal subject of King George, he spent several years in England as chief representative of the colonies. There he became friends with many Britishers. When Franklin observed Parliament's plans for taxing the colonies, however, his loyalty to England faded. Elected in 1775 to the second Continental Congress, he was chosen to help write the Declaration of Independence.

During the American Revolution, Franklin's diplomatic skill won French support and aid that helped the colonists win the war. Franklin was rewarded with the first ambassadorship to France. In 1787, he helped to develop the Constitution of the United States.

Franklin's public spirit extended beyond politics. He founded the first public library in America, served as postmaster, organized Philadelphia's first fire company, improved streets, lighting, and sanitation, and reformed education. His genius was channeled into the field of science. His inventions include the Franklin stove, bifocals, and the lightning rod. Franklin's experiments with electricity were hailed worldwide.

From
The Autobiography

BENJAMIN FRANKLIN

Ben Franklin was a man of many talents. He was a scientist, a writer, a politician, and a printer. What experiences in his youth may have been responsible for the adult he became?

Dear Son:

Imagining it may be agreeable to you to know the circumstances of my life, many of which you are yet unacquainted with, and expecting a week's uninterrupted leisure in my present country retirement, I sit down to write them for you.

At ten years old, I was taken home to help my father in his business, which was that of a tallow chandler[1] and soap boiler. [This was] business he was not bred to but had assumed on his arrival in New England, because he found his dyeing trade, being in little request, would not maintain his family. Accordingly, I was employed in cutting wick for the candles, filling the molds for cast candles, attending the shop, going on errands, etc.

I disliked the trade and had a strong inclination to go to sea, but my father declared against it. However, living near the water, I was much in it and on it. I learned early to swim well and to manage boats; and when embarked with other boys, I was commonly allowed to govern, especially in any case of difficulty. Upon other occasions I was generally the leader among the boys and sometimes led them into scrapes, of which I will mention one instance as it shows an early projecting public spirit, tho' not then justly conducted.

There was a salt marsh that bounded part of the mill pond, on the edge of which at high water, we used to stand to fish for minnows. By much trampling we had made it a mere quagmire. My proposal was to build a wharf there for us to stand upon, and I showed my comrades a large heap of stones which were intended for a new house near the marsh and which would very well suit our purpose. Accordingly, in the evening when the workmen were gone home, I assembled a number of my playfellows. We worked diligently, sometimes two or three to a stone, till we brought them all to make our little wharf. The next morning the workmen were surprised at missing the stones, which had formed our wharf; enquiry was made. We were discovered, complained of; several of us were corrected by our fathers, and tho' I demonstrated the utility of our work, mine convinced me that that which was not honest could not be truly useful.

I never knew either my father or mother to have any sickness but that of which they died, he at eighty-nine and she at eighty-five years of

---

1. **tallow chandler**, one who makes and/or sells candles.

age. They lie buried together at Boston, where I some years since placed a marble stone over their grave with this inscription:

> Josiah Franklin
> And Abiah his wife
> Lie here interred.
> They lived lovingly together in wedlock
> Fifty-five years.
> Without an estate or any gainful employment,
> By constant labour and industry,
> With God's blessing,
> They maintained a large family
> Comfortably;
> And brought up thirteen children,
> And seven grandchildren
> Reputably.
> From this instance, Reader,
> Be encouraged to diligence in thy calling,
> And distrust not Providence.
> He was a pious and prudent man,
> She a discreet and virtuous woman.
> Their youngest son,
> In filial regard to their memory,
> Places this stone.
>
> J. F. born 1655—Died 1744—age 89.
> A. F. born 1667—Died 1752—85.

From my infancy I was passionately fond of reading, and all the little money that came into my hands was laid out in the purchasing of books. This bookish inclination at length determined my father to make me a printer, though he had already one son (James) of that profession. I liked it much better than that of my father, but still had a hankering for the sea. To prevent the effect of such an inclination, my father was impatient to have me bound to my brother. I stood out some time, but at last was persuaded and signed the indenture,[2] when I was yet but twelve years old. I was to serve as apprentice till I was twenty-one years of age, only I was to be allowed journeyman's wages during the last year. In a little time I made a great progress in the business and became a useful hand to my brother.

My brother had in 1720 or '21 begun to print a newspaper. It was the second that appeared in America and was called *The New England Courant*. The only one before it was *The Boston Newsletter*. I remember his being dissuaded by some of his friends from the undertaking as not likely to succeed, one newspaper being in their judgment enough for America. At this time, 1771, there are not less than five-and-twenty. He went on, however, with the undertaking; I was employed to carry the papers to the customers, after having worked in composing the types and printing off the sheets. He had some ingenious men among his friends who amused themselves by writing little pieces for this paper, which gained it credit and made it more in demand; and these gentlemen often visited us. Hearing their conversations and their accounts of the approval their papers were received with, I was excited to try my hand among them. But being still a boy and suspecting that my brother would object to printing anything of mine in his paper if he knew it to be mine, I contrived to disguise my hand; and writing an anonymous paper, I put it at night under the door of the printing house. It was found in the

---

2. **indenture**, a contract binding a person to work for another for a given length of time. After serving this apprenticeship, the person becomes a journeyman.

Benjamin Franklin, 1767, DAVID MARTIN.
Copyright © 1982 White House Historical Association,
Washington, D.C.

morning and communicated to his writing friends when they called in as usual. They read it, commented on it in my hearing, and I had the exquisite pleasure of finding it met with their approval. In their different guesses at the author, none were named but men of some character among us for learning and ingenuity. I suppose now that I was rather lucky in my judges and that perhaps they were not really so very good as I then believed them to be. Encouraged, however, by this attempt, I wrote and sent in the same way to the press several other pieces, which were equally approved, and I kept my secret till my small fund of sense for such performances was pretty well exhausted, and then I revealed it,

when I began to be considered a little more by my brother's acquaintance. However, that did not quite please him as he thought that it tended to make me too vain.

This might be one occasion of the differences we began to have about this time. Though a brother, he considered himself as my master and me as his apprentice, and accordingly expected the same services from me as he would from another. I thought he degraded me too much in some he required of me, who from a brother expected more indulgence. Our disputes were often brought before our father, and I was either generally in the right or else a better pleader, because the judgment was generally in my favour.

Moral Perfection

It was about this time I conceived the bold and arduous project of arriving at moral perfection. I wished to live without committing any fault at any time; I would conquer all that either natural inclination, custom, or company might lead me into. As I knew, or thought I knew, what was right and wrong, I did not see why I might not *always* do the one and avoid the other. But I soon found I had undertaken a task of more difficulty than I had imagined. While my attention was taken up and care employed in guarding against one fault, I was often surprised by another. I included under thirteen names of virtues all that at that time occurred to me as necessary or desirable, and followed each with a short precept which fully expressed the extent I gave to its meaning.

These names of virtues with their precepts were:

1. **Temperance.** Eat not to dullness. Drink not to elevation.
2. **Silence.** Speak not but what may benefit others or yourself. Avoid trifling conversation.
3. **Order.** Let all your things have their places. Let each part of your business have its time.
4. **Resolution.** Resolve to perform what you ought. Perform without fail what you resolve.
5. **Frugality.** Make no expense but to do good to others or yourself; i.e., waste nothing.
6. **Industry.** Lose no time. Be always employed in something useful. Cut off all unnecessary actions.
7. **Sincerity.** Use no hurtful deceit. Think innocently and justly; and, if you speak, speak accordingly.
8. **Justice.** Wrong none by doing injuries or omitting the benefits that are your duty.
9. **Moderation.** Avoid extremes. Forbear resenting injuries so much as you think they deserve.
10. **Cleanliness.** Tolerate no uncleanness in body, clothes or habitation.
11. **Tranquillity.** Be not disturbed at trifles or at accidents common or unavoidable.
12. **Chastity.** Rarely use venery but for health or offspring, never to dullness, weakness, or the injury of your own or another's peace or reputation.
13. **Humility.** Imitate Jesus and Socrates.[3]

I judged it would be well not to distract my attention by attempting the whole at once but to fix it on one of them at a time, and when I should be master of that, then to proceed to another, and so on till I should have gone thro' the thirteen. And as the previous acquisition of some might facilitate the acquisition of certain others, I arranged them with that view as they stand above.

I made a little book in which I allotted a page for each of the virtues. I ruled each page with red ink so as to have seven columns, one for each day of the week, marking each column with a letter for the day. I crossed these columns with twelve red lines, marking the beginning of each line with the first letter of one of the virtues, on which line and in its proper column I might mark by a little black

---

3. **Socrates**, a Greek teacher and philosopher who lived approximately 470–399 B.C.

spot every fault I found upon examination to have been committed respecting that virtue upon that day.

I determined to give a week's strict attention to each of the virtues successively. Thus

Form of the Pages

	S	M	T	W	T	F	S
T							
S	••	•		•		•	
O	•	•	•		•	•	•
R			•		•		
F		•		•			
I			•				
S							
J							
M							
Cl.	•						
T							
C							
H							

TEMPERANCE

Eat not to dullness.
Drink not to elevation.

in the first week my great guard was to avoid even the least offence against temperance, leaving the other virtues to their ordinary chance, only marking every evening the faults of the day. Thus if in the first week I could keep my first line marked "T." clear of spots, I supposed the habit of that virtue so much strengthened and its opposite weakened that I might venture extending my attention to include the next, and for the following week keep both lines clear of spots. Proceeding thus to the last, I could go through a course complete in thirteen weeks, and four courses in a year. So I should have (I hoped) the encouraging pleasure of seeing on my pages the progress I made in virtue by clearing successively my lines of their spots. In the end, by a number of courses, I should be happy in viewing a clean book after a thirteen weeks' daily examination. On the whole, though, I never arrived at the perfection I had been so ambitious of obtaining but fell far short of it. Yet I was by the endeavour a better and a happier man than I otherwise should have been if I had not attempted it.

Developing Comprehension Skills

1. What happened to Franklin and his friends after they built the wharf out of stones?

2. Reread what Franklin wrote for his parents' gravestone. Based on these words, how do you think Franklin felt about his parents?

3. Franklin became an apprentice to his brother. Why did Franklin's father make him a printer's apprentice? What would Franklin rather have done?

4. What caused problems between Franklin and his brother? How did Franklin feel about this relationship?

5. Which of the virtues on Franklin's list would be easiest for most people to follow? Which would be most difficult? Why?

Reading Literature

1. **Identifying Autobiography.** A story that a person writes about his or her own life is called an **autobiography**. What words tell the reader that Franklin is writing this story from his own point of view? What does the reader learn about Franklin from his autobiography that might not be found in a biography?

2. **Understanding the Narrator.** Franklin demonstrates to the reader the kind of person he is by telling about his personal experiences. Each of the statements below was taken from Franklin's autobiography. What does each statement tell you about Franklin directly? What additional information can you infer about Franklin from each statement?

   a. Upon other occasions I was generally the leader among the boys and sometimes led them into scrapes. . . .

   b. . . . all the little money that came into my hands was laid out in the purchasing of books.

   c. But being still a boy and suspecting that my brother would object to printing anything of mine in his paper. . . I contrived to disguise my hand; and writing an anonymous paper, I put it at night under the door. . . .

   d. I wished to live without committing any fault at any time.

3. **Recognizing Audience.** Writers usually have a specific audience in mind as they write. To help you identify Franklin's audience, look at the first line of Franklin's autobiography. To whom is it addressed? Do you think Franklin might have had a different audience in mind, as well? Explain what evidence led you to this conclusion.

4. **Identifying an Adage.** Franklin was a master at writing **adages**, or short sayings that contain practical, useful ideas. One adage that Franklin included in his autobiography is "that which was not honest could not be truly useful." What does that adage mean?

Developing Vocabulary Skills

Recognizing Terms from Specialized Fields. Every technical field develops its own special language. These terms, called **jargon**, are used by people in the field. Little by little, the terms sometimes become used outside that field. For example, the computer terms *software, microprocessor,* and *program* have become part of the general vocabulary.

In his autobiography, Benjamin Franklin uses specialized terms from the fields of candle-making and printing. Find three examples of terms from each field. Define each one.

Developing Writing Skills

1. **Presenting Your Opinion.** An opinion is a statement that cannot be proved true. A sound opinion, however, is one that can be supported by facts. What is your opinion of Franklin's search for moral perfection? Do you think any human being could achieve the goals Franklin set for himself? Write a paragraph that states your opinion. Support your opinion with reasons, facts, or examples from your own experience.

2. **Describing an Autobiographical Event.** Autobiographies usually include events and incidents that were of great importance in the writer's life. Through these events, the writer may have learned something important about himself or herself.

Write a paragraph or composition relating a memorable incident in your life.

Pre-Writing. Select an event from your life that you remember well. The event may have taught you something about yourself or about life in general.

Jot down details you remember about the event. Try to recall exactly what happened. Next, put the ideas in **chronological order**. This is the order in which the events occurred. Now review the list. Make sure that you have included enough details.

Writing. Begin your autobiographical event by giving background information. Include only the information that the reader will need to understand the event.

Then, using your list, describe what happened. Include the details on your list. You may also include new details that you think about as you write. Choose words that help the reader picture the event. Finally, write a conclusion that shows why the event was important to you.

Revising. Have you included enough information so that your reader understands what happened? Do your details create a vivid picture of the event? Are the events presented in a clear order? Be sure that you have described the event so that your conclusion makes sense.

Developing Skills in Critical Thinking

Recognizing the Fallacy of Stacking. A fallacy is a mistake in reasoning. You must be aware of common fallacies so that you can recognize them in the speaking and writing of others.

The **fallacy of stacking** occurs when a writer tells only those things he or she wants the reader to know. The writer does not mention things that might show the reader another side of the subject.

In his autobiography, Benjamin Franklin tells only certain facts about his life and accomplishments. What impression did he want his readers to have of him?

Now refer to an encyclopedia, *The Oxford Companion to American Literature, The Dictionary of American Biography*, or *Who Was Who in America: Historical Volume 1607–1896* to locate additional information on Franklin's life. What additional facts did you learn about Franklin's life? Why do you think he failed to mention these facts in his autobiography?

Developing Skills in Speaking and Listening

Doing an Oral Interpretation. An **oral interpretation** is the reading of a piece of literature to an audience. As the speaker reads, he or she tries to capture the author's original feelings.

Present an oral interpretation of your own. Choose a short portion of this selection, or of another selection that you have enjoyed. Read the selection to yourself several times. Pay attention to the author's ideas and feelings.

Now, practice the selection out loud. Do not read in a monotone. Try instead to use the rhythm, feeling, and tone of normal speech. Work to create mood by raising or lowering your voice. You might also vary the speed with which you read.

Pay attention to punctuation. Pause at commas and periods. This will give your listeners time to think about your words.

When you feel comfortable with the selection, present your oral interpretation to your audience.

Poor Richard's Almanack, *by Benjamin Franklin, was the most popular publication in America from 1732 to 1758. Why do you think so many people enjoyed it?*

Epigrams from *Poor Richard's Almanack*

BENJAMIN FRANKLIN

1   He that cannot obey cannot command.

2   He that lies down with dogs shall rise up with fleas.

3   If you would be loved, love and be lovable.

4   Keep your eyes wide open before marriage, half shut afterwards.

5   Love your neighbor; yet don't pull down your hedge.

6   Three may keep a secret, if two of them are dead.

7   Lost time is never found again.

8   Be slow in choosing a friend, slower in changing.

9   Well done is better than well said.

10 God helps them that help themselves.

11 Diligence is the mother of good luck.

12 Being ignorant is not so much shame, as being unwilling to learn.

13 When the well's dry, we know the worth of water.

14 A long life may not be good enough, but a good life is long enough.

15 If you would keep your secret from an enemy, tell it not to a friend.

16 Don't count your chickens before they are hatched.

17 If you'd have a good servant that you like, serve yourself.

18 A friend in need is a friend indeed.

19 Fish and visitors smell in three days.

20 He that falls in love with himself will have no rivals.

21 Never leave that till tomorrow, which you can do today.

22 He that goes a borrowing goes a sorrowing.

23 Little strokes fell great oaks.

24 Early to bed, and early to rise, makes a man healthy, wealthy, and wise.

Magnetic Dispensary, 1790, SAMUEL COLLINGS. Library Company of Philadelphia, Pennsylvania.

Developing Comprehension Skills

1. According to "Poor Richard," what must a person do to earn the love of others?

2. Hedges may be used to divide property and maintain privacy. What does Franklin mean when he says that you should love your neighbor, but keep your hedges?

3. In which two epigrams does Franklin refer to secrets? Does he think that people can be trusted with secrets?

4. What is Franklin saying about luck in epigram 11?

5. According to Franklin, what is worse than ignorance?

6. Which epigrams do you think are most useful for people today? Which do you think do not apply today? Explain your answer.

Reading Literature

1. **Appreciating Proverbs.** A **proverb**, or adage, is a short saying that contains practical advice. What advice about friends does Franklin give in *Poor Richard's Almanack*? Do you agree with Franklin's opinion? Why or why not?

2. **Identifying the Audience.** Ben Franklin used the name Poor Richard Saunders when he wrote the *Almanack*. Is this an ordinary or a fancy name? Now consider both this name and the type of advice the almanac contains. Do they give you a hint as to who the intended audience was?

3. **Appreciating Humor.** Many of the epigrams in *Poor Richard's Almanack* are humorous. Why do you think Franklin sometimes chose to give serious advice in a humorous way? In your opinion, is the advice in the humorous epigrams as worthwhile as the advice in the serious epigrams? Explain your answer.

4. **Understanding Implied Metaphor.** A **metaphor** is a type of comparison. It involves two unlike things that have something in common. A metaphor states that one thing is another, as in the phrase "hard work is the best medicine."

   Sometimes a metaphor is less clear. It simply implies, or suggests, a comparison. In one of Franklin's epigrams, a dry well and water are used in an implied comparison. What might Franklin be comparing to them? Do you think this is an effective comparison? Why or why not?

Developing Vocabulary Skills

Recognizing Formal and Informal English. Within standard English, there are two levels of language: formal and informal. As you know, **formal English** is serious and dignified. It uses long words and sentences. It is proper for formal speeches, public documents, academic papers, and similar writing. **Informal English** is simpler, more casual, and more personal. It is used every day in talking and writing to friends, as well as to general audiences. Its sentences are shorter, and its vocabulary is simpler. It often uses contractions and clipped words.

Look carefully at the sayings from *Poor Richard's Almanack*. They are written in informal standard English. Choose any four of the sayings and write them more formally. Keep the same idea, but remember to use a more serious tone and a more dignified vocabulary.

Example:

   He that lies down with dogs shall rise up with fleas.

A person who associates with question-able individuals may find that he or she is tainted by the relationship.

Developing Writing Skills

1. **Writing About Values.** A value is a standard or quality that people think is important. For example, honesty and loyalty can both be part of a person's values. People reveal their values through the way they act and by the advice they give others. Based on the selections you have read, write a brief essay that identifies and explains what Franklin thought was important in life.

    Pre-Writing. Think of everything you have read by Franklin. List the qualities that seem important to him. For example, his epigrams show his feelings about honesty and about hard work. After completing your list, choose three or four items that you think were most important to Ben Franklin.

    Writing. In your first sentence, briefly present the values you will focus on in your essay. Then explain how Franklin showed the importance of that value to him. Use passages from the selections to support your statements.

    Revising. Ask a classmate to check your essay to make sure you have clearly described Franklin's values. Have you explained how you know the values were important to him? Now read your essay aloud to yourself. Do the sentences and ideas flow smoothly? Finally, check your writing for correct spelling, grammar, and punctuation.

2. **Developing an Idea with an Anecdote.** A short, entertaining personal story is called an **anecdote.** Anecdotes can teach as well as entertain. Select one of Franklin's epigrams that you think contains good advice. In one paragraph, write an anecdote that proves the value of the advice.

Developing Skills in Study and Research

Using the Almanac. An **almanac** is a reference book that contains information and data on many subjects. Almanacs are published and updated each year. *Poor Richard's Almanack* was similar to other almanacs of the 1700's. It contained calendars, locations of hotels, maps, names of rulers and kings, dates of eclipses, special holidays, and fairs. It also contained rules of health, recipes, rhymes, descriptions of historical events, and proverbs.

Examine a modern almanac in the reference section of your library. Look at the almanac's table of contents, which is found in the front of the book. Make a list of the information that can be found in the modern almanac. How does it differ from that in *Poor Richard's Almanack*? Do you think the almanacs of the 1700's served a different purpose than today's almanacs? Explain your answer.

Benjamin Franklin Hurls His Defiance at an Old Comrade

Philad^a July 5, 1775

Mr. Strahan,

    You are a Member of Parliament, and one of that Majority which has doomed my Country to Destruction.—You have begun to burn our Towns and murder our People.—Look upon your hands!—They are stained with the Blood of your Relations!—You and I were long Friends:—You are now my Enemy,— and

                I am
                    Yours,
                        B. Franklin

Developing Comprehension Skills

1. Why is the date of the letter important?

2. Who is William Strahan? What sort of relationship had he once had with Franklin?

3. Why is Strahan now an enemy?

4. Do you think Franklin makes his point with this letter? Explain your answer.

Reading Literature

1. **Recognizing Loaded Language.** A writer's tone can often be determined by considering the words and phrases used. In this letter, Franklin uses loaded language such as "doomed." **Loaded language** is language that appeals to emotion rather than reason.

    What other loaded language does Franklin use in this letter? How does this language affect the tone of the letter?

2. **Appreciating Double Meaning.** Franklin seems to end his letter in the usual, respectful manner: *I am Yours, B. Franklin.* However, there is a second meaning to Franklin's words. Read the letter aloud. Do not pause at the end of the last line of the letter. What else was Franklin saying to his old friend?

Benjamin Franklin Hurls His Defiance   *81*

On Being Learned

BENJAMIN FRANKLIN

SETTING A PURPOSE *This brief statement shows Franklin at his cleverest, using humor to make a point. What wisdom does this quotation reveal?*

He was so learned that he could name a horse in nine languages; so ignorant that he bought a cow to ride on.

Developing Comprehension Skills

1. How is the person Franklin speaks about in the quotation intelligent? How is he ignorant?

2. Does Franklin seem to prefer practical knowledge or formal education? Explain your answer.

3. Is it important that the reader knows what particular person Franklin is speaking about? Why or why not?

4. In your opinion, is humor an effective way for Franklin to make his point about knowledge? Why or why not?

Reading Literature

1. **Recognizing Quotations.** A **quotation** is a statement that is so well expressed that it is remembered and repeated frequently. Why do you think "On Being Learned" has become a famous quotation? Could it apply to a person today as well as to a person in Franklin's era?

2. **Identifying Tone.** An author's attitude toward his or her subject is the **tone** of the selection. What is Franklin's attitude toward the learned man described in his quotation? What clues in the quotation lead you to your conclusion?

Benjamin Franklin Writes His Own Epitaph

The Body of
B. Franklin,
Printer,
Like the Cover of an old Book,
Its Contents torn out,
And Stript of its Lettering and Gilding,
Lies here, Food for Worms.
But the Work shall not be wholly lost:
For it will, as he believ'd, appear once more,
In a new and more perfect Edition,
Corrected and amended
By the Author.
He was born Jan. 6 1706
Died   17

Ben Franklin's epitaph. Beinecke Rare Book and Manuscript Library, Yale University, New Haven, Connecticut.

Developing Comprehension Skills

1. To what does Franklin compare himself? Why do you think he used this comparison?

2. What is "the Work" referred to in the epitaph?

3. What is the "new and more elegant Edition"? Who is "the Author"?

4. Do you think his epitaph is a good one? Why or why not?

Reading Literature

1. **Identifying an Epitaph.** An **epitaph** is a statement written on a tombstone. An epitaph often tells something memorable about the person buried there. Usually it is written by someone else. Why do you think Franklin wrote his own epitaph?

2. **Appreciating Extended Metaphor.** A metaphor is a direct comparison between two unlike things. An **extended metaphor** continues the comparison throughout a selection. In what way is Franklin's epitaph an extended metaphor?

Developing Vocabulary Skills

Understanding Standard and Nonstandard English. Nonstandard English, as you have learned, does not follow traditional rules of spelling, usage, and mechanics. Rules for proper usage, spelling, and mechanics, however, have changed over the years. What was standard English in Benjamin Franklin's time may be considered nonstandard English today.

Look at Franklin's letter to William Strahan, and at the epitaph Franklin wrote. Find one or more examples of each of the following that would be judged nonstandard today:

1. spelling   2. punctuation   3. capitalization

Developing Writing Skills

1. **Writing a Character Sketch.** A **character sketch** is a brief description of a person. It presents the person's background, thoughts, actions, and traits. A character sketch may also include an evaluation of the person by the writer. Write a character sketch of Benjamin Franklin, based on your reading.

    Pre-Writing. Review each of Franklin's selections. List any facts about his background, thoughts, actions, and traits that you feel show the kind of man he was. Take notes on the passages where you find each item in your list. You might group the items under headings, as follows:

Background facts	Thoughts
came from a large family	in favor of separating from England

Actions	Traits
experimented with electricity	showed leadership qualities early in life

    Writing. Write the first draft of your character sketch. Include Franklin's name and a general statement about the kind of man he was in the opening sentence of the first paragraph. This is your main idea sentence, sometimes called a **thesis statement**. Continue your character sketch with paragraphs based on each group from your list. Use the details from your list to support the topic sentence in each paragraph. As you write each paragraph, add any new details you think of.

    Revising. Ask the following questions as you revise your character sketch:

    Does each paragraph begin with a topic sentence?

Is each topic sentence supported with enough details?

Are there enough details to present an accurate, interesting picture of Franklin?

Are the spelling, grammar, and punctuation correct?

After revising, prepare a clean, final copy.

2. **Writing an Epitaph.** Write your own epitaph. Remember that an epitaph may say something positive about a person's career, family, or special interests. An epitaph is usually only a few, well-chosen sentences. After all, it must fit on a tombstone.

Developing Skills in Study and Research

Using *Bartlett's Familiar Quotations.* The reference book *Bartlett's Familiar Quotations* contains thousands of famous quotations. For each quotation, the book lists the author's name and the title of the literary work in which the quotation was first written.

To find a quotation when you know the author, look for the author's name in the index. The index lists authors' last names alphabetically. You can then find the first page number on which quotations by that author appear.

Following the quotation, you will find the title and date of the work that the quotation comes from. Or, instead of a title or a date, you may find the letters "Ib." This means that you should look for the title at the end of the quotation before it.

Use *Bartlett's Familiar Quotations* to find three additional quotations by Ben Franklin. Write the quotations and the titles and dates of the works in which they first appeared.

From
The Crisis

THOMAS PAINE

SETTING A PURPOSE

Thomas Paine was a political writer who was strongly in favor of the American Revolution. He wrote The Crisis *to lift the morale of the American soldiers. How does Paine appeal to emotions in this essay?*

These are the times that try men's souls. The summer soldier and the sunshine patriot will, in this crisis, shrink from the service of his country; but he that stands it *now*, deserves the love and thanks of man and woman. Tyranny, like hell, is not easily conquered; yet we have this consolation with us, that the harder the conflict, the more glorious the triumph. What we obtain too cheap, we esteem too lightly: it is dearness only that gives everything its value. Heaven knows how to put a proper price upon its goods; and it would be strange indeed if so celestial an article as FREEDOM should not be highly rated. Britain, with an army to enforce her tyranny, has declared that she has a right (*not only to* TAX) but "to BIND *us in* ALL CASES WHATSOEVER"; and if being *bound in that manner* is not slavery, then is there not such a thing as slavery upon earth. Even the expression is impious; for so unlimited a power can belong only to God. . . .

I have as little superstition in me as any man living; but my secret opinion has ever been, and still is, that God Almighty will not give up a people to military destruction, or leave them unsupportedly to perish, who have so earnestly and so repeatedly sought to avoid the calamities of war, by every decent method which wisdom could invent. Neither have I so much of the infidel in me as to suppose that He has relinquished the government of the world, and given us up to the care of devils; and as I do not, I cannot see on what grounds the king of Britain can look up to heaven for help against us: a common murderer, a highwayman, or a housebreaker, has as good a pretense as he. . . .

Not a place upon earth might be so happy as America. Her situation is remote from all the wrangling world, and she has nothing to do but to trade with them. A man can distinguish himself between temper and principle: and I am as confident as I am that God governs the world, that America will never be happy till she gets clear of foreign dominion.

Developing Comprehension Skills

1. *The Crisis* was written in 1776. How does the title describe the situation then?

2. Who are the "summer soldier" and the "sunshine patriot"? How do they differ from a true patriot?

3. Does Paine think that the colonists have tried to avoid war?

4. To what does Paine compare the King of England?

5. According to Paine, why might America be a happy land? Do you agree with him? Explain your answer.

Reading Literature

1. **Achieving Purpose.** Rhetoric is the art of using words to achieve a purpose. Paine wrote *The Crisis* when the war was going badly for the colonists. It was handed out as a pamphlet and was read to George Washington's starving troops at Valley Forge just before Christmas in 1776. What effect do you think Paine wanted his words to have? Do you think Paine achieved his purpose?

2. **Recognizing Appeals to Emotion.** Writers think carefully about the words they use. A writer may use words that appeal to a reader's reason, or logic. Or, the writer may use words that appeal to a reader's emotions. In this excerpt from *The Crisis* Paine uses words such as *tyranny, hell, freedom, God, slavery,* and *common murderer* to support his points. Do these words appeal to reason or emotion? Do you think Paine could have been more effective in his appeal if he had simply presented facts and used more reasonable language? Explain your answer.

Developing Vocabulary Skills

Reviewing Levels of Language. You have learned the differences between standard English and nonstandard English. You also know that there are two levels of standard English, formal and informal.

Look at the following passages based on selections you have studied so far in this chapter. Label each passage formal, informal, or nonstandard.

1. What then is the American, this new man?

2. From idleness, dependence, poverty, and useless labor, he has passed to toils for which he will be amply rewarded.

3. When the well's dry, we know the worth of water.

4. Yeah, he'd already decided I wasn't gonna be no sailor.

5. Tyranny, like hell, is not easily conquered; yet we have this consolation with us, that the harder the conflict, the more glorious the triumph.

Developing Writing Skills

1. **Examining a Title.** The title of Thomas Paine's appeal to the American Revolutionary soldiers is *The Crisis.* In a paragraph, explain the problems facing the American colonies in 1776. Use an encyclopedia or history text to find your information. Which specific problems does Paine mention? How does he think these problems might be solved?

2. **Persuading an Audience.** Successful persuasion is built on sound opinions. Sound opinions are supported by facts. Write a paragraph on a subject that you feel strongly

about. Try to persuade the reader to think the same way you do about your subject.

Pre-Writing. Choose a topic about which you feel strongly. Write a sentence stating your opinion. Then think of several reasons that you can use to persuade your audience. List facts, examples, or personal experiences to support each reason.

Writing. Begin with a clear statement of your opinion or belief. Present your opinions and supporting facts in the order of their importance. Using this method, you arrange your details so that your strongest reason appears last. That way, you will leave your audience with the most convincing reason.

Revising. As you revise, check to see that you have supported your opinions with facts. Check also to see if you have arranged your details in the order of their importance. Then, ask a classmate to read your para-graph. Is your writing convincing? What more could you include to support your opinion successfully?

Developing Skills in Critical Thinking

Identifying Loaded Language. Loaded language appeals to a person's emotions rather than to reason. Loaded language is often used in place of facts to persuade readers and listeners. There are two kinds of loaded language: **snarl words** and **purr words**. A snarl word creates a negative feeling. *Lazy, dull,* and *cheap* are examples of snarl words. A purr word creates a positive reaction. *Hard-working, freedom,* and *love* are purr words.

This selection from *The Crisis* by Thomas Paine uses several snarl words and purr words. Find at least two of each. Explain the emotions associated with each word.

The Declaration of Independence

THOMAS JEFFERSON

SETTING A PURPOSE | *Thomas Jefferson was the chief author of the* Declaration of Independence. *The Declaration clearly states the reasons why the colonies separated from England. Which of these reasons are most convincing?*

In Congress, July 4, 1776

When, in the course of human events, it becomes necessary for one people to dissolve the political bands which have connected them with another, and to assume, among the powers of the earth, the separate and equal station to which the laws of nature and of nature's God entitle them, a decent respect to the opinions of mankind requires that they should declare the causes which impel them to the separation.

We hold these truths to be self-evident:— That all men are created equal; that they are endowed by their Creator with certain unalienable rights; that among these are life, liberty, and the pursuit of happiness. That, to secure these rights, governments are instituted among men, deriving their just powers from the consent of the governed; that, whenever any form of government becomes destructive of these ends, it is the right of the people to alter or to abolish it, and to institute new government, laying its foundation on such principles, and organizing its powers in such form, as to them shall seem most likely to effect their safety and happiness. Prudence, indeed, will dictate that governments long established should not be changed for light and transient causes; and, accordingly, all experience hath shown that mankind are more disposed to suffer, while evils are sufferable, than to right themselves by abolishing the forms to which they are accustomed. But, when a long train of abuses and usurpations, pursuing invariably the same object, evinces a design to reduce them under absolute despotism, it is their right, it is their duty, to throw off such government, and to provide new guards for their future security. Such has been the patient sufferance of these colonies; and such is now the necessity that constrains them to alter their former systems of government. The history of the present King of Great Britain is a history of repeated injuries and usurpations, all having in direct object the establishment of an absolute tyranny over these States. To prove this, let facts be submitted to a candid world.

He has refused his assent to laws the most wholesome and necessary for the public good.

He has forbidden his Governors to pass laws of immediate and pressing importance, unless suspended in their operation till his assent should be obtained; and when so suspended, he has utterly neglected to attend to them.

He has refused to pass other laws for the accommodation of large districts of people, unless those people would relinquish the right of representation in the legislature—a right inestimable to them, and formidable to tyrants only.

He has called together legislative bodies at places unusual, uncomfortable, and distant from the depository of their public records, for the sole purpose of fatiguing them into compliance with his measures.

He has dissolved representative houses repeatedly, for opposing, with manly firmness, his invasions on the rights of the people.

He has refused for a long time, after such dissolutions, to cause others to be elected; whereby the legislative powers, incapable of annihilation, have returned to the people at large for their exercise; the State remaining, in the meantime, exposed to all the dangers of invasion from without, and convulsions within.

He has endeavored to prevent the population of these States; for that purpose obstructing the laws for the naturalization of foreigners; refusing to pass others to encourage their migrations hither, and raising the conditions of new appropriations of lands.

He has obstructed the administration of justice, by refusing his assent to laws for establishing judiciary powers.

He has made judges dependent on his will alone, for the tenure of their offices, and the amount and payment of their salaries.

He has erected a multitude of new offices, and sent hither swarms of officers to harass our people, and eat out their substance.

He has kept among us, in times of peace, standing armies, without the consent of our legislatures.

He has affected to render the military independent of and superior to the civil power.

He has combined with others to subject us to a jurisdiction foreign to our constitution, and unacknowledged by our laws; giving his assent to their acts of pretended legislation:

The Congress Voting Independence, late 18th century, ROBERT EDGE PINE/EDWARD SAVAGE.
Historical Society of Pennsylvania, Philadelphia.

For quartering large bodies of armed troops among us;

For protecting them, by a mock trial, from punishment for any murders which they should commit on the inhabitants of these States;

For cutting off our trade with the world;

For imposing taxes on us without consent;

For depriving us, in many cases, of the benefits of trial by jury;

For transporting us beyond the seas to be tried for pretended offences;

For abolishing the free system of English laws in a neighboring province, establishing therein an arbitrary government, and enlarging its boundaries, so as to render it at once an example and fit instrument for introducing the same absolute rule into these colonies;

For taking away our charters, abolishing our most valuable laws, and altering fundamentally the forms of our governments;

For suspending our own legislatures, and declaring themselves invested with power to legislate for us in all cases whatsoever.

He has abdicated government here, by declaring us out of his protection, and waging war against us.

He has plundered our seas, ravaged our coasts, burnt our towns, and destroyed the lives of our people.

He is at this time transporting large armies of foreign mercenaries to complete the works of death, desolation, and tyranny, already begun with circumstances of cruelty and perfidy scarcely paralleled in the most barbarous ages, and totally unworthy the head of a civilized nation.

He has constrained our fellow citizens, taken captive on the high seas, to bear arms against their country, to become the executioners of their friends and brethren, or to fall themselves by their hands.

He has excited domestic insurrections amongst us, and has endeavored to bring on the inhabitants of our frontiers, the merciless Indian savages, whose known rule of warfare is an undistinguished destruction of all ages, sexes, and conditions.

In every state of these oppressions, we have petitioned for redress, in the most humble terms: our repeated petitions have been answered only by repeated injury. A prince, whose character is thus marked by every act which may define a tyrant, is unfit to be the ruler of a free people.

Nor have we been wanting in attentions to our British brethren. We have warned them, from time to time, of attempts by their legislature to extend an unwarrantable jurisdiction over us. We have reminded them of the circumstances of our emigration and settlement here. We have appealed to their native justice and magnanimity; and we have conjured them, by the ties of our common kindred, to disavow these usurpations, which would inevitably interrupt our connections and correspondence. They, too, have been deaf to the voice of justice and of consanguinity. We must, therefore, acquiesce in the necessity, which denounces our separation, and hold them, as we hold the rest of mankind, enemies in war, in peace friends.

WE, THEREFORE, THE REPRESENTATIVES OF THE UNITED STATES OF AMERICA, in General Congress assembled, appealing to the Supreme Judge of the world for the rectitude of our intentions, do, in the name and by the authority of the good people of these colonies, solemnly publish and declare, That these United Colonies are, and of right ought to be, FREE AND INDEPENDENT STATES; that they are absolved from all allegiance to the British crown, and that all political connection between them and the state of Great Britain, is and ought to be, totally dissolved; and that, as free and independent states, they have full power to levy war, conclude peace, contract alliances, establish commerce, and to do all other acts and things which independent states may of right do. And, for the support of this declaration, with a firm reliance on the protection of Divine Providence, we mutually pledge to each other our lives, our fortunes, and our sacred honor.

Developing Comprehension Skills

1. According to this document, what must people do when declaring their independence from another country?

2. According to Jefferson, what three rights do all people have?

3. Whom does Jefferson blame for most of the colonies' problems? According to Jefferson, what was this person trying to do?

4. How did the British government respond to the "repeated petitions" of the American colonists?

5. Did the colonists have good reasons for separating from England? Could they have tried another solution before beginning a revolution? Explain your answer.

6. The language in a document such as the Declaration of Independence must be powerful and memorable. Do you think the language in the Declaration of Independence fits this description? Use passages from the Declaration to support your answer.

Reading Literature

1. **Understanding Political Documents.** A political document often helps a reader to remember important events in the history of a people or nation. What is the subject of the Declaration of Independence? Why has this document become famous?

2. **Recognizing Purpose.** A political document may be written to inform, describe, or persuade. It may even be intended to accomplish all of these purposes. What is the main purpose of the Declaration of Independence? What clues in the document lead you to this conclusion?

3. **Using Punctuation To Aid Understanding.** The Declaration of Independence contains many long sentences. Commas, colons, and semicolons are used to divide the sentences into shorter thoughts. By paying attention to these marks, the writing becomes easier to understand. For example, the first eight lines of the second paragraph contain six different ideas. Each idea is separated from the others by a punctuation mark. Locate and list these six ideas.

4. **Identifying Loaded Language.** Loaded language is language that appeals to a person's emotions. Political writers and speakers often use loaded language to sway the thinking of their audience. For example, in paragraph 27, Jefferson uses the words *death*, *desolation*, *tyranny*, *cruelty*, and *barbarous*. To what emotions do these words appeal? Locate other examples of loaded language in paragraphs 28, 29, and 30. What effect was Jefferson trying to achieve with each word?

Developing Vocabulary Skills

Recognizing Characteristics of Formal English. The Declaration of Independence is a formal government document. Therefore, it was appropriate for Thomas Jefferson to write it in formal English. Its vocabulary is difficult and its sentences are long and complex. The tone is serious and dignified.

Rewrite the following passages from the Declaration of Independence in informal standard English. Then decide how the language changes the effect.

1. Prudence, indeed, will dictate that governments long established should not be changed for light and transient causes. . . .

2. He has combined with others to subject us to a jurisdiction foreign to our constitutions, and unacknowledged by our laws. . . .

3. We hold these truths to be self evident:— That all men are created equal; that they are endowed by their Creator with certain unalienable rights. . . .

4. But, when a long train of abuses and usurpations, pursuing invariably the same object, evinces a design to reduce them under absolute despotism, it is their right, it is their duty, to throw off such government. . . .

Developing Writing Skills

1. **Writing a Paraphrase.** When you write a **paraphrase**, you restate someone else's ideas in your own words. The paraphrase covers the ideas in the original version, but often makes them easier to understand. Here is a paraphrase of the first paragraph of the Declaration of Independence:

> One country may break its ties with another country. It does this so that it can be separate and equal according to God's law. When a country does separate from another, the first country should give its reasons for doing so.

Write a paraphrase of the last paragraph of the Declaration of Independence. Explain the original idea in your own words.

2. **Writing a Declaration.** A persuasive document like the Declaration of Independence is written because a problem exists that needs attention. Write a declaration of your own. First, select a problem that you think needs attention. You may desire a change of some sort in your community, family, or job. You might even want to write about a larger problem, one of local or national importance.

Pre-Writing. State the issue or problem you have chosen. Then make notes about the problem. What has caused it? What makes it unacceptable? Why do you want the problem corrected? Finally, jot down ideas about how you propose to solve the problem.

Writing. Use your notes to write a first draft of your declaration. Begin with a statement of the problem. Tell who is affected by the problem. Provide more background information if necessary. Next, state reasons why this problem must be dealt with. Your document may use one- and two-sentence paragraphs to achieve this. If you wish, use the Declaration of Independence, paragraphs 3–29, as a model. Be sure your causes and reasons are clear.

The last section should state your solution to the problem. It should be a forceful paragraph. You may wish to use language that appeals to the emotions to make your point.

Revising. Ask a classmate to read your declaration to you. Are the problem, the reasons for changing, and the solution easy to understand? Have you used emotional language carefully? Have you used formal language? Add any additional causes and reasons that will help make your declaration more persuasive. Make a clean, final copy.

Developing Skills in Study and Research

Using Skimming and Scanning. When you study literature and other written materials, you can use several types of reading. Each type has a specific purpose.

One method of fast reading, **skimming**, is used to get a general idea of a selection. It is also the first step in the SQ3R study method. When skimming a selection, move your eyes quickly over the material. Glance at titles, subtitles, headings, pictures, and graphic aids. Do not read every word. Also look at the first and last sentences of paragraphs. In this way, you can find out what a selection is about without reading it closely. Skim Chapter 5, beginning on page 131. What are some of the subjects that you will read about in the chapter?

Another fast reading technique is scanning. **Scanning** is used to find specific information quickly. To scan, you move your eyes quickly across a line or down the page. As you scan, look for key words and phrases that tell you that you are near the information you need. When you find such clues, stop scanning and begin to read slowly and carefully.

Use scanning to find answers to the following questions about the Declaration of Independence. After answering each question, note the key word or phrase that you found while scanning.

1. What right do the people have when a government becomes destructive?

2. What has happened to taxes in the colonies?

3. What did the king do about laws for the naturalization of foreigners?

4. What has happened to trial by jury?

5. What do the colonists pledge to each other?

Developing Skills in Speaking and Listening

Discussing Historic Ideas. The ideas and arguments presented in the Declaration of Independence were indeed revolutionary. No people had ever before demanded such freedom and criticized a government so harshly. Reread the second paragraph of the Declaration. Think about the ideas in this paragraph. Then discuss the following questions with a small group of classmates:

1. What might people think of these ideas today?

2. If people did not know these ideas were from the Declaration of Independence, might they think the ideas sound radical or extreme?

3. Would people be likely to support a political party favoring these ideas today?

When discussing ideas, be sure to allow each person in the group the opportunity to speak. Remember, group discussion requires good listening as well as speaking. One person in each group might take notes on ideas expressed. These ideas can then be presented to the entire class.

A Letter from Thomas Jefferson to His Daughter

In a letter to his daughter, Thomas Jefferson suggests a plan of education. What does this plan say about Jefferson's attitude toward his daughter?

THOMAS JEFFERSON

To Martha Jefferson

Annapolis, Nov. 28, 1783

My dear Patsy,

After four days journey I arrived here without any accident and in as good health as when I left Philadelphia. The conviction that you would be more improved in the situation I have placed you than if still with me has solaced me on my parting with you, which my love for you has rendered a difficult thing. The skills which I hope you will acquire under the tutors I have provided for you will render you more worthy of my love, and if they cannot increase it they will prevent its diminution. . . .

With respect to the distribution of your time the following is what I should approve:

from 8 to 10 o'clock practice music.
from 10 to 1 dance one day and draw another.
from 1 to 2 draw on the day you dance, and write a letter the next day.
from 3 to 4 read French.
from 4 to 5 exercise yourself in music.
from 5 till bedtime read English, write &c.

Communicate this plan to Mrs. Hopkinson and if she approves of it pursue it. . . . I expect you will write to me by every post. Inform me what books you read, what tunes you

Maria with Dog Under a Tree, about 1845, artist unknown.
Colby College Museum, Waterville, Maine.

learn, and inclose me your best copy of every lesson in drawing. Write also one letter every week either to your Aunt Eppes, your Aunt Skipwith, your Aunt Carr, or the little lady from whom I now inclose a letter, and always put the letter you so write under cover to me. Take care that you never spell a word wrong. Always before you write a word consider how it is spelled, and if you do not remember it, turn to a dictionary. It produces great praise to a lady to spell well.

I have placed my happiness on seeing you good and accomplished, and no distress which this world can now bring on me could equal that of your disappointing my hopes. If you love me, then, strive to be good under every situation and to all living creatures, and to acquire those accomplishments which I have put in your power, and which will go far towards ensuring you the warmest love of your affectionate father,

Th. Jefferson

P.S. Keep my letters and read them at times, so that you may always have present in your mind those things which will endear you to me.

Developing Comprehension Skills

1. Why did Jefferson leave Patsy in Philadelphia?

2. What subjects does Jefferson suggest Patsy study? What subjects are not mentioned? Does this say something about Jefferson's attitude toward women? Explain your answer.

3. How does Jefferson pressure Patsy to do well?

4. How would you rate Jefferson's plan for each school day? How does it compare with your own school plan?

Reading Literature

1. **Appreciating the Language of Letters.** Some letters can be serious and formal. Such letters are often used in business and government communications. For example, Franklin's letter to William Strahan was formal in both language and tone.

Jefferson's letter to Patsy is much more casual. How do the two letters differ? Why would Jefferson's style in this letter not have been appropriate for Franklin's purpose?

2. **Identifying Tone.** The attitude a writer takes toward a subject is the **tone**. What is the tone of Jefferson's letter? What words and phrases provide clues to Jefferson's attitude?

3. **Inferring Character.** When you infer, you make a guess based on information you already know. Jefferson's letter reveals the type of parent he is. From his message to his daughter, would you call him a trusting parent? Is he a demanding one? Can you think of other terms to describe him? What does the message in the P.S. tell you about Jefferson as a parent?

Developing Vocabulary Skills

Recognizing Traits of Informal English. You have seen how Jefferson's letter differed from Franklin's letter to William Strahan. Now examine how Jefferson adjusted his own level of language for two different purposes. In the Declaration of Independence, Jefferson uses serious, dignified, formal English. Here he uses more personal, informal English.

Explain how this letter and the Declaration of Independence differ in the following ways:

1. audience
2. purpose
3. sentence length
4. use of informal expressions
5. structure and organization

Developing Writing Skills

1. **Contrasting Ideas.** Contrast Jefferson's idea of education for a lady in 1783 with today's ideas about education. Remember, when you contrast two subjects, you are looking for differences. Use Jefferson's letter to Patsy as your source of information. Begin with a clear topic sentence. It should tell the readers that today's idea of education for a woman is different from Jefferson's idea. Then, support the topic sentence with several examples of these differences. Arrange supporting ideas in order of importance, saving the most important difference for last.

2. **Writing a Personal Plan.** Jefferson's letter to his daughter outlined his plans for her education. Compose a plan of education or training for yourself. Your plan may deal with formal education or on-the-job training. Discuss in the plan what you want to learn, why you want to learn it, and a schedule that will allow you to reach your goal.

   Pre-Writing. First, determine your goal. What skill or knowledge are you seeking? Then decide what you must accomplish to reach your goal. Jot down all the details that you feel must be included in your study or training. Also note the amount of time each part of the process will require.

   Writing. Begin your plan with a topic sentence. This sentence should introduce the goal you have set. Tell why this goal is important to you. Then, explain your plan in detail. You might write a very detailed schedule, as Jefferson did for Patsy. Or, you might simply explain why each part of the study or training program is necessary.

   Revising. As you read your plan once again, ask yourself these questions:

   Will each part of my plan help to achieve my goal?
   Is each part of the plan necessary?
   Have I explained each part of the plan in detail?

Developing Skills in Speaking and Listening

Dramatizing a Character. Imagine that you are Patsy Jefferson, or Patsy's "brother." How would you reply to your father's letter if you were talking to him in person? Prepare a brief oral response telling your father what you think of his plans for Patsy's education. Remember that the year is 1783. Consider what a young person's attitude toward parents and family relationships would be at that time. Do these attitudes differ from the attitudes today?

As you give your reply, let your face and posture emphasize your feelings and ideas.

The Letters of Abigail and John Adams

Before he became President, John Adams helped write the Declaration of Independence. While John was away, letters kept him and his wife in touch. What do you learn of their relationship through these letters?

Abigail Adams to John

March 31, 1776

. . . I long to hear that you have declared an independency—and, by the way, in the new code of laws, which I suppose it will be necessary for you to make, I desire you would remember the ladies, and be more generous and favorable to them than [were] your ancestors. Do not put such unlimited power into the hands of the husbands. Remember many men would be tyrants if they could. If particular care and attention is not paid to the ladies, we are determined to [instigate] a rebellion, and will not hold ourselves bound by any laws in which we have no voice or representation.

That some men are naturally tyrannical is a truth so thoroughly established as to admit of no dispute. But such of you as wish to be happy willingly give up the harsh title of master for the more tender and endearing one of friend. Why, then, not put it out of the power of the vicious and the lawless to use us with cruelty and indignity. . . ? Men of sense in all ages abhor those customs which treat us only as the vassals of men. Regard us then as human beings, placed by providence under your protection, and in imitation of the Supreme Being make use of that power only for our happiness.

Abigail Adams (detail), 1766, BENJAMIN BLYTH. Massachusetts Historical Society, Boylston.

John Adams to Abigail

April 14, 1776

As to your extraordinary code of laws, I cannot but laugh. We have been told that our struggle has loosened the bands of government everywhere. That children and apprentices were disobedient—that schools and colleges were grown turbulent—that Indians slighted their guardians and slaves grew insolent to their masters. But your letter was the first intimation that another tribe more numerous and powerful than all the rest [had] grown discontented. This is rather too coarse a compliment, but you are so saucy, I won't blot it out.

Depend upon it, we know better than to repeal our masculine systems. Although they are in full force, you know they are little more than theory. We dare not exert our power in its full latitude. We are obliged to go fair and softly, and in practice, you know, we are the subjects. We have only the name of masters, and rather than give up this, which would completely subject us to the despotism of the petticoat, I hope General Washington, and all our brave heroes would fight.

John Adams (detail), 1766, BENJAMIN BLYTH. Massachusetts Historical Society, Boylston.

Developing Comprehension Skills

1. What does Abigail ask of her husband as he works on the Declaration of Independence?

2. What arguments does Abigail give to support her request?

3. What is "the tribe" that John Adams says has grown discontented? Why does he say that men should not give in to this tribe?

4. Do you think John loved Abigail? Did he respect her? What clues in his letter lead you to your conclusion?

5. What is John's attitude towards Abigail's suggestion? Do you think he treated it less seriously than she would have liked?

6. Look again at the Declaration of Independence. Does it seem to reflect Abigail's wishes? What else do you think she would have liked to include?

Reading Literature

1. **Appreciating the Tone of a Letter.** Clues to the writer's tone, or attitude, are often found

in the words chosen by the writer. What is the tone of Abigail's letter? What is the tone of John's letter? What words or phrases provide clues to the tone of each letter? Can the tone of a letter be humorous yet serious at the same time? Explain your answer.

2. **Understanding Audience and Purpose.** Most letters are written with only one person in mind. These are personal letters. How can you tell that John's letter to Abigail was personal? What is it about both of these letters that makes them appealing to a larger audience? How would you feel about others reading your personal letters? Explain your reasons.

3. **Appreciating Humorous Exaggeration.** A way a writer can create humor or make a point is through exaggeration. For example, Abigail writes that women might rebel if care and attention are not given to them. Does she really believe in a possible revolution by women? How does John use exaggeration in his letter to create a humorous mood in the first paragraph?

Developing Vocabulary Skills

Identifying Colloquial Expressions. A colloquial expression is a word or phrase that is common in informal speaking or writing. One type of colloquialism is the **idiom**. This is a word or phrase that has a meaning other than what the actual words suggest. For example, the phrase *lost my head* has nothing to do with an accident.

John Adams, in his letter to his wife, uses the colloquialism "the petticoat" when he refers to women. Examples of more modern colloquialisms are *josh*, *hold out for*, *horse sense*, and *pull someone's leg*.

Explain the meanings of the following colloquialisms. You may need to use a dictionary. Write down a more formal word that has the same meaning.

1. buddy
2. pesky
3. up the creek
4. hotfoot
5. missed the boat
6. monkeyshine
7. slip-up
8. sizzler
9. straight
10. shrimp
11. pussyfoot
12. had an earful

Developing Writing Skills

1. **Contrasting Ideas.** A contrast points out the differences between two or more things or ideas. Write a paragraph contrasting Abigail Adams with Jefferson's "ideal" woman.

Pre-Writing. Reread Abigail Adams's letter to her husband. From the ideas in her letter, you should be able to infer, or guess, the type of woman she was. For example, was Abigail Adams shy or outspoken? Was she independent? Was she intelligent? List the traits you identify. Then list the qualities or traits that Jefferson might expect a lady to have. Reread Jefferson's letter to his daughter to refresh your memory. Finally, compare your two lists.

Writing. Begin your paragraph with a topic sentence that states the main idea of your paragraph about Abigail Adams. Then, in the remainder of the paragraph, explain *how* she was different from Jefferson's ideal. Develop the topic sentence with at least three differences. Support each idea with passages from the letters.

Revising. As you revise, work in an editing group with some of your classmates. One person could check to see that you have clearly explained the differences between Abigail Adams and Jefferson's ideal woman. Another could check to see that your ideas flow smoothly. A third could proofread the draft for errors. Use the comments from each of your readers to write a clean, final copy.

2. **Writing a Letter.** Imagine the next letter that Abigail Adams might have written to John after reading his letter of April 14, 1776. In this letter, respond to John's statement that women are really in charge. Before you write, think about the tone of your letter. Will it be serious, light, or both?

Developing Skills in Critical Thinking

Recognizing Overgeneralizations. A **generalization** is a broad statement based upon several specific facts. Suppose, for example, that you observed a certain kind of automobile in a garage for repairs. The next day you observed another car of the same make in the garage for repairs. If this happened several more times, you might make this generalization: "Brand X automobiles often need repairs."

An **overgeneralization** is a broad generalization about people, things, or ideas. It is usually based upon an insufficient number of facts. For example, if you said "*All* Brand X automobiles are unreliable," you would be making an overgeneralization. Certainly not all cars of any type break down. The word *all* is a clue to an overgeneralization. So are words such as *every*, *none*, *always*, and *never*. Whenever possible, generalizations should be modified with such words as *most*, *some*, *often*, and *seldom*. Otherwise the statements may be unfair or harmful.

What overgeneralizations are made by Abigail and John Adams in their letters? Why are they overgeneralizations? Why might they be harmful?

Letter from Abigail to John Adams, dated March 31, 1776 (detail). Massachusetts Historical Society, Boylston.

Chapter 3 Review

Using Your Skills in Reading Literature

The following is part of a letter from the revolutionary period. It was written from Valley Forge on December 23, 1777. George Washington wrote the letter after his leadership had been criticized. Read the paragraph. Then explain the purpose and the tone of the letter. Use punctuation clues to help you find idea groups as you read.

> As a proof of the little benefit received from a clothier-general, and as a further proof of the inability of an army, under the circumstances of this, to perform the common duties of soldiers, . . . we have, by a field-return this day made, no less than two thousand eight hundred and ninety-eight men now in camp unfit for duty, because they are barefoot and otherwise naked. . . . Our numbers fit for duty, from the hardships and exposures they have undergone, particularly on account of blankets (numbers having been obliged, and still are, to sit up all night by fires, instead of taking comfortable rest in a natural and common way), have decreased near two thousand men.

Using Your Comprehension Skills

The following passage is from the story "The Devil and Daniel Webster" that you will read in Chapter Five. Read the passage carefully. Tell which statements are fact and which are opinion. Decide if the passage contains slanted writing. If so, which words have strong connotations?

> There was a man named Jabez Stone, lived at Cross Corners, New Hampshire. He wasn't a bad man to start with, but he was an unlucky man. If he planted corn, he got borers; if he planted potatoes, he got blight. He had good enough land, but it didn't prosper him; he had a decent wife and children, but the more children he had, the less there was to feed them. If stones cropped up in his neighbor's field, boulders boiled up in his; if he had a horse with the spavins, he'd trade it for one with the staggers and give something extra. There's some folks bound to be like that, apparently. But one day Jabez Stone got sick of the whole business.

Using Your Vocabulary Skills

Read the following sentences from Chapter Five. Identify each sentence as formal, informal, or nonstandard English. Then rewrite the nonstandard and the formal sentences to make them standard informal English.

1. After that, all of a sudden, things began to pick up and prosper for Jabez Stone.

2. "Well, I admit I made time," said Jabez.

3. That was Miser Stevens' voice! And he ain't dead! You can't tell me he is!

4. "Sir," said I, "or Madam, truly your forgiveness I implore."

5. Why should we live with such hurry and waste of life?

6. Such has been the patient sufferance of the women under this government, and such is now the necessity which constrains them to demand the equal station to which they are entitled.

Using Your Writing Skills

Choose one of the writing assignments below.

1. Much of the literature of the revolutionary period deals with political and social change. Choose three such selections from this chapter. Explain the type of reform each author is asking for. Also tell how successful you think the writing was.

2. The revolutionary period was a time of national crisis. Action was taken to solve the country's problems. Think about a personal problem or crisis that you have experienced. Write a composition telling about your experience. Also, tell about any actions that you took to solve your problem.

Using Your Skills in Study and Research

Use the SQ3R method to study the selections by Benjamin Franklin. Then decide in what ways the method helped you to learn the material.

CHAPTER FOUR

Techniques Writers Use

Bursting Star, about 1885, ELIZABETH MOHLER and MARY MARTZALL. Mennonite pieced quilt. Courtesy of American Hurrah Antiques, New York.

Using the Sounds of Language

A good writer thinks about more than what a word means. He or she also considers how a word sounds. The sound of a well-chosen word can strengthen a mood or make an idea more forceful. The sounds of words can also create a musical quality in a piece of writing. In this chapter, you will learn about the following ways that writers use the sounds of language:

alliteration	consonance	rhythm
assonance	rhyme	onomatopoeia

Seascape, 1906, THOMAS MORAN. The Brooklyn Museum, gift of the Executors of the Estate of Colonel Michael Friedsam. New York.

Alliteration

> **Alliteration** is the repetition of a consonant sound at the beginning of words.
>
> Examples:　<u>r</u>ipped and <u>r</u>agged　　<u>s</u>teal the <u>s</u>cene
> 　　　　　　<u>l</u>ost <u>l</u>ove　　　　　<u>g</u>reedily <u>g</u>rasped

Alliteration in Prose.　Alliteration is one of the most common techniques in writing. Many phrases that use alliteration, such as "wild and woolly" and "do or die," have become familiar in everyday speech. Writers can add to their readers' enjoyment by using alliteration. Writers can also use alliteration to emphasize important words in a sentence. Notice how the repetition of sounds calls attention to words in these examples:

Every sweet has its sour, every evil its good.
> —Ralph Waldo Emerson, "Compensation"

Fondly do we hope—fervently do we pray—that this mighty scourge of war may speedily pass away.
> —Abraham Lincoln, Second Inaugural Address

Life is made up of marble and mud.
> —Nathaniel Hawthorne, *The House of the Seven Gables*

Alliteration in Poetry.　Poets can call attention to certain words in a line of poetry by using alliteration. They can also use alliteration to create a pleasant, rhythmic effect. In the following poetic lines, notice how alliteration is used to emphasize words and to create rhythm:

Give me the splendid silent sun with all his beams full-dazzling!
> —Walt Whitman, "Give Me the Splendid Silent Sun"

Love, leave me like the light,
　The gently passing day;
> —Countee Cullen, "If You Should Go"

Alliteration also can add to the mood of a poem. If a poet repeats soft, melodious sounds, a calm or dignified mood can result. If harsh, hard sounds are repeated, on the other hand, the mood can become tense or excited. In this poem, alliteration of the *s*, *l*, and *f* sounds adds to a hushed, peaceful mood:

> Softer be they than slippered sleep
> the lean lithe deer
> the fleet flown deer.
>
> > —e. e. cummings, "All in green went my love riding"

Exercises: Using Alliteration

A. Identify the consonant sounds that are repeated in the following examples. Try to see how the alliteration emphasizes ideas, creates rhythm, or contributes to mood.

1. The slow steps that made the movement piled up and piled up until the continent was crossed.
   > —John Steinbeck, "The Leader of the People"

2. The men and women richly sang
   In land of gold and green and red,
   The bells of merriment richly rang.
   > —Gwendolyn Brooks, "The Womanhood"

3. Happy is the house that shelters a friend.
   > —Ralph Waldo Emerson, "Friendship"

4. The soul selects her own society,
   Then shuts the door.
   > —Emily Dickinson, "The Soul Selects Her Own
   > Society"

B. Write several sentences describing a special tradition. Use alliteration at least twice to emphasize ideas or to add to a mood.

Assonance

> **Assonance** is the repetition of the same vowel sound within words.
>
> Examples: l<u>ow</u> m<u>oa</u>n   g<u>e</u>t r<u>ea</u>dy, g<u>e</u>t s<u>e</u>t

Assonance in Prose.   Like alliteration, assonance can both strengthen ideas and create a musical feeling. Assonance can also make certain words stand out in a sentence. In this sentence, for example, assonance calls attention to two important words:

> These are the times that try men's souls . . . .
>
> —Thomas Paine, "The Crisis"

Assonance can also emphasize a mood. For example, repeating the long vowels *i*, *e*, and *o* in this passage creates a feeling of freedom:

> High above everything, the wheel of fields, house, and cabins, and the deep road surrounding like a moat to keep them in, was the turning sky . . . . Even in the house the earth was sweet to breathe.
>
> —Eudora Welty, "Livvie"

In contrast, the repetition of clipped, short vowel sounds at the end of this sentence from the same story creates a trapped feeling:

> And sound asleep while all this went around him that was his, Solomon was like a little still spot in the middle.

Notice that alliteration is also used in the above example. Alliteration and assonance often work together to create a mood or emphasize ideas.

Assonance in Poetry.   Poets, too, repeat vowel sounds to stress words or ideas. Assonance can also be used simply to add a musical quality to a poem. Finally, assonance can help to set the mood of a poem. In general, long vowel sounds suggest either a free, joyful mood or an eerie mood. Short vowel sounds usually suggest a harsher, tighter, or more delicate mood.

Notice the assonance of the long vowel sounds in the following example. What effect does this create for the reader?

He who, from zone to zone,
Guides through the boundless sky thy certain flight,
In the long way that I must tread alone,
    Will lead my steps aright.

> —William Cullen Bryant, "To a Waterfowl"

Notice the different effect that the assonance of short vowel sounds has in the following poem:

Night's brittle song, sliver-thin
Shatters into a billion fragments
Of quiet shadows

> —Frank Marshall Davis, "Four Glimpses of Night"

Exercises: Using Assonance

A. Find the examples of assonance in the following selections.

1. Then the valley of ashes opened out on both sides of us.
   > —F. Scott Fitzgerald, *The Great Gatsby*

2. I am Anne Rutledge who sleeps beneath these weeds,
   Beloved in life of Abraham Lincoln,
   > —Edgar Lee Masters, *Spoon River Anthology*

3. As for me, give me liberty or give me death.
   > —Patrick Henry, *The Call to Arms*

4. Alone with only wind, with only ice,
   The moss is growing, clinging to the stone;
   > —Owen Dodson, "Epitaph for a Negro Woman"

B. Write two descriptive sentences that include assonance of long vowel sounds. Then write two more sentences that contain assonance of short vowel sounds. Try to use the assonance to create a specific mood.

Consonance

> **Consonance** is the repetition of consonant sounds within and at the end of words.
>
> Examples: la<u>t</u>e a<u>t</u> nigh<u>t</u>   ha<u>r</u>d-hea<u>r</u>ted
>   sho<u>r</u>t and swee<u>t</u>   fi<u>r</u>e and wate<u>r</u>

Consonance in Prose. Writers can use consonance to make words stand out or to link related words together. Notice the important words, for example, that are linked by the repetition of the consonant *l* sound in the following sentence:

> Chicago seemed an unreal city whose mythical houses were built of slabs of black coal wreathed in palls of gray smoke . . . .
> —Richard Wright, *American Hunger*

In this example, consonance of the *r* sound not only emphasizes words, but also creates a rhythm, or regular movement:

> The crash. The attic smashing into kitchen and parlor. The parlor into cellar, cellar into sub-cellar.
> —Ray Bradbury, "There Will Come Soft Rains"

Consonance is often used along with assonance and alliteration to create a powerful effect. Can you find examples of the other two devices in the above examples?

Consonance in Poetry. Poets use consonance both for re-creating sounds and for emphasizing words. Consonance can add a musical quality and rhythm to poetry. Notice how consonance adds rhythm to the poems that follow:

> And come to the front door mother, here's a letter from thy dear son,
> —Walt Whitman, "Come Up from the Fields, Father"

> I turned aside and bowed my head and wept.
> —Claude McKay, "The Tropics in New York"

In the next example, repetition of the *sh* sound helps create the sound of fish swishing by. Both consonance and alliteration are used to emphasize important words:

> birches like zebra fish
> flash by in a pack.
>
> —Anne Sexton, "The Fortress"

Exercise: Using Consonance

Find examples of consonance in each example below. Try to explain how consonance helps to create rhythm and stress important ideas.

1. The good and the bad and the worst and the best
   Have gone to their eternal rest.
   > —Edgar Allan Poe, "The City in the Sea"

2. Our tragedy today is a general and universal physical fear so long sustained by now that we can even bear it.
   > —William Faulkner, Nobel Prize Acceptance Speech

3. Avoid the reeking herd,
       Shun the polluted flock,
   Live like that stoic bird
       The eagle of the rock.
   > —Elinor Wylie, "The Eagle and the Mole"

4. Except when he was steering a big log down the mountain to his mill he had never known such a thrilling sense of mastery.
   > —Edith Wharton, *Ethan Frome*

Rhyme

Rhyme is the repetition of sounds at the ends of words. Rhyme may involve one or more syllables.

> Example: Listen my children, and you shall hear
> Of the midnight ride of Paul Revere
> —Henry Wadsworth Longfellow,
> "Paul Revere's Ride"

Rhyme in Prose.   Rhyme is not common in prose. It is used mainly in poetry, where sound is very important. However, rhyme is sometimes used to make sayings or proverbs easy to remember. For example:

> He that would live in peace and at ease, must not speak all he knows, nor judge all he sees.
> —Benjamin Franklin, *Poor Richard's Almanack*

Occasionally, rhyme is used to call attention to an idea in prose. In the following dialogue, for example, the rhyming of *light* and *night* emphasizes two important ideas:

> "I am of those who like to stay late at the café," the older waiter said. "With all those who do not want to go to bed. With all those who need a light for the night."
> —Ernest Hemingway, "A Clean, Well-Lighted Place"

Rhyme makes this ending to a famous short story effective and memorable:

> Ah, Bartleby! Ah, humanity!
> —Herman Melville, "Bartleby, the Scrivener"

Rhyme in Poetry.   Rhyme helps to make poetry musical and pleasant to hear. Usually, rhyme occurs at the ends of lines. The pattern of this end rhyme is called the **rhyme scheme** of the poem.

Letters are used to label the rhyme scheme of a poem. Each rhyming sound is assigned a different letter. Lines that rhyme are given the same letter. Notice how this was done in the following poem:

The railroad track is miles away	*a*
And the day is loud with voices speaking,	*b*
Yet there isn't a train goes by all day	*a*
But I hear its whistle shrieking.	*b*

—Edna St. Vincent Millay, "Travel"

Sometimes rhyme is not exact. In that case, it is known as **off-rhyme**. The last words of these lines are examples of off-rhyme:

For of all sad words of tongue or pen,	*a*
The saddest are these: "It might have been!"	*a*

—John Greenleaf Whittier, "Maud Muller"

While end rhyme is the most common kind of rhyme, sometimes words within a line rhyme. This kind of rhyme is called **internal rhyme**. In the following lines of poetry, for example, *trip* and *ship* rhyme:

The ship is anchored safe and sound, its voyage closed and done,
From fearful trip the victor ship comes home with object won:

—Walt Whitman, "O Captain! My Captain!"

Exercises: Using Rhyme

A. Identify the rhyme scheme of each excerpt.

1. And o'er his heart a shadow
    Fell as he found
    No spot of ground
  That looked like Eldorado.
            —Edgar Allan Poe, "Eldorado"

2. Chained in the market-place he stood,
    A man of giant frame,
  Amid the gathering multitude
    That shrunk to hear his name.
            —William Cullen Bryant, "The African Chief"

B. Write a four-line poem using the *a b c b* rhyme scheme.

Rhythm

> **Rhythm** is the pattern of stressed (/) and unstressed (⌣) syllables in a sentence or a line of poetry. The pattern is shown by marking syllables with these symbols, as follows:
>
> Example: There is no frigate like a book
> To take us lands away,
>
> —Emily Dickinson, "A Book"

Rhythm in Prose. The rhythm of prose follows the natural rhythms of speech. Of course, writers try to match the rhythm of their writing to the mood of their subject matter. Pauses, punctuation, and many stressed syllables all slow down the rhythm, for example. Short words and brief sentences speed it up. Notice how the writer uses a slow rhythm to build suspense in this story:

> I turned—I gasped for breath. For a moment, I experienced all the pangs of suffocation; I became blind, and deaf, and giddy; and then, some invisible fiend, I thought, struck me with his broad palm up on the back. The long-imprisoned secret burst forth from my soul.
>
> —Edgar Allan Poe, "The Imp of the Perverse"

Rhythm in Poetry. Through the use of rhythm, poets can bring out the mood and meaning of a poem. For example, a quick rhythm with many unaccented syllables suggests excitement and movement. A slow rhythm with many accents and pauses, on the other hand, seems dignified or sorrowful.

Notice how many unaccented syllables create a lively pace in this poem:

Quick!
Empty the offices
rush all the lecture halls
Abandon the copying machines
burst out   —Eve Merriam, "Blue Alert"

In the next poem, a slow rhythm results from many accented syllables and long vowel sounds. The measured pace creates a thoughtful, peaceful mood:

The woods are lovely, dark and deep,
But I have promises to keep,
And miles to go before I sleep.

> —Robert Frost, "Stopping by Woods on a Snowy
> Evening"

Exercises: Using Rhythm

A. Describe the rhythm in this poem. How does it reflect the ideas that are presented?

I wake to sleep, and take my waking slow.
I feel my fate in what I cannot fear.
I learn by going where I have to go.

> —Theodore Roethke, "The Waking"

B. In the following selection, how does the writer use the rhythms of language to suggest the movement of a bullfight?

The bull's tail went up and he charged, and Romero moved his arms ahead of the bull, wheeling, his feet firmed. The dampened, mud-weighted cape swung open and full as a sail fills, and Romero pivoted with it just ahead of the bull. At the end of the pass they were facing each other again. Romero smiled. The bull wanted it again . . . .

> —Ernest Hemingway, *The Sun Also Rises*

C. Copy the poem on page 38. Mark the stressed and unstressed syllables.

Onomatopoeia

> **Onomatopoeia** is the use of words that imitate sounds.
>
> Examples: buzz, meow, splat, vroom, rat-a-tat

Onomatopoeia in Prose.   When prose writers describe sounds, they often use words that imitate those sounds. These words may have begun as echoic, or sound-imitating words. They may also have been invented by a writer to suggest a sound. Find the onomatopoeia in the following example:

> As the craft plopped her stern down again the spray splashed past them. . . . There was a long, loud swishing astern of the boat.
>
> —Stephen Crane, "The Open Boat"

Onomatopoeia in Poetry.   Onomatopoeia can add excitement to the sound of a poem. Notice how one poet suggests sounds in this poem:

> You can hear her holler and whine and cry.
> Her voice is thin and her moan is high,
> And her cackling laugh or her barking cold
> Bring terror to the young and old.
>
> —Margaret Walker, "Molly Means"

Exercises: Using Onomatopoeia

A. Find the onomatopoeia in the following sentences and lines:

1. The rattle and bang of the frying pan was grating horribly on my nerves.
   —Jack London, *Sea Wolf*

2. And where the bugs buzz by in private cars
   Across old peach cans and old jelly jars.
   —Gwendolyn Brooks, "The Birth in a Narrow Room"

B. Use onomatopoeia in three sentences to imitate the sounds of three machines or three animals. Use actual echoic words or invent your own.

Using Figures of Speech

Writers often use words in a special way to create their own unique vision of the world. An imaginative and powerful way to express an idea or describe something is by using **figurative language**. In this section, you will learn about the following figures of speech:

simile   personification
metaphor   hyperbole

Character Before the Sun, 1968, JOAN MIRÓ. The Joan Miró Foundation, Barcelona. Copyright © 1985 A.D.A.G.P., Paris/V.A.G.A., New York.

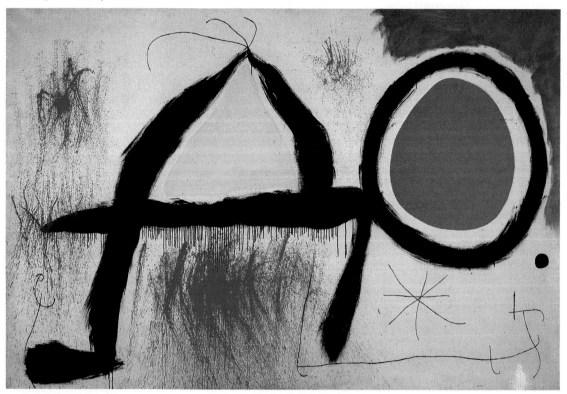

Simile

> A **simile** is a comparison between two unlike things. It uses the words *like* or *as*.
>
> Examples: The ball shot over home plate like a white bullet.
> Vacation went by as fast as a flea's wink.

Similes in Prose. With a simile, a writer can help readers to see things in a fresh, original way. Often, a simile creates an actual picture, or image, in the reader's mind. A good simile may seem surprising at first, because the things it compares are so different. However, this difference allows the one or two similarities to have an even greater impact.

What is compared in the following examples? How do the similes create a picture? What characteristics of the subject does each one stress?

The craft pranced and reared and plunged like an animal. As each wave came and she rose for it, she seemed like a horse making at a fence, outrageously high.

—Stephen Crane, "The Open Boat"

Your true dull minds are preferred for public employ . . . your keen intellects, like razors, being considered too sharp for common service.

—Washington Irving, *Knickerbocker's History of New York*

. . . the land and the brush and the houses and the trees were silver-grey and black like a photograph negative. . . .

—John Steinbeck, "The Red Pony"

Similes can also add to the mood of a piece of writing. In the following example, a simile helps to create a pleasant feeling:

The pillow rose and floated under her, pleasant as a hammock in a light wind.

—Katherine Ann Porter, "The Jilting of Granny Weatherall"

Similes in Poetry. In poetry, too, similes help to create striking sensory images. They also help the reader experience the mood of the poem. Try to see the images that the similes create in the following poems.

> A storm half out to sea kept turning around like a dog trying to settle himself on a rug:
>
> —John Updike, "Wash"

> Grass nibbling inward
> Like green fire
>
> —Mark Van Doren, "Farmer Barn Lot"

Exercises: Using Similes

A. Explain the two unlike things that are compared in each of the following similes.

1. Arithmetic is where numbers fly like pigeons in and out of your head.
   —Carl Sandburg, "Arithmetic"
2. The men were thrown into space like a dozen wriggling silverfish.
   —Ray Bradbury, "Kaleidoscope"
3. Her face is closed as a nut,
   closed as a careful snail
   or a thousand-year-old seed.
   —Elizabeth Bishop, "House Guest"

B. Write three similes about a single subject. Try to choose comparisons that are surprising, yet meaningful. You may want to write about one of the following: a skyscraper, a telephone, a siren, a desert, a breeze.

Metaphor

A **metaphor** is a figure of speech comparing two unlike things that have something in common. Unlike similes, metaphors do not use the words *like* or *as*.

Examples: Nature's calling cards are blooming in the garden.
The train is a needle plunging into the fabric of night.

Metaphors in Prose.   Prose writers frequently use metaphors to describe something in an unusual way. Metaphors can often express more meaning than a direct statement. They also may suggest a mood and leave a lasting image. In the following metaphor, what do two unlike things have in common?

Beauty without grace is the hook without the bait.
—Ralph Waldo Emerson, "Beauty"

Notice how writers emphasize their ideas through metaphors in the following examples:

A whale ship was my Yale College and my Harvard.
—Herman Melville, *Moby Dick*

He had considered a visit to their weed-strewn graves but hadn't the heart at the last minute. The past was a wound in the head.
—Bernard Malamud, *The Fixer*

Metaphors in Poetry.   Poetry, too, contains metaphors that present ideas, feelings, and images vividly. In these examples, notice what is compared and what makes the comparison fitting:

the brittle treacherous bright
streets
of memory
—e.e. cummings, "Along the little treacherous bright streets"

I'm sorry that country is not in working order.
I'm sorry that planet is out of service.

> —Eve Merriam, "I'm sorry said the machine"

An **extended metaphor** compares two subjects in a number of ways.
The following extended metaphor compares parts of a person to geographical areas:

The Heart is the capital of the Mind,
The Mind is a single State;
The Heart and the Mind together make
A single continent.

> —Emily Dickinson, "The Heart Is the Capital of
> the Mind"

Exercises: Using Metaphors

A. Explain the comparison in each of the following metaphors. What makes
each comparison a good one?

1. Mountains are earth's undecaying monuments.
> —Nathaniel Hawthorne, *Sketches from Memory*

2. Time is a sandpile we run our fingers in.
> —Carl Sandburg, "Hotel Girl"

3.   The last cobwebs
   of fog in the
   black firtrees are flakes
   of white ash in the world's hearth.
   > —Denise Levertov, "The Depths"

B. Write three original metaphors. You might begin by asking yourself to what
you can compare the following: friends, headlights, rain, fire, music, laughter,
watermelon. Your answers may suggest ideas for metaphors.

Personification

Personification is another kind of comparison. It gives human qualities to an object, an animal, an idea, or a place.

Examples: The ocean swallowed the small boat.
One lonely star looked down from the sky.

Personification in Prose. Personification can create a strong, surprising picture in a reader's mind. It can also help to set a mood or emphasize an idea. Notice what is personified in the following examples.

Habit is habit, and not to be flung out of the window by any man, but coaxed downstairs a step at a time.
—Mark Twain, *Pudd'nhead Wilson*

Slang is a language that rolls up its sleeves, spits on its hands, and goes to work. —Carl Sandburg

No barrier of the senses shuts me out from the sweet, gracious discourse of my book-friends. They talk to me without embarrassment or awkwardness. —Helen Keller, *The Story of My Life*

Personification in Poetry. Personification can have a powerful effect on a poem. It can add to the mood and meaning. It can also allow the reader to "see" something that might not otherwise be visible. What non-human things are given human traits in these poems?

Hog Butcher for the World,
Tool Maker, Stacker of Wheat,
Player with the Railroads and the Nation's Freight Handler;
Stormy, husky, brawling,
City of the Big Shoulders.
—Carl Sandburg, "Chicago"

A narrow wind complains all day
How some one treated him:
—Emily Dickinson, "The Sky Is Low, the
Clouds Are Mean"

Exercises: Using Personification

A. Explain what is personified in each of the following examples. Describe the mood that is created.

1. The starred and stately nights seemed haughty dames in jewelled velvets, nursing at home in lonely pride the memory of their absent conquering Earls, the golden helmeted suns!
   —Herman Melville, *Moby Dick*

2. There is a Reaper whose name is Death,
      And, with his sickle keen,
   He reaps the bearded grain at a breath,
      And the flowers that grow between.
                    —Henry Wadsworth Longfellow, "The Reaper
                       and the Flowers"

3. I like trees because they seem more resigned to the way they have to live than other things do.
   —Willa Cather, *O Pioneers!*

B. Use personification as you write descriptions of two of the following. Think carefully about what aspects can be compared to a human.

a car	a streetlamp	a spider	a ferris wheel
a jukebox	a stereo	an onion	a vending machine

Hyperbole

> **Hyperbole** is exaggeration. It creates a striking impression that is sometimes humorous.
>
> Examples:　The speaker droned on forever.
> 　　　　　　I'm melting in this heat.

Hyperbole in Prose. Hyperbole is used most often in humorous writing. It can surprise readers, often with a funny and wildly exaggerated image. The following example of hyperbole is from a tall tale about Paul Bunyan and Babe, the blue ox:

> Hitched onto the end of this wiggly road, which by luck was on a level stretch, Babe . . . kept going until he pulled her straight.

Hyperbole can also be used to make a point. What idea does exaggeration emphasize in these examples:

> A mob's a monster; heads enough but no brains.
> 　　　—Benjamin Franklin, *Poor Richard's Almanack*

> You can fool all of the people some of the time, and some of the people all of the time, but you cannot fool all the people all of the time.
> 　　　—Abraham Lincoln

Hyperbole in Poetry. Humorous poetry often uses hyperbole. It may create the kind of ridiculous image typical of a tall tale.

> He could fiddle all the bugs off a sweet-potato vine.
> 　　　—Stephen Vincent Benét, "The Mountain
> 　　　　Whippoorwill"

Hyperbole jolts readers with a surprising image. It can be used to get readers' attention and to highlight an idea, as in these examples:

> To make a prairie it takes a clover and a bee,
> One clover, and a bee,
> 　　　—Emily Dickinson, "To Make a Prairie"

I think that I shall never see
A billboard lovely as a tree.
Indeed, unless the billboards fall
I'll never see a tree at all.

    —Ogden Nash, "Song of the Open Road"

Exercises: Using Hyperbole

A. Explain what is exaggerated in each of the following passages. What is the purpose of each example of hyperbole?

1. Soap and education are not as sudden as a massacre, but they are more deadly.   —Mark Twain, "The Facts Concerning the Recent Resignation"

2. A door is what a dog is perpetually on the wrong side of.
    —Ogden Nash, "A Dog's Best Friend Is His Illiteracy"

3. A sensational event was changing from the brown suit to the gray the contents of his pockets. He was earnest about these objects. They were of eternal importance, like baseball or the Republican party.
    —Sinclair Lewis, *Babbitt*

4. Then if my friendships break and bend,
   There's little need to cry
The while I know that every foe
   Is faithful till I die.
    —Dorothy Parker, "The Leal"

B. Write your own hyperbole. While it may have a humorous effect, write it to make a point.

Chapter 4 *Review*

Understanding the Sounds of Language

Read each of the following passages carefully. Find examples of alliteration, assonance, consonance, rhyme, rhythm, and onomatopoeia. Then explain how each technique helps the reader to understand or appreciate the selection.

1. Forget me for a month, a year,
       But, oh, beloved, think of me
    When unexpected beauty burns
       Like sudden sunlight on the sea.

    —Sara Teasdale, "Vignettes Overseas: Off Algiers"

2. The gondola rumbled and lurched into the shed at the top; an attendant opened the door, and there was a howling mixed of wind and of boys whooping to keep warm.

    —John Updike, "Man and Daughter in the Cold"

Understanding Figures of Speech

In the following selections, find at least one example of each of the following figures of speech: simile, metaphor, personification, hyperbole. Explain each figure of speech and the idea it emphasizes.

1. the wise trees
    stand sleeping in the cold.

    —William Carlos Williams, "Winter Trees"

2. Bill wrestled the bear and tossed it around until the bear put its paws over its head and begged for mercy. Bill couldn't talk yet, but he patted the bear to show that he didn't have any hard feelings. After that, the bear followed Bill around like a big, flat-footed puppy.

    —"Pecos Bill," retold by Adrien Stoutenburg

3. It is morning, I awake from a bed of silence,
    Shining I rise from the starless waters of sleep.

    —Conrad Aiken, "Morning Song from 'Senlin' "

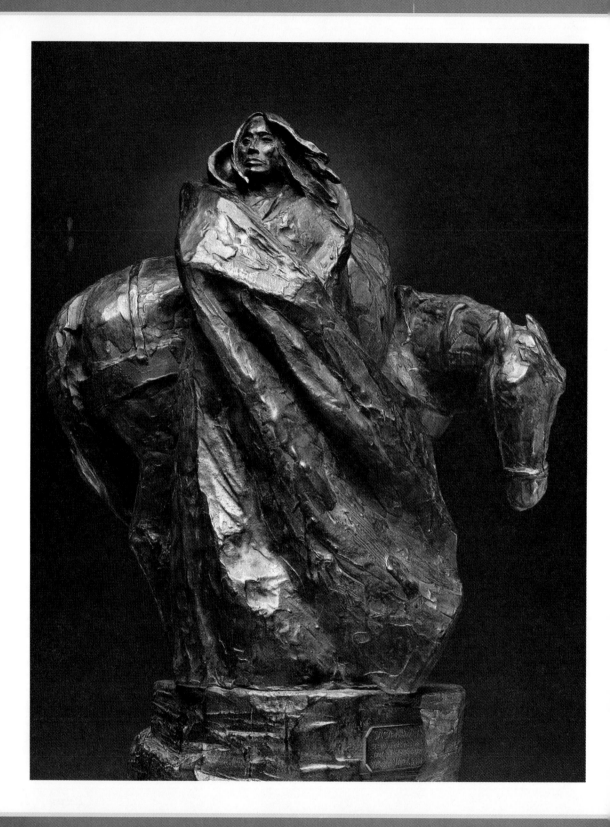

CHAPTER FIVE

The Early National Period (1800—1855)

Sacagawea with Pack Horse, 1978, HARRY JACKSON.
Copyright © Harry Jackson 1985. Photograph by Marcello Bertoni,
© WFS, Inc. 1985. Cody, Wyoming.

Historical Background
The Early National Period (1800–1855)

The Growth of a Nation

With the struggle for independence over, Americans in the early 1800's turned their attention to the problems and challenges of a developing nation. One of the most obvious changes was in the growth of the country itself.

In 1803, Thomas Jefferson persuaded Congress to approve the Louisiana Purchase. As a result of this agreement with France, the area of the United States was doubled. In 1804, Meriwether Lewis and William Clark set out to explore the vast territory west of the Mississippi River, all the way to the Pacific Ocean. The information they collected helped to open up the western frontier for settlement.

The War of 1812 also helped to open up the western frontier. This war was fought between the United States and Britain over shipping rights. However, the situation was often used as an excuse to push Native Americans from an increasingly attractive frontier. By the end of the war, the Native Americans had been forced much farther west.

1800	1805	1810	1815	1820	1825	1830

Literature

- **1814** *Lewis and Clark Expedition Journal* published
- **1819** Washington Irving publishes first volume of short stories, *The Sketch Book*
- **1823** James Fenimore Cooper publishes *The Pioneers*
- **1830** Oliver Wendell Holmes writes poem "Old Ironsides"

History

- **1801** Thomas Jefferson becomes President
- **1803** U.S. purchases Louisiana Territory from France
- **1804** Lewis and Clark begin exploration of Louisiana Territory
- **1812** U.S. goes to war with Britain in War of 1812
- **1820** Missouri Compromise bans slavery in parts of new territories
- **1828** Andrew Jackson elected President
- **1830** Congress passes the Indian Removal Act

By 1820, the Union had grown to include twenty-three states. As the young nation grew, so did the political power of the common people—those who did not own property. The election of Andrew Jackson as President in 1828 also was a victory for the common people. Jackson's motto was "Let the people rule."

During this time, pioneers continued to push the frontier still farther westward. By 1850, they had reached the Pacific coast. The westward expansion meant that more and more Native Americans were being driven from their lands. Many of them fought back, resulting in bloody battles between Indians and settlers.

During the 1840's, the United States gained even more new territory. In 1845, Congress voted to annex, or add, Texas to the Union. More land was gained in 1846 when Britain agreed to give the southern part of the Oregon territory to the United States. Following the Mexican-American War, Mexico gave the United States all its land between Texas and the Pacific Ocean.

The Development of a National Culture

As the country itself expanded, tremendous growth also occurred in the nation's social and cultural life. The movement for free public education began. Opposition to slavery grew. The women's rights movement also began during this time.

Finally, this period saw great advances in literature and the arts. American writers and artists began to develop their own styles rather than imitate European models. By 1855, a truly American literature had finally developed.

1835	1840	1845	1850	1855	1860	1865

■ **1840** Edgar Allan Poe publishes *Tales of the Grotesque and Arabesque*

■ **1841** Ralph Waldo Emerson publishes essay "Self-Reliance"

■ **1850** Nathaniel Hawthorne publishes *The Scarlet Letter*

■ **1851** Herman Melville publishes *Moby Dick*

■ **1852** Harriet Beecher Stowe publishes *Uncle Tom's Cabin*

■ **1854** Henry David Thoreau publishes *Walden*

1837 Massachusetts establishes first state board of education

1846 Britain gives the southern part of Oregon territory to U.S.

1846 Mexican-American War breaks out

1848 Elizabeth Cady Stanton helps organize first women's rights convention at Seneca Falls, New York

Reading Literature

The American Romantics

Along with the amazing growth of the nation came a tremendous development in literature. Increasingly, American writers looked to themselves rather than to Europe for topics and for inspiration.

American Romanticism

At the beginning of the 1800's, a movement called Romanticism began in Europe. The Romantics believed that too much emphasis had been placed on reason. Instead, they felt that emotion should be stressed over reason, and nature over society. The Romantics celebrated the value of the individual. Folk tales, legends, and the supernatural also interested Romantic writers.

The ideas of the Romantics seemed extremely well suited to the mood and ideals of the country. Closeness to nature and the importance of the individual were important themes of American life. The optimism of the Romantics also seemed well suited to the hopeful attitude of the young, growing country.

Not surprisingly, the first important writers of the 1800's were Romantics. They included James Fenimore Cooper and Washington Irving. Cooper captured the country's imagination with a series of five novels about life on the New York frontier. Irving's most famous works include "The Legend of Sleepy Hollow" and "Rip Van Winkle." These were German folk tales that Irving retold using American settings. Irving's use of the supernatural in these stories was clearly in the Romantic tradition.

The Fireside Poets, another group of Romantic writers, included Henry Wadsworth Longfellow and Oliver Wendell Holmes. Generally, their poetry was humorous, morally uplifting, or romantic. Families often read these poems aloud while sitting around the fireplace.

The Transcendentalist writers also were part of the Romantic tradition. American Transcendentalism (tran'sen den't'l iz'm) was a movement that developed in the 1830's in the Boston area. Its followers believed that there are kinds of knowledge that transcend, or go beyond, reason and experience. Thus, Transcendentalists urged people to have faith in their own "inner lights." Like other Romantics, they focused on the individual and looked to nature for inspiration.

Ralph Waldo Emerson and Henry David Thoreau are the most famous of the Transcendentalist writers. Emerson was an essayist, poet, philosopher, and leader in the Transcendental movement. He believed in a basic unity between human beings and nature. Emerson thought that the cares of everyday living often prevented people from recognizing this unity. Thoreau, a follower of Emerson, removed himself from most everyday cares when he went to live alone at Walden Pond in Massachussetts. This experience allowed him to test Emerson's ideas about self-reliance. It also resulted in the book *Walden,* one of the great works of American literature.

Edgar Allan Poe, Herman Melville, and Nathaniel Hawthorne also belonged to the Romantic tradition. But unlike the early Romantics and the Transcendentalists, these three giants of the period did not express a hopeful outlook. Instead, their work probed the darker side of human nature.

Poe is ranked among the greatest American short story writers and poets. In fact, he and Nathaniel Hawthorne are credited with inventing the modern short story form.

Hawthorne wrote novels as well as short stories. *The Scarlet Letter,* published in 1850, is considered by some to be the first truly symbolic novel. Herman Melville, author of *Moby-Dick,* was the other great American novelist of the mid-1800's.

The Achievement of American Literature

By 1855, American Literature had clearly come into its own. Just thirty-five years before, the British critic Sydney Smith had scorned American writers, saying: "Literature the Americans have none . . . it is all imported." But by 1855, a truly national literature had developed. These writers experimented with old literary forms and even invented a new one—the short story. The literature of social protest also grew during this period. Antislavery literature and the women's rights movement appealed to the conscience of the nation. American writers produced masterpieces that ranked with the best works in world literature. By 1855, American literature had gained respectability. It was now a literary force to be reckoned with.

Comprehension Skills

Relationships Between Ideas

Have you ever tried to state a difficult idea in only one or two sentences? It is almost impossible to do. Professional writers face the same problem. They usually provide many supporting details. As you read, you must pay attention to how these ideas work together.

Understanding Main Idea and Supporting Details

Writers organize their ideas into paragraphs. The most important idea in each paragraph is called the main idea.

> During the 1840's, the United States gained even more new territory. In 1845, Congress voted to add Texas to the Union. More land was gained in 1846 when Britain gave the southern part of the Oregon territory to the United States. Following the Mexican-American War, Mexico gave the United States all its land between Texas and the Pacific Ocean.

In this paragraph, the main idea is stated in the first sentence. A sentence that states the main idea is called the **topic sentence.** The other sentences develop the main idea with facts, statistics, examples, or anecdotes. Some paragraphs do not have a topic sentence. The reader must infer the main idea from the supporting details.

Understanding Cause and Effect

Events in narrative or explanatory writing are often related by cause and effect. That is, one event may be a cause, or reason, for an effect, or result. Identify the cause and the effect in the following sentences.

> In 1803, Thomas Jefferson persuaded Congress to approve the Louisiana Purchase. As a result of this agreement with France, the area of the United States was doubled.

As a result signals a cause-and-effect relationship. Other words that signal cause-and-effect relationships include *because, for, finally, then, after, before, now, soon, next, since,* and *at last.*

Writers do not always use key words to signal cause-and-effect relationships. However, you still can recognize a cause-and-effect relationship by noticing when one event is responsible for a second event.

Sometimes you must look deeper to find a cause-and-effect relationship because the cause or effect is not stated directly. Such a relationship is called **implied cause and effect.** Look at the following poem:

> as my eyes
> > look over the prairie
> > > I feel summer in the spring

You are not told directly what causes the speaker to "feel summer in the spring." However, you can infer, or guess, that the speaker sees summer flowers or a change in the color that signals the changing seasons.

Exercises: Understanding Relationships Between Ideas

A. Find the main idea of the following paragraph by Henry David Thoreau. Then tell how the other sentences in the paragraph support the main idea.

> Our life is frittered away by detail. An honest man has hardly need to count more than his ten fingers, or in extreme cases he may add his ten toes, and lump the rest. Simplicity, simplicity, simplicity! I say, let your affairs be as two or three, and not a hundred or a thousand; instead of a million count half a dozen, and keep your accounts on your thumb-nail.

B. In each item below, tell which event is the cause and which is the effect.

1. As Rip approached the village he met a number of people, but none of whom he knew, which somewhat surprised him, for he had thought himself acquainted with every one in the country round.

2. I went to the woods because I wished to live deliberately.

3. I think it was his eye! . . . Whenever it fell upon me, my blood ran cold; and so . . . I made up my mind to take the life of the old man. . . .

4. And the biggest case Dan'l argued never got written in the books, for he argued it against the devil, nip and tuck, and no holds barred.

$\mathcal{V}$ocabulary Skills

Context Clues

Whenever you read, you use many different skills. One of these skills involves finding the meaning of unfamiliar words by using *context clues*.

Context means the sentences and paragraphs in which a word appears. Clues to the meaning of a word often can be found in its context.

Definition Clues and Restatement Clues. To help you understand the meaning of a new word, a writer will sometimes **define** it directly.

Euphony is the pleasing or agreeable nature of a sound.

At other times, the writer may **restate** the word in a different way.

Rip's *torpor,* or listlessness, angered his wife.

Several key words and phrases can tell you when a word is being defined or restated. These include *or, is called, that is, who is,* or *in other words*.

In addition, the writer may use punctuation marks to signal that the word is being restated. The restatement can be set off from the rest of the sentence by a comma, a pair of commas, a dash, a pair of dashes, or parentheses.

Synonyms and Antonyms. Sometimes a word is used in context with its synonym. A **synonym** is a word that has the same or almost the same meaning as another. If you recognize the synonym, you can figure out the new word.

I could not bear their *dissembling,* their lying, any longer.

In this case, the word *lying* is a synonym for *dissembling*.

Antonyms can also provide helpful clues. An **antonym** is a word that has an opposite meaning.

Women held *subordinate* positions. They seldom had positions of authority.

Here, *subordinate* and *authority* are opposites.

Examples. An unfamiliar word is sometimes followed by one or more **examples.** By looking at examples, you can often get a good idea of the meaning of the unknown word. At other times, the unfamiliar word itself is used as an example. Then you can determine the meaning from the familiar word it illustrates. Look at this example:

Conifers like the pine, yew, and fir create seeds in the form of cones.

From the examples, you know that a conifer is a type of tree.
Several key words and phrases signal examples. Here are some of the more common ones:

like	such as	for example	this
other	especially	for instance	these

Comparison and Contrast Clues. Writers often use **comparisons** to make the meaning of a word clear. These comparisons are signaled by key words such as *like, also, in addition, as, similar to, both,* and *than.*

His movements were *ungainly,* similar to those of a new-born colt.

A **contrast clue** shows how two ideas are different. Key words that signal contrast are *not, unlike, in contrast to,* and *different from.*

The hike was *arduous,* unlike the pleasant stroll he had in mind.

In this sentence, you can tell that the *arduous* hike contrasts with the pleasant stroll. Therefore, *arduous* means "hard" or "difficult."

Exercise: Using Context Clues

Determine the meaning of each underlined word by using context clues.

1. His <u>rubicund</u> face looked like a glowing red balloon.
2. The people treated Daniel Webster as though he were a great <u>patriarch</u> like Abraham, Isaac, or Jacob.
3. The man hid all evidence of the crime between the <u>scantlings</u>, or supporting timbers, of the wall.
4. He knew he could never <u>dissever</u> his soul from the soul of Annabel Lee. The two would always be united.
5. He fished in the <u>tarn</u> by his cottage and in other nearby mountain lakes.

Prayer at Sunrise

ZUÑI INDIAN

SETTING A PURPOSE

The early Zuñi Indians were desert farmers. What do these farmers offer the sun father? What do they want from him?

Now this day,
My sun father,
Now that you have come out standing
    to your sacred place,
That from which we draw the water
    of life,
Prayer meal,
Here I give to you.
Your long life,
Your old age,
Your waters,
Your seeds,
Your riches,
Your power,
Your strong spirit,
All these to me may you grant.

Cosmic Hands, 1980, LINDA LOMAHAFTEWA
(Hopi). Private Collection.

Developing Comprehension Skills

1. To whom is the poem "Prayer at Sunrise" addressed?

2. The "sacred place" of the sun father is the sky. What, then, is "the water of life"?

3. What does the speaker give to the sun? What does the speaker ask for in return?

4. If the word *sunrise* had not been in the title, how would you know that the time for this prayer is sunrise?

5. The speaker offers a gift to the deity on high, in exchange for benefits. Are these the same benefits you would want? Explain.

Reading Literature

1. **Recognizing a Prayer.** A **prayer** is a special request made to a god or other object of worship. The prayer is part of the **oral tradition** of a people. Oral tradition refers to the myths, legends, folktales, and stories that are passed on by word of mouth.

"Prayer at Sunrise" has special importance for the Zuñi. Why would they repeat this prayer every morning?

2. **Identifying Personification.** The figure of speech that gives human traits to non-human things is called **personification**. For example, you could say "the stars smiled down from the heavens." Native Americans often personified things within nature. In "Prayer at Sunrise," how is the sun personified?

3. **Using Punctuation To Aid Understanding.** In poetry, words within sentences are often written in an order that is different from regular speech. Punctuation can give the reader important clues to the meaning of a sentence in poetry. For example, without the period at the end of line 6, how might the meaning of "Prayer at Sunrise" change?

Read the poem aloud, pausing as each punctuation mark indicates. How do commas and periods help you understand the sentences and the meaning of the prayer?

Spring Song

Native Americans often use tribal songs to express their feelings aloud. What feelings are expressed in the following songs?

OJIBWA INDIAN

as my eyes
   look over the prairie
      I feel the summer in the spring

Darkness Song

IROQUOIS INDIAN

We wait in the darkness!
Come, all ye who listen,
Help in our night journey:
Now no sun is shining;
Now no star is glowing;
Come show us the pathway:
The night is not friendly;
She closes her eyelids;
The moon has forgot us,
We wait in the darkness!

Iroquois face mask of basswood and horsehair, 1920–25. Photograph by Peter Furst.

Developing Comprehension Skills

1. What does the speaker of "Spring Song" mean by "I feel the summer in the spring"?

2. What do you think the speaker might see on the prairie in spring?

3. Who is being addressed in "Darkness Song"? Who is speaking?

4. "We wait in the darkness!" says the speaker of "Darkness Song." What do you think the people are waiting for?

5. Why is the night "not friendly"?

6. In your opinion, what type of relationship do Native Americans seem to have with nature? Do you think modern-day Americans have the same relationship? Explain.

Reading Literature

1. **Understanding Songs.** A song is a form of oral literature. It allows the speaker to express feelings aloud. Melodies and rhythm are used to emphasize these feelings.

   Read the two songs aloud. What feeling do you think inspired the singer in each tribal song? What sort of melody and rhythm would you expect each song to have?

2. **Appreciating Imagery.** Description that appeals to the senses is known as **imagery**. Imagery helps readers to see, hear, feel, taste, or smell the things that are described. Find two examples of imagery in these songs. What pictures do they create in your mind?

3. **Analyzing Personification.** Personification, you will recall, gives human traits to non-human things. Line 9 of "Darkness Song" contains an example of personification: "The moon has forgot us." Find one other example of personification in "Darkness Song." What is personified? How does this help create a strong image for the reader?

4. **Identifying Mood.** The **mood** of a work of literature is the feeling it creates in the reader. What moods are created in the two tribal songs? How do they differ? Which words and images in the two songs are important for creating mood?

Developing Vocabulary Skills

Understanding Synonyms. Sometimes an unfamiliar word is presented with its synonym in context. A **synonym** is a word that has the same or almost the same meaning as another word. Look at the following example:

> Every star was *sacred* to our people, and every blade of grass was holy.

You may not know the meaning of the word *sacred*. However, the word *holy* is a synonym. It has a meaning that is similar to that of the word *sacred*.

Each of the sentences below contains a synonym for the underlined word. The synonym is a word from one of the poems you just read. Find the synonym. Then use it to determine the meaning of the underlined word.

1. The patriarch of the tribe was a type of father to his people.

2. The wealth in nature created the feeling of affluence that Native Americans had.

3. The vitality of the spring flowers inspired the poet; life sparkled all around her.

4. Each individual prayed that the gods would bestow their blessings and grant the requests of the tribe.

5. The <u>specter</u> of night frightened the waiting <u>warriors</u>. Like all spirits, however, it disappeared with the dawn.

Developing Writing Skills

1. **Using Contrast.** Both "Spring Song" and "Darkness Song" are tribal songs, passed down for generations. How do these songs differ? Write one paragraph contrasting the two songs.

    Pre-Writing. Reread the songs. Think about the purpose, mood, and language of each song. Make notes on the differences between the two songs. Organize your notes by grouping ideas together. For example, keep all ideas related to purpose together. Do the same thing for ideas related to mood and to language.

    Writing. Write a topic sentence summarizing the main differences between "Spring Song" and "Darkness Song." Then explain each aspect of the difference in detail. Support each idea with details from the songs.

    Revising. Read your paragraph carefully. Have you contrasted the songs in at least two ways? Have you used specific details to support your ideas? Have you included only differences between the songs? Improve your paragraph by making needed changes. Then make a clean final copy.

2. **Writing a Song.** Write a brief song that shows your feelings about a change in seasons. Include sensory details to describe the change of seasons. Try to create a definite mood.

Developing Skills in Speaking and Listening

Listening to Recordings. A library contains more than books. It may also contain an audio-visual collection. This collection can include records, tapes, films, slides, and video cassettes.

Use the audio-visual index in your library to find recordings of Native American songs, chants, or prayers. Listen carefully to the sound of these works. What is the melody of each like? the mood? the beat? How are instruments and voices used to give the piece rhythm? How does this music differ from music you are more familiar with? Compare your conclusions with those of other students in your class.

Rip Van Winkle

WASHINGTON IRVING

SETTING A PURPOSE | *Rip Van Winkle spends most of his time trying to escape from his wife and his chores. At one point, however, he escapes for twenty years. What changes occur while he is gone?*

Whoever has made a voyage up the Hudson must remember the Kaatskill mountains. They are a dismembered branch of the great Appalachian family, and are seen away to the west of the river, swelling up to a noble height, and lording it over the surrounding country. Every change of season, every change of weather, indeed, every hour of the day, produces some change in the magical hues and shapes of these mountains, and they are regarded by all the good wives, far and near, as perfect barometers. When the weather is fair and settled, they are clothed in blue and purple, and print their bold outlines on the clear evening sky; but, sometimes, when the rest of the landscape is cloudless, they will gather a hood of gray vapors about their summits, which, in the last rays of the setting sun, will glow and light up like a crown of glory.

At the foot of these fairy mountains, the voyager may have descried the light smoke curling up from a village, whose shingle-roofs gleam among the trees, just where the blue tints of the upland melt away into the fresh green of the nearer landscape. It is a little village of great antiquity, having been founded by some of the Dutch colonists, in the early times of the province, just about the beginning of the government of the good Peter Stuyvesant[1] (may he rest in peace!), and there were some of the houses of the original settlers standing within a few years, built of small yellow bricks brought from Holland, having latticed windows and gable fronts, surmounted with weather-cocks.

In that same village, and in one of these very houses (which, to tell the precise truth, was sadly time-worn and weather-beaten), there lived many years since, while the country was yet a province of Great Britain, a simple good-natured fellow of the name of Rip Van Winkle. He was a descendant of the Van Winkles who figured so gallantly in the chivalrous days of Peter Stuyvesant, and accompanied him to the siege of Fort Christina. He inherited, however, but little of the martial character of his ancestors. I have observed that he was a simple good-natured man; he was, moreover, a kind neighbor, and an obedient hen-pecked husband. Indeed, to the latter circumstance might be owing that meekness of spirit which gained him such universal popularity; for those men are most apt to be obsequious and conciliating

---

1. **Peter Stuyvesant**, (1610?–1672) the last Dutch governor of New Netherland, an area that included part of present-day New York and surrounding states.

abroad, who are under the discipline of shrews at home. Their tempers, doubtless, are rendered pliant and malleable in the fiery furnace of domestic tribulation; and a curtain lecture is worth all the sermons in the world for teaching the virtues of patience and long-suffering. A termagant wife may, therefore, in some respects, be considered a tolerable blessing; and if so, Rip Van Winkle was thrice blessed.

Certain it is that he was a great favorite among all the good wives of the village, who, as usual, with the amiable sex, took his part in all family squabbles; and never failed, whenever they talked those matters over in their evening gossipings, to lay all the blame on Dame Van Winkle. The children of the village, too, would shout with joy whenever he approached. He assisted at their sports, made their playthings, taught them to fly kites and shoot marbles, and told them long stories of ghosts, witches, and Indians. Whenever he went dodging about the village, he was surrounded by a troop of them, hanging on his skirts, clambering on his back, and playing a thousand tricks on him with impunity; and not a dog would bark at him throughout the neighborhood.

The great error in Rip's composition was an insuperable aversion to all kinds of profitable labor. It could not be from the want of assiduity or perseverance; for he would sit on a wet rock, with a rod as long and heavy as a Tartar's lance, and fish all day without a murmur, even though he should not be encouraged by a single nibble. He would carry a fowling-piece on his shoulder for hours together, trudging through woods and swamps, and up hill and down dale, to shoot a few squirrels or wild pigeons. He would never refuse to assist a neighbor even in the roughest toil, and was a foremost man at all country frolics for husking Indian corn, or building stone-fences; the women of the village, too, used to employ him to run their errands, and to do such little odd jobs as their less obliging husbands would not do for them. In a word Rip was ready to attend to anybody's business but his own; but as to doing family duty, and keeping his farm in order, he found it impossible.

In fact, he declared it was of no use to work on his farm; it was the most pestilent little piece of ground in the whole country; every thing about it went wrong, and would go wrong, in spite of him. His fences were continually falling to pieces; his cow would either go astray, or get among the cabbages; weeds were sure to grow quicker in his fields than anywhere else; the rain always made a point of setting in just as he had some outdoor work to do; so that though his patrimonial estate had dwindled away under his management, acre by acre, until there was little more left than a mere patch of Indian corn and potatoes, yet it was the worst conditioned farm in the neighborhood.

His children, too, were as ragged and wild as if they belonged to nobody. His son Rip, an urchin begotten in his own likeness, promised to inherit the habits, with the old clothes of his father. He was generally seen trooping like a colt at his mother's heels, equipped in a pair of his father's cast-off galligaskins, which he had much ado to hold up with one hand, as a fine lady does her train in bad weather.

Rip Van Winkle, however, was one of those happy mortals, of foolish, well-oiled dispositions, who take the world easy, eat white bread or brown, whichever can be got with least thought or trouble, and would rather starve on a penny than work for a pound. If left to himself, he would have whistled life away in perfect contentment; but his wife kept continually dinning in his ears about his idleness, his carelessness, and the ruin he was bringing on his family. Morning, noon, and night, her tongue was incessantly going, and everything he said or did was sure to produce a torrent of household eloquence. Rip had but one way of replying to all lectures of the kind, and that, by frequent use, had grown into a habit. He shrugged his shoulders, shook his head, cast up his eyes, but said nothing. This, however, always provoked a fresh volley from his wife; so that he was fain to draw off his forces, and take to the outside of the house— the only side which, in truth, belongs to a hen-pecked husband.

Rip's sole domestic adherent was his dog Wolf, who was as much hen-pecked as his master; for Dame Van Winkle regarded them as companions in idleness, and even looked upon Wolf with an evil eye, as the cause of his master's going so often astray. True it is, in all points of spirit befitting an honorable dog, he was as courageous an animal as ever scoured the woods—but what courage can withstand the ever-during and all-besetting terrors of a woman's tongue? The moment Wolf entered the house his crest fell, his tail drooped to the ground, or curled between his legs, he sneaked about with a gallows air, casting many a sidelong glance at Dame Van Winkle, and at the least flourish of a broomstick or ladle, he would fly to the door with a yelp.

Times grew worse and worse with Rip Van Winkle as years of matrimony rolled on; a tart temper never mellows with age, and a sharp tongue is the only edged tool that grows keener with constant use. For a long while he used to console himself, when driven from home, by frequenting a kind of perpetual club of the sages, philosophers, and other idle personages of the village; which held its sessions on a bench before a small inn, designated by a rubicund portrait of His Majesty George the Third. Here they used to sit in the shade through a long lazy summer's day, talking listlessly over village gossip, or telling endless sleepy stories about nothing. But it would have been worth any statesman's money to have heard the profound discussions that sometimes took place, when by chance an old newspaper fell into their hands from some passing traveller. How solemnly they would listen to the contents, as drawled out by Derrick Van Bummel, the schoolmaster, a dapper learned little man, who was not to be daunted by the most gigantic word in the dictionary; and how sagely they would deliberate upon public events some months after they had taken place.

The opinions of this junto were completely controlled by Nicholas Vedder, a patriarch of the village, and landlord of the inn, at the door of which he took his seat from morning till night, just moving sufficiently to avoid the sun and keep in the shade of a large tree; so that the neighbors could tell the hour by his movements as accurately as by a sun-dial. It is true he was rarely heard to speak, but smoked his pipe incessantly. His adherents, however (for every great man has his adherents), perfectly understood him, and knew how to gather his opinions. When any thing that was read or related displeased him, he was observed to smoke his pipe vehemently, and to send forth short, frequent and angry puffs; but when pleased, he would inhale the smoke slowly and tranquilly, and emit it in light and placid clouds; and sometimes, taking the pipe from his mouth, and letting the fragrant vapor curl about his nose, would gravely nod his head in token of perfect approbation.

From even this stronghold the unlucky Rip was at length routed by his termagant wife, who would suddenly break in upon the tranquility of the assemblage and call the members all to naught; nor was that august personage, Nicholas Vedder himself, sacred from the daring tongue of this terrible virago, who charged him outright with encouraging her husband in habits of idleness.

Poor Rip was at last reduced almost to despair; and his only alternative, to escape from the labor of the farm and clamor of his wife, was to take gun in hand and stroll away into the woods. Here he would sometimes seat himself at the foot of a tree, and share the contents of his wallet with Wolf, with whom he sympathized as a fellow-sufferer in persecution. "Poor Wolf," he would say, "thy mistress leads thee a dog's life of it; but never mind, my lad, whilst I live thou shalt never want a friend to stand by thee!" Wolf would wag his tail, look wistfully in his master's face, and if dogs can feel pity I verily believe he reciprocated the sentiment with all his heart.

In a long ramble of the kind on a fine autumnal day, Rip had unconsciously scrambled to one of the highest parts of the Kaatskill mountains. He was after his favorite sport of squirrel shooting, and the still solitudes had echoed and re-echoed with the reports of his gun. Panting and fatigued, he threw himself,

late in the afternoon, on a green knoll, covered with mountain herbage, that crowned the brow of a precipice. From an opening between the trees he could overlook all the lower country for many a mile of rich woodland. He saw at a distance the lordly Hudson, far, far below him, moving on its silent but majestic course, with the reflection of a purple cloud, or the sail of a lagging bark, here and there sleeping on its glassy bosom, and at last losing itself in the blue highlands.

On the other side he looked down into a deep mountain glen, wild, lonely, and shagged, the bottom filled with fragments from the impending cliffs, and scarcely lighted by the reflected rays of the setting sun. For some time Rip lay musing on this scene; evening was gradually advancing; the mountains began to throw their long blue shadows over the valleys; he saw that it would be dark long before he could reach the village, and he heaved a heavy sigh when he thought of encountering the terrors of Dame Van Winkle.

As he was about to descend, he heard a voice from a distance, hallooing, "Rip Van Winkle! Rip Van Winkle!" He looked round, but could see nothing but a crow winging its solitary flight across the mountain. He thought his fancy must have deceived him, and turned again to descend, when he heard the same cry ring through the still evening air; "Rip Van Winkle! Rip Van Winkle!"—at the same time Wolf bristled up his back, and giving a low growl, skulked to his master's side, looking fearfully down into the glen. Rip now felt a vague apprehension stealing over him; he looked anxiously in the same direction, and perceived a strange figure slowly toiling up the rocks, and bending under the

Scene on the Hudson (Rip van Winkle), 1845, JAMES HAMILTON. National Museum of American Art, Smithsonian Institution, museum purchase. Washington, D.C.

weight of something he carried on his back. He was surprised to see any human being in this lonely and unfrequented place, but supposing it to be some one of the neighborhood in need of his assistance, he hastened down to yield it.

On nearer approach he was still more surprised at the singularity of the stranger's appearance. He was a short square-built old fellow, with thick bushy hair, and a grizzled beard. His dress was of the antique Dutch fashion—a cloth jerkin strapped round the waist—several pair of breeches, the outer one of ample volume, decorated with rows of buttons down the sides, and bunches at the

knees. He bore on his shoulder a stout keg, that seemed full of liquor, and made signs for Rip to approach and assist him with the load. Though rather shy and distrustful of this new acquaintance, Rip complied with his usual alacrity; and mutually relieving one another, they clambered up a narrow gully, apparently the dry bed of a mountain torrent. As they ascended, Rip every now and then heard long rolling peals, like distant thunder, that seemed to issue out of a deep ravine, or rather cleft, between lofty rocks, toward which their rugged path conducted. He paused for an instant, but supposing it to be the muttering of one of those transient thunder-showers which often take place in mountain heights, he proceeded. Passing through the ravine, they came to a hollow, like a small amphitheatre, surrounded by perpendicular precipices, over the brinks of which impending trees shot their branches, so that you only caught glimpses of the azure sky and the bright evening cloud. During the whole time Rip and his companion had labored on in silence; for though the former marvelled greatly what could be the object of carrying a keg of liquor up this wild mountain, yet there was something strange and incomprehensible about the unknown, that inspired awe and checked familiarity.

On entering the amphitheatre, new objects of wonder presented themselves. On a level spot in the centre was a company of odd-looking personages playing at nine-pins. They were dressed in a quaint outlandish fashion; some wore short doublets, others jerkins, with long knives in their belts, and most of them had enormous breeches, of similar style with that of the guide's. Their visages, too, were peculiar: one had a large beard, broad face, and small piggish eyes: the face of another seemed to consist entirely of nose, and was surmounted by a white sugar-loaf hat set off with a little red cock's tail. They all had beards, of various shapes and colors. There was one who seemed to be the commander. He was a stout old gentleman, with a weather-beaten countenance; he wore a laced doublet, broad belt and hanger, high-crowned hat and feather, red stockings, and high-heeled shoes, with roses in them. The whole group reminded Rip of the figures in an old Flemish painting, in the parlor of Dominie Van Shaick, the village parson, and which had been brought over from Holland at the time of the settlement.

What seemed particularly odd to Rip was, that though these folks were evidently amusing themselves, yet they maintained the gravest faces, the most mysterious silence, and were, withal, the most melancholy party of pleasure he had ever witnessed. Nothing interrupted the stillness of the scene but the noise of the balls, which, whenever they were rolled, echoed along the mountains like rumbling peals of thunder.

As Rip and his companion approached them, they suddenly desisted from their play, and stared at him with such fixed statue-like gaze, and such strange, uncouth, lack-lustre countenances, that his heart turned within him, and his knees smote together. His companion now emptied the contents of the keg into large flagons, and made signs to him to wait upon the company. He obeyed with fear and trembling; they quaffed the liquor in profound silence, and then returned to their game.

By degrees Rip's awe and apprehension subsided. He even ventured, when no eye was fixed upon him, to taste the beverage, which he found had much of the flavor of excellent Hollands. He was naturally a thirsty soul, and was soon tempted to repeat the draught. One taste provoked another; and he reiterated his visits to the flagon so often that at length his senses were overpowered, his eyes swam in his head, his head gradually declined, and he fell into a deep sleep.

On waking, he found himself on the green knoll whence he had first seen the old man of the glen. He rubbed his eyes—it was a bright sunny morning. The birds were hopping and twittering among the bushes, and the eagle was wheeling aloft, and breasting the pure mountain breeze. "Surely," thought Rip, "I have not slept here all night." He recalled the occurrences before he fell asleep. The strange man with a keg of liquor—the mountain ravine—the wild retreat among the rocks—the woe-begone party at nine-pins—the flagon— "Oh! that flagon! that wicked flagon!" thought Rip—"what excuse shall I make to Dame Van Winkle!"

He looked round for his gun, but in place of the clean well-oiled fowling-piece, he found an old firelock lying by him, the barrel incrusted with rust, the lock falling off, and the stock worm-eaten. He now suspected that the grave roysters of the mountain had put a trick upon him, and, having dosed him with liquor, had robbed him of his gun. Wolf, too, had disappeared, but he might have strayed away after a squirrel or partridge. He whistled after him and shouted his name, but all in vain; the echoes repeated his whistle and shout, but no dog was to be seen.

He determined to revisit the scene of the last evening's gambol, and if he met with any of the party, to demand his dog and gun. As he rose to walk, he found himself stiff in the joints, and wanting in his usual activity. "These mountain beds do not agree with me," thought Rip, "and if this frolic should lay me up with a fit of the rheumatism, I shall have a blessed time with Dame Van Winkle." With some difficulty he got down into the glen: he found the gully up which he and his companion had ascended the preceding evening; but to his astonishment a mountain stream was now foaming down it, leaping from rock to rock, and filling the glen with babbling murmurs. He, however, made shift to scramble up its sides, working his toilsome way through thickets of birch, sassafras, and witch-hazel, and sometimes tripped up or entangled by the wild grapevines that twisted their coils or tendrils from tree to tree, and spread a kind of network in his path.

At length he reached to where the ravine had opened through the cliffs to the amphitheatre; but no traces of such opening remained. The rocks presented a high impenetrable wall over which the torrent came tumbling in a sheet of feathery foam, and fell into a broad deep basin, black from the shadows of the surrounding forest. Here, then, poor Rip was brought to a stand. He again called and whistled after his dog; he was only answered by the cawing of a flock of idle crows, sporting high in air about a dry tree that overhung a sunny precipice; and who, secure in their elevation, seemed to look down and scoff at the poor man's perplexities. What was to be done? The morning was passing away, and Rip felt famished for want of his breakfast. He grieved to give up his dog and gun; he dreaded to meet his wife; but it would not do to starve among the mountains. He shook his head, shouldered the rusty firelock, and, with a heart full of trouble and anxiety, turned his steps homeward.

As he approached the village he met a number of people, but none whom he knew, which somewhat surprised him, for he had thought himself acquainted with every one in the country round. Their dress, too, was of a different fashion from that to which he was accustomed. They all stared at him with equal marks of surprise, and whenever they cast their eyes upon him, invariably stroked their chins. The constant recurrence of this gesture induced Rip, involuntarily, to do the same, when, to his astonishment, he found his beard had grown a foot long!

He had now entered the skirts of the village. A troop of strange children ran at his heels, hooting after him, and pointing at his gray beard. The dogs, too, not one of which he recognized for an old acquaintance, barked at him as he passed. The very village was altered; it was larger and more populous. There were rows of houses which he had never seen before, and those which had been his familiar haunts had disappeared. Strange names were over the doors—strange faces at the windows—every thing was strange. His mind now misgave him; he began to doubt whether both he and the world around him were not bewitched. Surely this was his native village, which he had left but the day before. There stood the Kaatskill mountains—there ran the silver Hudson at a distance—there was every hill and dale precisely as it had always been—Rip was sorely perplexed—"That flagon last night," thought he, "has addled my head!"

It was with some difficulty that he found the way to his own house, which he approached with silent awe, expecting every moment to hear the shrill voice of Dame Van Winkle. He found the house gone to decay—the roof fallen in, the windows shattered, and the doors off the hinges. A half-starved dog that looked like Wolf was skulking about it. Rip called him by name, but the cur snarled, showed his teeth, and passed on. This was an unkind cut indeed—"My very dog," sighed poor Rip, "has forgotten me!"

He entered the house, which, to tell the truth, Dame Van Winkle had always kept in neat order. It was empty, forlorn, and apparently abandoned. This desolateness overcame all his connubial fears—he called loudly for his wife and children—the lonely chambers rang for a moment with his voice, and then all again was silence.

He now hurried forth, and hastened to his old resort, the village inn—but it too was gone. A large rickety wooden building stood in its place, with great gaping windows, some of them broken and mended with old hats and petticoats, and over the door was painted, "the Union Hotel, by Jonathan Doolittle." Instead of the great tree that used to shelter the quiet little Dutch inn of yore, there now was reared a tall naked pole, with something on the top that looked like a red night-cap, and from it was fluttering a flag, on which was a singular assemblage of stars and stripes—all this was strange and incomprehensible. He recognized on the sign, however, the ruby face of King George, under which he had smoked so many a peaceful pipe; but even this was singularly metamorphosed. The red coat was changed for one of blue and buff, a sword was held in the hand instead of a sceptre, the head was decorated with a cocked hat, and underneath was painted in large characters, GENERAL WASHINGTON.

There was, as usual, a crowd of folk about the door, but none that Rip recollected. The very character of the people seemed changed. There was a busy, bustling, disputatious tone about it, instead of the accustomed phlegm and drowsy tranquillity. He looked in vain for the sage Nicholas Vedder, with his broad face, double chin, and fair long pipe, uttering clouds of tobacco-smoke instead of idle speeches; or Van Bummel, the schoolmaster, doling forth the contents of an ancient newspaper. In place of these, a lean, bilious-looking fellow, with his pockets full of handbills, was haranguing vehemently about rights of citizens—elections—members of congress—liberty—Bunker's Hill—heroes of seventy-six—and other words, which were a perfect Babylonish jargon to the bewildered Van Winkle.

The appearance of Rip, with his long grizzled beard, his rusty fowling-piece, his uncouth dress, and an army of women and children at his heels, soon attracted the attention of the tavern politicians. They crowded round him, eyeing him from head to foot with great curiosity. The orator bustled up to him, and, drawing him partly aside, inquired "on which side he voted?" Rip stared in vacant stupidity. Another short but busy little fellow pulled him by the arm, and, rising on tiptoe, inquired in his ear, "Whether he was Federal or Democrat?" Rip was equally at a loss to comprehend the question; when a knowing, self-important old gentleman, in a sharp cocked hat, made his way through the crowd, putting them to the right and left with his elbows as he passed, and planting himself before Van Winkle, with one arm akimbo, the other resting on his cane, his keen eyes and sharp hat penetrating, as it were, into his very soul, demanded in an austere tone, "what brought him to the election with a gun on his shoulder, and a mob at his heels, and whether he meant to breed a riot in the village?"— "Alas! gentlemen," cried Rip, somewhat dismayed, "I am a poor quiet man and a loyal subject of the king, God bless him!"

Here a general shout burst from the bystanders—"A tory! a tory! a spy! a refugee! hustle him! away with him!" It was with great difficulty that the self-important man in the cocked hat restored order; and, having assumed a tenfold austerity of brow, demanded again of the unknown culprit, what he came there for, and whom he was seeking? The poor man humbly assured him that he meant no harm, but merely came there in search of some of his neighbors, who used to keep about the tavern.

"Well—who are they?—name them."

Rip bethought himself a moment, and inquired, "Where's Nicholas Vedder?"

There was a silence for a little while, when an old man replied, in a thin piping voice, "Nicholas Vedder! why, he is dead and gone these eighteen years! There was a wooden tombstone in the church-yard that used to tell all about him, but that's rotten and gone too."

"Where's Brom Dutcher?"

"Oh, he went off to the army in the beginning of the war; some say he was killed at the storming of Stony Point—others say he was drowned in a squall at the foot of Antony's Nose. I don't know—he never came back again."

"Where's Van Bummel, the schoolmaster?"

"He went off to the wars, too, was a great militia general, and is now in congress."

Rip's heart died away at hearing of these sad changes in his home and friends, and finding himself thus alone in the world. Every answer puzzled him too, by treating of such enormous lapses of time, and of matters which he could not understand: war—congress—Stony Point—he had no courage to ask after any more friends, but cried out in despair, "Does nobody here know Rip Van Winkle?"

"Oh, Rip Van Winkle!" exclaimed two or three, "Oh, to be sure! that's Rip Van Winkle yonder, leaning against the tree."

Rip looked, and beheld a precise counterpart of himself, as he went up the mountain: apparently as lazy, and certainly as ragged. The poor fellow was now completely confounded. He doubted his own identity, and whether he was himself or another man. In the midst of his bewilderment, the man in the cocked hat demanded to know who he was.

"God knows," exclaimed he, at his wit's end; "I'm not myself—I'm somebody else—that's me yonder—no—that's somebody else got into my shoes—I was myself last night, but I fell asleep on the mountain, and they've changed my gun, and every thing's changed, and I'm changed, and I can't tell what's my name, or who I am!"

The by-standers began now to look at each other, nod, wink significantly, and tap their fingers against their foreheads. There was a whisper, also, about securing the gun, and keeping the old fellow from doing mischief,

The Return of Rip van Winkle, about 1849, JOHN QUIDOR. National Gallery of Art, Andrew W. Mellon Collection. Washington, D.C.

at the very suggestion of which the self-important man in the cocked hat retired with some precipitation. At this critical moment a fresh comely woman pressed through the throng to get a peep at the gray-bearded man. She had a chubby child in her arms, which, frightened at his looks, began to cry. "Hush, Rip," cried she, "hush, you little fool; the old man won't hurt you." The name of the child, the air of the mother, the tone of her voice, all awakened a train of recollections in his mind. "What is your name, my good woman?" asked he.

"Judith Gardenier."

"And your father's name?"

"Ah, poor man, Rip Van Winkle was his name, but it's twenty years since he went away from home with his gun, and never has been heard of since—his dog came home without him; but whether he shot himself, or was carried away by the Indians, nobody can tell. I was then but a little girl."

Rip had but one question more to ask; but he put it with a faltering voice:

"Where's your mother?"

"Oh, she too had died but a short time since; she broke a blood-vessel in a fit of passion at a New-England peddler."

There was a drop of comfort, at least, in this intelligence. The honest man could contain himself no longer. He caught his daughter and her child in his arms. "I am your father!" cried he—"Young Rip Van Winkle once—old Rip Van Winkle now! Does nobody know poor Rip Van Winkle?"

All stood amazed, until an old woman, tottering out from among the crowd, put her hand to her brow, and peering under it in his face for a moment, exclaimed, "Sure enough! it is Rip Van Winkle—it is himself! Welcome home again, old neighbor—Why, where have you been these twenty long years?"

Rip's story was soon told, for the whole twenty years had been to him but as one night. The neighbors stared when they heard it; some were seen to wink at each other, and put their tongues in their cheeks: and the self-important man in the cocked hat, who, when the alarm was over, had returned to the field, screwed down the corners of his mouth, and shook his head—upon which there was a general shaking of the head throughout the assemblage.

It was determined, however, to take the opinion of old Peter Vanderdonk, who was seen slowly advancing up the road. He was a descendant of the historian of that name, who wrote one of the earliest accounts of the province. Peter was the most ancient inhabitant of the village, and well versed in all the wonderful events and traditions of the neighborhood. He recollected Rip at once, and corroborated his story in the most satisfactory manner. He assured the company that it was a fact, handed down from his ancestor the historian, that the Kaatskill mountains had always been haunted by strange beings. That it was affirmed that the great Hendrick Hudson, the first discoverer of the river and country, kept a kind of vigil there every twenty years, with his crew of the Half-moon; being permitted in this way to revisit the scenes of his enterprise, and keep a guardian eye upon the river, and the great city called by his name. That his father had once seen them in their old Dutch dresses playing at nine-pins in a hollow of the mountain; and that he himself had heard, one summer afternoon, the sound of their balls, like distant peals of thunder.

To make a long story short, the company broke up, and returned to the more important concerns of the election. Rip's daughter took him home to live with her; she had a snug, well-furnished house, and a stout cheery farmer for a husband, whom Rip recollected for one of the urchins that used to climb upon his back. As to Rip's son and heir, who was the ditto of himself, seen leaning against the tree, he was employed to work on the farm; but evinced an hereditary disposition to attend to any thing else but his business.

Rip now resumed his old walks and habits; he soon found many of his former cronies, though all rather the worse for the wear and tear of time; and preferred making friends among the rising generation, with whom he soon grew into great favor.

Having nothing to do at home, and being arrived at that happy age when a man can be idle with impunity, he took his place once more on the bench at the inn door, and was reverenced as one of the patriarchs of the village, and a chronicle of the old times "before the war." It was some time before he could get into the regular track of gossip, or could be made to comprehend the strange events that had taken place during his torpor. How that there had been a revolutionary war—that the country had thrown off the yoke of old England—and that, instead of being a subject of his Majesty George the Third, he was now a free citizen of the United States. Rip, in fact, was no politician; the changes of states and empires made but little impression on him; but there was one species of despotism under which he had long groaned, and that was—petticoat government. Happily that was at an end; he had got his neck out of the yoke of matrimony, and could go in and out whenever he pleased, without dreading the tyranny of Dame Van Winkle. Whenever her name was mentioned, however, he shook his head, shrugged his shoulders, and cast up his eyes; which might pass either for an expression of resignation to his fate, or joy at his deliverance.

He used to tell his story to every stranger that arrived at Mr. Doolittle's hotel. He was observed, at first, to vary on some points every time he told it, which was, doubtless, owing to his having so recently awaked. It at last settled down precisely to the tale I have related, and not a man, woman, or child in the neighborhood, but knew it by heart. Some always pretended to doubt the reality of it, and insisted that Rip had been out of his head, and that this was one point on which he always remained flighty. The old Dutch inhabitants, however, almost universally gave it full credit. Even to this day they never hear a thunderstorm of a summer afternoon about the Kaatskill, but they say Hendrick Hudson and his crew are at their game of nine-pins; and it is a common wish of all hen-pecked husbands in the neighborhood, when life hangs heavy on their hands, that they might have a quieting draught out of Rip Van Winkle's flagon.

Developing Comprehension Skills

1. What problems does Rip Van Winkle have at home?

2. What is the one "great error," or flaw, in Rip's character?

3. Briefly describe Rip's experience with the strange little men.

4. When Rip wakes up, what clues tell him that a great deal of time has passed? What historical events occurred during the twenty years that Rip slept?

5. What is Rip's reaction when he learns his wife has died? Why does he wait to learn of his wife's fate before identifying himself?

6. "Rip Van Winkle" is said to be among the first examples of a true American literature. In your opinion, what elements of the story make it distinctly American?

Reading Literature

1. **Understanding Folklore.** Many of Irving's stories are based on folklore. **Folklore** includes the stories, legends, customs, and beliefs of a group of people. Folklore is passed on orally from generation to generation. What early New York legend does Irving use in the story of "Rip Van Winkle"?

2. **Appreciating Descriptions of Setting.** The place and the time where the action of a story happens is the **setting.** Washington Irving was one of the first writers to vividly portray American settings. Find a paragraph in the story that describes a particular setting in detail. What sensory details within the paragraph help you to picture it clearly? What does the setting teach you about the people, buildings, and customs of the time?

3. **Analyzing Characterization.** The way a character is revealed in a story is called **characterization**.

   One way that Irving characterizes Rip Van Winkle is through the reactions of other characters to him. What is revealed about Rip by the reactions of his wife? of his neighbors? of the village children?

4. **Identifying Mood.** Mood, as you recall, is the feeling that a work of literature creates in a reader. Washington Irving immediately sets a mood in the introductory paragraph of "Rip Van Winkle." What is the mood of the story? How does the "magical" description of the mountains contribute to mood?

5. **Understanding History Through Literature.** Some literature mixes fact with fiction. Imaginary characters may be set against actual events in the past. Early literature is important because it provides us with another way of looking at historical events.

   In "Rip Van Winkle," what major event in American history does Rip awaken to discover? How is Irving's presentation of the event different from one you would find in a history book?

Developing Vocabulary Skills.

Identifying Word Meanings with Synonyms. **Synonyms**, as you know, are words with similar meanings. You may be able to learn the meaning of an unfamiliar word by finding a synonym in context. The synonym may be in the same sentence, or in a different sentence, as in the following example:

> The team members were extremely assiduous. The coach had never had such hard-working athletes.

While you may not recognize the word *assiduous*, the adjective *hard-working* is a synonym. It provides the meaning of the word *assiduous*.

The following sentences contain words from "Rip Van Winkle." Look for a synonym for each underlined word. Then write down both the synonym and the meaning of the underlined word.

1. Rip's tribulations at home were many, but his troubles never seemed to interfere with his social life in the village.
2. People were attracted to Rip's conciliating nature. His winning manner appealed to everyone but his wife.
3. He tried to avoid Dame Van Winkle's incessant demands, but they were indeed endless.
4. The villagers often sought the approbation of Nicholas Vedder. His approval was important to all of the tavern philosophers.
5. Rip viewed the strange-looking men with apprehension. He soon realized the reason for his uneasiness.
6. Everything in the village had metamorphosed; even the topics of conversation had changed.

Developing Writing Skills

1. **Analyzing Theme.** The main idea that a writer tries to communicate to a reader is called the **theme** of a piece of writing. Some people have said that the character of Rip Van Winkle represents America. Rip awoke to discover many changes in his life. America, also, experienced many changes during those twenty years. In one paragraph, explain why you agree or disagree with this interpretation.

2. **Writing Fiction.** Rip Van Winkle sleeps for twenty years. Imagine that you fell asleep twenty years ago and awoke just today. Write two or three paragraphs describing what you have missed in the past twenty years.

   Pre-Writing. Imagine what it would be like to wake up after sleeping twenty years. Make notes describing what you would see. Remember, you might not have seen some things before. How would you describe them? How would you react to them? Group related notes and ideas together. Then put your notes into a logical order.

   Writing. As you write, arrange your ideas so that the reader has a clear picture of the things you are describing. Use specific sensory details in your descriptions. Show your surprise at what you have missed.

   Revising. Work with someone in order to improve your paper. Ask the person to comment on how well you describe the various things you see. Are your descriptions vivid? Have you expressed your feelings clearly?

Developing Skills in Study and Research

Using the Encyclopedia. Use an encyclopedia to find information about one of the following historical figures or topics:

Henry Hudson
Peter Stuyvesant
Bunker Hill
King George III
Federal and Democratic parties
Storming of Stony Point

How were each of these figures or topics used in "Rip Van Winkle"?

The Devil and Daniel Webster

STEPHEN VINCENT BENÉT

It's a story they tell in the border country, where Massachusetts joins Vermont and New Hampshire.

Yes, Dan'l Webster's dead—or, at least, they buried him. But every time there's a thunderstorm around Marshfield,[1] they say you can hear his rolling voice in the hollows of the sky. And they say that if you go to his grave and speak loud and clear, "Dan'l Webster—Dan'l Webster!" the ground'll begin to shiver and the trees begin to shake. And after a while you'll hear a deep voice saying, "Neighbor, how stands the Union?" Then you better answer: the Union stands as she stood, rock-bottomed and copper-sheathed, one and indivisible, or he's liable to rear right out of the ground. At least, that's what I was told when I was a youngster.

You see, for a while, he was the biggest man in the country. He never got to be President, but he was the biggest man. There were thousands that trusted in him right next to God Almighty, and they told stories about him and all the things that belonged to him that were like the stories of patriarchs and such. They said when he stood up to speak, stars and stripes came right out in the sky, and once he spoke against a river and made it sink into the ground. They said when he walked the woods with his fishing rod, Killall, the trout would jump out of the streams right into his pockets, for they knew it was no use putting up a fight against him; and, when he argued a case, he could turn on the harps of the blessed and the shaking of the earth underground. That was the kind of man he was, and his big farm up at Marshfield was suitable to him. The chickens he raised were all white meat down through the drumsticks, the cows were tended like children, and the big ram he called Goliath had horns with a curl like a morning-glory vine and could butt through an iron door. But Dan'l wasn't one of your gentlemen farmers; he knew all the ways of the land, and he'd be up by candlelight to see that the chores got done. A man with a mouth like a mastiff, a brow like a mountain, and eyes like burning anthracite—that was Dan'l Webster in his prime. And the biggest case he argued never got written down in the books, for he argued it against the devil, nip and tuck, and no holds

---

1. **Marshfield**, a small town located southeast of Boston, where Daniel Webster had a farm.

Daniel Webster (Black Dan), 1835, FRANCIS ALEXANDER. Hood Museum of Art, Dartmouth College, gift of Dr. George C. Shattuck. Hanover, New Hampshire.

barred. And this is the way I used to hear it told:

There was a man named Jabez Stone, lived at Cross Corners, New Hampshire. He wasn't a bad man to start with, but he was an unlucky man. If he planted corn, he got borers; if he planted potatoes, he got blight. He had good enough land, but it didn't prosper him; he had a decent wife and children, but the more children he had, the less there was to feed them. If stones cropped up in his neighbor's field, boulders boiled up in his; if he had a horse with the spavins, he'd trade it for one with the staggers and give something extra. There's some folks bound to be like that, apparently. But one day Jabez Stone got sick of the whole business.

He'd been plowing that morning and he'd just broke the plowshare on a rock that he could have sworn hadn't been there yesterday. And, as he stood looking at the plowshare, the off horse began to cough—that ropy kind of cough that means sickness and horse doctors. There were two children down with the measles, his wife was ailing, and he had a whitlow on his thumb. It was about the last straw for Jabez Stone. "I vow," he said, and he looked around him kind of desperate—"I vow it's enough to make a man want to sell his soul to the devil! And I would, too, for two cents!"

Then he felt a kind of queerness come over him at having said what he'd said; though, naturally, being a New Hampshireman, he wouldn't take it back. But, all the same, when it got to be evening and, as far as he could see, no notice had been taken, he felt relieved in his mind, for he was a religious man. But notice is always taken, sooner or later, just like the Good Book says. And, sure enough, the next day, about suppertime, a soft-spoken, dark-dressed stranger drove up in a handsome buggy and asked for Jabez Stone.

Well, Jabez told his family it was a lawyer, come to see him about a legacy. But he knew who it was. He didn't like the looks of the stranger, nor the way he smiled with his teeth. They were white teeth, and plentiful—some say they were filed to a point. And he didn't like it when the dog took one look at the stranger and ran away howling, with his tail between his legs. But having passed his word, more or less, he stuck to it, and they went out behind the barn and made their bargain. Jabez Stone had to prick his finger to sign, and the stranger lent him a silver pen. The wound healed clean, but it left a little white scar.

After that, all of a sudden, things began to pick up and prosper for Jabez Stone. His cows got fat and his horses sleek, his crops were the envy of the neighborhood, and lightning might strike all over the valley, but it wouldn't strike his barn. Pretty soon, he was one of the prosperous people of the county; they asked him to stand for selectman,[2] and he stood for it; there began to be talk of running him for state senate. All in all, you might say the Stone family was as happy and contented as cats in a dairy. And so they were, except for Jabez Stone.

He'd been contented enough, the first few years. It's a great thing when bad luck turns; it drives most other things out of your head. True, every now and then, especially in rainy weather, the little white scar on his finger would give him a twinge. And once a year, punctual as clockwork, the stranger with the handsome buggy would come driving by. But the sixth year, the stranger lighted, and, after that, his peace was over for Jabez Stone.

The stranger came up through the lower field, switching his boots with a cane—they were handsome black boots, but Jabez Stone never liked the look of them, particularly the toes. And, after he'd passed the time of day, he said, "Well, Mr. Stone, you're a hummer! It's a very pretty property you've got here, Mr. Stone."

"Well, some might favor it and others might not," said Jabez Stone, for he was a New Hampshireman.

"Oh, no need to decry your industry!" said the stranger, very easy, showing his teeth in a smile. "After all, we know what's been done, and it's been according to contract. So when—ahem—the mortgage falls due next year, you shouldn't have any regrets."

"Speaking of that mortgage, mister," said Jabez Stone, and he looked around for help to the earth and the sky, "I'm beginning to have one or two doubts about it."

"Doubts?" said the stranger, not quite so pleasantly.

"Why, yes," said Jabez Stone. "This being the U.S.A. and me always having been a religious man." He cleared his throat and got bolder. "Yes, sir," he said, "I'm beginning to have considerable doubts as to that mortgage holding in court."

"There's courts and courts," said the stranger, clicking his teeth. "Still, we might as well have a look at the original document." And he hauled out a big black pocketbook, full of papers. "Sherwin, Slater, Stevens, Stone," he muttered. "I, Jabez Stone, for a term of seven years—Oh, it's quite in order."

But Jabez Stone wasn't listening, for he saw something else flutter out of the black pocketbook. It was something that looked like a moth, but it wasn't a moth. And as Jabez Stone stared at it, it seemed to speak to him in a small sort of piping voice, terrible small and thin, but terrible human.

"Neighbor Stone!" it squeaked. "Neighbor Stone! Help me! I beg you, help me!"

But before Jabez Stone could stir hand or foot, the stranger whipped out a big bandanna handkerchief, caught the creature in it, just like a butterfly, and started tying up the ends of the bandanna.

"Sorry for the interruption," he said. "As I was saying—"

2. **selectman**, one of a board of officers in New England chosen annually to manage town affairs.

But Jabez Stone was shaking all over like a scared horse.

"That's Miser Stevens' voice!" he said, in a croak. "And you've got him in your handkerchief!"

The stranger looked a little embarrassed.

"Yes, I really should have transferred him to the collecting box," he said with a simper, "but there were some rather unusual specimens there and I didn't want them crowded. Well, well, these little contretemps will occur."

"I don't know what you mean by contertan," said Jabez Stone, "but that was Miser Stevens' voice! And he ain't dead! You can't tell me he is! He was just as spry and mean as a woodchuck, Tuesday!"

"In the midst of life—"[3] said the stranger, kind of pious. "Listen!" Then a bell began to toll in the valley, and Jabez Stone listened, with the sweat running down his face. For he knew it was tolled for Miser Stevens and that he was dead.

"These long-standing accounts," said the stranger with a sigh; "one really hates to close them. But business is business."

He still had the bandanna in his hand, and Jabez Stone felt sick as he saw the cloth struggle and flutter.

"Are they all as small as that?" he asked hoarsely.

"Small?" said the stranger. "Oh, I see what you mean. Why, they vary." He measured Jabez Stone with his eyes, and his teeth showed. "Don't worry, Mr. Stone," he said. "You'll go with a very good grade. I wouldn't trust you outside the collecting box. Now, a man like Dan'l Webster, of course—well, we'd have to build a special box for him, and

even at that, I imagine the wingspread would astonish you. He'd certainly be a prize. I wish we could see our way clear to him. But, in your case, as I was saying—"

"Put that handkerchief away!" said Jabez Stone, and he began to beg and to pray. But the best he could get at the end was a three years' extension, with conditions.

But till you make a bargain like that, you've got no idea of how fast four years can run. By the last months of those years, Jabez Stone's known all over the state and there's talk of running him for governor—and it's dust and ashes in his mouth. For every day, when he gets up, he thinks, "There's one more night gone," and every night when he lies down, he thinks of the black pocketbook and the soul of Miser Stevens, and it makes him sick at heart. Till, finally, he can't bear it any longer, and, in the last days of the last year, he hitches up his horse and drives off to seek Dan'l Webster. For Dan'l Webster was born in New Hampshire, only a few miles from Cross Corners, and it's well known that he has a particular soft spot for old neighbors.

It was early in the morning when he got to Marshfield, but Dan'l was up already, talking Latin to the farm hands and wrestling with the ram, Goliath, and trying out a new trotter and working up speeches to make against John C. Calhoun.[4] But when he heard a New Hampshireman had come to see him, he dropped

---

3. **"In the midst of life—"**, "In the midst of life we are in death." A quotation from "The Burial of the Dead" in *The Book of Common Prayer.*
4. **John C. Calhoun**, an American statesman who served as Vice-President from 1825–1832. He was known as a great orator from the South, as Webster was from the North.

everything else he was doing, for that was Dan'l's way. He gave Jabez Stone a breakfast that five men couldn't eat, went into the living history of every man and woman in Cross Corners, and finally asked him how he could serve him.

Jabez Stone allowed that it was a kind of mortgage case.

"Well, I haven't pleaded a mortgage case in a long time, and I don't generally plead now, except before the Supreme Court," said Dan'l, "but if I can, I'll help you."

"Then I've got hope for the first time in ten years," said Jabez Stone, and told him the details.

Dan'l walked up and down as he listened, hands behind his back, now and then asking a question, now and then plunging his eyes at the floor, as if they'd bore through it like gimlets. When Jabez Stone had finished telling his story, Dan'l puffed out his cheeks and blew. Then he turned to Jabez Stone, and a smile broke over his face like the sunrise over Monadnock.

"You've certainly given yourself the devil's own row to hoe, Neighbor Stone," he said, "but I'll take your case."

"You'll take it?" said Jabez Stone, hardly daring to believe.

"Yes," said Dan'l Webster. "I've got about seventy-five other things to do and the Missouri Compromise[5] to straighten out, but I'll take your case. For if two New Hampshire-men aren't a match for the devil, we might as well give the country back to the Indians."

---

5. **Missouri Compromise**, a Congressional Act passed in 1820 that attempted to settle the question of slavery in the newly established Western States.

Then he shook Jabez Stone by the hand and said, "Did you come down here in a hurry?"

"Well, I admit I made time," said Jabez.

"You'll go back faster," said Dan'l Webster, and he told 'em to hitch up Constitution and Constellation to the carriage. They were matched grays with one white forefoot, and they stepped like greased lightning.

Well, I won't describe how excited and pleased the whole Stone family was to have the great Dan'l Webster for a guest, when they finally got there. Jabez Stone had lost his hat on the way, blown off when they overtook a wind, but he didn't take much account of that. But after supper he sent the family off to bed, for he had most particular business with Mr. Webster. Mrs. Stone wanted them to sit in the front parlor, but Dan'l Webster knew front parlors and said he preferred the kitchen. So it was there they sat, waiting for the stranger, with a jug on the table between them and a bright fire on the hearth—the stranger being scheduled to show up on the stroke of midnight, according to specification.

Well, most men wouldn't have asked for better company than Dan'l Webster and a jug. But with every tick of the clock Jabez Stone got sadder and sadder. His eyes roved round, and though he sampled the jug, you could see he couldn't taste it. Finally, on the stroke of 11:30, he reached over and grabbed Dan'l Webster by the arm.

"Mr. Webster, Mr. Webster!" he said, and his voice was shaking with fear and a desperate courage. "For God's sake, Mr. Webster, harness your horses and get away from this place while you can!"

"You've brought me a long way, neighbor, to tell me you don't like my company," said

Dan'l Webster, quite peaceable, pulling at the jug.

"Miserable wretch that I am!" groaned Jabez Stone. "I've brought you a devilish way, and now I see my folly. Let him take me if he wills. I don't hanker after it, I must say, but I can stand it. But you're the Union's stay and New Hampshire's pride! He mustn't get you, Mr. Webster! He mustn't get you!"

Dan'l Webster looked at the distracted man, all gray and shaking in the firelight, and laid a hand on his shoulder.

"I'm obliged to you, Neighbor Stone," he said gently. "It's kindly thought of. But there's a jug on the table and a case in hand. And I never left a jug or a case half finished in my life."

And just at that moment there was a sharp rap on the door.

"Ah," said Dan'l Webster, very coolly, "I thought your clock was a trifle slow, Neighbor Stone." He stepped to the door and opened it. "Come in!" he said.

The stranger came in—very dark and tall he looked in the firelight. He was carrying a box under his arm—a black, japanned box with little air holes in the lid. At the sight of the box, Jabez Stone gave a low cry and shrank into a corner of the room.

"Mr. Webster, I presume," said the stranger very polite, but with his eyes glowing like a fox's deep in the woods.

"Attorney of record for Jabez Stone," said Dan'l Webster, but his eyes were glowing too. "Might I ask your name?"

"I've gone by a good many," said the stranger carelessly. "Perhaps Scratch will do for the evening. I'm often called that in these regions."

Then he sat down at the table and poured himself a drink from the jug. The liquor was cold in the jug, but it came steaming into the glass.

"And now," said the stranger, smiling and showing his plentiful, white teeth, "I shall call upon you, as a law-abiding citizen, to assist me in taking possession of the property that is rightfully mine."

Well, with that the argument began—and it went hot and heavy. At first, Jabez Stone had a flicker of hope, but when he saw Dan'l Webster being forced back at point after point, he just sat scrunched in his corner, with his eyes on that japanned box. For there wasn't any doubt as to the deed or the signature—that was the worst of it. Dan'l Webster twisted and turned and thumped his fist on the table, but he couldn't get away from that. He offered to compromise the case; the stranger wouldn't hear of it. He pointed out the property had increased in value, and state senators ought to be worth more; the stranger stuck to the letter of the law. He was a great lawyer, Dan'l Webster, but we know who's the King of Lawyers, as the Good Book tells us, and it seemed as if, for the first time, Dan'l Webster had met his match.

Finally, the stranger yawned a little. "Your spirited efforts on behalf of your client do you credit, Mr. Webster," he said, "but if you have no more arguments to adduce, I'm rather pressed for time—" and Jabez Stone shuddered.

Dan'l Webster's brow looked dark as a thundercloud: "Pressed or not, you shall not have this man!" he thundered. "Mr. Stone is an American citizen, and no American citizen may be forced into the service of a foreign prince. We fought England for that in '12[6] and we'll fight all hell for it again!"

"Foreign?" said the stranger. "And who calls me a foreigner?"

"Well, I never yet heard of the dev—of your claiming American citizenship," said Dan'l Webster with surprise.

"And who with better right?" said the stranger, with one of his terrible smiles. "When the first wrong was done to the first Indian, I was there. When the first slaver put out for the Congo, I stood on her deck. Am I not in your books and stories and beliefs, from the first settlements on? Am I not spoken of, still, in every church in New England? 'Tis true the North claims me for a Southerner, and the South for a Northerner, but I am neither. I am merely an honest American like yourself—and of the best descent—for, to tell the truth, Mr. Webster, though I don't like to boast of it, my name is older in this country than yours."

"Aha!" said Dan'l Webster, with the veins standing out in his forehead. "Then I stand on the Constitution! I demand a trial for my client!"

"The case is hardly one for an ordinary court," said the stranger, his eyes flickering. "And, indeed, the lateness of the hour—"

"Let it be any court you choose, so it is an American judge and an American jury!" said Dan'l Webster in his pride. "Let it be the quick or the dead; I'll abide the issue!"

"You have said it," said the stranger, and pointed his finger at the door. And with that,

and all of a sudden, there was a rushing of wind outside and a noise of footsteps. They came, clear and distinct, through the night. And yet, they were not like the footsteps of living men.

"In God's name, who comes by so late?" cried Jabez Stone, in an ague of fear.

"The jury Mr. Webster demands," said the stranger, sipping at his boiling glass. "You must pardon the rough appearance of one or two; they will have come a long way."

And with that the fire burned blue and the door blew open and twelve men entered.

If Jabez Stone had been sick with terror before, he was blind with terror now. For there was Walter Butler, the Loyalist, who spread fire and horror through the Mohawk Valley in the times of the Revolution; and there was Simon Girty, the renegade, who saw white men burned at the stake and whooped with the Indians to see them burn. His eyes were green, like a catamount's, and the stains on his hunting shirt did not come from the blood of the deer. King Philip[7] was there, wild and proud as he had been in life, with the great gash in his head that gave him his death wound, and cruel Governor Dale,[8] who broke men on the wheel. There was Morton of Merry Mount, who so vexed the Plymouth Colony, with his flushed, loose, handsome face and his hate of the godly. There was Teach, the bloody pirate, with his black beard curling on his breast. The Reverend John Smeet, with his strangler's hands and his

---

6. **in '12**, a reference to the War of 1812 which was partially caused by the English forcing Americans to serve in the British navy.

7. **King Philip**, an Indian chief who started an uprising against white settlers in 1675. He was killed in 1676.
8. **Governor Dale**, the British Governor of the Virginia colony from 1611–1616. His rule was considered cruel and harsh.

Geneva gown, walked as daintily as he had to the gallows. The red print of the rope was still around his neck, but he carried a perfumed handkerchief in one hand. One and all, they came into the room with the fires of hell still upon them, and the stranger named their names and their deeds as they came, till the tale of twelve was told. Yet the stranger had told the truth—they had all played a part in America.

"Are you satisfied with the jury, Mr. Webster?" said the stranger mockingly, when they had taken their places.

The sweat stood upon Dan'l Webster's brow, but his voice was clear.

"Quite satisfied," he said. "Though I miss General Arnold from the company."

"Benedict Arnold is engaged upon other business," said the stranger, with a glower. "Ah, you asked for a justice, I believe."

He pointed his finger once more, and a tall man, soberly clad in Puritan garb, with the burning gaze of the fanatic, stalked into the room and took his judge's place.

"Justice Hathorne is a jurist of experience," said the stranger. "He presided at certain witch trials once held in Salem. There were others who repented of the business later, but not he."

"Repent of such notable wonders and undertakings?" said the stern old justice. "Nay, hang them—hang them all!" And he muttered to himself in a way that struck ice into the soul of Jabez Stone.

Then the trial began, and, as you might expect, it didn't look anyways good for the defense. And Jabez Stone didn't make much of a witness in his own behalf. He took one look at Simon Girty and screeched, and they

had to put him back in his corner in a kind of swoon.

It didn't halt the trial, though; the trial went on, as trials do. Dan'l Webster had faced some hard juries and hanging judges in his time, but this was the hardest he'd ever faced, and he knew it. They sat there with a kind of glitter in their eyes, and the stranger's smooth voice went on and on. Every time he'd raise an objection, it'd be "Objection sustained," but whenever Dan'l objected, it'd be "Objection denied." Well, you couldn't expect fair play from a fellow like this Mr. Scratch.

It got to Dan'l in the end, and he began to heat, like iron in the forge. When he got up to speak, he was going to flay that stranger with every trick known to the law, and the judge and jury too. He didn't care if it was contempt of court or what would happen to him for it. He didn't care any more what happened to Jabez Stone. He just got madder and madder, thinking of what he'd say. And yet, curiously enough, the more he thought about it, the less he was able to arrange his speech in his mind.

Till, finally, it was time for him to get up on his feet, and he did so, all ready to bust out with lightnings and denunciations. But before he started, he looked over the judge and jury for a moment, such being his custom. And he noticed the glitter in their eyes was twice as strong as before, and they all leaned forward. Like hounds just before they get the fox, they looked, and the blue mist of evil in the room thickened as he watched them. Then he saw what he'd been about to do, and he wiped his forehead, as a man might who's just escaped falling into a pit in the dark.

For it was him they'd come for, not only Jabez Stone. He read it in the glitter of their

Trial Scene, 1860–63, DAVID GILMORE BLYTHE. Memorial Art Gallery of the University of Rochester, Marian Stratton Gould Fund. New York.

eyes and in the way the stranger hid his mouth with one hand. And if he fought them with their own weapons, he'd fall into their power; he knew that, though he couldn't have told you how. It was his own anger and horror that burned in their eyes; and he'd have to wipe that out or the case was lost. He stood there for a moment, his black eyes burning like anthracite. And then he began to speak.

He started off in a low voice, though you could hear every word. They say he could call on the harps of the blessed when he chose. And this was just as simple and easy as a man could talk. But he didn't start out by condemning or reviling. He was talking about the things that make a country a country, and a man a man.

And he began with the simple things that everybody's known and felt—the freshness of a fine morning when you're young, and the taste of food when you're hungry, and the new day that's every day when you're a child. He took them up and he turned them in his hands. They were good things for any man. But without freedom, they sickened. And when he talked of those enslaved, and the

The Devil and Daniel Webster   167

sorrows of slavery, his voice got like a big bell. He talked of the early days of America and the men who had made those days. It wasn't a spread-eagle speech, but he made you see it. He admitted all the wrong that had ever been done. But he showed how, out of the wrong and the right, the suffering and the starvations, something new had come. And everybody had played a part in it, even the traitors.

Then he turned to Jabez Stone and showed him as he was—an ordinary man who'd had hard luck and wanted to change it. And, because he'd wanted to change it, now he was going to be punished for all eternity. And yet there was good in Jabez Stone, and he showed that good. He was hard and mean, in some ways, but he was a man. There was sadness in being a man, but it was a proud thing too. And he showed what the pride of it was till you couldn't help feeling it. Yes, even in hell, if a man was a man, you'd know it. And he wasn't pleading for any one person any more, though his voice rang like an organ. He was telling the story and the failures and the endless journey of mankind. They got tricked and trapped and bamboozled, but it was a great journey. And no demon that was ever foaled could know the inwardness of it—it took a man to do that.

The fire began to die on the hearth and the wind before morning to blow. The light was getting gray in the room when Dan'l Webster finished. And his words came back at the end to New Hampshire ground, and the one spot of land that each man loves and clings to. He painted a picture of that, and to each one of that jury he spoke of things long forgotten. For his voice could search the heart, and that was his gift and his strength. And to one, his voice was like the forest and its secrecy, and to

another like the sea and the storms of the sea; and one heard the cry of his lost nation in it, and another saw a little harmless scene he hadn't remembered for years. But each saw something. And when Dan'l Webster finished, he didn't know whether or not he'd saved Jabez Stone. But he knew he'd done a miracle. For the glitter was gone from the eyes of judge and jury, and, for the moment, they were men again, and knew they were men.

"The defense rests," said Dan'l Webster, and stood there like a mountain. His ears were still ringing with his speech, and he didn't hear anything else till he heard Judge Hathorne say, "The jury will retire to consider its verdict."

Walter Butler rose in his place and his face had a dark, gay pride on it.

"The jury has considered its verdict," he said, and looked the stranger full in the eye. "We find for the defendant, Jabez Stone."

With that, the smile left the stranger's face, but Walter Butler did not flinch.

"Perhaps 'tis not strictly in accordance with the evidence," he said, "but even the damned may salute the eloquence of Mr. Webster."

With that, the long crow of a rooster split the gray morning sky, and judge and jury were gone from the room like a puff of smoke and as if they had never been there. The stranger turned to Dan'l Webster, smiling wryly. "Major Butler was always a bold man," he said. "I had not thought him quite so bold. Nevertheless, my congratulations, as between two gentlemen."

"I'll have that paper first, if you please," said Dan'l Webster, and he took it and tore it into four pieces. It was queerly warm to the touch. "And now," he said, "I'll have you!"

and his hand came down like a bear trap on the stranger's arm. For he knew that once you bested anybody like Mr. Scratch in fair fight, his power on you was gone. And he could see that Mr. Scratch knew it too.

The stranger twisted and wriggled, but he couldn't get out of that grip. "Come, come, Mr. Webster," he said, smiling palely. "This sort of thing is ridic—ouch!—is ridiculous. If you're worried about the costs of the case, naturally, I'd be glad to pay—"

"And so you shall!" said Dan'l Webster, shaking him till his teeth rattled. "For you'll sit right down at that table and draw up a document, promising never to bother Jabez Stone nor his heirs or assigns nor any other New Hampshireman till doomsday! For any hades we want to raise in this state, we can raise ourselves, without assistance."

"Ouch!" said the stranger. "Ouch! Well, they never did run very big to the barrel, but—ouch!—I agree!"

So he sat down and drew up the document. But Dan'l Webster kept his hand on his coat collar all the time.

"And, now, may I go?" said the stranger, quite humble, when Dan'l'd seen the document was in proper and legal form.

"Go?" said Dan'l, giving him another shake. "I'm still trying to figure out what I'll do with you. For you've settled the costs of the case, but you haven't settled with me. I think I'll take you back to Marshfield," he said, kind of reflective. "I've got a ram there named Goliath that can butt through an iron door. I'd kind of like to turn you loose in his field and see what he'd do."

Well, with that the stranger began to beg and to plead. And he begged and he pled so humble that finally Dan'l, who was naturally kindhearted, agreed to let him go. The stranger seemed terrible grateful for that and said, just to show they were friends, he'd tell Dan'l's fortune before leaving. So Dan'l agreed to that, though he didn't take much stock in fortunetellers ordinarily.

But, naturally, the stranger was a little different. Well, he pried and he peered at the lines in Dan'l's hands. And he told him one thing and another that was quite remarkable. But they were all in the past.

"Yes, all that's true, and it happened," said Dan'l Webster. "But what's to come in the future?"

The stranger grinned, kind of happily, and shook his head. "The future's not as you think it," he said. "It's dark. You have a great ambition, Mr. Webster."

"I have," said Dan'l firmly, for everybody knew he wanted to be President.

"It seems almost within your grasp," said the stranger, "but you will not attain it. Lesser men will be made President and you will be passed over."

"And, if I am, I'll still be Daniel Webster," said Dan'l. "Say on. What else do you see in the future?"

"You have two strong sons," said the stranger, shaking his head. "You look to found a line. But each will die in war and neither reach greatness."

"Live or die, they are still my sons," said Dan'l Webster. "Say on."

"You have made great speeches," said the stranger. "You will make more."

"Ah," said Dan'l Webster.

"But the last great speech you make will turn many of your own against you," said the stranger. "They will call you Ichabod;[9] they will call you by other names. Even in New England some will say you have turned your coat and sold your country, and their voices will be loud against you till you die."

"So it is an honest speech, it does not matter what men say," said Dan'l. Then he looked at the stranger and their glances locked.

"One question," he said. "I have fought for the Union all my life. Will I see that fight won against those who would tear it apart?"

"Not while you live," said the stranger, grimly, "but it will be won. And after you are dead, there are thousands who will fight for your cause, because of words that you spoke."

"Why, then, you long-barreled, slab-sided, lantern-jawed, fortunetelling note-shaver!"

---

9. **Ichabod**, the name of a poem by John Greenleaf Whittier. The poem was critical of Webster's role in the passage of a bill that many felt was pro-slavery.

said Dan'l Webster, with a great roar of laughter, "be off with you to your own place before I put my mark on you! For, by the thirteen original colonies I'd go to the Pit itself to save the Union!"

And with that he drew back his foot for a kick that would have stunned a horse. It was only the tip of his shoe that caught the stranger, but he went flying out of the door with his collecting box under his arm.

"And now," said Dan'l Webster, seeing Jabez Stone beginning to rouse from his swoon, "let's see what's left in the jug, for it's dry work talking all night. I hope there's pie for breakfast, Neighbor Stone."

But they say that whenever the devil comes near Marshfield, even now, he gives it a wide berth. And he hasn't been seen in the state of New Hampshire from that day to this. I'm not talking about Massachusetts or Vermont.

Developing Comprehension Skills

1. Who was the stranger? What was the bargain he made with Jabez Stone?

2. Why does Daniel Webster agree to take Stone's case? What does this show about Webster?

3. Why do you think the devil agreed to a trial? What kind of men does he choose for the jury?

4. Just before Webster spoke to the jury, he felt as if he had "just escaped falling into a pit in the dark." What did he realize after looking over the judge and jury?

5. How does Daniel Webster win over the jury? What is the point of his speech?

6. In your opinion, does Daniel Webster live up to his reputation as described on page 159? What is his special power?

Reading Literature

1. **Recognizing Folklore.** "Rip Van Winkle," and "The Devil and Daniel Webster" are both based on folklore. What clues at the beginning of "The Devil and Daniel Webster" show that it is based on folklore? In what region did this tale originate?

2. **Making Inferences About Character.** An inference, you remember, is a conclusion based on specific facts. Make an inference about Daniel Webster's character from each of the following statements:

  a. It was early in the morning . . . but Dan'l was up already, talking Latin to the farm hands and wrestling with the ram, Goliath, and trying out a new trotter and working up speeches. . . .

  b. "So it is an honest speech, it does not matter what men say," said Dan'l. . . .

  c. . . . by the thirteen original colonies I'd go to the Pit itself to save the Union!

3. **Appreciating Local Color.** Writers sometimes add local color to their writing to add interest. **Local color** includes the traits, characters' speech, and mannerisms of a certain region. Benét uses local color throughout his story. He does this by characterizing the people of New Hampshire. For example, he writes, ". . . being a New Hampshireman, he wouldn't take it back." What trait of a New Hampshireman is Benét describing? Locate other passages where Benét uses the phrase "New Hampshireman." Identify the supposed character trait revealed in each.

4. **Identifying the Author's Purpose.** The entire story "The Devil and Daniel Webster" builds up to the line ". . . even the damned may salute the eloquence of Mr. Webster." Explain the importance of that statement in the story. What does the line indicate about Benét's purpose in writing the story?

Developing Vocabulary Skills

Using Definition and Restatement Clues. One type of context clue is a **definition** or **restatement** clue. This kind of clue reveals the meaning of an unfamiliar word by defining it or stating it in a slightly different way.

Certain key words may signal a definition or a restatement clue. Some of these words are *or, is, is called, that is, who is, which is,* or *in other words.* A writer may also use certain punctuation marks as signals. These include commas, dashes, and parentheses. Read the following sentence:

The boats were laden, or loaded, with supplies.

You can determine the meaning of *laden* because it is restated for you. Notice, too, how commas signal the restatement.

The underlined words in the following sentences are taken from "The Devil and Daniel Webster." Determine the meaning of each by using context clues. Write the meaning of the word and tell what words or punctuation marks acted as signals.

1. Daniel had eyes that burned like anthracite —a type of coal.

2. A legacy is money or property left to someone by an ancestor.

3. Jabez Stone was so unlucky that he would trade a horse with spavins, a bone disease, for one that was even worse.

4. The stranger made Jabez Stone a prosperous man. In other words, Stone became quite successful and well-to-do.

5. Unfortunately, the dark stranger was extremely punctual—he made it a point to be on time whether people wanted him to be or not.

6. Simon Girty was a renegade, a traitor who had fought against his own people.

Developing Writing Skills

1. **Using Comparison.** Both "The Devil and Daniel Webster" and "Rip Van Winkle" tell of fantastic events. Both contain elements of folklore. In a well-developed paragraph, explain these and other similarities between the two stories. Give examples of each similarity.

2. **Developing an Argument.** Daniel Webster develops a powerful argument to persuade Scratch's jury to free Stone. In a brief composition, develop a persuasive argument of your own. Your topic should be an issue related to your school.

   Pre-Writing. Think of a school issue about which you feel strongly. You may wish to defend a school policy, for example. You may also want to argue for a needed change. State your position, and make notes on your reasons for it. Add specific examples and facts that support your viewpoint. Organize your notes in logical order. You might want to build, for instance, to your most persuasive reason.

   Writing. Write an introduction that catches the reader's attention and clearly states your opinion. Each paragraph in the body of your composition should develop a single main idea, or reason. That idea should be stated in the topic sentence.

   Develop each paragraph with examples, reasons, and facts listed in your notes. The concluding paragraph should summarize your main ideas and restate your position.

   Revising. Reread your composition carefully. Look for reasons that are not well supported and add the needed information. Use transitional words such as *because, since,* and *therefore* to state your reasons.

Developing Skills in Critical Thinking

1. **Understanding Transfer.** Speakers and writers sometimes try to persuade their audiences through a technique known as transfer. **Transfer** occurs when someone tries to create strong feelings in others by linking one idea with another, unrelated idea. For example, a car manufacturer might mention America and baseball during a commercial in order to create strong positive feelings in the viewers.

   Explain how Daniel Webster used transfer in his speech addressing the jury. Use passages from the story to support your answer.

2. **Recognizing the Error of Stacking.** The error of stacking occurs when only one side of a situation is presented. The speaker or writer purposely leaves out important facts. Do you think Daniel Webster left out important facts about Jabez Stone during his speech to the jury? Explain.

Focus on

EDGAR ALLAN POE
1809–1849

Edgar Allan Poe (detail), about 1847. Daguerreotype probably by Gabriel Harrison. The Edgar Allan Poe collection of Cliff and Michele Krainik, Washington, D.C.

The artistic genius of Edgar Allan Poe was never appreciated during his lifetime. Nevertheless, his dreams and talents helped to steer American literature onto a new course. A versatile writer, Poe is known for his abilities as a short story writer, a poet, and a critic.

Together with Nathaniel Hawthorne, Poe is credited with shaping and defining the short story form. Poe's essays about the short story helped to set standards for short story writers everywhere. Poe insisted on the importance of a unified impression, or a single effect, on the reader. He also felt that the story should be short enough to be read in one sitting.

Poe's short stories are imaginative and often sorrowful. He is best known for his eerie horror tales. "The Tell-Tale Heart" in this chapter (page 174) is a fine example of Poe's ability to draw the reader into a suspenseful mood. Poe is also said to have developed the modern detective story.

Poe turned to short story writing to earn a living, but his first and fiercest love was for poetry. Many of his poems including "Annabel Lee," (page 187) and "The Raven," (page 181) are memorable for their haunting themes and music-like structure.

Unfortunately, Poe's personal life was marred by tragedy. Poe was raised by foster parents, Mr. and Mrs. John Allan of Richmond, Virginia. His relationship with John Allan, a wealthy merchant, was one of continuing quarrels. Eventually, Allan disowned him.

In 1835, Poe married his 13-year-old cousin Virginia Clemm. Sadly, she died in 1847. Poe himself began to sicken after her death. During this time, however, he wrote some fine work, including "Annabel Lee," which may have been inspired by the death of his young wife. Poe himself died on October 7, 1849. His tomb lay unmarked by a gravestone for twenty-six years.

Although Poe's life ended in loneliness and disappointment, his writing shone forth as a bright beginning in literature. His short stories and poetry had lasting influence on both American and European writers.

The Tell-Tale Heart

EDGAR ALLAN POE

A man has committed a murder. As he describes his crime, see if you agree with his statement that he is sane.

True!—nervous—very, very dreadfully nervous I had been and am; but why *will* you say that I am mad? The disease had sharpened my senses—not destroyed—not dulled them. Above all was the sense of hearing acute. I heard all things in the heaven and in the earth. I heard many things in hell. How, then, am I mad? Hearken! and observe how healthily—how calmly I can tell you the whole story.

It is impossible to say how first the idea entered my brain; but once conceived, it haunted me day and night. Object there was none. Passion there was none. I loved the old man. He had never wronged me. He had never given me insult. For his gold I had no desire. I think it was his eye! yes, it was this! One of his eyes resembled that of a vulture—a pale blue eye, with a film over it. Whenever it fell upon me, my blood ran cold; and so by degrees—very gradually—I made up my mind to take the life of the old man, and thus rid myself of the eye forever.

Now this is the point. You fancy me mad. Madmen know nothing. But you should have seen *me*. You should have seen how wisely I proceeded—with what caution—with what foresight—with what dissimulation I went to work! I was never kinder to the old man than during the whole week before I killed him. And every night, about midnight, I turned the latch of his door and opened it—oh, so gently! And then, when I had made an opening sufficient for my head, I put in a dark lantern, all closed, closed, so that no light shone out, and then I thrust in my head. Oh, you would have laughed to see how cunningly I thrust it in! I moved it slowly—very, very slowly, so that I might not disturb the old man's sleep. It took me an hour to place my whole head within the opening so far that I could see him as he lay upon his bed. Ha!—would a madman have been so wise as this? And then, when my head was well in the room, I undid the lantern cautiously—oh, so cautiously—cautiously (for the hinges creaked)—I undid it just so much that a single thin ray fell upon the vulture eye. And this I did for seven long nights—every night just at midnight—but I found the eye always closed; and so it was impossible to do the work; for it was not the old man who vexed me, but his Evil Eye. And every morning, when the day broke, I went boldly into the chamber, and spoke courageously to him, calling him by name in a hearty tone, and inquiring how he had passed the night. So you see he would have been a very profound old man, indeed, to suspect that every night, just at twelve, I looked in upon him while he slept.

Upon the eighth night I was more than usually cautious in opening the door. A watch's minute hand moves more slowly than did mine. Never before that night had I *felt* the extent of my own powers—of my sagacity. I could scarcely contain my feelings of triumph. To think that there I was, opening the door, little by little, and he not even to dream of my secret deeds or thoughts. I fairly chuckled at the idea; and perhaps he heard me; for he moved on the bed suddenly, as if startled. Now you may think that I drew back—but no. His room was as black as pitch with the thick darkness (for the shutters were close fastened, through fear of robbers), and so I knew that he could not see the opening of the door, and I kept pushing it on steadily, steadily.

I had my head in, and was about to open the lantern, when my thumb slipped upon the tin fastening, and the old man sprang up in the bed, crying out—"Who's there?"

I kept quite still and said nothing. For a whole hour I did not move a muscle, and in the meantime I did not hear him lie down. He was still sitting up in the bed listening;—just as I have done, night after night, hearkening to the death watches in the wall.

Presently I heard a slight groan, and I knew it was the groan of mortal terror. It was not a groan of pain or of grief—oh, no!—it was the low stifled sound that arises from the bottom of the soul when overcharged with awe. I knew the sound well. Many a night, just at midnight, when all the world slept, it has welled up from my own bosom, deepening, with its dreadful echo, the terrors that distracted me. I say I knew it well. I knew what the old man felt, and pitied him, although I chuckled at heart. I knew that he had been lying awake ever since the first slight noise, when he had turned in the bed. His fears had been ever since growing upon him. He had been trying to fancy them causeless, but could not. He had been saying to himself—"It is nothing but the wind in the chimney—it is only a mouse crossing the floor," or "it is merely a cricket which has made a single chirp." Yes, he had been trying to comfort himself with these suppositions; but he had found all in vain. *All in vain*; because Death, in approaching him, had stalked with his black shadow before him, and enveloped the victim. And it was the mournful influence of the unperceived shadow that caused him to feel—although he neither saw nor heard—to *feel* the presence of my head within the room.

When I had waited a long time, very patiently, without hearing him lie down, I resolved to open a little—a very, very little crevice in the lantern. So I opened it—you cannot imagine how stealthily, stealthily—until, at length, a single dim ray, like the thread of the spider, shot from out the crevice and full upon the vulture eye.

It was open—wide, wide open—and I grew furious as I gazed upon it. I saw it with perfect distinctness—all a dull blue, with a hideous veil over it that chilled the very marrow in my bones; but I could see nothing else of the old man's face or person: for I had directed the ray as if by instinct, precisely upon the damned spot.

And now have I not told you that what you mistake for madness is but over-acuteness of the senses?—now, I say, there came to my

Seated Man, 1949, ALBERTO GIACOMETTI.
The Morton Neumann Family Collection.

ears a low, dull, quick sound, such as a watch makes when enveloped in cotton. I knew *that* sound well too. It was the beating of the old man's heart. It increased my fury, as the beating of a drum stimulates the soldier into courage.

But even yet I refrained and kept still. I scarcely breathed. I held the lantern motionless. I tried how steadily I could maintain the ray upon the eye. Meantime the hellish tattoo of the heart increased. It grew quicker and quicker, and louder and louder every instant. The old man's terror *must* have been extreme! It grew louder, I say, louder every moment!—do you mark me well? I have told you that I am nervous: so I am. And now at the dead hour of the night, amid the dreadful silence of that old house, so strange a noise as this excited me to uncontrollable terror. Yet, for some minutes longer I refrained and stood still. But the beating grew louder, louder! I thought the heart must burst. And now a new anxiety seized me—the sound would be heard by a neighbor! The old man's hour had come! With a loud yell, I threw open the lantern and leaped into the room. He shrieked once—once only. In an instant I dragged him to the floor, and pulled the heavy bed over him. I then smiled gaily, to find the deed so far done. But, for many minutes, the heart beat on with a muffled sound. This, however, did not vex me; it would not be heard through the wall. At length it ceased. The old man was dead. I removed the bed and examined the corpse. Yes, he was stone, stone dead. I placed my hand upon the heart and held it there many minutes. There was no pulsation. He was stone dead. His eye would trouble me no more.

If still you think me mad, you will think so no longer when I describe the wise precautions I took for the concealment of the body. The night waned, and I worked hastily, but in silence. First of all I dismembered the corpse. I cut off the head and the arms and the legs.

I then took up three planks from the flooring of the chamber, and deposited all between the scantlings. I then replaced the boards so cleverly, so cunningly, that no human eye—not even *his*—could have detected anything wrong. There was nothing to wash out—no stain of any kind—no blood-spot whatever. I had been too wary for that. A tub had caught all—ha! ha!

When I had made an end to these labors, it was four o'clock—still dark as midnight. As the bell sounded the hour, there came a knocking at the street door. I went down to open it with a light heart,—for what had I *now* to fear? There entered three men, who introduced themselves, with perfect suavity, as officers of the police. A shriek had been heard by a neighbor during the night; suspicion of foul play had been aroused; information had been lodged at the police office, and they (the officers) had been deputed to search the premises.

I smiled,—for *what* had I to fear? I bade the gentlemen welcome. The shriek, I said, was my own in a dream. The old man, I mentioned, was absent in the country. I took my visitors all over the house. I bade them search—search *well*. I led them, at length, to *his* chamber. I showed them his treasures, secure, undisturbed. In the enthusiasm of my confidence, I brought chairs into the room, and desired them *here* to rest from their fatigues, while I myself, in the wild audacity of my perfect triumph, placed my own seat upon the very spot beneath which reposed the corpse of the victim.

The officers were satisfied. My *manner* had convinced them. I was singularly at ease. They sat, and while I answered cheerily, they chatted familiar things. But, ere long, I felt myself getting pale and wished them gone. My head ached, and I fancied a ringing in my ears: but still they sat and still chatted. The ringing became more distinct:—it continued and became more distinct: I talked more freely to get rid of the feeling: but it continued and gained definitiveness—until, at length, I found that the noise was *not* within my ears.

No doubt I now grew *very* pale;—but I talked more fluently, and with a heightened voice. Yet the sound increased—and what could I do? It was *a low, dull, quick sound—much such a sound as a watch makes when enveloped in cotton*. I gasped for breath—and yet the officers heard it not. I talked more quickly—more vehemently; but the noise steadily increased. I arose and argued about trifles, in a high key and with violent gesticulations, but the noise steadily increased. Why *would* they not be gone? I paced the floor to and fro with heavy strides, as if excited to fury by the observation of the men—but the noise steadily increased. Oh God! what *could* I do? I foamed—I raved—I swore! I swung the chair upon which I had been sitting, and grated it upon the boards, but the noise arose over all and continually increased. It grew louder—louder—*louder!* And still the men chatted pleasantly, and smiled. Was it possible they heard not? Almighty God!—no, no! They heard!—they suspected!—they *knew!*—they were making a mockery of my horror!—this I thought, and this I think. But anything was better than this agony! Anything was more tolerable than this derision! I could bear those hypocritical smiles no longer! I felt that I must scream or die!—and now—again!—hark! louder! louder! *louder!*

"Villains!" I shrieked, "dissemble no more! I admit the deed!—tear up the planks!—here, here!—it is the beating of his hideous heart!"

Developing Comprehension Skills

1. Why does the narrator want to kill the old man?

2. After the narrator kills the old man, how does he conceal the body?

3. What evidence does the narrator present to prove that he has a keen sense of hearing? Do you believe he actually heard everything he says he did? Explain.

4. Why does the narrator confess to his crime? Before he confesses, do you think that the police suspected him of the crime? Find passages that support your opinion.

5. Do you think the murdered man's heart was really beating loudly? Could there have been some other explanation?

6. The narrator insists that he is sane. What reasons does he give? Do you think he proves his point? Explain.

Reading Literature

1. **Understanding the Short Story.** A **short story** is a piece of fiction short enough to be read at one sitting. A short story has a **plot**, which is the series of events that unfolds as the result of some struggle. A short story also has **characters**, or people involved in the action. A third element of the short story is the setting. The **setting** is where and when a story takes place.

   Edgar Allan Poe is credited with developing a definition of what a short story should be. He believed that the purpose of a story was to create a single strong effect upon the reader's mind and feelings. Every event and word in the story should help create that effect.

   How well does "The Tell-Tale Heart" fit Poe's definition of a short story? What effect do you think he was trying to create?

2. **Identifying Mood.** Poe is probably best known for his tales of horror. Look again at "The Tell-Tale Heart." What parts did you find most terrifying? Study one of those passages carefully. How did Poe use words, sentence length, and tone to create the mood of horror?

3. **Analyzing Point of View.** "The Tell-Tale Heart" is told from the **first-person point of view**. In first-person narration, the narrator is a character involved in the action. How does this point of view affect "The Tell-Tale Heart"? Would the story have been different if it had been told by a character outside the action? Explain.

4. **Recognizing Suspense.** The tension created when the reader does not know the outcome of a situation is called **suspense**. As the reader waits, the tension mounts. Find a passage in "The Tell-Tale Heart" that you find especially suspenseful. Describe the situation. What makes it suspenseful?

5. **Recognizing Irony.** The contrast between what appears to be true and what actually is true is known as **irony**. One type of irony occurs when the reader understands something that a character in the story does not. In "The Tell-Tale Heart," the narrator attempts to show that he is sane. Find passages where he tries to prove that he is sane. What is ironic about his arguments?

6. **Analyzing Style.** Poe uses several different techniques to create the frantic, crazed speech of the narrator. Find examples of each of the following methods:
   a. broken sentences
   b. exclamations
   c. punctuation
   How does each add to the overall effect?

Developing Vocabulary Skills

Recognizing Antonyms. You have learned that a word can be used in context with its synonym. Sometimes a word can be used with its antonym. **Antonyms** are words with opposite meanings. An antonym can reveal the meaning of an unfamiliar word by telling you what it does not mean.

Read the following sentences. The word *dull* is an antonym of *acute*. By using *dull* as a clue you should be able to determine that the meaning of *acute* is "sharp or keen."

My senses were far from dull.
They were so *acute* that I could
   hear his heart beat.

The underlined word in each sentence below has been taken from "The Tell-Tale Heart." Write down the word and its antonym. Then, use the antonym to determine the meaning of the underlined word. Write the definition.

1. Although the old man's manner soothed him, the narrator was becoming increasingly vexed by the vulture's eye.

2. The officers conversed quietly, but the narrator's words were spoken more and more vehemently.

3. Although the officers were sincere, the narrator insisted that they were being hypocritical.

4. With audacity, the narrator placed his chair directly over the floorboards that concealed the old man's body. He was proud that he felt no cowardice.

5. The narrator showed no signs of awkwardness. He greeted the officers with suavity.

6. Instead of becoming indistinct, the beating of the old man's heart became more definitive.

Developing Writing Skills

1. **Analyzing Conflict.** A **conflict** is a struggle between opposing forces. The conflict may be **external**. In that case, it is between the character and nature, the character and society, or the character and another character. The conflict may also be **internal**, or within the mind of the character.

   "The Tell-Tale Heart" contains several conflicts. Some are internal and some are external. In your opinion, what is the main conflict? In one paragraph explain that conflict. Use specific examples and quotations to support your opinion.

2. **Using the First-Person Point of View.** A reader is able to see things differently in a story if it is told by a character who is part of the action. Adapt a well-known story so that it is told from the first-person point of view.

Pre-Writing. Choose a famous story to adapt in first person. You might wish to use "Rip Van Winkle" or "The Devil and Daniel Webster." Put yourself in the main character's place. Imagine how the character would describe events that happen. Make notes for your retelling of the story. Organize these notes in chronological order.

Writing. Use the pronouns *I* and *me* as you retell the story from the first-person point of view. Use a style of writing that reflects the character's personality. For example, if you are telling Daniel Webster's story you might use a more difficult vocabulary than you would for Rip Van Winkle.

Revising. Does your retelling give a new slant to the original story? Does it let readers see events from the character's point of view? Does it reveal the personality of the main character? If necessary, improve your story with more information that shows the character's viewpoint.

Developing Skills in Speaking and Listening

Presenting an Oral Interpretation. Oral interpretation is the oral reading of a piece of literature. A well-planned interpretation can bring the literature to life. Here are some guidelines for oral interpretation:

1. Before presenting an interpretation, read the piece until you are familiar with it. Look for words or sentences you want to emphasize. Find places where pauses or a different tone of voice would be effective.

2. Practice reading the piece out loud. Pronounce your words clearly. Make sure your tone of voice fits what you are saying.

3. Control the speed of your reading. Pause before something important, for example. Slow down at suspenseful points.

4. Use facial expressions and gestures to help create the mood or to emphasize important ideas.

Present an oral interpretation of three or four paragraphs from "The Tell-Tale Heart." Try to capture the mood in your interpretation. Also, try to convey the narrator's mad state of mind.

The Raven

EDGAR ALLAN POE

SETTING A PURPOSE

A man trying to forget his sorrow is visited by an evil-looking raven. By the end of this poem, what is the ominous meaning of the raven's one word, "Nevermore"?

Once upon a midnight dreary, while I pondered, weak and weary,
Over many a quaint and curious volume of forgotten lore—
While I nodded, nearly napping, suddenly there came a tapping,
As of someone gently rapping, rapping at my chamber door.
" 'Tis some visitor," I muttered, "tapping at my chamber door—   5
    Only this and nothing more."

Ah, distinctly I remember it was in the bleak December,
And each separate dying ember wrought its ghost upon the floor.
Eagerly I wished the morrow—vainly I had sought to borrow
From my books surcease of sorrow—sorrow for the lost Lenore—   10
For the rare and radiant maiden whom the angels name Lenore—
    Nameless *here* forevermore.

And the silken, sad, uncertain rustling of each purple curtain
Thrilled me—filled me with fantastic terrors never felt before;
So that now, to still the beating of my heart, I stood repeating,   15
" 'Tis some visitor entreating entrance at my chamber door—
Some late visitor entreating entrance at my chamber door—
    This it is and nothing more."

Presently my soul grew stronger; hesitating then no longer,
"Sir," said I, "or Madam, truly your forgiveness I implore;   20
But the fact is I was napping, and so gently you came rapping,
And so faintly you came tapping, tapping at my chamber door,
That I scarce was sure I heard you"—here I opened wide the door—
    Darkness there and nothing more.

Deep into that darkness peering, long I stood there wondering, fearing,   25
Doubting, dreaming dreams no mortal ever dared to dream before;
But the silence was unbroken, and the stillness gave no token,
And the only word there spoken was the whispered word "Lenore?"
This I whispered, and an echo murmured back the word "Lenore!"—
     Merely this and nothing more.   30

Back into the chamber turning, all my soul within me burning,
Soon again I heard a tapping somewhat louder than before.
"Surely," said I, "surely that is something at my window lattice;
Let me see, then, what thereat is, and this mystery explore—
Let my heart be still a moment and this mystery explore—   35
     'Tis the wind and nothing more!"

Open here I flung the shutter, when, with many a flirt and flutter,
In there stepped a stately Raven of the saintly days of yore;
Not the least obeisance made he; not a minute stopped or stayed he;
But, with mien of lord or lady, perched above my chamber door—   40
Perched upon a bust of Pallas just above my chamber door—
     Perched, and sat, and nothing more.

Then this ebon bird beguiling my sad fancy into smiling,
By the grave and stern decorum of the countenance it wore,
"Though thy crest be shorn and shaven, thou," I said, "art sure no craven,   45
Ghastly grim and ancient Raven wandering from the Nightly shore—
Tell me what thy lordly name is on the Night's Plutonian shore!"
     Quoth the Raven, "Nevermore."

Much I marveled this ungainly fowl to hear discourse so plainly,
Though its answer little meaning—little relevancy bore;   50
For we cannot help agreeing that no living human being
Ever yet was blessed with seeing bird above his chamber door—
Bird or beast upon the sculptured bust above his chamber door,
     With such name as "Nevermore."

But the Raven, sitting lonely on the placid bust, spoke only   55
That one word, as if his soul in that one word he did outpour.
Nothing further than he uttered, not a feather then he fluttered—
Till I scarcely more than muttered, "Other friends have flown before—

On the morrow *he* will leave me, as my Hopes have flown before."
    Then the bird said, "Nevermore."   60

Startled at the stillness broken by reply so aptly spoken,
"Doubtless," said I, "what it utters is its only stock and store
Caught from some unhappy master whom unmerciful Disaster
Followed fast and followed faster till his songs one burden bore—
Till the dirges of his Hope that melancholy burden bore   65
    Of 'Never—nevermore.' "

But the Raven still beguiling all my fancy into smiling,
Straight I wheeled a cushioned seat in front of bird and bust and door;
Then, upon the velvet sinking, I betook myself to linking
Fancy unto fancy, thinking what this ominous bird of yore—   70
What this grim, ungainly, ghastly, gaunt, and ominous bird of yore
    Meant in croaking, "Nevermore."

This I sat engaged in guessing, but no syllable expressing
To the fowl, whose fiery eyes now burned into my bosom's core;
This and more I sat divining, with my head at ease reclining   75
On the cushion's velvet lining that the lamp-light gloated o'er,
But whose velvet violet lining with the lamp-light gloating o'er
     She shall press, ah, nevermore!

Then, methought, the air grew denser, perfumed from an unseen censer
Swung by seraphim whose footfalls tinkled on the tufted floor.   80
"Wretch," I cried, "thy God hath lent thee—by these angels he hath
    sent thee
Respite—respite and nepenthe from thy memories of Lenore!
Quaff, oh quaff this kind nepenthe and forget this lost Lenore!"
     Quoth the Raven, "Nevermore."   85

"Prophet!" said I, "thing of evil!—prophet still, if bird or devil!—
Whether Tempter sent, or whether tempest tossed thee here ashore,
Desolate yet all undaunted, on this desert land enchanted—
On this home by horror haunted—tell me truly, I implore—
Is there—*is* there balm in Gilead?¹—tell me—tell me, I implore!"   90
     Quoth the Raven, "Nevermore."

"Prophet!" said I, "thing of evil—prophet still, if bird or devil!
By that Heaven that bends above us—by that God we both adore—
Tell this soul with sorrow laden if, within the distant Aidenn,²
It shall clasp a sainted maiden whom the angels name Lenore—   95
Clasp a rare and radiant maiden whom the angels name Lenore!"
     Quoth the Raven, "Nevermore."

"Be that word our sign of parting, bird or fiend!" I shrieked,
    upstarting—
"Get thee back into the tempest and the Night's Plutonian shore!   100
Leave no black plume as a token of that lie thy soul hath spoken!
Leave my loneliness unbroken! quit the bust above my door!
Take thy beak from out my heart, and take thy form from off my door!"
     Quoth the Raven, "Nevermore."

---

1. **balm in Gilead**, a soothing cream made in Gilead, a region in Palestine; relief from suffering.
2. **Aidenn**, an Arabic word for Eden or heaven.

And the Raven, never flitting, still is sitting, still is sitting
On the pallid bust of Pallas just above my chamber door;
And his eyes have all the seeming of a demon's that is dreaming,
And the lamp-light o'er him streaming throws his shadow on the floor;
And my soul from out that shadow that lies floating on the floor
        Shall be lifted—nevermore!

Developing Comprehension Skills

1. By reading, what is the speaker trying to forget?

2. What is the speaker's first reaction to the raven? How does his attitude change?

3. The only word the raven speaks is *nevermore*. What effect does this word have on the speaker?

4. Why does the speaker tell the raven to leave in the second to the last stanza? Why does the speaker remain sorrowful at the end of the poem?

5. Do you think Poe has succeeded in creating a memorable poem in "The Raven"? Do you believe the speaker comes alive as a real person? Explain your answer.

Reading Literature

1. **Understanding Poetry.** According to William Wordsworth, a famous poet, poetry is "the spontaneous overflow of powerful feelings." What strong feelings are evident in "The Raven"?

2. **Appreciating End Rhyme.** Edgar Allan Poe's "The Raven" has unmistakable sound appeal. One reason for this is the use of end rhyme. **End rhyme** occurs at the end of a line of poetry. Look at each stanza, or group of lines. Which lines contain end rhyme? Which lines do not contain end rhyme?

3. **Recognizing Internal Rhyme.** Besides end rhyme, "The Raven" also has internal rhyme. **Internal rhyme** is rhyme within a line. For example, in the first line the words *dreary* and *weary* rhyme. Which lines in each stanza contain internal rhyme?

4. **Recognizing Alliteration and Consonance.** Other sound devices that Poe uses are alliteration and consonance. **Alliteration** refers to the repetition of beginning consonant sounds. For example, in the phrase "weak and weary" the *w* sound is repeated. **Consonance** is the repetition of consonant sounds within and at the ends of words. Both alliteration and consonance may be used to call attention to important words or to emphasize sounds. Find examples of both types of sound devices in these lines:

    a. And the silken sad uncertain rustling of each purple curtain

    b. Not a feather then he fluttered

    c. What this grim, ungainly, ghastly, gaunt, and ominous bird of yore

Find two other examples of alliteration within "The Raven."

5. **Appreciating Assonance.** The repetition of vowel sounds within different words is known as **assonance**. An example is the repetition of the *o* sound in "forgiveness I implore." The long *o* sound helps to create a mood of sadness. Find two examples of assonance in "The Raven."

6. **Understanding Symbolism.** A **symbol** is something that stands for, or represents, something beyond itself. For example, the color white might represent goodness or purity. Poe uses the raven as a symbol. What does it symbolize? What might the shadow of the raven symbolize?

7. **Analyzing Repetition.** When a word or group of words is repeated in a selection, the writer is using **repetition**. Poets use repetition to emphasize an important idea to connect ideas, or to create a sound effect. Find two examples of word repetition. Explain the purpose of each.

Developing Vocabulary Skills

Reviewing Context Clues. The underlined words in the following sentences are taken from "The Raven." Write the meaning of each word. Then, explain which method you used to figure out each definition.

1. The man was searching for a surcease—a temporary end—to his grief.

2. The face on the bust of Pallas was placid, totally unlike the narrator's frantic expression.

3. The Raven promised no respite from his memories nor relief from loneliness.

4. An ominous sign is one that predicts evil.

5. He longed for some kind of balm for his soul, something that would refresh and comfort him.

Developing Writing Skills

1. **Explaining an Interpretation.** Who do you think is responsible for the raven's sorrowful message of "Nevermore"? You may think that the bird is at fault for the sad message. On the other hand, the man may be responsible because he phrases questions knowing that the answer will be "Nevermore." In one paragraph, state your interpretation, or opinion, and support it.

   Pre-Writing. Reread "The Raven." Draw a conclusion about who is responsible for the sad message of "Nevermore." Make notes on the reasons for your interpretation. Jot down passages, or quotes, that support your opinion. Organize your notes in logical order.

   Writing. State your interpretation of the poem in a clear topic sentence. Remember to give support to your opinion with specific examples and quotations. Conclude with a "clincher" sentence that ties the paragraph together.

   Revising. Ask someone else to read your paragraph. Ask the person if he or she finds anything that is unclear. If so, make the necessary changes so your meaning is clear.

2. **Writing a Parody.** A **parody** is an imitation of a work of literature. Its purpose may be humor, criticism, or praise. Write a parody of "The Raven." In your parody, substitute a different subject. Make your parody about three stanzas long.

| *This sad love poem was inspired by Poe's wife Virginia. What happened to the young Annabel Lee?*

Annabel Lee

EDGAR ALLAN POE

It was many and many a year ago,
    In a kingdom by the sea,
That a maiden there lived whom you may know
    By the name of Annabel Lee;
And this maiden she lived with no other thought   5
    Than to love and be loved by me.

She was a child and *I* was a child,
    In this kingdom by the sea,
But we loved with a love that was more than love—
    I and my Annabel Lee—   10
With love that the wingéd seraphs of Heaven
    Coveted her and me.

And this was the reason that, long ago,
    In this kingdom by the sea,
A wind blew out of a cloud by night   15
    Chilling my Annabel Lee;
So that her highborn kinsmen came
    And bore her away from me,
To shut her up in a sepulchre
    In this kingdom by the sea.   20

The angels, not half so happy in Heaven,
    Went envying her and me:—
Yes!—that was the reason (as all men know,
    In this kingdom by the sea)
That the wind came out of the cloud, chilling   25
    And killing my Annabel Lee.

Virginia Clemm, Poe's child-bride, on her deathbed, January 31, 1847.
The Edgar Allan Poe Museum, Richmond, Virginia.

But our love it was stronger by far than the love
   Of those who were older than we—
   Of many far wiser than we—
And neither the angels in Heaven above   30
   Nor the demons down under the sea,
Can ever dissever my soul from the soul
   Of the beautiful Annabel Lee:—

For the moon never beams, without bringing me dreams
   Of the beautiful Annabel Lee:—   35
And the stars never rise but I see the bright eyes
   Of the beautiful Annabel Lee:
And so, all the night-tide, I lie down by the side
Of my darling, my darling, my life and my bride,
   In her sepulchre there by the sea—   40
   In her tomb by the side of the sea.

Study for Eos, 1973, WILL BARNET.
Collection of Katherine Kuh, New York.
Photograph by Otto Nelson.

Developing Comprehension Skills

1. Who is the speaker of the poem? How does he feel about Annabel Lee?

2. What kind of love did the speaker and Annabel Lee have? How did it differ from other people's love?

3. According to the speaker, who is responsible for Annabel Lee's death? What seems to be the actual cause of death?

4. What is the speaker's life like after Annabel Lee's death?

5. What things in nature remind the speaker of Annabel Lee?

6. The introduction states that "Annabel Lee" is a sad love poem. Do you agree? Explain.

Reading Literature

1. **Understanding the Author's Motivation.** The **author's motivation** is his or her purpose for writing the selection. The purpose of many poems is to express strong feelings. In "Annabel Lee" the speaker expresses his feelings about the death of a young woman. Why might Poe have written such a poem? What event in his personal life might have inspired "Annabel Lee"?

2. **Analyzing Stanzas.** Each stanza of a poem is like a paragraph. The stanza develops a single main idea. How many stanzas are there in "Annabel Lee"? What is the main idea of each stanza? State it briefly.

3. **Appreciating Alliteration.** Alliteration, you will recall, is the repetition of beginning consonant sounds. An example is the repetition of the *s* sound in the poem's final line, "by the side of the sea." Find two other examples of alliteration in the poem.

4. **Analyzing Assonance.** Besides alliteration, Poe also uses assonance in "Annabel Lee." Assonance, you remember, is the repetition of vowel sounds in different words. In this phrase, for example, the long *i* sound is repeated: "my life and my bride." Find two other examples of assonance in the poem.

5. **Analyzing Repetition.** Poe uses repetition throughout "Annabel Lee." It is used to emphasize important ideas and to unify the poem. For example, in "But we loved with a love that was more than love," the word *love* is repeated three times. Why do you think Poe repeats this word? Find two other examples of repetition within a stanza.

6. **Appreciating Style.** "Annabel Lee" begins almost like a fairy tale. What words and images does Poe use to create this effect? How do the sounds and rhythm of the poem add to this feeling? Now reread the last two lines of the poem. How do they depart from the earlier style? Why do you think Poe made such a drastic change?

Developing Vocabulary Skills

Using Example Clues. Instead of simply stating the meaning of a word, a writer may give examples. From these examples, you may be able to discover the meaning of the unfamiliar word. Here is an example.

> It could not be for want of . . . *perseverance*; for he would sit on a wet rock . . . and fish all day without a murmur, even though he should not be encouraged by a single nibble.

From this sentence, you can figure out from the fishing example that *perseverance* must have to do with dedication and patience. Words that often signal examples as context clues are *for instance, for example, such as, like, including, these, especially*, and *other*.

The underlined words in the following sentences are from the selections you have read. Read each sentence carefully, and look for the example clue. Use the clue to determine the meaning of the underlined word. Write the word and its meaning.

1. The strangers all wore cloth <u>jerkins</u>; two wore short brown jackets, and a third wore a moss-colored vest.

2. "Their <u>visages</u>, too, were peculiar: one had a large broad face and small piggish eyes: the face of another seemed to consist almost entirely of nose."

3. To provide evidence of his <u>acute</u> hearing, the murderer explained that he could hear the beating of the old man's heart.

4. The narrator felt that they <u>mocked</u> his terror because they sat and chatted and joked.

5. Burial tombs, such as mausoleums and <u>sepulchers</u>, were dark shadows in the gloom of the cemetery.

Developing Writing Skills

1. **Using Comparison.** Although "Annabel Lee" is a love poem and "The Raven" is a poem of gloom, both are similar in some ways. Write three paragraphs comparing the poems. Consider speaker, mood, and sound techniques.

   Pre-Writing. Reread the two poems closely. Observe how the speakers, moods, and sound techniques of the two poems are alike. Make notes under these three headings.

   Writing. Develop each grouping of ideas into a paragraph. Each paragraph should center on one area of similarity: speaker, mood, or sound. Write a topic sentence for each paragraph. Support it with specific examples and quotations from the poems.

   Revising. Check to see that each paragraph has a topic sentence. See if each paragraph has specific examples and quotations to give support. Omit any ideas that are unrelated. Clarify any confusing sentences.

2. **Using Figurative Language.** You have seen that "Annabel Lee" begins like a fairy tale. "It was many and many a year ago, In a kingdom by the sea." Poe's use of the word *kingdom*, however, is figurative. It is not meant to be taken as real or as fact. It is meant, instead, to suggest the special joy of the speaker and Annabel Lee's young love. In one paragraph, describe a place that seems wonderful or special to you. Describe it with figurative language that makes it seem special or fantastic.

Developing Skills in Study and Research

Doing Biographical Research. There are several specialized biographical references that contain articles about authors. Some of these are: *American Authors, 1600–1900, Oxford Companion to American Literature*, and *Reader's Encyclopedia of American Literature*. Use these biographical references to find out about Edgar Allan Poe's life and how it relates to his work. Take notes on the important facts of Poe's life. Add to your information with an encyclopedia article, too. Share your information with other students in your class.

Old Ironsides

OLIVER WENDELL HOLMES

SETTING A PURPOSE

Old Ironsides was the nickname of the ship Constitution, *which took part in the War of 1812. The ship was about to be destroyed when this poem was written. How does the speaker feel about Old Ironsides?*

Ay, tear her tattered ensign down!
   Long has it waved on high,
And many an eye has danced to see
   That banner in the sky;
Beneath it rung the battle shout,
   And burst the cannon's roar;—
The meteor of the ocean air
   Shall sweep the clouds no more!

Her deck once red with heroes' blood,
   Where knelt the vanquished foe,
When winds were hurrying o'er the flood,
   And waves were white below,
No more shall feel the victor's tread,
   Or know the conquered knee;—
The harpies of the shore shall pluck
   The eagle of the sea!

Oh, better that her shattered hulk
   Should sink beneath the wave;
Her thunders shook the mighty deep,
   And there should be her grave;
Nail to the mast her holy flag,
   Set every threadbare sail,
And give her to the god of storms,
   The lightning and the gale!

Constitution and Guerrière, date unknown, attributed to THOMAS BIRCH.
United States Naval Academy Museum, Annapolis, Maryland.

Developing Comprehension Skills

1. Holmes writes, "tear her tattered ensign down!" Do you think he really wants the ship to be destroyed? How can you tell?

2. What does Holmes tell the reader about the ship's history?

3. What does Holmes think is a fitting fate for Old Ironsides? Why?

4. Why do you think Holmes feels so strongly about Old Ironsides? Is there any historic object in the United States today that would arouse a similar public reaction? Explain.

Reading Literature

1. **Understanding the Author's Purpose.** "Old Ironsides" reveals the strong feelings that Oliver Wendell Holmes had for the *Constitution*. Often a writer will choose to write an essay or letter to express feelings about a particular subject. Why do you suppose Holmes chose to use poetry in his effort to save the *Constitution*?

2. **Analyzing the Stanza.** A stanza, you will recall, is a group of lines that forms a unit in poetry. The stanza is similar to a paragraph. Each contains a main idea. "Old Ironsides"

is made up of three stanzas. Briefly state the main idea contained in each.

3. **Understanding Metaphor.** A metaphor, as you know, is a comparison between two unlike things. Metaphors do not use the words *like* or *as*. Find the following metaphors in the poem.

   a. The meteor of the ocean air
   b. The eagle of the sea

   What is each metaphor describing? Do you think each one is a good comparison?

4. **Recognizing Personification.** You have learned that personification gives human traits to objects, ideas, or animals. Which words in "Old Ironsides" show that Holmes personifies the ship? How does personification help to make Holmes's poem persuasive?

Developing Vocabulary Skills

Understanding Synonyms and Antonyms. Synonyms are words that have nearly the same meaning. Notice these synonyms from "Old Ironsides":

> Ay, tear her tattered *ensign* down!
>   Long has it waved on high,
> And many an eye has danced to see
>   That *banner* in the sky;

The words *ensign* and *banner* are synonyms.
   Locate the following paragraphs or passages. Then answer the questions related to each.

1. "Annabel Lee," page 187. Reread the last two lines of Poe's poem. The same idea is presented in each of the two lines. Which word in the second line is a synonym for sepulchre?

2. "The Tell-Tale Heart," page 174. In the first paragraph, Poe states that his senses had been sharpened. What word in the paragraph did he use to show the opposite idea?

3. "The Tell-Tale Heart," page 177. In the first paragraph, what phrase acts as a synonym for dismembered? In the next paragraph, what is a synonym for cleverly?

4. "The Devil and Daniel Webster," page 168. Reread the last three sentences of paragraph 2. What do you think bamboozled means? Which word gave you a clue?

5. "Rip Van Winkle," page 145. Reread the right-hand column. The author describes Rip's meekness in his relationship with his wife. What two other words does he use to describe that characteristic? How does the word meekness help you understand their meaning?

6. "Rip Van Winkle," page 148. At the top of the right-hand column, the author says that Rip saw the lordly Hudson. What synonym for lordly does he use in the same sentence?

Developing Writing Skills

1. **Writing Persuasion.** Holmes's poem "Old Ironsides," was so persuasive that the *Constitution* was saved from destruction. Write a persuasive composition on one of these topics or on one of your choosing:

   Why families should unplug their TVs
   Why people should listen to rock/jazz/
     folksongs
   Why young people should avoid peer
     pressure
   Why every school should have a student
     newspaper

   Pre-Writing. Choose a topic. Determine the purpose of your writing. Decide what you want it to accomplish. Then, identify your audience. This is important. It will tell you what objections you will have to overcome. It may also tell you which reasons would be most effective. Jot down notes and logical reasons to support your topic. For each reason, list facts, examples, and incidents that you can use to support your idea. Arrange your notes in logical order. For this type of composition you will probably want to build up to the strongest reason.

Writing. Write an introduction that states the main point of your composition. Make the introduction lively by using a quotation, a startling fact, or a description. Use each reason as the topic sentence of a paragraph. Support each reason with evidence listed in your notes. Close with a strong summary.

Revising. Ask someone else to read your composition. Ask the person what is most and least persuasive about your composition. You may have to provide more logical reasons, or better evidence, to improve your paper. Ask the person if any sentences are unclear or vague. Rewrite them to make them more precise.

2. **Using Figurative Language.** You have seen that Holmes uses powerful language to make his point. Some of this language is figurative. It is not meant to be taken as real or fact. For example, Holmes refers to the *Constitution* as the "meteor of the ocean air" and "the eagle of the sea." In one paragraph, describe a place or thing that has special meaning for you. Use figurative language in your description to emphasize your subject's unique qualities.

Developing Skills in Critical Thinking

Recognizing Emotional Appeals. Because "Old Ironsides" aroused deep feelings, public reaction forced officials to spare the ship. The poem appeals strongly to emotions through the use of flag-waving. **Flag-waving** is an emotional appeal that associates a cause with patriotism. Find words in "Old Ironsides" that appeal to the idea of patriotism.

Killed at the Ford

HENRY WADSWORTH LONGFELLOW

SETTING A PURPOSE *Longfellow's son, Charles, was wounded while serving in the Army of the Potomac. That fact might have inspired the following poem. What is Longfellow's attitude toward war?*

He is dead, the beautiful youth,
The heart of honor, the tongue of truth,
He, the life and light of us all,
Whose voice was blithe as a bugle-call,
Whom all eyes followed with one consent,   5
The cheer of whose laugh, and whose pleasant word,
Hushed all murmurs of discontent.

Only last night, as we rode along,
Down the dark of the mountain gap,
To visit the picket-guard at the ford,   10
Little dreaming of any mishap,
He was humming the words of some old song:
"Two red roses he had on his cap,
And another he bore at the point of his sword."

Sudden and swift a whistling ball   15
Came out of a wood, and the voice was still;
Something I heard in the darkness fall,
And for a moment my blood grew chill;
I spake in a whisper, as he who speaks
In a room where some one is lying dead;   20
But he made no answer to what I said.

We lifted him up to his saddle again,
And through the mire and the mist and the rain
Carried him back to the silent camp,
And laid him as if asleep on his bed;   25

And I saw by the light of the surgeon's lamp
Two white roses upon his cheeks,
And one, just over his heart, blood-red!

And I saw in a vision how far and fleet
That fatal bullet went speeding forth,   30
Till it reached a town in the distant North,
Till it reached a house in a sunny street,
Till it reached a heart that ceased to beat
Without a murmur, without a cry;
And a bell was tolled, in that far-off town,   35
For one who had passed from cross to crown,
And the neighbors wondered that she should die.

Developing Comprehension Skills

1. The first stanza gives details that reveal the youth's personality. What was the young person like?

2. What did the speaker hear fall in the darkness?

3. How do the circumstances of the boy's death make it especially tragic?

4. How do you think the speaker was affected by the boy's death?

5. Besides the dead boy, who is the bullet's other victim? How did the bullet cause her death, too?

6. In "Killed at the Ford," Longfellow gives a personal view of one person's death in war. Do you think he could have shown the horror of war more clearly if he had described the deaths of many people? Explain your answer.

Reading Literature

1. **Analyzing Theme.** In a work of literature, the main idea about life is called the **theme**. In "Killed at the Ford," Longfellow comments on war. What is the theme of the poem? What do you think Longfellow's purpose was in writing the poem?

2. **Recognizing Metaphor.** In line 3, explain the metaphor: "the life and light of us all." What things are being compared? What do these comparisons tell about the boy?

3. **Using Contrast.** In the second stanza, Longfellow presents the song the boy was singing when he was killed. Later Longfellow repeats the words of the song, but with some variation. Identify the stanza where the song is repeated. How does it differ from the song in stanza two? Why is this contrast effective?

4. **Analyzing Repetition.** In the fifth stanza, Longfellow repeats the phrase "Till it reached." With each repetition, Longfellow focuses on a different, and specific, object. How does the repetition help to show the impact of the bullet on the boy's mother?

5. **Identifying Symbols.** In many religions, the cross and the crown represent hardships and suffering. Longfellow uses *cross* and *crown* in line 36. Read stanza five. Then, explain why *cross* and *crown* are symbolic.

American infantry uniforms and equipment used during the Revolutionary War.
West Point Museum; Fort Ticonderoga Museum; New York State Office of Parks, Recreation and Historic Preservation; Palisades Region Headquarters State Historic Site and the H. Charles Barron collections. Courtesy of *American Heritage* Publishing Co., Inc, New York. Photograph by Arnold Newman.

Life is full of many different types of journeys. Where is the traveler in this poem going?

The Tide Rises, the Tide Falls

HENRY WADSWORTH LONGFELLOW

The tide rises, the tide falls,
The twilight darkens, the curlew calls;
Along the sea-sands damp and brown
The traveler hastens toward the town,
　And the tide rises, the tide falls.

Darkness settles on roofs and walls,
But the sea, the sea in the darkness calls;
The little waves, with their soft, white hands,
Efface the footprints in the sands,
　And the tide rises, the tide falls.

The morning breaks; the steeds in their stalls
Stamp and neigh, as the hostler calls;
The day returns, but nevermore
Returns the traveler to the shore,
　And the tide rises, the tide falls.

Orange Sunset Waning Low, 1897, WILLIAM TROST RICHARDS. Time Inc., Washington, D.C.

Developing Comprehension Skills

1. What is the setting of this poem? Where is the traveler heading?

2. What happens to the footprints the traveler leaves behind?

3. This poem may be telling about something other than one person's walk down a beach. If so, what might the journey represent? Why won't the traveler be returning?

4. In your opinion, is this a sad poem or does it create some other kind of mood? Explain your answer.

Reading Literature

1. **Understanding Symbolic Meaning.** This poem makes sense on a **literal,** or surface,

level. However, it can be read on a **symbolic** level as well. This means that each detail of the poem stands for something beyond itself.

The journey in this poem could represent our journey through life. If so, what details in the first stanza could show that the traveler is close to death? In the second stanza, which images tell the reader that death has occurred? Finally, what might the third stanza suggest about what goes on in the rest of the world after a person's death?

2. **Recognizing Symbols.** You know that "The Tide Rises, the Tide Falls" can be read on a symbolic level. In particular, what might the tide be a symbol of? Why is it fitting that the tide erases the traveler's footprints?

3. **Appreciating Repetition.** Which phrase is repeated four times in this poem? How does this refrain add to the meaning of the poem? Remember to keep the symbolic meaning of the tide in mind.

4. **Appreciating Form.** Examine the rhyme scheme of this poem. Then read it aloud and listen to the rhythm. Would you say that this poem has a regular or irregular form? Why do you think the poet chose this kind of form for this particular poem?

Developing Vocabulary Skills

Recognizing Comparison Clues. Another type of context clue is the comparison. In a **comparison clue** the writer compares the unfamiliar word with other, more familiar words.

Words that signal comparisons include *like, as, similar to, also, in the same way, related,* and *another.*

The meaning of the word *efface* in "The Tide Rises, the Tide Falls" could be given through a

The Tide Rises, the Tide Falls 199

comparison clue. Look at the following sentence:

> The waves *efface* the footprints in the sand in the same way an eraser removes chalk marks.

The comparison clue leads the reader to discover that *efface* means "to erase" or "to rub or wipe out."

The underlined words in the following sentences are taken from selections you have read. Use comparison clues to determine the meaning of each underlined word. Write the word and its meaning.

1. Holmes feared that Old Ironsides would be plucked like a slaughtered bird.
2. The murderer moved as stealthily as a wolf stalking his prey.
3. Soon the danger ebbed, much like the retreating water after a flood.
4. Rip's character was as malleable as soft clay.
5. The beating heart made muffled sounds— much like that of a watch enveloped in cotton.

Developing Writing Skills

1. **Using Comparison and Contrast.** Both poems by Longfellow, "Killed at the Ford" and "The Tide Rises, the Tide Falls," concern a person's death. Do they present similar or different views of death? In two paragraphs, compare and contrast the tone and mood of these poems.

   Pre-Writing. Reread the poems closely. Compare and contrast the tone and mood of the poems. Examine the ideas in the poems as well as the word choice, sound, and rhythm. List examples and quotations that show similarities or differences. Group similar ideas together. Choose a logical order to present your ideas.

   Writing. In each paragraph, expand on one similarity or difference between the poems. Write a topic sentence to summarize the main idea of each paragraph. Use specific examples and quotations as support.

   Revising. Does each paragraph deal with a single idea? Have you found enough similarities or differences to fully develop your paragraphs? Will your reader be able to follow your ideas? Make changes if necessary.

2. **Writing Fiction.** Find a newspaper account that reports a dramatic event in a dry, factual manner. Then, as Longfellow did in "Killed at the Ford," write a fictional account of the event. Pretend you were present while the event was taking place. Tell how one person was directly affected. For example, you might read an article about unemployment and write about an imaginary character seeking work. Submit the news report with your fictional story.

Developing Skills in Critical Thinking

Making Inferences. An inference is a conclusion based on facts. The speaker in "Killed at the Ford" describes the death of the young soldier and its effect on others. Although the speaker says little about himself, the reader can draw conclusions about the type of individual he is.

Read the poem again. Based on the speaker's words, what kind of person is he? Explain.

From
Self-Reliance

RALPH WALDO EMERSON

Ralph Waldo Emerson was a great thinker and writer. The ideas of Emerson have inspired generations of readers. Where does Emerson advise you to look for direction in your life?

There is a time in every man's education when he arrives at the conviction that envy is ignorance; that imitation is suicide; that he must take himself for better, for worse, as his portion; that though the wide universe is full of good, no kernel of nourishing corn can come to him but through his toil bestowed on that plot of ground which is given to him to till.

Trust thyself: every heart vibrates to that iron string. Accept the place the divine providence has found for you, the society of your contemporaries, the connection of events. Great men have always done so, and confided themselves childlike to the genius of their age, betraying their perception that the absolutely trustworthy was seated at their heart, working through their hands, predominating in all their being.

Whoso would be a man, must be a nonconformist. He who would gather immortal palms must not be hindered by the name of goodness, but must explore if it be goodness. Nothing is at last sacred but the integrity of your own mind. Absolve you to yourself, and you shall have the suffrage of the world. I remember an answer which when quite young I was prompted to make to a valued adviser who was wont to importune me with the dear old doctrines of the church. On my saying, "What have I to do with the sacredness of traditions, if I live wholly from within?" my friend suggested,—"But these impulses may be from below, not from above." I replied, "They do not seem to me to be such; but if I am the Devil's child, I will live then from the Devil." No law can be sacred to me but that of my nature. Good and bad are but names very readily transferable to that or this; the only right is what is after my constitution; the only wrong what is against it.

What I must do is all that concerns me, not what the people think. This rule, equally arduous in actual and in intellectual life, may serve for the whole distinction between greatness and meanness. It is the harder because you will always find those who think they know what is your duty better than you know it. It is easy in the world to live after the world's opinion; it is easy in solitude to live after our own; but the great man is he who in the midst of the crowd keeps with perfect sweetness the independence of solitude.

For nonconformity the world whips you with its displeasure. And therefore a man must know how to estimate a sour face. The by-standers look askance on him in the public street or in the friend's parlor. If this aversion had its origin in contempt and resistance like his own he might well go home with a sad countenance; but the sour faces of the multitude, like their sweet faces, have no deep cause, but are put on and off as the wind blows and a newspaper directs.

The other terror that scares us from self-trust is our consistency; a reverence for our past act or word because the eyes of others have no other data for computing our orbit than our past acts, and we are loth to disappoint them.

A foolish consistency is the hobgoblin of little minds, adored by little statesmen and philosophers and divines. With consistency a great soul has simply nothing to do. He may as well concern himself with his shadow on the wall. Speak what you think now in hard words and to-morrow speak what to-morrow thinks in hard words again, though it contradict every thing you said to-day.—"Ah, so you shall be sure to be misunderstood."—Is it so bad then to be misunderstood? Pythagoras was misunderstood, and Socrates, and Jesus, and Luther, and Copernicus, and Galileo, and Newton, and every pure and wise spirit that ever took flesh. To be great is to be misunderstood.

Ralph Waldo Emerson, 1885. The New-York Historical Society, New York.

Insist on yourself; never imitate. Your own gift you can present every moment with the cumulative force of a whole life's cultivation; but of the adopted talent of another you have only an extemporaneous half possession. That which each can do best, none but his Maker can teach him. No man yet knows what it is, nor can, till that person has exhibited it. Where is the master who could have taught Shakespeare? Where is the master who could have instructed Franklin, or Washington, or Bacon, or Newton? Every great man is a unique.

Developing Comprehension Skills

1. Emerson writes, "Trust thyself: every heart vibrates to that iron string." What does he mean?

2. Emerson says that *good* and *bad* are just names or labels attached to different things. What does he consider the only good, or right, thing? the only wrong?

3. According to Emerson, "It is easy in the world to live after the world's opinion." What does he mean?

4. Consistency involves following the same pattern or routine. According to Emerson, what disadvantage is there in consistency?

5. How does Emerson define greatness?

6. If Emerson were alive today, what would he think of fads in fashion? of television commentators? of political parties?

Reading Literature

1. **Understanding Essays.** A brief, nonfiction composition that expresses an opinion on a subject is called an **essay**. An essay may be formal or informal. A **formal essay** is serious, dignified, impersonal, and carefully organized. On the other hand, the **informal essay** is casual, personal, and looser in structure. The passages you have just read come from an essay by Emerson called "Self-Reliance." Do you think Emerson's essay is formal or informal? Why?

2. **Understanding Transcendentalism.** Transcendentalism (tran' sen den't'l iz'm) was a philosophy, or way of thinking. It was especially popular among certain thinkers and writers in nineteenth-century New England. Transcendentalists believed that God was in humans. They also believed that people became more spiritual by being close to nature. In addition, Transcendentalists believed strongly in the importance of the individual. They encouraged self-confidence. What elements of Transcendentalism are shown in "Self-Reliance"?

3. **Identifying Theme.** In his writings Emerson expresses many ideas about life. What is the main theme of "Self-Reliance"? State it in one sentence.

Developing Vocabulary Skills

Recognizing Contrast Clues. You have learned that a writer can explain a word by comparing it to a similar word or idea. In the same way, a writer can explain a word by showing how it is different from another word or idea. This is called a **contrast clue**. The contrast tells you what the word does *not* mean. Here is an example:

> He preferred to be among his *contemporaries*, as opposed to those older or younger than himself.

In this sentence, the word *contemporaries* is contrasted to *those older or younger than himself.* Therefore, *contemporaries* must mean people of the same age. The key phrase that alerted you to a contrast is "as opposed to." Other words and phrases that signal contrast clues are the following: *but, although, however, on the other hand, yet, different from, in contrast to, unlike,* and *not.*

The underlined words in the following sentences come from the selection you have just read. Look for contrast clues to figure out the meaning of each underlined word. Write the word and its meaning.

1. Emerson feels that all great people are <u>non-conformists</u>, unlike most of us who tend to follow the crowd.

2. To follow one's own desires is actually an <u>arduous</u> task, not a natural or easy one.

3. Is it more important to be <u>consistent</u> or to remain open to a change of mind or opinion?

4. Emerson felt that we should not be "<u>hindered</u> by the name of goodness," but should instead feel free to explore what goodness is.

5. It is easy to keep an opinion in <u>solitude</u>, but it is hard to do so in a crowd.

6. Sometimes we hold too much <u>reverence</u> for our past actions. On the other hand, we sometimes feel only disrespect.

Developing Writing Skills

1. **Supporting an Opinion.** Emerson expresses opinions about self-trust, conformity, greatness, and consistency. Choose a statement by Emerson with which you strongly agree or disagree. Write a composition defending your opinion on the subject. Include specific reasons to support your opinion.

2. **Writing About a Personal Experience.** Emerson wrote, "For nonconformity the world whips you with its displeasure." Think of a time when you chose to "insist on yourself." How did others react to your decision? Tell about your experience in a well-planned composition.

   Pre-Writing. Decide on an incident to write about. How did you fail to conform? Why didn't you conform? How were you treated as a result? Jot down ideas related to these questions. Each of these ideas will be developed later in a separate paragraph.

   Writing. Begin with an introduction that uses Emerson's quotation about nonconformity. Develop individual paragraphs related to the various aspects of your experience. You might present these events in chronological, or time, order. Connect ideas and explanations smoothly and logically.

   Revising. Ask someone to read your composition. Does he or she think you have given enough information? Was your tone, or feelings about the experience, clearly expressed? Ask if the person has suggestions for improving the composition.

Developing Skills in Speaking and Listening

Holding a Panel Discussion. A panel discussion is an informal discussion among a small group of people. Some purposes for holding such discussions include sharing information, solving problems, and planning courses of action. Hold a panel discussion in your class and share ideas about one of the following statements:

1. Whoso would be a man, must be a nonconformist.

2. No law can be sacred to me but that of my nature.

3. A foolish consistency is the hobgoblin of little minds.

Students on the panel should begin by comparing ideas on what the statement means. They should also offer their opinions on whether Emerson is right. If you are on the panel, be courteous and listen to what others say. Try to understand the other person's point of view. When you wish to take part in the discussion, express your ideas briefly but clearly.

Emerson could express a great deal of truth in a brief sentence. What ideas and suggestions does he offer in the following sayings?

Epigrams

RALPH WALDO EMERSON

I think no virtue goes with size.

The only way to have a friend is to be one.

The true test of civilization is, not the census, nor the size of cities, nor the crops—no, but the kind of man the country turns out.

What is a weed? A plant whose virtues have not yet been discovered.

Hitch your wagon to a star.

To be great is to be misunderstood.

Nothing great was ever achieved without enthusiasm.

The reward of a thing well done is to have done it.

We boil at different degrees.

Keep cool; it will be all one a hundred years hence.

Developing Comprehension Skills

1. According to Emerson, what is "the only way to have a friend"?

2. The "true test" of a civilization, according to Emerson, is "the kind of man the country turns out." What does he mean?

3. Emerson describes a weed as "A plant whose virtues have not yet been discovered." If the weed represents a person, what possibility exists in each individual?

4. "The reward of a thing well done is to have done it," Emerson says. Do you think Emerson places importance on material things? What sorts of things give him satisfaction?

5. Emerson says that "Nothing great was ever achieved without enthusiasm." Do you agree?

Reading Literature

1. **Understanding Epigrams.** A brief saying that expresses a truth about life is called an **epigram**. A large portion of Emerson's writing contains epigrams. Reread "Self-Reliance." Find three statements that could be considered epigrams.

2. **Explaining Metaphors.** Several of Emerson's epigrams make their points through metaphor. Read epigrams five and nine

again. What is Emerson comparing in each metaphor? Why do you think he chose to make these comparisons?

Developing Vocabulary Skills

Using Antonyms. Antonyms, you recall, are words that have opposite meanings. The use of an antonym as a context clue can give the meaning of the word by telling what it is not.

In the epigrams you have read by Emerson he speaks of being virtuous. If you were not sure of the meaning of virtuous, an antonym might have been helpful. Read the following:

His life was virtuous. He never committed a deed that could be considered *sinful*.

The word *sinful* is an antonym of the word *virtuous*. Therefore, you should be able to conclude that virtue is related to goodness.

For each of the following, write an antonym. Then, try using the original word and the antonym in a sentence. The antonym should help provide the meaning of the first word.

valuable	dejected	sincere
superior	generous	luxury
fascinating	supernatural	delicate

Developing Writing Skills

1. **Supporting an Opinion.** Choose one of the epigrams by Emerson. Write a brief composition explaining why you agree or disagree with it.

   Pre-Writing. Decide on the epigram you will use. Think carefully about why you agree or disagree with it. Write down your reasons. Also jot down all the facts, examples, and incidents you can think of that will lend support to your reasons. You may look into history and current events, as well as your own experience.

   Writing. Write an introduction that includes Emerson's quotation and your opinion of it. In each paragraph that follows, develop one reason to support your opinion. Include the examples, facts, and incidents you have noted. Tie your composition together by summarizing your opinion in the concluding paragraph.

   Revising. How convincing is your composition? Would it be stronger if you added more evidence or different reasons? Are your reasons easy to understand? Make changes that are needed to improve your writing.

2. **Writing Epigrams.** Write your own epigrams by completing the following statements. Try to use a metaphor in at least one.

   a. The best gift is . . .
   b. A true friend is . . .
   c. Plant your hopes . . .

Developing Skills in Study and Research

Finding Epigrams. Sometimes you may want to find meaningful epigrams to use in a speech or a piece of writing. *Bartlett's Familiar Quotations* in your library can help you to find quotations by many authors. An index in this reference work lists quotations by subject. Quotations are also indexed by author.

Use *Bartlett's Familiar Quotations* to find three excellent epigrams for each of these subjects: friendship, education, and beauty. Then use *Bartlett's* to find three more epigrams by Emerson. Share these epigrams with the class.

Concord was the site of the second battle between the British and the American colonists in 1775. Over sixty years later, why does Emerson want that battle to be remembered?

Concord Hymn
Sung at the Completion of the Battle Monument, July 4, 1837

RALPH WALDO EMERSON

By the rude bridge that arched the flood,
  Their flag to April's breeze unfurled,
Here once the embattled farmers stood
  And fired the shot heard round
  the world.

The foe long since in silence slept;
  Alike the conqueror silent sleeps;
And Time the ruined bridge has swept
  Down the dark stream which seaward
  creeps.

The Fight on Lexington Common, *April 19, 1775,* 1898, HOWARD PYLE. The Delaware Art Museum, the Howard Pyle Collection. Wilmington.

On this green bank, by this soft stream,
  We set to-day a votive stone;
That memory may their deed redeem,
  When, like our sires, our sons are gone.

Spirit, that made those heroes dare
  To die, and leave their children free,
Bid Time and Nature gently spare
  The shaft we raise to them and thee.

Developing Comprehension Skills

1. Why did the people gather at Concord on July 4, 1837?

2. The colonists, writes Emerson, "fired the shot heard round the world." In what way was the shot heard everywhere?

3. Since the time of the battle, several changes have taken place. What has happened to the soldiers? What has happened to the bridge?

4. In the final stanza, what is the shaft that is being raised? What does the speaker ask of the "Spirit, that made those heroes dare to die"?

5. What is Emerson's opinion of the "embattled farmers"? How can you tell?

6. "Concord Hymn" was written for the dedication of a war memorial. How appropriate do you think the poem is for this occasion?

Reading Literature

1. **Understanding Hymns.** A poem expressing praise and emotion is called a **hymn**. It is intended to be sung. The praise may be directed to God or to famous people. Why is it appropriate, then, that Emerson entitled his poem "Concord Hymn"?

2. **Recognizing Tone.** The tone in "Concord Hymn" is quite easy to determine. What is the tone? What words help you to identify it?

3. **Identifying Alliteration.** "Concord Hymn" contains several examples of alliteration. For example, in the first stanza the *f* sound is repeated in several different words. What beginning consonant sound is repeated most often in stanzas two and three? How does this sound add to the meaning of the poem?

4. **Analyzing Hyperbole.** Hyperbole is a statement that is greatly exaggerated. Emerson uses hyperbole when he describes "the shot heard round the world." What is exaggerated? What idea was Emerson emphasizing through this exaggeration?

5. **Identifying Rhyme Scheme.** You will remember that rhyme scheme is the pattern of end rhyme in a poem. In addition, you will recall that the pattern is determined by assigning a letter of the alphabet to each line. Lines that rhyme are given the same letter. Determine the rhyme scheme in "Concord Hymn."

Developing Vocabulary Skills

1. **Understanding Multiple Meanings.** As you know, context clues can help you determine the correct meaning of a word for a particular sentence. For example, the word *rude* has several different meanings. Read the following line from "Concord Hymn."

By the *rude* bridge that arched the flood. . . .

Which of the following meanings does *rude* have in the poem?

a. rough, violent, or harsh (*a rude awakening*)
b. vulgar; impolite (*a rude reply*)
c. crude or rough in form (*a rude shack*)
d. showing little skill (*a rude drawing*)

For each of the above definitions, write a sentence using that particular meaning. Make sure the context suggests the meaning of *rude* that you intend.

2. **Using Multiple Meanings.** Look at the words below. Each one is from "Concord Hymn." Look up each word in the dictionary. Write the meaning of the word as it is used in the poem. Then write a second definition for the word. Use the word in a sentence that shows this second meaning of the word.

fired   free   bank   deed   spare

Developing Writing Skills

1. **Analyzing Poetry.** In "Concord Hymn" Emerson speaks of time and nature. Both have an effect on the way things change. In a paragraph, explain the importance of time and nature in "Concord Hymn."

2. **Writing a Tribute.** "Concord Hymn" is an example of a tribute. A **tribute** is a work that praises and honors someone or something. In the poem, Emerson shows his admiration for the Concord soldiers and their contribution to America. Think of someone who has made a significant contribution in history, science, or the arts. Write a tribute to that person.

Pre-Writing. To get ideas for your subject, think about historical and social leaders, as well as public figures. When you decide on a person, make notes on that person's contributions. If your subject is a historical figure, you may need to do research. Identify two or three qualities to praise, and jot down incidents that show these qualities. Make an outline to organize your ideas.

Writing. In your introductory paragraph, explain what makes your subject worthy of praise. In other paragraphs describe the individual's qualities and traits. Also, give details about his or her accomplishments. Follow your outline. In your concluding paragraph, tell what kind of inspiration the person provides.

Revising. Work with a partner. Ask the person for suggestions on how to make your tribute more meaningful. Make sure that you have used language that praises the individual.

Developing Skills in Study and Research

Using Historical Reference Works. Libraries have specialized reference works that contain information on historical topics. They include the following:

Great Events from History (American Series)
Harper's Encyclopedia of United States History
Dictionary of American History
Encyclopedia of the American Revolution

Use three historical reference works to find information on the Battle of Concord. Share your information with the class.

From
Walden

HENRY DAVID THOREAU

Henry David Thoreau left his job in a factory and spent two years in a cabin near Walden Pond. What was the purpose of this experiment, as suggested by these excerpts?

Where I Lived and What I Lived For

When first I took up my abode in the woods, that is, began to spend my nights as well as days there, which, by accident, was on Independence Day, or the Fourth of July, 1845, my house was not finished for winter, but was merely a defence against the rain, without plastering or chimney, the walls being of rough, weather-stained boards, with wide chinks, which made it cool at night. The upright white hewn studs and freshly planed door and window casings give it a clean and airy look, especially in the morning, when its timbers were saturated with dew, so that I fancied that by noon some sweet gum would exude from them.

The only house I had been the owner of before, if I except a boat, was a tent, which I used occasionally when making excursions in the summer, and this is still rolled up in my garret; but the boat, after passing from hand to hand, has gone down the stream of time. With this more substantial shelter about me, I had made some progress toward settling in the world.

For the first week, whenever I looked out on the pond it impressed me like a tarn high up on the side of a mountain, its bottom far above the surface of other lakes, and, as the sun arose, I saw it throwing off its nightly clothing of mist, and here and there, by degrees, its soft ripples or its smooth reflecting surface was revealed, while the mists, like ghosts, were stealthily withdrawing in every direction into the woods, as at the breaking up of some nocturnal conventicle. The very dew seemed to hang upon the trees later into the day than usual, as on the sides of mountains.

Every morning was a cheerful invitation to make my life of equal simplicity, and I may say innocence, with Nature herself. I got up early and bathed in the pond; that was a religious exercise, and one of the best things which I did. The morning is the most memorable season of the day.

I went to the woods because I wished to live deliberately, to front only the essential facts of life, and see if I could not learn what it had to teach, and not, when I came to die, discover that I had not lived. I did not wish to live what was not life, living is so dear; nor did I wish to practise resignation, unless it was quite necessary. I wanted to live deep and suck out all the marrow of life, to live so sturdily and Spartan-like as to put to rout all that was not life, to cut a broad swath and shave close, to drive life into a corner, and reduce it to its lowest terms, and, if it proved to be mean, why then to get the whole and genuine meanness of it, and publish its meanness to the world; or if it were sublime, to know it by experience, and be able to give a true account of it in my next excursion. For most men, it appears to me, are in a strange uncertainty about it, whether it is of the devil or of God, and have *somewhat hastily* concluded that it is the chief end of man here to "glorify God and enjoy him forever."

Still we live meanly, like ants. Our life is frittered away by detail. An honest man has hardly need to count more than his ten fingers, or in extreme cases he may add his ten toes, and lump the rest. Simplicity, simplicity, simplicity! I say, let your affairs be as two or three, and not a hundred or a thousand; instead of a million count half a dozen, and keep your accounts on your thumbnail. Simplify, simplify. Instead of three meals a day, if it be necessary eat but one; instead of a hundred dishes, five; and reduce other things in proportion.

Why should we live with such hurry and waste of life? We are determined to be starved before we are hungry. Men say that a stitch in time saves nine, and so they take a thousand stitches to-day to save nine to-morrow. As for *work*, we haven't any of any consequence.

Time is but the stream I go a-fishing in. I drink at it; but while I drink I see the sandy bottom and detect how shallow it is. Its thin current slides away, but eternity remains. I would drink deeper; fish in the sky, whose bottom is pebbly with stars. I cannot count

one. I know not the first letter of the alphabet. I have always been regretting that I was not as wise as the day I was born. The intellect is a cleaver; it discerns and rifts its way into the secret of things. I do not wish to be any more busy with my hands than is necessary. My head is hands and feet. I feel all my best faculties concentrated in it. My instinct tells me that my head is an organ for burrowing, as some creatures use their snout and fore paws, and with it I would mine and burrow my way through these hills. I think that the richest vein is somewhere hereabouts; so by the divining-rod and thin rising vapors I judge; and here I will begin to mine.

Solitude

I have never felt lonesome, or in the least oppressed by a sense of solitude, but once, and that was a few weeks after I came to the woods. For an hour, I doubted if the near neighborhood of man was not essential to a serene and healthy life. To be alone was something unpleasant. But I was at the same time conscious of a slight insanity in my mood, and seemed to foresee my recovery. In the midst of a gentle rain while these thoughts prevailed, I was suddenly sensible of the sweet and beneficent society in Nature. Every little pine needle expanded and swelled with sympathy and befriended me. I was so distinctly made aware of the presence of something kindred to me, even in scenes which we are accustomed to call wild and dreary, and also that the nearest of blood to me and humanest was not a person nor a villager, that I thought no place could ever be strange to me again.

Some of my pleasantest hours were during the long rainstorms in the spring or fall, which confined me to the house for the afternoon as well as the forenoon. Early twilight ushered in long evenings in which many thoughts had time to take root and unfold themselves.

Men frequently say to me, "I should think you would feel lonesome down there, and want to be nearer to folks, rainy and snowy days and nights especially." I am tempted to reply to such, This whole earth which we inhabit is but a point in space. How far apart, think you, dwell the two most distant inhabitants of yonder star, the breadth of whose disk cannot be appreciated by our instruments? Why should I feel lonely? is not our planet in the Milky Way? This which you put seems to me not to be the most important question. What sort of space is that which separates a man from his fellows and makes him solitary? I have found that no exertion of the legs can bring two minds much nearer to one another. What do we want most to dwell near to? Not to many men surely, the depot, the post-office, the barroom, the meeting-house, the school-house, the grocery, Beacon Hill, or the Five Points, where men most congregate, but to the perennial source of our life, whence in all our experience we have found that to issue, as the willow stands near the water and sends out its roots in that direction. This will vary with different natures, but this is the place where a wise man will dig his cellar.

The Pond in Winter

After a still winter night I awoke. There was dawning Nature, in whom all creatures live, looking in my broad windows with serene and satisfied face. I awoke to Nature and daylight. The snow lying deep on the earth dotted with young pines, and the very slope of the hill on which my house is placed, seemed to say, Forward!

Then to my morning work. First I take an axe and pail and go in search of water, if that be not a dream. After a cold and snowy night it needed a divining rod to find it. Every winter the liquid and trembling surface of the pond, which was so sensitive to every breath, and reflected every light and shadow, becomes solid to the depth of a foot or a foot and a half, so that it will support the heaviest teams, and perchance the snow covers it to an equal depth, and it is not to be distinguished from any level field. Standing on the snow-covered plain, as if in a pasture amid the hills, I cut my way first through a foot of snow, and then a foot of ice, and open a window under my feet, where, kneeling to drink, I look down into the quiet parlor of the fishes, pervaded by a softened light as through a window of ground glass, with its bright sanded floor the same as in summer. There a perennial waveless serenity reigns as in the amber twilight sky, corresponding to the cool and even temperament of the inhabitants. Heaven is under our feet as well as over our heads.

Spring

One attraction in coming to the woods to live was that I should have leisure and opportunity to see the Spring come in. . . .

The change from storm and winter to serene and mild weather, from dark and sluggish hours to bright and elastic ones, is a memorable crisis which all things proclaim. It is seemingly instantaneous at last. Suddenly an influx of light filled my house, though the evening was at hand, and the clouds of winter still overhung it, and the eaves were dripping

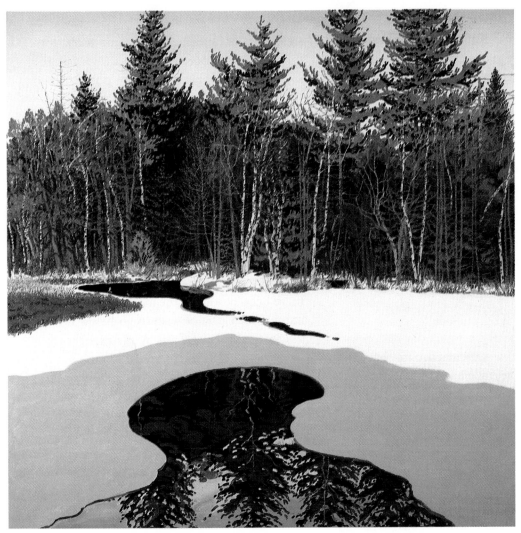

Pond Pass, 1974, NEIL WELLIVER. Federal Reserve Bank of Boston. Courtesy of Marlborough Galleries, New York.

with sleety rain. I looked out the window, and lo! where yesterday was cold gray ice there lay the transparent pond already calm and full of hope as in a summer evening, reflecting a summer evening sky in its bosom, though none was visible overhead, as if it had intelligence with some remote horizon.

Early in May, the oaks, hickories, maples, and other trees, just putting out amidst the pine woods around the pond, imparted a brightness like sunshine to the landscape, especially in cloudy days, as if the sun were breaking through mists and shining faintly on the hillsides here and there. On the third or fourth of May I saw a loon in the pond, and during the first week of the month I heard the whippoorwill, the brown-thrasher, the veery, the wood-pewee, the chewink, and other birds. I had heard the wood-thrush long before. The phoebe had already come once more and looked in at my door and window, to see if my house was cavern-like enough for her, sustaining herself on humming wings with clinched talons, as if she held by the air, while she surveyed the premises. The sulphur-like pollen of the pitch pine soon covered the pond and the stones and rotten wood along the shore, so that you could have collected a barrelful. And so the seasons went rolling on into summer, as one rambles into higher and higher grass.

Thus was my first year's life in the woods completed: and the second year was similar to it. I finally left Walden September 6th, 1847.

Conclusion

I left the woods for as good a reason as I went there. Perhaps it seemed to me that I had several more lives to live, and could not spare any more time for that one. It is remarkable how easily and insensibly we fall into a par-ticular route, and make a beaten track for ourselves. I had not lived there a week before my feet wore a path from my door to the pond-side; and though it is five or six years since I trod it, it is still quite distinct. It is true, I fear that others may have fallen into it, and so helped to keep it open. The surface of the earth is soft and impressible by the feet of men; and so with the paths which the mind travels. How worn and dusty, then, must be the highways of the world, how deep the ruts of tradition and conformity! I did not wish to take a cabin passage, but rather to go before the mast and on the deck of the world, for there I could best see the moonlight amid the mountains. I do not wish to go below now.

I learned this, at least, by my experiment; that if one advances confidently in the direction of his dreams, and endeavors to live the life which he has imagined, he will meet with a success unexpected in common hours.

Developing Comprehension Skills

1. Why did Thoreau go to the woods? What did he hope to learn there?

2. Thoreau believes in simplicity. While at Walden, how did Thoreau simplify his style of living?

3. "I did not wish to live what was not life," Thoreau writes. What does he mean?

4. When speaking of work, Thoreau says "we haven't any of any consequence." What did he mean? Do you agree? Explain.

5. Thoreau says he felt lonesome only once while at Walden Pond. Being with other humans didn't matter. What became more important to Thoreau than physical closeness to people?

6. Thoreau says humans "make a beaten track." Explain what Thoreau means. What can be done to avoid making such a track?

Reading Literature

1. **Understanding Essays.** You recall that essays may be formal or informal. Formal essays are impersonal, serious, and tightly structured. Informal essays are more personal, casual, and loosely organized. Would

you consider Thoreau's *Walden* formal or informal? Explain.

2. **Analyzing Metaphors.** Thoreau uses a metaphor when he says, "Time is but the stream I go a-fishing in." Time is being compared to a stream. What qualities does this comparison give to Time? Do you think it is an effective comparison?

3. **Understanding Symbols.** A symbol is a person, place, or thing that represents something beyond itself. Morning, for example, may symbolize rebirth in *Walden*. How is the symbolism of spring similar? What might the pond symbolize to Thoreau?

4. **Understanding Transcendentalism.** Thoreau, like Emerson, was a Transcendentalist. Like other Transcendentalists, Thoreau believed that individuals could become close to God through nature. Explain how these statements illustrate Transcendentalism:
   a. I got up early and bathed in the pond; that was a religious exercise.
   b. I was suddenly sensible of the sweet and beneficent society in Nature.
   c. Heaven is under our feet as well as over our heads.

5. **Recognizing Structure.** Thoreau structures his record of the Walden experiment around the seasons of the year. He begins his account in the summer of 1845 and ends it in the spring of 1847. Why do you think Thoreau uses the cycle of the seasons to arrange his writing?

Developing Vocabulary Skills

Reviewing Context Clues. In this chapter you learned that the meaning of an unfamiliar word can often be found in context. You have also learned how to use the following context clues: definition or restatement clues, synonyms, antonyms, comparison clues, contrast clues, and example clues. In addition, you have learned how to infer the meaning of a word from your understanding of an entire passage.

The following sentences are from the selections you have read in this chapter. Use context clues to determine the meaning of each underlined word. Write the word and its meaning. Also, write the words or ideas from the sentence that helped you to determine the meaning.

1. Times grew worse and worse with Rip Van Winkle as years of matrimony rolled on; a tart temper never mellows with age. . . .

2. . . . he was observed to smoke his pipe vehemently, and to send forth short, frequent and angry puffs; but when he pleased, he would inhale the smoke slowly and tranquilly.

3. Let him take me if he wills. I don't hanker after it, I must say, but I can stand it.

4. If this aversion had its origin in contempt and resistance like his own he might well go home with a sad countenance; but the sour faces of the multitude, like their sweet faces, have no deep cause. . . .

5. . . . I was suddenly sensible of the sweet and beneficent society in Nature. Every little pine needle . . . befriended me.

6. There a perennial waveless serenity reigns as in the amber twilight sky, corresponding to the cool and even temperament of the inhabitants.

7. The surface of the earth is soft and impressible by the feet of men. . . .

Developing Writing Skills.

1. **Using Comparison.** Thoreau's ideas in *Walden* are similar in many ways to Emerson's in "Self-Reliance." Emerson said that "Whoso would be a man, must be a nonconformist." The same person should learn to trust himself. How does Thoreau's stay at Walden Pond put Emerson's theories into practice? Explain in a brief composition.

   Pre-Writing. Review the main points of Emerson's essay. Then consider similarities in Thoreau's and Emerson's ideas. Make notes on the similarities and on how Thoreau puts each idea into practice. Decide on the best order for presenting your ideas. The order of their importance might be one possibility.

   Writing. Develop an introductory paragraph stating that Emerson and Thoreau have similar ideas. In addition, mention that Thoreau put these ideas into practice. In each body paragraph, focus on one belief that both men share. Explain it, and use quotations from "Self-Reliance" and *Walden* to clarify it. Tell how Thoreau puts the ideas into practice. In the concluding paragraph, summarize the main ideas.

   Revising. Have you used quotations to make Thoreau's and Emerson's ideas clear? Have you proved that the two men shared similar beliefs? Have you told how Thoreau put each belief into practice? Check to see that each paragraph has a topic sentence that states the main idea of that paragraph.

2. **Supporting an Opinion.** Does the "simple life" that Thoreau leads at Walden Pond appeal to you? In one paragraph, state your opinion and tell your reasons.

Developing Skills in Critical Thinking

Distinguishing Fact from Opinion. Nonfiction can include opinions as well as facts. A careful reader can tell the difference. A fact is something that can be proven true. It can be proven by observation or through reference to an encyclopedia. An opinion is a belief about something and cannot be proven. Opinions often contain **judgment** words such as *best, worst, beautiful*, and *talented*. Decide which of these statements from *Walden* are facts and which are opinions:

1. The morning is the most memorable season of the day.
2. First I take an axe and pail and go in search of water. . . .
3. On the third or fourth of May I saw a loon in the pond. . . .
4. Still we live meanly, like ants. Our life is frittered away by detail.

Developing Skills in Speaking and Listening

Giving an Oral Presentation. Henry David Thoreau and Ralph Waldo Emerson had strong views on many subjects. Not everyone, however, would agree with their views. With a partner, stage a conversation involving either Thoreau or Emerson and someone with opposing views. The other person may be real or fictional. For your conversation, choose one of the following topics, or one of your own.

1. wilderness camping
2. reading the classics
3. protest demonstrations
4. pollution

The Declaration of Women's Rights

ELIZABETH CADY STANTON

SETTING A PURPOSE | *Elizabeth Cady Stanton organized the first women's rights convention in 1848. There she presented this declaration. What rights, according to Stanton, had women been denied?*

When in the course of human events, it becomes necessary for one portion of the family of man to assume among the people of the earth a position different from that which they have hitherto occupied, but one to which the laws of nature and of nature's God entitle them, a decent respect to the opinions of mankind requires that they should declare the causes that impel them to such a course.

Theory of Equality and Natural Rights

We hold these truths to be self-evident: that all men and women are created equal; that they are endowed by their Creator with certain inalienable rights; that among these are life, liberty, and the pursuit of happiness; that to secure these rights governments are instituted, deriving their just powers from the consent of the governed. Whenever any form of government becomes destructive of these ends, it is the right of those who suffer from it to refuse allegiance to it, and to insist upon the institution of a new government, laying its foundation on such principles, and organizing its powers in such form, as to them shall seem most likely to effect their safety and happiness. Prudence, indeed, will dictate that governments long established should not be changed for light and transient causes; and accordingly all experience hath shown that mankind are more disposed to suffer, while evils are sufferable, than to right themselves by abolishing the forms to which they were accustomed. But when a long train of abuses and usurpations, pursuing invariably the same object evinces a design to reduce them under absolute despotism, it is their duty to throw off such government, and to provide new guards for their future security. Such has been the patient sufferance of the women under this government, and such is now the necessity which constrains them to demand the equal station to which they are entitled.

The history of mankind is a history of repeated injuries and usurpations on the part of man toward woman, having in direct object the establishment of an absolute tyranny over her. To prove this let facts be submitted to a candid [impartial] world.

Legal Inequality

He has never permitted her to exercise her inalienable right to the elective franchise.

The executive committee of the First International Council for Women in 1888. Elizabeth Cady Stanton is seated, fourth from left. Susan B. Anthony is seated, second from left. Culver Pictures, New York.

He has compelled her to submit to laws, in the formation of which she had no voice.

He has withheld from her rights which are given to the most ignorant and degraded men—both natives and foreigners.

Having deprived her of this first right of a citizen, the elective franchise, thereby leaving her without representation in the halls of legislation, he has oppressed her on all sides.

Oppression in Marriage

He has made her, if married, in the eye of the law, civilly dead.

He has taken from her all right in property, even to the wages she earns.

He has made her, morally, an irresponsible being, as she can commit many crimes with impunity, provided they be done in the presence of her husband. In the covenant of marriage, she is compelled to promise obedience to her husband, he becoming, to all intents and purposes, her master—the law giving him power to deprive her of her liberty, and administer chastisement [punishment].

He has so framed the laws of divorce, as to what shall be the proper causes, and in case of separation, to whom the guardianship of the children shall be given, as to be wholly regardless of the happiness of women—the law, in all cases, going upon a false supposition of the supremacy of man, and giving all power into his hands.

After depriving her of all rights as a married woman, if single, and the owner of property, he has taxed her to support a government which recognizes her only when her property can be made profitable to it.

Denial of Opportunity

He has monopolized nearly all the profitable employments, and from those she is permitted to follow, she receives but a scanty remuneration [payment]. He closes against her all the avenues to wealth and distinction which he considers most honorable to himself. As a teacher of theology, medicine, or law, she is not known.

He has denied her the facilities for obtaining a thorough education, all colleges being closed against her.

He allows her in Church, as well as state, but a subordinate position, claiming Apostolic authority for her exclusion from the ministry, and, with some exceptions, from any public participation in the affairs of the Church.

He has created a false public sentiment by giving to the world a different code of morals for men and women, by which moral delinquencies which exclude women from society, are not only tolerated, but deemed of little account in man.

He has usurped the prerogative of Jehovah [God] himself, claiming it as his right to assign for her a sphere of action, when that belongs to her conscience and to her God.

He has endeavored, in every way that he could, to destroy her confidence in her own powers, to lessen her self-respect, and to make her willing to lead a dependent and abject life.

Demands and Determination

Now, in view of this entire disfranchisement of one half the people of this country, their social and religious degradation—in view of the unjust laws above mentioned, and because women do feel themselves aggrieved, oppressed, and fraudulently deprived of their most sacred rights, we insist that they have immediate admission to all the rights and privileges which belong to them as citizens of the United States.

In entering upon the great work before us, we anticipate no small amount of misconception, misrepresentation, and ridicule; but we shall use every instrumentality within our power to effect our object. We shall employ agents, circulate tracts, petition the state and national legislatures, and endeavor to enlist the pulpit and the press in our behalf. We hope this convention will be followed by a series of conventions embracing every part of the country.

Developing Comprehension Skills

1. Stanton's document resembles a more famous declaration. What declaration does it resemble? Where does it begin to differ in wording from the original?

2. According to Stanton, what attitude do men have toward women?

3. According to Stanton, what rights have women been denied in marriage? in careers? as citizens?

4. In the last paragraph, Stanton states the reaction she expects her declaration to receive. Do you think she was right?

5. A large portion of Stanton's declaration describes the ways women are treated by men. Do you think she gives a negative view of men? Is she too harsh in her descriptions?

Reading Literature

1. **Understanding the Author's Purpose.** Elizabeth Cady Stanton probably had several purposes for writing her declaration. Do you think the primary purpose of Stanton's declaration is to inform, criticize, persuade, or demand? Which statement in the declaration best summarizes Stanton's purpose?

2. **Recognizing Parody.** A parody is an imitation of a serious work of literature. It may be written to criticize, to praise, or to entertain with humor. "The Declaration of Women's Rights" could be taken as a parody of a famous document. Considering Stanton's purpose, would this document be an especially fitting one to imitate?

3. **Making Inferences About a Writer.** From the way a piece of literature is written you can make inferences about its writer. An inference, as you know, is a logical conclusion based on facts. Find passages that allow you to draw inferences about Stanton. How would you describe her? What character traits did she have?

4. **Analyzing Repetition.** As Stanton lists the rights denied women, she begins each paragraph with the words "He has." What does the repetition of these words emphasize? How does it make her speech effective?

Developing Vocabulary Skills

Determining Methods for Identifying Word Meanings. As you read, you should be aware of context clues used by a writer. However, many times a writer may not provide context clues to the meaning of a word. If you are unsure of a word's meaning, then you should use a dictionary or glossary.

The following sentences contain underlined words taken from "The Declaration of Women's Rights." Try to use context clues to determine the meaning of each word. If, however, there is no context clue, write *dictionary* and the dictionary meaning of the word.

1. Despotism is a state or country ruled by absolute authority and power.
2. Unlike the usurpations women suffered in the past, they now have the right to a college education and are able to obtain high-paying jobs.
3. Some of women's rights include franchise, the right to property, and equal employment opportunity.
4. It has not been the privilege or the prerogative of women to hold high offices in most religions.

Developing Writing Skills

1. **Writing an Explanation.** Elizabeth Cady Stanton names many ways that women, in 1848, were denied their rights. How many of these rights have women gained since Stanton's time? How much of what Stanton says is still true today? Write a composition explaining how much progress has been made in the area of women's rights.

   Pre-Writing. List the rights that Stanton says women were denied. Decide which ones women still don't have today. You may need to do research on women's legal rights. For your composition, use the organization that Stanton uses. First, discuss citizen's rights. Then cover marriage rights, and finally rights of opportunity. Group your notes accordingly.

   Writing. Begin with an introductory paragraph that states your views related to the progress in women's rights since 1848.

   Your body paragraphs will involve putting your notes in sentence form. Also, fill in details. As you write use transitional words and phrases to tie ideas together. End your composition with a short conclusion.

   Revising. Read your composition to a small group of listeners. Ask them if you have given a thorough update in each area of women's rights. Ask if anyone sees any errors in your ideas.

2. **Writing a Declaration.** Elizabeth Cady Stanton developed a declaration of rights for a group that was discriminated against. Develop your own declaration for a minority that you feel is treated unfairly. Include logical reasons why the group deserves the rights you demand.

Developing Skills in Study and Research

Finding Statistics. You can find facts and statistics by using sources in the reference section of your library. One important source is an almanac. It contains current facts and statistics on many topics. Other sources for statistics are the annual *Statistical Abstract of the United States* and Bureau of the Census reports.

Use these sources to find out the following about changes in the status of women:

1. change in the percentage of women with a college education

2. changes in women's average income levels

3. changes in the number of women in professional and managerial occupations

Developing Skills in Critical Thinking

1. **Evaluating Support for an Opinion.** A sound opinion is one that is well supported with facts. Elizabeth Cady Stanton states the opinion that men have established "an absolute tyranny" over women. What evidence does Stanton give to prove her opinion? Does she support her opinion well with facts? Explain.

2. **Recognizing Loaded Language.** Words that create powerful positive or negative feelings are **loaded words**. The use of such words can sway or affect people's attitudes about a particular subject. Your feelings about a person may be affected positively or negatively. For example, what would your reaction be if someone was described as confident? as conceited?

   Find words in Stanton's essay that suggest positive ideas and negative ideas.

Chapter 5 Review

Using Your Skills in Reading Literature

The following paragraph is from Edgar Allan Poe's "Ligeia." Read the paragraph carefully. Explain what mood you think is created in the passage. Then tell how the word choice and point of view help create this mood.

> An hour thus elapsed when (could it be possible?) I was a second time aware of some vague sound issuing from the region of the bed. I listened—in extremity of horror. The sound came again—it was a sigh. Rushing to the corpse, I saw—distinctly saw—a tremor upon the lips. In a minute afterward they relaxed, disclosing a bright line of the pearly teeth.

Using Your Comprehension Skills

This is a paragraph from Frederick Douglass's autobiography from Chapter Six. It tells of the years when he was a slave to the Auld family. What is the main idea in the paragraph? Find the topic sentence, and tell how the sentences in the paragraph support the main idea. Explain.

> When I went into their family, it was the abode of happiness and contentment. The mistress of the house was a model of affection and tenderness. Her fervent piety and watchful uprightness made it impossible to see her without thinking and feeling—"that woman is a Christian." There was no sorrow nor suffering for which she had not a tear, and there was no innocent joy for which she had not a smile. She had bread for the hungry, clothes for the naked, and comfort for every mourner that came within her reach. Slavery soon proved its ability to divest her of these excellent qualities and her home of its early happiness.

Using Your Vocabulary Skills

The underlined words in the following sentences are from Chapter Six. In each sentence, there is a context clue to help you define the underlined word. For each sentence, give the meaning of the underlined word. In addition, identify the kind of context clue you find: definition or restatement, synonym, antonym, comparison, contrast, or example.

1. He stepped gingerly, testing cautiously for each foothold.
2. The once angelic face of the young soldier now had a diabolical look.
3. The clamor on the hill included shouts of the officers, crashing of volleys, and cheers of the soldiers.
4. Farquhar's executioners gesticulated at him, just as the captain motioned toward the soldiers.
5. A sentinel, that is, a guard, of the Union army stood at either end of the bridge.

Using Your Writing Skills

Choose one of the writing assignments below.

1. The Early National Period was the beginning of a truly American literature. It stressed Romanticism, which emphasized emotion, nature, and individualism.

    Choose a poem, a story, and a nonfiction piece from this chapter. In a composition, discuss the aspects of Romanticism that you find.

2. Choose one of the following people who especially appeals to you: Henry David Thoreau, Elizabeth Cady Stanton, or Daniel Webster. Write a story in which that person sleeps for 150 years and wakes in modern America. Use first-person point of view in your story.

Using Your Skills in Critical Thinking

Elizabeth Cady Stanton argues that women in the nineteenth century were treated as inferior. Search the selections in this chapter for evidence to support or disprove Stanton's opinion.

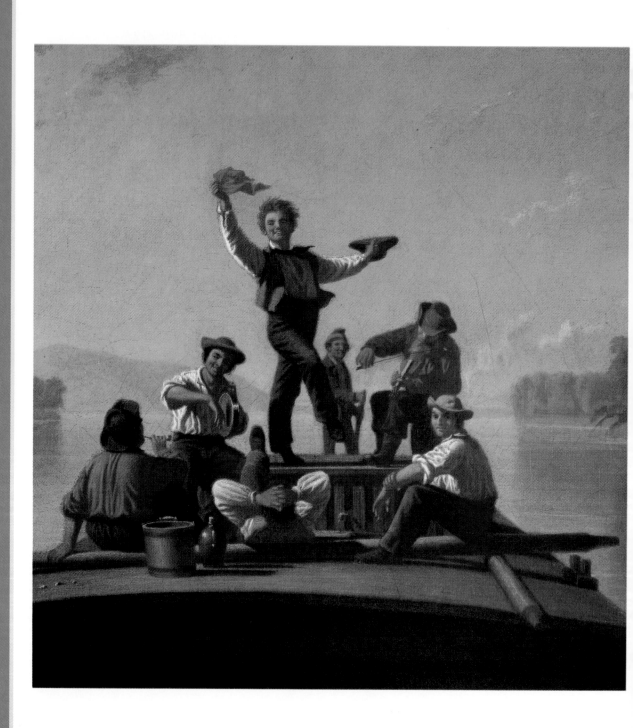

CHAPTER SIX

The Late Nineteenth Century (1855–1900)

The Jolly Flatboatmen (detail), 1848, GEORGE CALEB BINGHAM. Terra Museum of American Art, Daniel J. Terra Collection. Evanston, Illinois.

Historical Background
The Late Nineteenth Century (1855–1900)

By 1855, the United States covered a vast territory that stretched from coast to coast. The country's economy was growing and expanding. However, a dark cloud lurked on the horizon: the problem of slavery.

The Civil War

The growth and expansion of the United States during the 1840's led to an explosive question: Would the new territories and states formed from these lands be slave or would they be free? This question divided the nation, and social and economic problems added to the growing tension between the Northern and the Southern states. Finally, in 1860 and 1861, a total of eleven Southern states seceded, or withdrew, from the Union and formed the Confederate States of America.

The Civil War began in 1861 and lasted until 1865. The North eventually won the war. Slavery was abolished, and the Union was preserved. But the cost of the war was extremely high. Well over half a million Americans died in the war. Equally important, the Civil War created feelings of bitterness between Northerners and Southerners.

	1855	1860	1865	1870	1875
Literature	1855 Walt Whitman publishes first edition of his book of poems, *Leaves of Grass* 1855 Frederick Douglass publishes revised version of his autobiography		1863 Abraham Lincoln delivers The Gettysburg Address 1865 Robert E. Lee writes "Farewell to His Army"	1869 Bret Harte publishes "The Outcasts of Poker Flat"	
History		1858 Lincoln and Douglas debate in Illinois 1861 Civil War begins	1863 Lincoln issues Emancipation Proclamation 1865 John Wilkes Booth assassinates Abraham Lincoln	1876 Alexander Graham Bell invents the telephone	

Westward Migration

The discovery of gold in California in 1848 had brought many people to the Far West. More mining settlements grew up when the Comstock Lode of silver was discovered in Nevada in 1859. Following the Civil War, the Homestead Act of 1862 encouraged settlement in the Great Plains.

By 1890, the American frontier was a thing of the past. The end of the frontier also meant an end to the Native American way of life. The United States government began forcing Native Americans onto reservations. The Indians lost not only their tribal lands but also an entire way of life.

Industrial Growth and Expansion

Great changes took place in American industry following the Civil War. In manufacturing, hand labor was largely replaced by machine production. A new nationwide rail system meant that the products of industry could be sold throughout the country. The new industries were concentrated in Northern cities. Thousands of workers, many of them new immigrants, moved to the cities to find work in these industries.

In 1900, the United States had become an industrial giant. However, the laboring classes shared in little of the wealth created by the growth of industry. The gap between the rich and the poor widened, especially in the cities.

Nationalism and Regionalism

Following the Civil War, a sense of national identity began to develop. Improvements in transportation and communication helped to promote a sense of national unity. Many newspapers and magazines now carried information about national events. The bitter division between the North and the South gradually began to heal.

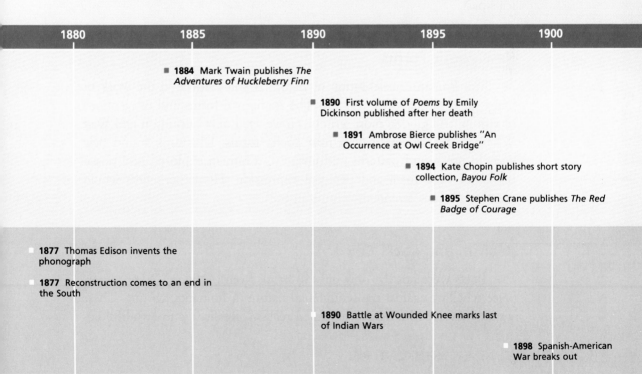

1880　1885　1890　1895　1900

1884 Mark Twain publishes *The Adventures of Huckleberry Finn*

1890 First volume of *Poems* by Emily Dickinson published after her death

1891 Ambrose Bierce publishes "An Occurrence at Owl Creek Bridge"

1894 Kate Chopin publishes short story collection, *Bayou Folk*

1895 Stephen Crane publishes *The Red Badge of Courage*

1877 Thomas Edison invents the phonograph

1877 Reconstruction comes to an end in the South

1890 Battle at Wounded Knee marks last of Indian Wars

1898 Spanish-American War breaks out

Reading Literature

Realism and Naturalism

The Civil War marked a break with the Romantic past. Writers looked to new ways of treating those subjects.

The Literature of the Civil War

Like the Revolutionary era, the Civil War era produced important political documents. These documents include The Gettysburg Address and The Emancipation Proclamation, both written by Abraham Lincoln. The argument over slavery and states' rights was carried on in speeches, debates, letters, essays, and newspaper articles.

The Civil War influenced other forms of writing as well. It appears as a theme in the poetry of Walt Whitman. It also provided the raw materials for the realistic fiction of Stephen Crane and Ambrose Bierce. Their graphic descriptions of war help re-create a nightmare from America's past.

New Poetic Forms

The Romantic celebration of nature is still evident in the work of many poets of the Civil War era. The traditional forms and conventions of writing still guided most writers. However, Emily Dickinson and Walt Whitman experimented with new poetic forms. Dickinson found new ways to use sound patterns and imagery. Whitman explored new possibilities of both form and personal expression. His experiments would greatly influence twentieth-century poets.

Realism and Local Color

Poets were not the only ones to break from tradition. Other writers were rebelling against the sentimental nature of Romantic writing. These writers developed a new style, called realism. **Realism** is the truthful imitation of real life. It uses clear, direct language to present ordinary, everyday events. This style reflects the careful look that many Americans were taking at their growing country.

As America developed a national identity, people also began to take pride in the particular region in which they lived. A movement called **regionalism** developed around this feeling. This movement focused attention on the unique character of the various regions of the country.

Writers such as Mark Twain and Bret Harte began writing in a style that came to be known as **local-color** realism. These writers portrayed in accurate detail the characters, speech, customs, and attitudes of their particular regions of the country. Twain, for example, often wrote about life on and around the Mississippi River. His masterpieces, *The Adventures of Tom Sawyer* and *The Adventures of Huckleberry Finn,* are excellent examples of local-color realism.

During the late 1800's, such local-color realists as Mary E. Wilkins Freeman and Kate Chopin continued to write in the regionalist tradition. Freeman's short stories and novels were set in New England. Chopin wrote about the Cajuns, Creoles, blacks, and Indians of Louisiana.

Naturalism

A type of writing called **naturalism** also developed during the second half of the 1800's. It can be described as an extreme form of realism. Like the realist, the naturalist tried to portray people and events accurately. But unlike the realists, naturalists believed that people have no control over their fates. They felt that human beings are simply victims of their surroundings and of their own drives and desires. Stephen Crane, author of *The Red Badge of Courage,* was one of the first Americans to write in the naturalist style.

Comprehension Skills

Literal and Figurative Language

Language can sometimes be read or interpreted on a literal level. The word *literal* means "exact," or "not exaggerated." **Literal language** uses the exact, or familiar, meanings of words. When writers use literal language, they expect the reader to take the idea at face value. For example:

> A man stood upon a railroad bridge in northern Alabama, looking down into the swift water twenty feet below.

This sentence can be understood using the ordinary meanings of the words.

Interpreting Figurative Language

Figurative language is language that requires the reader to look beyond the usual meanings of the words. Read the following example of figurative language. In it, Frederick Douglass, a former slave, is trying to explain how knowledge made him aware of some ugly truths:

> This knowledge opened my eyes to the horrible pit and revealed the teeth of the frightful dragon that was ready to pounce upon me.

Obviously, Douglass does not really see a dragon. He is using figurative language to show the reader how frightening what he learned was to him.

One reason writers use figurative language is to create vivid images in the minds of readers. These images can add a great deal to the feeling, or mood, of a piece. Poets in particular depend on figurative language to create mental pictures for the audience. Look at the following lines of a poem by Walt Whitman. They describe cavalry riding through a forest.

> A line in long array where they wind between green
>   islands,
> They take a serpentine course, their arms flash
>   in the sun

A writer may also use figurative language to emphasize an important point. For example, read the following description of the difference between the white man and the Native American:

> They are like the grass that covers the vast prairies. My people are few, and resemble the scattering trees of a storm-swept plain.

Sometimes language makes no sense on a literal level. Then you will know that you must look for the deeper meaning. At other times, language can be read on both a literal and figurative level. In these cases you must be careful not to miss either meaning.

Exercises: Understanding Literal and Figurative Language

A. Is the language in each of the following items literal or figurative?

1. He plunged in among the big spruce trees. The trail was faint.
   A foot of snow had fallen since the last sled had passed over.
2. If I die here, the wind,
   The wind rushing over the prairie,
   The wind will take me home.
3. The Brain—is wider than the Sky—
4. He was a man, and as a man he knew
   Love, separation, sorrow, joy and death.
5. when i go on the hunt
   my wife goes in my heart

B. Study the figurative language in each of the following examples. Then tell whether the writer is trying to create an image, stress a point, or both.

1. When a gun was fired, a red streak as round as a log flashed by in the heavens, like a monstrous bolt of lightning.
2. There was a time when our people covered the whole land as the waves of the wind-ruffled sea cover its shell-paved floor.
3. Such horses are the jewels of the horseman's hands and thighs.
4. Fame is a bee,
   It has a song—
   It has a sting—
   Ah, too, it has a wing.

$\mathcal{V}$ocabulary Skills

Word Parts

Three basic types of word parts are base words, prefixes, and suffixes. The **base word** is a word to which other parts may be added. A **prefix** is a word part added on to the beginning of a base word. A **suffix** is a word part added to the end of a base word. When you find an unfamiliar word, try to unlock its meaning by studying the individual parts.

Prefixes

Below are some of the most commonly used prefixes.

Prefix	Meaning	Example
com-, con-	with; together	composition
de-	down; away from	depart
ex-	out of; from	exchange
extra-	beyond	extrasensory
im-, in-	in, into	immigrant, indoor
mis-	wrong	misjudge
re-	again; back	reorganize
sub-	under	submarine

Prefix	Meaning	Example
in-, ir-, im-, il-, dis-, un-, non-	"not" or "the opposite of"	il + logical = illogical (not logical)

Suffixes

Two of the most helpful groups of suffixes to know are adjective suffixes and noun suffixes. **Adjective suffixes** can be used to make describing words. **Noun suffixes** can be used to make words that stand for a state of being or quality. See the following:

Adjective Suffixes

Suffix	Meaning	Example
-able, -ible	capable of being	profitable
-ful	full of, having	cheerful
-ish	like, tending toward	feverish
-less	without	expressionless
-ory	having the nature of	contradictory

Noun Suffixes

Suffix	Example	Suffix	Example
-ance, -ence	resistance	-hood	brotherhood
-er, -or, -ist, -ian	director	-ness	weariness

Latin and Greek Roots

A **root** contains the word's basic meaning.

Latin Roots	Meaning	Greek Roots	Meaning
capt	take	auto	self
cred	believe	bio	life
dic, dict	say	chron	time
fac, fec	make	graph, gram	write
port	send or carry	logos	word, thought
scrit, script	write		
spec	see		
voc, vok	speak		

Exercise: Using Word Parts To Determine Meaning

Identify the base words, prefixes, suffixes, and roots in the words below.

1. compress
2. emergence
3. substandard
4. spectator
5. vocalist
6. convertible
7. creditable
8. chronic

The Gettysburg Address

ABRAHAM LINCOLN

SETTING A PURPOSE | *In 1863, part of the Gettysburg battlefield was set aside as a cemetery. Abraham Lincoln delivered this speech during the dedication. What does Lincoln think we can learn from those who lost their lives in this battle?*

Four score and seven years ago our fathers brought forth on this continent, a new nation, conceived in liberty, and dedicated to the proposition that all men are created equal.

Now we are engaged in a great civil war, testing whether that nation, or any nation so conceived and so dedicated, can long endure. We are met on a great battlefield of that war. We have come to dedicate a portion of that field, as a final resting place for those who here gave their lives that that nation might live. It is altogether fitting and proper that we should do this.

But, in a larger sense, we cannot dedicate—we cannot consecrate—we cannot hallow—this ground. The brave men, living and dead, who struggled here, have consecrated it, far above our poor power to add or detract. The world will little note, nor long remember what we say here, but it can never forget what they did here. It is for us the living, rather, to be dedicated here to the unfinished work which they who fought here have thus far so nobly advanced. It is rather for us to be here dedicated to the great task remaining before us—that from these honored dead we take increased devotion to that cause for which they gave the last full measure of devotion—that we here highly resolve that these dead shall not have died in vain—that this nation, under God, shall have a new birth of freedom—and that government of the people, by the people, for the people, shall not perish from the earth.

Developing Comprehension Skills

1. Lincoln opens his speech with a reference to the nation's founding fathers. What beliefs of the founding fathers does Lincoln mention in his speech?

2. According to Lincoln, what was the test the American people faced in the Civil War?

3. Why is it "fitting and proper" that the battlefield be dedicated?

4. Lincoln emphasizes that the living should dedicate themselves to the "unfinished work" that the soldiers began. What is this "unfinished work"?

5. To what kind of government is Lincoln committed?

6. Lincoln says Americans can learn from the example set by "these honored dead." What can Americans today learn from those who died at Gettysburg? Explain.

Reading Literature

1. **Identifying Tone.** Tone, you remember, is the author's attitude toward what is being said. What is Lincoln's tone in "The Gettysburg Address" regarding the sacrifice of the dead? What words reveal this tone?

2. **Appreciating Parallelism.** Parallelism is an effective speech device. When a writer uses **parallelism**, he or she presents several phrases or sentences that follow an identical structure, or form. Parallelism is used to emphasize main ideas. In the last paragraph, for example, Lincoln uses parallelism in "of the people, by the people, and for the people." In this case, the parallelism emphasizes the idea of democracy. Find another example of parallelism in Lincoln's speech. What ideas are emphasized?

3. **Analyzing Word Choice.** Many times in this speech, Lincoln uses words or phrases that would seem unusual in everyday speech. For example, rather than say "eighty-seven years ago" Lincoln uses the phrase "Four score and seven years ago." Provide a more common word or phrase for the following:

a. a final resting place
b. shall not perish from the earth

Why do you think Lincoln chose the more unusual phrases? What effect would the common words or phrases have if they had been used in the speech?

4. **Appreciating Allusions.** An **allusion** is a reference to a well-known person, place, or event. An allusion may be used to provide the reader or listener with a deeper understanding of the main ideas.

Lincoln opens his speech with an allusion to the founding of the nation in 1776. How does this allusion add meaning to the speech?

Letter to Mrs. Bixby

ABRAHAM LINCOLN

When Abraham Lincoln became President, he did not lose his concern for others. What does this letter reveal about Abraham Lincoln, the man?

Executive Mansion, Washington,
November 21, 1864

MRS. BIXBY, Boston, Massachusetts:

Dear Madam:

I have been shown in the files of the War Department a statement of the Adjutant-General of Massachusetts that you are the mother of five sons who have died gloriously on the field of battle. I feel how weak and fruitless must be any words of mine which should attempt to beguile you from the grief of a loss so overwhelming. But I cannot refrain from tendering to you the consolation that may be found in the thanks of the Republic they died to save. I pray that our Heavenly Father may assuage the anguish of your bereavement, and leave you only the cherished memory of the loved and lost, and the solemn pride that must be yours to have laid so costly a sacrifice upon the altar of freedom.

Yours very sincerely and respectfully,
Abraham Lincoln

Developing Comprehension Skills

1. How did Abraham Lincoln learn of Mrs. Bixby's loss? According to the letter, how did her sons die?

2. Why do you suppose Lincoln wrote this letter to Mrs. Bixby?

3. Does it seem as though Lincoln understood the woman's grief? Explain.

4. Lincoln wrote, "I feel how weak and fruitless must be any words of mine which should attempt to beguile you from the grief of a loss so overwhelming." In your own words, explain what Lincoln meant.

5. What source of comfort does Lincoln think Mrs. Bixby can find in her loss?

6. Do you think that this letter consoled Mrs. Bixby? Why or why not?

Reading Literature

1. **Using Letters.** To learn more about an individual, it is helpful to read letters that he or she has written. Letters can reveal the ideas, beliefs, and personality of an individual. Which passages in Lincoln's letter reveal his concern for others? his devotion to God? his humbleness?

2. **Analyzing Word Choice.** Many times a writer or speaker chooses one word over another because of the additional meaning it can provide. A carefully selected word can give a great deal of power to a statement. What word, in each of the following phrases, gives power, or additional meaning, to the statement?

   a. died gloriously
   b. the Republic they died to save
   c. anguish of your bereavement
   d. cherished memory

3. **Explaining Metaphor.** A **metaphor**, as you know, is a comparison between unlike things. A metaphor does not use *like* or *as*. Examine Lincoln's metaphor in the last sentence: "to have laid so costly a sacrifice upon the altar of freedom." What things are being compared? How does this metaphor add to the meaning?

First Virginia Regiment at the time of Harper's Ferry, October, 1859. The Valentine Museum, Richmond, Virginia.

Letter to Mrs. Bixby 237

The Emancipation Proclamation was an historic document that led to the end of slavery in the United States. Who was affected by the proclamation?

From

The Emancipation Proclamation

ABRAHAM LINCOLN

On the first day of January, in the year of our Lord one thousand eight hundred and sixty-three, all persons held as slaves within any state or designated part of a state, the people whereof shall then be in rebellion against the United States, shall be then, thenceforward, and forever, free; and the Executive Government of the United States, including the military and naval authority thereof, will recognize and maintain the freedom of such persons, and will do no act or acts to repress such persons, or any of them, in any efforts they may make for their actual freedom.

Old Couple Looking at a Portrait of Lincoln, about 1892, HENRY OSSAWA TANNER. National Museum of American Art, Smithsonian Institution, gift of Norman Robbins. Washington, D.C.

Developing Comprehension Skills

1. What was the date of "The Emancipation Proclamation"?

2. The proclamation says that slaves shall be set free within certain states, "the people whereof shall then be in rebellion against the United States." What states are being described in this particular passage?

3. What does "The Emancipation Proclamation" guarantee to former slaves?

4. "The Emancipation Proclamation" had an affect on both the slave and the slaveowner. How do you suppose the slaves felt upon hearing the proclamation? the slaveowners? Explain.

Reading Literature

1. **Understanding a Proclamation.** A **proclamation** is a statement that officially announces something. What is the official announcement contained in "The Emancipation Proclamation"?

2. **Analyzing Language.** "The Emancipation Proclamation" contains formal language. Formal language is often used in situations that are serious, dignified, or ceremonial. The sentences are usually longer and the vocabulary can be difficult. Formal language is used more often in writing than in speaking. For example, formal language is often used in professional journals, legal papers, business reports, and many textbooks.

   Which words in "The Emancipation Proclamation" would you consider formal? Why did Lincoln use these words? Explain.

3. **Using Punctuation To Aid Understanding.** The passage which you read from "The Emancipation Proclamation" is one sentence. Punctuation can help you understand the ideas in this sentence. What are the two main ideas that are separated by the use of the semicolon? How do commas help you understand the ideas in this complicated sentence?

Epigrams

ABRAHAM LINCOLN

SETTING A PURPOSE | *These epigrams reflect the wisdom and wit of Abraham Lincoln. What can you learn from each short selection?*

A man that has no faults has pesky virtues.

I don't know who my grandfather was; I am much more concerned to know what his grandson will be.

Developing Comprehension Skills

1. How does Lincoln feel about the man that has no faults? How can you tell?

2. What does Lincoln mean by his first epigram? Do you think he is being serious? Explain.

3. Who is the grandson Lincoln talks about in the second epigram? What is Lincoln curious to see?

4. Lincoln seems to suggest, in the second epigram, that some people place too much importance on ancestry. Can a concern about one's ancestors ever be unhealthy or dangerous? Explain.

Reading Literature

1. **Recognizing Epigrams.** A brief, witty saying that expresses a truth about life is called an **epigram**. What ideas about life are expressed in Lincoln's epigrams? Do you consider them truths? Explain.

2. **Appreciating Humor.** How does the rural slang term *pesky* add to the humor of the first epigram? Is there any humor in the second epigram? Explain.

Developing Vocabulary Skills

1. **Identifying Word Parts.** In this chapter you will learn how to discover the meaning of a

word by analyzing its parts. The three basic types of word parts are base words, prefixes, and suffixes.

A complete word to which another word part can be added is called a **base word**. A **prefix** is a word part added to the beginning of a base word. A **suffix** is a word part added to the end of a base word.

Make three columns on your paper. Label them *Prefix*, *Base Word*, *Suffix*. For each word, list its word parts in the appropriate column, as shown below.

Example: inactivity

Prefix	Base Word	Suffix
in-	active	-ity

Notice that the spelling of the base word changed when the ending was added. If a word has no prefix or suffix, write 0 in that column.

a. government
b. detraction
c. transcontinental
d. preconceived
e. unforgetful
f. endurable
g. remeasure
h. unperishable
i. powerful
j. unfitting

2. **Using Prefixes.** A word part that is added to the beginning of a word is called a **prefix**. Several commonly used prefixes have the meaning "not" or "the opposite of." They include the following:

dis-   im-   ir-
non-   in-   un-

The following words, or their base words, are taken from "The Gettysburg Address" and "Letter to Mrs. Bixby." Use one of the prefixes shown above to change the word to its opposite. Then, use each word in a sentence that shows you understand the meaning. Refer to the dictionary if necessary.

a. sincerely
b. respectfully
c. gloriously
d. honorable
e. proper
f. measurable
g. resolvable
h. assemble
i. governmental
j. consolable

Developing Writing Skills

1. **Explaining an Idea.** Lincoln's "Gettysburg Address" reveals his firm belief in democracy. In one paragraph, define democracy. Then, in two or three additional paragraphs, explain the democratic ideas expressed in "The Gettysburg Address."

    Pre-Writing. Using a dictionary and a history textbook, develop a definition of democracy. Include in your definition specific characteristics of democracy that separate it from other types of government. Next, reread "The Gettysburg Address." List all the ideas that support your definition of democracy. Organize your notes in a logical sequence. You might go from the general to the specific.

    Writing. In one paragraph, define democracy. In the second paragraph, summarize the ideas in "The Gettysburg Address" that relate to democracy.

    Revising. Is your definition thorough and accurate? Do your passages from "The Gettysburg Address" tie in to this definition? Have you given your readers enough information so that they understand the word you are defining as well as you do? Make changes if necessary.

2. **Writing a Diary Entry.** Imagine that you are Mrs. Bixby and have just received the letter from President Lincoln. Write a diary entry explaining your reaction and feelings after reading the letter.

3. **Writing a Paraphrase.** A paraphrase, as you know, is the rewording of a work. Write a paraphrase of "The Emancipation Proclamation" by using simpler language. See page 94 for more information on how to write a paraphrase.

Developing Skills in Study and Research

Researching Letters. During the time he was President, Lincoln wrote many letters. The majority of these letters have been collected and published. You can locate these collections by looking under *Letters* in the card catalog of the library. In addition, you can check in the biography section. Many of these collections have the call number 921.

Locate a collection of Lincoln's letters. Find letters addressed to his family, victims of war, generals, or other politicians. What do these letters reveal about Lincoln? Share your findings with the class.

Developing Skills in Critical Thinking

1. **Recognizing Emotional Appeals.** Often a speaker will attempt to influence or persuade an audience by appealing to their emotions. The subjects of Lincoln's speech are emotional topics: life, death, war, and liberty. Which passages appeal to the emotions?

2. **Recognizing Absolute Words.** Words that are used to refer to every event or thing of a kind are called **absolute words**. Some common absolute words are *all, every, everybody, none,* and *never.* "The Emancipation Proclamation" declares that the government will not repress those set free "in any effort they make for their actual freedom." What is the absolute word in this passage? Can you think of some problems this wording could cause?

Developing Skills in Speaking and Listening

Using Voice to Create Mood. Form small groups within your class. Choose one member to read "The Gettysburg Address" aloud. Another member of the group should be the "director," coaching the "actor" in volume, pace, and pauses. Other group members can offer suggestions.

From
Robert E. Lee

STEPHEN VINCENT BENÉT

SETTING A PURPOSE | *Robert E. Lee was the commander of the Confederate Army during the Civil War. According to Stephen Vincent Benét, what made Lee a great leader?*

Robert E. Lee, 1898, GUSTAVE KRUELL.
The Metropolitan Museum of Art, bequest of Allen Munn, 1924. (24.90.1135). New York.

And now at last,
Comes Traveller and his master. Look at them well.
The horse is an iron-grey, sixteen hands high,
Short back, deep chest, strong haunch, flat legs,
    small head,   5
Delicate ear, quick eye, black mane and tail,
Wise brain, obedient mouth.
                Such horses are
The jewels of the horseman's hands and thighs,
They go by the word and hardly need the rein.   10
They bred such horses in Virginia then,
Horses that were remembered after death
And buried not so far from Christian ground
That if their sleeping riders should arise
They could not witch them from the earth again   15
And ride a printless course along the grass
With the old manage and light ease of hand.
The rider now.
        He too, is iron-grey,
Though the thick hair and thick, blunt-pointed beard   20
Have frost in them.
        *   *   *   *   *
The man was loved, the man was idolized,
The man had every just and noble gift.
He took great burdens and he bore them well,

Believed in God but did not preach too much,   25
Believed and followed duty first and last
With marvellous consistency and force,
Was a great victor, in defeat as great,
No more, no less, always himself in both,
Could make men die for him but saved his men   30
Whenever he could save them—was most kind
But was not disobeyed—was a good father,
A loving husband, a considerate friend:
Had little humor, but enough to play
Mild jokes that never wounded, but had charm,   35
Did not seek intimates, yet drew men to him,
Did not seek fame, did not protest against it,
Knew his own value without pomp or jealousy
And died as he preferred to live—sans phrase,[1]
With commonsense, tenacity and courage.   40

         *   *   *   *   *

He was a man, and as a man he knew
Love, separation, sorrow, joy and death.
He was a master of the tricks of war,
He gave great strokes and warded strokes as great.   45
He was the prop and pillar of a State,
The incarnation of a national dream,
And when the State fell and the dream dissolved
He must have lived with bitterness itself—
But what his sorrow was and what his joy,
And how he felt in the expense of strength,   50
And how his heart contained its bitterness,
He will not tell us.

---

1. **sans phrase**, French: without words. In this case, simply and
   without fanfare.

Developing Comprehension Skills

1. Benét's poem contains two descriptions. One focuses on Robert E. Lee. What does the second description focus on?

2. How did Lee react to great burdens?

3. Benét says Lee "was a great victor, in defeat as great." What does he mean?

4. According to Benét, Lee "was a man." Because of this, what were some of the things Lee knew, or felt?

5. In the final stanza, what is it that Lee "will not tell us"? Why won't he tell us?

6. In the poem Benét reveals his admiration for the many qualities of Robert E. Lee. Do you think it is possible for one person to have so many fine qualities? If Benét is exaggerating, why might he have done so?

Reading Literature

1. **Understanding Purpose.** Benét's poem describes, in detail, the admirable qualities of Lee. What do you think Benét's purpose was in describing Lee in this manner? What purpose did he have in writing the poem?

2. **Explaining Metaphors.** Benét uses several metaphors in his descriptions of Robert E. Lee and Traveller. These comparisons help create vivid descriptions. Explain the meaning of the following metaphors used in the poem. What additional meaning does each one add to the ideas Benét is expressing?

   a. Such horses are / The jewels of the horseman's hands and thighs

   b. He was the prop and pillar of a State

3. **Analyzing the Use of Contrast.** In his poem, Benét shows two sides to several aspects of Lee's character. He does this through the use of contrast. For example, Lee "Did not seek intimates, yet drew men to him." Locate two other phrases that use contrast to describe Lee. What do you think Benét was trying to show by using contrasts?

4. **Identifying Mood.** While paying tribute to Lee, Benét creates a specific mood. What feelings does the poem create in the reader? What phrases help to create the mood?

Developing Vocabulary Skills

Using Prefixes To Determine Word Meaning. The underlined word in each sentence below was formed from a base word and a prefix that is listed on page 232. Write each underlined word and give the meaning of the prefix. Then, write the meaning of the entire word.

1. Robert E. Lee's dedication to the cause he fought for was never <u>misinterpreted.</u>

2. Lee was a man of <u>extraordinary</u> strength and personal courage.

3. Lee felt <u>compassion,</u> but never pity, for the soldiers he led.

4. Lee's <u>readjustment</u> period was long and painful.

5. Lee <u>rededicated</u> himself to peacetime goals.

6. To this day, his contributions to his cause cannot be <u>devalued.</u>

Developing Writing Skills

1. **Using Comparison.** "Robert E. Lee" contains descriptions of Lee and his horse, Traveller. There are several similarities between the two. Write a paragraph comparing Lee and Traveller. Use passages from the poem to give support to your paragraph.

2. **Writing a Character Sketch.** Think of a person you admire. Write a character sketch of that person, describing his or her admirable qualities. Use specific incidents and examples to create an accurate and vivid description of the individual.

Pre-Writing. Choose a person to describe. Identify that person's most admirable qualities. List specific details, examples, and incidents that illustrate these qualities. Organize your notes by grouping ideas related to the same quality. Decide on an order for presenting your ideas. For example, you might begin with the most obvious qualities and work toward the hidden ones.

Writing. Develop an introduction that states your purpose in writing the character sketch. Then, describe the person's qualities. Provide enough details, examples, and incidents to make your description vivid. In addition, try to create a specific tone. End your composition with a good, well stated conclusion.

Revising. Read your composition. Does it give an accurate description of the individual? Have you presented enough details to bring the subject to life? Also, is your admiration for the person evident? Make changes, if necessary. Then write a clean final copy.

Developing Skills in Critical Thinking

Drawing Conclusions. Benét does not tell the reader what Lee's reaction was to losing the Civil War. In fact, he says that Lee himself never revealed what he felt. However, Benét does give enough information so that the reader can make a logical conclusion. What passages in the poem, and especially in the final stanza, give clues as to how Lee might have felt after losing the war?

Developing Skills in Speaking and Listening

Presenting a Choral Reading. Work with several other students to do a group reading of "Robert E. Lee." Analyze the poem together. Look for idea groups that could be presented by different speakers. Should some lines be presented by several people? Do certain lines require a gentler voice, or a stronger one? Are there individual words that should be emphasized? Assign parts, and practice reading your poem aloud. Make sure one speaker blends into the next smoothly. When you are satisfied with your reading, present the poem to the class.

Frederick Douglass was a slave who later gained his freedom. He then worked hard to try to eliminate slavery. What events in his childhood shaped his beliefs and attitudes?

From

My Bondage and My Freedom

FREDERICK DOUGLASS

I lived in the family of Master Hugh, at Baltimore, seven years, during which time—as the almanac makers say of the weather—my condition was variable. The most interesting feature of my history here was my learning to read and write, under somewhat marked disadvantages. In attaining this knowledge, I was compelled to resort to indirections by no means congenial to my nature and which were really humiliating to me. My mistress—who had begun to teach me—was suddenly checked in her benevolent design by the strong advice of her husband. In faithful compliance with this advice, the good lady had not only ceased to instruct me herself, but had set her face as a flint against my learning to read by any means. It is due, however, to my mistress to say that she did not adopt this course in all its stringency at the first. She either thought it unnecessary or she lacked the depravity indispensable to shutting me up in mental darkness. It was at least necessary for her to have some training and some hardening in the exercise of the slaveholder's prerogative to make her equal to forgetting my human nature and character, and to treating me as a thing destitute of a moral or an intellectual nature. Mrs. Auld—my mistress—was a most kind and tenderhearted woman; and, in the humanity of her heart and the simplicity of her mind, she set out, when I first went to live with her, to treat me as she supposed one human being ought to treat another . . . .

I was human, and she, dear lady, knew and felt me to be so. How could she then treat me as a brute, without a mighty struggle with all the noble powers of her own soul. That struggle came, and the will of the husband was victorious. Her noble soul was overthrown.

When I went into their family, it was the abode of happiness and contentment. The mistress of the house was a model of affection and tenderness. Her fervent piety and watchful uprightness made it impossible to see her without thinking and feeling—"that woman is a Christian." There was no sorrow nor suffering for which she had not a tear, and there was no innocent joy for which she had not a smile. She had bread for the hungry, clothes for the naked, and comfort for every mourner that came within her reach. Slavery soon proved its ability to divest her of these excellent qualities and her home of its early happiness . . . .

In ceasing to instruct me, she must begin to justify herself *to* herself; and, once consenting to take sides in such a debate, she was riveted to her position. One needs very little knowledge of moral philosophy to see *where* my mistress now landed. She finally became even more violent in her opposition to my learning to read than was her husband himself. She was not satisfied with simply doing as *well* as her husband had commanded her, but seemed resolved to better his instruction. Nothing appeared to make my poor mistress—after her turning toward the downward path— more angry than seeing me, seated in some nook or corner, quietly reading a book or a newspaper. I have had her rush at me with the utmost fury, and snatch from my hand such newspaper or book, with something of the wrath and consternation which a traitor might be supposed to feel on being discovered in a plot by some dangerous spy.

Seized with a determination to learn to read at any cost, I hit upon many expedients to accomplish the desired end. The plea which I mainly adopted, and the one by which I was most successful, was that of using my young white playmates, whom I met in the street, as teachers. I used to carry, almost constantly, a copy of Webster's spelling book in my pocket; and, when sent on errands, or when play time was allowed me, I would step, with my young friends, aside, and take a lesson in spelling. I generally paid my *tuition fee* to the boys with bread, which I also carried in my pocket. For a single biscuit, any of my hungry little comrades would give me a lesson more valuable to me than bread. Not every one, however, demanded this consideration, for there were those who took pleasure in teaching me

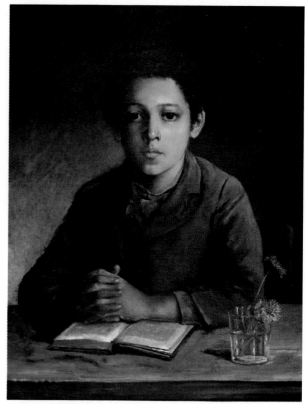

A Difficult Task, 1887, FLORENCE WOLF GOTTHOLD. Montrose Galleries, Bethesda, Maryland.

whenever I had a chance to be taught by them. I am strongly tempted to give the names of two or three of those little boys as a slight testimonial of the gratitude and affection I bear them, but prudence forbids; not that it would injure me, but it might possibly embarrass them; for it is almost an unpardonable offense to do any thing, directly or indirectly, to promote a slave's freedom in a slave state. It is enough to say of my warm-hearted little playfellows that they lived on Philpot Street very near Durgin & Bailey's shipyard.

Although slavery was a delicate subject, and very cautiously talked about among grownup people in Maryland, I frequently talked about it—and that very freely—with the white boys. I would sometimes say to them, while seated on a curb stone or a cellar door, "I wish I could be free, as you will be when you get to be men. You will be free, you know, as soon as you are twenty-one and can go where you like, but I am a slave for life. Have I not as good a right to be free as you have?" Words like these, I observed, always troubled them; and I had no small satisfaction in wringing from the boys, occasionally, that fresh and bitter condemnation of slavery that springs from nature, unseared and unperverted. Of all consciences, let me have those to deal with which have not been bewildered by the cares of life. I do not remember ever to have met with a *boy*, while I was in slavery, who defended the slave system; but I have often had boys to console me with the hope that something would yet occur by which I might be made free. Over and over again, they have told me that "they believed *I* had as good a right to be free as *they* had," and that "they did not believe God ever made anyone to be a slave." The reader will easily see that such little conversations with my playfellows had no tendency to weaken my love of liberty nor to render me contented with my condition as a slave.

When I was about thirteen years old and had succeeded in learning to read, every increase of knowledge, especially respecting the free states, added something to the almost intolerable burden of the thought—"I am a slave for life." To my bondage I saw no end. It was a terrible reality, and I shall never be able to tell how sadly that thought chafed my young spirit. Fortunately, or unfortunately, about this time in my life, I had made enough money to buy what was then a very popular schoolbook, the *Columbian Orator*. I bought this addition to my library of Mr. Knight on Thames street, Fell's Point, Baltimore, and paid him fifty cents for it. I was first led to buy this book by hearing some little boys say that they were going to learn some little pieces out of it for the Exhibition. This volume was indeed a rich treasure, and every opportunity afforded me, for a time, was spent in diligently perusing it. . . . The dialogue and the speeches were all redolent of the principles of liberty, and poured floods of light on the nature and character of slavery. . . . I was no longer the light-hearted, gleesome boy, full of mirth and play, as when I landed first at Baltimore. Knowledge had come. . . .

This knowledge opened my eyes to the horrible pit and revealed the teeth of the frightful dragon that was ready to pounce upon me, but it opened no way for my escape. I have often wished myself a beast or a bird—anything, rather than a slave. I was wretched and gloomy beyond my ability to describe. I was too thoughtful to be happy. It was this everlasting thinking which distressed and tormented me; and yet there was no getting rid of the subject of my thoughts. All nature was redolent of it. My spirit was roused to eternal wakefulness. Liberty! the inestimable birthright of every man had for me converted every object into an asserter of this great right. It was heard in every sound and beheld in every object. It was ever present to torment me with a sense of my wretched condition. The more beautiful and charming were the smiles of nature, the more horrible and desolate was my condition. I saw nothing without seeing it, and I heard nothing without hearing it. I do not exaggerate when I say that it looked from every star, smiled in every calm, breathed in every wind, and moved in every storm.

I have no doubt that my state of mind had something to do with the change in the treatment adopted by my once kind mistress toward me. I can easily believe that my leaden, downcast, and discontented look was very offensive to her. Poor lady! She did not know my trouble, and I dared not tell her. Could I have freely made her acquainted with the real state of my mind and given her the reasons therefor, it might have been well for both of us. Her abuse of me fell upon me like the blows of the false prophet upon his donkey; she did not know that an *angel* stood in the way;[1] and—such is the relation of master and slave—I could not tell her. Nature had made us *friends*; slavery made us *enemies*. My interests were in a direction opposite to hers, and we both had our private thoughts and plans. She aimed to keep me ignorant; and I resolved

to know, although knowledge only increased my discontent. My feelings were not the result of any marked cruelty in the treatment I received; they sprung from the consideration of my being a slave at all. It was *slavery*—not its mere *incidents*—that I hated. I had been cheated. I saw through the attempt to keep me in ignorance; I saw that slaveholders would have gladly made me believe that they were merely acting under the authority of God in making a slave of me and in making slaves of others, and I treated them as robbers and deceivers. The feeding and clothing me well could not atone for taking my liberty from me. The smiles of my mistress could not remove the deep sorrow that dwelt in my young bosom. Indeed these, in time, came only to deepen my sorrow. She had changed; and the reader will see that I had changed too. We were both victims to the same overshadowing evil—*she* as mistress, *I* as slave. I will not censure her harshly; she cannot censure me, for she knows I speak but the truth, and have acted in my opposition to slavery, just as she herself would have acted in a reverse of circumstances.

---

1. **blows . . . way**, A biblical reference (Numbers 22: 21–35) in which a donkey is being beaten by her master, but cannot go forward because an angel blocks the way.

Developing Comprehension Skills

1. Why did Mrs. Auld stop teaching Frederick Douglass to read? How did her attitude toward Douglass change?

2. Why do you think the Aulds believed that education for a slave was wrong?

3. Douglass writes of Mrs. Auld, "We were both victims to the same overshadowing evil— *she* as mistress, *I* as slave." According to Douglass, why is slavery bad for both slave and slaveholder?

4. What was the tuition fee Douglass paid to the white boys who helped him to read?

5. Douglass says the white boys "believed *I* had as good a right to be free as *they* had." The children seemed able to see the injustice of

slavery. Why do you think children view things differently than adults?

6. Knowledge made Douglass "wretched and gloomy beyond my ability to describe." What knowledge had this effect?

Reading Literature

1. **Understanding Autobiography.** The story of a person's life, written by that person, is called an **autobiography**. In an autobiography, the writer describes experiences that were significant in his or her life. In the selection you have read about Douglass, what seems to have been the most significant event in his childhood? Why do you think it affected him so strongly?

2. **Analyzing Point of View.** Autobiographies are almost always told from the first-person point of view. The author uses the pronouns *I* and *me*. This point of view offers the reader the opportunity to share and understand the experiences of the author.

   What can you learn from Douglass's autobiography that you probably would not learn in a biography told by someone else?

3. **Recognizing Conflict.** The struggle that a character faces is the **conflict** in a story. This conflict may be between two characters. It may also be between the character and society, or between the character and nature. Sometimes, however, the conflict is within the character.

   What type of conflicts did Douglass face? Which do you think were the most difficult for him?

4. **Identifying Theme.** You will recall that the theme in a work of literature is the main idea.

What does Douglass's writing tell about the effects of slavery on an individual? Locate two passages related to this theme.

5. **Analyzing Characterization.** You remember that the way a character is revealed in a selection is called **characterization**. With **direct characterization**, character is told directly by the author. In **indirect characterization**, character is revealed by the way a person thinks, acts, or speaks.

   Frederick Douglass reveals the character of Mrs. Auld through direct description. He says she "was a most kind and tender-hearted woman." What actions of Mrs. Auld indirectly prove that this is true? Which actions contradict this?

Developing Vocabulary Skills

Using Prefixes To Unlock Meaning. The underlined words in the following sentences are taken from *My Bondage and My Freedom*. Determine the meaning of each by using your knowledge of prefixes. Write the meaning of each word and check it with the dictionary.

1. Douglass had a feeling of <u>indirection</u> in his life until he discovered books.

2. As a <u>precaution</u>, he did not tell Mrs. Auld that he was continuing his studies.

3. At that time, education of a slave was considered an <u>unpardonable</u> offense.

4. Unfortunately, Mrs. Auld could not hope to remain <u>unperverted</u> by the times in which she lived.

5. The new knowledge brought Douglass <u>inestimable</u> joy and a great deal of pain.

6. The more he learned, however, the more <u>discontented</u> he became with his situation.

7. Douglass knew that he could not <u>retrace</u> his life, nor did he want to.

Developing Writing Skills

1. **Analyzing the Writer.** The experiences described in an autobiography tell the reader a great deal about the author. Many of the author's character traits are revealed directly by the author. The incidents he or she chooses to write about also tell something about the writer. Write a composition that analyzes Douglass's character.

   Pre-Writing. Talk with your classmates about what makes Douglass a unique person. Then decide on three characteristics to analyze in your composition. For each characteristic, list incidents, examples, or quotations from *My Bondage and My Freedom* that reveal the trait. Organize your notes in a logical sequence. You may want to lead up to the most important trait.

   Writing. Write an introduction that states your topic. Make sure it also gains your reader's attention. You might do this by stating an interesting fact about Douglass or by asking an interesting question. Develop each characteristic of Douglass in a separate paragraph. Include examples and quotations from the autobiography to illustrate each characteristic. The conclusion should summarize the kind of person Douglass was.

   Revising. Work with an editing partner. Ask your partner for suggestions to improve your composition. Have your partner check for the following: logical organization, well-developed ideas, word choice. Make changes in the areas where improvement is needed.

2. **Writing an Autobiographical Story.** In the selection you have read, Douglass describes the changes that took place in his relationship with Mrs. Auld. Write an autobiographical story that tells the changes that occurred in one of your relationships with someone. The person may be a friend, a family member, a teacher, or anyone else of your choosing. Be sure to tell how you felt. Why was the incident so important to you?

Developing Skills in Study and Research

Using the Card Catalog. Use the card catalog to find a biography of Frederick Douglass. Skim the index or table of contents to find the section of the book that covers Douglass's childhood with the Aulds. Read this section carefully. How does this account compare with Douglass's version? How can you explain these differences?

Developing Skills in Critical Thinking

Identifying Judgment Words. Words that strongly label something as good or bad are called **judgment words**. *Vicious, magnificent,* and *beautiful,* for example, are judgment words. When a speaker or writer uses a judgment word that person is expressing an opinion. He or she should be prepared to support the opinion with facts.

What judgment words does Douglass use in describing Mrs. Auld and her husband? What judgment words does Douglass use to describe slavery? Does he provide any facts to back up these judgments?

An Occurrence at Owl Creek Bridge

AMBROSE BIERCE

SETTING A PURPOSE | *Peyton Farquhar is to be hanged by the Union Army. While the rope is around his neck, he thinks of a way to escape. Will he succeed?*

1

A man stood upon a railroad bridge in northern Alabama, looking down into the swift water twenty feet below. The man's hands were behind his back, the wrists bound with a cord. A rope closely encircled his neck. It was attached to a stout cross-timber above his head and the slack fell to the level of his knees. Some loose boards laid upon the sleepers supporting the metals of the railway supplied a footing for him and his executioners—two private soldiers of the Federal army, directed by a sergeant who in civil life may have been a deputy sheriff. At a short remove upon the same temporary platform was an officer in the uniform of his rank, armed. He was a captain. A sentinel at each end of the bridge stood with his rifle in the position known as "support," that is to say, vertical in front of the left shoulder, the hammer resting on the forearm thrown straight across the chest—a formal and unnatural position, enforcing an erect carriage of the body. It did not appear to be the duty of these two men to know what was occurring at the center of the bridge; they merely blockaded the two ends of the foot planking that traversed it.

Beyond one of the sentinels nobody was in sight; the railroad ran straight away into a forest for a hundred yards, then, curving, was lost to view. Doubtless there was an outpost farther along. The other bank of the stream was open ground—a gentle acclivity topped with a stockade of vertical tree trunks, loopholed for rifles, with a single embrasure through which protruded the muzzle of a brass cannon commanding the bridge. Midway of the slope between bridge and fort were the spectators—a single company of infantry in line, at "parade rest," the butts of the rifles on the ground, the barrels inclining slightly backward against the right shoulder, the hands crossed upon the stock. A lieutenant stood at the right of the line, the point of his sword upon the ground, his left hand resting upon his right. Excepting the group of four at the center of the bridge, not a man moved. The company faced the bridge, staring stonily, motionless. The sentinels, facing the banks of the stream, might have been statues to adorn the bridge. The captain stood with folded arms, silent, observing the work of his subordinates, but making no sign. Death is a dignitary who when he comes announced is to be received with formal manifestations of respect, even by those most familiar with him. In the code of military etiquette, silence and fixity are forms of deference.

The man who was engaged in being hanged was apparently about thirty-five years of age. He was a civilian, if one might judge from his habit, which was that of a planter. His features were good—a straight nose, firm mouth, broad forehead, from which his long, dark hair was combed straight back, falling behind his ears to the collar of his well-fitting frock coat. He wore a mustache and pointed beard, but no whiskers; his eyes were large and dark gray, and had a kindly expression which one would hardly have expected in one whose neck was in the hemp. Evidently this was no vulgar assassin. The liberal military code makes provision for hanging many kinds of persons, and gentlemen are not excluded.

The preparations being complete, the two private soldiers stepped aside and each drew away the plank upon which he had been standing. The sergeant turned to the captain, saluted and placed himself immediately behind that officer, who in turn moved apart one pace. These movements left the condemned man and the sergeant standing on the two ends of the same plank; which spanned three of the cross-ties of the bridge. The end upon which the civilian stood almost, but not quite, reached a fourth. This plank had been held in place by the weight of the captain; it was now held by that of the sergeant. At a signal from the former, the latter would step aside, the plank would tilt and the condemned man go

An Occurrence at Owl Creek Bridge. From the 1962 film, directed by Robert Enrico. Courtesy National Film Archive, London, England.

down between two ties. The arrangement commended itself to his judgment as simple and effective. His face had not been covered nor his eyes bandaged. He looked a moment at his "unsteadfast footing," then let his gaze wander to the swirling water of the stream racing madly beneath his feet. A piece of dancing driftwood caught his attention and his eyes followed it down the current. How slowly it appeared to move! What a sluggish stream!

He closed his eyes in order to fix his last thoughts upon his wife and children. The water, touched to gold by the early sun, the brooding mists under the banks at some distance down the stream, the fort, the soldiers, the piece of drift—all had distracted him. And now he became conscious of a new disturbance. Striking through the thought of his dear ones was a sound which he could neither ignore nor understand, a sharp, distinct, metallic percussion like the stroke of a blacksmith's hammer upon the anvil; it had the same ringing quality. He wondered what it was, and whether immeasurably distant or nearby—it seemed both. Its recurrence was regular, but as slow as the tolling of a death knell. He awaited each stroke with impatience and—he knew not why—apprehension. The intervals of silence grew progressively longer; the delays became maddening. With their greater infrequency the sounds increased in strength and sharpness. They hurt his ear like the thrust of a knife; he feared he would shriek. What he heard was the ticking of his watch.

He unclosed his eyes and saw again the water below him. "If I could free my hands," he thought, "I might throw off the noose and spring into the stream. By diving I could evade the bullets and, swimming vigorously, reach the bank, take to the woods and get away home. My home, thank God, is as yet outside their lines; my wife and little ones are still beyond the invader's farthest advance."

As these thoughts, which have here to be set down in words, were flashed into the doomed man's brain rather than evolved from it, the captain nodded to the sergeant. The sergeant stepped aside.

2

Peyton Farquhar was a well-to-do planter, of an old and highly respected Alabama family. Being a slave-owner, and like other slave owners a politician, he was naturally an original secessionist and ardently devoted to the Southern cause. Circumstances of an imperious nature, which it is unnecessary to relate here, had prevented him from taking service with the gallant army that had fought the disastrous campaigns ending with the fall of Corinth, and he chafed under the inglorious restraint, longing for the release of his energies, the larger life of the soldier, the opportunity for distinction. That opportunity, he felt, would come, as it comes to all in war time. Meanwhile he did what he could. No service was too humble for him to perform in aid of the South, no adventure too perilous for him to undertake if consistent with the character of a civilian who was at heart a soldier, and who in good faith and without too much qualification assented to at least a part of the frankly villainous dictum that all is fair in love and war.

One evening while Farquhar and his wife were sitting on a rustic bench near the entrance to his grounds, a gray-clad soldier rode up to the gate and asked for a drink of water. Mrs. Farquhar was only too happy to serve him with her own white hands. While she was fetching the water, her husband approached the dusty horseman and inquired eagerly for news from the front.

"The Yanks are repairing the railroads," said the man, "and are getting ready for another advance. They have reached the Owl Creek bridge, put it in order and built a stockade on the north bank. The commandant has issued an order, which is posted everywhere, declaring that any civilian caught interfering with the railroad, its bridges, tunnels, or trains will be summarily hanged. I saw the order."

"How far is it to the Owl Creek bridge?" Farquhar asked.

"About thirty miles."

"Is there no force on this side of the creek?"

"Only a picket post half a mile out, on the railroad, and a single sentinel at this end of the bridge."

"Suppose a man—a civilian and student of hanging—should elude the picket post and perhaps get the better of the sentinel," said Farquhar, smiling. "What could he accomplish?"

The soldier reflected. "I was there a month ago," he replied. "I observed that the flood of last winter had lodged a great quantity of driftwood against the wooden pier at this end of the bridge. It is now dry and would burn like tow."

The lady had now brought the water, which the soldier drank. He thanked her ceremoniously, bowed to her husband and rode away. An hour later, after nightfall, he repassed the plantation, going northward in the direction from which he had come. He was a Federal scout.

3

As Peyton Farquhar fell straight downward through the bridge, he lost consciousness and was as one already dead. From this state he was awakened—ages later, it seemed to him—by the pain of a sharp pressure upon his throat, followed by a sense of suffocation. Keen, poignant agonies seemed to shoot from his neck downward through every fiber of his body and limbs. These pains appeared to flash along well-defined lines of ramification and to beat with an inconceivably rapid periodicity. They seemed like streams of pulsating fire heating him to an intolerable temperature. As to his head, he was conscious of nothing but a feeling of fullness—of congestion. These sensations were unaccompanied by thought. The intellectual part of his nature was already effaced; he had power only to feel, and feeling was torment. He was conscious of motion. Encompassed in a luminous cloud, of which he was now merely the fiery heart, without material substance, he swung through unthinkable arcs of oscillation, like a vast pendulum. Then all at once, with terrible suddenness, the light about him shot upward with the noise of a loud plash; a frightful roaring was in his ears, and all was cold and dark. The power of thought was restored; he knew that the rope had broken and he had fallen into the stream. There was no additional strangulation; the noose about his neck was already suffocating him and kept the water from his lungs. To die of hanging at the bottom of a river!—the idea seemed to him ludicrous. He opened his eyes in the darkness and saw above him a gleam of light, but how distant, how inaccessible! He was still sinking, for the light became fainter and fainter until it was a mere glimmer. Then it began to grow and brighten, and he knew that he was rising toward the surface—knew it with reluctance, for he was now very comfortable. "To be hanged and drowned," he thought, "that is not so bad; but I do not wish to be shot. No; I will not be shot; that is not fair."

He was not conscious of an effort, but a sharp pain in his wrist apprised him that he was trying to free his hands. He gave the struggle his attention, as an idler might observe the feat of a juggler, without interest in the outcome. What splendid effort!—what magnificent, what superhuman strength! Ah, that was a fine endeavor! Bravo! The cord fell away; his arms parted and floated upward, the hands dimly seen on each side in the growing light. He watched them with a new interest as first one and then the other pounced upon the noose at his neck. They tore it away and thrust it fiercely aside, its undulations resembling those of a water-snake. "Put it back, put it back!" He thought he shouted these words to his hands, for the undoing of the noose had been succeeded by the direst pang that he had yet experienced. His neck ached horribly; his brain was on fire; his heart, which had been fluttering faintly, gave a great leap, trying to force itself out at his mouth. His whole body was racked and wrenched with an insupportable anguish! But his disobedient hands gave no heed to the command. They beat the water vigorously with quick, downward strokes, forcing him to the surface. He felt his head emerge; his eyes were blinded by the sunlight;

his chest expanded convulsively, and with a supreme and crowning agony his lungs engulfed a great draught of air, which instantly he expelled in a shriek!

He was now in full possession of his physical senses. They were, indeed, preternaturally keen and alert. Something in the awful disturbance of his organic system had so exalted and refined them that they made record of things never before perceived. He felt the ripples upon his face and heard their separate sounds as they struck. He looked at the forest on the bank of the stream, saw the individual trees, the leaves, and the veining of each leaf—saw the very insects upon them: the locusts, the brilliant-bodied flies, the gray spiders stretching their webs from twig to twig. He noted the prismatic colors in all the dewdrops upon a millon blades of grass. The humming of the gnats that danced above the eddies of the stream, the beating of the dragon-flies' wings, the strokes of the water-spiders' legs, like oars which had lifted their boat—all these made audible music. A fish slid along beneath his eyes, and he heard the rush of its body parting the water.

He had come to the surface facing down the stream; in a moment the visible world seemed to wheel slowly round, himself the pivotal point, and he saw the bridge, the fort, the soldiers upon the bridge, the captain, the sergeant, the two privates, his executioners. They were in silhouette against the blue sky. They shouted, pointing at him. The captain had drawn his pistol, but did not fire; the others were unarmed. Their movements were grotesque and horrible, their forms gigantic.

Suddenly he heard a sharp report and something struck the water smartly within a few inches of his head, spattering his face with spray. He heard a second report, and saw one of the sentinels with his rifle at his shoulder, a light cloud of blue smoke rising from the muzzle. The man in the water saw the eye of the man on the bridge gazing into his own through the sights of the rifle. He observed that it was a gray eye and remembered having read that gray eyes were keenest, and that all famous marksmen had them. Nevertheless, this one had missed.

A counter-swirl had caught Farquhar and turned him half round; he was again looking into the forest on the bank opposite the fort. The sound of a clear, high voice in a monotonous singsong now rang out behind him and came across the water with a distinctness that pierced and subdued all other sounds, even the beating of the ripples in his ears. Although no soldier, he had frequented camps enough to know the dread significance of that deliberate, drawling, aspirated chant; the lieutenant on shore was taking a part in the morning's work. How coldly and pitilessly—with what an even, calm intonation, presaging, and enforcing tranquillity in the men—with what accurately measured intervals fell those cruel words:

"Attention, company! . . . Shoulder arms! . . . Ready! . . . Aim! . . . Fire!"

Farquhar dived—dived as deeply as he could. The water roared in his ears like the voice of Niagara, yet he heard the dulled thunder of the volley and, rising again toward the surface, met shining bits of metal, singularly flattened, oscillating slowly downward. Some of them touched him on the face and hands, then fell away, continuing their descent. One lodged between his collar and neck;

it was uncomfortably warm and he snatched it out.

As he rose to the surface, gasping for breath, he saw that he had been a long time under water; he was perceptibly farther down stream—nearer to safety. The soldiers had almost finished reloading; the metal ramrods flashed all at once in the sunshine as they were drawn from the barrels, turned in the air, and thrust into their sockets. The two sentinels fired again, independently and ineffectually.

The hunted man saw all this over his shoulder; he was now swimming vigorously. His brain was as energetic as his arms and legs; he thought with the rapidity of lightning.

"The officer," he reasoned, "will not make that martinet's error a second time. It is as easy to dodge a volley as a single shot. He has probably already given the command to fire at will. God help me, I cannot dodge them all!"

An appalling plash within two yards of him was followed by a loud, rushing sound, *diminuendo*,[1] which seemed to travel back through the air to the fort and died in an explosion which stirred the very river to its deeps! A rising sheet of water curved over him, fell down upon him, blinded him, strangled him! The cannon had taken a hand in the game. As he shook his head free from the commotion of the smitten water, he heard the deflected shot humming through the air ahead, and in an instant it was cracking and smashing the branches in the forest beyond.

"They will not do that again," he thought; "the next time they will use a charge of grape.[2]

---

1. **diminuendo**, a gradual decrease in loudness.
2. **grape**, (grapeshot) a cluster of small iron balls fired from a cannon in one shot.

I must keep my eye upon the gun; the smoke will apprise me—the report arrives too late; it lags behind the missile. That is a good gun."

Suddenly he felt himself whirled round and round—spinning like a top. The water, the banks, the forests, the now distant bridge, fort and men—all were commingled and blurred. Objects were represented by their colors only; circular horizontal streaks of color—that was all he saw. He had been caught in a vortex and was being whirled on with a velocity of advance and gyration that made him giddy and sick. In a few moments he was flung upon the gravel at the foot of the left bank of the stream—the southern bank—and behind a projecting point which concealed him from his enemies. The sudden arrest of his motion, the abrasion of one of his hands on the gravel, restored him, and he wept with delight. He dug his fingers into the sand, threw it over himself in handfuls and audibly blessed it. It looked like diamonds, rubies, emeralds; he could think of nothing beautiful which it did not resemble. The trees upon the bank were giant garden plants; he noted a definite order in their arrangement, inhaled the fragrance of their blooms. A strange, roseate light shone through the spaces among their trunks and the wind made in their branches the music of aeolian harps. He had no wish to perfect his escape—was content to remain in that spot until retaken.

A whiz and rattle of grapeshot among the branches above his head roused him from his dream. The baffled cannoner had fired him a random farewell. He sprang to his feet, rushed up the sloping bank and plunged into the forest.

All that day he traveled, laying his course by the rounding sun. The forest seemed interminable: nowhere did he discover a break in it, not even a woodman's road. He had not known that he lived in so wild a region. There was something uncanny in the revelation.

By nightfall he was fatigued, footsore, famishing. The thought of his wife and children urged him on. At last he found a road which led him in what he knew to be the right direction. It was as wide and straight as a city street, yet it seemed untraveled. No fields bordered it, no dwelling anywhere. Not so much as the barking of a dog suggested human habitation. The black bodies of the trees formed a straight wall on both sides, terminating on the horizon in a point, like a diagram in a lesson in perspective. Overhead, as he looked up through this rift in the wood, shone great golden stars looking unfamiliar and grouped in strange constellations. He was sure they were arranged in some order which had a secret and malign significance. The wood on either side was full of singular noises, among which—once, twice, and again—he distinctly heard whispers in an unknown tongue.

His neck was in pain and lifting his hand to it he found it horribly swollen. He knew that it had a circle of black where the rope had bruised it. His eyes felt congested; he could no longer close them. His tongue was swollen with thirst; he relieved its fever by thrusting it forward from between his teeth into the cold air. How softly the turf had carpeted the untraveled avenue—he could no longer feel the roadway beneath his feet!

Doubtless, despite his suffering, he had fallen asleep while walking, for now he sees another scene—perhaps he has merely recovered from a delirium. He stands at the gate of his own home. All is as he left it, and all bright and beautiful in the morning sunshine. He must have traveled the entire night. As he pushes open the gate and passes up the wide white walk, he sees a flutter of female garments; his wife, looking fresh and cool and sweet, steps down from the veranda to meet him. At the bottom of the steps she stands waiting, with a smile of ineffable joy, an attitude of matchless grace and dignity. Ah, how beautiful she is! He springs forward with extended arms. As he is about to clasp her he feels a stunning blow upon the back of the neck; a blinding white light blazes all about him with a sound like the shock of a cannon— then all is darkness and silence!

Peyton Farquhar was dead; his body, with a broken neck, swung gently from side to side beneath the timbers of the Owl Creek bridge.

Developing Comprehension Skills

1. Why are the Union soldiers on the bridge?

2. How does Peyton Farquhar think he can "escape"?

3. Farquhar is a Southerner. What keeps him from joining the Confederate forces? In what way was the scout warning the people of the district?

4. Farquhar notices many small things when he reaches the surface of the stream. His senses "made record of things never before perceived." What are some of the things that Farquhar notices in detail? Why is he suddenly so aware of those details?

5. Where does Farquhar plan to go after escaping from the soldiers? What thoughts "urged him on"?

6. At the end of the story, what does the reader find out about Farquhar's "escape"?

7. Bierce's story has a surprise ending. Was the ending predictable? Explain. In your opinion, was the ending believable? Explain your reasons.

Reading Literature

1. **Appreciating the Surprise Ending.** An unexpected turn of events at the end of a story is called a **surprise ending**. How does Bierce surprise the reader of "An Occurrence at Owl Creek Bridge"? Were there any clues within the story that things might not be as they seem?

2. **Inferring Character Traits.** The character of Peyton Farquhar is revealed in a variety of ways. The reader can draw conclusions about him from his outward appearance, his actions, and his thoughts. Explain what each

of these descriptions reveals about Farquhar:

a. . . . his long, dark hair was combed straight back, falling behind his ears to the collar of his well-fitting frock coat. . . . his eyes were large and dark gray, and had a kindly expression. . . .

b. No service was too humble for him to perform in aid of the South, no adventure too perilous for him to undertake if consistent with the character of a civilian who was at heart a soldier. . . .

c. He closed his eyes in order to fix his last thoughts upon his wife and children.

3. **Analyzing Point of View.** The way the narrator tells the story is called **point of view**. In "An Occurrence at Owl Creek Bridge," Ambrose Bierce uses **third-person limited** point of view. However, the narrator is both objective and subjective.

With both approaches, the narrator tells the action using the pronouns *he*, *she*, and *they*. However, in third-person objective narration, the narrator reports only facts. Thoughts and feelings are not revealed. In third-person subjective narration, the narrator tells events from one character's viewpoint, and that character's thoughts and feelings are revealed.

The first three paragraphs of "An Occurrence at Owl Creek Bridge," for example, are told by an objective narrator. Only facts are revealed. Where does Bierce begin using a subjective narrator? Why do you think he switches? Where does the story return to objective narration? What effect does this have on our understanding?

4. **Identifying Flashback.** A scene or event that happened before the beginning of a story, or

at an earlier point, is called a **flashback**. A writer will generally include a flashback to reveal information from a character's past. What part of "An Occurrence at Owl Creek Bridge" is a flashback? What information is revealed about Peyton Farquhar?

5. **Identifying Plot Sequence.** The events in this story are not told in the order in which they occur. To see the order of events clearly, it is helpful to make a time line. A **time line** is a way of showing the events of a story in chronological order. To make a time line, begin by drawing a straight line. Then place a dot on the line for each important event in the story. Make a time line and arrange the major events in the order in which they took place. Next to each dot, write a few words describing the event. Make a separate line to show the events of the dream.

events of dream

first event   second event   etc.   final event

Developing Vocabulary Skills

Recognizing Adjective Suffixes. A word part placed at the end of a base word to form a new word is called a **suffix**. Suffixes that change words to adjectives—words that describe—are called **adjective suffixes**. You studied some of these suffixes on page 233. Other common adjective suffixes are listed below.

Suffix	Meaning	Example
-al	of; having the nature of	accidental
-ic	having to do with	historic
-ive	of; having to do with	expensive
-like	like	childlike
-ous	full of; having	courageous
-some	tending to	bothersome

The column on the right lists words from "An Occurrence at Owl Creek Bridge." These words use adjective suffixes, as well as prefixes you already know. Match the words with their definitions by writing the correct number of the definition next to the letter of the word.

1. full of ceremony; formal
2. having involuntary contractions
3. not having glory or honor
4. having to do with a prism
5. full of evil
6. not able to be reached
7. not able to be imagined
8. slow and inactive like a slug
9. a turning point, like a pivot
10. not able to be supported

a. sluggish
b. inglorious
c. ceremonious
d. prismatic
e. inaccessible
f. pivotal
g. convulsive
h. insupportable
i. inconceivable
j. villainous

Developing Writing Skills

1. **Evaluating the Surprise Ending.** In "An Occurrence at Owl Creek Bridge" the reader is led to believe that Farquhar has escaped. However, Ambrose Bierce surprises the reader at the end of the story by announcing that Farquhar is dead.

How does Bierce effectively mislead the reader with Farquhar's escape? In one or two paragraphs, explain why the ending is an effective surprise.

Pre-Writing. Jot down details of Farquhar's escape that make it believable. How do these elements of the story help Bierce in creating a surprise ending? Organize your notes around several main ideas. For example, you might include the vivid sensory details in one group, and Farquhar's thoughts in another.

Writing. State your purpose for writing. Then explain how Bierce effectively takes the reader by surprise. Use passages from the story to support your point. Include a sentence at the end that summarizes the main idea of your paper.

Revising. Check your ideas. Does each paragraph have a good topic sentence? Do all of your details help to develop the main ideas of your paragraph? Make changes if necessary. Then, make a clean, final copy.

2. **Describing an Object.** When Farquhar supposedly surfaces in the water, Bierce says that his senses are unusually keen. Farquhar sees such small things as the veins on leaves and dewdrops upon blades of grass. Carefully observe and study a small object. Use your senses to discover more about the object. Then write a detailed description of the object. Be sure to include precise, vivid details that appeal to more than one sense.

Developing Skills in Critical Thinking

Separating the Possible from the Impossible. "An Occurrence at Owl Creek Bridge" contains many details that may not make sense. For example, Farquhar was under water, supposedly, for an extremely long time. He should have drowned. What are some other events in the story that probably couldn't have taken place? Explain why you think they are unreal.

Developing Skills in Speaking and Listening

Presenting a News Story. Imagine that you are a newscaster. Prepare a newscast in which you report the events that occurred at Owl Creek Bridge. Remember to report only the facts of the incidents and the events that lead up to it. Before you present your report, observe a newscaster on television. Notice the newscaster's tone of voice, facial expressions, and use of eye contact. Try to apply the effective speaking techniques you observed in the newscaster.

A Mystery of Heroism

STEPHEN CRANE

The dark uniforms of the men were so coated with dust from the incessant wrestling of the two armies that the regiment almost seemed a part of the clay bank which shielded them from the shells. On the top of the hill a battery was arguing in tremendous roars with some other guns, and to the eye of the infantry the artillerymen, the guns, the caissons, the horses, were distinctly outlined upon the blue sky. When a piece was fired, a red streak as round as a log flashed low in the heavens, like a monstrous bolt of lightning. The men of the battery wore white duck trousers, which somehow emphasized their legs; and when they ran and crowded in little groups at the bidding of the shouting officers, it was more impressive than usual to the infantry.

Fred Collins, of A Company, was saying, "Thunder! I wisht I had a drink. Ain't there any water round here?" Then somebody yelled, "There goes th' bugler!"

As the eyes of half the regiment swept in one machine-like movement, there was an instant's picture of a horse in a great convulsive leap of a death-wound and a rider leaning back with a crooked arm and spread fingers before his face. On the ground was the crimson terror of an exploding shell, with fibers of flame that seemed like lances. A glittering bugle swung clear of the rider's back as fell headlong the horse and the man. In the air was an odor as from a conflagration.

Sometimes they of the infantry looked down at a fair little meadow which spread at their feet. Its long green grass was rippling gently in a breeze. Beyond it was the grey form of a house half torn to pieces by shells and by the busy axes of soldiers who had pursued firewood. The line of an old fence was now dimly marked by long weeds and by an occasional post. A shell had blown the well-house to fragments. Little lines of grey smoke ribboning upward from some embers indicated the place where had stood the barn.

From beyond a curtain of green woods there came the sound of some stupendous scuffle, as if two animals of the size of islands were fighting. At a distance there were occasional appearances of swift-moving men, horses, batteries, flags; and with the crashing of infantry volleys were heard, often, wild cheers. In the midst of it all Smith and Ferguson, two privates of A Company, were engaged in a heated discussion which involved the greatest questions of the national existence.

The battery on the hill presently engaged in a frightful duel. The white legs of the gunners scampered this way and that way, and the officers redoubled their shouts. The guns, with their demeanors of stolidity and courage, were typical of something infinitely self-possessed in this clamor of death that swirled around the hill.

One of a "swing" team[1] was suddenly smitten quivering to the ground, and his maddened brethren dragged his torn body in their struggle to escape from this turmoil and danger. A young soldier astride one of the leaders swore and fumed in his saddle and furiously jerked at the bridle. An officer screamed out an order so violently that his voice broke and ended the sentence in a falsetto shriek.

The leading company of the infantry regiment was somewhat exposed, and the colonel ordered it moved more fully under the shelter of the hill. There was the clank of steel against steel.

A lieutenant of the battery rode down and passed them, holding his right arm carefully in his left hand. And it was as if this arm was not at all a part of him, but belonged to another man. His sober and reflective charger went slowly. The officer's face was grimy and perspiring, and his uniform was tousled as if he had been in direct grapple with an enemy. He smiled grimly when the men stared at him. He turned his horse toward the meadow.

Collins, of A Company, said, "I wisht I had a drink. I bet there's water in that there ol' well yonder!"

"Yes; but how you goin' to git it?"

For the little meadow which intervened was now suffering a terrible onslaught of shells. Its green and beautiful calm had vanished utterly. Brown earth was being flung in monstrous handfuls. And there was a massacre of the young blades of grass. They were being torn, burned, obliterated. Some curious fortune of the battle had made this gentle little meadow the object of the red hate of the shells, and each one as it exploded seemed like an imprecation in the face of a maiden.

The wounded officer who was riding across this expanse said to himself: "Why, they couldn't shoot any harder if the whole army was massed here!"

A shell struck the grey ruins of the house, and as, after the roar, the shattered wall fell in fragments, there was a noise which resembled the flapping of shutters during a wild gale of winter. Indeed, the infantry paused in the shelter of the bank appeared as men standing upon a shore contemplating a madness of the sea. The angel of calamity had under its glance the battery upon the hill. Fewer white-legged men labored about the guns. A shell had smitten one of the pieces, and after the flare, the smoke, the dust, the wrath of this blow were gone, it was possible to see white legs stretched horizontally upon the ground. And at that interval to the rear where it is the business of battery horses to stand with their noses to the fight, awaiting the command to drag their guns out of the destruction, or into it, or wheresoever these incomprehensible humans demanded with whip and spur—in this line of passive and dumb spectators, whose fluttering hearts yet would not let them forget the iron laws of man's control of them—in this rank of brute-soldiers there had been relentless and hideous carnage. From

---

1. **"swing" team**, the middle pair of a six-horse team.

the ruck of bleeding and prostrate horses, the men of the infantry could see one animal raising its stricken body with its forelegs and turning its nose with mystic and profound eloquence toward the sky.

Some comrades joked Collins about his thirst. "Well, if yeh want a drink so bad, why don't yeh go git it?"

"Well, I will in a minnet, if yeh don't shut up!"

A lieutenant of artillery floundered his horse straight down the hill with as little concern as if it were level ground. As he galloped past the colonel of the infantry, he threw up his hand in swift salute. "We've got to get out of that," he roared angrily. He was a black-bearded officer, and his eyes, which resembled beads, sparkled like those of an insane man. His jumping horse sped along the column of infantry.

The fat major, standing carelessly with his sword held horizontally behind him and with his legs far apart, looked after the receding horseman and laughed. "He wants to get back with orders pretty quick, or there'll be no batt'ry left," he observed.

The wise young captain of the second company hazarded to the lieutenant-colonel that the enemy's infantry would probably soon attack the hill, and the lieutenant-colonel snubbed him.

A private in one of the rear companies looked out over the meadow, and then turned to a companion and said, "Look there, Jim!" It was the wounded officer from the battery, who some time before had started to ride across the meadow, supporting his right arm carefully with his left hand. This man had encountered a shell, apparently, at a time

when no one perceived him, and he could now be seen lying face downward with a stirruped foot stretched across the body of his dead horse. A leg of the charger extended slantingly upward, precisely as stiff as a stake. Around this motionless pair the shells still howled.

There was a quarrel in A Company. Collins was shaking his fist in the faces of some laughing comrades. "Dern yeh! I ain't afraid t' go. If yeh say much, I will go!"

"Of course, yeh will! You'll run through that there medder, won't yeh?"

Collins said, in a terrible voice: "You see now!"

At this ominous threat his comrades broke into renewed jeers.

Collins gave them a dark scowl, and went to find his captain. The latter was conversing with the colonel of the regiment.

"Captain," said Collins, saluting and standing at attention—in those days all trousers bagged at the knees—"Captain, I want t' get permission to go git some water from that there well over yonder!"

The colonel and the captain swung about simultaneously and stared across the meadow. The captain laughed. "You must be pretty thirsty, Collins?"

"Yes, sir, I am."

"Well—ah," said the captain. After a moment, he asked, "Can't you wait?"

"No, sir."

The colonel was watching Collins's face. "Look here, my lad," he said, in a pious sort of voice—"Look here, my lad"—Collins was not a lad—"don't you think that's taking pretty big risks for a little drink of water?"

"I dunno," said Collins uncomfortably. Some of the resentment toward his companions, which perhaps had forced him into this affair, was beginning to fade. "I dunno w'ether 'tis."

The colonel and the captain contemplated him for a time.

"Well," said the captain finally.

"Well," said the colonel, "if you want to go, why, go."

Collins saluted. "Much obliged t' yeh."

As he moved away the colonel called after him. "Take some of the other boys' canteens with you, an' hurry back, now."

"Yes, sir, I will."

The colonel and the captain looked at each other then, for it had suddenly occurred that they could not for the life of them tell whether Collins wanted to go or whether he did not.

They turned to regard Collins, and as they perceived him surrounded by gesticulating comrades, the colonel said, "Well, by thunder! I guess he's going."

Collins appeared as a man dreaming. In the midst of all the excited talk of his company mates, he maintained a curious silence.

Guerrilla Warfare, Civil War, 1862, ALBERT BIERSTADT. The Century Association, New York.

They were very busy in preparing him for his ordeal. When they inspected him carefully, it was somewhat like the examination that grooms give a horse before a race; and they were amazed, staggered, by the whole affair. Their astonishment found vent in strange repetitions.

"Are yeh sure a-goin'?" they demanded again and again.

"Certainly I am," cried Collins at last, furiously.

He strode sullenly away from them. He was swinging five or six canteens by their cords. It seemed that his cap would not remain firmly on his head, and often he reached and pulled it down over his brow.

There was a general movement in the compact column. The long animal-like thing moved slightly. Its four hundred eyes were turned upon the figure of Collins.

"Well, sir, if that ain't th' derndest thing! I never thought Fred Collins had the blood in him for that kind of business."

"What's he goin' to do, anyhow?"

"He's goin' to that well there after water."

"We ain't dyin' of thirst, are we? That's foolishness."

"Well, somebody put him up to it, an' he's doin' it."

"Say, he must be a desperate cuss."

When Collins faced the meadow and walked away from the regiment, he was vaguely conscious that a chasm, the deep valley of all prides, was suddenly between him and his comrades. It was provisional, but the provision was that he return as a victor. He had blindly been led by quaint emotions, and laid himself under an obligation to walk squarely up to the face of death.

But he was not sure that he wished to make a retraction, even if he could do so without shame. As a matter of truth, he was sure of very little. He was mainly surprised.

It seemed to him supernaturally strange that he had allowed his mind to maneuvre his body into such a situation. He understood that it might be called dramatically great.

However, he had no full appreciation of anything, excepting that he was actually conscious of being dazed. He could feel his dulled mind groping after the form and color of this incident. He wondered why he did not feel some keen agony of fear cutting his sense like a knife. He wondered at this, because human expression had said loudly for centuries that men should feel afraid of certain things, and that all men who did not feel this fear were phenomena—heroes.

He was, then, a hero. He suffered that disappointment which we would all have if we discovered that we were ourselves capable of those deeds which we most admire in history and legend. This, then, was a hero. After all, heroes were not much.

No, it could not be true. He was not a hero. Heroes had no shames in their lives, and, as for him, he remembered borrowing fifteen dollars from a friend and promising to pay it back the next day, and then avoiding that friend for ten months. When, at home, his mother had aroused him for the early labor of his life on the farm, it had often been his fashion to be irritable, childish, diabolical; and his mother had died since he had come to the war.

He saw that, in this matter of the well, the canteens, the shells, he was an intruder in the land of fine deeds.

He was now about thirty paces from his comrades. The regiment had just turned its many faces toward him.

From the forest of terrific noises there suddenly emerged a little uneven line of men. They fired fiercely and rapidly at distant foliage on which appeared little puffs of white smoke. The spatter of skirmish firing was added to the thunder of the guns on the hill. The little line of men ran forward. A color-sergeant fell flat with his flag as if he had slipped on ice. There was hoarse cheering from this distant field.

Collins suddenly felt that two demon fingers were pressed into his ears. He could see nothing but flying arrows, flaming red. He lurched from the shock of this explosion, but he made a mad rush for the house, which he viewed as a man submerged to the neck in a boiling surf might view the shore. In the air little pieces of shell howled, and the earth-quake explosions drove him insane with the menace of their roar. As he ran the canteens knocked together with a rhythmical tinkling.

As he neared the house, each detail of the scene became vivid. He was aware of some bricks of the vanished chimney lying on the sod. There was a door which hung by one hinge.

Rifle bullets called forth by the insistent skirmishers came from the far-off bank of foliage. They mingled with the shells and the pieces of shells until the air was torn in all directions by hootings, yells, howls. The sky was full of fiends who directed all their wild rage at his head.

When he came to the well, he flung himself face downward and peered into its darkness. There were furtive silver glintings some feet from the surface. He grabbled one of the canteens and, unfastening its cap, swung it down by the cord. The water flowed slowly in with an indolent gurgle.

And now, as he lay with his face turned away, he was suddenly smitten with the terror. It came upon his heart like the grasp of claws. All the power faded from his muscles. For an instant he was no more than a dead man.

The canteen filled with a maddening slowness, in the manner of all bottles. Presently he recovered his strength and addressed a screaming oath to it. He leaned over until it seemed as if he intended to try to push water into it with his hands. His eyes as he gazed down into the well shone like two pieces of metal, and in their expression was a great appeal and a great curse. The stupid water derided him.

There was the blaring thunder of a shell. Crimson light shone through the swift-boiling smoke, and made a pink reflection on part of the wall of the well. Collins jerked out his arm and canteen with the same motion that a man would use in withdrawing his head from a furnace.

He scrambled erect and glared and hesitated. On the ground near him lay the old well bucket, with a length of rusty chain. He lowered it swiftly into the well. The bucket struck the water and then, turning lazily over, sank. When, with hand reaching tremblingly over hand, he hauled it out, it knocked often against the walls of the well and spilled some of its contents.

In running with a filled bucket, a man can adopt but one kind of gait. So, through this terrible field over which screamed practical angels of death, Collins ran in the manner of a farmer chased out of a dairy by a bull.

His face went staring white with anticipating—anticipation of a blow that would whirl him around and down. He would fall as he had seen other men fall, the life knocked out of them so suddenly that their knees were no more quick to touch the ground than their heads. He saw the long blue line of the regiment, but his comrades were standing looking at him from the edge of an impossible star. He was aware of some deep wheel ruts and hoofprints in the sod beneath his feet.

The artillery officer who had fallen in this meadow had been making groans in the teeth of the tempest of sound. These futile cries, wrenched from him by his agony, were heard only by shells, bullets. When wild-eyed Collins came running, this officer raised himself. His face contorted and blanched from pain, he was about to utter some great beseeching cry. But suddenly his face straightened, and he called: "Say, young man, give me a drink of water, will you?"

Collins had no room amid his emotions for surprise. He was made from the threats of destruction.

"I can't!" he screamed, and in his reply was a full description of his quaking apprehension. His cap was gone and his hair was riotous. His clothes made it appear that he had been dragged over the ground by the heels. He ran on.

The officer's head sank down, and one elbow crooked. His foot in its brass-bound stirrup still stretched over the body of his horse, and the other leg was under the steed.

But Collins turned. He came dashing back.

His face had now turned grey, and in his eyes was all terror. "Here it is! here it is!"

The officer was as a man gone in drink. His arm bent like a twig. His head drooped as if his neck were of willow. He was sinking to the ground, to lie face downward.

Collins grabbed him by the shoulder. "Here it is. Here's your drink. Turn over. Turn over, man, for God's sake!"

With Collins hauling at his shoulder, the officer twisted his body and fell with his face turned toward that region where lived the unspeakable noises of the swirling missiles. There was the faintest shadow of a smile on his lips as he looked at Collins. He gave a sigh, a little primitive breath like that from a child.

Collins tried to hold the bucket steadily, but his shaking hands caused the water to splash all over the face of the dying man. Then he jerked it away and ran on.

The regiment gave him a welcoming roar. The grimed faces were wrinkled in laughter.

His captain waved the bucket away. "Give it to the men!"

The two genial, skylarking young lieutenants were the first to gain possession of it. They played over it in their fashion.

When one tried to drink, the other teasingly knocked his elbow. "Don't Billie! You'll make me spill it," said the one. The other laughed.

Suddenly there was an oath, the thud of wood on the ground, and a swift murmur of astonishment among the ranks. The two lieutenants glared at each other. The bucket lay on the ground, empty.

Developing Comprehension Skills

1. Briefly describe the area where the story takes place. Where are the troops? Where are the house and the meadow?

2. How do Collins's fellow soldiers treat him? Why does he go for the water?

3. What is Collins's concept of a hero? Why is he disappointed to think of himself as a hero?

4. When does Collins finally feel fear? What actions by Collins reveal the fact that he is afraid?

5. Why do you think Collins runs back to give the artillery officer a drink? Do you think this qualifies Collins as a hero? Explain.

6. "A Mystery of Heroism" contains several ideas and views of what a hero is. What is your definition of a hero? Is your definition similar to ideas in the story? Explain.

Reading Literature

1. **Recognizing Conflict.** An internal conflict, as you know, is a struggle within a character. In "A Mystery of Heroism," two internal conflicts exist for Collins. One involves getting the water. What second decision must Collins make?

2. **Identifying Figures of Speech.** In Chapter 4 you learned that writers use figures of speech to make their stories colorful and lively. Decide whether each of the following phrases uses simile, metaphor, or personification. Then explain how these descriptions add additional meaning to the ideas being presented.

   a. a curtain of green woods
   b. a battery was arguing in tremendous roars
   c. fibers of flame that seemed like lances

Find two other figures of speech and explain why you think they are especially effective.

3. **Recognizing Realism.** Writing that presents people and things as they really appear to be in life is called **realism**. Stephen Crane never saw the Civil War, but he is able to create a very real picture of it. Read Crane's description of battle in the third and fourth paragraphs. What makes it believable and realistic?

4. **Examining Dialect.** The language that is characteristic of a certain people or region is called **dialect**. Dialect results from differences in vocabulary, grammar, and pronunciation. Everyone speaks some sort of dialect.

   What evidence do you see that the following portion of dialogue was written to show a specific dialect?

   > Collins, of A Company, said, "'I wisht I had a drink. I bet there's water in that there ol' well yonder!"

5. **Understanding the Title.** The story "A Mystery of Heroism" suggests that heroism is neither simple nor easily understood. For example, heroism is different from what Fred Collins expected. Why is the word *mystery* appropriate for the title of Crane's story?

Developing Vocabulary Skills

Using Noun Suffixes. Suffixes that make nouns out of the base word are called **noun suffixes**. The noun suffixes listed below mean "one who does something" or "that which does something."

Suffix	Example	Word Meaning
-ant, -ent	informant	one who informs
-ary	missionary	one sent on a mission

-eer	auctioneer	one who auctions
-er, -or	astronomer	one who studies astronomy
-ician	beautician	one who beautifies
-ist	journalist	one who writes

The following sentences are from selections you have read. Find the word or words in each sentence that have a suffix meaning "one who." Write each word and its meaning.

1. He was a civilian, if one might judge from his habit, which was that of a planter.

2. Being a slave-owner, and like other slave-owners a politician, he was naturally an original secessionist and ardently devoted to the Southern cause.

3. The baffled cannoneer had fired him a random farewell.

4. Death is a dignitary, who when he comes announced is to be received with formal manifestations of respect, even by those familiar with him.

5. Rifle bullets called forth by the insistent skirmishers came from the far-off bank of foliage.

Developing Writing Skills

1. **Analyzing Suspense.** Suspense, as you know, is the feeling of tension created when a reader does not know the outcome of a story. In one or more paragraphs, explain how Stephen Crane creates suspense in "A Mystery of Heroism."

   Pre-Writing. Review the story. Note passages that are especially suspenseful. Look for the devices that Crane uses to create suspense. What tricks does he use to delay the outcome? Write down these techniques, along with several examples. Organize your notes in a logical order. You may wish to arrange details in order of importance, or in chronological order.

   Writing. Begin with a topic sentence that makes a general statement about the suspense in the story. Or, write a general statement about how Crane creates suspense. Then, explain each technique that Crane uses. Use specific examples to illustrate each technique. Write a conclusion that repeats or summarizes your main ideas.

   Revising. Read your paragraph aloud. Are the ideas presented in a clear, logical order? Have you given specific examples from the story? Make changes if necessary.

2. **Analyzing Symbolism.** A symbol, as you know, is something that stands for something else. In "A Mystery of Heroism," different colors are used to symbolize different ideas. Green, for example, may represent life. On the other hand, red may represent violence or death. Choose one color that is repeated throughout the story. What does the color symbolize? Write one or two paragraphs showing how the color is used throughout the story. In each example, try to explain the color's symbolic importance as well.

Developing Skills in Speaking and Listening

Creating Sound Effects. With a partner, present a passage from "A Mystery of Heroism." Have your partner read the passage aloud, trying to create mood while you add excitement by using sound effects.

Many of Walt Whitman's poems present scenes from war. In the following poem, what details are mentioned in the description of the cavalry?

Cavalry Crossing a Ford

WALT WHITMAN

A line in long array where they wind betwixt green islands,
They take a serpentine course, their arms flash in the sun—hark to the
    musical clank,
Behold the silvery river, in it the splashing horses loitering stop to
    drink,
Behold the brown-faced men, each group, each person a picture, the
    negligent rest on the saddles,
Some emerge on the opposite bank, others are just entering the ford—
    while,
Scarlet and blue and snowy white,
The guidon flags flutter gayly in the wind.

Developing Comprehension Skills

1. What is being described in this poem?

2. What are the "green islands" between which the cavalry marches?

3. Line 2 mentions "arms" that "flash in the sun." The arms, however, are not human. What "arms" are being described?

4. What do the colors in the next to last line describe?

5. Whitman tries to present a vivid picture of the cavalry to his readers. Do you think he succeeds? Explain.

Reading Literature

1. **Understanding Poetry.** Most poetry has regular rhythm and arrangement of lines. Walt Whitman's poetry was considered shocking in his time because it did not have regular rhyme, rhythm, or line length. This kind of poetry is **free verse**. How does the form of "Cavalry Crossing a Ford" differ from that of other poems you have read so far? Why does the poem still fit the definition of poetry?

2. **Understanding Metaphor.** What metaphors are used to describe the cavalry?

Beat! Beat! Drums!

WALT WHITMAN

Beat! beat! drums!—blow! bugles! blow!
Through the windows—through doors—burst like a ruthless force,
Into the solemn church, and scatter the congregation,
Into the school where the scholar is studying;
Leave not the bridegroom quiet—no happiness must he have now with   5
    his bride,
Nor the peaceful farmer any peace, ploughing his field or gathering his
    grain,
So fierce you whirr and pound you drums—so shrill you bugles blow.

Beat! beat! drums!—blow! bugles! blow!   10
Over the traffic of cities—over the rumble of wheels in the streets;
Are beds prepared for sleepers at night in the houses? no sleepers must
    sleep in those beds,
No bargainers' bargains by day—no brokers or speculators—would
    they continue?   15
Would the talkers be talking? would the singer attempt to sing?
Would the lawyer rise in the court to state his case before the judge?
Then rattle quicker, heavier drums—you bugles wilder blow.

Beat! beat! drums!—blow! bugles! blow!
Make no parley—stop for no expostulation,   20
Mind not the timid—mind not the weeper or prayer,
Mind not the old man beseeching the young man,
Let not the child's voice be heard, nor the mother's entreaties,
Make even the trestles to shake the dead where they lie awaiting the
    hearses,   25
So strong you thump O terrible drums—so loud you bugles blow.

Funeral of the Anarchist Galli, 1911, CARLO CARRA. Oil on canvas 6'6 ¼" x 8'6".
The Museum of Modern Art, bequest of Lillie P. Bliss. New York.

Developing Comprehension Skills

1. In each stanza of the poem, who is disturbed by the drums and bugles?

2. Why do these drums have such a disturbing effect? What do they represent?

3. In the third stanza, why do you think people are weeping and praying?

4. What do you think the old man in the last stanza is asking for? the child? the mother? Are they being listened to?

5. "Beat! Beat! Drums!" describes the effect that war has on people. What do you suppose Whitman's attitude was toward war? Do you think he successfully gets that attitude across to the reader of his poem? Explain.

Reading Literature

1. **Analyzing Repetition.** Repetition may be used to highlight an idea or make a point. A phrase or line that is repeated throughout a poem is called a **refrain**. What is the refrain in "Beat! Beat! Drums!"? How does the repetition of the refrain help to create mood?

   Notice, too, the last line in each stanza. What is repeated? What changes? Why do you think Whitman did this?

2. **Analyzing Alliteration.** Whitman uses alliteration throughout "Beat! Beat! Drums!" Find three examples where beginning consonant sounds are repeated. What effect does each sound have in the poem?

Walt Whitman believed that people could learn from nature. How does nature inspire the speaker in the following poem?

When I Heard the Learn'd Astronomer

WALT WHITMAN

When I heard the learn'd astronomer,
When the proofs, the figures, were ranged in columns before me,
When I was shown the charts and diagrams, to add, divide, and
    measure them,
When I sitting heard the astronomer where he lectured with much
    applause in the lecture-room,
How soon unaccountable I became tired and sick,
Till rising and gliding out I wander'd off by myself,
In the mystical moist night air, and from time to time,
Look'd up in perfect silence at the stars.

Developing Comprehension Skills

1. What objects does the astronomer use in his lecture about the universe?

2. How is his lecture received by the audience? by the speaker?

3. Where does the speaker go? What does he do?

4. What does the speaker seem to understand about nature that the astronomer and the audience do not? Do you think most people today are like the speaker or like the astronomer? Explain your answer.

Reading Literature

1. **Appreciating Contrast.** In "When I Heard the Learn'd Astronomer," Walt Whitman contrasts the lecture hall at the beginning of the poem with the outdoors. What differences exist between the two settings? How does Whitman help emphasize those differences?

2. **Understanding Theme.** In "When I Heard the Learn'd Astronomer," Whitman shows two ways of viewing the world. According to Whitman, what are the two ways of viewing

nature? Which approach do you think he considers superior? Explain.

3. **Recognizing Verbal Irony.** Irony, as you recall, is the contrast between what appears to be true and what is actually true. In **verbal irony**, a writer says one thing but means something entirely different. Whitman refers to the astronomer as "learn'd." Is he? What is Whitman's attitude toward the astronomer?

4. **Appreciating Language.** In "When I Heard the Learn'd Astronomer," Whitman uses the word "mystical." The word describes something that is spiritual or supernatural. Why do you suppose Whitman chose the word "mystical"?

Developing Vocabulary Skills

Using Noun Suffixes. Some noun suffixes create abstract words. **Abstract words** describe a state of being or a quality. For example, *boredom* is the state of being bored. *Cleverness* is the quality that makes a person clever. You learned about some noun suffixes on page 271. Other noun suffixes that make abstract words are listed below.

Suffix	Example
-ation, -ition	imagination, condition
-ice	cowardice
-ity	sanity
-ment	bewilderment
-ship	companionship

The following base words are from Whitman's poems. Use the suffixes above to create abstract words. Use the word you created in an original sentence. You may need to check the dictionary for the correct spelling and meaning.

1. solemn		5. ruthless
2. oppose		6. state
3. speculate		7. timid
4. sick		8. measure

Developing Writing Skills

1. **Contrasting Mood.** Mood is the feeling that a work of literature creates. Both "Cavalry Crossing the Ford" and "Beat! Beat! Drums!" describe war. The mood, however, is quite different in each one. What is the mood in "Cavalry Crossing a Ford"? in "Beat! Beat! Drums!"?

2. **Using Personification.** In "Beat! Beat! Drums!" Whitman personifies, or gives human traits to, the drums. The drums are addressed directly and are described as if they were alive. Write a brief poem of your own, giving a lifeless object human qualities.

   Pre-Writing. Decide on an object to personify. Think of several things about the object that resemble human features. For example, you might think of a scissors' cutting edges as jaws and its handles as eyes. Jot down descriptions of the object's "human" traits. Then, write down details about the object in action. Decide on a situation in which the object could be involved.

   Writing. Write a description of your object in action. Personify the object as you describe it. Use words that would normally be used to describe people. Use vivid sensory details. Arrange your description in poetic lines. You may use rhyme if you wish.

   Revising. Read your poem aloud. Have you given your object human qualities? Are your descriptions vivid? Have you created a clear image for the reader of the poem? Make any changes that are necessary to improve the description.

3. **Relating Poetry to Personal Experience.** The speaker in "When I Heard the Learn'd Astronomer" is moved when he looks at the stars. Write a description of something in nature that has had the same effect on you. As you describe your experience, use sensory details that appeal to more than one sense.

Developing Skills in Critical Thinking

1. **Appreciating Connotations.** The true meaning of a word is its **denotation**. The feelings and ideas linked with a word are its **connotations**. Whitman chose words carefully to create a certain feeling. In "Beat! Beat! Drums!" what verbs and adjectives are used to describe the drums and what they do? What connotations do these words have? What are the connotations of the verbs and adjectives that describe the people? What do the connotations of these words add to the meaning of the poem?

2. **Identifying Unstated Opinions.** Sometimes opinions are implied rather than stated directly. This means that opinions are only suggested or hinted at. In "When I Heard the Learn'd Astronomer," Walt Whitman gives his opinion of science without stating it directly. Explain how he indirectly makes his opinion known.

Now look at the other poems by Whitman. Can you identify any other unstated opinions?

Developing Skills in Speaking and Listening

Interpreting a Poem. "Beat! Beat! Drums!" is very much a "sound poem." Its meaning is clearer when the poem is read aloud. Read "Beat! Beat! Drums!" aloud to the class. As you read, pay attention to punctuation to help you pause in the right places. In addition, emphasize the alliteration and onomatopoeia to accurately create the intended sound effects. Vary your tone of voice to emphasize mood. Don't speak in a monotone. Raise or lower your voice in appropriate places.

Focus on

EMILY DICKINSON
1830–1886

Today, Emily Dickinson is considered one of the greatest American poets. During her lifetime, however, only seven of her poems appeared. After she died in 1886, nearly eighteen hundred poems were found. Many were in a locked box, neatly tied in packets.

When Dickinson's verse was first made public, it became immensely popular. While she lived and wrote, however, she kept to herself. After attending Mount Holyoke Female Seminary and Amherst Academy, she made her home in Amherst the center of her world.

Although after 1862 Emily Dickinson lived in seclusion, her poems range far and wide. They treat large, universal issues, such as love, loss, nature, and faith. One of her most common themes is death, which she examines from various points of view.

Considering the calm surface of her life, Dickinson's poems are surprisingly intense in feeling. Some critics describe them as "explosive." They reveal a woman with a mind of her own, a love of nature, and a deep faith.

What else sets Emily Dickinson apart as a poet? "Her great gift was for poetic thought," said critic F. O. Matthiessen. Besides her ideas, her style also makes her outstanding. It marks a departure from the traditional poetry of her period. Her poems are short yet vividly expressed. Her figures of speech are fresh and original. A playful sense of humor shines through. She often treats difficult ideas with simple, familiar images. She uses the simple rhythms of the church hymns she knew, but she adds a fresh twist with off-rhymes, or words that do not rhyme exactly. In such departures from traditional forms, her poems prepared readers for the freedom of modern poetry.

Critics point to Emily Dickinson and Walt Whitman as the leading poets of the nineteenth century. Their experiments with sound and form opened new possibilities for other writers. Poet Archibald MacLeish said: "Emily locked away in a chest a voice which cries to all of us of our common life and love and death and fear and wonder."

Several of Emily Dickinson's poems are unusual, creative definitions. How does she define the brain in the following poem?

The Brain Is Wider Than the Sky

EMILY DICKINSON

The Brain—is wider than the Sky—
For—put them side by side—
The one the other will contain
With ease—and You—beside—

The Brain is deeper than the sea—
For—hold them—Blue to Blue—
The one the other will absorb—
As Sponges—Buckets—do—

The Brain is just the weight of God—
For—Heft them—Pound for Pound—
And they will differ—if they do—
As Syllable from Sound—

Study of Cirrus Clouds, about 1821, JOHN CONSTABLE. By courtesy of the Board of Trustees of the Victoria and Albert Museum, London.

Developing Comprehension Skills

1. In the first stanza, what can the brain "contain with ease" besides the sky?

2. What is the brain compared to in the second stanza?

3. What do you suppose the speaker means by "The Brain is just the weight of God."

4. Dickinson lived all her life in Amherst, Massachusetts. Nevertheless, she wrote more than 1,700 poems describing many different things. Based on this poem, how was she able to do this?

Reading Literature

1. **Recognizing Parallelism.** Parallelism, you remember, occurs when a writer expresses ideas of equal worth in the same grammatical form, or structure. In "The Brain Is Wider Than the Sky," for example, Dickinson uses the same form in the first line of each stanza. Find another example of parallelism in the poem. What effect does using this technique have on the poem?

2. **Understanding Simile.** Find the simile that compares the brain to a sponge. How is the brain like a sponge? Is this an effective simile?

3. **Analyzing Stanzas.** Many of Dickinson's poems are brief, one-stanza poems. In "The Brain Is Wider Than the Sky," she uses stanzas like paragraphs to focus on three different ideas. What is the main idea of each stanza in this poem?

During her lifetime, only seven of Emily Dickinson's poems were published. Judging from this poem, do you think this bothered her?

Fame Is a Bee

EMILY DICKINSON

Fame is a bee.
    It has a song—
It has a sting—
    Ah, too, it has a wing.

Developing Comprehension Skills

1. What three things does fame have in common with a bee?

2. Dickinson says that fame has a song. Do you think that the song is one of happiness or sorrow?

3. How can fame "sting" a person?

4. According to Dickinson, fame also has a "wing." What do you suppose she is saying about fame? Do you agree?

Reading Literature

1. **Identifying Tone.** Emily Dickinson reveals her attitude about fame in four short lines. What is this attitude?

2. **Analyzing Metaphors.** In "Fame Is a Bee," Dickinson uses metaphor to show the similarities between two unlike things. Why do you suppose Dickinson chose a bee for her metaphor? Why is the comparison a good one?

*There are many ways of looking
at the world. According to Emily
Dickinson, what role does faith
have in the way some people
see things?*

"Faith" Is a Fine Invention

EMILY DICKINSON

"Faith" is a fine invention
When Gentlemen can *see*—
But *Microscopes* are prudent
In an Emergency.

Developing Comprehension Skills

1. How is faith defined in line 1?

2. The word *see* may have more than one meaning in this poem. What are some possible meanings?

3. Faith, according to Dickinson, is one way "Gentlemen" can view the world. If *gentlemen* is replaced by *society,* is the poem's meaning clearer? When does Dickinson feel microscopes are appropriate? Do you agree?

Reading Literature

1. **Recognizing Lyric Poems.** A **lyric poem** presents a single speaker who expresses thoughts and feelings. These thoughts and feelings can be related to a variety of subjects.

Explain why the three poems by Dickinson can be considered lyric poems.

2. **Identifying Tone.** The ideas that Dickinson expresses in this poem can be very serious ones. Is this how Dickinson treats the subject? Explain your answer.

Developing Vocabulary Skills

Reviewing Prefixes and Suffixes. Review the following lists of word parts and their meanings. You may need to check pages 232, 233, 241, 262, 271, and 277 if you are unsure of meanings. Below the lists are words taken from the selections you have read. For each, choose a prefix, a suffix, or both in order to form a new word. Make as many different words as you can.

Use the dictionary if you need help in forming or spelling the words correctly.

Prefixes	Suffixes	
im-	-able	-ic
in-	-al	-ition
non-	-ance	-ity
pre-	-ant	-ive
re-	-ation	-ness
super-	-er	-or
un-	-ible	-tion

1. contain
2. absorb
3. differ
4. strong
5. prudent
6. measure
7. perfect
8. observe
9. history
10. human

Developing Writing Skills

1. **Analyzing Theme.** Emily Dickinson's poems usually deal with such themes as love, death, and nature. All of her poems, however, deal with a basic idea about life. Determine the theme of one of the three poems you have just read. In a paragraph, explain the theme and how Dickinson presents it. Use specific passages from the poem for support.

2. **Writing an Imaginative Definition.** Fame is an **abstract** idea. This means it can neither be seen nor touched. In "Fame Is a Bee," Dickinson explains the nature of fame by comparing it to something concrete. A bee *can* be seen and touched.

   Choose an abstract noun, such as *love, loneliness, success,* or *hope.* Write a paragraph in which you define the abstract noun by comparing it to something concrete.

Pre-Writing. Decide on the term you will define. Jot down characteristics about the noun you have chosen. Then, use your imagination to think of something concrete with the same characteristics. Try to choose an item that makes a point about the abstract noun. Make notes on how the two are similar.

Writing. In your topic sentence, compare the abstract noun with the concrete noun, as Dickinson does in "Fame Is a Bee." Identify the similarities, and explain each one. Use the ideas from your notes. Make sure that your readers will understand the comparison.

Revising. Have you identified at least three similarities between the abstract noun and the concrete noun? Do your ideas flow smoothly from one similarity to the next? You may need to add transitions that show addition or similarity. Try to use some of the following transitions: *moreover, also, in addition, besides, likewise,* and *similarly.*

Developing Skills in Critical Thinking

Recognizing the Need To Define Terms. Often a word has a variety of meanings. In Dickinson's poem " 'Faith' Is a Fine Invention," *see* has different meanings. Readers may interpret the poem differently if they apply different meanings to the word *see.*

Write down your definition for each of the following words: *fair, strike, off, smart,* and *sharp.* Compare your definitions with your classmates. How are they similar? How are they different? Look in the dictionary for still other definitions. How could these differences affect your understanding of a piece of writing? Explain.

Death is a subject that appears many times in Emily Dickinson's poetry. What attitude toward death is expressed in the following poem?

Because I Could Not Stop for Death

EMILY DICKINSON

Because I could not stop for Death—
He kindly stopped for me—
The Carriage held but just Ourselves—
And Immortality.

We slowly drove—He knew no haste   5
And I had put away
My labor and my leisure too,
For His Civility—

We passed the School, where Children strove
At Recess—in the Ring—   10
We passed the Field of Gazing Grain—
We passed the Setting Sun—

Or rather—He passed Us—
The Dews drew quivering and chill—
For only Gossamer, my Gown—   15
My Tippet[1]—only Tulle—

We paused before a House that seemed
A Swelling of the Ground—
The Roof was scarcely visible—
The Cornice—in the Ground—   20

---

1. **Tippet**, a scarf-like garment for the neck and shoulders.

Since then—'tis Centuries—and yet
Feels shorter than the Day
I first surmised the Horses' Heads
Were toward Eternity—

Developing Comprehension Skills

1. Who stopped for the speaker?

2. Why do you suppose the speaker was unable to stop for death?

3. In the third stanza, what three things does the carriage pass?

4. What details in the fourth stanza suggest that the speaker is not ready to die? Do you think most people are unprepared for death?

5. What is the "House" described in the fifth stanza? What details help you to answer this question?

Reading Literature

1. **Recognizing Personification.** In this poem, death is personified, or given human qualities. What are some of the qualities given to death? Is death portrayed as a cruel or gentle person? What might this say about the speaker's view of death?

2. **Identifying Symbols.** A symbol, you recall, is something that stands for something else. In the third stanza, the carriage passes playing children, fields of grain, and the setting sun. What stage of life might each represent? What makes each one a fitting symbol?

3. **Understanding Theme.** In the first and last stanzas of "Because I Could Not Stop for Death," the speaker seems to be making a comment about time. In the first stanza the speaker was too busy to stop for death. What is her view of time in the last stanza? What is the main idea about death and time expressed in the poem?

The Bustle in a House

EMILY DICKINSON

The Bustle in a House
The Morning after Death
Is solemnest of industries
Enacted upon Earth—

The Sweeping up the Heart
And putting Love away
We shall not want to use again
Until Eternity.

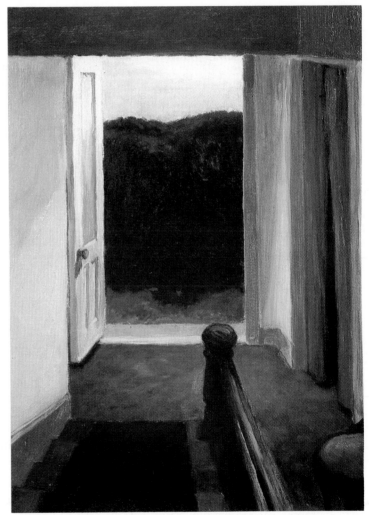

Stairway, about 1925, EDWARD HOPPER. Oil on wood, 16" x 11⅞". Whitney Museum of American Art, bequest of Josephine N. Hopper. New York.

Developing Comprehension Skills

1. According to Dickinson, what is the "solemnest of industries"?

2. Why do you suppose a heart would need "sweeping up"? Why would love be put away?

3. Do you think this poem presents an accurate version of how people react following the death of a loved one? Explain.

Reading Literature

1. **Understanding Metaphor.** In "The Bustle in a House," to what does Dickinson compare "the Sweeping up the Heart"? Why is this an effective metaphor?

2. **Recognizing Off-Rhyme.** End rhymes that are not exact are called **off-rhymes**. In "The Bustle in a House," the rhyming of *Death* and *Earth* is one example of off-rhyme. Find another example of off-rhyme in the poem.

Developing Vocabulary Skills

Reviewing Context Clues. The sentences below contain words taken from selections in this chapter. Write the meaning of each underlined word. Tell which kind of context clue you used: definition or restatement, example, comparison, contrast, synonym, or antonym.

1. General Lee commended his men for their actions; he also praised his officers for their assistance.

2. Douglass felt that his owner's order was ludicrous, unlike the sensible decisions she usually gave.

3. The ramifications, or results, of the proclamation were quite clear.

4. The Gettysburg Address was eloquent, strangely like a poem in the middle of a war.

5. He was furious about the soldiers' indolent behavior. They let rust form on their weapons, were careless about their uniforms, and marched in a sort of sloppy shuffle.

Developing Writing Skills

1. **Using Comparison and Contrast.** Both "The Bustle in a House" and "Because I Could Not Stop for Death" deal with death. Write a brief composition comparing and contrasting these two poems.

   Pre-Writing. Review both poems. Make notes on similarities and differences between such things as content, tone, and mood. It may help to discuss the poems with your classmates.

   Writing. Use the ideas from your notes to compare and contrast the two poems. You may explain first the similarities and then the differences. Or you may compare and contrast the poems first in one area and then another. Use specific quotations from the poems to support your ideas.

   Revising. Ask someone else to check the organization of your composition. If necessary, delete unrelated ideas and put related ideas together. Have you used transitional words and phrases so that your ideas flow smoothly? Have you supported your ideas?

2. **Using Figurative Language.** In "The Bustle in a House," Dickinson compares an emotional task to a domestic chore. Write a brief unrhymed poem of your own that compares an emotional process, such as growing up, to a domestic task, such as watering flowers.

Rain-in-the-Face

CHARLES A. EASTMAN

SETTING A PURPOSE | *In 1905, Charles Eastman interviewed the Sioux warrior Rain-in-the-Face. What new views of history do you get by seeing it through the eyes of this Native American?*

The noted Sioux warrior, Rain-in-the-Face, whose name once carried terror to every part of the frontier, died at his home on the Standing Rock reserve in North Dakota on September 14, 1905. About two months before his death I went to see him for the last time, where he lay upon the bed of sickness from which he never rose again, and drew from him his life-history.

It had been my experience that you cannot induce an Indian to tell a story, or even his own name, by asking him directly.

"Friend," I said, "even if a man is on a hot trail, he stops for a smoke! In the good old days, before the charge there was a smoke. At home, by the fireside, when the old men were asked to tell their brave deeds, again the pipe was passed. So come, let us smoke now to the memory of the old days!"

He took of my tobacco and filled his long pipe, and we smoked.

The old man lay upon an iron bedstead, covered by a red blanket, in a corner of the little log cabin. He was all alone that day; only an old dog lay silent and watchful at his master's feet.

Finally he looked up and said with a pleasant smile:

"True, friend; it is the old custom to retrace one's trail before leaving it forever! I know that I am at the door of the spirit home.

"I was born near the forks of the Cheyenne River, about seventy years ago. My father was not a chief; my grandfather was not a chief, but a good hunter and a feastmaker. On my mother's side I had some noted ancestors, but they left me no chieftainship. I had to work for my reputation.

"When I was a boy, I loved to fight," he continued. "In all our boyish games I had the name of being hard to handle, and I took much pride in the fact.

"I was about ten years old when we encountered a band of Cheyennes. They were on friendly terms with us, but we boys always indulged in sham fights on such occasions, and this time I got in an honest fight with a Cheyenne boy older than I. I got the best of the boy, but he hit me hard in the face several times, and my face was all spattered with blood and streaked where the paint had been washed away. The Sioux boys whooped and yelled:

" 'His enemy is down, and his face is spattered as if with rain! Rain-in-the-Face! His name shall be Rain-in-the-Face!'

Rain in the Face, before 1900. Smithsonian Institution, N.A.A., Washington, D.C. Photo 44821A. Photograph possibly by F. Jay Haynes.

"Afterwards, when I was a young man, we went on a warpath against the Gros Ventres. We stole some of their horses, but were overtaken and had to abandon the horses and fight for our lives. I had wished my face to represent the sun when partly covered with darkness, so I painted it half black, half red. We fought all day in the rain, and my face was partly washed and streaked with red and black: so again I was christened Rain-in-the-Face. We considered it an honorable name.

"I had been on many warpaths, but was not especially successful until about the time the Sioux began to fight with the white man. One of the most daring attacks that we ever made was at Fort Totten, North Dakota, in the summer of 1866.

"Hóhay, the Assiniboine captive of Sitting Bull, was the leader in this raid. Wapáypay, the Fearless Bear, who was afterward hanged at Yankton, was the bravest man among us. He dared Hóhay to make the charge. Hóhay accepted the challenge, and in turn dared the other to ride with him through the agency and right under the walls of the fort, which was well garrisoned and strong.

"Wapáypay and I in those days called each other 'brother-friend.' It was a life-and-death vow. What one does the other must do; and that meant that I must be in the forefront of the charge, and if he is killed, I must fight until I die also!

"I prepared for death. I was painted as usual like an eclipse of the sun, half black and half red."

His eyes gleamed and his face lighted up remarkably as he talked, pushing his black hair back from his forehead with a nervous gesture.

"Now the signal for the charge was given! I started even with Wapáypay, but his horse was faster than mine, so he left me a little behind as we neared the fort. This was bad for me, for by that time the soldiers had somewhat recovered from the surprise and were aiming better.

"Their big gun talked very loud, but my Wapáypay was leading on, leaning forward on his fleet pony like a flying squirrel on a smooth log! He held his rawhide shield on the right side, a little to the front, and so did I. Our warwhoop was like the coyotes singing in the evening, when they smell blood!

"The soldiers' guns talked fast, but few were hurt. Their big gun was like a toothless old dog, who only makes himself hotter the more noise he makes," he remarked.

"How much harm we did I do not know, but we made things lively for a time; and the white men acted as people do when a swarm of angry bees get into camp. We made a successful retreat, but some of the reservation Indians followed us yelling, until Hóhay told them that he did not wish to fight with the captives of the white man, for there would be no honor in that. There was blood running down my leg, and I found that both my horse and I were slightly wounded.

"Some two years later we attacked a fort west of the Black Hills [Fort Phil Kearny, Wyoming]. It was there we killed one hundred soldiers. [The military reports say eighty men, under the command of Captain Fetterman—not one left alive to tell the tale!] Nearly every band of the Sioux nation was represented in that fight—Red Cloud, Spotted Tail, Crazy Horse, Sitting Bull, Big Foot, and all our great chiefs were there. Of course such men as I were then comparatively unknown. However, there were many noted young warriors, among them Sword, the younger Young-Man-Afraid, American Horse [afterward chief], Crow King, and others.

"This was the plan decided upon after many councils. The main war party lay in ambush, and a few of the bravest young men were appointed to attack the woodchoppers who were cutting logs to complete the building of the fort. We were told not to kill these men, but to chase them into the fort and retreat slowly, defying the white men; and if the soldiers should follow, we were to lead them into the ambush. They took our bait exactly as we had hoped! It was a matter of a very few minutes, for every soldier lay dead in a shorter time than it takes to annihilate a small herd of buffalo.

"This attack was hastened because most of the Sioux on the Missouri River and eastward had begun to talk of suing for peace. But even this did not stop the peace movement. The very next year a treaty was signed at Fort Rice, Dakota Territory, by nearly all the Sioux chiefs, in which it was agreed on the part of the Great Father in Washington that all the country north of the Republican River in Nebraska, including the Black Hills and the Big Horn Mountains, was to be always Sioux country, and no white man should intrude upon it without our permission. Even with this agreement Sitting Bull and Crazy Horse were not satisfied, and they would not sign.

"Up to this time I had fought in some important battles, but had achieved no great deed. I was ambitious to make a name for myself. I joined war parties against the Crows, Mandans, Gros Ventres, and Pawnees, and gained some little distinction.

"It was when the white men found the yellow metal in our country, and came in great numbers, driving away our game, that we took up arms against them for the last time. I must say here that the chiefs who were loudest for war were among the first to submit and accept reservation life. Spotted Tail was a great warrior, yet he was one of the first to yield, because he was promised by the Chief Soldiers that they would make him chief of all the Sioux. Ugh! He would have stayed with Sitting Bull to the last had it not been for his ambition.

"About this time we young warriors began to watch the trails of the white men into the Black Hills, and when we saw a wagon coming we would hide at the crossing and kill them all without much trouble. We did this to discourage the whites from coming into our country without our permission. It was the duty of our Great Father at Washington, by the agreement of 1868, to keep his white children away.

"During the troublesome time after this treaty, which no one seemed to respect, either white or Indian [but the whites broke it first], I was like many other young men—much on the warpath, but with little honor. I had not yet become noted for any great deed. Finally, Wapáypay and I way-laid and killed a white soldier on his way from the fort to his home in the east.

"There were a few Indians who were liars, and never on the warpath, playing 'good Indian' with the Indian agents and the war chiefs at the forts. Some of this faithless set betrayed me, and told more than I ever did. I was seized and taken to the fort near Bismarck, North Dakota [Fort Abraham Lincoln], by a brother [Tom Custer] of the Long-Haired War Chief, and imprisoned there. These same lying Indians, who were selling their services as scouts to the white man, told me that I was to be shot to death, or else hanged upon a tree. I answered that I was not afraid to die.

"However, there was an old soldier who used to bring my food and stand guard over me—he was a white man, it is true, but he had an Indian heart! He came to me one day and unfastened the iron chain and ball with which they had locked my leg, saying by signs and what little Sioux he could muster:

" 'Go, friend! take the chain and ball with you. I shall shoot, but the voice of the gun will lie.'

"When he had made me understand, you may guess that I ran my best! I was almost over the bank when he fired his piece at me several times but I had already gained cover and was safe. I have never told this before, and would not, lest it should do him an injury, but he was an old man then, and I am sure he must be dead long since. That old soldier taught me that some of the white people have hearts," he added, quite seriously.

"I went back to Standing Rock in the night, and I had to hide for several days in the woods, where food was brought to me by my relatives. The Indian police were ordered to retake me, and they pretended to hunt for me, but really they did not, for if they had found me I would have died with one or two of them, and they knew it! In a few days I departed with several others, and we rejoined the hostile camp on the Powder River and made some trouble for the men who were building the great iron track north of us [Northern Pacific].

"In the spring the hostile Sioux got together again upon the Tongue River. It was one of the greatest camps of the Sioux that I ever saw. There were some Northern Cheyennes with us, under Two Moon, and a few Santee Sioux, renegades from Canada, under Inkpaduta, who had killed white people in

Iowa long before. We had decided to fight the white soldiers until no warrior should be left."

At this point Rain-in-the-Face took up his tobacco pouch and began again to fill his pipe.

"Of course the younger warriors were delighted with the prospect of a great fight! Our scouts had discovered piles of oats for horses and other supplies near the Missouri River. They had been brought by the white man's fire-boats. Presently they reported a great army about a day's travel to the south, with Shoshone and Crow scouts.

"There was excitement among the people, and a great council was held. Many spoke. I was asked the condition of those Indians who had gone upon the reservation, and I told them truly that they were nothing more than prisoners. It was decided to go out and meet Three Stars [General Crook] at a safe distance from our camp.

"We met him on the Little Rosebud. I believe that if we had waited and allowed him to make the attack, he would have fared no better than Custer. He was too strongly fortified where he was, and I think, too, that he was saved partly by his Indian allies, for the scouts discovered us first and fought us first, thus giving him time to make his preparations. I think he was more wise than brave! After we had left that neighborhood he might have pushed on and connected with the Long-Haired Chief. That would have saved Custer and perhaps won the day.

"When we crossed from Tongue River to the Little Big Horn, on account of the scarcity of game, we did not anticipate any more trouble. Our runners had discovered that Crook had retraced his trail to Goose Creek, and we did not suppose that the white men

would care to follow us farther into the rough country.

"Suddenly the Long-Haired Chief appeared with his men! It was a surprise."

"What part of the camp were you in when the soldiers attacked the lower end?" I asked.

"I had been invited to a feast at one of the young men's lodges [a sort of club]. There was a certain warrior who was making preparations to go against the Crows, and I had decided to go also," he said.

"While I was eating my meat we heard the war cry! We all rushed out, and saw a warrior riding at top speed from the lower camp, giving the warning as he came. Then we heard the reports of the soldiers' guns, which sounded differently from the guns fired by our people in battle.

"I ran to my teepee and seized my gun, a bow, and a quiver full of arrows. I already had my stone war club, for you know we usually carry those by way of ornament. Just as I was about to set out to meet Reno, a body of soldiers appeared nearly opposite us, at the edge of a long line of cliffs across the river.

"All of us who were mounted and ready immediately started down the stream toward the ford. There were Ogallalas, Minneconjous, Cheyennes, and some Unkpapas, and those around me seemed to be nearly all very young men.

" 'Behold, there is among us a young woman!' I shouted. 'Let no young man hide behind her garment!' I knew that would make those young men brave.

"The woman was Tashenamani, or Moving Robe, whose brother had just been killed in the fight with Three Stars. Holding her brother's war staff over her head, and leaning forward upon her charger, she looked as pretty as a bird. Always when there is a woman in the charge, it causes the warriors to vie with one another in displaying their valor," he added.

"The foremost warriors had almost surrounded the white men, and more were continually crossing the stream. The soldiers had dismounted, and were firing into the camp from the top of the cliff."

"My friend, was Sitting Bull in this fight?" I inquired.

"I did not see him there, but I learned afterward that he was among those who met Reno, and that was three or four of the white man's miles from Custer's position. Later he joined the attack upon Custer, but was not among the foremost.

"When the troops were surrounded on two sides, with the river on the third, the order came to charge! There were many very young men, some of whom had only a war staff or a stone war club in hand, who plunged into the column, knocking the men over and stampeding their horses.

"The soldiers had mounted and started back, but when the onset came they dismounted again and separated into several divisions, facing different ways. They fired as fast as they could load their guns, while we used chiefly arrows and war clubs. There seemed to be two distinct movements among the Indians. One body moved continually in a circle, while the other rode directly into and through the troops.

"Presently some of the soldiers remounted and fled along the ridge toward Reno's position; but they were followed by our warriors, like hundreds of blackbirds after a hawk.

A larger body remained together at the upper end of a little ravine, and fought bravely until they were cut to pieces. I had always thought that white men were cowards, but I had a great respect for them after this day.

"It is generally said that a young man with nothing but a war staff in his hand broke through the column and knocked down the leader very early in the fight. We supposed him to be the leader, because he stood up in full view, swinging his big knife [sword] over his head, and talking loud. Some one unknown afterwards shot the chief, and he was probably killed also; for if not, he would have told of the deed, and called others to witness it. So it is that no one knows who killed the Long-Haired Chief [General Custer].

"After the first rush was over, coups were counted as usual on the bodies of the slain. You know four coups [or blows] can be counted on the body of an enemy, and whoever counts the first one [touches it for the first time] is entitled to the 'first feather.'

"There was an Indian here called Appearing Elk, who died a short time ago. He was slightly wounded in the charge. He had some of the weapons of the Long-Haired Chief, and the Indians used to say jokingly after we came upon the reservation that Appearing Elk must have killed the Chief, because he had his sword! However, the scramble for plunder did not begin until all were dead. I do not think he killed Custer, and if he had, the time to claim the honor was immediately after the fight.

"Many lies have been told of me. Some say that I killed the Chief, and others that I cut out the heart of his brother [Tom Custer], because he had caused me to be imprisoned. Why, in that fight the excitement was so great that we scarcely recognized our nearest friends! Everything was done like lightning. After the battle we young men were chasing horses all over the prairie, while the old men and women plundered the bodies; and if any mutilating was done, it was by the old men.

"I have lived peaceably ever since we came upon the reservation. No one can say that Rain-in-the-Face has broken the rules of the Great Father. I fought for my people and my country. When we were conquered I remained silent, as a warrior should. Rain-in-the-Face was killed when he put down his weapons before the Great Father. His spirit was gone then; only his poor body lived on, but now it is almost ready to lie down for the last time. Ho, hechetu! [It is well.]"

The Mist Between the Day and Night, 1985, EARL BISS. Courtesy of Paul Zueger, Gallery One, Denver, Colorado.

Developing Comprehension Skills

1. How did Eastman persuade Rain-in-the-Face to tell his life history?

2. Rain-in-the-Face received his name following two incidents early in his life. What were the two incidents?

3. Why might the Indians have felt justified in attacking white settlers and soldiers?

4. How did Rain-in-the-Face become a prisoner at Fort Lincoln? How did he escape? What two things did he learn from this entire incident?

5. Who was the Long-Haired Chief who surprised the Sioux at Little Big Horn? What was the outcome of that battle?

6. How does Rain-in-the-Face explain his lack of knowledge about who killed Custer or whom he fought? Do you think this is probably true? Why or why not?

7. How does Rain-in-the-Face defend his reservation life after his surrender? What does he mean when he says "Rain-in-the-Face was killed when he put down his weapons before the Great Father"?

Reading Literature

1. **Understanding the Interview.** A meeting in which one person asks another about his or her opinions and activities is called an **interview**. Its purpose is to obtain information and reveal something about the personality of the person being interviewed.

   What qualities of Rain-in-the-Face are revealed in this interview conducted by Eastman? What can you learn from this interview that might be missing from other accounts of Rain-in-the-Face?

2. **Understanding History Through Literature.** This story is a Sioux warrior's account of the Native American struggle. It is a story seldom seen in history books. The conflict between white settlers and Native Americans is usually told from the settlers' point of view. How has this conflict been described in the past? Have you learned something new from this account?

3. **Appreciating Similes.** In his story, Rain-in-the-Face uses several similes. What two things are compared in each of the following similes? What do these similes tell you about the Sioux relationship with nature?

   a. Our warwhoop was like the coyotes singing in the evening when they smell blood.
   b. she was as pretty as a bird
   c. the soldiers were followed by our warriors, like hundreds of blackbirds after a hawk

Developing Vocabulary Skills

Recognizing Latin Roots. Another way of developing your vocabulary is to become familiar with roots. A **root** is the part of a word that contains its basic meaning. Unlike base words, roots cannot stand alone. They are used with prefixes and suffixes to form words. A great many roots used in the English language come from Latin and Greek.

Here are some common Latin roots:

Root	Meaning	Example
cede, ceed, cess	go, yield	precede
dorm	sleep	dormitory
duc, duct	lead	conduct
mit, miss	send	transmit
pon, pos, posit	put, place	deposit
trude	thrust	protrude

The following sentences contain words from "Rain-in-the-Face." Explain how the Latin root provides the basic meaning of each underlined word. Explain how the root meaning combines with the meaning of the suffix to make a complete word. You may use a dictionary.

1. Many people can trace their <u>ancestry</u> to the Indians.

2. After he was betrayed by another Indian, Rain-in-the-Face was held <u>captive</u>.

3. Most of the settlers felt no guilt about <u>intruding</u> on the Indians' land.

4. Many agreements for peace were <u>submitted</u> for approval, but few were accepted.

5. The Indians looked forward to the <u>prospect</u> of regaining their territory.

Developing Writing Skills

1. **Analyzing Character Traits.** Rain-in-the-Face possessed many qualities that made him a great leader and a famous warrior. Make a list of the personal traits revealed by Rain-in-the-Face in his interview. Then, choose one which you feel made him a respected leader and warrior. Write a paragraph in which you describe this trait. Use passages and evidence from the interview to give support to your writing.

2. **Narrating a Personal Experience.** Rain-in-the-Face describes several incidents when he felt he was brave. Have you had an experience when you were called upon to display courage? In two paragraphs, describe your experience.

   Pre-Writing. Think of instances when you faced some danger in a courageous way. It may have been physical danger. Or, it may have been a temptation that you faced and overcame. Choose one such incident. Make notes about the incident. List events in chronological order, the order in which they happened.

   Writing. In the first paragraph, describe the incident. When and where did it happen? Who else was involved? What event started the incident? Be specific.

   In the second paragraph describe how you responded to the danger. What actions did you take? How did you feel? Use transitional words such as *first*, *then*, and *finally*. Also, describe your events precisely. Use strong verbs and adjectives.

   Revising. Ask someone to read your two paragraphs. Does he or she feel you have clearly described the situation? If not, you may need to change the details or add new ones. Add details that help clear up the *who*, *what*, *when*, *where*, and *how* of your story. Check to be sure you have included all important events in chronological order.

Developing Skills in Study and Research

Using SQ3R. A good way to study "The Sioux Woman," page 299, is to use the SQ3R method. This method, you remember, consists of five steps: survey, question, read, recite, and review. You may wish to read page 68 for a detailed explanation of these steps.

Use the first two parts of this method on "The Sioux Woman." Complete the remaining steps when you study the selection.

I Kill Her Enemies

NORMAN H. RUSSELL

SETTING A PURPOSE | *Many people believe that Native American men thought they were far superior to the women. What relationship exists between the speaker and his wife in this contemporary poem?*

i wear the blanket of my wife
she wears the bracelet i have made
i raised the sheep
she dug the turquoise
i teach the son she gave me
she cooks the food i gave her
my wife paints me for war
i kill her enemies

when i go on the hunt
my wife goes in my heart
when my wife stays in the hogan
i also stay in her heart

we are two
we are one.

Developing Comprehension Skills

1. What object made by his wife does the speaker wear? What object made by him does she wear?

2. In the first stanza, what three tasks does the speaker perform? What tasks does his wife perform?

3. What is the relationship between the speaker and his wife? How do you know?

4. What view of marriage is expressed in the last two lines? Do you find this particular view of marriage surprising? Explain.

Reading Literature

Recognizing Parallelism. Parallelism, you may recall, is presenting ideas of equal importance in identical structures, or forms. In "I Kill Her Enemies," ideas are expressed in a "subject, verb, object" pattern as in the following examples:

    s   v   o
    i   wear   the blanket

    s   v   o
    she wears the bracelet

How does the use of parallelism highlight the speaker's view of marriage? Explain.

The Sioux Woman

MARI SANDOZ

SETTING A PURPOSE *An old Sioux saying states that "the honor of the people lies in the moccasin tracks of the women." How does the Sioux woman's daily behavior reflect the values of her tribe?*

A Sioux maiden saw modesty, moderation, and poised reserve the approved pattern of life all around her. She learned, often very early, that to the Sioux, courtesy is making others feel pleasant and warm as with the sunlight upon them. Face must be saved, but first of all the face of others. "If one shames himself by rudeness to you, then you must make yourself seem to deserve it all, and more."

The small girl saw the women manage the life of the lodge in their quiet and gentle way although some Sioux women were good taunters of enemy warriors and of their own if they seemed laggard.

Ceremony

There were some Sioux women in public life—famous healers and herbalists and a few holy ones who sometimes gave advice, mainly about ceremonials and religious duties and personal perplexities. Like the holy men, they were generally good listeners. . . . Often a woman was required by the medicine man's healing because health to the Indians seemed a thing of balance, a basic wholeness, and restoring it needed the two halves, the man and a woman helper. Women and girls, too, sometimes made vows of special ordeal or sacrifice in times of sickness, famine or great war danger. . . . They fulfilled these in the proper way, perhaps even in the rigors of the sun dance. They held chieftainships when bands lost all their men of leadership stature, as in the great scourges and in the later Sioux wars, when so many good men died. . . .

Watching and Learning

The little Sioux girl learned about life, about birth and death, as her brother did, in the natural way, long before she realized their full meaning—a realization that came to her gradually, like growth in the sleep of night, without shock or a sense of betrayal by pretty stories and pretenses.

When war parties went out the young girl stood behind the women making their songs and dances for the strong heart, for hope and for victory. She covered her head with her robe or blanket in the keening [mourning] for those who did not return, or those who had to be borne to the trees or the death scaffold from other dying. She sat with the women at work or went with the berry pickers, the turnip diggers and the herb gatherers. Evenings she joined the water carriers, shy with

A Sioux Man and Woman, 1898, GERTRUDE KÄSEBIER. The Library of Congress, Washington, D.C.

the boys and young men who seemed so ordinary during the day and so strange in the evening sun. She learned to shoot the small bow of the children and the women, and to carry a short butcher knife in her belt, ready for work and for defense if it was needed against enemies and any who would molest her, for among the Sioux a woman had the duty of defending herself at all cost against attack. . . .

Becoming a Woman

Every Sioux maiden went through a "Coming of Age" ceremony. Friends of the mother came to bathe the daughter, dress her and seat her in the honored place of the lodge usually set up for the purpose, with prominent ones beside her. Here the girl received congratulations, gifts, and songs of praise and promise, and an elaborate oration from a wise man of the village, who outlined the duties of a woman of the Sioux. First there was the long harangue [speech] on the greatness of the tribe and then about the girl's family and her duties to them, repeating the reminder: the honor of the people lies in the moccasin tracks of the women. "Walk the good road, my daughter, and the buffalo herds wide and dark as cloud shadows moving over the prairie will follow you, the spring full of the yellow calves, the fall earth shaking with the coming of the fat ones, their robes thick and warm as the sun on the lodge door. Be dutiful, respectful, gentle and modest, my daughter. And proud walking. If the pride and the virtue of the women are lost, the spring will come but the buffalo trails will turn to grass. Be strong, with the warm, strong heart of the earth. No people goes down until their women are weak and dishonored, or dead upon the ground. Be strong and bless the strength of the Great Powers within you and all around you."

Developing Comprehension Skills

1. What is the Sioux definition of courtesy?

2. Sioux women played an important role in the healing ceremonies. How did the Sioux woman help the medicine man? Why were the women necessary to proper healing?

3. What does the author mean when she says that the little Sioux girl learned about life "in the natural way . . . without . . . pretty stories and pretenses"?

4. In his speech during the "Coming of Age" ceremony, what specific qualities did the village wise man encourage a girl to develop? What did he mean when he told her to be "proud walking"?

5. The village wise man says that "No people goes down until their women are weak and dishonored, or dead upon the ground." Why might this be so? Why would a tribe's strength be in its women and not its leaders or warriors?

Reading Literature

1. **Analyzing Expository Writing.** Writing that provides explanations is known as **expository writing**. There are three basic types of expository writing. In one type, the writer explains a process, or how to do something. In the second type, the writer presents a definition. The third type of expository writing presents reasons about why something is, or should be. Which type of expository writing best describes "The Sioux Woman"? Give reasons for your choice.

2. **Making Inferences About Character.** Although this piece is called "The Sioux Woman," the reader can also draw several conclusions about the Sioux man from the facts provided. The reader is told of the various tasks and duties expected of the Sioux women. From this information, what conclusions can you make about the Sioux man? How did he view the Sioux woman? Explain your answer.

3. **Recognizing Mood.** Mood, as you recall, is the feeling a writer creates for a reader. What is the mood of "The Sioux Woman"? What phrases help to create the mood?

Developing Vocabulary Skills

Learning Latin Roots. You have already studied some Latin roots on page 233 and 296.

Here are some others that will help you determine the meaning of unfamiliar words.

Root	Meaning	Example
lumen	light	luminous
manus	hand	manage
pendere	to hang	suspend
vers, vert	turn	invert
visus	see	visible

Each of the following words was formed by combining prefixes and suffixes with the Latin roots above. Use your knowledge of word parts to determine the meaning of each word. Check the dictionary for the exact meaning.

1. pendant
2. vocation
3. subversion
4. manual
5. inscription
6. luminary
7. revision
8. conversion
9. deportation
10. benefactor

Developing Skills in Writing

1. **Writing an Analysis.** Both "I Kill Her Enemies" and "The Sioux Woman" present similar views of how the woman was treated in certain tribes. Write a paragraph in which you explain the attitude toward women that is presented in the selections. Use specific details for support.

2. **Writing a Definition.** "The Sioux Woman" provides the reader with a definition of what the Sioux woman was. In a paragraph, write your definition of the modern American man or woman.

   Pre-Writing. A good definition puts the subject in a broad category and then shows the particular characteristics of the subject. Jot down details which will help you to develop a complete and accurate definition. You will probably want to include facts, examples, and statistics. Your definition should move from general to specific.

   Writing. Define the subject clearly and completely in the topic sentence. Then, provide the specific details that will develop the definition. Write an ending sentence that provides a strong summary of your definition. Use transitional words like "for example" or "furthermore" to connect your ideas.

   Revising. Read your rough draft. Does your topic sentence clearly state your definition? Have you used some specific details to develop your definition? Have you used transitional words to tie your ideas together? Do you provide a good summary? Make any changes that will improve your work. Then make a clean, final copy.

Developing Skills in Study and Research

Checking the Accuracy of Facts. Expository writing presents the reader with many factual statements. A careful researcher would check to make sure the statements are correct. To check the accuracy, the researcher may use different sources.

Choose several statements from "The Sioux Woman" and check them for accuracy. If possible, go to the library and obtain a copy of *These Were the Sioux* by Mari Sandoz. Check to see if it contains a bibliography. This is a list of sources the author used to gather facts. It will tell you where Sandoz found her information. If the book is not available, use other library sources such as the encyclopedia, and card catalog. Try to prove the accuracy of as many facts as you can from "The Sioux Woman."

| *One of the most famous Sioux leaders was Sitting Bull. How did he feel as he came to the end of his life?*

The Last Song of Sitting Bull, the Teton Sioux

SIOUX INDIAN

A warrior
I have been.
Now
It is all over.
A hard time
I have.

After Many Years of Warfare, 1907, JOSEPH HENRY SHARP. Courtesy of Fenn Galleries, Ltd., Santa Fe, New Mexico.

Developing Comprehension Skills

1. What has Sitting Bull been during his life?

2. Sitting Bull says, "It is all over." What do you suppose he is describing?

3. This poem is very short. Was it still able to express the ideas of Sitting Bull? Explain.

Reading Literature

1. **Identifying Mood.** The mood of a poem is the feeling you get when reading it. What is the mood of this poem? What words and phrases help to create that mood?

2. **Recognizing Tone.** "The Last Song of Sitting Bull" was written as he neared the end of life. What do you suppose his attitude was toward dying?

Few of us want to die away from the things we know and love. How does the speaker in this poem learn to accept the situation?

Song of a Man About To Die in a Strange Land

OJIBWA INDIAN

If I die here in a strange land,
If I die in a land not my own,
Nevertheless, the thunder,
The rolling thunder,
Will take me home.   5

If I die here, the wind,
The wind rushing over the prairie,
The wind will take me home.

The wind and the thunder,
They are the same everywhere,   10
What does it matter, then,
If I die here in a strange land?

Developing Comprehension Skills

1. What is the speaker sorrowing over in the first two lines?

2. What situation might have resulted in the speaker's being away from "home" and about to die?

3. Where does the speaker say that he will be taken? What two elements of nature will take him there?

4. In the last stanza, why does it no longer matter to him if he should die in a strange land? Is his attitude a good one? Could it be applied today?

Reading Literature

1. **Appreciating Repetition in Oral Literature.** As you know, much Native American literature was passed down orally from generation to generation. Often repetition was used to create rhythm, mood, and meaning. Explain how repetition creates rhythm, mood, and meaning in "Song of a Man About To Die in a Strange Land."

2. **Recognizing Internal Conflict.** Internal conflict, you will recall, is the struggle within a character that he or she must face. What internal conflict exists for the speaker in "Song of a Man About To Die"? How is it solved?

There Is No Death

CHIEF SEATTLE

SETTING A PURPOSE | *In this speech, Chief Seattle expresses his belief that the Native Americans will never die. How will his people continue to live in the world of the whites?*

Yonder sky that has wept tears of compassion on our fathers for centuries untold, and which, to us, looks eternal, may change. Today is fair, tomorrow it may be overcast with clouds. My words are like the stars that never change. What Seattle says, the great chief in Washington can rely upon, with as much certainty as our paleface brothers can rely upon the return of the seasons.

The son of the White Chief says that his father sends us greetings of friendship and good will. This is kind, for we know he has little need of our friendship in return, because his people are many. They are like the grass that covers the vast prairies. My people are few, and resemble the scattering trees of a storm-swept plain. . . .

There was a time when our people covered the whole land as the waves of the wind-ruffled sea cover its shell-paved floor. But that time has long since passed away with the greatness of tribes now almost forgotten. I will not mourn over our untimely decay, nor reproach my paleface brothers with hastening it. . . .

Your religion was written on tablets of stone, by the iron finger of your God, lest you forget it. The red men could never remember it or comprehend it. Our religion is the traditions of our ancestors, the dreams of our old men, given them by the Great Spirit, and the visions of our sachems, and is written in the hearts of our people. . . .

Every part of this country is sacred to my people. Every hillside, every valley, every plain and grove has been hallowed by some fond memory or some sad experience of my tribe. Even the rocks which seem to lie dumb as they swelter in the sun . . . thrill with memories of past events connected with the fate of my people. . . .

The braves, fond mothers, glad-hearted maidens, and even little children, who lived here . . . still love these solitudes. Their deep fastnesses at eventide grow shadowy with the presence of dusty spirits. When the last red man shall have perished from the earth and his memory among the white men shall have become a myth, these shores shall swarm with the invisible dead of my tribe. . . .

At night when the streets of your cities and villages shall be silent, and you think them deserted, they will throng with the returning hosts that once filled and still love this beautiful land.

The white man will never be alone. Let him be just and deal kindly with my people, for the dead are not altogether powerless. Dead, did I say? There is no death, only a change of worlds.

Developing Comprehension Skills

1. According to Chief Seattle, what things change? What is the one thing that will never change? Why is this statement important to the rest of what he says?

2. Seattle feels the White Chief does not need the friendship of the Indians. Why?

3. According to Seattle, how is the religion of the whites different from the Indian's religion? What is Seattle saying about the importance of religion to the two groups?

4. Why are the hillsides, valleys, and other parts of the natural landscape sacred places for the Indians?

5. Seattle says that "The white man will never be alone." How will the American Indian continue to be present in the white man's world?

6. Seattle says, "There is no death, only a change of worlds." Do you find this view of death comforting? Explain.

Reading Literature

1. **Identifying the Purpose of a Speech.** A **speech** is the oral presentation of ideas. Like any presentation, it must have a purpose and be directed at a specific audience. Who is the audience for Chief Seattle's speech? How do you know? Look carefully at the last paragraph of the speech. What do you think Seattle was trying to accomplish?

2. **Analyzing Tone.** What is the tone of Chief Seattle's speech? Does this attitude stay the same throughout or does it change? Support your answer with examples.

3. **Appreciating Similes.** In his speech, Seattle uses similes to show the difference between the Indians and the white man. Find the simile in paragraph two that describes the white man. Then, find the simile in paragraph three that describes the Indian. How does the use of similes stress the differences between the two peoples?

4. **Understanding Allusion.** You may recall that an **allusion** is a reference to a person, place, or event outside a work of literature. Seattle speaks of "tablets of stone." What biblical event does this allude to?

Developing Vocabulary Skills

1. **Understanding Greek Roots.** Many English words come from Greek roots as well as Latin roots. An understanding of Greek roots can help you to determine the meaning of many new words. You learned several Greek roots on page 233. Here are some others:

Root	Meaning	Example
log, leg	speak, say	epilogue
logy	study of	geology
phil	loving, fond	philosophy
phon	sound	phonograph
soph	wise	sophisticated

Write another example for each root.

2. **Using Greek Roots.** Find the Greek roots in each of the following underlined words. Write the meaning of the roots and of the whole word. You may use your dictionary.

   a. A chronology of the nineteenth century would show many periods of growth and change.

   b. The autobiography of Rain-in-the-Face gives a different view of the conflict between the settlers and Native Americans.

c. The <u>logistics</u> of the attack were up to the chief.

d. <u>Telegraph</u> wires soon stretched across the prairies, signaling the end of an era.

Developing Writing Skills

1. **Writing a Summary.** The selections you have read deal with different views of death. Write a paragraph summarizing the Native American's ideas on death. Use specific examples from the selections for support.

2. **Writing a Description of a Setting.** Chief Seattle claims that many natural settings are considered holy and memorable by his people. Think of some natural setting that is special in your memory and write a paragraph describing it.

   Pre-Writing. Choose a place that has special meaning for you. Recreate the place in your mind. What do you see? What do you hear? What smells are present? What can you taste or touch? Take notes on these details. Then organize them logically. You might use spatial order. That is, describe your place from top to bottom, from near to far, from left to right, or in some other suitable order.

   Writing. In your topic sentence tell how you discovered this place. Then, use your list of details to describe the scene. Use precise words that appeal to the senses. For example, if you are describing trees you might describe the leaves as *velvety* or *smooth*. In addition, use transitional phrases like "at the top" or "to the right" to help your readers picture the scene.

   Revising. Reread your paragraph. Use this checklist to find areas for improvement:

   > Have I named the place and told how I found it?
   > Have I used precise words that appeal to the senses?
   > Are my details arranged in spatial order?
   > Have I used appropriate transitions?

   Revise your paragraph as needed. Then write a final, clean copy.

Developing Skills in Critical Thinking

Recognizing the Error of Stereotype. A **stereotype** is a type of faulty generalization. A stereotype wrongly states that an entire group shares certain characteristics. For example, you might meet an unfriendly salesperson in a store and decide that all salespeople are rude. This would be an unfair stereotype.

What are some of the typical ways that Native Americans have been stereotyped? Based on the selections you have read, what truths contradict the stereotypes?

Focus on

MARK TWAIN
1835–1910

Samuel Langhorne Clemens (Mark Twain), (detail). 1935, FRANK E. LARSON. National Portrait Gallery, Smithsonian Institution, gift of the artist. Washington, D.C.

Samuel Langhorne Clemens adopted the pen name Mark Twain at age twenty-eight. He did so with the goal of "making all God's creatures laugh." And laugh they did. On the lecture circuit, Twain dazzled audiences with sparkling wit. In books and sketches, he amused readers with frontier humor and biting satire. For these reasons, Mark Twain is known as one of America's greatest humorists.

Samuel Clemens grew up in the "sleepy" small town of Hannibal, Missouri. As a boy, his heroes were riverboat pilots. After working for several years as a printer, Mark Twain finally lived out his childhood dream by becoming a riverboat pilot.

His experiences on the steamboat affected his life—and his name. In Mississippi riverboat jargon, "mark twain" refers to water that is two fathoms deep, or safe enough to travel. As Twain rose to fame and fortune, the name Mark Twain kept him in touch with his roots along the Mississippi River.

Twain's greatest works, including *The Adventures of Huckleberry Finn, The Adventures of Tom Sawyer,* and *Life on the Mississippi,* were written between 1869 and 1889. *The*

Adventures of Huckleberry Finn (1884) is considered by some critics to be the greatest American novel.

In 1870, Twain married Olivia Langdon and settled down in Connecticut. He had become a businessman of the "Gilded Age." His books sold well, but he lost his money in unsound business investments. In 1894, he went bankrupt.

He set out on a worldwide lecture tour to pay his debts. Later, after his wife and his daughter Olivia died, he became increasingly bitter. Twain's later works are still sharp and clever, but they lack the light touch that made him so popular. Twain died in 1910 at the age of seventy-four.

For generations, Twain captured hearts with good-natured humor and keen observations. The spirit of America breathes through his best works: a love of fun, a commitment to democracy, and a hatred of injustice.

From
The Adventures of Huckleberry Finn

MARK TWAIN

Preface

Persons attempting to find a motive in this narrative will be prosecuted; persons attempting to find a moral in it will be banished; persons attempting to find a plot in it will be shot.

By Order of the Author,
Per G.G., Chief of Ordnance

The Grangerfords Take Me In

I made a safe landing, and clumb up the bank. I couldn't see but a little ways, but I went poking along over rough ground for a quarter of a mile or more, and then I run across a big old-fashioned double log house before I noticed it. I was going to rush by and get away, but a lot of dogs jumped out and went to howling and barking at me, and I knowed better than to move another peg.

In about a minute somebody spoke out of a window without putting his head out, and says:

"Be done, boys! Who's there?"

I says:

"It's me."

"Who's me?"

"George Jackson, sir."

"What do you want?"

"I don't want nothing, sir. I only want to go along by, but the dogs won't let me."

"What are you prowling around here this time of night for—hey?"

"I warn't prowling around, sir; I fell overboard off the steamboat."

"Oh, you did, did you? Strike a light there, somebody. What did you say your name was?"

"George Jackson, sir. I'm only a boy."

"Look here, if you're telling the truth you needn't be afraid—nobody 'll hurt you. But don't try to budge; stand right where you are. Rouse out Bob and Tom, some of you, and fetch the guns. George Jackson, is there anybody with you?"

"No, sir, nobody."

I heard the people stirring around in the house now, and see a light. The man sung out:

"Snatch that light away, Betsy, you old fool—ain't you got any sense? Put it on the floor behind the front door. Bob, if you and Tom are ready, take your places."

"All ready."

"Now, George Jackson, do you know the Shepherdsons?"

"No, sir; I never heard of them."

"Well, that may be so, and it mayn't. Now, all ready. Step forward, George Jackson. And mind, don't you hurry—come mighty slow. If there's anybody with you, let him keep back—if he shows himself he'll be shot. Come along now. Come slow; push the door open yourself—just enough to squeeze in, d'you hear?"

I didn't hurry; I couldn't if I'd-a-wanted to. I took one slow step at a time and there warn't a sound, only I thought I could hear my heart. The dogs were as still as the humans, but they followed a little behind me. When I got to the three log doorsteps I heard them unlocking and unbarring and unbolting. I put my hand on the door and pushed it a little and a little more till somebody said, "There, that's enough—put your head in." I done it, but I judged they would take it off.

The candle was on the floor, and there they all was, looking at me, and me at them, for about a quarter of a minute: Three big men with guns pointed at me, which made me wince, I tell you; the oldest, gray and about sixty, the other two thirty or more—all of them fine and handsome—and the sweetest

The Nooning, about 1872, WINSLOW HOMER. Wadsworth Atheneum, the Ella Gallup Sumner and Mary Catlin Sumner Collection. Hartford, Connecticut.

old gray-headed lady, and back of her two young women which I couldn't see right well. The old gentleman says:

"There; I reckon it's all right. Come in."

As soon as I was in the old gentleman he locked the door and barred it and bolted it, and told the young men to come in with their guns, and they all went in a big parlor that had a new rag carpet on the floor, and got together in a corner that was out of the range of the front windows—there warn't none on the side. They held the candle, and took a good look at me, and all said, "Why, *he* ain't a Shepherdson—no, there ain't any Shepherd-son about him." Then the old man said he hoped I wouldn't mind being searched for arms, because he didn't mean no harm by it—it was only to make sure. So he didn't pry into my pockets, but only felt outside with his hands, and said it was all right. He told me to make myself easy and at home, and tell all about myself; but the old lady says:

"Why, bless you, Saul, the poor thing's as wet as he can be; and don't you reckon it may be he's hungry?"

"True for you, Rachel—I forgot."

So the old lady says:

"Betsy" (this was a servant woman), "you fly around and get him something to eat as quick as you can, poor thing; and one of you girls go and wake up Buck and tell him—oh, here he is himself. Buck, take this little stranger and get the wet clothes off from him and dress him up in some of yours that's dry."

Buck looked about as old as me—thirteen or fourteen or along there, though he was a little bigger than me. He hadn't on anything but a shirt, and he was very frowzy-headed. He came in gaping and digging one fist into his eyes, and he was dragging a gun along with the other one. He says:

"Ain't they no Shepherdsons around?"

They said, no, 'twas a false alarm.

"Well," he says, "if they'd 'a' ben some, I reckon I'd 'a' got one."

They all laughed, and Bob says:

"Why, Buck, they might have scalped us all, you've been so slow in coming."

"Well, nobody come after me, and it ain't right. I'm always kept down; I don't get no show."

"Never mind, Buck, my boy," says the old man, "you'll have show enough, all in good time, don't you fret about that. Go 'long with you now, and do as your mother told you."

When we got up-stairs to his room he got me a coarse shirt and a roundabout and pants of his, and I put them on. While I was at it he asked me what my name was, but before I could tell him he started to tell me about a bluejay and a young rabbit he had catched in the woods day before yesterday, and he asked me where Moses was when the candle went out. I said I didn't know; I hadn't heard about it before, no way.

"Well, guess," he says.

"How'm I going to guess," says I, "when I never heard tell of it before?"

"But you can guess, can't you? It's just as easy."

"*Which* candle?" I says.

"Why, any candle," he says.

"I don't know where he was," says I; "where was he?"

"Why, he was in the *dark*! That's where he was!"

"Well, if you knowed where he was, what did you ask me for?"

"Why, blame it, it's a riddle, don't you see? Say, how long are you going to stay here? You got to stay always. We can just have booming times—they don't have no school now. Do you own a dog? I've got a dog—and he'll go in the river and bring out chips that you throw in. Do you like to comb up Sundays, and all that kind of foolishness? You bet I don't, but ma she makes me. Confound these ole britches! I reckon I'd better put 'em on, but I'd ruther not, it's so warm. Are you all ready? All right. Come along, old hoss."

Cold corn-pone, cold corn-beef, butter and buttermilk—that is what they had for me down there, and there ain't nothing better that ever I've come across yet. Buck and his ma and all of them smoked cob pipes, except the servant woman, which was gone, and the two young women. They all smoked and talked, and I eat and talked. The young women had quilts around them, and their hair down their backs. They all asked me questions, and I told them how pap and me and all the family was living on a little farm down at the bottom of Arkansaw, and my sister Mary Ann run off and got married and never was heard of no more, and Bill went to hunt them and he warn't heard of no more, and Tom and Mort died, and then there warn't nobody but just me and pap left, and he was just trimmed down to nothing, on account of his troubles; so when he died I took what there was left, because the farm didn't belong to us, and started up the river, deck passage, and fell overboard; and that was how I come to be here. So they said I could have a home there as long as I wanted it. Then it was most daylight and everybody went to bed, and I went to bed with Buck, and when I waked up in the morning, drat it all, I had forgot what my name was. So I laid there about an hour trying to think, and when Buck waked up I says:

"Can you spell, Buck?"

"Yes," he says.

"I bet you can't spell my name," says I.

"I bet you what you dare I can," says he.

"All right," says I, "go ahead."

"G-e-o-r-g-e J-a-x-o-n—there now," he says.

"Well," says I, "you done it, but I didn't think you could. It ain't no slouch of a name to spell—right off without studying."

I set it down, private, because somebody might want *me* to spell it next, and so I wanted to be handy with it and rattle it off like I was used to it.

It was a mighty nice family, and a mighty nice house, too. I hadn't seen no house out in the country before that was so nice and had so much style. It didn't have an iron latch on the front door, nor a wooden one with a buckskin string, but a brass knob to turn, the same as houses in town. There warn't no bed in the parlor, nor a sign of a bed; but heaps of parlors in towns has beds in them. There was a big fireplace that was bricked on the bottom, and the bricks was kept clean and red by pouring water on them and scrubbing them with another brick; sometimes they wash them over with red water-paint that they call Spanish-brown, same as they do in town. They had big brass dog-irons[1] that could hold up a saw-log. There was a clock on the middle of the mantelpiece, with a picture of a town painted on the bottom half of the glass front,

---

1. **dog-irons**, andirons; metal supports that hold wood in a fireplace.

and a round place in the middle of it for the sun, and you could see the pendulum swinging behind it. It was beautiful to hear that clock tick; and sometimes when one of these peddlers had been along and scoured her up and got her in good shape, she would start in and strike a hundred and fifty before she got tuckered out. They wouldn't took any money for her.

Well, there was a big outlandish parrot on each side of the clock, made out of something like chalk, and painted up gaudy. By one of the parrots was a cat made of crockery, and a crockery dog by the other; and when you pressed down on them they squeaked, but didn't open their mouths nor look different nor interested. They squeaked through underneath. There was a couple of big wild-turkey-wing fans spread out behind those things. On the table in the middle of the room was a kind of a lovely crockery basket that had apples and oranges and peaches and grapes piled up in it, which was much redder and yellower and prettier than real ones is, but they warn't real because you could see where pieces had got chipped off and showed the white chalk, or whatever it was, underneath.

This table had a cover made out of a beautiful oilcloth, with a red and blue spread-eagle painted on it, and a painted border all around. It come all the way from Philadelphia, they said. There was some books, too, piled up perfectly exact, on each corner of the table. One was a big family Bible full of pictures. One was *Pilgrim's Progress*, about a man that left his family, it didn't say why. I read considerable in it now and then. The statements was interesting, but tough. Another was *Friendship's Offering*, full of beautiful stuff and poetry; but I didn't read the poetry. Another was Henry Clay's Speeches, and another was Dr. Gunn's *Family Medicine*, which told you all about what to do if a body was sick or dead. There was a hymn-book, and a lot of other books. And there was nice split-bottom chairs, and perfectly sound, too—not bagged down in the middle and busted, like an old basket.

They had pictures hung on the walls—mainly Washingtons and Lafayettes, and battles, and Highland Marys, and one called "Signing the Declaration." There was some that they called crayons, which one of the daughters which was dead made her own self when she was only fifteen years old. They was different from any pictures I ever seen before—blacker, mostly, than is common. One was a woman in slim black dress, belted small under the armpits, with bulges like a cabbage in the middle of the sleeves, and a large black scoop-shovel bonnet with a black veil, and white slim anklets crossed about with black tape, and very wee black slippers, like a chisel, and she was leaning pensive on a tombstone on her right elbow, under a weeping willow, and her other hand hanging down her side holding a white handkerchief and a reticule, and underneath the picture it said "Shall I Never See Thee More Alas." Another one was a young lady with her hair all combed up straight to the top of her head, and knotted there in front of a comb like a chair-back, and she was crying into a handkerchief and had a dead bird laying on its back in her other hand with its heels up, and underneath the picture it said "I Shall Never Hear Thy Sweet Chirrup More Alas." There was one where a young lady was at a window looking up at the moon, and tears running down her cheeks; and she had an open letter in one hand with black sealing-wax showing on one edge of it and she was mashing a locket with a chain to it against her mouth, and underneath the picture it said "And Art Thou Gone Yes Thou Art Gone Alas." These was all nice pictures, I reckon, but I didn't somehow seem to take to them, because if ever I was down a little they always give me the fan-tods. Everybody was sorry she died, because she had laid out a lot more of these pictures to do, and a body could see by what she had done what they had lost. But I reckoned that with her disposition she was having a better time in the graveyard. She was at work on what they said was her greatest picture when she took sick, and every day and every night it was her prayer to be allowed to live till she got it done, but she never got the chance. It was a picture of a young woman in a long white gown, standing on the rail of a bridge all ready to jump off, with her hair all down her back, and looking up to the moon, with the tears running down her face, and she had two arms folded across her breast, and two arms stretched out in front, and two more reaching up toward the moon—and the idea was to see which pair would look best and then scratch out all the other arms; but as I was saying, she died before she got her mind made up, and now they kept this picture over the head of the bed in her room, and every time her birthday come they hung flowers on it. Other times it was hid with a little curtain. The young woman in the picture had a kind of a nice sweet face, but there was so many arms it made her look too spidery, seemed to me.

This young girl kept a scrap-book when she was alive, and used to paste obituaries and accidents and cases of patient suffering in it out of the *Presbyterian Observer*, and write poetry after them out of her own head. It was very good poetry. This is what she wrote about a boy by the name of Stephen Dowling Bots that fell down a well and was drownded:

ODE TO STEPHEN DOWLING BOTS, DEC'D

And did young Stephen sicken,
    And did young Stephen die?
And did the sad hearts thicken,
    And did the mourners cry?

No; such was not the fate of
    Young Stephen Dowling Bots;
Though sad hearts round him thickened,
    'Twas not from sickness' shots.

No whooping-cough did rack his frame,
    Nor measles drear with spots;
Not these impaired the sacred name
    Of Stephen Dowling Bots.

Despised love struck not with woe
    That head of curly knots,
Nor stomach troubles laid him low,
    Young Stephen Dowling Bots.

O no. Then list with tearful eye,
    Whilst I his fate do tell.
His soul did from this cold world fly
    By falling down a well.

They got him out and emptied him;
    Alas it was too late;
His spirit was gone for to sport aloft
    In the realms of the good and great.

If Emmeline Grangerford could make poetry like that before she was fourteen, there ain't no telling what she could 'a' done by and

Mourning Picture for the Cutlers, early 19th century, artist unknown. Private collection.
Reproduced from *Small Folk* by permission of E.P. Dutton, New York.

by. Buck said she could rattle off poetry like nothing. She didn't ever have to stop to think. He said she would slap down a line, and if she couldn't find anything to rhyme with it would just scratch it out and slap down another one, and go ahead. She warn't particular; she could write about anything you choose to give her to write about just so it was sadful. Every time a man died, or a woman died, or a child died, she would be on hand with her "tribute" before he was cold. She called them tributes. The neighbors said it was the doctor first, then Emmeline, then the undertaker—the under-taker never got in ahead of Emmeline but once, and then she hung fire on a rhyme for the dead person's name, which was Whistler. She warn't ever the same after that; she never complained, but she kinder pined away and did not live long. Poor thing, many's the time I made myself go up to the little room that used to be hers and get out her poor old scrap-book and read in it when her pictures had been aggravating me and I had soured on her a little. I liked all that family, dead ones and all, and warn't going to let anything come between us. Poor Emmeline made poetry about all the dead people when she was alive, and it didn't seem right that there warn't nobody to make some about her now she was gone; so I tried to sweat out a verse or two myself, but I couldn't seem to make it go somehow. They kept Emmeline's room trim and nice, and all the things fixed in it just the way she liked to have them when she was alive, and nobody ever slept there. The old lady took care of the room herself, though there was plenty of servants, and she sewed there a good deal and read her Bible there mostly.

Well, as I was saying about the parlor, there was beautiful curtains on the windows; white, with pictures painted on them of castles with vines all down the walls, and cattle coming down to drink. There was a little old piano, too, that had tin pans in it, I reckon, and nothing was ever so lovely as to hear the young ladies sing "The Last Link is Broken" and play "The Battle of Prague" on it. The walls of all the rooms was plastered, and most had carpets on the floors, and the whole house was whitewashed on the outside.

It was a double house, and the big open place betwixt them was roofed and floored, and sometimes the table was set there in the middle of the day, and it was a cool, comfortable place. Nothing couldn't be better. And warn't the cooking good, and just bushels of it too!

Developing Comprehension Skills

1. According to the preface, which would be more dangerous: attempting to find a motive, attempting to find a moral, or attempting to find a plot in this story?

2. Why was Huck unable to run past the "big old-fashioned double log house"?

3. Why do the Grangerfords ask Huck if he knows the Shepherdsons?

4. Huck has the ability to lie creatively. How does he use this ability in his dealings with the Grangerfords? Find several examples.

5. What does Huck find impressive about the Grangerfords' house? With what does he compare it? What do his reactions reveal about his background?

6. How can you tell that no one actually read the books stacked on the Grangerfords' table?

7. What did Huck attempt to do in honor of Emmeline that no one else had ever done for her? What do you learn about Huck from this action?

8. Sometimes a reader sees things that a character does not. Huck thinks the Grangerford house has "style." Do you agree?

Reading Literature

1. **Understanding a Preface.** An introductory statement to a book is called a **preface**. A preface usually tells the subject, purpose, or plan of the story.

   Mark Twain was impatient with people who ruin the pleasure of reading by inventing a book's purpose. From his preface, how do you think he wants this novel to be read?

2. **Understanding the Narrator.** The story of *Huckleberry Finn* is told by Huck himself. Is he experienced in the ways of the world, or is he innocent and lacking in knowledge? Find details to support your answer. Why do you think Twain chose this type of narrator?

3. **Recognizing Satire.** Writing that ridicules, or pokes fun at, foolish ideas or customs is called **satire.** For example, Twain ridicules people like Emmeline Grangerford and their amateurish poetry. In what way does Twain ridicule the lifestyle of the Grangerfords? Why do you suppose he does so?

4. **Appreciating Dialect. Dialect,** you recall, is language that is characteristic of a certain people or region. It includes differences in vocabulary, grammar, and pronunciation. Writers often use dialect to create a realistic character that fits a particular setting.

    In this selection, Twain uses many examples of dialect such as "clumb," "knowed" and "if they'd 'a' ben some." Find other examples of dialect from the selection. Does dialect add to or take away from your enjoyment of the story? Explain your answer.

5. **Recognizing Humor.** Humor can often result when somebody says or does something unexpected. Or, it can result when somebody says or does something in an exaggerated way. For example, Huck's reaction to Buck's riddle is humorous because of his complete inability to understand the joke.

    Find another example of humor in the selection. Is it humorous mostly because something is unexpected or because something is exaggerated?

Developing Vocabulary Skills

Learning More Greek Roots. Review the Greek roots you studied on pages 233 and 306. Then study these additional roots.

Root	Meaning	Example
anthropos	man	anthropology
biblos	book	Bible
geos	earth	geography
metron	measure	metrics
micro	small	microscopic
pathos	to feel, suffer	apathy
psyche	soul	psychiatry
tele	far off	telegram

Use your knowledge of Greek roots to determine the meaning of each of the words below. You may have to refer to the lists on pages 233 and 306. Then write a second example for each of the Greek roots listed above.

1. philanthropy
2. geologist
3. chronometer
4. anthropologist
5. pathology
6. bibliography
7. microorganism
8. psychotherapy
9. telepathy
10. geophysics

Developing Writing Skills

1. **Analyzing a Character Trait.** A **character trait** is a quality that a character shows through actions, statements, or thoughts. One of Huck's character traits is his cleverness. For example, he uses a clever method to find out the false name he gave to the Grangerfords. In a paragraph, describe another one of Huck's character traits.

    Pre-Writing. Make a list of character traits that you learn about Huckleberry Finn from reading the story. Choose one trait as the subject of your paragraph. Write down several details from the story that demonstrate this trait.

Writing. Use your pre-writing notes to write a rough draft of your paragraph. Begin your paragraph with a strong topic sentence that tells the trait you are describing. Follow your topic sentence with at least two details that prove Huck had this trait. Use passages from the selection to support the details you use.

Revising. Read your rough draft. Did you limit your paragraph to one character trait? Does the topic sentence tell what the paragraph is about? Did you choose the best details to support your topic sentence? That is, do your details show that Huck had the trait you chose? When you have revised the content of your paragraph, check your grammar, spelling, and punctuation.

2. **Describing a Setting.** The Grangerfords' home reveals a great deal about the personality of the owners. Write a paragraph in which you describe a room that you feel reflects the personality of its owner. Arrange your details in spatial order, such as left to right, or top to bottom. Be sure to state what you feel this room tells you about its owner.

Developing Skills in Study and Research

Using Literary Reference Books. "The Grangerfords Take Me In" is a chapter from the novel *The Adventures of Huckleberry Finn*. If you want to find out a little more about what happens in the rest of that novel, you can use a reference like *The Oxford Companion to American Literature*. This valuable reference work contains brief summaries of the most famous works in American literature, as well as other valuable information about American authors and their works.

Find this reference book in your library, and look up "Huckleberry Finn." Read the entry and take notes to report on in class.

Developing Skills in Speaking and Listening

1. **Using Audio-Visual Aids.** Many of Mark Twain's stories have been recorded on records and tapes. Find such a recording and play it in class. Some recordings the class might enjoy include the following:

Short Stories of Mark Twain. CMS Records SMS531. (1968) (read by Salem Ludwig).
Mark Twain Stories. Caedmon CDL 51027. (1965) (read by Walter Brennan).
Mark Twain Tonight. Columbia 052019, 2030. (1959–61) (read by Hal Holbrook).
Mark Twain's America. Caedmon CDL 52064. (1971) (read by Will Geer).

Listen carefully for ways in which the actors make the recording come alive. If an actor is playing two characters, how does he make his voice different? Does he make the dialect sound natural? How does he vary his speed, pitch, and volume to build excitement?

2. **Interpreting Dialect.** Select a passage from "The Grangerfords Take Me In" that contains dialogue. With a partner read the passage aloud. Try to make the characters come alive through the use of dialect. Pay close attention to pronunciation. This will help you create a believable character.

The Boys' Ambition

MARK TWAIN
From Life on the Mississippi

SETTING A PURPOSE

Life on the Mississippi describes Twain's true-life adventures on that mighty river. As you read this excerpt, look for ways in which the Mississippi became a central force in Twain's life.

When I was a boy, there was but one permanent ambition among my comrades in our village on the west bank of the Mississippi River. That was, to be a steamboatman. We had transient ambitions of other sorts, but they were only transient.

When a circus came and went, it left us all burning to become clowns; the first minstrel show that came to our section left us all suffering to try that kind of life; now and then we had a hope that if we lived and were good, God would permit us to be pirates. These ambitions faded out, each in its turn; but the ambition to be a steamboatman always remained.

Once a day a cheap, gaudy packet arrived upward from St. Louis, and another downward from Keokuk. Before these events, the day was glorious with expectancy; after them, the day was a dead and empty thing. Not only the boys, but the whole village, felt this. After all these years I can picture that old time to myself now, just as it was then: the white town drowsing in the sunshine of a summer's morning; the streets empty, or pretty nearly so; one or two clerks sitting in front of the Water

Samuel Clemens's pilot license. The Mariner's Museum, Newport News, Virginia.

*A Steamboat Race on the
Mississippi (between the* Baltic
and Diana*)*. 1859. Printed by
GEORGE F. FULLER. Missouri
Historical Society, Saint Louis.

Street stores, with their splint-bottomed chairs tilted back against the wall, chins on breasts, hats slouched over their faces, a-sleep—with shingle shavings enough around to show what broke them down; a sow and a litter of pigs loafing along the sidewalk, doing a good business in watermelon rinds and seeds; two or three lonely little freight piles scattered about the "levee"; a pile of "skids" on the slope of the stone-paved wharf, and the fragrant town drunkard asleep in the shadow of them; two or three wood flats at the head of the wharf, but nobody to listen to the peaceful lapping of the wavelets against them; the great Mississippi, the majestic, the magnificent Mississippi, rolling its mile-wide tide along, shining in the sun; the dense forest away on the other side; the "point" above the town, and the "point" below, bounding the river-glimpse and turning it into a sort of sea, and

My father was a justice of the peace, and I supposed he possessed the power of life and death over all men and could hang anybody that offended him. This was distinction enough for me as a general thing; but the desire to be a steamboatman kept intruding, nevertheless. I first wanted to be a cabin boy, so that I could come out with a white apron on and shake a tablecloth over the side, where all my old comrades could see me; later I thought I would rather be the deck hand who stood on the end of the stage plank with the coil of rope in his hand, because he was particularly conspicuous. But these were only daydreams,— they were too heavenly to be contemplated as real possibilities. By and by one of our boys went away. He was not heard of for a long time. At last he turned up as apprentice engineer or "striker" on a steamboat. This thing shook the bottom out of all my Sunday-school teachings. That boy had been notoriously worldly, and I just the reverse; yet he was exalted to this eminence, and I left in obscurity and misery. There was nothing generous about this fellow in his greatness. He would always manage to have a rusty bolt to scrub while his boat tarried at our town, and he would sit on the inside guard and scrub it, where we could all see him and envy him and loathe him. And whenever his boat was laid up he would come home and swell around the town in his blackest and greasiest clothes, so that nobody could help remembering that he was a steamboatman; and he used all sorts of steamboat technicalities in his talk, as if he were so used to them that he forgot common people could not understand them. He would speak of the "labboard" side of a horse in an easy, natural way that would make one wish he

withal a very still and brilliant and lonely one. Presently a film of dark smoke appears above one of those remote "points"; instantly a Negro drayman, famous for his quick eye and prodigious voice, lifts up the cry, "S-t-e-a-m-boat a-comin'!" and the scene changes! The town stirs, the clerks wake up, a furious clatter of drays follows, every house and store pours out a human contribution, and all in a twinkling the dead town is alive and moving.

was dead. And he was always talking about "St. Looy" like an old citizen; he would refer casually to occasions when he "was coming down Fourth Street," or when he was "passing by the Planter's House," or when there was a fire and he took a turn on the brakes of "the old Big Missouri"; and then he would go on and lie about how many towns the size of ours were burned down there that day. Two or three of the boys had long been persons of consideration among us because they had been to St. Louis once and had a vague general knowledge of its wonders, but the day of their glory was over now. They lapsed into a humble silence, and learned to disappear when the ruthless "cub" engineer approached. This fellow had money, too, and hair oil. Also an ignorant silver watch and a showy brass watch chain. He wore a leather belt and used no suspenders. If ever a youth was cordially admired and hated by his comrades, this one was. No girl could withstand his charms. He "cut out" every boy in the village. When his boat blew up at last, it diffused a tranquil contentment among us such as we had not known for months. But when he came home the next week, alive, renowned, and appeared in church all battered up and bandaged, a shining hero, it seemed to us that the partiality of Providence for an undeserving reptile had reached a point where it was open to criticism.

This creature's career could produce but one result, and it speedily followed. Boy after boy managed to get on the river. The minister's son became an engineer. The doctor's and the postmaster's sons became "mud clerks"; the wholesale liquor dealer's son became a barkeeper on a boat; four sons of the chief merchant, and two sons of the county judge, became pilots. Pilot was the grandest position of all. The pilot, even in those days of trivial wages, had a princely salary—from a hundred and fifty to two hundred and fifty dollars a month, and no board to pay. Two months of his wages would pay a preacher's salary for a year. Now some of us were left disconsolate. We could not get on the river—at least our parents would not let us.

So by and by I ran away. I said I never would come home again till I was a pilot and could come in glory. But somehow I could not manage it. I went meekly aboard a few of the boats that lay packed together like sardines at the long St. Louis wharf, and very humbly inquired for the pilots, but got only a cold shoulder and short words from mates and clerks. I had to make the best of this sort of treatment for the time being, but I had comforting daydreams of a future when I should be a great and honored pilot, with plenty of money, and could kill some of these mates and clerks and pay for them.

Developing Comprehension Skills

1. What was the permanent ambition of Twain and his friends while they were boys? What were some of the boys' transient, or passing, ambitions? What did all of these dreams have in common?

2. Briefly describe a typical day in Twain's town before the steamboat arrives. How does this scene change when the drayman cries "S-t-e-a-m-boat a-comin'!"?

3. Briefly describe the first boy from Twain's group who got a job on a steamboat. Why did this event cause Twain to question his Sunday school teachings?

4. What daydream comforted Twain after he ran away and awaited his chance to become a pilot?

5. Twain's selection deals with boyhood ambitions. How do the ambitions described by Twain compare to the ambitions of youngsters today? Explain.

Reading Literature

1. **Analyzing Nonfiction.** Writing that tells about real people, places, and events is called **nonfiction.** Unlike fiction, nonfiction is largely concerned with factual information. However, the writer may shape the information according to his or her purpose.

   How is *Life on the Mississippi* similar to the *Huckleberry Finn* selection? How are the two selections different? Does the fact that *Life on the Mississippi* is nonfiction add to its enjoyment? Explain.

2. **Appreciating Local Color.** **Local color** is the speech, mannerisms, dress, customs, and attitudes of a particular region of the country. Writers use it to create a vivid picture of one area. What examples of local color do you find in this selection by Twain?

3. **Understanding the Author's Purpose.** When an author begins to write, he has a certain purpose in mind. For example, the purpose may be to provide information, persuade, or entertain. What do you think Twain's purpose was in writing this piece? To decide, ask yourself what effect it had on you.

4. **Analyzing Tone.** What do you believe is Twain's tone, or attitude, in this selection from *Life on the Mississippi*? Point out words and phrases from the selection which you feel reflect this tone. Does the tone stay the same throughout the selection, or does it change? Explain your answer.

5. **Recognizing Symbols.** A symbol, you recall, is a person, place, or thing that represents something beyond itself. The American flag, for example, is a symbol for the United States as well as patriotism and love of country. In this selection, both the Mississippi River and the steamboat are very important to young Twain. What do you think each represents for him? Give reasons for your answer.

6. **Appreciating Sensory Images.** When describing a scene, a writer sometimes tries to make a picture more realistic by including details that appeal to the five senses. Reread the third paragraph of this selection, which describes the town and the river. What details appeal to the sense of sight? hearing? smell? taste? touch?

Developing Vocabulary Skills

Using Greek and Latin Prefixes. There is a special group of Greek and Latin prefixes that refers to numbers or amounts. Several of these prefixes are shown below.

Prefix	Meaning	Example
mono-, uni-	one	monotone
di-, bi-, duo-	two	biannual
tri-	three	tripod
quad-	four	quadrangle
pent-	five	pentagon
deca-, deci-	ten	decathlon
poly-, multi-	many	polygon
semi-	half	semiphore
pan-, omni-	all	omnipotent
cent-	hundred	century

Use your understanding of these word parts, as well as others you have studied, to answer the following questions. Use a dictionary if necessary.

1. Did riverboats have a monopoly on the dreams of young Twain?

2. Before the steamboat arrived, was there a polyphony of sound in the town?

3. Was Chief Seattle probably bilingual or did he most likely need an interpreter?

4. Do you think the effect of the white settlers seemed omnipresent to the Native Americans?

5. If a "score" is twenty, how many decades does Lincoln refer to at the beginning of the Gettysburg Address?

Developing Skills in Writing

1. **Understanding the Writer.** This selection tells us a great deal about Twain's background, childhood, and personal feelings. From this piece, what would you guess were two or three things Twain loved best in life? What things particularly seemed to annoy him? How do you think the events of his boyhood influenced the kinds of things he chose to write about? Write a paragraph discussing these questions.

2. **Writing About Career Ambitions.** Twain tells us that his career ambition was to become a pilot on a steamboat. Write a paragraph or composition in which you reveal your ambition. Include your reasons for choosing this career, and events or people in your past that might have influenced you.

   Pre-Writing. Write down the career or occupational goal you hope to reach some day. Write notes on how you became interested in that career. You should do some research on the career, also. Your guidance counselor or librarian can help you find sources of information. Take notes on the good points of the career you have chosen. Organize your pre-writing notes logically. For example, you might put background information in one group, personal reasons for your choice in another, and facts and statistics in a third group.

   Writing. In one of your opening sentences, name your career goal and show its importance to you. Tell how you became interested in this particular career. Then, give your reasons for choosing that career. Try to make your reasons as specific as possible. Arrange these in order of importance. Be sure to use transitional words like *first*, *next*, and *finally* to connect your ideas, and show their importance.

Revising. Read your first draft. Have you told the reader exactly what your ambition is? Have you included specific reasons to show why you chose a particular career? Do these reasons include facts and statistics from your research? Does your use of transitional words and phrases make the order of importance clear? Make changes if necessary.

Developing Skills in Study and Research

Finding Career Information. *The Occupational Outlook Handbook* is a reference book that is issued yearly by the United States Department of Labor. It lists major occupations and gives information on such things as salaries, working conditions, entrance requirements, and job outlook.

Find *The Occupational Outlook Handbook* in your school library or counseling department.

Find the listing for an occupation that you might like to pursue. List some details about the career such as salary, benefits, and the education necessary to enter that career. You might compare and contrast some details of your career with other people in your class.

Developing Skills in Speaking and Listening

Listening for Sounds. Twain makes his world come alive for the reader by describing its everyday sounds. For example, he describes the lapping of the wavelets against the wood flats, the drayman's cry of "S-t-e-a-m-boat a-comin'," and the furious clatter of drays. What does *your* world sound like? Spend at least five minutes listening carefully to the sounds around you. Make detailed notes on what you hear. What sounds are soothing? Which ones are harsh? Do any sounds surprise you? If so, which ones?

An Encounter with an Interviewer

MARK TWAIN

SETTING A PURPOSE | *As Mark Twain traveled around the world lecturing, he was interviewed by many journalists. In the following fictional interview, how does Twain finally "get even" with some of these interviewers?*

The nervous dapper, "peart" young man took the chair I offered him, and said he was connected with the "Daily Thunderstorm" and added,—

"Hoping it's no harm, I've come to interview you."

"Come to what?"

"*Interview* you."

"Ah! I see. Yes—yes. Um! Yes—yes. I see."

I was not feeling bright that morning. Indeed, my powers seemed a bit under a cloud. However, I went to the bookcase, and when I had been looking six or seven minutes, I found I was obliged to refer to the young man. I said,—

"How do you spell it?"

"Spell what?"

"Interview."

"Oh my goodness! what do you want to spell it for?"

"I don't want to spell it; I want to see what it means."

"Well, this is astonishing, I must say. I can tell you what it means, if you—if you—"

"Oh, all right! That will answer, and much obliged to you, too."

"In, *in*, ter, *ter*, *in*ter—"

"Then you spell it with an *I*?"

"Why, certainly!"

"Oh, that is what took me so long."

"Why, my *dear* sir, what did *you* propose to spell it with?"

"Well, I—I—hardly know. I had the Unabridged, and I was ciphering around in the back end, hoping I might tree her among the pictures. But it's a very old edition."

"Why, my friend, they wouldn't have a *picture* of it in even the latest e— My dear sir, I beg your pardon, I mean no harm in the world, but you do not look as—as—intelligent as I had expected you would."

"Oh, don't mention it! It has often been said, and by people who would not flatter and who could have no inducement to flatter, that I am quite remarkable in that way. Yes—yes; they always speak of it with rapture."

"I can easily imagine it. But about this interview. You know it is the custom, now, to interview any man who has become notorious."

"Indeed, I had not heard of it before. It must be very interesting. What do you do it with?"

From a series of photographs called *Progress of a Moral Purpose* by Samuel Langhorne Clemens.
Manuscripts Department, Lilly Library, Indiana University, Bloomington.

"Ah, well—well—well—this is disheartening. It *ought* to be done with a club in some cases; but customarily it consists in the interviewer asking questions and the interviewed answering them. It is all the rage now. Will you let me ask you certain questions calculated to bring out the salient points of your public and private history?"

"Oh, with pleasure,—with pleasure. I have a very bad memory, but I hope you will not mind that. That is to say, it is an irregular memory,—singularly irregular. Sometimes it goes in a gallop, and then again it will be as much as a fortnight passing a given point. This is a great grief to me."

"Oh, it is no matter, so you will try to do the best you can."

"I will. I will put my whole mind on it."

"Thanks. Are you ready to begin?"

"Ready."

Q. How old are you?

A. Nineteen, in June.

Q. Indeed! I would have taken you to be thirty-five or six. Where were you born?

A. In Missouri.

Q. When did you begin to write?

A. In 1836.

Q. Why, how could that be, if you are only nineteen now?

A. I don't know. It does seem curious, somehow.

Q. It does, indeed. Whom do you consider the most remarkable man you ever met?

A. Aaron Burr.[1]

Q. But you never could have met Aaron Burr, if you are only nineteen years—

A. Now, if you know more about me than I do, what do you ask me for?

Q. Well, it was only a suggestion—nothing more. How did you happen to meet Burr?

A. Well, I happened to be at his funeral one day, and he asked me to make less noise and—

Q. But, good heavens! If you were at his funeral, he must have been dead; and if he was dead, how could he care whether you made a noise or not?

---

1. **Aaron Burr**, (1756–1836) Vice-President of the United States (1801–05). A controversial figure who killed Alexander Hamilton in a duel and was tried and acquitted for treason.

A. I don't know. He was always a particular kind of man that way.

Q. Still, I don't understand it at all! You say he spoke to you, and that he was dead.

A. I didn't say he was dead.

Q. But, wasn't he dead?

A. Well, some said he was, some said he wasn't.

Q. What did you think?

A. Oh, it was none of my business! It wasn't any of my funeral.

Q. Did you—However, we can never get this matter straight. Let me ask about something else. What was the date of your birth?

A. Monday, October 31st, 1693.

Q. What! Impossible! That would make you a hundred and eighty years old. How do you account for that?

A. I don't account for it at all.

Q. But you said at first you were only nineteen, and now you make yourself out to be one hundred and eighty. It is an awful discrepancy.

A. Why, have you noticed that? (Shaking hands.) Many a time it has seemed to me like a discrepancy, but somehow I couldn't make up my mind. How quick you notice a thing!

Q. Thank you for the compliment, as far as it goes. Had you, or have you, any brothers or sisters?

A. Eh! I—I—I think so—yes—but I don't remember.

Q. Well, this is the most extraordinary statement I ever heard!

A. Why, what makes you think that?

Q. How could I think otherwise? Why, look here! Who is this a picture of on the wall? Isn't that a brother of yours?

A. Oh! yes, yes, yes! Now you remind me of it, that *was* a brother of mine. That's William—*Bill* we called him. Poor old Bill!

Q. Why? Is he dead; then?

A. Ah! well, I suppose so. We never could tell. There was a great mystery about it.

Q. That is sad, very sad. He disappeared, then?

A. Well, yes, in a sort of general way. We buried him.

Q. *Buried* him. *Buried* him, without knowing whether he was dead or not?

A. Oh, no! Not that. He was dead enough.

Q. Well, I confess that I can't understand this. If you buried him, and you knew he was dead—

A. No! no! We only thought he was.

Q. Oh, I see! He came to life again?

A. I bet he didn't.

Q. Well, I never heard anything like this. *Somebody* was dead. *Somebody* was buried. Now, where was the mystery?

A. Ah! that's just it! That's it exactly. You see, we were twins,—defunct and I,—and we got mixed in the bath-tub when we were only two weeks old, and one of us was drowned. But we didn't know which. Some think it was Bill. Some think it was me.

Q. Well, that *is* remarkable. What do *you* think?

A. Goodness knows! I would give whole worlds to know. This solemn, this awful mystery has cast a gloom over my whole life. But I will tell you a secret now, which I never have revealed to any creature before. One of us had a peculiar mark—a large mole on the back of his left hand; that was *me. That child was the one that was drowned!*

Q. Very well, then, I don't see that there is any mystery about it, after all.

A. You don't? Well, I do. Anyway, I don't see how they could ever have been such a blundering lot as to go and bury the wrong child. But, 'sh—don't mention it where the family can hear of it. Heaven knows they have heart-breaking troubles enough without adding this.

Q. Well, I believe I have got material enough for the present, and I am very much obliged to you for the pains you have taken. But I was a good deal interested in that account of Aaron Burr's funeral. Would you mind telling me what particular circumstance it was that made you think Burr was such a remarkable man?

A. Oh! it was a mere trifle! Not one man in fifty would have noticed it at all. When the sermon was over, and the procession all ready to start for the cemetery, and the body all arranged nice in the hearse, he said he wanted to take a last look at the scenery, and so he *got up and rode with the driver—*

Then the young man reverently withdrew. He was very pleasant company, and I was sorry to see him go.

Developing Comprehension Skills

1. Why do you suppose the young man was "nervous" about interviewing Twain?

2. What is your first clue that Twain may be trying to make a fool out of the interviewer?

3. Who does Twain say is the most remarkable man he ever met? Why does this answer upset the interviewer?

4. What is the mystery concerning Twain and his twin brother? How does the interviewer's response show that Twain has him completely under control? Explain your answer.

5. The interviewer says he has "got material enough for the present." Is this possible? Why or why not?

Reading Literature

1. **Appreciating Satire.** Satire, you recall, is writing that ridicules, or pokes fun at, foolish ideas or customs. "An Encounter with an Interviewer" is an example of satire. What is Twain ridiculing? Why do you think he does so? Explain your answer.

2. **Analyzing Narration.** The narrator in "An Encounter with an Interviewer" is the person being interviewed. What can the reader learn about the narrator from the interview? Is he a fool, or is he extremely clever? Explain.

Developing Vocabulary Skills

Understanding Word Families. Sometimes a single root is used in many different words. These related words make up a word family. If you know the meaning of one root, you can often figure out the meanings of many words.

Each sentence on the following page has an underlined word with a Greek or Latin root. Write the word on your paper. Underline the root and give the meaning of the root. Then create a word family for that word by writing as many related words as you can.

1. Frederick Douglass decided to <u>proceed</u> with his studies despite the disapproval of the Aulds.

2. Lincoln and other <u>luminaries</u> attended the dedication of the Gettysburg battlefield.

3. Before Farquhar could <u>submit</u> any information, he was captured by Union soldiers.

4. When Twain attempted to <u>diversify</u> and go into business, he met with failure.

Developing Skills in Writing

1. **Analyzing Mood.** As you read "An Encounter with an Interviewer," what feeling, or mood, did you experience? How did Twain create that particular mood? In a well written paragraph, identify the mood created by Twain in this selection. Use examples from the piece for support.

2. **Describing a Person.** In this selection, Twain presented himself as quite an eccentric. An eccentric is a person who seems somewhat odd or unusual in his or her appearance or conduct. Write a paragraph or composition in which you describe the most eccentric person you have known.

    Pre-Writing. Think of an unusual person you know. What characteristics separate this person from others? Make notes on his or her appearance. What is unusual about it? Now think about less obvious details. Does he or she have any unusual mannerisms, habits, or ideas?

    Writing. Begin your description by introducing your character. Try to spark your reader's interest with an unusual detail or idea. Then give additional details about the person you are describing. You might present your details in order of importance, from the most striking or noticeable to the one that is least obvious. Use specific verbs and adjectives that will vividly describe the person for your readers.

    Revising. Have someone else read your paragraph and give his or her impression of the character you have described. Did you get ideas across that you wanted to? If not, you may have to add details that enable you to do so. Do your adjectives help paint a clear and vivid picture? Make any necessary changes.

Developing Skills in Speaking and Listening

Conducting an Interview. Interviews can help you find new ideas or information. Conduct an interview with someone you find interesting or unusual. You might interview a person who is not well known by others. Before conducting the interview, study the following guidelines:

1. Make an appointment for the interview.

2. If possible, do some basic research on the person so you can ask informed questions.

3. Prepare eight to ten questions in advance to get the information you need.

4. Arrive on time for your appointment.

5. Begin asking your questions. Pay close attention to what the person says. Follow up on interesting points with additional questions.

6. Take notes on the person's manner and appearance as well as on the answers.

7. Be courteous.

Epigrams

MARK TWAIN

SETTING A PURPOSE *Mark Twain often used humor to teach people or to remind them of their shortcomings. What does Twain tell people in each of the following epigrams?*

Don't Copy Cat

Don't, like the cat, try to get more out
of an experience than there is in it.
The cat, having sat upon a hot stove lid,
Will not sit upon a hot stove lid again.
Nor upon a cold stove lid.

Wisdom

When I was a boy of fourteen, my father
was so ignorant I could hardly stand to have
the old man around. But when I got to be
twenty-one I was astonished at how much the
old man had learned in seven years.

Developing Comprehension Skills

1. After sitting on a hot stove lid, what idea does the cat have about stove lids in general?

2. What is a "copy cat"? Do you think this is a good title for this piece? Why or why not?

3. When Twain was fourteen, what opinion did he have of his father? How did this opinion change when Twain became twenty-one?

4. Who really changed in those seven years, Twain or his father? Explain your answer.

5. Do you think most teen-agers share the young Twain's opinion about fathers? Do you think they will also share his later conclusion?

Reading Literature

1. **Recognizing Epigrams.** An **epigram**, you may recall, is a brief, witty statement that expresses a truth about life. What lesson is Twain trying to teach in "Don't Copy Cat"?

2. **Understanding Analogies.** When a writer uses an **analogy**, he or she explains an idea by relating it to something else. For example, a writer might talk about the complex nature of the brain by comparing it to a computer. Why do you think Twain used a cat to make his point in "Don't Copy Cat"? Would his lesson have been more or less effective if the saying simply read "Do not try to get more out of an experience than there is in it"?

Developing Vocabulary Skills

Identifying Word Parts and Their Meanings. The following list of words contains some of the prefixes, suffixes, and Greek and Latin roots you have learned in this chapter. Write the meaning of each important word part. Then write the meaning of the whole word.

1. contradiction
2. monologue
3. microbiology
4. consensus
5. dictograph
6. illumination

Developing Writing Skills

1. **Appreciating Humor.** Twain's humor could be light at times, and very sharp and biting at others. Write a composition in which you explore the different types of humor Twain used in the selections in this chapter. Use passages from the stories and epigrams to support your ideas.

2. **Writing an Epigram.** In his epigrams, Twain was able to remind people of their shortcomings. Write an epigram in which you point out a human shortcoming. Try to make your epigram humorous.

   Pre-Writing. Think of an experience that made you change your mind about someone or something. On a piece of paper make three columns. In the first column, make notes about your old opinion or belief. Why did you have this opinion? In the second column, make notes about the events that prompted you to question your belief. In the third column, make notes about your new opinion. What is it? How is your behavior different because of it?

   Writing. Using the information from the three columns, write a three-paragraph composition. In the first paragraph, describe your old opinion. Be sure you use past tense verbs. In the second paragraph, tell how you happened to question your belief. Arrange these details in chronological order. In the third paragraph, describe your new opinion and its effect on you. Use present tense verbs.

   Revising. Ask a classmate to read your composition and write down these things: your original opinion, your new opinion, and what happened to make you change your opinion. Read what he or she wrote. If it does not match what you think you said, revise your work.

Developing Skills in Critical Thinking

1. **Recognizing the Error of Overgeneralization.** In "Don't Copy Cat," the cat makes an overgeneralization. "*Many* dogs have fleas" is an example of a generalization. When the generalization is so broad that it covers people, places, things, and events that it should not cover, it is an overgeneralization. An example is "*All* dogs have fleas."

   In "Don't Copy Cat," what overgeneralization did the cat make? What was the result of this overgeneralization? In general, how can overgeneralizations affect your actions?

2. **Making Inferences.** Because an epigram is so short, it may be necessary for the reader to make inferences to understand it. In other words, the reader must draw conclusions from facts that are given by the writer.

   What inferences can you make about Twain's relationship with his father when he was twenty-one? What do you think happened to Twain during the years between age fourteen and age twenty-one?

To Build a Fire

JACK LONDON

SETTING A PURPOSE | *Imagine a place where winter is seven months long. The Klondike, a region of northern Canada, is such a place. Why is this setting so important in the following story?*

Day had broken cold and gray, exceedingly cold and gray, when the man turned aside from the main Yukon[1] trail and climbed the high earth-bank, where a dim and little-travelled trail led eastward through the fat spruce timberland. It was a steep bank, and he paused for breath at the top, excusing the act to himself by looking at his watch. It was nine o'clock. There was no sun nor hint of sun, though there was not a cloud in the sky. It was a clear day, and yet there seemed an intangible pall over the face of things, a subtle gloom that made the day dark, and that was due to the absence of sun. This fact did not worry the man. He was used to the lack of sun. It had been days since he had seen the sun, and he knew that a few more days must pass before that cheerful orb, due south, would just peep above the sky line and dip immediately from view.

The man flung a look back along the way he had come. The Yukon lay a mile wide and hidden under three feet of ice. On top of this ice were as many feet of snow. It was all pure white, rolling in gentle undulations where the ice jams of the freeze-up had formed. North and south, as far as his eye could see, it was unbroken white, save for a dark hairline that curved and twisted from around the spruce-covered island to the south, and that curved and twisted away into the north, where it disappeared behind another spruce-covered island. This dark hairline was the trail—the main trail—that led south five hundred miles to the Chilcoot Pass, Dyea, and salt water; and that led north seventy miles to Dawson, and still on to the north a thousand miles to Nulato, and finally to St. Michael, on the Bering Sea, a thousand miles and a half a thousand more.

But all this—the mysterious, far reaching hairline trail, the absence of sun from the sky, the tremendous cold, and the strangeness and weirdness of it all—made no impression on the man. It was not because he was long used to it. He was a newcomer in the land, a *chechaquo,* and this was his first winter. The trouble with him was that he was without imagination. He was quick and alert in the things of life, but only in the things, and not in the significances. Fifty degrees below zero

---

1. **Yukon**, a territory of NW Canada, east of Alaska; also a river flowing through this territory.

meant eighty-odd degrees of frost. Such fact impressed him as being cold and uncomfortable, and that was all. It did not lead him to meditate upon his frailty as a creature of temperature, and upon man's frailty in general, able only to live within certain narrow limits of heat and cold; and from there on it did not lead him to the conjectural field of immortality and man's place in the universe. Fifty degrees below zero stood for a bite of frost that hurt and that must be guarded against by the use of mittens, ear flaps, warm moccasins, and thick socks. Fifty degrees below zero was to him just precisely fifty degrees below zero. That there should be anything more to it than that was a thought that never entered his head.

As he turned to go on, he spat speculatively. There was a sharp explosive crackle that startled him. He spat again. And again, in the air, before it could fall to the snow, the spittle crackled. He knew that at fifty below spittle crackled on the snow, but this spittle had crackled in the air. Undoubtedly it was colder than fifty below—how much colder he did not know. But the temperature did not matter. He was bound for the old claim on the left fork of Henderson Creek, where the boys were already. They had come over across the divide from the Indian Creek country, while he had come the roundabout way to take a look at the possibilities of getting out logs in the spring from the islands in the Yukon. He would be in to camp by six o'clock; a bit after dark, it was true, but the boys would be there, a fire would be going, and a hot supper would be ready. As for lunch, he pressed his hand against the protruding bundle under his jacket. It was also under his shirt, wrapped up

in a handkerchief and lying against the naked skin. It was the only way to keep the biscuits from freezing. He smiled agreeably to himself as he thought of those biscuits, each cut open and sopped in bacon grease, and each enclosing a generous slice of fried bacon.

He plunged in among the big spruce trees. The trail was faint. A foot of snow had fallen since the last sled had passed over, and he was glad he was without a sled, travelling light. In fact, he carried nothing but the lunch wrapped in the handkerchief. He was surprised, however, at the cold. It certainly was cold, he concluded, as he rubbed his numb nose and cheekbones with his mittened hand. He was a warm-whiskered man, but the hair on his face did not protect the high cheekbones and the eager nose that thrust itself aggressively into the frosty air.

At the man's heels trotted a dog, a big native husky, the proper wolf dog, graycoated and without any visible or temperamental difference from its brother, the wild wolf. The animal was depressed by the tremendous cold. It knew that it was no time for travelling. Its instinct told it a truer tale than was told to the man by the man's judgment. In reality, it was not merely colder than fifty below zero; it was colder than sixty below, than seventy below. It was seventy-five below zero. Since the freezing point is thirty-two above zero, it meant that one hundred and seven degrees of frost obtained. The dog did not know anything about thermometers. Possibly in its brain there was no sharp consciousness of a condition of very cold such as was in the man's brain. But the brute had its instinct. It experienced a vague but menacing apprehension that subdued it and made it

Canadian Rockies, 1967, REUBEN TAM. "A Thing of Beauty," the Gallery at Waiohai, Kauai, Hawaii.

slink along at the man's heels, and that made it question eagerly every unwonted movement of the man as if expecting him to go into camp or to seek shelter somewhere and build a fire. The dog had learned fire, and it wanted fire, or else to burrow under the snow and cuddle its warmth away from the air.

The frozen moisture of its breathing had settled on its fur in a fine powder of frost, and especially were its jowls, muzzle, and eyelashes whitened by its crystalled breath. The man's red beard and mustache were likewise frosted, but more solidly, the deposit taking the form of ice and increasing with every warm, moist breath he exhaled. Also, the man was chewing tobacco, and the muzzle of ice held his lips so rigidly that he was unable to clear his chin when he expelled the juice. The result was that a crystal beard of the color and solidity of amber was increasing its length on his chin. If he fell down it would shatter itself, like glass, into brittle fragments. But he did not mind the appendage. It was the penalty all tobacco chewers paid in that country, and he had been out before in two cold snaps. They had not been so cold as this, he knew, but by the spirit thermometer at Sixty Mile he knew they had been registered at fifty below and at fifty-five.

He held on through the level stretch of woods for several miles, crossed a wide flat, and dropped down a bank to the frozen bed of a small stream. This was Henderson Creek, and he knew he was ten miles from the forks. He looked at his watch. It was ten o'clock. He was making four miles an hour, and he calculated that he would arrive at the forks at half-past twelve. He decided to celebrate that event by eating his lunch here.

The dog dropped in again at his heels, with a tail drooping discouragement, as the man swung along the creek bed. The furrow of the old sled trail was plainly visible, but a dozen inches of snow covered the marks of the last runners. In a month no man had come up or down that silent creek. The man held steadily on. He was not much given to thinking, and just then particularly he had nothing to think about save that he would eat lunch at the forks and that at six o'clock he would be in camp with the boys. There was nobody to talk to; and, had there been, speech would have been impossible because of the ice muzzle on his mouth. So he continued monotonously to chew tobacco and to increase the length of his amber beard.

Once in a while the thought reiterated itself that it was very cold and that he had never experienced such cold. As he walked along he rubbed his cheekbones and nose with the back of his mittened hand. He did this automatically, now and again changing hands. But, rub as he would, the instant he stopped his cheekbones went numb, and the following instant the end of his nose went numb. He was

sure to frost his cheeks; he knew that, and experienced a pang of regret that he had not devised a nose strap of the sort Bud wore in cold snaps. Such a strap passed across the cheeks, as well, and saved them. But it didn't matter much, after all. What were frosted cheeks? A bit painful, that was all; they were never serious.

Empty as the man's mind was of thoughts, he was keenly observant, and he noticed the changes in the creek, the curves and bends and timber jams, and always he sharply noted where he placed his feet. Once, coming around a bend, he shied abruptly, like a startled horse, curved away from the place where he had been walking, and retreated several paces back along the trail. The creek he knew was frozen clear to the bottom—no creek could contain water in that arctic winter—but he knew also that there were springs that bubbled out from the hillsides and ran along under the snow and on top the ice of the creek. He knew that the coldest snaps never froze these springs, and he knew likewise their danger. They were traps. They hid pools of water under the snow that might be three inches deep, or three feet. Sometimes a skin of ice half an inch thick covered them, and in turn was covered by the snow. Sometimes there were alternate layers of water and ice skin, so that when one broke through he kept on breaking through for a while, sometimes wetting himself to the waist.

That was why he had shied in such panic. He had felt the give under his feet and heard the crackle of a snow-hidden ice skin. And to get his feet wet in such a temperature meant trouble and danger. At the very least it meant delay, for he would be forced to stop and build a fire, and under its protection to bare his feet while he dried his socks and moccasins. He stood and studied the creek bed and its banks, and decided that the flow of water came from the right. He reflected awhile, rubbing his nose and cheeks, then skirted to the left, stepping gingerly and testing the footing for each step. Once clear of the danger, he took a fresh chew of tobacco and swung along at his four-mile gait.

In the course of the next two hours he came upon several similar traps. Usually the snow above the hidden pools had a sunken, candied appearance that advertised the danger. Once again, however, he had a close call; and once, suspecting danger, he compelled the dog to go on in front. The dog did not want to go. It hung back until the man shoved it forward, and then it went quickly across the white, unbroken surface. Suddenly it broke through, floundered to one side, and got away to firmer footing. It had wet its forefeet and legs, and almost immediately the water that clung to it turned to ice. It made quick efforts to lick the ice off its legs, then dropped down in the snow and began to bite out the ice that had formed between the toes. This was a matter of instinct. To permit the ice to remain would mean sore feet. It did not know this. It merely obeyed the mysterious prompting that arose from the deep crypts of its being. But the man knew, having achieved a judgment on the subject, and he removed the mitten from his right hand and helped tear out the ice particles. He did not expose his fingers more than a minute, and was astonished at the swift numbness that smote them. It certainly was cold. He pulled on the mitten hastily, and beat the hand savagely across his chest.

At twelve o'clock the day was at its brightest. Yet the sun was too far south on its winter journey to clear the horizon. The bulge of the earth intervened between it and Henderson Creek, where the man walked under a clear sky at noon and cast no shadow. At half-past twelve, to the minute, he arrived at the forks of the creek. He was pleased at the speed he had made. If he kept it up, he would certainly be with the boys by six. He unbuttoned his jacket and shirt and drew forth his lunch. The action consumed no more than a quarter of a minute, yet in that brief moment the numbness laid hold of the exposed fingers. He did not put the mitten on, but, instead, struck the fingers a dozen sharp smashes against his leg. Then he sat down on a snow-covered log to eat. The sting that followed upon the striking of his fingers against his leg ceased so quickly that he was startled. He had no chance to take a bite of biscuit. He struck the fingers repeatedly and returned them to the mitten, baring the other hand for the purpose of eating. He tried to take a mouthful, but the ice muzzle prevented. He had forgotten to build a fire and thaw out. He chuckled at his foolishness, and as he chuckled he noted the numbness creeping into the exposed fingers. Also, he noted that the stinging which had first come to his toes when he sat down was already passing away. He wondered whether the toes were warm or numb. He moved them inside the moccasins and decided that they were numb.

He pulled the mitten on hurriedly and stood up. He was a bit frightened. He stamped up and down until the stinging returned into the feet. It certainly was cold, was his thought. That man from Sulphur Creek had spoken the truth when telling how cold it sometimes got in the country. And he had laughed at him at the time! That showed one must not be too sure of things. There was no mistake about it, it *was* cold. He strode up and down, stamping his feet and threshing his arms, until reassured by the returning warmth. Then he got out matches and proceeded to make a fire. From the undergrowth, where high water of the previous spring had lodged a supply of seasoned twigs, he got his firewood. Working carefully from a small beginning, he soon had a roaring fire, over which he thawed the ice from his face and in the protection of which he ate his biscuits. For the moment the cold of space was outwitted. The dog took satisfaction in the fire, stretching out close enough for warmth and far enough away to escape being singed.

When the man had finished, he filled his pipe and took his comfortable time over a smoke. Then he pulled on his mittens, settled the ear flaps of his cap firmly about his ears, and took the creek trail up the left fork. The dog was disappointed and yearned back toward the fire. This man did not know cold. Possibly all the generations of his ancestry had been ignorant of cold, of real cold, of cold one hundred and seven degrees below freezing point. But the dog knew; all its ancestry knew, and it had inherited the knowledge. And it knew that it was not good to walk abroad in such fearful cold. It was the time to lie snug in a hole in the snow and wait for a curtain of cloud to be drawn across the face of outer space whence this cold came. On the other hand, there was no keen intimacy between the dog and the man. The one was the toil slave of the other, and the only caresses it had ever received were the caresses of the whip lash

and of harsh and menacing throat sounds that threatened the whip lash. So the dog made no effort to communicate its apprehension to the man. It was not concerned in the welfare of the man; it was for its own sake that it yearned back toward the fire. But the man whistled, and spoke to it with the sound of whip lashes, and the dog swung in at the man's heels and followed after.

The man took a chew of tobacco and proceeded to start a new amber beard. Also, his moist breath quickly powdered with white his mustache, eyebrows, and lashes. There did not seem to be so many springs on the left fork of the Henderson, and for half an hour the man saw no signs of any. And then it happened. At a place where there were no signs, where the soft, unbroken snow seemed to advertise solidity beneath, the man broke through. It was not deep. He wet himself halfway to the knees before he floundered out to the firm crust.

He was angry, and cursed his luck aloud. He had hoped to get into camp with the boys at six o'clock, and this would delay him an hour, for he would have to build a fire and dry out his footgear. This was imperative at that low temperature—he knew that much; and he turned aside to the bank, which he climbed. On top, tangled in the underbrush about the trunks of several small spruce trees, was a high-water deposit of dry firewood— sticks and twigs, principally, but also larger portions of seasoned branches and fine, dry, last year's grasses. He threw down several large pieces on top of the snow. This served for a foundation and prevented the young flame from drowning itself in the snow it otherwise would melt. The flame he got by touching a match to a small shred of birch bark that he took from his pocket. This burned even more readily than paper. Placing it on the foundation, he fed the young flame with wisps of dry grass and dry twigs.

He worked slowly and carefully, keenly aware of his danger. Gradually, as the flame grew stronger, he increased the size of the twigs with which he fed it. He squatted in the snow, pulling the twigs out from their entanglement in the brush and feeding directly to the flame. He knew there must be no failure. When it is seventy-five below zero, a man must not fail in his first attempt to build a fire—that is, if his feet are wet. If his feet are dry, and he fails, he can run along the trail for half a mile and restore his circulation. But the circulation of wet and freezing feet cannot be restored by running when it is seventy-five below. No matter how fast he runs, the wet feet will freeze the harder.

All this the man knew. The old-timer on Sulphur Creek had told him about it the previous fall, and now he was appreciating the advice. Already all sensation had gone out of his feet. To build the fire he had been forced to remove his mittens, and the fingers had quickly gone numb. His pace of four miles an hour had kept his heart pumping blood to the surface of his body and to all the extremities. But the instant he stopped, the action of the pump eased down. The cold of space smote the unprotected tip of the planet, and he, being on that unprotected tip, received the full force of the blow. The blood of his body recoiled before it. The blood was alive, like the dog, and like the dog it wanted to hide away and cover itself up from the fearful cold. So long as he walked four miles an hour, he pumped that blood, willy-nilly, to the surface; but now it ebbed away and sank down into the recesses of his body. The extremities were the first to feel its absence. His wet feet froze the faster, and his exposed fingers numbed the faster, though they had not yet begun to freeze. Nose and cheeks were already freezing, while the skin of all his body chilled as it lost its blood.

But he was safe. Toes and nose and cheeks would be only touched by the frost, for the fire was beginning to burn with strength. He was feeding it with twigs the size of his finger. In another minute he would be able to feed it with branches the size of his wrist, and then he could remove his wet footgear, and, while it dried, he could keep his naked feet warm by the fire, rubbing them at first, of course, with snow. The fire was a success. He was safe. He remembered the advice of the old-timer on Sulphur Creek, and smiled. The old-timer had been very serious in laying down the law that no man must travel alone in the Klondike after fifty below. Well, here he was; he had had the accident; he was alone; and he had saved himself. Those old-timers were rather womanish, some of them, he thought. All a man had to do was to keep his head, and he was all right. Any man who was a man could travel alone. But it was surprising, the rapidity with which his cheeks and nose were freezing. And he had not thought his fingers could go lifeless in so short a time. Lifeless they were, for he could scarcely make them move together to grip a twig, and they seemed remote from his body and from him. When he touched a twig, he had to look and see whether or not he had hold of it. The wires were pretty well down between him and his finger ends.

All of which counted for little. There was the fire, snapping and crackling and promising life with every dancing flame. He started to untie his moccasins. They were coated with ice; the thick German socks were like sheaths of iron halfway to the knees; and the moccasin strings were like rods of steel all twisted and knotted as by some conflagration. For a moment he tugged with his numb fingers, then, realizing the folly of it, he drew his sheath knife.

But before he could cut the strings, it happened. It was his own fault or, rather, his mistake. He should not have built the fire under the spruce tree. He should have built it in the open. But it had been easier to pull the twigs from the brush and drop them directly on the fire. Now the tree under which he had done this carried a weight of snow on its boughs. No wind had blown for weeks, and each bough was fully freighted. Each time he had pulled a twig he had communicated a slight agitation to the tree—an imperceptible agitation, so far as he was concerned, but an agitation sufficient to bring about the disaster. High up in the tree one bough capsized its load of snow. This fell on the boughs beneath, capsizing them. This process continued, spreading out and involving the whole tree. It grew like an avalanche, and it descended without warning upon the man and the fire, and the fire was blotted out! Where it had burned was a mantle of fresh and disordered snow.

The man was shocked. It was as though he had just heard his own sentence of death. For a moment he sat and stared at the spot where the fire had been. Then he grew very calm. Perhaps the old-timer on Sulphur Creek was right. If he had only had a trail mate he would have been in no danger now. The trail mate could have built the fire. Well, it was up to him to build the fire over again, and this second time there must be no failure. Even if he succeeded, he would most likely lose some toes. His feet must be badly frozen by now, and there would be some time before the second fire was ready.

Such were his thoughts, but he did not sit and think them. He was busy all the time they were passing through his mind. He made a new foundation for a fire, this time in the open, where no treacherous tree could blot it out. Next he gathered dry grasses and tiny twigs from the high-water flotsam. He could not bring his fingers together to pull them out, but he was able to gather them by the handful. In this way he got many rotten twigs and bits of green moss that were undesirable, but it was the best he could do. He worked methodically, even collecting an armful of the larger branches to be used later when the fire gathered strength. And all the while the dog sat and watched him, a certain yearning wistfulness in its eyes, for it looked upon him as the fire provider, and the fire was slow in coming.

When all was ready, the man reached in his pocket for a second piece of birch bark. He knew the bark was there, and, though he could not feel it with his fingers, he could hear its crisp rustling as he fumbled for it. Try as he would, he could not clutch hold of it. And all the time, in his consciousness, was the knowledge that each instant his feet were freezing. This thought tended to put him in a panic, but he fought against it and kept calm. He pulled on his mittens with his teeth, and threshed his arms back and forth, beating his hands with all his might against his sides. He did this sitting down, and he stood up to do it; and all the while the dog sat in the snow, its wolf brush of a tail curled around warmly over its forefeet, its sharp wolf ears pricked forward intently as it watched the man. And the man, as he threshed with his arms and hands, felt a surge of envy as he regarded the creature that was warm and secure in its natural covering.

After a time he was aware of the first far-away signals of sensation in his beaten fingers. The faint tingling grew stronger till it evolved into a stinging ache that was excruciating, but which the man hailed with satisfaction. He stripped the mitten from his right hand and fetched forth the birch bark. The exposed fingers were quickly going numb again. Next he brought out his bunch of sulphur matches. But the tremendous cold had already driven the life out of his fingers. In his effort to separate one match from the others, the whole bunch fell in the snow. He tried to pick it out of the snow, but failed. The dead fingers could neither touch nor clutch. He was very careful. He drove the thought of his freezing feet, and nose, and cheeks, out of his mind, devoting his whole soul to the matches. He watched, using the sense of vision in place of that of touch, and when he saw his fingers on each side of the bunch, he closed them—that is, he willed to close them, for the wires were down, and the fingers did not obey. He pulled the mitten on the right hand, and beat it fiercely against his knee. Then, with both mittened hands, he scooped the bunch of matches, along with much snow, into his lap. Yet he was no better off.

After some manipulation he managed to get the bunch between the heels of his mittened

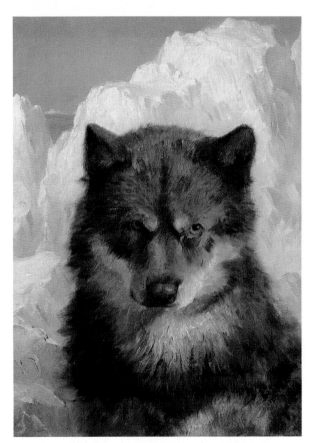

Ossisuak, about 1861, FREDERIC EDWIN CHURCH. Private collection.

hands. In this fashion he carried it to his mouth. The ice crackled and snapped when by a violent effort he opened his mouth. He drew the lower jaw in, curled the upper lip out of the way, and scraped the bunch with his upper teeth in order to separate a match. He succeeded in getting one, which he dropped on his lap. He was no better off. He could not pick it up. Then he devised a way. He picked it up in his teeth and scratched it on his leg. Twenty times he scratched before he succeeded in lighting it. As it flamed he held it with his teeth to the birch bark. But the burning brimstone went up his nostrils and into his lungs, causing him to cough spasmodically. The match fell into the snow and went out.

The old-timer on Sulphur Creek was right, he thought in the moment of controlled despair that ensued: after fifty below, a man should travel with a partner. He beat his hands, but failed in exciting any sensation. Suddenly he bared both hands, removing the mittens with his teeth. He caught the whole bunch between the heels of his hands. His arm muscles not being frozen enabled him to press the hand heels tightly against the matches. Then he scratched the bunch along his leg. It flared into flame, seventy sulphur matches at once! There was no wind to blow them out. He kept his head to one side to escape the strangling fumes, and held the blazing bunch to the birch bark. As he so held it, he became aware of sensation in his hand. His flesh was burning. He could smell it. Deep down below the surface he could feel it. The sensation developed into pain that grew acute. And still he endured it, holding the flame of the matches clumsily to the bark that would not light readily because his own burning hands were in the way, absorbing most of the flame.

At last, when he could endure no more, he jerked his hands apart. The blazing matches fell sizzling into the snow, but the birch bark was alight. He began laying dry grasses and the tiniest twigs on the flame. He could not pick and choose, for he had to lift the fuel between the heels of his hands. Small pieces of rotten wood and green moss clung to the twigs, and he bit them off as well as he could with his teeth. He cherished the flame carefully and awkwardly. It meant life, and it must not perish. The withdrawal of blood from the surface of his body now made him begin to shiver, and he grew more awkward. A large piece of green moss fell squarely on the little fire. He tried to poke it out with his fingers, but his shivering frame made him poke too far, and he disrupted the nucleus of the little fire, the burning grasses and tiny twigs separating and scattering. He tried to poke them together again, but in spite of the tenseness of the effort, his shivering got away with him, and the twigs were hopelessly scattered. Each twig gushed a puff of smoke and went out. The fire provider had failed. As he looked apathetically about him, his eyes chanced on the dog, sitting across the ruins of the fire from him, in the snow, making restless, hunching movements, slightly lifting one forefoot and then the other, shifting its weight back and forth on them with wistful eagerness.

The sight of the dog put a wild idea into his head. He remembered the tale of the man, caught in a blizzard, who killed a steer and crawled inside the carcass, and so was saved. He would kill the dog and bury his hands in the warm body until the numbness went out of them. Then he could build another fire. He spoke to the dog, calling it to him; but in his voice was a strange note of fear that frightened the animal, who had never known the man to speak in such way before. Something was the matter, and its suspicious nature sensed danger—it knew not what danger, but somewhere, somehow, in its brain arose an apprehension of the man. It flattened its ears down at the sound of the man's voice, and its restless, hunching movements and the liftings and shiftings of its forefeet became more pronounced; but it would not come to the man. He got on his hands and knees and crawled toward the dog. This unusual posture again excited suspicion, and the animal sidled mincingly away.

The man sat up in the snow for a moment and struggled for calmness. Then he pulled on his mittens, by means of his teeth, and got upon his feet. He glanced down at first in order to assure himself that he was really standing up, for the absence of sensation in his feet left him unrelated to the earth. His erect position in itself started to drive the webs of suspicion from the dog's mind; and when he spoke peremptorily, with the sound of whip lashes in his voice, the dog rendered its customary allegiance and came to him. As it came within reaching distance, the man lost his control. His arms flashed out to the dog, and he experienced genuine surprise when he discovered that his hands could not clutch, that there was neither bend nor feeling in the fingers. He had forgotten for the moment that they were frozen and that they were freezing more and more. All this happened quickly, and before the animal could get away, he encircled its body with his arms. He sat down in the snow, and in this fashion held the dog, while it snarled and whined and struggled.

But it was all he could do, hold its body encircled in his arms and sit there. He realized that he could not kill the dog. There was no way to do it. With his helpless hands he could neither draw nor hold his sheath knife nor throttle the animal. He released it, and it plunged wildly away, with tail between its legs, and still snarling. It halted forty feet away and surveyed him curiously, with ears sharply pricked forward.

The man looked down at his hands in order to locate them, and found them hanging on the ends of his arms. It struck him as curious that one should have to use his eyes in order to find out where his hands were. He began threshing his arms back and forth, beating the mittened hands against his sides. He did this for five minutes, violently, and his heart pumped enough blood up to the surface to put a stop to his shivering. But no sensation was aroused in the hands. He had an impression that they hung like weights on the ends of his arms, but when he tried to run the impression down, he could not find it.

A certain fear of death, dull and oppressive, came to him. This fear quickly became poignant as he realized that it was no longer a mere matter of freezing his fingers and toes, or of losing his hands and feet, but that it was a matter of life and death with the chances against him. This threw him into a panic, and he turned and ran up the creek bed along the old, dim trail. The dog joined in behind and kept up with him. He ran blindly, without intention, in fear such as he had never known in his life. Slowly, as he plowed and floundered through the snow, he began to see things again—the banks of the creek, the old timber jams, the leafless aspens, and the sky. The running made him feel better. He did not shiver. Maybe, if he ran on, his feet would thaw out; and anyway, if he ran far enough, he would reach camp and the boys. Without doubt he would lose some fingers and toes and some of his face; but the boys would take care of him, and save the rest of him when he got there. And at the same time there was another thought in his mind that said he would never get to the camp and the boys; that it was too many miles away, that the freezing had too great a start on him, and that he would soon be stiff and dead. This thought he kept in the background and refused to consider. Sometimes it pushed itself forward and demanded to be heard, but he thrust it back and strove to think of other things.

It struck him as curious that he could run at all on feet so frozen that he could not feel them when they struck the earth and took the weight of his body. He seemed to skim along above the surface, and to have no connection with the earth. Somewhere he had seen a winged Mercury, and he wondered if Mercury felt as he felt when skimming over the earth.

His theory of running until he reached camp and the boys had one flaw in it: he lacked the endurance. Several times he stumbled, and finally he tottered, crumpled up, and fell. When he tried to rise, he failed. He must sit and rest, he decided, and next time he would merely walk and keep on going. As he sat and regained his breath, he noted that he was feeling quite warm and comfortable. He was not shivering, and it even seemed that a warm glow had come to his chest and trunk. And yet, when he touched his nose or cheeks, there was no sensation. Running would not thaw them out. Nor would it thaw out his hands and feet. Then the thought came to him that the frozen portions of his body must be extending. He tried to keep this thought down, to forget it, to think of something else; he was aware of the panicky feeling that it caused, and he was afraid of the panic. But the thought asserted itself, and persisted, until it produced a vision of his body totally frozen. This was too much, and he made another wild run along the trail. Once he slowed down to a walk, but the thought of the freezing extending itself made him run again.

And all the time the dog ran with him, at his heels. When he fell down a second time, it curled its tail over its forefeet and sat in front of him, facing him, curiously eager and intent. The warmth and security of the animal angered him, and he cursed it till it flattened down its ears appeasingly. This time the shivering came more quickly upon the man. He was losing in his battle with the frost. It was creeping into his body from all sides. The thought of it drove him on, but he ran no more than a hundred feet, when he staggered and pitched headlong. It was his last panic. When he had recovered his breath and control, he sat up and entertained in his mind the conception of meeting death with dignity. However, the conception did not come to him in such terms. His idea of it was that he had been making a fool of himself, running around like a chicken with its head cut off—such was the simile that occurred to him. Well, he was bound to freeze anyway, and he might as well take it decently. With this new-found peace of mind came the first glimmerings of drowsiness. A good idea, he thought, to sleep off to death. It was like taking an anesthetic. Freezing was not so bad as people thought. There were lots worse ways to die.

He pictured the boys finding his body the next day. Suddenly he found himself with them, coming along the trail and looking for himself. And, still with them, he came around a turn in the trail and found himself lying in the snow. He did not belong with himself any more, for even then he was out of himself, standing with the boys and looking at himself in the snow. It certainly was cold, was his thought. When he got back to the States he could tell the folks what real cold was. He drifted on from this to a vision of the old-timer on Sulphur Creek. He could see him quite clearly, warm and comfortable, and smoking a pipe.

"You were right, old hoss; you were right," the man mumbled to the old-timer of Sulphur Creek.

Then the man drowsed off into what seemed to him the most comfortable and satisfying sleep he had ever known. The dog sat facing him and waiting. The brief day drew to a close in a long, slow twilight. There were no signs of a fire to be made, and besides, never in the dog's experience had it known a man to sit like that in the snow and make no fire. As the twilight drew on, its eager yearning for the fire mastered it, and with a great lifting and shifting of forefeet, it whined softly, then flattened its ears down in anticipation of being chidden by the man. But the man remained silent. Later the dog whined loudly. And still later it crept close to the man and caught the scent of death. This made the animal bristle and back away. A little longer it delayed, howling under the stars that leaped and danced and shone brightly in the cold sky. Then it turned and trotted up the trail in the direction of the camp it knew, where were the other food providers and fire providers.

Developing Comprehension Skills

1. In the beginning of the story, the man is described as "quick and alert in the things of life, but only in the things and not the significances." What does this mean? How does his inability to understand "significances" affect what happens to him?

2. Early in the journey, how does the man think about the cold? How does his attitude toward the cold change as his journey continues?

3. What are the "traps" the man must look out for? Why does he build a fire? Why is he forced to build a second one?

4. Describe the man's relationship with the dog. Do you think the man could have survived if this relationship had been different? Explain your answer.

5. What advice did the man receive from the old-timer on Sulphur Creek? How does his attitude toward this advice change as the story progresses?

6. With what attitude does the man finally face death? Does this attitude surprise you? Explain your answer.

Reading Literature

1. **Making Inferences About Character.** Character can be revealed through the thoughts and actions of a person. What can you learn about the man in "To Build a Fire" from his thoughts and actions? What facts lead you to the conclusions you made?

2. **Appreciating Setting.** Setting can be used to help an author develop the action and events of the story. The setting of "To Build a

Fire" is important to the plot. What is this setting? What are the most important aspects of this setting? Why are they crucial to the story?

3. **Recognizing Foreshadowing.** Hints or clues that prepare the reader for events that will occur later in the story are called **fore-shadowing**. Jack London provides several clues to indicate what will happen to the main character in his story.

   Point out at least three examples of foreshadowing in "To Build a Fire." For example, how does the description of daybreak in the first paragraph foreshadow later events?

4. **Appreciating Suspense.** The reader of "To Build a Fire" feels tension and excitement as he or she becomes involved in the story. The reader is anxious to know if the man will survive. How does Jack London delay the answer to this question? What passages are especially suspenseful?

Developing Vocabulary Skills

Finding Meaning from Word Parts and Context Clues. The following sentences come from "To Build a Fire." Use your knowledge of word parts and context clues to decide on the meaning of each underlined word. Write the meaning of the word. Then tell whether you used context clues, word parts, or both to determine meaning.

1. He was a newcomer in the land, a chechaquo, and this was his first winter.

2. As he turned to go, he spat speculatively.

3. So he continued monotonously to chew tobacco and to increase the length of his amber beard.

4. Its instinct told it a truer tale than was told to the man by the man's judgment.

5. The one was the toil slave of the other, and the only caresses it had ever received were the caresses of the whip lash and of harsh and menacing throat sounds that threatened the whip lash.

6. The blood of his body recoiled before it. The blood was alive, like the dog, and like the dog it wanted to hide away and cover itself up from the fearful cold.

7. After some manipulation he managed to get the bunch between the heels of his mittened hands.

8. Once in a while the thought reiterated itself that it was very cold and that he had never experienced such cold.

9. Once, coming around a bend, he shied abruptly, like a startled horse . . . .

10. The extremities were the first to feel its absence.

Developing Writing Skills

1. **Evaluating Conflicts.** The main character in "To Build a Fire" experiences several conflicts. These conflicts are both internal and external. **Internal conflicts** are struggles within the character. **External conflicts**, on the other hand, are struggles between characters or between a character and some force in nature.

   Write a composition in which you describe the conflicts that exist for the main character in London's story.

   Pre-Writing. Make a list of the various conflicts that the man experiences. Which are internal? Which are external? Jot down details related to each. How does the man deal with each conflict? Make notes on this also. Choose a way of organizing your notes. You may wish to describe minor conflicts first and then build to the major conflict in the story.

Writing. Write an introductory paragraph that captures your reader's interest and tells what your composition is about. Then, begin describing the various conflicts in the story. As you describe each, use passages and evidence from the story to give support to your writing. Be sure you tell how the man deals with each conflict also. Use transitional words and phrases as you move from one conflict to the next.

Revising. Reread your paper. Check to see that your paragraphs contain specific conflicts. Is each conflict summarized clearly? Are these supported with passages and evidence from the story? Did you tell how the conflict was dealt with?

2. **Describing a Conflict.** The main character in "To Build a Fire" must struggle with the forces of nature. He does not survive. In a few paragraphs, describe a struggle that you, or someone you know, had with some force in nature. Provide vivid descriptions. In addition, tell about the feelings your main character experienced during the conflict. How did this person survive the conflict?

Developing Skills in Study and Research

Using Biographical References. Your library contains several reference books that are excellent sources for finding information about the lives of famous Americans, both living and dead. Some of the most popular sources are *Webster's Biographical Dictionary*, the *Dictionary of American Biography*, and *Current Biography*. Consider which of these works would be best for finding information about the life of Jack London. Locate the book in your library. Then take notes on the following points:

1. Describe London's education.
2. List some jobs he held.
3. List some places he traveled.
4. List two of his most famous works.

Chapter 6 *R*eview

Using Your Skills in Reading Literature

Read this paragraph from Mark Twain's frontier tale "The Celebrated Jumping Frog of Calaveras County." In it, Simon Wheeler tells a long story about Jim Smiley, who loved to bet. Read the paragraph carefully and answer the questions that follow.

> Well, thish-yer Smiley had rat terriers, and chicken cocks, and tomcats and all them kind of things, till you couldn't rest, and you couldn't fetch nothing for him to bet on but he'd match you. He ketched a frog one day, and took him home, and said he calk'lated to edercate him; and so he never done nothing for three months but set in his back yard and learn that frog to jump.

1. How does Twain make the story realistic in its use of language?
2. What can you infer about Simon Wheeler? about Jim Smiley?
3. What is the tone of Wheeler's story?

Using Your Comprehension Skills

Explain the following figurative language from Chapter Seven. Tell why you think the writer used figurative rather than literal language: for description, to convey feeling, or to emphasize an idea.

1. An October wind vanished among the moaning trees.
2. Janet's and Robert's and Tom's faces were pink, now blue, now white with fountains of soft fire.
3. An old lady cleared her throat like a sheep bleating.
4. Along the highway the cars of the migrant people crawled out like bugs.

Using Your Vocabulary Skills

The following sentences are from Chapter Seven. Use your knowledge of word parts to explain the meaning of the underlined words.

1. The woman stood looking at him with a <u>mistrustful</u> eye.

2. . . . and the neat, the <u>unbelievably</u> trim lines of the house itself. . . .

3. For ten seconds let us regard with discreet scrutiny some <u>inconsequential</u> object in the other direction.

4. Jim stopped inside the door, as <u>immovable</u> as a setter at the scent of quail.

5. Linda Stewart's parents would have gone <u>unsuspectingly</u> ahead with their lives, ...

6. The <u>fogginess</u> seemed to rise in her throat again.

Using Your Writing Skills

Choose one of the writing assignments below.

1. The literature of this period moved away from Romanticism and toward realism. Choose a selection from this chapter that you find extremely realistic. Discuss how this realism is achieved.

2. Write a letter to one of the authors in this chapter. Respond to the writer's ideas, and discuss your own ideas on the subject.

Using Your Skills in Critical Thinking

Several selections in this chapter were influenced by the Civil War or the Native American struggle. Identify these selections. Then draw conclusions about each author's opinion of the conflict. List specific judgment words, emotional appeals, or descriptive details that help to reveal the writer's opinion.

CHAPTER SEVEN

Twentieth Century Fiction

OPTIONS FOR RESPONDING

Activity Ideas

As you read:
- In a reading log, write quotations that reveal the qualities of the main characters; record your responses to these quotations as well.
- Identify the most dramatic event in each story, and write a newspaper headline.
- Record the actions of the characters on a calendar or in an appointment book.
- Graph your emotional response as you read each story.
- List questions you might ask a character in an interview.

After you read:
- Write a script for a scene that takes place after the ending of a story.
- For each main character, fill out a chart with the following categories: dog, car, music, hobby, sport, TV show, comic strip.
- Imagine that you are an editor who must cut one story from this chapter; argue for your choice orally or in writing.
- In overlapping circles show two characters' similarities and differences.
- Create montages that capture the settings of the stories.
- Seat ten characters at five tables of two, and then choose one pair and either write a dialogue or perform a dialogue with a partner.

City Street, 1955, DAVID PARK. Sheldon Memorial Art Gallery, University of Nebraska, Howard S. Wilson Memorial Collection, Lincoln.

Wars and Economic Depression

The industrial expansion that began in the late 1800's continued into the twentieth century. As America's industrial power grew, so did its military strength and its influence in world affairs. This eventually led to the United States' involvement in World War I. The two million American soldiers who fought in the war helped to ensure victory for the Allies in 1918.

Great changes took place in the decade following World War I. During this era, often called the *Roaring Twenties*, the American economy experienced spectacular growth. The good times did not last long, however. The stock market crashed in 1929, leading to the Great Depression of the 1930's.

The United States entered World War II in 1941 after the Japanese bombed Pearl Harbor. As in World War I, America played a key role in the Allied victory. The atomic bombs that the United States dropped on Japan in 1945 finally ended the war. They also ushered in the nuclear age.

1900	1910	1920	1930	1940

Literature

■ **1913** Robert Frost publishes first volume of poetry

■ **1914** Carl Sandburg publishes poem "Chicago"

■ **1916** Eugene O'Neill has his first play staged by Provincetown Players

■ **1926** Langston Hughes publishes first book of poems

■ **1926** Ernest Hemingway publishes *The Sun Also Rises*

■ **1929** William Faulkner publishes *The Sound and the Fury*

■ **1930** Katherine Anne Porter publishes *Flowering Judas*

■ **1939** John Steinbeck publishes *The Grapes of Wrath*

■ **1941** Eudora Welty publishes first collection of stories

1945 Richard Wright publishes *Black Boy* ■

History

■ **1901** McKinley assassinated; Theodore Roosevelt becomes President

■ **1917** U.S. enters World War I

1920 19th Amendment grants women the right to vote ■

■ **1929** Stock market crashes, beginning the Great Depression

■ **1932** Franklin Delano Roosevelt is elected President

1941 U.S. enters World War II ■

1945 U.S. drops two atomic bombs on ■ Japan, ending World War II

1945 United Nations is organized ■

Post War America

The years following World War II were a period of increased prosperity for most Americans. There were dark spots, however. From 1950 to 1953, the United States was involved in the Korean War. Back at home, there were different kinds of conflicts. The problem of racial discrimination led to the civil rights movement of the 1950's and 60's. Under the leadership of such reformers as Dr. Martin Luther King, Jr., much progress was made in ensuring equal rights for all Americans.

The 1960's also were marked by political assassinations and protests. President John F. Kennedy was felled by an assassin's bullets in 1963. Dr. King and presidential hopeful Robert Kennedy both were assassinated in 1968. The Vietnam War divided the country.

The 1970's were an era of political scandals. The Watergate scandal resulted in the resignation of President Richard Nixon in 1974. Two years later, the nation celebrated its 200th birthday. This event marked the beginning of a time of healing.

A Time of Growth and Change

The twentieth century has been a period of rapid growth and change for the United States. The population has grown from about 76 million in 1900 to over 226 million today. The country has changed from a rural to an urban nation. Advances in science, technology, and medicine have opened whole new worlds. Women and minorities have gained more rights. Not surprisingly, much of the literature of the twentieth century reflects the excitement and anxieties of modern life. It shows American writers at their finest—shining with imagination, wit, social concern, and emotion.

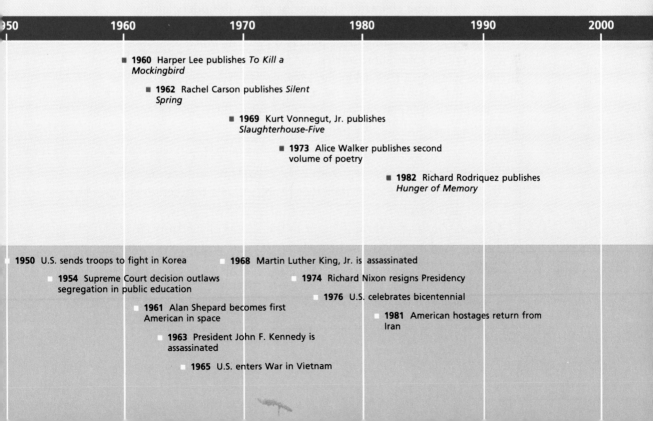

950   1960   1970   1980   1990   2000

- **1960** Harper Lee publishes *To Kill a Mockingbird*
- **1962** Rachel Carson publishes *Silent Spring*
- **1969** Kurt Vonnegut, Jr. publishes *Slaughterhouse-Five*
- **1973** Alice Walker publishes second volume of poetry
- **1982** Richard Rodriquez publishes *Hunger of Memory*

- **1950** U.S. sends troops to fight in Korea
- **1954** Supreme Court decision outlaws segregation in public education
- **1961** Alan Shepard becomes first American in space
- **1963** President John F. Kennedy is assassinated
- **1965** U.S. enters War in Vietnam
- **1968** Martin Luther King, Jr. is assassinated
- **1974** Richard Nixon resigns Presidency
- **1976** U.S. celebrates bicentennial
- **1981** American hostages return from Iran

Reading Literature

Short Stories

A **short story** is a work of fiction short enough to be read at one sitting. In most short stories, the writer focuses on only a few characters and one important event or set of events.

Major Elements of the Short Story

The major elements in a short story are characters, setting, and plot.

Characters. The characters in a short story are the people or animals who take part in the action. The **major characters** are the most important characters in the story. The other characters are called **minor characters.** Short story writers communicate information about characters by describing their actions, appearance, thoughts, or words. A character may be static or dynamic. A **static** character does not change over the course of a story. A **dynamic** character changes, or grows in understanding.

Setting. The **setting** is the time and place in which the action of the story occurs. In some short stories, the setting is a very important element. In others, it is simply the background against which the story takes place.

Plot. The **plot** is the sequence of events in a story. In many short stories, the plot follows this pattern:

> **Introduction:** The writer presents the characters and setting.
> **Rising Action:** The characters face problems as a conflict, or struggle, develops.
> **Climax:** This is the turning point in the action of the story.
> **Falling Action:** Following the climax, events follow their logical course to the end of the story.
> **Resolution:** The action of the story is completed. Any questions that remain usually are answered.

Other Elements of the Short Story

Other important elements in a short story include **point of view** and **theme.**

Point of View. A short story may be told from several points of view. In the **first-person point of view,** the narrator, or person telling the story, is a character in the story. He or she describes the action using the pronouns *I* and *we.* When the narrator is not a character in the story, the story is written from the **third-person point of view.** The third-person point of view can be either limited or omniscient.

In a story written from the **third-person limited** point of view, the narrator presents the events as they are seen or experienced by only one person. In contrast, the narrator of a story written from the **third-person omniscient** point of view knows everything that happens. This narrator also knows the thoughts and feelings of all the characters.

Theme. The **theme** of a short story is the main idea or message that the writer wishes to share with the reader. In most short stories, the theme is not stated directly. However, you usually can figure out the theme by thinking about the events in the story.

Different readers sometimes find different themes in the same story. This is not surprising, since each person brings different experiences to the story. Also, many stories have more than one theme.

How To Read a Short Story

1. Allow yourself enough time to read the story carefully.
2. Identify the narrator. Is this person a character, or is he or she relating the events from outside the story? Ask yourself how this point of view might affect the way events are presented in the story.
3. Pay close attention to details, since most short story writers choose every word and sentence carefully to create a particular effect. Is the writer trying to create a particular mood? Can you figure out the tone by studying the writer's choice of words and details?
4. After reading the story, try to figure out its main idea, or theme. Remember that some stories have more than one theme.

Comprehension Skills

Tone, Mood, and Emphasis

Reading is a process that asks you to do more than understand the writer's words and sentences. You must understand the writer's tone, or attitude. You also need to identify the mood the writer creates. Finally, you must identify the important ideas in a selection. To do this, you should be familiar with the methods a writer may use to emphasize ideas.

Tone

The writer's attitude toward a subject or a character is the **tone** of the piece. Depending on the words the writer chooses, the tone may be humorous, angry, serious, bitter, or carefree, for example. To determine the tone in a piece of writing, think carefully about the writer's choice of words. For example, what is the writer's tone in the following passage from "A Visit of Charity"? Does she seem to approve or disapprove of the characters?

> "I'm a Campfire Girl . . . . I have to pay a visit to some old lady," she told the nurse at the desk. This was a woman in a white uniform who looked as if she were cold; she had close-cut hair which stood up on the very top of her head exactly like a sea wave. Marian, the little girl, did not tell her that this visit would give her a minimum of only three points in her score.

Mood

The **mood** is the feeling you get as you read a piece of writing. For example, you may feel sad, relaxed, frightened, confused, or joyful. Sometimes the mood is the same as the tone of the writer; sometimes it is very different.

To create a mood, writers consider both the **denotations** and the **connotations** of the words they choose. That is, they consider both the dictionary definitions and the thoughts and feelings that the words bring to mind.

In addition to choosing words carefully, a writer also must select details that reinforce the mood. For example, imagine that a writer is trying to create a mood of loneliness. Which of the following phrases would help?

| a cheery fire | the loud ticking of a clock | an empty beach |
| a silent house | a pleasant hum of voices | a beautiful snowfall |

Emphasis

Writers use a variety of techniques to place emphasis, or stress, on particular ideas in a piece of writing. One of these techniques is repetition. Another technique involves using sentences of varying lengths.

Writers also emphasize certain ideas by devoting more space to them. The placement of ideas can indicate their importance as well. Another way to emphasize an idea is by choosing unusual words to describe it.

Look at the following sentence from "The Far and the Near." How does the writer emphasize the sameness of the engineer's routine?

> Every day for more than twenty years, as the train had approached this house, the engineer had blown on the whistle, and every day . . . a woman had appeared on the back porch of the little house and waved to him.

Exercise: Recognizing Tone, Mood, and Emphasis

Read the following passage. Then answer the questions that follow it.

> On the outskirts of a little town upon a rise of land that swept back from the railway there was a tidy little cottage of white boards, trimmed vividly with green blinds. To one side of the house there was a garden neatly patterned with plots of growing vegetables, and an arbor for the grapes which ripened late in August. Before the house there were three mighty oaks which sheltered it in their clean and massive shade in summer, and to the other side there was border of gay flowers. The whole place had an air of tidiness, thrift, and modest comfort.

1. Would you describe the tone as approving or as critical?
2. What is the mood of the passage?
3. Which words and details in the passage help to create this mood?
4. What techniques are used to emphasize the main idea?

$\mathcal{V}$ocabulary Skills

Inference and Word Meaning

You have learned that the context of an unfamiliar word often provides clues to its meaning. Here is a review of the clues you have studied:

Definition or Restatement: A word is defined or restated.
Synonym: A word that means the same or nearly the same as the unfamiliar word is provided in context.
Antonym: A word that means the opposite of the new word is given.
Example: An unfamiliar word or term is followed by several examples, or the unfamiliar word itself is given as an example.
Comparison: An unfamiliar word is compared to a familiar idea.
Contrast: An unfamiliar word is contrasted to a familiar idea.

Word Parts

Knowing the meanings of different word parts can also help you figure out the definitions of new words. For example:

Prefixes		Latin Roots	
retro-	backward	spect, spic	to look at
pro-	forward	ced	to go

From a knowledge of these word parts you can determine that *proceed* means "to go forward" and *retrospect* means "to look backward."

Inference

Sometimes the meaning of an unfamiliar word cannot be determined by using the methods shown above. There may not be any specific context clues or recognizable word part to provide meaning.

Despite these problems, it may still be possible for you to figure out the meaning of the unfamiliar word. You can do this by studying the entire passage in which the word appears. From the main idea of the passage, you may be able to infer, or draw a conclusion about, the meaning of the unknown word. Read the following paragraph:

> And now his own voice sounded unreal and ghastly to him as he tried to explain his presence, to tell her who he was and the reason he had come. But he *faltered* on, fighting stubbornly against the horror of regret, confusion, disbelief that surged up in his spirit . . . .

From the passage you can tell that the man is confused and upset. Therefore, you can infer that *faltered* means "hesitated."

Often, no one method of determining word meaning will give you the definition of a word. In such a case, use all three methods, if necessary, to unlock meaning. Look at the following example:

> That year our father did something so unusual that he was no longer an *inconspicuous* person in town.

The words "no longer" in this sentence signal a contrast. Therefore, *inconspicuous* somehow contrasts with the main idea of the unusual action of the father. The word parts give you the ideas of *not* (in), *with* (con), *spic* (see), and *having* (ous). From all these clues, you can infer that *inconspicuous* means "not easy to be seen or noticed" or "not readily attracting attention."

Exercise: Choosing the Best Way To Find Word Meaning

Read each of these sentences from selections you will be studying. Then write the definition of the underlined word as you understand it.

1. So now Della's long brown hair fell about her, rippling and shining like a <u>cascade</u> of brown water.
2. He was a <u>pensioned</u> servant of his company with no more work to do.
3. . . . the version of the little house . . . had become fixed in the mind of the engineer as something beautiful and <u>enduring</u>, something beyond all change and ruin.
4. He did not look like a shepherd or <u>herdsman</u>.
5. Don and Helen Crane were two of the most infatuated young parents she have ever known, she thought <u>indulgently</u>.

The Gift of the Magi

People often give and receive presents that cost a great deal. Is the most valuable gift, however, also the most expensive?

O. HENRY

One dollar and eighty-seven cents. That was all. And sixty cents of it was in pennies. Pennies saved one and two at a time by bulldozing the grocer and the vegetable man and the butcher until one's cheek burned with silent imputation of parsimony[1] that such close dealing implied. Three times Della counted it. One dollar and eighty-seven cents. And the next day would be Christmas.

There was clearly nothing to do but flop down on the shabby little couch and howl. So Della did it. Which instigates the moral reflection that life is made up of sobs, sniffles, and smiles, with sniffles predominating.

While the mistress of the home is gradually subsiding from the first stage to the second, take a look at the home. A furnished flat at eight dollars per week. It did not exactly beggar description, but it certainly had that word on the lookout for the mendicancy squad.[2]

In the vestibule below was a letter box into which no letter would go, and an electric button from which no mortal finger could coax a ring. Also appertaining thereunto was a card bearing the name "Mr. James Dillingham Young."

The "Dillingham" had been flung to the breeze during a former period of prosperity when its possessor was being paid thirty dollars per week. Now, when the income was shrunk to twenty dollars, the letters of "Dillingham" looked blurred, as though they were thinking seriously of contracting to a modest and unassuming D. But whenever Mr. James Dillingham Young came home and reached his flat above he was called "Jim" and greatly hugged by Mrs. James Dillingham Young, already introduced to you as Della. Which is all very good.

Della finished her cry and attended to her cheeks with the powder rag. She stood by the window and looked out dully at a gray cat walking a gray fence in a gray backyard. Tomorrow would be Christmas Day, and she had only one dollar and eighty-seven cents with which to buy Jim a present. She had been saving every penny she could for months, with this result. Twenty dollars a week doesn't go far. Expenses had been greater than she had calculated. They always are. Only one dollar and eighty-seven cents to buy a present for

---

1. **imputation of parsimony**, the feeling that one is being accused of stinginess.
2. **mendicancy squad**, law officers who kept the streets free of beggars.

Jim. Her Jim. Many a happy hour she had spent planning for something nice for him. Something fine and rare and sterling—something just a little bit near to being worthy of the honor of being owned by Jim.

There was a pier glass between the windows of the room. Perhaps you have seen a pier glass in an eight-dollar flat. A very thin and very agile person may, by observing his reflection in a rapid sequence of longitudinal strips, obtain a fairly accurate conception of his looks. Della, being slender, had mastered the art.

Suddenly she whirled from the window and stood before the glass. Her eyes were shining brilliantly, but her face had lost its color within twenty seconds. Rapidly she pulled down her hair and let it fall to its full length.

Now there were two possessions of the James Dillingham Youngs in which they both took a mighty pride. One was Jim's gold watch that had been his father's and his

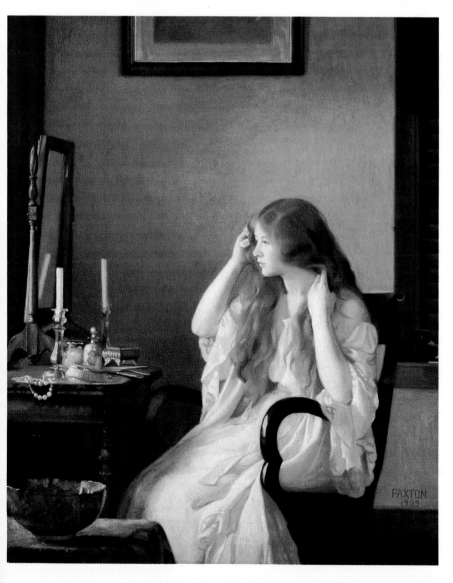

Girl Combing Her Hair, 1909,
WILLIAM McGREGOR PAXTON.
Private collection.

grandfather's. The other was Della's hair. Had the Queen of Sheba lived in the flat across the air shaft, Della would have let her hair hang out the window someday to dry, just to depreciate Her Majesty's jewels and gifts. Had King Solomon been the janitor, with all his treasures piled up in the basement, Jim would have pulled out his watch every time he passed, just to see him pluck at his beard from envy.

So now Della's beautiful hair fell about her, rippling and shining like a cascade of brown waters. It reached below her knee and made itself almost a garment for her. And then she did it up again nervously and quickly. Once she faltered for a minute and stood still while a tear or two splashed on the worn red carpet.

On went her old brown jacket; on went her old brown hat. With a whirl of skirts and with the brilliant sparkle still in her eyes, she fluttered out the door and down the stairs to the street.

Where she stopped the sign read: "Mme. Sofronie. Hair Goods of All Kinds." One flight up Della ran—and collected herself, panting. Madame, large, too white, chilly, hardly looked the "Sofronie."

"Will you buy my hair?" asked Della.

"I buy hair," said Madame. "Take yer hat off and let's have a sight at the looks of it."

Down rippled the brown cascade.

"Twenty dollars," said Madame, lifting the mass with a practiced hand.

"Give it to me quick," said Della.

Oh, and the next two hours tripped by on rosy wings. Forget the hashed metaphor. She was ransacking the stores for Jim's present.

She found it at last. It surely had been made for Jim and no one else. There was no other like it in any of the stores, and she had turned all of them inside out. It was a platinum fob chain simple and chaste in design, properly proclaiming its value by substance alone and not by meretricious ornamentation—as all good things should do. It was even worthy of The Watch. As soon as she saw it she knew that it must be Jim's. It was like him. Quietness and value—the description applied to both. Twenty-one dollars they took from her for it, and she hurried home with the eighty-seven cents. With that chain on his watch Jim might be properly anxious about the time in any company. Grand as the watch was, he sometimes looked at it on the sly on account of the old leather strap that he used in place of a chain.

When Della reached home her intoxication gave way a little to prudence and reason. She got out her curling irons and lighted the gas and went to work repairing the ravages made by generosity added to love. Which is always a tremendous task, dear friends—a mammoth task.

Within forty minutes her head was covered with tiny, close-lying curls that made her look wonderfully like a truant schoolboy. She looked at her reflection in the mirror long, carefully, and critically.

"If Jim doesn't kill me," she said to herself, "before he takes a second look at me, he'll say I look like a Coney Island chorus girl. But what could I do—oh! what could I do with a dollar and eighty-seven cents?"

At seven o'clock the coffee was made and the frying pan was on the back of the stove hot and ready to cook the chops.

Jim was never late. Della doubled the fob chain in her hand and sat on the corner of the table near the door that he always entered. Then she heard his step on the stair away down on the first flight, and she turned white for just a moment. She had a habit of saying little silent prayers about the simplest every-day things, and now she whispered, "Please, God, make him think I am still pretty."

The door opened and Jim stepped in and closed it. He looked thin and very serious. Poor fellow, he was only twenty-two—and to be burdened with a family! He needed a new overcoat and he was without gloves.

Jim stopped inside the door, as immovable as a setter at the scent of quail. His eyes were fixed upon Della; and there was an expression in them that she could not read, and it terrified her. It was not anger, nor surprise, nor disapproval, nor horror, nor any of the sentiments that she had been prepared for. He simply stared at her fixedly with that peculiar expression on his face.

Della wriggled off the table and went to him.

"Jim, darling," she cried, "don't look at me that way. I had my hair cut off and sold it because I couldn't have lived through Christmas without giving you a present. It'll grow out again—you won't mind, will you? I just had to do it. My hair grows awfully fast. Say 'Merry Christmas!' Jim, and let's be happy. You don't know what a nice—what a beautiful, nice gift I've got for you."

"You've cut off your hair?" asked Jim laboriously, as if he had not arrived at that patent fact yet even after the hardest mental labor.

"Cut it off and sold it," said Della. "Don't you like me just as well, anyhow? I'm me without my hair, ain't I?"

Jim looked about the room curiously.

"You say your hair is gone?" he said, with an air almost of idiocy.

"You needn't look for it," said Della. "It's sold, I tell you—sold and gone, too. It's Christmas Eve, boy. Be good to me, for it went for you. Maybe the hairs of my head were numbered," she went on with a sudden serious sweetness, "but nobody could ever count my love for you."

Out of his trance Jim seemed quickly to wake. He enfolded his Della. For ten seconds let us regard with discreet scrutiny some inconsequential object in the other direction. Eight dollars a week or a million a year—what is the difference? A mathematician or a wit would give you the wrong answer. The Magi[3] brought valuable gifts, but that was not among them. This dark assertion will be illuminated later on.

Jim drew a package from his overcoat pocket and threw it upon the table.

"Don't make any mistake, Dell," he said, "about me. I don't think there's anything in the way of a haircut or a shave or a shampoo that could make me like my girl any less. But if you'll unwrap that package you may see why you had me going awhile at first."

White fingers and nimble tore at the string and paper. And then an ecstatic scream of joy; and then, alas! a quick feminine change to hysterical tears and wails, necessitating the immediate employment of all the comforting powers of the lord of the flat.

For there lay The Combs—the set of combs, side and back, that Della had wor-

---

3. **The Magi**, the three wise men who brought gifts to the infant Jesus.

shiped for long in a Broadway window. Beautiful combs, pure tortoise shell, with jeweled rims—just the shade to wear in the beautiful vanished hair. They were expensive combs, she knew, and her heart had simply craved and yearned over them without the least hope of possession. And now they were hers, but the tresses that should have adorned the coveted adornments were gone.

But she hugged them to her bosom, and at length she was able to look up with dim eyes and a smile and say, "My hair grows so fast, Jim!"

And then Della leaped up like a little singed cat and cried, "Oh, oh!"

Jim had not yet seen his beautiful present. She held it out to him eagerly upon her open palm. The dull precious metal seemed to flash with a reflection of her bright and ardent spirit.

"Isn't it a dandy, Jim? I hunted all over town to find it. You'll have to look at the time a hundred times a day now. Give me your watch. I want to see how it looks on it."

Instead of obeying Jim tumbled down on the couch and put his hands under the back of his head and smiled.

"Della," said he, "let's put our Christmas presents away and keep 'em awhile. They're too nice to use just at present. I sold the watch to get the money to buy your combs. And now suppose you put the chops on."

The Magi, as you know, were wise men—wonderfully wise men—who brought gifts to the Babe in the manger. They invented the art of giving Christmas presents. Being wise, their gifts were no doubt wise ones, possibly bearing the privilege of exchange in case of duplication. And here I have lamely related to you the uneventful chronicle of two foolish children in a flat who most unwisely sacrificed for each other the greatest treasures of their house. But in a last word to the wise of these days let it be said that of all who give gifts these two were the wisest. Of all who give and receive gifts, such as they are wisest. Everywhere they are wisest. They are the Magi.

Developing Comprehension Skills

1. Briefly describe the way Della and Jim live. Use details and phrases from the story.

2. How would you describe Della and Jim's relationship? Find details in the story that support your answer.

3. What are Della and Jim's most prized possessions?

4. How do Jim and Della raise the money for each other's gifts? What is ironic about this?

5. O. Henry calls Della and Jim "foolish children" who "of all who give gifts these two were the wisest." Do you consider Della and Jim "foolish" or "wise"? Explain.

Reading Literature

1. **Recognizing a Fable.** A story that teaches a lesson about human nature is called a **fable**. The lesson it teaches is called a **moral**. Sometimes the writer does not write the moral. He

or she wants the reader to think about the events that happened and to figure out the lesson. Why could "The Gift of the Magi" be considered a fable? What is the moral?

2. **Understanding Plot.** The sequence of events in a story is called the **plot**. In many short stories, the plot follows the same general plan. The elements of that plan are:

 Introduction. This comes at the beginning of the story. The **introduction** presents the characters, setting, and the conflict.

 Rising Action. The **rising action** presents complications, or additional difficulties, the characters must face.

 Climax. The turning point in the story is called the **climax**. It often involves an important event, decision, or discovery.

 Falling Action. The action that takes place after the climax is called the **falling action**. It leads, in a logical manner, to the conclusion.

 Resolution. The last part of the plot is called the **resolution**. The loose ends are tied up and the story ends.

 Below is the skeleton of a plot diagram. Draw these lines on your own paper. Place the events of "The Gift of the Magi" in their correct positions on the chart. More than one event may be placed in each position.

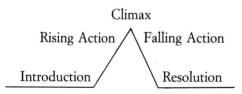

Climax
Rising Action Falling Action
Introduction Resolution

3. **Analyzing Characterization.** A writer often reveals a character through **indirect description**. With this technique, the reader learns about the character from his or her words and actions. Below are several statements about Della. What personality traits are revealed in each one?

 a. There was clearly nothing to do but flop down on the shabby little couch and howl. So Della did it.

 b. Many a happy hour she had spent planning for something nice for him.

 c. She had a habit of saying little silent prayers about the simplest everyday things, and now she whispered, "Please, God, make him think I am still pretty."

4. **Analyzing Narration.** In "The Gift of the Magi," the narrator, or person telling the story, often speaks directly to the reader. For example, the narrator says, "I have lamely related to you the uneventful chronicle of two foolish children . . . ."

 Find other examples where the narrator speaks to the reader. How does this influence the tone of the story?

5. **Appreciating the Surprise Ending.** O. Henry is considered by many to be "the master of the surprise ending." Careful reading shows that O. Henry hinted at the ending in "The Gift of the Magi." Find specific passages that suggest the outcome.

Developing Vocabulary Skills

 Reviewing Synonyms. Synonyms are often given in context as clues to unfamiliar words. A synonym is a word that means the same or nearly the same as another word.

 The following sentences or groups of sentences are from "The Gift of the Magi." Find the synonym of each underlined word. Other parts of the sentence may provide clues. Write the underlined word, its synonym, and any other clues you used to infer the meaning of the word. Then write the meaning as you understand it.

1. It was a platinum fob chain, simple and <u>chaste</u> in design, properly proclaiming its value by substance alone . . . .

2. When Della reached home her intoxication gave way a little to <u>prudence</u> and reason.

3. Which is always a tremendous task, dear friends—a <u>mammoth</u> task.

4. She looked at her reflection in the mirror long, carefully, and <u>critically</u>.

5. And then an <u>ecstatic</u> scream of joy; and then, alas! a quick <u>feminine</u> change to hysterical tears and <u>wails</u>, . . .

Developing Writing Skills

1. **Understanding Theme.** "The Gift of the Magi" isn't simply a story about gift-giving. The main idea that O. Henry wants to get across to his readers deals with love and selflessness. Write a paragraph in which you discuss the theme of this story.

2. **Changing the Point of View.** The events in "The Gift of the Magi" are presented as experienced by Della. The reader sees her actions but not Jim's.

   In a well-organized paper, describe Jim's day as he makes the decision to buy Della's present. You can put him in any situation you wish, but it must not contradict the information contained in the story.

   Pre-Writing. List the activities that Jim performed during the day. Next to each activity, jot down notes which indicate what his thoughts might have been.

Arrange the activities and thoughts in chronological order. This is the order in which they happened.

Compare your list to the story. Remember that what he does in your paper must agree with what happens in the story.

Writing. Begin your paper with a topic sentence that introduces Jim and puts him in a setting. You may want to start with his leaving the apartment. Then, describe his day. Explain what he does and what he thinks about.

End with a concluding sentence that has him opening the door and seeing Della. The ending will be the same as the one in the original story.

Revising. Revise your paper by following these guidelines:

Make certain that your events are in chronological order.
Check to see that the introduction and concluding sentences are effective.
Proofread carefully for correct grammar usage and mechanics.
Prepare your final copy, including any corrections you have made.

Developing Skills in Study and Research

Researching Allusions. As you recall, O. Henry uses allusion when he mentions the Magi. He also uses allusion when mentioning the Queen of Sheba and King Solomon. Using an encyclopedia for information, find out who these people were.

How does understanding these allusions add to your enjoyment of the story? What additional ideas was O. Henry suggesting about the events and characters?

A Visit of Charity

EUDORA WELTY

SETTING A PURPOSE | *The word "charity" comes from the Latin word* caritas, *meaning "love." Does love motivate Marian's actions in the following story?*

It was mid-morning—a very cold, bright day. Holding a potted plant before her, a girl of fourteen jumped off the bus in front of the Old Ladies' Home, in the outskirts of town. She wore a red coat, and her straight yellow hair was hanging down loose from the pointed white cap all the little girls were wearing that year. She stopped for a moment beside one of the prickly dark shrubs with which the city had beautified the Home, and then proceeded slowly toward the building, which was of whitewashed brick and reflected the winter sunlight like a block of ice. As she walked vaguely up the steps she shifted the small pot from hand to hand; then she had to set it down and remove her mittens before she could open the heavy door.

"I'm a Campfire Girl. . . . I have to pay a visit to some old lady," she told the nurse at the desk. This was a woman in a white uniform who looked as if she were cold; she had close-cut hair which stood up on the very top of her head exactly like a sea wave. Marian, the little girl, did not tell her that this visit would give her a minimum of only three points in her score.

"Acquainted with any of our residents?" asked the nurse. She lifted one eyebrow and spoke like a man.

"With any old ladies? No—but—that is, any of them will do," Marian stammered. With her free hand she pushed her hair behind her ears, as she did when it was time to study Science.

The nurse shrugged and rose. "You have a nice *multiflora cineraria* there," she remarked as she walked ahead down the hall of closed doors to pick out an old lady.

There was loose, bulging linoleum on the floor. Marian felt as if she were walking on the waves, but the nurse paid no attention to it. There was a smell in the hall like the interior of a clock. Everything was silent until, behind one of the doors, an old lady of some kind cleared her throat like a sheep bleating. This decided the nurse. Stopping in her tracks, she first extended her arm, bent her elbow, and leaned forward from the hips—all to examine the watch strapped to her wrist; then she gave a loud double-rap on the door.

"There are two in each room," the nurse remarked over her shoulder.

"Two what?" asked Marian without thinking. The sound like a sheep's bleating almost made her turn around and run back.

One old woman was pulling the door open in short, gradual jerks, and when she saw the nurse a strange smile forced her old face dangerously awry. Marian, suddenly propelled by the strong, impatient arm of the nurse, saw next the side-face of another old woman, who was lying in bed with a cap on and a counterpane drawn up to her chin.

"Visitor," said the nurse, and after one more shove she was off up the hall.

Marian stood tongue-tied; both hands held the potted plant. The old woman, still with that terrible, square smile (which was a smile of welcome) stamped on her bony face, was waiting. . . . Perhaps she said something. The old woman in bed said nothing at all, and she did not look around.

Suddenly Marian saw a hand, quick as a bird claw, reach up in the air and pluck the white cap off her head. At the same time, another claw to match drew her all the way into the room, and the next moment the door closed behind her.

"My, my, my," said the old lady at her side.

Marian stood enclosed by a bed, a washstand and a chair; the tiny room had altogether too much furniture. Everything smelled wet—even the bare floor. She held onto the back of the chair, which was wicker and felt soft and damp. Her heart beat more and more slowly, her hands got colder and colder, and she could not hear whether the old women were saying anything or not. She could not see them very clearly. How dark it was! The window shade was down, and the only door was shut. Marian looked at the ceiling. . . . It was like being caught in a robber's cave, just before one was murdered.

"Did you come to be our little girl for a while?" the first robber asked.

Then something was snatched from Marian's hand—the little potted plant.

"Flowers!" screamed the old woman. She stood holding the pot in an undecided way. "Pretty flowers," she added.

Then the old woman in bed cleared her throat and spoke. "They are not pretty," she said, still without looking around, but very distinctly.

Marian suddenly pitched against the chair and sat down in it.

"Pretty flowers," the first old woman insisted. "Pretty—pretty. . . ."

Marian wished she had the little pot back for just a moment—she had forgotten to look at the plant herself before giving it away. What did it look like?

"Stinkweeds," said the other old woman sharply. She had a bunchy white forehead and red eyes like a sheep. Now she turned them toward Marian. The fogginess seemed to rise in her throat again, and she bleated, "Who—are—you?"

To her surprise, Marian could not remember her name. "I'm a Campfire Girl," she said finally.

"Watch out for the germs," said the old woman like a sheep, not addressing anyone in particular.

"One came out last month to see us," said the first old woman.

A sheep or a germ? wondered Marian dreamily, holding onto the chair.

"Did not!" cried the other old woman.

"Did so! Read to us out of the Bible, and we enjoyed it!" screamed the first.

"Who enjoyed it!" said the woman in bed. Her mouth was unexpectedly small and sorrowful, like a pet's.

"We enjoyed it," insisted the other. "You enjoyed it—I enjoyed it."

"We all enjoyed it," said Marian, without realizing that she had said a word.

The first old woman had just finished putting the potted plant high, high on the top of the wardrobe, where it could hardly be seen from below. Marian wondered how she had ever succeeded in placing it there, how she could ever have reached so high.

"You mustn't pay any attention to old Addie," she now said to the little girl. "She's ailing today."

"Will you shut your mouth?" said the woman in bed. "I am not."

"You're a story."

"I can't stay but a minute—really, I can't," said Marian suddenly. She looked down at the wet floor and thought that if she were sick in here they would have to let her go.

With much to-do the first old woman sat down in a rocking chair—still another piece of furniture!—and began to rock. With the fingers of one hand she touched a very dirty

Last Sickness, 1952, ALICE NEEL.
Collection of Richard and Hartley Neel. Courtesy of Robert Miller Gallery, New York.

cameo pin on her chest. "What do you do at school?" she asked.

"I don't know . . ." said Marian. She tried to think but she could not.

"Oh, but the flowers are beautiful," the old woman whispered. She seemed to rock faster and faster; Marian did not see how anyone could rock so fast.

"Ugly," said the woman in bed.

"If we bring flowers—" Marian began, and then fell silent. She had almost said that if Campfire Girls brought flowers to the Old Ladies' Home, the visit would count one extra point, and if they took a Bible with them on the bus and read it to the old ladies, it counted double. But the old woman had not listened, anyway; she was rocking and watching the other one, who watched back from the bed.

"Poor Addie is ailing. She has to take medicine—see?" she said, pointing a horny finger at a row of bottles on the table, and rocking so high that her black comfort shoes lifted off the floor like a little child's.

"I am no more sick than you are," said the woman in bed.

"Oh yes you are!"

"I just got more sense than you have, that's all," said the other old woman, nodding her head.

"That's only the contrary way she talks when *you all* come," said the first old lady with sudden intimacy. She stopped the rocker with a neat pat of her feet and leaned toward Marian. Her hand reached over—it felt like a petunia leaf, clinging and just a little sticky.

"Will you hush! Will you hush!" cried the other one.

Marian leaned back rigidly in her chair.

"When I was a little girl like you, I went to school and all," said the old woman in the same intimate, menacing voice. "Not here—another town. . . ."

"Hush!" said the sick woman. "You never went to school. You never came and you never went. You never were anywhere—only here. You never were born! You don't know anything. Your head is empty, your heart and hands and your old black purse are all empty, even that little old box that you brought with you you brought empty—you showed it to me. And yet you talk, talk, talk, talk, talk all the time until I think I'm losing my mind. Who are you? You're a stranger—a perfect stranger! Don't you know you're a stranger? Is it possible that they have actually done a thing like this to anyone—sent them in a stranger to talk, and rock, and tell away her whole long rigmarole? Do they seriously suppose that I'll be able to keep it up, day in, day out, night in, night out, living in the same room with a terrible old woman—forever?"

Marian saw the old woman's eyes grow bright and turn toward her. This old woman was looking at her with despair and calculation on her face. Her small lips suddenly dropped apart, and exposed a half circle of false teeth with tan gums.

"Come here, I want to tell you something," she whispered. "Come here!"

Marian was trembling, and her heart nearly stopped beating altogether for a moment.

"Now, now, Addie," said the first old woman. "That's not polite. Do you know what's really the matter with old Addie today?" She, too, looked at Marion; one of her eyelids drooped low.

"The matter?" the child repeated stupidly. "What's the matter with her?"

"Why, she's mad because it's her birthday!" said the first old woman, beginning to rock again and giving a little crow as though she had answered her own riddle.

"It is not, it is not!" screamed the old woman in bed. "It is not my birthday, no one knows when that is but myself, and will you please be quiet and say nothing more, or I'll go straight out of my mind!" She turned her eyes toward Marian again, and presently she said in the soft, foggy voice, "When the worst comes to the worst, I ring this bell, and the nurse comes." One of her hands was drawn out from under the patched counterpane—a thin little hand with enormous black freckles. With a finger which would not hold still she pointed to a little bell on the table among the bottles.

"How old are you?" Marian breathed. Now she could see the old woman in bed very closely and plainly, and very abruptly, from all sides, as in dreams. She wondered about her—she wondered for a moment as though there was nothing else in the world to wonder about. It was the first time such a thing had happened to Marian.

"I won't tell!"

The old face on the pillow, where Marian was bending over it, slowly gathered and collapsed. Soft whimpers came out of the small open mouth. It was a sheep that she sounded like—a little lamb. Marian's face drew very close, the yellow hair hung forward.

"She's crying!" She turned a bright, burning face up to the first old woman.

"That's Addie for you," the old woman said spitefully.

Marian jumped up and moved toward the door. For the second time, the claw almost touched her hair, but it was not quick enough. The little girl put her cap on.

"Well, it was a real visit," said the old woman, following Marian through the doorway and all the way out into the hall. Then from behind she suddenly clutched the child with her sharp little fingers. In an affected, high-pitched whine she cried, "Oh, little girl, have you a penny to spare for a poor old woman that's not got anything of her own? We don't have a thing in the world—not a penny for candy—not a thing! Little girl, just a nickel—a penny—"

Marian pulled violently against the old hands for a moment before she was free. Then she ran down the hall, without looking behind her and without looking at the nurse, who was reading *Field & Stream* at her desk. The nurse, after another triple motion to consult her wrist watch, asked automatically the question put to visitors in all institutions: "Won't you stay and have dinner with *us*?"

Marian never replied. She pushed the heavy door open into the cold air and ran down the steps.

Under the prickly shrub she stopped and quickly, without being seen, retrieved a red apple she had hidden there.

Her yellow hair under the white cap, her scarlet coat, her bare knees all flashed in the sunlight as she ran to meet the big bus rocketing through the street.

"Wait for me!" she shouted. As though at an imperial command, the bus ground to a stop.

She jumped on and took a big bite out of the apple.

Developing Comprehension Skills

1. Why does Marian go to the Old Ladies' Home?

2. When asked if she is acquainted with any of the residents, Marian replies, "With any old ladies? No . . . any of them will do." How does this statement reveal Marian's attitude toward the women in the home?

3. The two old women react differently to the potted plant Marian brings them. How does each react? What do their reactions tell you about them?

4. The last thing Marian does is bite into an apple. What does that action tell us about her feelings toward her visit?

5. Do you think Marian's attitude toward the two women is typical of a fourteen-year-old? Why or why not?

Reading Literature

1. **Identifying Theme.** Throughout the story the residents in the home are referred to as "old ladies" or "old women." Only one is identified by name. Are the residents of the home treated as individuals? What, then, do you suppose the main idea of the story is?

2. **Understanding Mood.** The setting of a story often creates a particular mood. What is the mood in "A Visit of Charity"? How does the description of the Old Ladies' Home help to create this mood? Explain.

3. **Appreciating Point of View.** "A Visit of Charity" is told from the third-person limited point of view. The writer presents the events as experienced by only one character. Who is the character through whom Eudora Welty tells the story? Why do you suppose she

chose this character? How does it affect the story?

4. **Understanding Imagery.** Imagery, you recall, is a description that appeals to your senses. An author may describe something so clearly that you can taste, hear, smell, feel, or see it.

In "A Visit of Charity," the author compares the old women to sheep. Find three examples where this image is presented in the story. How does the imagery help you to picture the women? What does it tell you about both the women and Marian?

Developing Vocabulary Skills

Inferring Word Meanings. To infer means to draw a conclusion from specific facts. If you find no context clues to an unfamiliar word, look for specific information that provides hints to meaning. Consider this example:

> One of the old ladies spoke in a *contrary* voice as she contradicted everything the other lady had to say.

The fact that one old woman contradicted the other tells you that *contrary* means disagreeable.

The following sentences are from "A Visit of Charity." Read each one carefully, looking for information that would allow you to infer the meaning of the underlined word. Then write your definition of the word.

1. "With any old ladies? No—but—that is, any of them will do," Marian stammered.

2. Marian saw next the side-face of another old woman, even older, who was lying in bed with a cap on and a counterpane drawn up to her chin.

3. Poor Addie is <u>ailing</u>. She has to take medicine—see?

4. Is it possible that they have actually done a thing like this to anyone—sent them in a stranger to talk, and rock, and tell away her whole long <u>rigmarole</u>?

5. In an <u>affected</u>, high-pitched whine, she cried, "Oh, little girl, have you a penny to spare for a poor old woman that's not got anything of her own?"

Developing Writing Skills

1. **Contrasting Themes.** Write a paper in which you contrast the idea of giving in "The Gift of the Magi" and "A Visit of Charity." In your paper, discuss the differences between the "gifts," the motives of the givers, and the reactions of the receivers.

   Pre-Writing. Before making any notes, review the questions you have discussed for each story. Then, on paper, make a column for each story and put the story's title at the top of each column. Divide each column into thirds. Label one part "gifts," another "motives," and the third, "reactions." These are the three ideas you will discuss. Put down details from each story in the appropriate sections.

   Writing. Begin your paper with an introduction that states the titles of the stories and the topic you are discussing. Remember to put the titles in quotation marks.

   Organize the body of your paper into three different paragraphs. Each paragraph will contrast one of the three ideas: "gifts," "motives," and "reactions." Refer to your notes as you write.

End with a strong conclusion that ties together everything you have written.

   Revising. Reread your paper aloud. Often, you will hear mistakes in sentence structure and in usage that you might not see. Keep a pen or pencil handy as you read so you can mark places that need improvement.

   After reading your paper, think again about organization. Have you kept related ideas together in the same part of the paragraph? Then, prepare a final copy.

2. **Creating a Setting.** An important part of creating a story is creating a setting. An appropriate setting often creates a particular mood. In "A Visit of Charity," the Old Ladies' Home creates the mood. Write a description of a place that brings out a particular feeling in you. Try to convey that mood in your writing. Use vivid verbs and adjectives to help you.

Developing Skills in Speaking and Listening

Holding a Group Discussion. A small group discussion can be used to share ideas and solve problems. In a small group, discuss how society treats the elderly. If possible, the group should try to answer this question: Does "A Visit of Charity" give an accurate picture of how the elderly are treated?

In order for the discussion to be successful, everyone should contribute ideas. Listen politely to the opinions of others. Remember that the purpose of a small group discussion is to discuss, not argue.

At the end of your discussion, have one person summarize the ideas that were presented.

The Far and the Near

THOMAS WOLFE

On the outskirts of a little town upon a rise of land that swept back from the railway there was a tidy little cottage of white boards, trimmed vividly with green blinds. To one side of the house there was a garden neatly patterned with plots of growing vegetables, and an arbor for the grapes which ripened late in August. Before the house there were three mighty oaks which sheltered it in their clean and massive shade in summer, and to the other side there was a border of gay flowers. The whole place had an air of tidiness, thrift, and modest comfort.

Every day, a few minutes after two o'clock in the afternoon, the limited express between two cities passed this spot. At that moment the great train, having halted for a breathing-space at the town near by, was beginning to lengthen evenly into its stroke, but it had not yet reached the full drive of its terrific speed. It swung into view deliberately, swept past with a powerful swaying motion of the engine, a low smooth rumble of its heavy cars upon pressed steel, and then it vanished in the cut. For a moment the progress of the engine could be marked by heavy bellowing puffs of smoke that burst at spaced intervals above the edges of the meadow grass, and finally noth-

ing could be heard but the solid clacking tempo of the wheels receding into the drowsy stillness of the afternoon.

Every day for more than twenty years, as the train had approached this house, the engineer had blown on the whistle, and every day, as soon as she heard this signal, a woman had appeared on the back porch of the little house and waved to him. At first she had a small child clinging to her skirts, and now this child had grown to full womanhood, and every day she, too, came to the porch and waved.

The engineer had grown old and gray in service. He had driven his great train, loaded with its weight of lives, across the land ten thousand times. His own children had grown up and married, and four times he had seen before him on the tracks the ghastly dot of tragedy converging like a cannon ball to its eclipse of horror at the boiler head—a light spring wagon filled with children, with its clustered row of small stunned faces; a cheap automobile stalled upon the tracks, set with the wooden figures of people paralyzed with fear; a battered hobo walking by the rail, too deaf and old to hear the whistle's warning; and a form flung past his window with a scream—all this the man had seen and

New York, New Haven and Hartford, 1931, EDWARD HOPPER. Indianapolis Museum of Art, Emma Harter Sweetser Fund.

known. He had known all the grief, the joy, the peril and the labor such a man could know; he had grown seamed and weathered in his loyal service, and now, schooled by the qualities of faith, courage, and humbleness that attended his labor, he had grown old, and had the grandeur and wisdom these men have.

But no matter what peril or tragedy he had known, the vision of the little house and the women waving to him with a brave free motion of the arm had become fixed in the mind of the engineer as something beautiful and enduring, something beyond all change and ruin, and something that would always be the same, no matter what mishap, grief or error might break the iron schedule of his days.

The sight of the little house and of these two women gave him the most extraordinary happiness he had ever known. He had seen them in a thousand lights, a hundred weathers. He had seen them through the harsh bare light of wintry gray across the brown and frosted stubble of the earth, and he had seen them again in the green luring sorcery of April.

He felt for them and for the little house in which they lived such tenderness as a man might feel for his own children, and at length the picture of their lives was carved so sharply in his heart that he felt that he knew their lives completely, to every hour and moment of the day, and he resolved that one day, when his years of service should be ended, he would go and find these people and speak at last with them whose lives had been so wrought into his own.

That day came. At last the engineer stepped from a train onto the station platform of the town where these two women lived. His years upon the rail had ended. He was a pensioned servant of his company, with no more work to do. The engineer walked slowly through the station and out into the streets of the town. Everything was as strange to him as if he had never seen this town before. As he walked on, his sense of bewilderment and confusion grew. Could this be the town he had passed ten thousand times? Were these the same houses he had seen so often from the high windows of his cab? It was all as unfamiliar, as disquieting as a city in a dream, and the perplexity of his spirit increased as he went on.

Presently the houses thinned into the straggling outposts of the town, and the street faded into a country road—the one on which the women lived. And the man plodded on slowly in the heat and dust. At length he stood before the house he sought. He knew at once that he had found the proper place. He saw the lordly oaks before the house, the flower beds, the garden and the arbor, and farther off, the glint of rails.

Yes, this was the house he sought, the place he had passed so many times, the destination he had longed for with such happiness. But now that he had found it, now that he was here, why did his hand falter on the gate; why had the town, the road, the earth, the very entrance to this place he loved turned unfamiliar as the landscape of some ugly dream? Why did he now feel this sense of confusion, doubt and hopelessness?

At length he entered by the gate, walked slowly up the path and in a moment more had mounted three short steps that led up to the porch, and was knocking at the door. Presently he heard steps in the hall, the door was opened, and a woman stood facing him.

And instantly, with a sense of bitter loss and grief, he was sorry he had come. He knew at once that the woman who stood there looking at him with a mistrustful eye was the same woman who had waved to him so many thousand times. But her face was harsh and pinched and meager; the flesh sagged wearily in sallow folds, and the small eyes peered at him with timid suspicion and uneasy doubt. All the brave freedom, the warmth and the affection that he had read into her gesture, vanished in the moment that he saw her and heard her unfriendly tongue.

And now his own voice sounded unreal and ghastly to him as he tried to explain his presence, to tell her who he was and the reason he had come. But he faltered on, fighting stubbornly against the horror of regret, confusion, disbelief that surged up in his spirit, drowning all his former joy and making his act of hope and tenderness seem shameful to him.

At length the woman invited him almost unwillingly into the house, and called her daughter in a harsh shrill voice. Then, for a brief agony of time, the man sat in an ugly little parlor, and he tried to talk while the two women stared at him with a dull, bewildered hostility, a sullen, timorous restraint.

And finally, stammering a crude farewell, he departed. He walked away down the path and then along the road toward town, and suddenly he knew that he was an old man. His heart, which had been brave and confident when it looked along the familiar vista of the rails, was now sick with doubt and horror as it saw the strange and unsuspected visage of an earth which had always been within a stone's throw of him, and which he had never seen or known. And he knew that all the magic of that bright lost way, the vista of that shining line, the imagined corner of that small good universe of hope's desire, was gone forever, could never be got back again.

Developing Comprehension Skills

1. Describe the event that has occurred "every day for more than twenty years."

2. Why did the engineer look forward to passing the little white cottage every day? Why did he want to visit the mother, daughter, and cottage after he retired?

3. When the woman answered the door, the engineer suddenly decided he should not have come. What "vanished in the moment that he saw her"?

4. As the engineer left the woman's house, "his heart, which had been brave and confident . . . was now sick with doubt and horror . . . ." What caused this change? What did he lose?

5. The image of the two women kept the engineer hopeful and happy. As a result, he believed that life had order and beauty. What dangers exist for people who place too much importance on dreams and ideas? Explain.

Reading Literature

1. **Relating the Theme to the Title.** The title of a story can often provide a clue to the theme. The title of this story involves distances. What do you think the main idea of Wolfe's story is? What is he saying about the dreams and visions that people have? What happens when dreams are examined too closely? How does the title relate to this theme?

2. **Recognizing Climax.** The climax is the turning point in the action of a story. The climax, too, often involves an important event, decision, or discovery. What is the turning point of "The Far and Near"?

3. **Appreciating Imagery.** The first two paragraphs of Wolfe's story are rich with imagery. These images appeal to the reader's senses of sight, sound, touch, taste, and smell.

   Find at least three descriptions that appeal to the senses. Which sense is affected by each?

Developing Vocabulary Skills

Inferring Meaning from Word Parts. Sometimes a familiar word part can give you a hint to the meaning of an unfamiliar word. If you combine this information with context, you can often infer the meaning of the word. Consider this example:

   The once familiar *visage* of the little house now seemed strange and confusing.

You know that the Latin root *vis* means "to see." From this and the context of the word, you can determine that *visage* refers to the appearance of something.

Here are some other Greek and Latin roots:

Root	Meaning	Example
chron (G.)	time	chronology
tim (L.)	fear	timid
sequ, secut (L.)	follow	sequel
put (L.)	think, reckon	reputation
verg (L.)	bend, turn	verge

The underlined words in these sentences come from selections you have read. First write down any word parts that can provide a clue to the meaning of the underlined word. Then use the context for additional help. Write down your definition of each underlined word, as well as the meaning of the familiar word part.

1. "... four times he had seen before him on the tracks the ghastly dot of tragedy converging like a cannonball ..."

2. The old man was uncomfortable under the timorous and sullen gaze of the two women.

3. He was confident as he looked along the familiar vista of the train rails.

4. Della saved pennies but hoped to avoid the imputation that she was miserly.

5. "For ten seconds, let us regard... some inconsequential object ..."

6. "And here I have lamely related to you the chronicle of two foolish children in a flat. .."

Developing Writing Skills

1. **Using Comparison and Contrast.** In "The Far and the Near," the main character has two visions of a house and the people who live there. Which details are the same from a distance as they are close up? Which details are different? Write two paragraphs in which you discuss the differences and similarities.

Pre-Writing. Scan the story for descriptions of the house and the women. Then, jot down details that describe the house and women as the engineer sees them from a distance. Secondly, take notes on the details the engineer sees when he visits. Determine which details are similar, and which ones are different. Group these details together. Decide on a method of presenting your findings. For example, you may wish to describe the details that are similar first and then the ones that are different.

Writing. State the purpose of your paper in your first sentence. This will tell your reader what the paper is about.

The first paragraph will be a comparison. Include details that you found to be the same. In the second paragraph, point out the differences between the distant and the near view. As you write each paragraph, use specific examples from the story to emphasize your point. Try to use transitional words to show how ideas are related. Conclude your paper with a summary statement.

Revising. Reread your paper. Did you stick to your topic? Have you used specific examples to show the similarities and differences? If your paper is confusing to you, it will be confusing to your readers. Make changes if necessary. Be sure the concluding sentence refers back to the purpose stated at the beginning of the paper.

2. **Writing a Letter.** The engineer unsuccessfully tried to explain to the woman why he was visiting. Imagine that you are the engineer. Write a letter to the woman explaining why you visited. Explain to the woman what she and her daughter have meant to you over the past twenty years.

Imagine being forced to leave your home. Where would you go? What would you do? In the following story, what will happen to one old man and the animals he loves?

Old Man at the Bridge

ERNEST HEMINGWAY

An old man with steel-rimmed spectacles and very dusty clothes sat by the side of the road. There was a pontoon bridge across the river and carts, trucks, and men, women, and children were crossing it. The mule-drawn carts staggered up the steep bank from the bridge with soldiers helping push against the spokes of the wheels. The trucks ground up and away heading out of it all and the peasants plodded along in the ankle deep dust. But the old man sat there without moving. He was too tired to go any farther.

It was my business to cross the bridge, explore the bridgehead beyond, and find out to what point the enemy had advanced. I did this and returned over the bridge. There were not so many carts now and very few people on foot, but the old man was still there.

"Where do you come from?" I asked him.

"From San Carlos," he said and smiled.

That was his native town and so it gave him pleasure to mention it and he smiled.

"I was taking care of animals," he explained.

"Oh," I said, not quite understanding.

"Yes," he said, "I stayed, you see, taking care of animals. I was the last one to leave the town of San Carlos."

He did not look like a shepherd nor a herdsman and I looked at his black dusty clothes and his gray dusty face and his steel-rimmed spectacles and said, "What animals were they?"

"Various animals," he said, and shook his head. "I had to leave them."

I was watching the bridge and the African-looking country of the Ebro Delta[1] and wondering how long now it would be before we would see the enemy, and listening all the while for the first noises that would signal that ever-mysterious event called contact, and the old man still sat there.

"What animals were they?" I asked.

"There were three animals altogether," he explained. "There were two goats and a cat and then there were four pairs of pigeons."

"And you had to leave them?" I asked.

"Yes. Because of the artillery. The captain told me to go because of the artillery."

"And you have no family?" I asked, watching the far end of the bridge where a few last carts were hurrying down the slope of the bank.

---

1. **Ebro Delta**, the area in northeastern Spain where the Ebro River empties into the Mediterranean Sea.

"No," he said, "only the animals I stated. The cat, of course, will be all right. A cat can look out for itself, but I cannot think what will become of the others."

"What politics have you?" I asked.

"I am without politics," he said. "I am seventy-six years old. I have come twelve kilometers now and I think now I can go no further."

"This is not a good place to stop," I said. "If you can make it, there are trucks up the road where it forks for Tortosa."

"I will wait a while," he said, "and then I will go. Where do the trucks go?"

"Towards Barcelona," I told him.

"I know no one in that direction," he said, "but thank you very much. Thank you again very much."

He looked at me very blankly and tiredly, then said, having to share his worry with someone, "The cat will be all right, I am sure. There is no need to be unquiet about the cat. But the others. Now what do you think about the others?"

Portrait of Patience Escalier,
1888, VINCENT van GOGH.
The Bridgeman Art Library/Art Resource,
New York

"Why, they'll probably come through it all right."

"You think so?"

"Why not?" I said, watching the far bank where now there were no carts.

"But what will they do under the artillery when I was told to leave because of the artillery?"

"Did you leave the dove cage unlocked?" I asked.

"Yes."

"Then they'll fly."

"Yes, certainly they'll fly. But the others. It's better not to think about the others," he said.

"If you are rested I would go," I urged. "Get up and try to walk now."

"Thank you," he said and got to his feet, swayed from side to side and then sat down backwards in the dust.

"I was taking care of animals," he said dully, but no longer to me. "I was only taking care of animals."

There was nothing to do about him. It was Easter Sunday and the Fascists[2] were advancing toward the Ebro. It was a gray overcast day with a low ceiling so their planes were not up. That and the fact that cats know how to look after themselves was all the good luck that old man would ever have.

---

2. **Fascists,** Spanish troops following the political beliefs and military leadership of General Francisco Franco; anyone believing in or practicing fascism.

Developing Comprehension Skills

1. Where is the old man when the narrator first sees him? Why does the narrator notice him?

2. The old man continually says, "I was taking care of animals." Why is this so important to him?

3. When the old man finds out the trucks are going to Barcelona, he says, "I know no one in that direction. . . ." What does that tell you about the old man's life?

4. Why doesn't the old man cross the bridge? Do you think he cannot cross it, or will not cross it?

5. What is "all the good luck" the old man will have? What do you think will happen to the old man?

6. The old man is "without politics" and "was only taking care of animals." How is the old man a victim of war? Does this story help you better understand the effects of war? Explain.

Reading Literature

1. **Inferring Setting.** Hemingway does not give a detailed, specific description of the setting. Instead, the reader has to infer the setting from the details that are given. Locate

details that help you answer the following questions:

Is the action set in a city or in the country?
What part of the world do you suppose the story takes place in?
What type of situation exists?

2. **Understanding Style.** Before becoming a successful novelist, Ernest Hemingway made his living as a journalist. His novels and short stories reflect the simple, direct style of a newspaper reporter. For example, his sentences are usually short and to the point. Why is this style of writing so appropriate to "Old Man at the Bridge"?

3. **Identifying Tone.** In "The Gift of the Magi," the tone is obvious because the narrator states his views directly. In "Old Man at the Bridge," however, Hemingway's attitudes are only suggested.

What do you suppose Hemingway's attitude is toward war? What details in the story support your answer?

4. **Understanding the Purpose of the Narrator.** The narrator, as you know, is the person from whose point of view the events in a story are told. Who is the narrator in "Old Man at the Bridge"? What is his job? What is the purpose of having the events told from his point of view? How would the story have been different if told by someone else? Explain your answer.

5. **Identifying Symbolism.** A bridge is a structure that allows people to cross over from one location to another. The bridge in Hemingway's story takes on additional meaning. How does it represent the old man's situation? What is the "bridge" that he must cross? Explain.

Developing Vocabulary Skills

Inferring the Correct Meaning. Each of the sentences below is from "Old Man at the Bridge." The underlined word in each sentence could have several meanings. By studying the passage in which the word appears, you may be able to infer the correct meaning.

Look up each word in the dictionary. Write the meaning that fits the sentence. Then write a second meaning for the word. Finally, write a sentence that uses the second meaning of the word.

1. An old man with steel-rimmed spectacles and very dusty clothes sat by the side of the road.

2. I was watching the bridge . . . and listening all the while for the first noises that would signal that ever mysterious event called contact. . . .

3. "I am without politics," he said.

4. "There is no need to be unquiet about the cat."

5. It was a gray overcast day with a low ceiling so their planes were not up.

Developing Writing Skills

1. **Evaluating an Introduction.** The introduction of a short story must give you information about the characters, setting, and possible conflicts. It must also capture the reader's interest.

In a well-organized paragraph, discuss the first two paragraphs of "Old Man at the Bridge." Tell why this is or isn't a good introduction.

Pre-Writing. Reread the first two paragraphs of the story. Then, look for details that provide information about the characters, setting, and conflicts. Jot down notes related to these details. What details, if any, catch the attention and interest of the reader? Make notes on these, also. Decide whether or not the introduction is a good one.

Writing. Begin with a clear topic sentence that reveals your evaluation of the introduction. Then, begin discussing the various elements of the introduction. As you explain each part, be certain to show why a particular detail is important. Why is the information necessary for the reader to know as he or she continues the story? How does it relate to later events? Use transitional words and phrases as you move from one point to the next. Write a strong concluding sentence that summarizes your opinion of the first two paragraphs of this story.

Revising. Exchange papers with a classmate. Each of you should consider the following questions as you read the other's paper:

> Are related ideas grouped together?
> Does the paper show an understanding of
>   what a short story introduction is?
> Are there specific details from the story?
>   If so, are direct quotes enclosed in quotation marks?

Write the final draft of your paper, making improvements suggested by your classmate.

2. **Writing an Introduction.** As you know, the introduction is an important part of a short story. A poorly written introduction can affect the entire selection.

Imagine that you are writing a short story about a character faced with an important decision. For example, your character may have to decide whether to tell a friend a painful truth, or leave that friend unaware. Write an introduction that will provide your readers with information about the characters, setting, and possible conflicts. Before you begin, spend some time thinking of a possible plot for the story. Only then can you write the introduction.

As you write, remember that you want the introduction to capture the interest of the reader. Use details that will help you achieve this purpose.

Developing Skills in Study and Research

Locating Biographical Information. Some of Hemingway's works are based on his own experiences. "Old Man at the Bridge," for example, is based on his experiences during the Spanish Civil War.

Use the card catalog to find biographies about Ernest Hemingway. A biography is indicated by a capital "B" on the left side of the card. Locate one or two of the books. Then, use the index or the table of contents to find sections on Hemingway's involvement in the Spanish Civil War. As you read this information in the book, take notes. Be prepared to share the following information with the class:

> What did Hemingway do during the Spanish
>   Civil War?
> How long was he in Spain?
> Which side did he support in the war? Why?

How are these experiences reflected in "Old Man at the Bridge"? Do you find any similarities between Hemingway and the narrator in the story? Explain.

Migrant People

JOHN STEINBECK
From The Grapes of Wrath

SETTING A PURPOSE | *In the 1930's, severe dust storms swept across the prairies. Many families left this "Dust Bowl" and journeyed to California. What does this selection from a novel reveal about their relationships and their dreams?*

The cars of the migrant people crawled out of the side roads onto the great cross-country highway, and they took the migrant way to the West. In the daylight they scuttled like bugs to the westward; and as the dark caught them, they clustered like bugs near to shelter and to water. And because they were lonely and perplexed, because they had all come from a place of sadness and worry and defeat, and because they were all going to a new mysterious place, they huddled together; they talked together; they shared their lives, their food, and the things they hoped for in the new country. Thus it might be that one family camped near a spring, and another camped for the spring and for company, and a third because two families had pioneered the place and found it good. And when the sun went down, perhaps twenty families and twenty cars were there.

In the evening a strange thing happened: the twenty families became one family, the children were the children of all. The loss of home became one loss, and the golden time in the West was one dream. And it might be that a sick child threw despair into the hearts of twenty families, of a hundred people; that a birth there in a tent kept a hundred people quiet and awestruck through the night and filled a hundred people with the birth-joy in the morning. A family which the night before had been lost and fearful might search its goods to find a present for a new baby. In the evening, sitting about the fires, the twenty were one. They grew to be units of the camps, units of the evenings and the nights. A guitar unwrapped from a blanket and tuned—and the songs, which were all of the people, were sung in the nights. Men sang the words, and women hummed the tunes.

Every night a world created, complete with furniture—friends made and enemies established; a world complete with braggarts and with cowards, with quiet men, with humble men, with kindly men. Every night relationships that make a world, established; and every morning the world torn down like a circus.

At first the families were timid in the building and tumbling worlds, but gradually the technique of building worlds became their technique. Then leaders emerged, then laws were made, then codes came into being. And as the worlds moved westward they were more complete and better furnished, for their builders were more experienced in building them.

The families learned what rights must be observed—the right of privacy in the tent; the right to keep the past black hidden in the heart; the right to talk and to listen; the right to refuse help or to accept, to offer help or to decline it; the right of son to court and daughter to be courted; the right of the hungry to be fed; the rights of the pregnant and the sick to transcend all other rights.

And the families learned, although no one told them, what rights are monstrous and must be destroyed: the right to intrude upon privacy, the right to be noisy while the camp slept, the right of seduction and theft and murder. These rights were crushed, because the little worlds could not exist for even a night with such rights alive.

And as the worlds moved westward, rules became laws, although no one told the families. It is unlawful to foul near the camp; it is unlawful in any way to foul the drinking water; it is unlawful to eat good rich food near one who is hungry, unless he is asked to share.

And the laws, the punishments—and there were only two—a quick and murderous fight or ostracism; and ostracism was the worst. For if one broke the laws his name and face went with him, and he had no place in any world, no matter where created.

The families moved westward, and the technique of building the worlds improved so that the people could be safe in their worlds; and the form was so fixed that a family acting in the rules knew it was safe in the rules.

There grew up government in the worlds, with leaders, with elders. A man who was wise found that his wisdom was needed in every camp; a man who was a fool could not change his folly with his world. And a kind of insurance developed in these nights. A man with food fed a hungry man, and thus insured himself against hunger. And when a baby died a pile of silver coins grew at the door flap, for a baby must be well buried, since it has had nothing else of life. An old man may be left in a potter's field,[1] but not a baby.

A certain physical pattern is needed for the building of a world—water, a river bank, a stream, a spring, or even a faucet unguarded. And there is needed enough flat land to pitch the tents, a little brush or wood to build the fires. If there is a garbage dump not too far off, all the better; for there can be found equipment—stove tops, a curved fender to shelter the fire, and cans to cook in and to eat from.

And the worlds were built in the evening. The people, moving in from the highways, made them with their tents and their hearts and their brains.

In the morning the tents came down, the canvas was folded, the tent poles tied along the running board, the beds put in place on the cars, the pots in their places. And as the families moved westward, the technique of building up a home in the evening and tearing it down with the morning light became fixed; so that the folded tent was packed in one place, the cooking pots counted in their box. And as the cars moved westward, each member of the family grew into his proper place,

---

1. **potter's field**, a burial place for poor people or those whose identity is unknown.

grew into his duties; so that each member, old and young, had his place in the car; so that in the weary, hot evenings, when the cars pulled into the camping places, each member had his duty and went to it without instruction: children to gather wood, to carry water; men to pitch the tents and bring down the beds; women to cook the supper and to watch while the family fed. And this was done without command. The families, which had been units of which the boundaries were a house at night, a farm by day, changed their boundaries. In the long hot light, they were silent in the cars moving slowly westward; but at night they integrated with any group they found.

Thus they changed their social life—changed as in the whole universe only man can change. They were not farm men any more, but migrant men. And the thought, the planning, the long staring silence that had gone out to the fields, went now to the roads, to the distance, to the West. That man whose mind had been bound with acres lived with narrow concrete miles. And his thought and his worry were not any more with rainfall, with wind and dust, with the thrust of the crops. Eyes watched the tires, ears listened to the clattering motors, and minds struggled with oil, with gasoline, with the thinning rubber between air and road. Then a broken gear was tragedy. Then water in the evening was the yearning, and food over the fire. Then health to go on was the need and strength to go on, and spirit to go on. The wills thrust westward ahead of them, and fears that had once apprehended drought or flood now lingered with anything that might stop the westward crawling. The camps became fixed—each a short day's journey from the last.

And on the road the panic overcame some of the families, so that they drove night and day, stopped to sleep in the cars, and drove on to the West, flying from the road, flying from movement. And these lusted so greatly to be settled that they set their faces into the West and drove toward it, forcing the clashing engines over the roads.

But most of the families changed and grew quickly into the new life. And when the sun went down—

Time to look out for a place to stop.

And—there's some tents ahead.

The car pulled off the road and stopped, and because others were there first, certain courtesies were necessary. And the man, the leader of the family, leaned from the car.

Can we pull up here an' sleep?

Why, sure, be proud to have you. What State you from?

Come all the way from Arkansas.

They's Arkansas people down that fourth tent.

That so?

And the great question, How's the water?

Well, she don't taste so good, but they's plenty.

Well, thank ya.

No thanks to me.

But the courtesies had to be. The car lumbered over the ground to the end tent, and stopped. Then down from the car the weary people climbed, and stretched stiff bodies. Then the new tent sprang up; the children went for water and the older boys cut brush or wood. The fires started and supper was put on to boil or to fry. Early comers moved over, and States were exchanged, and friends and sometimes relatives discovered.

Vian, Oklahoma, 1939, RUSSELL LEE. Library of Congress, Washington, D.C.

Oklahoma, huh? What county?

Cherokee.

Why, I got folks there. Know the Allens? They's Allens all over Cherokee. Know the Willises?

Why, sure.

And a new unit was formed. The dusk came, but before the dark was down the new family was of the camp. A word had been passed with every family. They were known people—good people.

I knowed the Allens all my life. Simon Allen, ol' Simon, had trouble with his first wife. She was part Cherokee. Purty as—as a black colt.

Sure, an' young Simon, he married a Rudolph, didn' he? That's what I thought. They went to live in Enid an' done well—real well.

Only Allen that ever done well. Got a garage.

When the water was carried and the wood cut, the children walked shyly, cautiously among the tents. And they made elaborate acquaintanceship gestures. A boy stopped near another boy and studied a stone, picked it up, examined it closely, spat on it, and rubbed it clean and inspected it until he forced the other to demand, What you got there?

And casually, Nothin'. Jus' a rock.

Well, what you lookin' at it like that for?

Thought I seen gold in it.

How'd you know? Gold ain't gold, it's black in a rock.

Sure, ever'body knows that.

I bet it's fool's gold, an' you figgered it was gold.

That ain't so, 'cause Pa, he's foun' lots a gold an' he tol' me how to look.

How'd you like to pick up a big ol' piece a gold?

Sa-a-ay! I'd git the bigges' piece a candy!

And young girls found each other and boasted shyly of their popularity and their prospects. The women worked over the fire, hurrying to get food to the stomachs of the family—pork if there was money in plenty, pork and potatoes and onions. Dutch-oven biscuits or cornbread, and plenty of gravy to go over it. Side-meat or chops and a can of boiled tea, black and bitter. Fried dough in drippings if money was slim, dough fried crisp and brown and the drippings poured over it.

Those families which were very rich or very foolish with their money ate canned beans and canned peaches and packaged bread and bakery cake; but they ate secretly, in their tents, for it would not have been good to eat such fine things openly. Even so, children eating their fried dough smelled the warming beans and were unhappy about it.

When supper was over the dishes dipped and wiped, the dark had come, and then the men squatted down to talk.

And they talked of the land behind them. I don' know what it's coming to, they said. The country's spoilt.

It'll come back though, on'y we won't be there.

Maybe, they thought, maybe we sinned some way we didn't know about.

Fella says to me, gov'ment fella, an' he says, she's gullied up on ya. Gov'ment fella. He says, if ya plowed 'cross the contour, she won't gully. Never did have no chance to try her. An' the new super' ain't plowin' 'cross the contour. Runnin' a furrow four miles long that ain't stoppin' or goin' aroun' Jesus Christ Hisself.

And they spoke softly of their homes: They was a little cool-house under the win'mill. Use' ta keep milk in there ta cream up, an' watermelons. Go in there midday when she was hotter'n a heifer, an' she'd be jus' as cool, as cool as you'd want. Cut open a melon in there an' she'd hurt your mouth, she was so cool. Water drippin' down from the tank.

They spoke of their tragedies: Had a brother Charley, hair as yella as corn, an' him a growed man. Played the 'cordeen nice too. He was harrowin'[2] one day an' he went up to clear his lines. Well, a rattlesnake buzzed an' them horses bolted an' the harrow went over Charley, an' the points dug into his guts an' his stomach, an' they pulled his face off an'— God Almighty!

They spoke of the future: Wonder what it's like out there?

Well, the pitchers sure do look nice. I seen one where it's hot an' fine, an' walnut trees an' berries; an' right behind, they's a tall up

---

2. **harrowin'**, (harrowing) pulling a heavy frame with spikes across a field to break up and level plowed ground.

mountain covered with snow. That was a pretty thing to see.

If we can get work it'll be fine. Won't have no cold in the winter. Kids won't freeze on the way to school. I'm gonna take care my kids don't miss no more school. I can read good, but it ain't no pleasure to me like with a fella that's used to it.

And perhaps a man brought out his guitar to the front of his tent. And he sat on a box to play, and everyone in the camp moved slowly in toward him, drawn in toward him. Many men can chord a guitar, but perhaps this man was a picker. There you have something—the deep chords beating, beating, while the melody runs on the strings like little footsteps. Heavy hard fingers marching on the frets. The man played and the people moved slowly in on him until the circle was closed and tight, and then he sang "Ten-Cent Cotton and Forty-Cent Meat." And the circle sang softly with him. And he sang "Why Do You Cut Your Hair, Girls?" And the circle sang. He wailed the song, "I'm Leaving Old Texas," that eerie song that was sung before the Spaniards came, only the words were Indian then.

And now the group was welded to one thing, one unit, so that in the dark the eyes of the people were inward, and their minds played in other times, and their sadness was like rest, like sleep. He sang the "McAlester Blues" and then, to make up for it to the older people, he sang "Jesus Calls Me to His Side." The children drowsed with the music and went into the tents to sleep, and the singing came into their dreams.

And after a while the man with the guitar stood up and yawned. Good night, folks, he said.

And they murmured, Good night to you.

And each wished he could pick a guitar, because it is a gracious thing. Then the people went to their beds, and the camp was quiet. And owls coasted overhead, and the coyotes gabbled in the distance, and into the camp skunks walked, looking for bits of food—waddling, arrogant skunks afraid of nothing.

The night passed, and with the first streak of dawn the women came out of the tents, built up the fires, and put the coffee to boil. And the men came out and talked softly in the dawn.

When you cross the Colorado river, there's the desert, they say. Look out for the desert. See you don't get hung up. Take plenty water, case you get hung up.

I'm gonna take her at night.

Me too. She'll cut the living Jesus outa you.

The families ate quickly, and the dishes were dipped and wiped. The tents came down. There was a rush to go. And when the sun arose, the camping place was vacant, only a little litter left by the people. And the camping place was ready for a new world in a new night.

But along the highway the cars of the migrant people crawled out like bugs, and the narrow concrete miles stretched ahead.

Developing Comprehension Skills

1. According to Steinbeck, the migrant people "huddled together; they talked together; they shared their lives, their food, and the things they hoped for. . . ." What reasons do they have for doing so?

2. What are the two punishments for breaking the laws of the camps? Which is the worse punishment? Why?

3. Steinbeck says that the courtesies people showed each other "had to be." Describe the nature of the courtesies. How would it have affected these little communities if the courtesies were not observed?

4. At night, in the camps, the separate families "became one family." What does Steinbeck mean? What characteristics of a family do you see in these groups?

5. The narrator says that these people "changed as . . . only man can change." Does the change seem positive or negative?

Reading Literature

1. **Identifying Theme.** The people described by Steinbeck had experienced tragedy and "were all going to a new mysterious place." Together they "became one family." What do you suppose Steinbeck is saying about hardship and the way it affects people?

2. **Analyzing Similes.** The author uses several similes to describe the migrant people. The first is his description of the cars being "like bugs." This comparison appears in the opening and closing paragraphs. What mental picture is created by this simile? Is the comparison a positive or negative one? Explain your answer.

What is being compared in each of the following similes? Why is each effective?

a. every morning the world [was] torn down like a circus

b. their sadness was like rest, like sleep

3. **Analyzing Punctuation Use.** Authors have a privilege most people don't: they can break the standard rules of punctuation to achieve a certain effect. In this selection, you probably noticed that Steinbeck does not use quotation marks to indicate conversation. Why do you think he did this? What might he be suggesting about his characters by not using quotation marks? Does the absence of the marks make the passages easier or more difficult to read? Explain your answers.

Developing Vocabulary Skills

Inferring Meaning of a Different Dialect. Often, a writer will try to re-create the dialect of a particular group. He or she does this by using the special vocabulary of the group and by showing pronunciation through unusual spelling. Reading dialect can be confusing. By using inference, however, you can usually figure out what is being said.

Look at the following sentences from "Migrant People." For each underlined word, write the correct spelling, if the spelling is not standard. Then, use the dictionary to find the meaning of any unfamiliar word or phrase. Finally, rewrite the sentence in your own words.

1. I bet it's fool's gold, an' you <u>figgered</u> it was gold.

2. It'll come back, <u>on'y</u> we won't be there.

3. <u>Fella</u> says to me, <u>gov'ment</u> fella, an' he says, she's <u>gullied up</u> on ya.

4. They was a little cool-house under the win'mill. Use' ta keep milk in there ta cream up, an' watermelons.

5. Had a brother Charley . . . Played the 'cordeen nice too.

Developing Writing Skills

1. **Analyzing Purpose.** What do you think Steinbeck's purpose was in writing "Migrant People"? Did he just want to tell about the journey of the migrants to California, or do you see another purpose? Write a composition explaining what you think Steinbeck's purpose was in writing "Migrant People." Develop your ideas with specific examples from the selection.

Pre-Writing. Before you begin writing, consider the following questions: How were you affected by "Migrant People"? Did you learn anything about the Dust Bowl or the people who lived there? Did you feel any compassion for them? Also, were any of their activities familiar to you?

Then, decide what you think the author's purpose or purposes were. Find details from the story that support your conclusions. Jot down your notes and ideas.

Writing. Use your pre-writing notes to write a rough draft of your composition. In your introduction, include a direct statement of what you think Steinbeck's purpose or purposes were. Also include the title of the selection and the author.

Show how Steinbeck achieved his purpose by organizing the body of your paper around the notes you made in the pre-writing activity. Make sure you have grouped your ideas logically.

Revising. As you reread your paper, remember that you, too, have a purpose to achieve. Ask yourself, "Have I clearly explained Steinbeck's purpose?" This will help you determine if you have given clear explanations and details.

2. **Making a Comparison.** When you say that something is a microcosm, you are saying that it represents something that is larger. The word *microcosm* means "small world." The United Nations, for example, is a microcosm of the world as a whole.

In what ways is the migrant society described by Steinbeck similar to the world as a whole? Write a composition in which you show how the campsites are microcosms. As you write, show how the different stages in the development of the camps resemble the organization of a society or a country.

Developing Skills in Speaking and Listening

Using Audio-Visual Resources. In "Migrant People," the main form of entertainment in the campsites was telling stories, listening to a guitar, and singing folk songs. Steinbeck even refers to specific songs that were sung.

Woody Guthrie was an American folk singer who was looked upon as the spokesman for the uprooted migrant people of the 1930's. In the audio-visual section of your library, locate one of his recordings. Listen to two songs, then take notes and answer the following questions:

How do Guthrie's songs reflect the concerns of the people you just read about? What specific words and phrases show these concerns? Do you think the songs had meaning only for the migrants? Why, or why not?

One-Shot Finch

HARPER LEE
From To Kill a Mockingbird

Atticus was feeble: he was nearly fifty. When Jem and I asked him why he was so old, he said he got started late, which we felt reflected upon his abilities and manliness. He was much older than the parents of our school contemporaries, and there was nothing Jem or I could say about him when our classmates said, "*My* father—"

Jem was football crazy. Atticus was never too tired to play keep-away, but when Jem wanted to tackle him Atticus would say, "I'm too old for that, son."

Our father didn't do anything. He worked in an office, not in a drugstore. Atticus did not drive a dump-truck for the county, he was not the sheriff, he did not farm, work in a garage, or do anything that could possibly arouse the admiration of anyone.

Besides that, he wore glasses. He was nearly blind in his left eye, and said left eyes were the tribal curse of the Finches. Whenever he wanted to see something well, he turned his head and looked from his right eye.

He did not do the things our schoolmates' fathers did: he never went hunting, he did not play poker or fish or drink or smoke. He sat in the living room and read.

When he gave us our air-rifles Atticus wouldn't teach us to shoot. Uncle Jack instructed us in the rudiments thereof; he said Atticus wasn't interested in guns. Atticus said to Jem one day, "I'd rather you shot at tin cans in the back yard, but I know you'll go after birds. Shoot all the bluejays you want, if you can hit 'em, but remember it's a sin to kill a mockingbird."

That was the only time I ever heard Atticus say it was a sin to do something, and I asked Miss Maudie about it.

"Your father's right," she said. "Mockingbirds don't do one thing but make music for us to enjoy. They don't eat up people's gardens, don't nest in corncribs, they don't do one thing but sing their hearts out for us. That's why it's a sin to kill a mockingbird."

"Miss Maudie, this is an old neighborhood, ain't it?"

"Been here longer than the town."

"Nome, I mean the folks on our street are all old. Jem and me's the only children. Mrs. Dubose is close on to a hundred and Miss Rachel's old and so are you and Atticus."

"I don't call fifty very old," said Miss Maudie tartly. "Not being wheeled around yet, am I? Neither's your father. But I must say Providence was kind enough to burn down that old mausoleum of mine, I'm too old to keep it up—maybe you're right, Jean Louise, this is a settled neighborhood. You've never been around young folks much, have you?"

"Yessum, at school."

"I mean young grown-ups. You're lucky, you know. You and Jem have the benefit of your father's age. If your father was thirty you'd find life quite different."

"I sure would. Atticus can't do anything. . . ."

"You'd be surprised," said Miss Maudie. "There's life in him yet."

"What can he do?"

"Well, he can make somebody's will so airtight can't anybody meddle with it."

"Shoot . . ."

"Well, did you know he's the best checkerplayer in this town? Why, down at the Landing when we were coming up, Atticus Finch could beat everybody on both sides of the river."

"Good Lord, Miss Maudie, Jem and me beat him all the time."

"It's about time you found out it's because he lets you. Did you know he can play a Jew's Harp?"[1]

This modest accomplishment served to make me even more ashamed of him.

"*Well . . .*" she said.

"Well, what, Miss Maudie?"

"Well nothing. Nothing—it seems with all that you'd be proud of him. Can't everybody play a Jew's Harp. Now keep out of the way of

the carpenters. You'd better go home, I'll be in my azaleas and can't watch you. Plank might hit you."

I went to the back yard and found Jem plugging away at a tin can, which seemed stupid with all the bluejays around. I returned to the front yard and busied myself for two hours erecting a complicated breastworks at the side of the porch, consisting of a tire, an orange crate, the laundry hamper, the porch chairs, and a small U.S. flag Jem gave me from a popcorn box.

When Atticus came home to dinner he found me crouched down aiming across the street. "What are you shooting at?"

"Miss Maudie's rear end."

Atticus turned and saw my generous target bending over her bushes. He pushed his hat to the back of his head and crossed the street. "Maudie," he called, "I thought I'd better warn you. You're in considerable peril."

Miss Maudie straightened up and looked toward me. She said, "Atticus, you are a devil from hell."

When Atticus returned he told me to break camp. "Don't you ever let me catch you pointing that gun at anybody again," he said.

I wished my father was a devil from hell. I sounded out Calpurnia on the subject. "Mr. Finch? Why, he can do lots of things."

"Like what?" I asked.

Calpurnia scratched her head. "Well, I don't rightly know," she said.

Jem underlined it when he asked Atticus if he was going out for the Methodists and Atticus said he'd break his neck if he did, he was just too old for that sort of thing. The Methodists were trying to pay off their church mortgage, and had challenged the Baptists to

---

1. **Jew's Harp**, a musical instrument held between the teeth that makes a twanging sound when plucked.

a game of touch football. Everybody in town's father was playing, it seemed, except Atticus. Jem said he didn't even want to go, but he was unable to resist football in any form, and he stood gloomily on the sidelines with Atticus and me watching Cecil Jacobs's father make touchdowns for the Baptists.

One Saturday Jem and I decided to go exploring with our air-rifles to see if we could find a rabbit or a squirrel. We had gone about five hundred yards beyond the Radley Place when I noticed Jem squinting at something down the street. He had turned his head to one side and was looking out of the corners of his eyes.

"Whatcha looking at?"

"That old dog down yonder," he said.

"That's old Tim Johnson, ain't it?"

"Yeah."

Tim Johnson was the property of Mr. Harry Johnson who drove the Mobile bus and lived on the southern edge of town. Tim was a liver-colored bird dog, the pet of Maycomb.

"What's he doing?"

"I don't know, Scout. We better go home."

"Aw Jem, it's February."

"I don't care, I'm gonna tell Cal."

We raced home and ran to the kitchen.

"Cal," said Jem, "can you come down the sidewalk a minute?"

"What for, Jem? I can't come down the sidewalk every time you want me."

"There's somethin' wrong with an old dog down yonder."

Calpurnia sighed. "I can't wrap up any dog's foot now. There's some gauze in the bathroom, go get it and do it yourself."

Jem shook his head. "He's sick, Cal. Something's wrong with him."

"What's he doin', trying to catch his tail?"

"No, he's doin' like this."

Jem gulped like a goldfish, hunched his shoulders and twitched his torso. "He's goin' like that, only not like he means to."

"Are you telling me a story, Jem Finch?" Calpurnia's voice hardened.

"No Cal, I swear I'm not."

"Was he runnin'?"

"No, he's just moseyin' along, so slow you can't hardly tell it. He's comin' this way."

Calpurnia rinsed her hands and followed Jem outside. "I don't see any dog," she said.

She followed us beyond the Radley Place and looked where Jem pointed. Tim Johnson was not much more than a speck in the distance, but he was closer to us. He walked erratically, as if his right legs were shorter than his left legs. He reminded me of a car stuck in a sandbed.

"He's gone lopsided," said Jem.

Calpurnia stared, then grabbed us by the shoulders and ran us home. She shut the wood door behind us, went to the telephone and shouted, "Gimme Mr. Finch's office!"

"Mr. Finch!" she shouted. "This is Cal. I swear to God there's a mad dog down the street a piece—he's comin' this way, yes sir, he's—Mr. Finch, I declare he is—old Tim Johnson, yes sir . . . yessir . . . yes—"

She hung up and shook her head when we tried to ask her what Atticus had said. She rattled the telephone hook and said, "Miss Eula May—now ma'am, I'm through talkin' to Mr. Finch, please don't connect me no more—listen, Miss Eula May, can you call Miss Rachel and Miss Stephanie Crawford and whoever's got a phone on this street and tell 'em a mad dog's comin'? Please ma'am!"

Calpurnia listened. "I know it's February, Miss Eula May, but I know a mad dog when I see one. Please ma'am hurry!"

Calpurnia asked Jem, "Radleys got a phone?"

Jem looked in the book and said no. "They won't come out anyway, Cal."

"I don't care, I'm gonna tell 'em."

She ran to the front porch, Jem and I at her heels. "You stay in that house!" she yelled.

Calpurnia's message had been received by the neighborhood. Every wood door within our range of vision was closed tight. We saw no trace of Tim Johnson. We watched Calpurnia running toward the Radley Place, holding her skirt and apron above her knees. She went up to the front steps and banged on the door. She got no answer, and she shouted, "Mr. Nathan, Mr. Arthur, mad dog's comin'! Mad dog's comin'!"

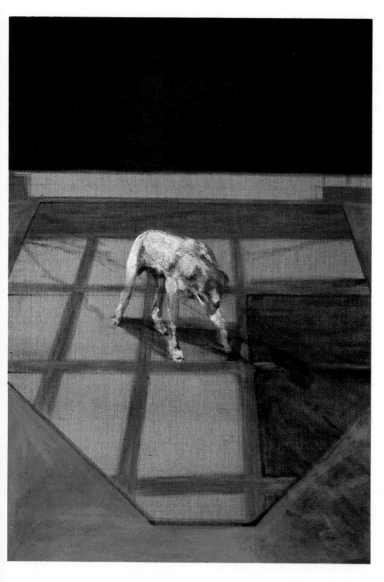

Dog, 1952, FRANCIS BACON. Oil on canvas, 6'6¼" x 54¼". The Museum of Modern Art, William A.M. Burden Fund, New York.

"She's supposed to go around in back," I said.

Jem shook his head. "Don't make any difference now," he said.

Calpurnia pounded on the door in vain. No one acknowledged her warning; no one seemed to have heard it.

As Calpurnia sprinted to the back porch a black Ford swung into the driveway. Atticus and Mr. Heck Tate got out.

Mr. Heck Tate was the sheriff of Maycomb County. He was as tall as Atticus, but thinner. He was long-nosed, wore boots with shiny metal eye-holes, boot pants and a lumber jacket. His belt had a row of bullets sticking in it. He carried a rifle. When he and Atticus reached the porch, Jem opened the door.

"Stay inside, son," said Atticus. "Where is he, Cal?"

"He oughta be here by now," said Calpurnia, pointing down the street.

"Not runnin', is he?" asked Mr. Tate.

"Naw sir, he's in the twitchin' stage, Mr. Heck."

"Should we go after him, Heck?" asked Atticus.

"We better wait, Mr. Finch. They usually go in a straight line, but you never can tell. He might follow the curve—hope he does or he'll go straight in the Radley back yard. Let's wait a minute."

"Don't think he'll get in the Radley yard," said Atticus. "Fence'll stop him. He'll probably follow the road. . . ."

I thought mad dogs foamed at the mouth, galloped, leaped and lunged at throats, and I thought they did it in August. Had Tim Johnson behaved thus, I would have been less frightened.

Nothing is more deadly than a deserted, waiting street. The trees were still, the mockingbirds were silent, the carpenters at Miss Maudie's house had vanished. I heard Mr. Tate sniff, then blow his nose. I saw him shift his gun to the crook of his arm. I saw Miss Stephanie Crawford's face framed in the glass window of her front door. Miss Maudie appeared and stood beside her. Atticus put his foot on the rung of a chair and rubbed his hand slowly down the side of his thigh.

"There he is," he said softly.

Tim Johnson came into sight, walking dazedly in the inner rim of the curve parallel to the Radley house.

"Look at him," whispered Jem. "Mr. Heck said they walked in a straight line. He can't even stay in the road."

"He looks more sick than anything," I said.

"Let anything get in front of him and he'll come straight at it."

Mr. Tate put his hand to his forehead and leaned forward. "He's got it all right, Mr. Finch."

Tim Johnson was advancing at a snail's pace, but he was not playing or sniffing at foliage: he seemed dedicated to one course and motivated by an invisible force that was inching him toward us. We could see him shiver like a horse shedding flies; his jaw opened and shut; he was alist, but he was being pulled gradually toward us.

"He's lookin' for a place to die," said Jem.

Mr. Tate turned around. "He's far from dead, Jem, he hasn't got started yet."

Tim Johnson reached the side street that ran in front of the Radley Place, and what remained of his poor mind made him pause and seem to consider which road he would take. He made a few hesitant steps and stopped in front of the Radley gate; then he tried to turn around, but was having difficulty.

Atticus said, "He's within range, Heck. You better get him before he goes down the side street—Lord knows who's around the corner. Go inside, Cal."

Calpurnia opened the screen door, latched it behind her, then unlatched it and held onto the hook. She tried to block Jem and me with her body, but we looked out from beneath her arms.

"Take him, Mr. Finch." Mr. Tate handed the rifle to Atticus; Jem and I nearly fainted.

"Don't waste time, Heck," said Atticus. "Go on."

"Mr. Finch, this is a one-shot job."

Atticus shook his head vehemently: "Don't just stand there, Heck! He won't wait all day for you—"

"For God's sake, Mr. Finch, look where he is! Miss and you'll go straight into the Radley house! I can't shoot that well and you know it!"

"I haven't shot a gun in thirty years—"

Mr. Tate almost threw the rifle at Atticus. "I'd feel mighty comfortable if you did now," he said.

In a fog, Jem and I watched our father take the gun and walk out into the middle of the street. He walked quickly, but I thought he moved like an underwater swimmer: time had slowed to a nauseating crawl.

When Atticus raised his glasses Calpurnia murmured, "Sweet Jesus help him," and put her hands to her cheeks.

Atticus pushed his glasses to his forehead; they slipped down, and he dropped them in the street. In the silence, I heard them crack.

Atticus rubbed his eyes and chin; we saw him blink hard.

In front of the Radley gate, Tim Johnson had made up what was left of his mind. He had finally turned himself around, to pursue his original course up our street. He made two steps forward, then stopped and raised his head. We saw his body go rigid.

With movements so swift they seemed simultaneous, Atticus's hand yanked a ball-tipped lever as he brought the gun to his shoulder.

The rifle cracked. Tim Johnson leaped, flopped over and crumpled on the sidewalk in a brown-and-white heap. He didn't know what hit him.

Mr. Tate jumped off the porch and ran to the Radley Place. He stopped in front of the dog, squatted, turned around and tapped his finger on his forehead above his left eye. "You were a little to the right, Mr. Finch," he called.

"Always was," answered Atticus. "If I had my 'druthers I'd take a shotgun."

He stooped and picked up his glasses, ground the broken lenses to powder under his heel, and went to Mr. Tate and stood looking down at Tim Johnson.

Doors opened one by one, and the neighborhood slowly came alive. Miss Maudie walked down the steps with Miss Stephanie Crawford.

Jem was paralyzed. I pinched him to get him moving, but when Atticus saw us coming he called, "Stay where you are."

When Mr. Tate and Atticus returned to the yard, Mr. Tate was smiling. "I'll have Zeebo collect him," he said. "You haven't forgot much, Mr. Finch. They say it never leaves you."

Atticus was silent.

"Atticus?" said Jem.

"Yes?"

"Nothin'."

"I saw that, One-Shot Finch!"

Atticus wheeled around and faced Miss Maudie. They looked at one another without saying anything, and Atticus got into the sheriff's car. "Come here," he said to Jem. "Don't you go near that dog, you understand? Don't go near him, he's just as dangerous dead as alive."

"Yes sir," said Jem. "Atticus—"

"What, son?"

"Nothing."

"What's the matter with you, boy, can't you talk?" said Mr. Tate, grinning at Jem. "Didn't you know your daddy's—"

"Hush, Heck," said Atticus, "let's go back to town."

When they drove away, Jem and I went to Miss Stephanie's front steps. We sat waiting for Zeebo to arrive in the garbage truck.

Jem sat in numb confusion, and Miss Stephanie said, "Uh, uh, uh, who'da thought of a mad dog in February? Maybe he wadn't mad, maybe he was just crazy. I'd hate to see Harry Johnson's face when he gets in from the Mobile run and finds Atticus Finch's shot his dog. Bet he was just full of fleas from somewhere—"

Miss Maudie said Miss Stephanie'd be singing a different tune if Tim Johnson was still coming up the street, that they'd find out soon enough, they'd send his head to Montgomery.

Jem became vaguely articulate: " 'd you see him, Scout? 'd you see him just standin' there? . . .'n' all of a sudden he just relaxed all over, an' it looked like that gun was a part of him . . . an' he did it so quick, like . . . I hafta aim for ten minutes 'fore I can hit somethin'. . . ."

Miss Maudie grinned wickedly. "Well now, Miss Jean Louise," she said, "still think your father can't do anything? Still ashamed of him?"

"Nome," I said meekly.

"Forgot to tell you the other day that besides playing the Jew's Harp, Atticus Finch was the deadest shot in Maycomb County in his time."

"Dead shot . . ." echoed Jem.

"That's what I said, Jem Finch. Guess you'll change *your* tune now. The very idea, didn't you know his nickname was Ol' One-Shot when he was a boy? Why, down at the Landing when he was coming up, if he shot fifteen times and hit fourteen doves he'd complain about wasting ammunition."

"He never said anything about that," Jem muttered.

"Never said anything about it, did he?"

"No ma'am."

"Wonder why he never goes huntin' now," I said.

"Maybe I can tell you," said Miss Maudie. "If your father's anything, he's civilized in his heart. Marksmanship's a gift of God, a talent—oh, you have to practice to make it perfect, but shootin's different from playing the piano or the like. I think maybe he put his gun down when he realized that God had given him an unfair advantage over most living things. I guess he decided he wouldn't shoot till he had to, and he had to today."

"Looks like he'd be proud of it," I said.

"People in their right minds never take pride in their talents," said Miss Maudie.

We saw Zeebo drive up. He took a pitchfork from the back of the garbage truck and gingerly lifted Tim Johnson. He pitched the dog onto the truck, then poured something from a gallon jug on and around the spot where Tim fell. "Don't yawl come over here for a while," he called.

When we went home I told Jem we'd really have something to talk about at school on Monday. Jem turned on me.

"Don't say anything about it, Scout," he said.

"What? I certainly am. Ain't everybody's daddy the deadest shot in Maycomb County."

Jem said, "I reckon if he'd wanted us to know it, he'da told us. If he was proud of it, he'da told us."

"Maybe it just slipped his mind," I said.

"Naw, Scout, it's something you wouldn't understand. Atticus is real old, but I wouldn't care if he couldn't do anything—I wouldn't care if he couldn't do a blessed thing."

Jem picked up a rock and threw it jubilantly at the carhouse. Running after it, he called back: "Atticus is a gentleman, just like me!"

Developing Comprehension Skills

1. Jem and Scout believe Atticus couldn't "do anything." What are some of the talents the children wish their father had?

2. Atticus tells Jem, "Shoot all the bluejays you want, if you can hit 'em, but remember it's a sin to kill a mockingbird." Why is it wrong to kill a mockingbird? What does this attitude reveal about Atticus? Explain your answer.

3. Why are the people afraid of Tim Johnson? How does Cal react when she sees the dog coming?

4. What is the reaction of the children when Sheriff Tate hands Atticus the gun? Why? What are their immediate reactions after Atticus shoots Tim Johnson?

5. Scout wants to tell all her friends about her father's feat. Why does Jem tell her to keep silent? How has Jem's opinion of his father changed since the beginning of the story?

6. Why do you suppose Atticus never told the children about his ability to shoot? Do you think his decision to keep it secret was a good one? Or, was it something he should have told them? Explain your answer.

Reading Literature

1. **Exploring Characterization.** There are several ways an author can reveal a character in a story. An author may reveal a character through 1) physical description, 2) dialogue, 3) character's actions, 4) the way other characters react to that person, or 5) the character's thoughts and feelings. Which methods does Harper Lee use to reveal Atticus's character? Find an example of each method.

2. **Identifying Suspense.** Tension, or suspense, in "One-Shot Finch" begins to build when Jem sees Tim Johnson in the distance.

He notices that the animal is acting oddly and gradually the tension builds. How does Harper Lee add to the growing suspense? How does she make the reader unsure of the outcome? Find specific examples.

3. **Recognizing the Climax.** As you know, the climax is the turning point of action in a story. It is the moment when interest is at its peak. What is the climax in "One-Shot Finch"? How does the event create a turning point in the children's relationship with their father?

4. **Identifying Symbolism.** The mockingbird mentioned in the story represents something other than itself. If the mockingbird symbolizes a person, what kind of person might it represent? Why would it be "a sin" to hurt such a person? Explain.

Developing Vocabulary Skills

Inferring Word Meaning. Carefully read the following sentences from the selection you just have read. Use specific information in each sentence to infer the meaning of the underlined word. On your paper, write the word and its meaning.

1. . . . Atticus wouldn't teach us to shoot. Uncle Jack instructed us in the rudiments thereof.

2. "Maudie," he called, "I thought I'd better warn you. You're in considerable peril."

3. He walked erratically, as if his right legs were shorter than his left legs.

4. "Mr. Finch, this is a one-shot job." Atticus shook his head vehemently.

5. With movements so swift they seemed simultaneous, Atticus's hand yanked a ball-tipped lever as he brought the gun to his shoulder.

6. Jem became vaguely articulate: " 'd you see him, Scout? 'd you see him just standin' there?"

Developing Writing Skills

1. **Analyzing the Relationship Between Characters.** What is the relationship that exists between Atticus and his children? Do you think it is a typical father/child relationship? Is it believable? In a composition, answer these questions. First, write a topic sentence that explains the purpose of the composition. Then, use specific details from the story to support your ideas.

2. **Writing an Autobiographical Incident.** In "One-Shot Finch," Scout tells about an incident from her childhood. As a result of the experience, she learns something new about her father.

   Describe an incident from your own life that revealed a new aspect of someone you know. The person might be a family member, a friend, or a classmate.

   Pre-Writing. Outline the most important events of the incident. Jot down where and when the incident took place. Who was involved? How did you view the person before? What caused you to see another side to that individual? Once you have made a list of these details, decide on an order in which to present them. It may be best to explain events in chronological order, the order in which they happened.

   Writing. Develop an introduction that will catch the attention of your reader and cause him or her to read your paper. For example, you might begin with a statement such as this: "I thought I really knew my brother. Did he surprise me!" Such an opening will arouse the reader's curiosity. Then, present the events of the incident. Be sure to be as specific as possible in describing it. Use words which help you present a clear, vivid picture for the reader.

Revising. Reread your paper. Have you presented all the details necessary to describe the incident clearly? Have you fully developed the character? Will your reader understand how you learned something new about someone you know? Remember, that is the purpose of the composition. After you have checked the content of your paper, check your grammar, capitalization, punctuation, and spelling. Make corrections as needed.

3. **Planning a Short Story.** As you know, the plot of a short story is made up of many different elements. So far, you have written an introduction for a short story, created a setting, and described a character. You have also developed a plot outline. Now, you can begin planning a story of your own.

First, use ideas from your journal, from your reading, from past experiences, or from your imagination to develop a general story idea. On a piece of paper, make a plot diagram for this story.

Identify your main characters, and create a specific setting. In addition, you will need to create conflicts for your main character, and decide how he or she will handle them.

Once you have decided on these important elements, jot down details that will help you develop each one. Do not worry about writing things out in detail at this time. Later you will be asked to tie all of the ideas together in a story. For now, just use your imagination to come up with ideas.

Developing Skills in Critical Thinking

Proving Statements of Fact. When a statement can be proven true it is a **fact**. An **opinion**, on the other hand, is a statement that can not be proven. Statements may be proven in a variety of ways. One way is through personal observation.

In "One-Shot Finch," Scout says, "Atticus can't do anything." What observations do the children make which at first seem to prove this statement? What observations do they make later in the story that disprove Scout's statement?

The Possibility of Evil

SHIRLEY JACKSON

Miss Adela Strangeworth came daintily along Main Street on her way to the grocery. The sun was shining, the air was fresh and clear after the night's heavy rain, and everything in Miss Strangeworth's little town looked washed and bright. Miss Strangeworth took deep breaths and thought that there was nothing in the world like a fragrant summer day.

She knew everyone in town, of course; she was fond of telling strangers—tourists who sometimes passed through the town and stopped to admire Miss Strangeworth's roses—that she had never spent more than a day outside this town in all her long life. She was seventy-one, Miss Strangeworth told the tourists, with a pretty little dimple showing by her lip, and she sometimes found herself thinking that the town belonged to her. "My grandfather built the first house on Pleasant Street," she would say, opening her blue eyes wide with the wonder of it. "This house, right here. My family has lived here for better than a hundred years. My grandmother planted these roses, and my mother tended them, just as I do. I've watched my town grow; I can remember when Mr. Lewis, Senior, opened the grocery store, and the year the river flooded out the shanties on the low road, and the excitement when some young folks wanted to move the park over to the space in front of where the new post office is today. They wanted to put up a statue of Ethan Allen"—Miss Strangeworth would frown a little and sound stern—"but it should have been a statue of my grandfather. There wouldn't have been a town here at all if it hadn't been for my grandfather and the lumber mill."

Miss Strangeworth never gave away any of her roses, although the tourists often asked her. The roses belonged on Pleasant Street, and it bothered Miss Strangeworth to think of people wanting to carry them away, to take them into strange towns and down strange streets. When the new minister came, and the ladies were gathering flowers to decorate the church, Miss Strangeworth sent over a great basket of gladioli; when she picked the roses at all, she set them in bowls and vases around the inside of the house her grandfather had built.

Walking down Main Street on a summer morning, Miss Strangeworth had to stop every minute or so to say good morning to someone or to ask after someone's health. When she came into the grocery, half a dozen people turned away from the shelves and the counters to wave at her or call out good morning.

"And good morning to you, too, Mr. Lewis," Miss Strangeworth said at last. The Lewis family had been in the town almost as long as the Strangeworths; but the day young Lewis left high school and went to work in the grocery, Miss Strangeworth had stopped calling him Tommy and started calling him Mr. Lewis, and he had stopped calling her Addie and started calling her Miss Strangeworth. They had been in high school together, and had gone to picnics together, and to high-school dances and basketball games; but now Mr. Lewis was behind the counter in the grocery, and Miss Strangeworth was living alone in the Strangeworth house on Pleasant Street.

"Good morning," Mr. Lewis said, and added politely, "Lovely day."

"It is a very nice day," Miss Strangeworth said, as though she had only just decided that it would do after all. "I would like a chop, please, Mr. Lewis, a small, lean veal chop. Are those strawberries from Arthur Parker's garden? They're early this year."

"He brought them in this morning," Mr. Lewis said.

"I shall have a box," Miss Strangeworth said. Mr. Lewis looked worried, she thought, and for a minute she hesitated, but then she decided that he surely could not be worried over the strawberries. He looked very tired indeed. He was usually so chipper, Miss Strangeworth thought, and almost commented; but it was far too personal a subject to be introduced to Mr. Lewis, the grocer, so she only said, "And a can of cat food and, I think, a tomato."

Silently, Mr. Lewis assembled her order on the counter, and waited. Miss Strangeworth looked at him curiously and then said, "It's Tuesday, Mr. Lewis. You forgot to remind me."

"Did I? Sorry."

"Imagine your forgetting that I always buy my tea on Tuesday," Miss Strangeworth said gently. "A quarter pound of tea, please, Mr. Lewis."

"Is that all, Miss Strangeworth?"

"Yes thank you, Mr. Lewis. Such a lovely day, isn't it?"

"Lovely," Mr. Lewis said.

Miss Strangeworth moved slightly to make room for Mrs. Harper at the counter. "Morning, Adela," Mrs. Harper said, and Miss Strangeworth said, "Good morning, Martha."

"Lovely day," Mrs. Harper said, and Miss Strangeworth said, "Yes, lovely," and Mr. Lewis, under Mrs. Harper's glance, nodded.

"Ran out of sugar for my cake frosting," Mrs. Harper explained. Her hand shook slightly as she opened her pocketbook. Miss Strangeworth wondered, glancing at her quickly, if she had been taking proper care of herself. Martha Harper was not as young as she used to be, Miss Strangeworth thought. She probably could use a good strong tonic.

"Martha," she said, "You don't look well."

"I'm perfectly all right," Mrs. Harper said shortly. She handed her money to Mr. Lewis, took her change and her sugar, and went out without speaking again. Looking after her, Miss Strangeworth shook her head slightly. Martha definitely did *not* look well.

Street in Iowa City, 1978, JOHN GORDON. Pillsbury Company, Minneapolis, Minnesota.

Carrying her little bag of groceries, Miss Strangeworth came out of the store into the bright sunlight and stopped to smile down on the Crane baby. Don and Helen Crane were really the two most infatuated young parents she had ever known, she thought indulgently, looking at the delicately embroidered baby cap and the lace-edged carriage cover.

"That little girl is going to grow up expecting luxury all her life," she said to Helen Crane.

Helen laughed. "That's the way we want her to feel," she said. "Like a princess."

"A princess can see a lot of trouble sometimes," Miss Strangeworth said dryly. "How old is Her Highness now?"

"Six months next Tuesday," Helen Crane said, looking down with rapt wonder at her child. "I've been worrying, though, about her. Don't you think she ought to move around more? Try to sit up, for instance?"

"For plain and fancy worrying," Miss Strangeworth said, amused, "give me a new mother every time."

"She just seems—slow," Helen Crane said.

"Nonsense. All babies are different. Some of them develop much more quickly than others."

"That's what my mother says." Helen Crane laughed, looking a little bit ashamed.

"I suppose you've got young Don all upset about the fact that his daughter is already six months old and hasn't yet begun to learn to dance?"

"I haven't mentioned it to him. I suppose she's just so precious that I worry about her all the time."

"Well, apologize to her right now," Miss Strangeworth said. "*She* is probably worrying about why you keep jumping around all the time." Smiling to herself and shaking her old head, she went on down the sunny street, stopping once to ask little Billy Moore why he wasn't out riding in his daddy's shiny new car; and talking for a few minutes outside the library with Miss Chandler, the librarian, about the new novels to be ordered and paid for by the annual library appropriation. Miss Chandler seemed absent-minded and very much as though she were thinking about something else. Miss Strangeworth noticed that Miss Chandler had not taken much trouble with her hair that morning, and sighed. Miss Strangeworth hated sloppiness.

Many people seemed disturbed recently, Miss Strangeworth thought. Only yesterday the Stewarts' fifteen-year-old Linda had run crying down her own front walk and all the way to school, not caring who saw her. People around town thought she might have had a fight with the Harris boy, but they showed up together at the soda shop after school as usual, both of them looking grim and bleak. Trouble at home, people concluded, and sighed over the problems of trying to raise kids right these days.

From halfway down the block, Miss Strangeworth could catch the heavy scent of her roses, and she moved a little more quickly. The perfume of roses meant home, and home meant the Strangeworth House on Pleasant Street. Miss Strangeworth stopped at her own front gate, as she always did, and looked with deep pleasure at her house, with the red and pink and white roses massed along the narrow lawn, and the rambler going up along the porch; and the neat, the unbelievably trim lines of the house itself, with its slimness and its washed white look. Every window sparkled, every curtain hung stiff and straight, and even the stones of the front walk were swept and clear. People around town wondered how old Miss Strangeworth managed to keep the house looking the way it did, and there was a legend about a tourist once mistaking it for the local museum and going all through the place without finding out about his mistake. But the town was proud of Miss Strangeworth and her roses and her house. They had all grown together.

Miss Strangeworth went up her front steps, unlocked her front door with her key, and went into the kitchen to put away her groceries. She debated about having a cup of tea and then decided that it was too close to midday dinnertime; she would not have the appetite for her little chop if she had tea now. Instead she went into the light, lovely sitting room, which still glowed from the hands of her mother and her grandmother, who had covered the chairs with bright chintz and hung the curtains. All the furniture was spare and shining, and the round hooked rugs on the floor had been the work of Miss Strangeworth's grandmother and her mother. Miss Strangeworth had put a bowl of her red roses on the low table before the window, and the room was full of their scent.

Miss Strangeworth went to the narrow desk in the corner and unlocked it with her key. She never knew when she might feel like writing letters, so she kept her notepaper inside and the desk locked. Miss Strangeworth's usual stationery was heavy and cream-colored, with STRANGEWORTH HOUSE engraved across the top; but, when she felt like writing her other letters, Miss Strangeworth used a pad of various-colored paper bought from the local newspaper shop. It was almost a town joke, that colored paper, layered in pink and green and blue and yellow; everyone in town bought it and used it for odd, informal notes and shopping lists. It was usual to remark, upon receiving a note written on a blue page, that so-and-so would be needing a new pad soon —here she was, down to the blue already. Everyone used the matching envelopes for tucking away recipes, or keeping odd little things in, or even to hold cookies in the school lunchboxes. Mr. Lewis sometimes gave them to the children for carrying home penny candy.

Although Miss Strangeworth's desk held a trimmed quill pen that had belonged to her grandfather, and a gold-frosted fountain pen that had belonged to her father, Miss Strangeworth always used a dull stub of pencil when she wrote her letters; and she printed them in a childish block print. After thinking for a minute, although she had been phrasing the letter in the back of her mind all the way home, she wrote on a pink sheet:

DIDN'T YOU EVER SEE AN IDIOT CHILD BEFORE? SOME PEOPLE JUST SHOULDN'T HAVE CHILDREN SHOULD THEY?

She was pleased with the letter. She was fond of doing things exactly right. When she made a mistake, as she sometimes did, or when the letters were not spaced nicely on the page, she had to take the discarded page to the kitchen stove and burn it at once. Miss Strangeworth never delayed when things had to be done.

After thinking for a minute, she decided that she would like to write another letter, perhaps to go to Mrs. Harper, to follow up the ones she had already mailed. She selected a green sheet this time and wrote quickly:

HAVE YOU FOUND OUT YET WHAT THEY WERE ALL LAUGHING ABOUT AFTER YOU LEFT THE BRIDGE CLUB ON THURSDAY? OR IS THE WIFE REALLY ALWAYS THE LAST ONE TO KNOW?

Miss Strangeworth never concerned herself with facts; her letters all dealt with the more negotiable stuff of suspicion. Mr. Lewis would never have imagined for a minute that his grandson might be lifting petty cash from the store register if he had not had one of Miss Strangeworth's letters. Miss Chandler, the librarian, and Linda Stewart's parents would have gone unsuspectingly ahead with their lives, never aware of possible evil lurking nearby, if Miss Strangeworth had not sent letters opening their eyes. Miss Strangeworth would have been genuinely shocked if there *had* been anything between Linda Stewart and the Harris boy; but, as long as evil existed unchecked in the world, it was Miss Strangeworth's duty to keep her town alert to it. It was far more sensible for Miss Chandler to wonder what Mr. Shelley's first wife had really died of than to take a chance on not knowing. There were so many wicked people in the world and only one Strangeworth left in the town. Besides, Miss Strangeworth liked writing her letters.

She addressed an envelope to Don Crane after a moment's thought, wondering curiously if he would show the letter to his wife, and using a pink envelope to match the pink paper. Then she addressed a second envelope, green, to Mrs. Harper. Then an idea came to her and she selected a blue sheet and wrote:

YOU NEVER KNOW ABOUT DOCTORS. REMEM-BER THEY'RE ONLY HUMAN AND NEED MONEY LIKE THE REST OF US. SUPPOSE THE KNIFE SLIPPED ACCIDENTALLY. WOULD DR. BURNS GET HIS FEE AND A LITTLE EXTRA FROM THAT NEPHEW OF YOURS?

She addressed the blue envelope to old Mrs. Foster, who was having an operation next month. She had thought of writing one more letter, to the head of the school board, asking how a chemistry teacher like Billy Moore's father could afford a new convertible, but, all at once, she was tired of writing letters. The three she had done would do for one day. She could write more tomorrow; it was not as though they all had to be done at once.

She had been writing her letters—sometimes two or three every day for a week, sometimes no more than one in a month—for the past year. She never got any answers, of course, because she never signed her name. If she had been asked, she would have said that her name, Adela Strangeworth, a name honored in the town for so many years, did not belong on such trash. The town where she lived had to be kept clean and sweet, but people everywhere were lustful and evil and degraded, and needed to be watched; the world was so large, and there was only one Strangeworth left in it. Miss Strangeworth sighed, locked her desk, and put the letters into her big black leather pocketbook, to be mailed when she took her evening walk.

She broiled her little chop nicely, and had a sliced tomato and a good cup of tea ready when she sat down to her midday dinner at the table in her dining room, which could be opened to seat twenty-two, with a second table, if necessary, in the hall. Sitting in the warm sunlight that came through the tall windows of the dining room, seeing her roses massed outside, handling the heavy, old silverware and the fine, translucent china, Miss Strangeworth was pleased; she would not have cared to be doing anything else. People must live graciously after all, she thought, and sipped her tea. Afterward, when her plate and cup and saucer were washed and dried and put back onto the shelves where they belonged, and her silverware was back in the mahogany silver chest, Miss Strangeworth went up the graceful staircase and into her bedroom, which was the front room overlooking the roses, and had been her mother's and her grandmother's. Their Crown Derby dresser set and furs had been kept there, their fans and silver-backed brushes and their own bowls of roses; Miss Strangeworth kept a bowl of white roses on the bed table.

She drew the shades, took the rose satin spread from the bed, slipped out of her dress and her shoes, and lay down tiredly. She knew that no doorbell or phone would ring; no one in town would dare to disturb Miss Strangeworth during her afternoon nap. She slept deep in the rich smell of roses.

After her nap she worked in her garden for a little while, sparing herself because of the heat; then she came in to her supper. She ate asparagus from her own garden, with sweet-butter sauce and a soft-boiled egg; and, while she had her supper, she listened to a late-evening news broadcast and then to a program of classical music on her small radio. After her dishes were done and her kitchen set in order, she took up her hat—Miss Strangeworth's hats were proverbial in the town; people believed that she had inherited them from her mother and her grandmother—and, locking the front door of her house behind her, set off on her evening walk, pocketbook under her arm. She nodded to Linda Stewart's father, who was washing his car in the pleasantly cool evening. She thought that he looked troubled.

There was only one place in town where she could mail her letters, and that was the new post office, shiny with red brick and silver letters. Although Miss Strangeworth had never given the matter any particular thought, she had always made a point of mailing her letters very secretly; it would, of course, not have been wise to let anyone see her mail them. Consequently, she timed her walk so she could reach the post office just as darkness was starting to dim the outlines of the trees and the shapes of people's faces, although no one could ever mistake Miss Strangeworth, with her dainty walk and her rustling skirts.

There was always a group of young people around the post office, the very youngest roller-skating upon its driveway, which went all the way around the building and was the only smooth road in town; and the slightly older ones already knowing how to gather in small groups and chatter and laugh and make great, excited plans for going across the street to the soda shop in a minute or two. Miss Strangeworth had never had any self-consciousness before the children. She did not feel that any of them were staring at her unduly or longing to laugh at her; it would have been most reprehensible for their parents to permit their children to mock Miss Strangeworth of Pleasant Street. Most of the children stood back respectfully as Miss Strangeworth passed, silenced briefly in her presence, and some of the older children greeted her, saying soberly, "Hello, Miss Strangeworth."

Miss Strangeworth smiled at them and quickly went on. It had been a long time since she had known the name of every child in town. The mail slot was in the door of the post office. The children stood away as Miss Strangeworth approached it, seemingly surprised that anyone should want to use the post office after it had been officially closed up for the night and turned over to the children. Miss Strangeworth stood by the door, opening her black pocketbook to take out the letters, and heard a voice which she knew at once to be Linda Stewart's. Poor little Linda was crying again, and Miss Strangeworth listened carefully. This was, after all, her town, and these were her people; if one of them was in trouble she ought to know about it.

"I can't tell you, Dave," Linda was saying— so she *was* talking to the Harris boy, as Miss Strangeworth had supposed—"I just *can't*. It's just *nasty*."

"But why won't your father let me come around any more? What on earth did I do?"

"I can't tell you. I just wouldn't tell you for *anything*. You've got to have a dirty, dirty mind for things like that."

"But something's happened. You've been crying and crying, and your father is all upset.

Why can't *I* know about it, too? Aren't I like one of the family?"

"Not any more, Dave, not any more. You're not to come near our house, again; my father said so. He said he'd horsewhip you. That's all I can tell you: You're not to come near our house any more."

"But I didn't *do* anything."

"Just the same, my father said . . ."

Miss Strangeworth sighed and turned away.

Roses on the Wall, 1874, GEORGE LAMBDIN. Courtesy of Mr. and Mrs. William C. Burt.

There was so much evil in people. Even in a charming little town like this one, there was still so much evil in people.

She slipped her letters into the slot, and two of them fell inside. The third caught on the edge and fell outside, onto the ground at Miss Strangeworth's feet. She did not notice it because she was wondering whether a letter to the Harris boy's father might not be of some service in wiping out this potential badness. Wearily Miss Strangeworth turned to go home to her quiet bed in her lovely house, and never heard the Harris boy calling to her to say that she had dropped something.

"Old lady Strangeworth's getting deaf," he said, looking after her and holding in his hand the letter he had picked up.

"Well, who cares?" Linda said. "Who cares any more, anyway?"

"It's for Don Crane," the Harris boy said, "this letter. She dropped a letter addressed to Don Crane. Might as well take it on over. We pass his house anyway." He laughed. "Maybe it's got a check or something in it, and he'd be just as glad to get it tonight instead of tomorrow."

"Catch old lady Strangeworth sending anybody a check," Linda said. "Throw it in the post office. Why do anyone a favor?" She sniffled. "Doesn't seem to me anybody around here cares about us," she said. "Why should we care about them?"

"I'll take it over anyway," the Harris boy said. "Maybe it's good news for them. Maybe they need something happy tonight, too. Like us."

Sadly, holding hands, they wandered off down the dark street, the Harris boy carrying Miss Strangeworth's pink envelope in his hand.

Miss Strangeworth awakened the next morning with a feeling of intense happiness, and for a minute wondered why, and then remembered that this morning three people would open her letters. Harsh, perhaps, at first, but wickedness was never easily banished, and a clean heart was a scoured heart. She washed her soft old face and brushed her teeth, still sound in spite of her seventy-one years, and dressed herself carefully in her sweet, soft clothes and buttoned shoes. Then, coming downstairs and reflecting that perhaps a little waffle would be agreeable for breakfast in the sunny dining room, she found the mail on the hall floor and bent to pick it up. A bill, the morning paper, a letter in a green envelope that looked oddly familiar. Miss Strangeworth stood perfectly still for a minute, looking down at the green envelope with the penciled printing, and thought: It looks like one of my letters. Was one of my letters sent back? No, because no one would know where to send it. How did this get here?

Miss Strangeworth was a Strangeworth of Pleasant Street. Her hand did not shake as she opened the envelope and unfolded the sheet of green paper inside. She began to cry silently for the wickedness of the world when she read the words:

LOOK OUT AT WHAT USED TO BE YOUR ROSES.

Developing Comprehension Skills

1. What kind of person is Miss Strangeworth, as described in the opening section of the story? How do the townspeople treat her?

2. Miss Strangeworth speaks politely to the people she meets. Do her actual thoughts match her speech and actions?

3. What types of letters does Miss Strangeworth send? How do you think the letters affect the people who receive them?

4. Miss Strangeworth thinks she is protecting the town from evil. Is Miss Strangeworth really exposing evil, or is she actually creating it? Explain your answer.

5. How does Don Crane learn that Miss Strangeworth has been writing the letters?

6. What is implied in the sentence "LOOK OUT AT WHAT USED TO BE YOUR ROSES"? Do you think Miss Strangeworth deserves such a harsh punishment? Why or why not?

Reading Literature

1. **Understanding Irony.** Like many of Shirley Jackson's stories, "The Possibility of Evil" uses irony to emphasize main ideas. Miss Strangeworth, for example, is not the person she appears to be. What is she really like?

   Another example of irony is the letters she sends. Miss Strangeworth believes she sends the letters to eliminate evil. What effect, however, do the letters have?

2. **Recognizing Change in Mood.** An author can often surprise his or her readers by suddenly changing mood. The quiet and peaceful mood in "The Possibility of Evil" suddenly becomes one of horror. When does this change take place? Find specific details that add to the peaceful mood in the first part of the story. What details contribute to the mood in the last part?

3. **Identifying Setting.** As you know, an appropriate setting can often help create a specific mood. What is the setting for "The Possibility of Evil"? How does this setting help in creating mood in the first part of the story? How does it emphasize the contrasting mood in the second part? Explain.

Developing Vocabulary Skills

Reviewing Ways To Determine Word Meaning. The following sentences are from "The Possibility of Evil." Read each sentence carefully. Look for context clues and word parts. Then, try to infer the meaning of each underlined word from the main idea of the passage. Write down each word and its meaning. Also, tell which clues you used to figure out the meaning.

1. He looked very tired indeed. He was usually so chipper.

2. People around town thought she might have had a fight with the Harris boy, but they showed up together at the soda shop after school as usual, both of them looking grim and bleak.

3. When she made a mistake . . . she had to take the discarded page to the kitchen stove and burn it at once.

4. . . . Linda Stewart's parents would have gone unsuspectingly ahead with their lives, never aware of possible evil lurking nearby . . . .

5. . . . handling the heavy, old silverware and the fine, translucent china, Miss Strangeworth was pleased.

6. . . . it would have been most <u>reprehensible</u> for their parents to permit their children to mock Miss Strangeworth of Pleasant Street.

7. . . . she was wondering whether a letter to the Harris boy's father might not be of some service in wiping out this <u>potential</u> badness.

8. . . . a clean heart was a <u>scoured</u> heart.

Developing Writing Skills

1. **Understanding Themes.** Things are not always as they appear to be. This is one of the main ideas in "A Possibility of Evil." It is also a theme in "One-Shot Finch." Write a two-paragraph composition showing how this theme exists in the stories.

   Pre-Writing. Jot down as many details as you can that relate to the theme. Your notes should deal with each character's appearance, and then with the actual person. Include details such as the words and actions of each character that reveal both sides of the person. You can also jot down notes on how characters view one another. For example, you could write down notes on how the townspeople view Miss Strangeworth.

   Writing. Begin with an introduction that presents the titles and themes of the stories. Then write a rough draft.

   There are several ways of organizing your composition. You might first write a paragraph about "The Possibility of Evil," and then a paragraph about "One-Shot Finch." Or, you might organize your composition so that the "appearances" are discussed in the first paragraph, and the "realities" in the second one. End your draft with a summary statement that restates your main idea.

   Revising. Read your draft carefully. Does your introduction include the titles of the two stories being compared? How well do your paragraphs develop this statement? Do the details you use clearly show how the stories develop the theme?

   Check your paper, also, for sentence fragments and run-on sentences. If you need to, correct these. Make a clean final copy to present to your teacher.

2. **Writing a Letter.** Miss Strangeworth writes short letters to the townspeople. In them she makes judgments and insinuations about the people and tells them what to do.

   Write a letter to Miss Strangeworth. In it, tell Miss Strangeworth what you think of her letter writing. Point out the effect her letters have on those who receive them.

Developing Skills in Study and Research

Using the Card Catalog. Short story collections are usually arranged in alphabetical order by author, and can be found in the 800 category. The card catalog will tell you exactly where the book can be found on the shelf.

Locate the author cards for Shirley Jackson in your library's card catalog. Write down the titles of one or more collections of short stories by Jackson. For each book, write down the call number from the corner of the card. Use this number to locate the book on the library shelves. If you have difficulty, ask the librarian to help. When you find the book, open to the table of contents in the front of the book. Choose one other story by Jackson to read and report on.

Time in Thy Flight

RAY BRADBURY

SETTING A PURPOSE | *Imagine a time when there are no more holidays and no celebrations. Imagine a world with no excitement or fantasy. What effect does this kind of world have on the children in this story?*

A wind blew the long years away past their hot faces.

The Time Machine stopped.

"Nineteen hundred and twenty-eight," said Janet. The two boys looked past her.

Mr. Fields stirred. "Remember, you're here to observe the behavior of these ancient people. Be inquisitive, be intelligent, observe."

"Yes," said the girl and the two boys in crisp khaki uniforms. They wore identical haircuts, had identical wristwatches, sandals, and coloring of hair, eyes, teeth, and skin.

"Shh!" said Mr. Fields.

They looked out at a little Illinois town in the spring of the year. A cool mist lay on the early morning streets.

Far down the street a small boy came running in the last light of the marble-cream moon. Somewhere a great clock struck 5 A.M. far away. Leaving tennis-shoe prints softly in the quiet lawns, the boy stepped near the invisible Time Machine and cried up to a high dark house window.

The house window opened. Another boy crept down the roof to the ground. The two boys ran off with banana-filled mouths into the dark cold morning.

"Follow them," whispered Mr. Fields. "Study their life patterns. Quick!"

Janet and William and Robert ran on the cold pavements of spring, visible now, through the slumbering town, through a park. All about, lights flickered, doors clicked, and other children rushed alone or in gasping pairs down a hill to some gleaming blue tracks.

"Here it comes!" The children milled about before dawn. Far down the shining tracks a small light grew seconds later into steaming thunder.

"What is it?" screamed Janet.

"A train, silly, you've seen pictures of them!" shouted Robert.

And as the Time children watched, from the train stepped gigantic gray elephants, steaming the pavements with their mighty waters, lifting question-mark nozzles to the cold morning sky. Cumbrous wagons rolled from the long freight flats, red and gold. Lions roared and paced in boxed darkness.

"Why—*this* must be a—circus!" Janet trembled.

"You think so? Whatever happened to them?"

Years of Fear, 1941, MATTA. Solomon R. Guggenheim Museum, New York.

"Like Christmas, I guess. Just vanished, long ago."

Janet looked around. "Oh, it's awful, isn't it."

The boys stood numbed. "It sure is."

Men shouted in the first faint gleam of dawn. Sleeping cars drew up, dazed faces blinked out at the children. Horses clattered like a great fall of stones on the pavement.

Mr. Fields was suddenly behind the children. "Disgusting, barbaric, keeping animals in cages. If I'd known this was here, I'd never let you come see. This is a terrible ritual."

"Oh, yes." But Janet's eyes were puzzled. "And yet, you know, it's like a nest of maggots. I want to study it."

"I don't know," said Robert, his eyes darting, his fingers trembling. "It's pretty crazy. We might try writing a thesis on it if Mr. Fields says it's all right. . ."

Mr. Fields nodded. "I'm glad you're digging in here, finding motives, studying this horror. All right—we'll see the circus this afternoon."

"I think I'm going to be sick," said Janet.

The Time Machine hummed.

"So that was a circus," said Janet, solemnly.

The trombone circus died in their ears. The last thing they saw was candy-pink trapeze people whirling while baking powder clowns shrieked and bounded.

"You must admit psychovision's better," said Robert slowly.

"All those nasty animal smells, the excitement." Janet blinked. "That's bad for children, isn't it? And those older people seated with the children. Mothers, fathers, they called them. Oh, that *was* strange."

Mr. Fields put some marks in his class grading book.

Janet shook her head numbly. "I want to see it all again. I've missed the motives somewhere. I want to make that run across town again in the early morning. The cold air on my face—the sidewalk under my feet—the circus train coming in. Was it the air and the early hour that made the children get up and run to see the train come in? I want to retrace the entire pattern. Why should they be excited? I feel I've missed out on the answer."

"They all smiled so much," said William.

"Manic-depressives," said Robert.

"What are summer vacations? I heard them talk about it." Janet looked at Mr. Fields.

"They spent their summers racing about like idiots, beating each other up," replied Mr. Fields seriously.

"I'll take our State Engineered summers of work for children anytime," said Robert, looking at nothing, his voice faint.

The Time Machine stopped again.

"The Fourth of July," announced Mr. Fields. "Nineteen hundred and twenty-eight. An ancient holiday when people blew each other's fingers off."

They stood before the same house on the same street but on a soft summer evening. Fire wheels hissed, on front porches laughing children tossed things out that went bang!

"Don't run!" cried Mr. Fields. "It's not war, don't be afraid!"

But Janet's and Robert's and William's faces were pink, now blue, now white with fountains of soft fire.

"We're all right," said Janet, standing very still.

"Happily," announced Mr. Fields, "they prohibited fireworks a century ago, did away with the whole messy explosion."

Children did fairy dances, weaving their names and destinies on the dark summer air with white sparklers.

"I'd like to do that," said Janet, softly. "Write my name on the air. See? I'd like that."

"What?" Mr. Fields hadn't been listening.

"Nothing," said Janet.

"Bang!" whispered William and Robert, standing under the soft summer trees, in shadow, watching, watching the red, white, and green fires on the beautiful summer night lawns. "Bang!"

October.

The Time Machine paused for the last time, an hour later in the month of burning leaves. People bustled into dim houses carrying pumpkins and corn shocks. Skeletons danced, bats flew, candles flamed, apples swung in empty doorways.

"Halloween," said Mr. Fields. "The acme of horror. This was the age of superstition, you know. Later they banned the Grimm Brothers, ghosts, skeletons, and all that claptrap. You children, thank God, were raised in an antiseptic world of no shadows or ghosts.

You had decent holidays like William C. Chatterton's Birthday, Work Day, and Machine Day."

They walked by the same house in the empty October night, peering in at the triangle-eyed pumpkins, the masks leering in black attics and damp cellars. Now, inside the house, some party children squatted telling stories, laughing!

"I want to be inside with them," said Janet at last.

"Sociologically, of course," said the boys.

"No," she said.

"What?" asked Mr. Fields.

"No, I just want to be inside, I just want to stay here, I want to see it all and be here and never be anywhere else, I want firecrackers and pumpkins and circuses, I want Christmases and Valentines and Fourths, like we've seen."

"This is getting out of hand . . ." Mr. Fields started to say.

But suddenly Janet was gone. "Robert, William, come on!" She ran. The boys leaped after her.

"Hold on!" shouted Mr. Fields. "Robert! William, I've got you!" He seized the last boy, but the other escaped. "Janet, Robert—come back here! You'll never pass into the seventh grade! You'll fail, Janet, Bob—*Bob*!"

An October wind blew wildly down the street, vanishing with the children off among moaning trees.

William twisted and kicked.

"No, not you, too, William, you're coming home with me. We'll teach those other two a lesson they won't forget. So they want to stay in the past, do they?" Mr. Fields shouted so everyone could hear. "All right, Janet, Bob, stay in this horror, in this chaos! In a few weeks you'll come sniveling back here to me. But I'll be gone! I'm leaving you here to go mad in this world!"

He hurried William to the Time Machine. The boy was sobbing. "Don't make me come back here on any more Field Excursions ever again, please, Mr. Fields, please—"

"Shut up!"

Almost instantly the Time Machine whisked away toward the future, toward the underground hive cities, the metal buildings, the metal flowers, the metal lawns.

"Good-bye, Janet, Bob!"

A great cold October wind blew through the town like water. And when it had ceased blowing it had carried all the children, whether invited or uninvited, masked or unmasked, to the doors of houses which closed upon them. There was not a running child anywhere in the night. The wind whined away in the bare treetops.

And inside the big house, in the candlelight, someone was pouring cold apple cider all around, to everyone, no matter *who* they were.

Developing Comprehension Skills

1. The children and teacher from the Time Machine are on a Field Excursion. What are they studying?

2. The children witness many different events. How do they react to what they see? Is each child affected in the same way?

3. How are the time travelers and their world different from the people and times they are studying? What accounts for these differences? Are there any similarities? Explain.

4. Explain Mr. Fields's warning to Janet and Bob: ". . . stay in this horror, in this chaos! . . . I'm leaving you here to go mad in this world!" Will they go mad? Give reasons for your answer.

5. Throughout the story Janet and Bob describe everything as terrible. Why do you suppose they want to stay? What attracts them? What is missing from their own world?

6. Do you consider any of our customs savage or cruel? Do you think society is heading toward the kind of future implied in this story? Explain.

Reading Literature

1. **Recognizing Science Fiction.** Writing that presents the possibilities of the future is called **science fiction**. The writer uses scientific facts, theories, and technology to create the story. In addition, imagination plays an important part in the writing of science fiction. How does "Time in Thy Flight" qualify as science fiction?

2. **Understanding Purpose and Theme.** As you know, an author usually has a particular purpose, or reason, for writing a story. Often he or she wishes to get an idea across to the reader. In "Time in Thy Flight," Ray Bradbury makes a comment about the role of science in society. Many human needs are taken care of by science and technology, but what else is important? Remember that Bradbury wrote this story in 1966. Is its message still appropriate today? Explain.

3. **Relating the Theme to the Title.** Often a writer will choose a title for a story from some other work. Read the following quote taken from Elizabeth Akers Allen's 1860 work, entitled, "Rock Me to Sleep." "Backward, turn backward, O Time, in your flight, / Make me a child again just for tonight!" How does the main idea of this passage relate to the theme and title of Bradbury's story? Why is "Time in Thy Flight" a good title?

4. **Understanding Internal Conflict.** When a character has a struggle within himself or herself it is called an **internal conflict**. Often it involves feelings and a decision the character must make. What decision must the children make? Why is this decision so difficult for them to make?

5. **Recognizing Irony.** Janet's response to the vanishing of Christmas and circuses is "Oh, it's awful, isn't it?" What two meanings might this statement have? Which do you consider the actual meaning? Why?

6. **Recognizing the Importance of Point of View.** The narrator, or person who tells the story, determines the point of view. With third-person point of view, the pronouns *he*, *she*, and *they* are used. The narrator remains distant and uninvolved.

   How would this story be different if it were told by one of the characters? Would the reader know too much, too soon? Explain your answer.

Developing Vocabulary Skills

Inferring the Meaning of Technical Terms. In science fiction, you often read passages that contain words from the vocabulary of an imaginary world or a specialized field. From context clues, word parts, and the main idea of the passage, you can often infer the meanings of these words. Use the skills you have developed to infer the meaning of the underlined words in these sentences from "Time in Thy Flight."

1. It's pretty crazy. We might try writing a thesis on it if Mr. Fields says it's all right . . .

2. "You must admit psychovision's better," said Robert slowly.

3. "They all smiled so much," said William. "Manic-depressives," said Robert.

4. "I want to be inside with them," said Janet at last. "Sociologically, of course," said the boys.

5. Almost instantly the Time Machine whisked away toward the future, toward the underground hive cities . . . .

Developing Writing Skills

1. **Contrasting Characters.** The Field Excursion in "Time in Thy Flight" reveals that Mr. Fields and Janet are not alike. In two paragraphs, describe the differences that exist between these two characters.

   Pre-Writing. On a piece of paper make two headings. Label one "Mr. Fields" and the other "Janet." Then, skim the story for details related to each character.

First, list traits of the characters. Then, list details that illustrate those traits. Organize your notes so that contrasting traits are put together.

   Writing. Your introduction should tell the reader that you are showing the differences between Janet and Mr. Fields. You might describe one of the characters in your first paragraph and the other in the second paragraph. Or, you could contrast the two characters trait by trait. Use examples and details from the story to give your writing support. Try to use transitional phrases like "on the other hand" and "contrary to" to show how ideas are related.

   Revising. Read your paper. Did you include only details that point out differences between the characters? Do you have enough details to support your topic sentences? If not, you may need to add more. Does your summary statement effectively conclude your paper? Does it remind the reader of your purpose?

2. **Using Imagination.** What would you do if you had one chance to use a Time Machine? Would you travel into the past or the future? Why? Imagine that you had such an opportunity. Then, write a paragraph describing your fantasy trip.

3. **Writing a Short Story.** Throughout this chapter, you have been completing different activities that will help you to write a short story. On page 401 you were asked to complete some pre-writing steps for a story. Now, use your notes to write a draft of your own original short story.

   As you write, you may think of additional things to add to the plot. Include these, but make sure that everything in your story works together. Concentrate on creating a good description of setting and character. Use words that will create specific images for your readers.

After you have written your story, be sure to spend time on revision. You may wish to form an editing group with your classmates to help with this stage.

Developing Skills in Critical Thinking

Recognizing Judgment Words. Judgment words, you will recall, express the attitudes of a writer or speaker toward a subject. Words such as *wonderful, terrible, beautiful,* and *ugly* reflect opinion. The use of such words can influence the opinions of others.

Mr. Fields uses judgment words when he describes the circus as "disgusting, barbaric." How does this influence the children's view of the circus? Find other examples of judgment words. How do they affect the children?

Developing Skills in Speaking and Listening

Preparing an Interview. The Time Machine crew is observing and investigating people of another time. Imagine that you are a member of a similar crew. Your assignment is to write an article about a person from another period in time. Decide whether you will interview someone from the past or the future. Then, develop a set of questions to ask this person. Avoid questions that can be answered with a "yes" or a "no." Ask questions that will help you discover what the person does, and what he or she likes and dislikes. Also, ask about government, sports, and entertainment. Add other questions which interest you.

After you have developed a set of questions, use them to interview a student in your class. This student should take on the role of the character you have imagined. When you have finished your interview, switch roles.

Chapter 7 *Review*

Using Your Skills in Reading Literature

The following is the opening of a short story, "Two Soldiers," by William Faulkner. Read it and answer the questions that follow.

> Me and Pete would go down to Old Man Killegrew's and listen to his radio. We would wait until after supper, after dark, and we would stand outside Old Man Killegrew's parlor window, and we could hear it because Old Man Killegrew's wife was deaf, and so he run the radio as loud as it would run, and so me and Pete could hear it plain as Old Man Killegrew's wife could, I reckon, even standing outside with the window closed.
>
> And that night I said, "What? Japanese? What's a pearl harbor?" and Pete said, "Hush."

1. From what point of view is the short story told?

2. What can you tell about the character of the narrator?

3. What details of the setting are given?

4. Do you see the beginning of a possible conflict?

Using Your Skills in Comprehension

Read the following passage and answer the questions.

> He stared at me with a massive scorn. "That's what I mean," he said. "You are a bonehead. You don't understand that a whole nation and a people are in this store."
>
> I looked uneasily toward the storeroom in the rear, almost expecting someone to emerge.
>
> "What about olives?" he cut the air with a sweep of his arm. "There are olives of many shapes and colors. Pointed black ones from Kalamata, oval ones from Amphissa, pickled green olives and sharp tangy yellow ones. Achilles carried black olives to Troy and after a day of savage battle leading his Myrmidons, he'd rest and eat cheese and ripe black olives such as these right here."

1. What is the tone of this passage?

2. What is the mood?

3. Which words and details help to create this mood?

4. How does the writer emphasize the main idea of the paragraph?

Using Your Vocabulary Skills

Read the following sentences from Chapter Eight. Infer the meaning of the underlined word. Then tell the meaning of the word.

1. With this faith we will be able to transform the jangling discords of our nation into a beautiful symphony of brotherhood.

2. Let the oppressed go free.

3. The swirling tendrils of food whirled like mist about his head.

4. If they liked me too well, they might be loath to drown me.

5. Thoreau, in an expansive mood, exulted, "What a rich book might be made about buds, including, perhaps, sprouts!"

Using Your Writing Skills

Choose one of the writing assignments below.

1. Many modern short stories focus on characters who have internal conflicts. These conflicts may help a character to grow. Choose four short stories in this chapter that portray internal conflict. Compare how the main characters' internal conflicts lead to growth.

2. Write a brief short story in which the main character faces and resolves one of the following internal conflicts:
   a. accepting a grandparent's move into the family home
   b. adjusting to a handicap
   c. facing up to a struggle over whether to follow the crowd

Using Your Skills in Critical Thinking

Find passages that describe the main character in one or two stories in this chapter. Examine the judgment words and connotations of the words used in the description. Decide if these words are mainly positive or mainly negative.

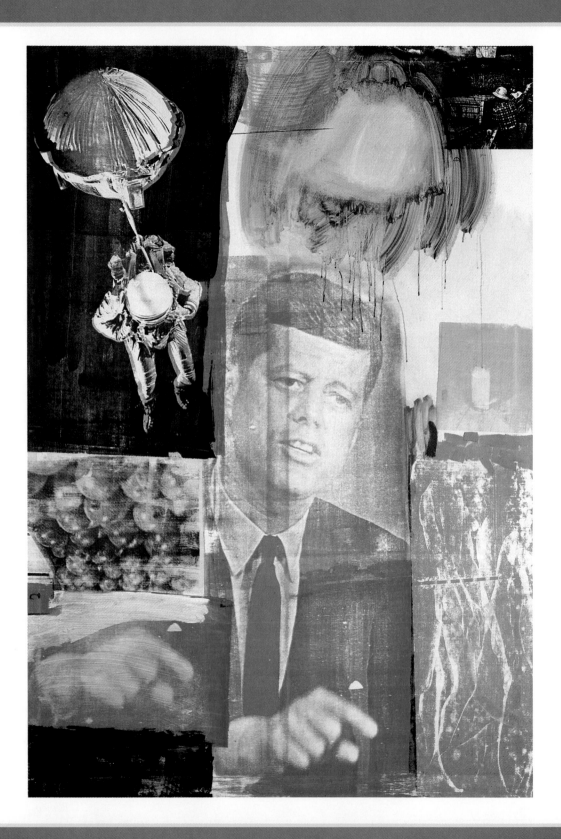

CHAPTER EIGHT

Twentieth Century Nonfiction

OPTIONS FOR RESPONDING

Activity Ideas

As you read:
- Decide which authors you would most like to have in your family, and later create a family tree showing where these people might fit.
- On a map, locate the places mentioned in the selections or associated with the writers.
- Choose some objects that would best represent each author or subject.
- Decide on the kind of music that would fit each selection.

After you read:
- Identify the product that each author might endorse, and create an ad.
- Clip newspaper articles on pollution.
- Survey your friends about the most pressing problems facing Americans today, then present your information on a chart.
- In a group, decide among the authors and subjects who would make the best class officers.
- Discuss which person in this chapter had the most interesting life and/or glamorous career.

Retroactive I, 1964, ROBERT RAUSCHENBERG. Wadsworth Atheneum, gift of Susan Morse Hilles, (1964.30), Hartford, Connecticut.

Reading Literature

Nonfiction

Nonfiction is writing that is based on facts rather than imagination. It tells about real people, places, and events. There are various types of nonfiction, each with its own style and purpose.

Types of Nonfiction

Letters. One of the oldest and most personal forms of nonfiction writing is the letter. People write letters for a variety of reasons. These include giving information; describing events, thoughts, and feelings; expressing opinions; and giving reasons. Letters often allow the reader to see history or world events in a much more personal way.

Journals. Journals are personal records, or diaries, of daily events. They are probably among the first kinds of writing. Like letters, they allow us to see situations through the eyes of someone who lived through them.

Biographies. A biography is a true account of a person's life. It relates important events in the person's life and usually attempts to explain the person's character. A good biography presents both positive and negative details. It allows the reader to draw his or her own conclusions.

Autobiographies. An autobiography is a book that a person writes about his or her own life. Since the writer is the main character in the story, an autobiography is written from the first-person point of view. This point of view allows the reader to get unique insights into the subject's character.

Speeches. Speeches are written to be read aloud. The success of a speech depends not only on the ideas presented but also on the skill of the speaker. To be effective, speeches must be well organized so that the listener or reader can easily follow the ideas and remember them later. Because of the oral nature of a speech, the writer may also use techniques such as repetition, alliteration, assonance, rhyme, and rhythm.

Essays. In an essay a writer expresses an opinion on a subject. An essay may inform, persuade, or entertain. The writer's tone, or attitude, can range from serious to humorous or lighthearted.

The Elements of Nonfiction

Like fiction, nonfiction writing may include the elements of character, setting, and plot. Refer to pages 354–355 for a review of these elements. Other elements of nonfiction are discussed below.

Point of View. Nonfiction writers often use the first-person point of view, which can be recognized by the use of the pronouns *I* and *we.* Letters, speeches, essays, and autobiographies usually are written from the first-person point of view. Other kinds of nonfiction, such as biographies and new articles, often use the third-person point of view. This point of view can be recognized by the use of the pronouns *he, she,* and *they.*

Purpose. Most nonfiction pieces are written to accomplish a specific purpose. This purpose may be to entertain, teach, persuade, or inform.

Organization. Nonfiction writing is organized using a variety of methods. The events in biographies and autobiographies often are organized according to chronological order. The ideas in speeches, letters, and essays often are arranged in the order of their importance.

Tone. The writer's tone, or attitude toward the subject, is an important element of nonfiction. The writer's choice of words determines the tone. The tone can help you decide what the writer hopes to accomplish.

How to Read Nonfiction

1. Identify the subject, the setting and the situation, if any.
2. Determine the point of view.
3. Identify the purpose of the selection.
4. Look for the organization the writer has used. Is the piece organized according to time order or logical order?
5. Be aware of the tone the writer uses in the piece.

Comprehension Skills

Purpose and Audience

Most writers carefully consider their purpose and audience before they begin to write. This allows them to choose facts and ideas that will help them to achieve their goal in writing a piece. It also allows writers to present ideas in a way that the audience can understand and accept. As a reader, you must be able to identify both the purpose and audience. Then you will better understand what the writer was trying to do. You will also be able to judge how successful he or she was.

Purpose

Writers have a variety of purposes, or reasons for writing. Sometimes a piece is meant to inform or persuade the reader. At other times, the purpose is to teach, to entertain, to relate personal experiences, or to express feelings. The writer's purpose influences his or her choice of words and ideas. It also influences the way in which the piece of writing is organized.

You can understand the writer's purpose by thinking about your own reaction to the piece. Did it entertain you or teach you something? Did it help you understand the writer's feelings about a subject or persuade you to agree with the author's opinion? By asking yourself these questions, you can determine the author's purpose for writing. You also can decide if the writer achieved his or her purpose.

Audience

Good writers give careful consideration to their audience—the people who will be reading their work. Writers consider the age of the audience, so that they can choose language that is neither too difficult nor too easy. Writers also consider how much or how little the audience knows about the topic. This affects both the amount and the difficulty of the information that is presented. In persuasive writing, the writer must consider the opinions and attitudes the readers have regarding the subject. Then, he or she can choose information that is most likely to be successful with this audience. In any piece of writing, the audience influences the method or methods the writer uses to develop and present information.

Exercises: Recognizing Purpose and Audience

A. Tell whether the purpose of each of these selections is to inform, to persuade, to teach, to entertain, to relate personal experiences, to explain an idea, or to express feelings. Some of the selections may have more than one purpose.

1. When the neighbors offered me food, I refused, already ashamed that so often in my life I had to be fed by strangers. And after I had been prevailed upon to eat I would eat as little as possible, feeling that some of the shame of charity would be taken away.

2. And so, my fellow Americans—ask not what your country can do for you—ask what you can do for your country.

3. America was founded by Columbus in 1492. This is an easy date to remember because it rhymes with "ocean blue," which was the color of the Atlantic in those days.

B. Identify the audience for each of the following selections.

1. Let every nation know, whether it wishes us well or ill, that we shall pay any price, bear any burden, meet any hardship, support any friend, oppose any foe to assure the survival and the success of liberty.
                    —John F. Kennedy

2. This is our hope. This is the faith with which I return to the South. With this faith we will be able to hew out of the mountain of despair a stone of hope. With this faith we will be able to transform the jangling discords of our nation into a beautiful symphony of brotherhood. With this faith we will be able to work together, to pray together, to struggle together, to go to jail together, to stand up for freedom together, knowing that we will be free one day.
                    —Dr. Martin Luther King, Jr.

$\mathcal{V}$ocabulary Skills

The Dictionary

You have learned how context clues, word parts, and inferences can help you to unlock word meaning. Sometimes, though, none of these methods helps. For example, look at this passage from *I Know Why the Caged Bird Sings:*

> Like women in English novels who walked the <u>moors</u> (whatever they were) with their loyal dogs racing at a respectful <u>distance</u>.

If it is not possible for you to figure out the meaning of *moor* through context clues, word parts, or inferences, however, you can turn to the dictionary for help.

You have already used the dictionary to find meanings and word origins. Following are other ways that the dictionary can help to strengthen your vocabulary skills.

Pronunciation. The respelling of a word shows its pronunciation. The respelling follows the entry word itself. A key to pronunciation shows what pronunciation symbols mean. There is a key at the beginning or end of the dictionary, as well as at the bottoms of pages.

Parts of Speech. The dictionary indicates the part of speech for each entry word with an abbreviation (*vi*—intransitive verb; *n.*—noun; *adj.*—adjective; *adv.*—adverb). If a word is used as more than one part of speech, definitions for each part are given after the abbreviation for that part.

> **mope** (mōp) *vi* **moped, mop′ing** [akin to M Du. *mopen,* Sw. dial. *mopa*] < to be gloomy, dull, apathetic, and dispirited— *vt.* **1.** to make gloomy, dull, etc.: used reflexively and in the passive **2.** to pass in gloom, dullness, etc. (with *away*)— *n.* **1.** a person who mopes or is inclined to mope **2.** [*pl.*] low spirits

Inflected Forms. A dictionary can also tell you if a word has any irregular forms. Verb parts, plurals, and comparative and superlative forms (*faster, fastest*) are all inflected forms of a word. They are listed in a dictionary if they are not formed in the usual way. In the entry for the verb *lie,* for example, irregular verb forms *lay, lain,* and *lying* are listed.

Idioms. Idioms are phrases that have a meaning that is different from the meanings of the individual words. For example, the phrase *under the weather* is an idiom. Idioms are also defined in a dictionary. These phrases are usually listed in the entry for the key word. For example, the phrase *break one's heart* would be found in the entry for the word *heart.*

Usage. A dictionary can also tell you the level of usage of a word. A word may be labeled *Colloquial* or *Slang,* for example. *Colloquial* means very informal, and *Slang* denotes nonstandard usage or word. Other usage labels include *Archaic,* or very old and rarely used, and *Obsolete,* or no longer used. *Poetic* and *Dialect* are other usage labels. *Poetic* refers to words used chiefly in poetry, and *Dialect* to regional terms. Sometimes only one of the definitions of a word is labeled as a certain level of usage.

Field Labels. Along with the general definitions of a word, a dictionary includes definitions that apply only in a specialized field, such as botany or baseball. The word *negative,* for example, has many general definitions. It also has specialized definitions in the fields of math, photography, medicine, biology, logic, and electricity.

Synonymies. Synonyms are words that have nearly the same meaning. A synonymy explains the fine differences of meaning between synonyms. A synonymy is usually found at the end of a dictionary entry.

Exercise: Using a Dictionary

Use a dictionary to define the following words. For each word, write the definition, respelling, and part of speech. Then use each word in a sentence.

1. aristocrat	6. invective	11. tremulous
2. sacrilegious	7. tribulation	12. dire
3. aura	8. creed	13. nonchalance
4. asunder	9. prodigious	14. sever
5. subversion	10. compulsion	15. malady

From
Black Boy

RICHARD WRIGHT

When he was young, Richard Wright lived with his brother and mother. The family was forced to move often. What difficulties did Richard experience as a child? Why was he often forced to prove himself?

My mother became too ill to work and I began to do chores in the neighborhood. My first job was carrying lunches to the men who worked in the roundhouse,[1] for which I received twenty-five cents a week. When the men did not finish their lunches, I would salvage what few crumbs remained. Later I obtained a job in a small café carting wood in my arms to keep the big stove going and taking trays of food to passengers when trains stopped for a half hour or so in a near-by station. I received a dollar a week for this work, but I was too young and too small to perform the duties; one morning while trying to take a heavily loaded tray up the steps of a train, I fell and dashed the tray of food to the ground.

Inability to pay rent forced us to move into a house perched atop high logs in a section of the town where flood waters came. My brother and I had great fun running up and down the tall, shaky steps.

Again paying rent became a problem and we moved nearer the center of town, where I found a job in a pressing shop, delivering clothes to hotels and sweeping floors.

Yet again we moved, this time to the outskirts of town, near a wide stretch of railroad tracks to which, each morning before school, I would take a sack and gather coal to heat our frame house, dodging in and out between the huge, black, puffing engines.

My mother, her health failing rapidly, spoke constantly now of Granny's home, of how ardently she wanted to see us grow up before she died. Already there had crept into her speech a halting, lisping quality that, though I did not know it, was the shadow of her future. I was more conscious of my mother now than I had ever been and I was already able to feel what being completely without her would mean. A slowly rising dread stole into me and I would look at my mother for long moments, but when she would look at me I would look away. Then real fear came as her illness recurred at shorter intervals. Time stood still. My brother and I waited, hungry and afraid.

---

1. **roundhouse**, a circular building with a turntable in the center, used for repairing and switching locomotives.

One morning a voice awakened me.

"Richard! Richard!"

I rolled out of bed. My brother came running into the room.

"Richard, you better come and see Mama. She's very sick," he said.

I ran into my mother's room and saw her lying upon her bed, dressed, her eyes open, her mouth gaped. She was very still.

"Mama!" I called.

She did not answer or turn her head. I reached forward to shake her, but drew back, afraid that she was dead.

"Mama!" I called again, my mind unable to grasp that she could not answer.

Finally I went to her and shook her. She moved slightly and groaned. My brother and I called her repeatedly, but she did not speak. Was she dying? It seemed unthinkable. My brother and I looked at each other; we did not know what to do.

"We better get somebody," I said.

I ran into the hallway and called a neighbor. A tall, black woman bustled out of a door.

"Please, won't you come and see my mama? She won't talk. We can't wake her up. She's terribly sick," I told her.

She followed me into our flat.

"Mrs. Wright!" she called to my mother.

My mother lay still, unseeing, silent. The woman felt my mother's hands.

"She ain't dead," she said. "But she's sick, all right. I better get some more of the neighbors."

Five or six of the women came and my brother and I waited in the hallway while they undressed my mother and put her to bed. When we were allowed back in the room, a woman said:

"Looks like a stroke to me."

"Just like paralysis," said another.

"And she's so young," someone else said.

My brother and I stood against a wall while the bustling women worked frantically over my mother. A stroke? Paralysis? What were those things? Would she die? One of the women asked me if there was any money in the house; I did not know. They searched through the dresser and found a dollar or two and sent for a doctor. The doctor arrived. Yes, he told us, my mother had suffered a stroke of paralysis. She was in a serious condition. She needed someone with her day and night; she needed medicine. Where was her husband? I told him the story and he shook his head.

"She'll need all the help that she can get," the doctor said. "Her entire left side is paralyzed. She cannot talk and she will have to be fed."

Later that day I rummaged through drawers and found Granny's address; I wrote to her, pleading with her to come and help us. The neighbors nursed my mother day and night, fed us and washed our clothes. I went through the days with a stunned consciousness, unable to believe what had happened. Suppose Granny did not come? I tried not to think of it. She *had* to come. The utter loneliness was now terrifying. I had been suddenly thrown emotionally upon my own. Within an hour the half-friendly world that I had known had turned cold and hostile. I was too frightened to weep. I was glad that my mother was not dead, but there was the fact that she would be sick for a long, long time, perhaps for the balance of her life. I became morose. Though I was a child, I could no longer feel as a child, could no longer react as a child. The desire for play was gone and I brooded, wondering if Granny would come and help us. I tried not to think of a tomorrow that was neither real nor wanted, for all tomorrows held questions that I could not answer.

When the neighbors offered me food, I refused, already ashamed that so often in my life I had to be fed by strangers. And after I had been prevailed upon to eat I would eat as little as possible, feeling that some of the shame of charity would be taken away. It pained me to think that other children were wondering if I were hungry, and whenever they asked me if I wanted food, I would say no, even though I was starving. I was tense during the days I waited for Granny, and when she came I gave up, letting her handle things, answering questions automatically, obeying, knowing that somehow I had to face things alone. I withdrew into myself.

I wrote letters that Granny dictated to her eight children—there were nine of them, including my mother—in all parts of the country, asking for money with which "to take Ella and her two little children to our home." Money came and again there were days of packing household effects. My mother was taken to the train in an ambulance and put on board upon a stretcher. We rode to Jackson in silence and my mother was put abed upstairs. Aunt Maggie came from Detroit to help nurse and clean. The big house was quiet. We spoke in lowered voices. We walked with soft tread. The odor of medicine hung in the air. Doctors came and went. Night and day I could hear my mother groaning. We thought that she would die at any moment.

Aunt Cleo came from Chicago. Uncle Clark came from Greenwood, Mississippi. Uncle Edward came from Carters, Mississippi. Uncle Charles from Mobile, Alabama. Aunt Addie from a religious school in Huntsville, Alabama. Uncle Thomas from Hazelhurst, Mississippi. The house had an expectant air and I caught whispered talk of "what is to become of her children?" I felt dread, knowing that others—strangers even though they were relatives—were debating my destiny. I had never seen my mother's brothers and sisters before and their presence made live again in me my old shyness. One day Uncle Edward called me to him and he felt my skinny arms and legs.

"He needs more flesh on him," he commented impersonally, addressing himself to his brothers and sisters.

I was horribly embarrassed, feeling that my life had somehow been full of nameless wrong, an unatonable guilt.

"Food will make him pick up in weight," Granny said.

Out of the family conferences it was decided that my brother and I would be separated, that it was too much of a burden for any one aunt or uncle to assume the support of both of us. Where was I to go? Who would take me? I became more anxious than ever. When an aunt or an uncle would come into my presence, I could not look at them. I was always reminding myself that I must not do anything that would make any of them feel they would not want me in their homes.

At night my sleep was filled with wild dreams. Sometimes I would wake up screaming in terror. The grownups would come running and I would stare at them, as though they were figures out of my nightmare, then go back to sleep. One night I found myself

My Brother, 1942, JOHN WILSON. Smith College Museum of Art, purchased 1943. Northampton, Massachusetts.

standing in the back yard. The moon was shining bright as day. Silence surrounded me. Suddenly I felt that someone was holding my hand. I looked and saw an uncle. He was speaking to me in a low, gentle voice.

"What's the matter, son?"

I stared at him, trying to understand what he was saying. I seemed to be wrapped in a kind of mist.

"Richard, what are you doing?"

I could not answer. It seemed that I could not wake up. He shook me. I came to myself and stared about at the moon-drenched yard.

"Where are we going?" I asked him.

"You were walking in your sleep," he said.

Granny gave me fuller meals and made me take naps in the afternoon and gradually my sleepwalking passed. The uneasy days and nights made me resolve to leave Granny's home as soon as I was old enough to support myself. It was not that they were unkind, but I knew that they did not have money enough to feed me and my brother. I avoided going into my mother's room now; merely to look at her was painful. She had grown very thin; she was still speechless, staring, quiet as stone.

One evening my brother and I were called into the front room where a conference of aunts and uncles was being held.

"Richard," said an uncle, "you know how sick your mother is?"

"Yes, sir."

"Well, Granny's not strong enough to take care of you two boys," he continued.

"Yes, sir," I said, waiting for his decision.

"Well, Aunt Maggie's going to take your brother to Detroit and send him to school."

I waited. Who was going to take me? I had wanted to be with Aunt Maggie, but I did not dare contest the decision.

"Now, where would you like to go?" I was asked.

The question caught me by surprise; I had been waiting for a fiat, and now a choice lay before me. But I did not have the courage to presume that anyone wanted me.

"Anywhere," I said.

"Any of us are willing to take you," he said.

Quickly I calculated which of them lived nearest to Jackson. Uncle Clark lived in Greenwood, which was but a few miles distant.

"I'd like to live with Uncle Clark, since he's close to the home here," I said.

"Is that what you really want?"

"Yes, sir."

Uncle Clark came to me and placed his hand upon my head.

"All right. I'll take you back with me and send you to school. Tomorrow we'll go and buy clothes."

My tension eased somewhat, but stayed with me. My brother was happy. He was going north. I wanted to go, but I said nothing.

A train ride and I was in yet another little southern town. Home in Greenwood was a four-room bungalow, comprising half of a double house that sat on a quiet shady road. Aunt Jody, a medium-sized, neat, silent, mulatto girl, had a hot supper waiting on the table. She baffled me with her serious, reserved manner; she seemed to be acting in conformity with a code unknown to me, and I assumed that she regarded me as a "wrong one," a boy who for some reason did not have a home; I felt that in her mind she would push me to the outskirts of life and I was awkward and self-conscious in her presence. Both Uncle Clark and Aunt Jody talked to me as though I were a grown-up and I wondered if I could do what was expected of me. I had always felt a certain warmth with my mother, even when we had lived in squalor; but I felt none here. Perhaps I was too apprehensive to feel any.

During supper it was decided that I was to be placed in school the next day. Uncle Clark and Aunt Jody both had jobs and I was told that at noon I would find lunch on the stove.

"Now, Richard, this is your new home," Uncle Clark said.

"Yes, sir."

"After school, bring in wood and coal for the fireplaces."

"Yes, sir."

"Split kindling and lay a fire in the kitchen stove."

"Yes, sir."

"Bring in a bucket of water from the yard so that Jody can cook in the mornings."

"Yes, sir."

"After your chores are done, you may spend the afternoon studying."

"Yes, sir."

I had never been assigned definite tasks before and I went to bed a little frightened. I lay sleepless, wondering if I should have come, feeling the dark night holding strange people, strange houses, strange streets. What would happen to me here? How would I get along? What kind of woman was Aunt Jody? How ought I act around here? Would Uncle Clark let me make friends with other boys? I awakened the next morning to see the sun shining into my room; I felt more at ease.

"Richard!" my uncle was calling me.

I washed, dressed, and went into the kitchen and sat wordlessly at the table.

"Good morning, Richard," Aunt Jody said.

"Oh, good morning," I mumbled, wishing that I had thought to say it first.

"Don't people say good morning where you come from?" she asked.

"Yes, ma'am."

"I thought they did," she said pointedly.

Aunt Jody and Uncle Clark began to question me about my life and I grew so self-conscious that my hunger left me. After breakfast, Uncle Clark took me to school, introduced me to the principal. The first half of the school day passed without incident. I sat looking at the strange reading book, following the lessons. The subjects seemed simple and I felt that I could keep up. My anxiety was still in me; I was wondering how I would get on with the boys. Each new school meant a new area of life to be conquered. Were the boys tough? How hard did they fight? I took it for granted that they fought.

At noon recess I went into the school grounds and a group of boys sauntered up to me, looked at me from my head to my feet, whispering among themselves. I leaned against a wall, trying to conceal my uneasiness.

"Where you from?" a boy asked abruptly.

"Jackson," I answered.

"How come they make you people so ugly in Jackson?" he demanded.

There was loud laughter.

"You're not any too good-looking yourself," I countered instantly.

"Aw!"

"You hear what he told 'im?"

"You think you're smart, don't you?" the boy asked, sneering.

"Listen, I ain't picking a fight," I said. "But if you want to fight, I'll fight."

"Hunh, hard guy, ain't you?"

"As hard as you."

"Do you know who you can tell that to?" he asked me.

"And you know who you can tell it back to?" I asked.

"Are you talking about my mama?" he asked, edging forward.

"If you want it that way," I said.

This was my test. If I failed now, I would have failed at school, for the first trial came not in books, but in how one's fellows took one, what value they placed upon one's willingness to fight.

"Take back what you said," the boy challenged me.

"Make me," I said.

The crowd howled, sensing a fight. The boy hesitated, weighing his chances of beating me.

"You ain't gonna take what that new boy said, is you?" someone taunted the boy.

The boy came close. I stood my ground. Our faces were four inches apart.

"You think I'm scared of you, don't you?" he asked.

"I told you what I think," I said.

Somebody, eager and afraid that we would not fight, pushed the boy and he bumped into me. I shoved him away violently.

"Don't push me!" the boy said.

"Then keep off me!" I said.

He was pushed again and I struck out with my right and caught him in the mouth. The crowd yelled, milled, surging so close that I could barely lift my arm to land a blow. When either of us tried to strike the other, we would be thrown off balance by the screaming boys. Every blow landed elicited shouts of delight. Knowing that if I did not win or make a good showing I would have to fight a new boy each day, I fought tigerishly, trying to leave a scar, seeking to draw blood as proof that I was not a coward, that I could take care of myself. The bell rang and the crowd pulled up apart. The fight seemed a draw.

In the classroom the boys asked me questions about myself; I was someone worth knowing. When the bell rang for school to be dismissed, I was set to fight again; but the boy was not in sight.

On my way home I found a cheap ring in the streets and at once I knew what I was going to do with it. The ring had a red stone held by tiny prongs which I loosened, took the stone out, leaving the sharp tiny prongs jutting up. I slid the ring on to my finger and shadow boxed. Now, by God, let a bully come and I would show him how to fight; I would leave a crimson streak on his face with every blow.

But I never had to use the ring. After I had exhibited my new weapon at school, a description of it spread among the boys. I challenged my enemy to another fight, but he would not respond. Fighting was not now necessary. I had been accepted.

Developing Comprehension Skills

1. Why did Richard's family move so often? What difficulties did this cause Richard?

2. How does his mother's stroke change Richard's life?

3. How does Richard feel about living with Aunt Jody and Uncle Clark? How is this life different from his life at home with his mother?

4. What does Wright mean when he says that "Each new school meant a new area of life to be conquered"?

5. Richard fought with another boy during his first day at the new school. Do you agree that Richard's action was necessary? Why or why not?

Reading Literature

1. **Appreciating Autobiography.** An **autobiography** is a true story that a person writes about his or her own life. Autobiographies can provide information about a person that other sources might overlook. What do you learn from Richard Wright about his experiences that you might not learn if someone else were telling the story?

2. **Identifying Conflict.** The struggle or problem that a character experiences in a situation

is called **conflict**. **External conflict** describes the struggle that a character has with other characters or situations. **Internal conflict** refers to the struggle that a character might have with his or her own feelings and thoughts.

What are the external and internal conflicts in this selection from *Black Boy*? Is each one solved or brought to some sort of conclusion? Explain your answer.

3. **Recognizing Mood.** Just as in fiction, nonfiction selections can create powerful feelings such as fear, loneliness, or anxiety in the reader.

Reread the passage on page 431 that follows Richard's account of writing a letter to Granny. Describe the mood that you experience. Note specific words and phrases that suggest this mood.

4. **Analyzing Characters.** Wright's autobiography describes Richard's ability to survive difficult situations. For example, Richard showed responsibility and the willingness to work hard when he took several odd jobs to support his family. Tell what traits helped Richard survive these situations:

a. his mother's illness
b. moving in with relatives
c. proving himself in a new school

Developing Vocabulary Skills

Using the Best Method To Determine Word Meaning. Many times you can infer the meaning of an unfamiliar word from its context or its word parts. At other times, however, you will need to use a dictionary to find the meaning of a new word.

Read each of the following sentences from *Black Boy*. Decide if you can use context clues and word parts to infer the meaning of the underlined word. If you cannot, you will have to look up the word in a dictionary. Using one of these methods, write down the meaning of each underlined word. Tell which method you used.

1. When the men did not finish their lunches, I would salvage what few crumbs remained.

2. My mother, her health failing rapidly, spoke constantly now of Granny's home, of how ardently she wanted to see us grow up before she died.

3. And after I had been prevailed upon to eat I would eat as little as possible, feeling that some of the shame of charity would be taken away.

4. I was horribly embarrassed, feeling that my life had somehow been full of nameless wrong, an unatonable guilt.

5. But I did not have the courage to presume that anyone wanted me.

6. I had always felt a certain warmth with my mother, even when we had lived in squalor; but I felt none here. Perhaps I was too apprehensive to feel any.

7. "Where you from?" a boy asked abruptly.

8. Every blow landed elicited shouts of delight.

Developing Writing Skills

1. **Determining Values.** Despite his many problems as a child, Richard Wright had a clear set of values. Values are the ways of living and acting that a person feels are important. Write a paragraph explaining what you think some of Wright's values were.

Think about the things that Richard thought were important. Consider his feelings about his mother and brother. Also consider the way he wanted others to think about him.

2. **Writing About an Autobiographical Event.** Write about a personal experience in which you had to struggle to succeed or survive in a difficult situation.

   Pre-Writing. Think about a difficult experience in which you had to struggle to succeed or survive. It may have taken place at home, at school, or at work. Jot down notes about what happened. Try to picture the event or situation in your mind as you write your notes. Think about words and phrases that capture the pictures you have in your mind. Don't forget to include feelings in your notes. When you finish, put your notes in chronological order, or time sequence.

   Writing. Use your notes to write a first draft of your story. Be sure that you write about only one event or situation. Include only that information related to that subject. Try to create vivid descriptions and a specific mood through careful word choice.

   Revising. Ask a friend to read your autobiographical incident. Have you included enough information to give a clear picture of what happened? Can your reader discover what your feelings were during the event? Based on what your reader tells you, revise your paper. Include any changes or additions that you think will improve your story.

Developing Skills in Critical Thinking

Drawing Conclusions from Facts. Every day, you draw conclusions based on facts. For example, before crossing a street you must first gather facts that allow you to decide if it is safe to cross.

Richard Wright had to draw conclusions based on the facts he observed. Think about the following facts Richard had to consider when he found his mother very ill:

Her health had been failing rapidly.
She lay still in bed with her eyes and her mouth open.
She did not answer when Richard called to her.

What does Richard conclude from these facts? What additional fact changes this conclusion?

Read the following paragraph about a fictional event. Then, study the conclusions following the paragraph. Decide which conclusions are based on the facts that are given in the paragraph.

I heard the tires screech as I walked down the steps of my house. A pick-up truck careened around the corner, jumped a curb, and hit a telephone pole in front of my neighbor's house. There was a crunch of metal and the shattering of glass. The truck came to rest with its back wheels resting in the neighbor's driveway. A yellow car backing out of the driveway stopped quickly before it reached the street. As a bearded man climbed out of the truck, a group of people gathered to see what had happened.

1. The accident caused no serious injuries.

2. The accident was caused by the driver turning the corner at a high speed.

3. The telephone pole had to be replaced.

4. The truck was damaged by the accident.

5. The neighbor was very angry with the driver of the pick-up truck.

From
Stelmark

HARRY MARK PETRAKIS

Many new Americans try to leave their old customs behind them. Discover how a plum, a fig, and an old storekeeper helped Harry Petrakis appreciate his heritage.

There was one storekeeper I remember above all others in my youth. It was shortly before I became ill, spending a good portion of my time with a motley group of varied ethnic ancestry. We contended with one another to deride the customs of the old country. On our Saturday forays into neighborhoods beyond our own, to prove we were really Americans, we ate hot dogs and drank Cokes. If a boy didn't have ten cents for this repast he went hungry, for he dared not bring a sandwich from home made of the spiced meats our families ate.

One of our untamed games was to seek out the owner of a pushcart or a store, unmistakably an immigrant, and bedevil him with a chorus of insults and jeers. To prove allegiance to the gang it was necessary to reserve our fiercest malevolence for a storekeeper or peddler belonging to our own ethnic background.

For that reason I led a raid on the small, shabby grocery of old Barba Nikos, a short, sinewy Greek who walked with a slight limp and sported a flaring, handlebar mustache.

We stood outside his store and dared him to come out. When he emerged to do battle, we plucked a few plums and peaches from the baskets on the sidewalk and retreated across the street to eat them while he watched. He waved a fist and hurled epithets at us in ornamental Greek.

Aware that my mettle was being tested, I raised my arm and threw my half-eaten plum at the old man. My aim was accurate and the plum struck him on the cheek. He shuddered and put his hand to the stain. He stared at me across the street, and although I could not see his eyes, I felt them sear my flesh. He turned and walked silently back into the store. The boys slapped my shoulders in admiration, but it was a hollow victory that rested like a stone in the pit of my stomach.

At twilight, when we disbanded, I passed the grocery alone on my way home. There was a small light burning in the store and the shadow of the old man's body outlined against the glass. Goaded by remorse, I walked to the door and entered.

The old man moved from behind the narrow wooden counter and stared at me. I wanted to turn and flee, but by then it was too late. As he motioned for me to come closer, I braced myself for a curse or a blow.

"You were the one," he said, finally, in a harsh voice.

Herb's Frames (detail), 1971,
BEN SCHONZEIT. Courtesy of
Nancy Hoffman Gallery, New York.

I nodded mutely.

"Why did you come back?"

I stood there unable to answer.

"What's your name?"

"Haralambos," I said, speaking to him in Greek.

He looked at me in shock. "You are Greek!" he cried. "A Greek boy attacking a Greek grocer!" He stood appalled at the immensity of my crime. "All right," he said coldly. "You are here because you wish to make amends." His great mustache bristled in concentration. "Four plums, two peaches," he said. "That makes a total of seventy-eight cents. Call it seventy-five. Do you have seventy-five cents, boy?"

I shook my head.

"Then you will work it off," he said. "Fifteen cents an hour into seventy-five cents makes"—he paused—"five hours of work. Can you come here Saturday morning?"

"Yes," I said.

"Yes, Barba Nikos," he said sternly. "Show respect."

"Yes, Barba Nikos," I said.

"Saturday morning at eight o'clock," he said. "Now go home and say thanks in your prayers that I did not loosen your impudent head with a solid smack on the ear." I needed no further urging and fled.

Saturday morning, still apprehensive, I returned to the store. I began by sweeping, raising clouds of dust in dark and hidden corners. I washed the windows, whipping the squeegee swiftly up and down the glass in a fever of fear that some member of the gang would see me. When I finished I hurried back inside.

For the balance of the morning I stacked cans, washed the counter, and dusted bottles of yellow wine. A few customers entered, and Barba Nikos served them. A little after twelve o'clock he locked the door so he could eat lunch. He cut himself a few slices of sausage, tore a large chunk from a loaf of crisp-crusted bread, and filled a small cup with a dozen black shiny olives floating in brine. He offered me the cup. I could not help myself and grimaced.

"You are a stupid boy," the old man said. "You are not really Greek, are you?"

"Yes, I am."

"You might be," he admitted grudgingly. "But you do not act Greek. Wrinkling your nose at these fine olives. Look around this store for a minute. What do you see?"

"Fruits and vegetables," I said. "Cheese and olives and things like that."

He stared at me with a massive scorn. "That's what I mean," he said. "You are a bonehead. You don't understand that a whole nation and a people are in this store."

I looked uneasily toward the storeroom in the rear, almost expecting someone to emerge.

"What about olives?" he cut the air with a sweep of his arm. "There are olives of many shapes and colors. Pointed black ones from Kalamata, oval ones from Amphissa,[1] pickled green olives and sharp tangy yellow ones. Achilles carried black olives to Troy and after a day of savage battle leading his Myrmidons,[2] he'd rest and eat cheese and ripe black olives such as these right here. You have heard of Achilles, boy, haven't you?"

"Yes," I said.

"Yes, Barba Nikos."

"Yes, Barba Nikos," I said.

He motioned at the row of jars filled with varied spices. "There is origanon there and basilikon and daphne and sesame and miantanos, all the marvelous flavorings that we have used in our food for thousands of years. The men of Marathon carried small packets of these spices into battle, and the scents reminded them of their homes, their families, and their children."

He rose and tugged his napkin free from around his throat. "Cheese, you said. Cheese! Come closer, boy, and I will educate your abysmal ignorance." He motioned toward a wooden container on the counter. "That glistening white delight is feta, made from goat's milk, packed in wooden buckets to retain the flavor. Alexander the Great[3] demanded it on his table with his casks of wine when he planned his campaigns."

He walked limping from the counter to the window where the piles of tomatoes, celery, and green peppers clustered. "I suppose all

---

1. **Kalamata . . . Amphissa**, cities in Greece.
2. **Myrmidons**, warriors from Thessaly, a region of eastern Greece, who fought under Achilles.
3. **Alexander the Great**, (356–323 B.C.) King of Macedonia and military conqueror who helped to spread Greek culture.

you see here are some random vegetables?" He did not wait for me to answer. "You are dumb again. These are some of the ingredients that go to make up a Greek salad. Do you know what a Greek salad really is? A meal in itself, an experience, an emotional involvement. It is created deftly and with grace. First, you place large lettuce leaves in a big, deep bowl." He spread his fingers and moved them slowly, carefully, as if he were arranging the leaves. "The remainder of the lettuce is shredded and piled in a small mound," he said. "Then comes celery, cucumbers, tomatoes sliced lengthwise, green peppers, origanon, green olives, feta, avocado, and anchovies. At the end you dress it with lemon, vinegar, and pure olive oil, glinting golden in the light."

He finished with a heartfelt sigh and for a moment closed his eyes. Then he opened one eye to mark me with a baleful intensity. "The story goes that Zeus himself created the recipe and assembled and mixed the ingredients on Mount Olympus one night when he had invited some of the other gods to dinner."

He turned his back on me and walked slowly again across the store, dragging one foot slightly behind him. I looked uneasily at the clock, which showed that it was a few minutes past one. He turned quickly and startled me. "And everything else in here," he said loudly. "White beans, lentils, garlic, crisp bread, kokoretsi, meatballs, mussels and clams." He paused and drew a deep, long breath. "And the wine," he went on, "wine from Samos, Santorini, and Crete, retsina and mavrodaphne, a taste almost as old as water . . . and then the fragrant melons, the pastries, yellow diples and golden loukoumades, the honey custard galatobouriko. Everything a

part of our history, as much a part as the exquisite sculpture in marble, the bearded warriors, Pan and the oracles at Delphi, and the nymphs dancing in the shadowed groves under Homer's[4] glittering moon." He paused, out of breath again, and coughed harshly. "Do you understand now, boy?"

He watched my face for some response and then grunted. We stood silent for a moment until he cocked his head and stared at the clock. "It is time for you to leave," he motioned brusquely toward the door. "We are square now. Keep it that way."

I decided the old man was crazy and reached behind the counter for my jacket and cap and started for the door. He called me back. From a box he drew out several soft, yellow figs that he placed in a piece of paper. "A bonus because you worked well," he said. "Take them. When you taste them, maybe you will understand what I have been talking about."

I took the figs and he unlocked the door and I hurried from the store. I looked back once and saw him standing in the doorway, watching me, the swirling tendrils of food curling like mist about his head.

I ate the figs late that night. I forgot about them until I was in bed, and then I rose and took the package from my jacket. I nibbled at one, then ate them all. They broke apart between my teeth with a tangy nectar, a thick sweetness running like honey across my tongue and into the pockets of my cheeks. In the morning when I woke, I could still taste and inhale their fragrance.

---

4. **Homer**, an early Greek poet, thought to be the author of *The Iliad* and *The Odyssey*.

I never again entered Barba Nikos' store. My spell of illness, which began some months later, lasted two years. When I returned to the streets I had forgotten the old man and the grocery. Shortly afterwards my family moved from the neighborhood.

Some twelve years later, after the war, I drove through the old neighborhood and passed the grocery. I stopped the car and for a moment stood before the store. The windows were stained with dust and grime, the interior bare and desolate, a store in a decrepit group of stores marked for razing so new structures could be built.

I have been in many Greek groceries since then and have often bought the feta and Kalamata olives. I have eaten countless Greek salads and have indeed found them a meal for the gods. On the holidays in our house, my wife and sons and I sit down to a dinner of steaming, buttered pilaf like my mother used to make and lemon-egg avgolemono and roast lamb richly seasoned with cloves of garlic. I drink the red and yellow wines, and for dessert I have come to relish the delicate pastries coated with honey and powdered sugar. Old Barba Nikos would have been pleased.

But I have never been able to recapture the halcyon flavor of those figs he gave me on that day so long ago, although I have bought figs many times. I have found them pleasant to my tongue, but there is something missing. And to this day I am not sure whether it was the figs or the vision and passion of the old grocer that coated the fruit so sweetly I can still recall their savor and fragrance after almost thirty years.

Developing Comprehension Skills

1. Why did the gang eat hot dogs and drink soft drinks? What was wrong with bringing a sandwich from home?

2. Why did the gang pester immigrant store owners?

3. Why does the narrator return to the grocery store in the evening? Why is the owner shocked to find that the boy is Greek?

4. Why does Barba Nikos explain olives, spices, and cheese in such detail to the narrator? What does he mean when he says ". . . a whole nation and a people are in this store"?

5. What was Barba Nikos trying to accomplish with Petrakis? Do you think he succeeded? Explain your answer.

6. How important is it for people to remember their heritage? Do you think it ever might be better to forget old customs and blend in with those around you?

Reading Literature

1. **Appreciating Tone.** You recall that a writer's tone is his or her attitude toward the subject. What is Petrakis's tone as he tells this incident from the point of view of the boy he

was? Do you notice a change in the tone at the end of the selection when Petrakis is speaking as an adult? How does he feel as he recalls the special flavor of the figs from years earlier?

2. **Understanding Theme.** An author's **theme** is the message that he or she wants the reader to think about. What message about ethnic background, or heritage does Petrakis want the reader to understand after reading this autobiographical account?

3. **Recognizing Allusions.** You remember that an **allusion** is a reference to a person or event in literature or history. For example, Barba Nikos alludes to *Achilles, Zeus, Mount Olympus,* and *the men of Marathon.* These are all references to people and places in Greek mythology. Why did Barba Nikos make these allusions when speaking to the narrator?

4. **Appreciating Similes.** Identify the simile or comparison in each passage below. Explain why it is appropriate or effective. You may need to reread the part of the selection to read the full paragraph in which it appears:

a. The boys slapped my shoulders in admiration, but it was a hollow victory that rested like a stone in the pit of my stomach. (page 439)

b. They broke apart between my teeth with a tangy nectar, a thick sweetness running like honey across my tongue . . . . (page 442)

Developing Vocabulary Skills

Using a Glossary. Some books, especially textbooks and technical books, have glossaries at the back. A **glossary** is an alphabetized listing of difficult terms, along with their definitions. You will often find a glossary helpful for understanding passages in a textbook.

Look at the glossary in the back of this book. Notice that it includes the more difficult or less commonly used words from the selections, along with their pronunciations, parts of speech, and definitions. Use the glossary to define the following words from *Stelmark.* On your paper, write down the definition for each word. Then use each word in a sentence.

1. deride	6. appall	11. baleful
2. bedevil	7. repast	12. desolate
3. motley	8. foray	13. decrepit
4. epithet	9. abysmal	14. halcyon
5. mettle	10. deftly	15. savor

Developing Writing Skills

1. **Analyzing the Importance of an Experience.** Richard Wright and Harry Mark Petrakis came from very different backgrounds. Despite this, the two men had something in common. Both learned lessons from their difficult childhoods that allowed them to become successful adults. Write a brief composition analyzing, or explaining, the lessons these two writers learned as children.

Pre-Writing. Scan both selections to find information on the backgrounds of Wright and Petrakis. Then think of some things that each writer learned as a child. Jot down notes on these lessons, as well as on the experiences that lead to them. When you have completed your list for each writer, arrange the items in order of importance. You might also look for similarities in the backgrounds and experiences of the two men.

Writing. Begin your analysis with a brief paragraph stating the purpose of your composition. The first paragraph should also mention the titles of the autobiographies. In one paragraph, provide some background about the two main characters. Then write at least one paragraph about each writer's childhood experiences. As you discuss these experiences, explain the lessons the writers learned as a result. Point out any similarities in the experiences and lessons. End your composition with a brief paragraph that summarizes your conclusions about the importance of the writers' childhoods.

Revising. Read your composition carefully. Does the introductory paragraph tell your purpose? Have you discussed important experiences from each writer's childhood? Have you explained the lesson the writers learned from their experiences? Did you end your composition with a strong conclusion? Make any changes or additions that will strengthen your analysis.

2. **Describing a Food.** Barba Nikos describes the Greek salad in great detail. He uses sensory words and phrases that make it so real that the reader can almost taste it. Reread the passage on page 442 to see how he does this. Then write a description of a food that you enjoy. It may be an ethnic specialty of your family or it may be some other favorite food. In any case, your job is to make the dish sound as appealing as possible. Use specific sensory words that describe the sight, smell, taste, and texture of the food.

Developing Skills in Study and Research

Using Reference Works. Petrakis makes several allusions to Greek mythology. Use different sources in the library to learn more about the characters and places listed below. Begin by looking in the subject index of the card catalog. Look for the topics GREEK MYTHOLOGY or MYTHOLOGY. Then look at the books listed there to get your information. The table of contents and index of the books you find will help you to locate the information you need. You may also refer to encyclopedias as well as specialized references suggested by the librarian.

Achilles	Troy
Myrmidons	Zeus
Mount Olympus	Nymphs
Pan	Delphi

Present a brief report on one character or place in Greek mythology. How does this new information affect your appreciation of Petrakis' story?

Of what value can a caring, older person be to a younger one? What was it about Mrs. Flowers that had such an impact on young Maya Angelou?

From

I Know Why the Caged Bird Sings

MAYA ANGELOU

For nearly a year, I sopped around the house, the Store, the school and the church, like an old biscuit, dirty and inedible. Then I met, or rather got to know, the lady who threw me my first life line.

Mrs. Bertha Flowers was the aristocrat of Black Stamps. She had the grace of control to appear warm in the coldest weather, and on the Arkansas summer days it seemed she had a private breeze which swirled around, cooling her. She was thin without the taut look of wiry people, and her printed voile dresses and flowered hats were as right for her as denim overalls for a farmer. She was our side's answer to the richest white woman in town.

Her skin was a rich black that would have peeled like a plum if snagged, but then no one would have thought of getting close enough to Mrs. Flowers to ruffle her dress, let alone snag her skin. She didn't encourage familiarity. She wore gloves too.

I don't think I ever saw Mrs. Flowers laugh, but she smiled often. A slow widening of her thin black lips to show even, small white teeth, then the slow effortless closing. When she chose to smile on me, I always wanted to thank her. The action was so graceful and inclusively benign.

She was one of the few gentlewomen I have ever known, and has remained throughout my life the measure of what a human being can be.

Momma had a strange relationship with her. Most often when she passed on the road in front of the Store, she spoke to Momma in that soft yet carrying voice, "Good day, Mrs. Henderson." Momma responded with "How you, Sister Flowers?"

Mrs. Flowers didn't belong to our church, nor was she Momma's familiar. Why on earth did she insist on calling her Sister Flowers? Shame made me want to hide my face. Mrs. Flowers deserved better than to be called Sister. Then, Momma left out the verb. Why not ask, "How *are* you, *Mrs.* Flowers?" With the unbalanced passion of the young, I hated her for showing her ignorance to Mrs. Flowers. It didn't occur to me for many years that they were as alike as sisters, separated only by formal education.

Although I was upset, neither of the women was in the least shaken by what I thought an unceremonious greeting. Mrs. Flowers would continue her easy gait up the hill to her little bungalow, and Momma kept on shelling peas or doing whatever had brought her to the front porch.

Occasionally, though, Mrs. Flowers would drift off the road and down to the Store and Momma would say to me, "Sister, you go on and play." As I left I would hear the beginning of an intimate conversation. Momma persistently using the wrong verb, or none at all.

"Brother and Sister Wilcox is sho'ly the meanest—" "Is," Momma? "Is"? Oh, please not "is," Momma, for two or more. But they talked, and from the side of the building where I waited for the ground to open up and swallow me, I heard the soft-voiced Mrs. Flowers and the textured voice of my grandmother merging and melting. They were interrupted from time to time by giggles that must have come from Mrs. Flowers (Momma never giggled in her life). Then she was gone.

She appealed to me because she was like people I had never met personally. Like women in English novels who walked the moors (whatever they were) with their loyal dogs racing at a respectful distance. Like the women who sat in front of roaring fireplaces, drinking tea incessantly from silver trays full of scones and crumpets. Women who walked over the "heath" and read morocco-bound books and had two last names divided by a hyphen. It would be safe to say that she made me proud to be Negro, just by being herself.

She acted just as refined as whitefolks in the movies and books and she was more beautiful, for none of them could have come near that warm color without looking gray by comparison.

It was fortunate that I never saw her in the company of powhitefolks. For since they tend to think of their whiteness as an evenizer, I'm certain that I would have had to hear her spoken to commonly as Bertha, and my image of her would have been shattered like the unmendable Humpty-Dumpty.

One summer afternoon, sweet-milk fresh in my memory, she stopped at the Store to buy provisions. Another Negro woman of her health and age would have been expected to carry the paper sacks home in one hand, but Momma said, "Sister Flowers, I'll send Bailey up to your house with these things."

She smiled that slow dragging smile, "Thank you, Mrs. Henderson. I'd prefer Marguerite, though." My name was beautiful when she said it. "I've been meaning to talk to her, anyway." They gave each other age-group looks.

Momma said, "Well, that's all right then. Sister, go and change your dress. You going to Sister Flowers's."

The chifforobe was a maze. What on earth did one put on to go to Mrs. Flowers' house? I knew I shouldn't put on a Sunday dress. It might be sacrilegious. Certainly not a house dress, since I was already wearing a fresh one. I chose a school dress, naturally. It was formal without suggesting that going to Mrs. Flowers' house was equivalent to attending church.

I trusted myself back into the Store.

"Now, don't you look nice." I had chosen the right thing, for once.

"Mrs. Henderson, you make most of the children's clothes, don't you?"

"Yes, ma'am. Sure do. Store-bought clothes ain't hardly worth the thread it take to stitch them."

"I'll say you do a lovely job, though, so neat. That dress looks professional."

Momma was enjoying the seldom-received compliments. Since everyone we knew (except Mrs. Flowers, of course) could sew competently, praise was rarely handed out for the commonly practiced craft.

"I try, with the help of the Lord, Sister Flowers, to finish the inside just like I does the outside. Come here, Sister."

I had buttoned up the collar and tied the belt, apron-like, in back. Momma told me to turn around. With one hand she pulled the strings and the belt fell free at both sides of my waist. Then her large hands were at my neck, opening the button loops. I was terrified. What was happening?

"Take it off, Sister." She had her hands on the hem of the dress.

"I don't need to see the inside, Mrs. Henderson, I can tell . . ." But the dress was over my head and my arms were stuck in the sleeves. Momma said, "That'll do. See here, Sister Flowers, I French-seams around the armholes." Through the cloth film, I saw the shadow approach. "That makes it last longer. Children these days would bust out of sheet-metal clothes. They so rough."

"That is a very good job, Mrs. Henderson. You should be proud. You can put your dress back on, Marguerite."

"No ma'am. Pride is a sin. And 'cording to the Good Book, it goeth before a fall."

"That's right. So the Bible says. It's a good thing to keep in mind."

I wouldn't look at either of them. Momma hadn't thought that taking off my dress in front of Mrs. Flowers would kill me stone dead. If I had refused, she would have thought I was trying to be "womanish." Mrs. Flowers had known that I would be embarrassed and that was even worse. I picked up the groceries and went out to wait in the hot sunshine. It would be fitting if I got a sunstroke and died before they came outside. Just dropped dead on the slanting porch.

There was a little path beside the rocky road, and Mrs. Flowers walked in front swinging her arms and picking her way over the stones.

She said, without turning her head, to me, "I hear you're doing very good school work, Marguerite, but that it's all written. The teachers report that they have trouble getting you to talk in class." We passed the triangular farm on our left and the path widened to allow us to walk together. I hung back in the separate unasked and unanswerable questions.

"Come and walk along with me, Marguerite." I couldn't have refused even if I wanted to. She pronounced my name so nicely. Or more correctly, she spoke each word with such clarity that I was certain a foreigner who didn't understand English could have understood her.

"Now no one is going to make you talk—possibly no one can. But bear in mind, language is man's way of communicating with his fellow man and it is language alone which separates him from the lower animals." That was a totally new idea to me, and I would need time to think about it.

"Your grandmother says you read a lot. Every chance you get. That's good, but not good enough. Words mean more than what is set down on paper. It takes the human voice to infuse them with the shades of deeper meaning."

I memorized the part about the human voice infusing words. It seemed so valid and poetic.

She said she was going to give me some books and that I not only must read them, I must read them aloud. She suggested that I try to make a sentence sound in as many different ways as possible.

"I'll accept no excuse if you return a book to me that has been badly handled." My imagination boggled at the punishment I would deserve if in fact I did abuse a book of Mrs. Flowers'. Death would be too kind and brief.

The odors in the house surprised me. Somehow I had never connected Mrs. Flowers with food or eating or any other common

Gwendolyn, about 1918, JOHN SLOAN. National Museum of American Art, Smithsonian Institution, gift of Mrs. John Sloan. Washington, D.C.

experience of common people. There must have been an outhouse, too, but my mind never recorded it.

The sweet scent of vanilla had met us as she opened the door.

"I made tea cookies this morning. You see, I had planned to invite you for cookies and lemonade so we could have this little chat. The lemonade is in the icebox."

It followed that Mrs. Flowers would have ice on an ordinary day, when most families in our town bought ice late on Saturdays only a few times during the summer to be used in the wooden ice-cream freezers.

She took the bags from me and disappeared through the kitchen door. I looked around the room that I had never in my wildest fantasies imagined I would see. Browned photographs leered or threatened from the walls and the white, freshly done curtains pushed against themselves and against the wind. I wanted to gobble up the room entire and take it to Bailey, who would help me analyze and enjoy it.

"Have a seat, Marguerite. Over there by the table." She carried a platter covered with a tea towel. Although she warned that she hadn't tried her hand at baking sweets for some time, I was certain that like everything else about her the cookies would be perfect.

They were flat round wafers, slightly browned on the edges and butter-yellow in the center. With the cold lemonade they were sufficient for childhood's lifelong diet. Remembering my manners, I took nice little lady-like bites off the edges. She said she had made them expressly for me and that she had a few in the kitchen that I could take home to my brother. So I jammed one whole cake in my mouth and the rough crumbs scratched the insides of my jaws, and if I hadn't had to swallow, it would have been a dream come true.

As I ate she began the first of what we later called "my lessons in living." She said that I must always be intolerant of ignorance but understanding of illiteracy. That some people, unable to go to school, were more educated and even more intelligent than college professors. She encouraged me to listen carefully to what country people called mother wit. That in those homely sayings was couched the collective wisdom of generations.

When I finished the cookies she brushed off the table and brought a thick, small book from the bookcase. I had read *A Tale of Two Cities* and found it up to my standards as a romantic novel. She opened the first page and I heard poetry for the first time in my life.

"It was the best of times and the worst of times . . . ." Her voice slid in and curved down through and over the words. She was nearly singing. I wanted to look at the pages. Were they the same that I had read? Or were there notes, music, lined on the pages, as in a hymn book? Her sounds began cascading gently. I knew from listening to a thousand preachers that she was nearing the end of her reading, and I hadn't really heard, heard to understand, a single word.

"How do you like that?"

It occurred to me that she expected a response. The sweet vanilla flavor was still on my tongue and her reading was a wonder in my ears. I had to speak.

I said, "Yes, ma'am." It was the least I could do, but it was the most also.

"There's one more thing. Take this book of

poems and memorize one for me. Next time you pay me a visit, I want you to recite."

I have tried often to search behind the sophistication of years for the enchantment I so easily found in those gifts. The essence escapes but its aura remains. To be allowed, no, invited, into the private lives of strangers, and to share their joys and fears, was a chance to exchange the Southern bitter wormwood for a cup of mead with Beowulf or a hot cup of tea and milk with Oliver Twist.[1] When I said aloud, "It is a far, far better thing that I do, than I have ever done . . ." tears of love filled my eyes at my selflessness.

On that first day, I ran down the hill and into the road (few cars ever came along it) and had the good sense to stop running before I reached the Store.

I was liked, and what a difference it made. I was respected not as Mrs. Henderson's grandchild or Bailey's sister but for just being Marguerite Johnson.

Childhood's logic never asks to be proved (all conclusions are absolute). I didn't question why Mrs. Flowers had singled me out for attention, nor did it occur to me that Momma might have asked her to give me a little talking to. All I cared about was that she had made tea cookies for *me* and read to *me* from her favorite book. It was enough to prove that she liked me.

Momma and Bailey were waiting inside the Store. He said, "My, what did she give you?" He had seen the books, but I held the paper sack with his cookies in my arms shielded by the poems.

Momma said, "Sister, I know you acted like a little lady. That do my heart good to see settled people take to you all. I'm trying my best, the Lord knows, but these days . . ." Her voice trailed off. "Go on in and change your dress."

In the bedroom it was going to be a joy to see Bailey receive his cookies.

---

1. **Southern . . . Twist**. The author compares her life to wormwood, a bitter oil, and contrasts it to mead, a honeyed drink. She escapes from reality by reading classic literature such as the epic poem *Beowulf* or *Oliver Twist* by Charles Dickens.

Developing Comprehension Skills

1. Marguerite says that Momma and Mrs. Flowers are as alike as sisters, separated only by formal education. How are Momma and Mrs. Flowers different? How are they alike?

2. What does Marguerite admire about Mrs. Flowers? How does she feel when she is around Mrs. Flowers?

3. What are some things that Momma does that irritate or embarrass the narrator? Do you think Marguerite has reason to be embarrassed?

4. What does Mrs. Flowers teach Marguerite about language and speaking? What does she teach Marguerite about "lessons in living"? Why was this last lesson so important?

5. Angelou says that Mrs. Flowers was the lady who "threw me my first life line." What do you think she meant by this?

6. Why do you think Mrs. Flowers took special interest in Marguerite? What qualities might she have seen in her? Do you think her time and interest were well spent? Explain your answer.

Reading Literature

1. **Understanding Characterization.** We learn about Mrs. Flowers's character through her actions, her words, and what others say about her. What character traits does she have? What actions, words, and comments by others point out the kind of person Mrs. Flowers is?

2. **Appreciating a Title.** The title of this selection is taken from a poem by Paul Laurence Dunbar entitled "Sympathy." In this poem, the poet tells of a song bird trapped in a cage. Why might Marguerite have used this title for her autobiography? In what ways did she feel trapped? In what other ways can Marguerite be compared to a song bird?

3. **Analyzing Theme.** Mrs. Flowers provided Marguerite with "lessons in living." What lessons did Marguerite learn? How are these ideas related to the story's theme, or main message?

4. **Recognizing Dialect.** Dialect is the way language is spoken by a particular group of people. Everyone speaks some sort of dialect. A person's dialect includes his or her pronunciation of words, vocabulary, and use of grammar. How is Momma's dialect sometimes different from that of Mrs. Flowers?

Why does this difference embarrass Marguerite?

Developing Vocabulary Skills

Understanding Usage Labels and Notes. You learned about the levels of language in Chapter Three. As you know, some words are quite formal, and others are informal. The dictionary has usage labels to show the level of a word or idiom. These are the labels that are usually used in a dictionary:

Usage	Meaning	Examples
Colloquial	Informal and conversational	neat trick, monkey business
Slang	Nonstandard, very informal	goof-off, mosey, yuck, beat it
Archaic	Rarely used	thine, withal
Dialect	Used in a certain region or by certain groups	reckon, varmint, do up right
Obsolete	No longer used	fulmine, lickerish
Poetic	Used chiefly in poetry	whene'er, oft, plaint

Usage labels may apply to the word itself or to only one sense of the word.

The following sentences are from *I Know Why the Caged Bird Sings.* Look at how each underlined word is used in its sentence. Then look up the usage labels and notes for the word in a dictionary. Is the use of the word colloquial, slang, archaic, dialect, obsolete, poetic, or nonstandard? Write your explanation, based on the usage labels and notes in the dictionary.

1. "Store-bought clothes <u>ain't</u> hardly worth the thread it take to stitch <u>them</u>."

2. "I try, with the help of the Lord, Sister Flowers, to finish the inside just <u>like</u> I does the outside."

3. "Children these days would <u>bust</u> out of sheet-metal clothes."

4. "<u>Sure</u> do."

5. . . . nor did it occur to me that Momma might have asked her to give me a little <u>talking to</u>.

Developing Writing Skills

1. **Supporting General Statements.** Mrs. Flowers gives Marguerite several pieces of wise advice. Explain and support one of these statements in a short composition.

   Be tolerant of ignorance but understanding of illiteracy.

   Listen carefully to mother wit, which is homely sayings that contain the collective wisdom of generations.

   Pre-Writing. Choose the statement that you find most interesting. Read the statement carefully. Jot down your own words and phrases to explain the statement. Then note several examples from the story or from your own knowledge and experience that help illustrate the statement.

   Writing. First, present the statement and provide some background of the story and characters it comes from. Then write your explanation of the meaning of the statement.

   Revising. Exchange papers with a classmate. Each of you should read the composition to decide how clear the explanation is. How well do the examples illustrate the idea in the statement? You can add more explanations and examples to your composition.

2. **Describing an Unforgettable Person.** Angelou described a personal hero in this selection. Think of a person who has influenced your life. Describe the effect he or she had on you.

Developing Skills in Study and Research

Using the SQ3R Study Method. Review the SQ3R study method on page 68. Then use the first two steps of the method to prepare for reading "The Legend of Amelia Earhart." Complete the last three steps as your teacher directs.

Developing Skills in Speaking and Listening

Reading Aloud. Mrs. Flowers gave advice to Marguerite about reading aloud.

As you speak, use your voice to give special meaning to words you use. Do this by raising or lowering the volume of your voice. Provide extra stress on certain words to add emphasis.

Read the sentence below six times. Use volume, stress, and pace to give the different meanings suggested below it.

I bought a new car today.

1. a statement

2. I bought it, not my parents.

3. a new one, not a used one

4. show excitement

5. as though it were nothing unusual, even though you know it is

6. as a boast

Use these same techniques whenever you read a story or poem aloud.

The Legend of Amelia Earhart

PETE HAMILL

Amelia Earhart was born in Atchison, Kansas, on July 24, 1897. Her father, Edwin, was a railroad lawyer, a small, precise man with a streak of brooding melancholy. Her mother, Amy Otis Earhart, the daughter of the most prominent judge in town, was by all accounts a remarkable woman: influenced by the first wave of American feminism, but still a prisoner of the rigid social codes of her day.

The marriage was tense from the beginning, as Judge Otis attempted to impose his will on the lives of his daughter and her husband. Earhart was away a lot, in his work as a claims agent, and sometimes he took his wife along with him. The result was that Amelia and her younger sister Muriel spent much of their childhood living with their grandparents. Amelia had a rich fantasy life, and lived adventurous summers exploring caves, playing baseball with equipment given to her by her father, reading Scott, Dickens, George Eliot; but she must have learned early that she was essentially alone.

"I was a horrid little girl," she said later. "Perhaps the fact that I was exceedingly fond of reading made me endurable. With a large library to browse in, I spent many hours not bothering anyone after I once learned to read."

The family moved to Des Moines in 1907, apparently to escape the domination of the grandparents, and on her tenth birthday, Amelia saw her first airplane. That day, her father took her to the Iowa State Fair. It was only five years after the Wright Brothers had first flown at Kitty Hawk (incidentally, with money provided by a Wright sister) and airplanes were a great curiosity. Amelia, however, was not impressed.

"It was a thing of rusty wire and wood," she wrote in 1937. "I was much more interested in an absurd hat made of an inverted peach-basket which I had just purchased for fifteen cents. . . . Today I loathe hats for more than a few minutes on the head and am sure I should pass by the niftiest creation if an airplane were anywhere around."

She went through six schools before finally graduating from Hyde Park High School in Chicago in 1916. In the yearbook she was described as "the girl in brown, who walks alone." Her mother then insisted on sending her to the Ogontz finishing school in Philadelphia, and she was at Ogontz in 1917 when the Americans entered the First World War. At Christmas she traveled to Toronto to visit her sister Muriel, who was then attending St. Margaret's School.

"Canada had been in the war four weary years—years the United States will never appreciate," Amelia wrote later. "Four men on crutches, walking together on King Street in Toronto that winter, was a sight which changed the course of existence for me."

Amelia quit the Ogontz school, and went to work as a nurse's aide for the Canadian Red Cross, caring for shell-shocked veterans. Much of her work was routine and boring, but the impact of sustained intimate contact with these wounded men was clearly profound; in later life, Amelia was a pacifist.

Toronto was also the place where she saw her second airplane, and its impact was considerably different from the one she saw when she was ten.

"A young woman friend and I had gone to the fair grounds to see an exhibition of stunt-flying by one of the aces[1] returned from the war," she remembered later. Amelia and her friend, dressed in their nurses' uniforms, moved to a clearing to get a better view. The pilot went through a repertory of stunts.

"After fifteen or twenty minutes of stunting, the pilot began to dive at the crowd," she wrote. "Looking back as a pilot I think I understand why. He was bored."

Then he saw Amelia and her friend in the open clearing, and started to swoop down on them, too. The friend broke and ran. Amelia stood still, watching the plane come at her.

"I remember the mingled fear and pleasure which surged over me as I watched that small plane at the top of its earthward swoop. Common sense told me that if something went wrong with the mechanism, or if the pilot lost control, he, the airplane, and I would be rolled up in a ball together. . . . I believe that little red airplane said something to me as it swished by."

First Flight

In the fall of 1919, Amelia moved to New York, and enrolled in a premed course at Columbia University, where she "started in to do the peculiar things they do who would be physicians. I fed orange juice to mice and dissected cockroaches." She took a heavy load of subjects, but she didn't forget flying.

In the summer of 1920, she went on vacation to California, where her parents had moved to start a new life after the death of her grandparents. On that trip, her father took her to an air meet. The planes were old wartime Jennies and Canucks, the pilots all members of that first swaggering generation of barnstormers.[2] The commercial airline industry had not yet been established; the skies were still empty. Amelia was enthralled.

"One thing I knew that day," she wrote, "I wanted to fly." She decided not to return to the university.

At first, she was too shy to ask about flying lessons, afraid that the all-male world of avia-

---

1. **ace**, a combat pilot who has destroyed many enemy planes.
2. **barnstormer**, a pilot who toured the country giving airplane rides and stunt flying exhibitions.

tion would snicker at the arrival of a woman in the ranks; she had her father ask on her behalf. He arranged for her to take a trial hop, as a passenger. "I am sure he thought one ride would be enough for me," she wrote later, "and he might as well act to cure me promptly."

The pilot was Frank Hawks, a slim, handsome man in the classic *macho* style, who was to become a famous aviator. Hawks insisted that another pilot accompany them on the flight in the event that Amelia turned out to be a "nervous lady." They flew out over the still smog-free green earth of Southern California, with the hills of Hollywood to one side and the vast blue Pacific on the other. Amelia was not a nervous lady. When the plane landed, she was determined to raise the five hundred dollars she would need for a twelve-hour course of instruction.

"Two things deterred me at that moment," she remembered. "One was the tuition fee to be wrung from my father, and the other the determination to look up a woman flier. . . . I felt I should be less self-conscious taking lessons with her, than with the men, who overwhelmed me with their capabilities."

The flier was Neta Snook, the first woman to graduate from the Curtiss School of Aviation, and a good instructor. Amelia took the first of twenty-eight jobs she was to hold in the next years—as a file clerk at the telephone company—in order to pay for her lessons, and Snook extended credit. Amelia, who had once taken a course in auto mechanics just to see what an automobile engine was made of, found herself as interested in the aircraft engines and design as she was in flying itself. When the phone company money did not

cover her expenses, she took another job, driving a truck for a sand and gravel company.

It was an exhilarating time, and Amelia soon was deeply involved in the life of airports. She learned to play rummy with the mechanics. She chopped her hair short, so that her leather helmet fitted snugly.

"I remember so well my first leather coat," she said later. "It was 1922. Somehow I'd contrived to save twenty dollars. With it I bought—at a very special sale—an elegant leather coat. *Patent* leather! Shiny and lovely. But suddenly I saw that it looked *too* new. How were people to think that I was a flier if I was wearing a flying coat that was brand-new? Wrinkles! That was it. There just had to be wrinkles. So—I slept in it for three nights to give my coat a properly veteran appearance."

Meanwhile, Neta Snook had gone broke and was forced to sell her plane. Amelia finally soloed under the guidance of a veteran named John Montijo. But even with her license in her pocket, she still did not know what to do with her life; the commercial aviation business was very young and there was no room in it for women.

Amelia studied photography and worked in a professional darkroom. She had a few secretarial jobs. She plowed all this money into the world of flying. In 1922, in a small open cockpit Kinner Canary, she flew to fourteen thousand feet, establishing her first world's record: highest altitude attained by a woman pilot.

Characteristically, she then tried to break her own record, and almost ended in disaster. "From the sight of cities and the glistening sea two miles below," she wrote about that dangerous attempt, "I plunged into a rolling

Amelia Earhart standing before her plane. The Bettmann Archive, New York.

bank of clouds. There was snow inside. It stung my face and plastered my goggles. At eleven thousand feet the snow changed to sleet, and at about twelve thousand, dense fog enveloped me. Unbelievably—until you've tried it—human sensations fail when one is thus 'blind.' Deprived of a horizon, a flier may lose the feel of his position in space. Was I flying one wing high? Was I turning? I couldn't be sure. I tried to keep the plane in flying trim, with one wish growing stronger every moment—to see the friendly earth

again. Spinning was the quickest way down my inexperience could suggest. And so I spun. Seconds seemed very long, until I saw clear weather several thousand feet above the world I knew."

On the ground, the man at the field was angry. "Show a little sense," he said. "Suppose the clouds had closed in until they touched the ground. We'd have had to dig you out in pieces."

"Yes," Amelia said. "I suppose you would."

Lady Lindy

One morning, Amelia Earhart received a phone call. The voice on the other end belonged to a press agent named Hilton H. Railey, and he wanted to know whether Amelia was interested in becoming the first woman to fly the Atlantic. At first she thought it was either a joke or a more sinister proposition; on at least two occasions bootleggers had asked her to fly a certain cargo from a certain place to a certain other place. She asked Railey for references. He was legitimate. One of his clients was Commander Richard E. Byrd.[3] She went to see Railey at his Boston office and started getting the full story.

He told her that a trimotored Fokker, the same airplane that Byrd flew to the South Pole, had recently been purchased by Mrs. Amy Guest. At first Mrs. Guest said that she wanted to fly the Atlantic herself, but her family objected. In those days, even after Lindbergh's[4] historic crossing, the flight was perilous; plane

---

3. **Richard E. Byrd**, (1888–1957), U.S. naval officer and Antarctic explorer.
4. **Charles A. Lindbergh**, (1902–1974), U.S. aviator who made the first non-stop solo flight across the Atlantic in 1927.

after plane had disappeared in the ocean. Radio equipment was primitive; so was weather information. De-icers had not been developed, so that some planes found themselves paralyzed with up to five hundred pounds of ice.

But Mrs. Guest was determined that a woman should fly the Atlantic. If she could not do it, then it should be someone else. She asked a friend, George Palmer Putnam, to find a suitable woman, and Putnam (whose family owned the publishing concern of G. P. Putnam's) had asked Railey to help. He poked around at Boston airports, and was told about the young woman from Denison House named Amelia Earhart. He was very impressed when he saw her: not by her obvious intelligence, or her more than five hundred hours of flying time, but by her physical resemblance to Charles Lindbergh. Visions of "Lady Lindy" bounced in his head. He reported this to Putnam, and an anxious Amelia was summoned to New York.

"I was interviewed by David T. Laymen, Jr. and John S. Phipps," she wrote, "and found myself in a curious situation. If they did not like me at all, or found me wanting in too many respects, I would be deprived of the trip. If they liked me too well, they might be loath to drown me. It was, therefore, necessary for me to maintain an attitude of impenetrable mediocrity. Apparently I did, because I was chosen."

The weeks that followed were nerve-racking. Amelia, who was to be paid absolutely nothing for the flight, was going only as a passenger. The pilot, a veteran named Wilmer "Bull" Stultz, was being paid twenty thousand dollars. His mechanic, Lou "Slim" Gordon, was to receive five thousand dollars.

But the Atlantic had already been flown; the true novelty of this flight was that its passenger was a woman. The sponsors did not want the rest of the world to know their plans, because someone carrying a woman might beat them across the Atlantic. The result was that Amelia was kept away from the airport, where Stultz and Gordon were working on the plane. Among other things, she wrote some "popping off" letters to her parents, in the event that the *Friendship*, as the plane was called, followed so many others into the Atlantic. The letters were sealed and not discovered until 1937.

> Dearest Dad:
>
> Hooray for the last grand adventure! I wish I had won, but it was worth while anyway. You know that. I have no faith we'll meet anywhere again, but I wish we might.
>
> Anyway, good-bye and good luck to you.
>
> Affectionately,
> your doter,
> Mill

To her mother she wrote: "Even though I have lost, the adventure was worth while. Our family tends to be too secure. My life has really been very happy, and I don't mind contemplating its end in the midst of it."

There was a third letter—to her sister Muriel—which was opened and shown to the press on the morning that Amelia and the *Friendship* took off from Boston Harbor.

> Dear Scrappy,
>
> I have tried to play for a large stake and if I succeed all will be well. If I don't, I shall be happy to pop off in the midst of such an adventure. My only regret would be leaving you and mother stranded for a while. . . .

Sam [Chapman] will tell you the whole story. Please explain all to mother. I couldn't stand the added strain of telling mother and you personally.

If reporters talk to you, say you knew, if you like . . .

Yours respectfully,
Sister

Throughout the days before departing Boston, the biggest problem was weather.

"When it was right in Boston, the mid-Atlantic was foreboding," Amelia wrote. "I have a memory of long gray days which had a way of dampening our spirits against our best efforts to be cheerful."

Finally, they departed Boston on June 3, 1928, only to find themselves bogged down for another two weeks in Trespassey, Newfoundland. Stultz could not eat fish, and existed on candy bars. They wandered around the tiny town, examined and reexamined the engines and pontoons, and waited for the weather to break. On the morning of the 17th, they finally took off. Amelia began to keep a detailed log of the flight, which later became a book, *20 Hours, 40 Minutes*. Some excerpts:

"Marvelous shapes in white stand out, some trailing shimmering veils. The clouds look like icebergs in the distance. . . . I think I am happy—sad admission of scant intellectual equipment."

"I am getting housemaid's knee kneeling here gulping beauty."

"How marvelous is a machine and the mind that made it. I am thoroughly occidental in this worship."

"Port motor coughing a bit. Sounds like water. We are going to go into, under, or over a storm. I don't like to, with one motor acting the way it is."

"Himmel! The sea! We are three thousand. Patchy clouds. We have been jazzing from one thousand to five thousand where we now are, to get out of clouds."

"Can't use radio at all. Coming down now in a rather clear spot. Twenty-five hundred feet. Everything sliding forward."

"8:50. Two Boats!!!!"

"Try to get bearing. Radio won't. One hour's gas. Mess. All craft cutting our course. Why?"

The answer to the "Why?" was land. They had made it across the Atlantic, and came down over the harbor of Burry Port, Wales. Amelia Earhart was famous.

The fame was sudden and all-encompassing. She was on all the front pages of the world, posing in a borrowed dress, smiling and giving credit for everything to Stultz and Gordon. As Railey had hoped, the papers started to call her "Lady Lindy." She was feted in London. Her arrival in New York brought the kind of ticker tape parades reserved for heroes. She was interviewed, photographed, mauled for autographs and souvenirs.

And waiting for her was George Palmer Putnam. He was a promoter, a gifted writer, a bit of a con man, who had been a newspaperman, Mayor of Bend, Oregon, and soldier before joining the family publishing firm. That was the era of adventure, and Putnam concentrated on the great books of exploration. His greatest coup was in signing Lindbergh to write *We* for $100,000, after the famous solo flight. Now he wanted Lady Lindy. Brash, complex, irritating, driven, Putnam was by all accounts a remarkable character. They were married in February, 1931.

Most of her public life is a matter of record, and in the years after her marriage, she lived most of her life in public. She broke record after record; she campaigned for Franklin Roosevelt and once took Eleanor up for a midnight ride; she spoke out on women's issues, looking for "the day when women . . . will be individuals free to live their lives as men are free."

Crossing the Atlantic

But Amelia always had something more personal to prove. "I wanted to make another flight alone," she wrote. "I wanted to justify myself to myself. I wanted to prove that I deserved at least a small fraction of the nice things said about me. . . . I already had the credit—heaped up and running over. I wanted to deposit a little security to make that credit good. Illogical? Perhaps. Most of the things we want are illogical."

The flight alone was to make up for the *Friendship*. She wanted to cross the Atlantic, flying the plane herself, with no one around to help. Again working in secret, to avoid the added pressure of heavy publicity, she took a Lockheed from Teterboro airport in New Jersey to Harbor Grace, Newfoundland. And on Friday, May 20, 1932, she took off. The journey was rough. Her altimeter failed, so that in fog she could not truly determine how close she was to the ocean. At one point, the plane iced up and went into a spin. "How long we spun I do not know. . . . As we righted and held level again, through the blackness below I could see the whitecaps too close for comfort."

Then a fire broke out in the manifold ring of her engine. "There was nothing to do about it," she said. "There was no use turning back. I couldn't land at Harbor Grace in the dark even if I could find my way. And I didn't want to roll up in a ball with all that gasoline. . . . So it seemed sensible to keep going."

The fire kept burning in the exhaust manifold, and she discovered she had a leaky fuel gauge. As the hours dragged on, she knew she would soon have to go down. And then she saw land. She circled over green hills, and landed in a pasture. Cows scattered in all directions, and a man came rushing out of a farmhouse.

"I've come from America," Amelia said.

"Do ye be tellin' me that now?" said Dan McCallion, and she knew she was in Ireland. She was exuberant. For the first time, after everything else she had done, Amelia Earhart felt that her fame was for real.

As she moved deeper into her own and the century's thirties, Amelia started to feel that time was beginning to run out. The old flying-by-the-seat-of-the-pants days were clearly over. The commercial giants were beginning to eat up or eliminate their smaller competitors. Amelia continued to set records, from Hawaii to Oakland, from Mexico City to Newark and more. She campaigned for Roosevelt in the 1936 election. She took a job as counselor in careers for women at Purdue University, and, with the financial help of Purdue, began to plan one last flight, in a Lockheed Electra fitted out as a flying laboratory. She wanted to fly around the world at the equator, a distance of 27,000 miles. Others had flown around the world but only via the shorter northern route.

"I have a feeling," she told a reporter in 1937, "that there is just about one more good flight left in my system, and I hope this trip is it."

Final Flight

The last flight remains mysterious to this day, shrouded in unsolved speculation. Was she on a secret reconnaissance trip for the government; an early intelligence pilot under orders from Roosevelt? Was she captured and imprisoned or killed by the Japanese? No one knows for sure. The first phase of this last adventure ended in March, 1937, when Amelia's overloaded Lockheed Electra crashed on the runway at Pearl Harbor. The plane was badly damaged, but Amelia was not injured. The plane was then taken apart by Lockheed engineers and shipped back to Burbank for repairs. It has never been determined exactly who paid for these repairs.

Between March and June, when the second phase started, a number of events took place. The route was altered, a fact noted by those who speculate about a reconnaissance mission. Instead of traveling around the world by going west, the route was changed to follow an Oakland-Miami-South America-Africa-Asia-Australia course, with the final 2,600-mile hop from Lae, New Guinea, to Howland Island in the mid-Pacific, the most dangerous part of the flight.

In addition, Fred Noonan became the sole navigator. Earlier, Amelia was helped by Paul Mantz on technical matters, and Captain Harry Manning was to be the navigator for part of the flight, with Noonan as his assistant. But Manning canceled after the Honolulu crash, and Mantz was busy on movie work.

Noonan was a legendary character in aviation. He had served as a maritime navigator, transport pilot, navigational instructor, manager of the Port-au-Prince airport in Haiti, and then inspector of all Pan Am airports. He had survived World War I torpedoing, and helped Pan Am map its routes across the Pacific. Nobody knew the Pacific better than Fred Noonan.

Noonan had lost his job with Pan Am because of his heavy drinking, but he had told friends that the flight with Amelia was to be a "second chance." And Amelia insisted she had faith in him.

The official story of the "Last Flight" is told in Amelia's book of that title (compiled by Putnam after her disappearance from letters, reports, and cables sent along the way). They took off from Miami on June 1 heading south to the equator and east around the world. After a month of grueling flight, they set out on the last lap of the journey. They never reached Howland Island.

There are many theories about the disappearance; writers have gone over the trail in considerable detail. Even Amelia's mother doubted the official version of events. In 1949, she said: "Amelia told me many things, but there were some things she couldn't tell me. I am convinced she was on some sort of a government mission, probably on verbal orders."

If Amelia was on a spy mission, it is most likely that she changed planes in Port Darwin, Australia, picking up another Lockheed Electra specially fitted with cameras. The political rationale for this theory includes Roosevelt's position then: he was unable to end the Depression and wanted heavy defense spending, but faced a Congress reluctant to spend money on guns when there were millions of unemployed Americans walking the streets. If Roosevelt could prove through photographs that Japan was building major naval bases on Saipan and Truk, he would get his defense bill. And in the event that Amelia and Noonan did not make it back, their disappearance would justify a massive sea-and-air search and the Americans could get their photographs anyway.

This in fact is precisely what happened. After the disappearance, a massive sea-and-air search was conducted, covering 400,000 square miles of the Pacific: some sixty-five airplanes were used; American ships moved freely through areas that were previously off limits. In January, Roosevelt got the largest peacetime naval spending bill of his first two administrations.

Meanwhile, there was genuine grief over Amelia's disappearance. Newspapers were full of the story. Tributes poured in. Statues were erected to her. Schools were named for her. After eighteen months, she was declared legally dead. Putnam married twice more, wrote some books, and died in 1950. The commercial airlines froze out women pilots, an event that might not have happened had Amelia still been around to lead a public fight. The old small planes went into the scrap heaps or the museums. Jets arrived. The DC-3

Amelia Earhart with her technical advisor, Paul Mantz (left) and the two navigators, Harry Manning and Fred Noonan in Honolulu, Hawaii, 1937. Wide World Photos, New York.

became the 707 which became the 747. Men landed on the moon. America had no women astronauts, and many years elapsed before there was even one women pilot of a major airline.

And yet, Amelia Earhart seems more alive and more relevant now than she has been since the days of her glory. Perhaps that is why rumors still drift to the surface: she is living in Japan, having survived a wartime concentration camp; she is living in New Jersey, still guarding the secret of her wartime mission by allowing the public to believe her dead. Like male heroes who were thought to live on after death, from Alexander through Zapata,[5] she fulfilled some need in us for the heroic spirit, and so we cannot quite bear to believe that she is gone.

---

5. **Alexander . . . Zapata**, Alexander the Great (356–323) a military conqueror and Emiliano Zapata (1879–1919) a Mexican revolutionary.

Developing Comprehension Skills

1. What was Amelia's childhood like? What effect did it have on her character?

2. What obstacles did Earhart have to overcome in order to become a flyer?

3. Just before Earhart crossed the Atlantic as a passenger, she wrote three letters to her family. Why do you think she wrote them?

4. Why did Earhart fly alone across the Atlantic after she had already achieved worldwide fame as the first woman passenger to cross that ocean? What does this tell you about her character?

5. According to the author, what is the most likely explanation for Earhart's "disappearance"?

6. What effect did Amelia Earhart have on women's role in aviation? Do you think that women would have been accepted in aviation sooner had she not "disappeared"? Why or why not?

Reading Literature

1. **Understanding Biography.** Unlike all of the other selections you have read in this chapter, the life story of Amelia Earhart is told by someone other than herself. How does this limit what the reader can learn about Amelia? On the other hand, what are the advantages of this method of telling a life story?

2. **Using Quotations.** The author of this biography chose to include several direct quotations by Amelia Earhart. For example, before Amelia's solo flight she says, "I wanted to justify myself to myself. I wanted to prove that I deserved at least a small fraction of the nice things said about me." What does Amelia's comment reveal about her? Find two other direct quotations in the biography. Why do you think the author decided to include quotations in this selection?

3. **Inferring Character Traits.** The reader can learn a great deal about Amelia through her

actions as well as her words. What character traits are revealed by each of the following incidents?

    a. Amelia takes twenty-eight jobs to pay for her flying lessons.

    b. She plays cards with the airport mechanics and sleeps in her leather coat to give it a veteran appearance.

    c. She tries to break her own records.

    d. She gives Noonan a second chance after he loses his job with Pan Am.

4. **Understanding History Through Literature.** This biography of Amelia Earhart mentions a number of important events in history. By reading the selection carefully, you should be able to find information about several famous people and events. Scan the selection to find answers to the following questions:

    a. What important event in aviation history took place at Kitty Hawk in the year 1903?

    b. In what year did the United States enter World War I?

    c. What expedition was Commander Richard E. Byrd famous for?

    d. Who was the first man to fly across the Atlantic?

    e. Amelia Earhart campaigned for which U.S. President in 1936?

5. **Understanding Objective and Subjective Writing. Objective writing** presents only the facts about a person or situation. **Subjective writing** includes the author's personal feelings and judgments. "The Legend of Amelia Earhart" is a mixture of both types of writing. Find passages that are strictly factual, or objective. Then find sections in which the author makes either positive or negative judgments about people and events.

Developing Vocabulary Skills

Understanding Symbols. The dictionary often uses symbols to give you information about a word. For example, in some dictionaries a star ☆ indicates an Americanism. An **Americanism** is a word or phrase that began in the United States. The dictionary also lists foreign words and phrases that are frequently used in the United States, such as *au contraire*. These are usually marked with the following symbol: ‡.

Look up the following words and phrases from "The Legend of Amelia Earhart": *jazzing* (under *jazz*), *Canuck*, *macho*, and *pop-off*. Which three are Americanisms? Which is a foreign word? Now look through your dictionary or go to the library and look through other dictionaries to find at least five more common Americanisms and five familiar foreign words and phrases.

Developing Writing Skills

1. **Writing a Biographical Summary.** "The Legend of Amelia Earhart" presents many details about Amelia's life. From this information, write a brief summary of her life.

    Pre-Writing. Begin by scanning the selection for the most important details about Amelia Earhart's life. Make a list of these details as you read. Then, group your ideas in the three categories shown below:

        early life
        public life
        major accomplishments

You may wish to organize the details in each category in chronological order.

    Writing. Write an introduction that will capture your reader's attention. For example, you may wish to begin with an interesting fact about Amelia's life. Begin each body paragraph with a good topic sentence. Then, follow the organization of your notes to develop each paragraph. As you write, try to focus on the highlights of Earhart's life. Be sure that your information is correct, especially when you mention dates.

Revising. Read your summary carefully. Did you begin each paragraph with a good topic sentence? Have you included the major accomplishments of Earhart's life? Are all of your facts correct? Check your work for errors in grammar, spelling, and punctuation. Then, make a clean final copy if necessary.

2. **Writing an Interview.** Imagine that you are a reporter living at the time of Amelia Earhart. You have been assigned to interview her after her first solo flight across the Atlantic in 1932.

Make a list of questions that you would like to ask Earhart. Try to capture the excitement of her accomplishment in your questions. Then, use the information in this selection along with your own imagination to answer these questions as Amelia Earhart might have.

Developing Skills in Study and Research

Using an Atlas. Amelia Earhart's final flight around the world was to follow "an Oakland-Miami-South America-Africa-Asia-Australia course. The final 2,600 mile hop was to be from Lae, New Guinea, to Howland Island in the mid-Pacific." Use the atlas to trace this flight as well as possible. At what point in her final journey was Amelia's plane lost?

Developing Skills in Critical Thinking

1. **Identifying Stereotypes.** A **stereotype** is an unfair generalization about people of a particular race, sex, religion, nationality, or social group. In "The Legend of Amelia Earhart," Amelia proves that many stereotypes about women are untrue. Skim the selection to find two stereotypes about women that Amelia proved to be untrue. Why do you think these stereotypes gained wide acceptance? Can you think of other stereotypes about men and women? Explain the problems with each one you mention.

2. **Understanding Cause and Effect Relationships.** A **cause and effect relationship** states that one thing happens because of something else. For example, suppose that as a result of a power failure, your lights go out. The power failure is the cause, and the loss of lights is the result.

What were the effects of the following situations and incidents in Amelia's life?
a. her family's move to Des Moines

b. her work as a nurse's aid in the Canadian Red Cross

c. her visit to an air meet when she was 22

Inaugural Address

JOHN F. KENNEDY

SETTING A PURPOSE

John F. Kennedy was sworn in as President of the United States in 1961. His inaugural address was delivered during a time of great tension in the world. What makes the speech such a memorable one?

We observe today not a victory of party but a celebration of freedom—symbolizing an end as well as a beginning—signifying renewal as well as change. For I have sworn before you and Almighty God the same solemn oath our forebears prescribed nearly a century and three-quarters ago.

The world is very different now. For man holds in his mortal hands the power to abolish all forms of human poverty and all forms of human life. And yet the same revolutionary beliefs for which our forebears fought are still at issue around the globe—the belief that the rights of man come not from the generosity of the state but from the hands of God.

We dare not forget today that we are the heirs of that first revolution. Let the word go forth from this time and place, to friend and foe alike, that the torch has been passed to a new generation of Americans—born in this century, tempered by war, disciplined by a hard and bitter peace, proud of our ancient heritage—and unwilling to witness or permit the slow undoing of those human rights to which this nation has always been committed, and to which we are committed today at home and around the world.

Let every nation know, whether it wishes us well or ill, that we shall pay any price, bear any burden, meet any hardship, support any friend, oppose any foe to assure the survival and the success of liberty.

This much we pledge—and more.

To those old allies whose cultural and spiritual origins we share, we pledge the loyalty of faithful friends. United, there is little we cannot do in a host of cooperative ventures. Divided, there is little we can do—for we dare not meet a powerful challenge at odds and split asunder.

To those new states whom we welcome to the ranks of the free, we pledge our word that one form of colonial control shall not have passed away merely to be replaced by a far more iron tyranny. We shall not always expect to find them supporting our view. But we shall always hope to find them strongly supporting their own freedom—and to remember that, in the past, those who foolishly sought power by riding the back of the tiger ended up inside.

To those people in the huts and villages of half the globe struggling to break the bonds of mass misery, we pledge our best efforts to help them help themselves, for whatever period is required—not because the Communists may be doing it, not because we seek their votes, but because it is right. If a free society cannot help the many who are poor, it cannot save the few who are rich.

To our sister republics south of our border, we offer a special pledge—to convert our good words into good deeds—in a new alliance for progress—to assist free men and free governments in casting off the chains of poverty. But this peaceful revolution of hope cannot become the prey of hostile powers. Let all our neighbors know that we shall join with them to oppose aggression or subversion anywhere in the Americas. And let every other power know that this hemisphere intends to remain the master of its own house.

To that world assembly of sovereign states, the United Nations, our last best hope in an age where the instruments of war have far outpaced the instruments of peace, we renew our pledge of support—to prevent it from becoming merely a forum for invective—to strengthen its shield of the new and the weak—and to enlarge the area in which its writ may run.

Finally, to those nations who would make themselves our adversary, we offer not a pledge but a request—that both sides begin anew the quest for peace before the dark

Portrait of John Fitzgerald Kennedy, 1967, JAMES WYETH. The John Fitzgerald Kennedy Presidential Library, Boston, Massachusetts. Copyright © 1967 James Wyeth.

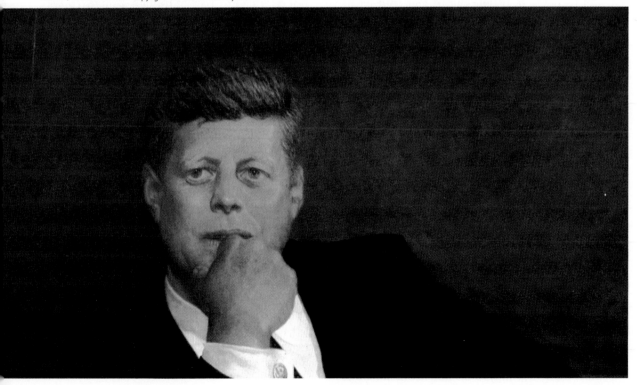

powers of destruction unleashed by science engulf all humanity in planned or accidental self-destruction. We dare not tempt them with weakness. For only when our arms are sufficient beyond doubt can we be certain beyond doubt that they will never be employed.

But neither can two great and powerful groups of nations take comfort from our present course—both sides overburdened by the cost of modern weapons, both rightly alarmed by the steady spread of the deadly atom, yet both racing to alter that uncertain balance of terror that stays the hand of mankind's final war.

So let us begin anew—remembering on both sides that civility is not a sign of weakness, and sincerity is always subject to proof. Let us never negotiate out of fear. But let us never fear to negotiate.

Let both sides explore what problems unite us instead of belaboring those problems which divide us.

Let both sides, for the first time, formulate serious and precise proposals for the inspection and control of arms—and bring the absolute power to destroy other nations under the absolute control of all nations.

Let both sides seek to invoke the wonders of science instead of its terrors. Together let us explore the stars, conquer the deserts, eradicate disease, tap the ocean depths, and encourage the arts and commerce.

Let both sides unite to heed in all corners of the earth the command of Isaiah—to "undo the heavy burdens . . . [and] let the oppressed go free."[1]

And if a beachhead of cooperation may push back the jungle of suspicion, let both sides join in creating a new endeavor, not a new balance of power but a new world of law, where the strong are just and the weak secure and the peace preserved.

All this will not be finished in the first 100 days. Nor will it be finished in the first 1,000 days, nor in the life of this administration, nor even perhaps in our lifetime on this planet. But let us begin.

In your hands, my fellow citizens, more than mine, will rest the final success or failure of our course. Since this country was founded, each generation of Americans has been summoned to give testimony to its national loyalty. The graves of young Americans who answered the call to service surround the globe.

Now the trumpet summons us again—not as a call to bear arms, though arms we need—not as a call to battle, though embattled we are—but a call to bear the burden of a long twilight struggle, year in and year out, "rejoicing in hope, patient in tribulation"[2]—a struggle against the common enemies of man: tyranny, poverty, disease and war itself.

Can we forge against these enemies a grand and global alliance, North and South, East and West, that can assure a more fruitful life for all mankind? Will you join in that historic effort?

In the long history of the world, only a few generations have been granted the role of defending freedom in its hour of maximum danger. I do not shrink from this responsibility—I welcome it. I do not believe that any of us would exchange places with any other

---

1. **undo . . . free**, a Biblical quote from Isaiah 58:6.
2. **rejoicing . . . tribulation**, a Biblical quote from Romans 12:12.

people or any other generation. The energy, the faith, the devotion which we bring to this endeavor will light our country and all who serve it—and the glow from that fire can truly light the world.

And so, my fellow Americans—ask not what your country can do for you—ask what you can do for your country.

My fellow citizens of the world—ask not what America will do for you but what together we can do for the freedom of man.

Finally, whether you are citizens of America or citizens of the world, ask of us here the same high standards of strength and sacrifice which we ask of you. With a good conscience our only sure reward, with history the final judge of our deeds, let us go forth to lead the land we love, asking His blessing and His help, but knowing that here on earth God's work must truly be our own.

Developing Comprehension Skills

1. John F. Kennedy begins his speech with a reference to the American Revolution. What similarity does Kennedy see between his time and 1776?

2. What promises does Kennedy make to friends? to new nations? to the United Nations?

3. What does Kennedy ask of the enemies of the United States? How can the U.S. and these countries achieve peace?

4. According to Kennedy, who will determine whether American efforts succeed or fail? Do you agree?

5. What does Kennedy ask of all Americans?

6. Do you think Kennedy's speech is an attempt to persuade or to please? Explain your answer.

Reading Literature

1. **Recognizing Persuasion.** Persuasive writing tries to convince people to think or act as the writer wishes them to. How does John F. Kennedy try to convince people that his plan of action is the right one? What reasons does he give? What persuasive techniques does he use?

2. **Appreciating a Strong Conclusion.** A persuasive piece, especially a speech, often ends with a call to action. Explain the call to action in the last three paragraphs of Kennedy's speech. What does Kennedy want people to do? Would his words have convinced you to act? Why or why not?

3. **Recognizing Theme.** A president's inaugural address usually contains a number of themes, or important ideas, that he wishes to

express. What were some of Kennedy's major concerns? How do you know that these subjects were important to him?

4. **Identifying Mood.** The mood of a speech is the feeling that it creates in the audience. What might have been the reaction of those who heard Kennedy's speech? What feelings did you have as you read the speech? Do you think people reading the speech might have a different reaction from those hearing the speech? Explain your answer.

5. **Appreciating Figurative Language.** In this speech, Kennedy often uses figurative language. **Figurative language** is the use of ordinary words in unusual ways. Writers use figurative language to get the reader to think about things in a new and fresh way.

Look at the following examples of figurative language. How does each speak of a familiar idea in a creative way? What mental picture might the audience have formed in response to each example?

a. . . . if a beachhead of cooperation may push back the jungle of suspicion, let both sides join in creating a new endeavor. . . .

b. The energy, the faith, the devotion which we bring to this endeavor will light our country and all who serve it—and the glow from that fire can truly light the world.

c. . . . this hemisphere intends to remain the master of its own house.

Developing Vocabulary Skills

Identifying Inflected Forms. The inflected forms of a word are the changes that occur when a word is used in a special way, such as in the plural form. The dictionary lists inflected forms

that are irregular, or not formed in the usual way. For example, the dictionary lists the following:

Irregular plurals of nouns. These plurals include such nouns as *mice* and *alumni*.

Irregular principal parts of verbs. For example, *broke*, *broken*, and *breaking* are listed after the entry word for *break*. When two inflected forms are given, the first is the form for the past tense and past participle, and the second is for the present participle. When three forms are given, the first is the past tense, the second is the past participle, and the third is the present participle.

Irregular comparative and superlative forms. These forms of adjectives and adverbs include such forms as *better* and *worst*.

The following is a dictionary listing for the word *easy*, which has irregular spellings for its comparative, *easier*, and its superlative, *easiest*:

eas·y (ē'zē) *adj.* **eas'i·er, eas'i·est**

The following words are from Kennedy's address. Use a dictionary to find the inflected form called for in parentheses. Write it on your paper.

1. swear (past tense)
2. forget (past participle)
3. well (comparative)
4. bear (past participle)
5. loyalty (plural)
6. split (past tense)
7. adversary (plural)
8. responsibility (plural)
9. steady (comparative)
10. sure (superlative)

Developing Writing Skills

1. **Supporting an Opinion.** Kennedy's most memorable statement from his Inaugural Address is "... ask not what your country can do for you—ask what you can do for your country."

   What did Kennedy mean by this statement? Do you think it is more important for a country to serve its citizens, or for citizens to serve their country? Write a composition explaining why you agree or disagree with Kennedy.

   Pre-Writing. Discuss this topic with classmates, teachers, or family members. Think carefully about your own opinion. Then write down the reasons for your opinion. For each reason, list supporting facts and ideas. Finally, organize your ideas. Order of importance is one good method to use.

   Writing. Write an introduction that presents Kennedy's quotation and gives your opinion of it. Use your organized notes to write for the body of the composition. Write one paragraph to develop each reason.

   Revising. Work with an editing partner to improve your writing. Check for a topic sentence in each paragraph. Have you developed each paragraph thoroughly? Have you taken out unrelated ideas? Does the conclusion sum up your main ideas?

2. **Writing a Speech.** Assume that you have been elected to an office in your school or organization. Write a brief speech to show the direction you will take in office. The speech should tell the direction or activities that you think are important for your group. It must also gather the support of students or members of your group.

Developing Skills in Critical Thinking

Identifying Emotional Appeals. An effective speaker may appeal to the listeners' emotions as well as to their reason. Kennedy uses two types of emotional appeals in his speech. One is known as a purr word. The other is called transfer. A **purr word** is a pleasant term that makes listeners react favorably. *Intelligent, exciting, marvelous, thoughtful,* and *beautiful* are all examples of purr words. **Transfer** is the association of positive feelings about one thing with some other unrelated thing or idea. For example, many political speakers stand in front of the American Flag, or by the statue of a national hero, when speaking. By doing this, they hope the audience will transfer positive feelings about these symbols to the speaker. Locate examples of each of these emotional appeals in Kennedy's speech. In your opinion, what effect did he hope to achieve with each example?

Developing Skills in Speaking and Listening

Using Audio-Visual Resources. Many libraries have recordings of Kennedy's Inaugural Address, as well as other speeches by Kennedy. The recordings in your library are indexed in a separate card catalog. Cards are alphabetized by title and subject. Each card has a call number, the title of the recording, and the subject. In addition, a card may tell you the name of the performer or speaker and when and where the recording was made. Finally, the card will tell you if the recording is a record or a cassette tape.

Find a recording of the Inaugural Address. Listen to it carefully. Compare listening to the speech with reading it. In what ways is the effect different?

From
I Have a Dream

MARTIN LUTHER KING, JR.

Five score years ago, a great American, in whose symbolic shadow we stand, signed the Emancipation Proclamation. This momentous decree came as a great beacon light of hope to millions of Negro slaves who had been seared in the flames of withering injustice. It came as a joyous daybreak to end the long night of captivity.

But one hundred years later, we must face the tragic fact that the Negro is still not free. One hundred years later, the life of the Negro is still sadly crippled by the manacles of segregation and the chains of discrimination. One hundred years later, the Negro lives on a lonely island of poverty in the midst of a vast ocean of material prosperity. One hundred years later the Negro still languishes in the corners of American society and finds himself an exile in his own land. So we have come here today to dramatize an appalling condition.

In a sense, we have come to our nation's capital to cash a check. When the architects of our republic wrote the magnificent words of the Constitution and the Declaration of Independence, they were signing a promissory note to which every American was to fall heir. This note was a promise that all men would be guaranteed the unalienable rights of life, liberty, and the pursuit of happiness . . . .

I say to you today, my friends, that in spite of the difficulties and frustrations of the moment, I still have a dream. It is a dream deeply rooted in the American dream.

I have a dream that one day this nation will rise up and live out the true meaning of its creed: "We hold these truths to be self-evident; that all men are created equal. . . ."

I have a dream that my four little children will one day live in a nation where they will not be judged by the color of their skin but by the content of their character.

I have a dream today . . . .

I have a dream that one day every valley shall be exalted, every hill and mountain shall be made low, the rough places will be made plains, and the crooked places will be made straight, and the glory of the Lord shall be revealed, and all flesh shall see it together.

This is our hope. This is the faith with which I return to the South. With this faith we will be able to hew out of the mountain of despair a stone of hope. With this faith we will be able to transform the jangling discords of our nation into a beautiful symphony of

(Above) Dr. King giving his "I Have a Dream" speech from the Lincoln Memorial, Washington, D.C. August 28, 1963. Magnum Photos, Inc., New York.

(Left) Dr. Martin Luther King, Jr., © Bob Adelman/Magnum Photos, Inc., New York.

brotherhood. With this faith we will be able to work together, to pray together, to struggle together, to go to jail together, to stand up for freedom together, knowing that we will be free one day.

This will be the day when all of God's children will be able to sing with new meaning, "My country 'tis of thee, sweet land of liberty, of thee I sing. Land where my fathers died, land of the pilgrim's pride, from every mountainside, let freedom ring."

And if America is to be a great nation, this must become true. So let freedom ring from the prodigious hilltops of New Hampshire. Let freedom ring from the mighty mountains of New York. Let freedom ring from the heightening Alleghenies of Pennsylvania!

Let freedom ring from the snowcapped Rockies of Colorado!

Let freedom ring from the . . . peaks of California!

But not only that; let freedom ring from Stone Mountain of Georgia!

Let freedom ring from Lookout Mountain of Tennessee!

Let freedom ring from every hill . . . of Mississippi.

From every mountainside, let freedom ring.

When we let freedom ring, when we let it ring from every village and every hamlet, from every state and every city, we will be able to speed up that day when all of God's children, black men and white men, Jews and Gentiles, Protestants and Catholics, will be able to join hands and sing in the words of the old Negro spiritual, "Free at last! Free at last! Thank God Almighty, we are free at last!"

Developing Comprehension Skills

1. What is the "tragic fact" Martin Luther King, Jr. mentions in this speech?

2. King says, ". . . we have come to our nation's capital to cash a check." What does he mean?

3. What is the "American dream" that King mentions? How is it related to King's dream?

4. What hopes does King's speech hold for the future of America? In your opinion, how realistic was King's dream? Explain your answer.

5. According to King, what must happen for America to become great?

6. How does the final paragraph of King's speech illustrate his dream?

Reading Literature

1. **Understanding Speeches.** A speech is meant to be delivered orally. Therefore, the writer chooses words for their sound and emotional impact, not only for their meaning. Because of this, a speech is more effective when it is heard than when it is read silently.

   How do you think Martin Luther King, Jr. would have delivered this speech? How do you think King would have emphasized the emotion and power behind his thoughts?

2. **Explaining Allusions.** King's speech opens with an allusion to Abraham Lincoln and the *Emancipation Proclamation.* Why do you think King makes that reference? In the passage that begins "every valley shall be exalted . . . ," King alludes to a passage in the Bible. Why might he have used this kind of allusion? Find one more allusion to a famous song, and another to a famous document. How does each strengthen King's speech?

3. **Identifying Repetition.** In his speech, King uses repetition to emphasize important ideas. For example, King repeats four times the opening phrase "I have a dream . . . ." He repeats nine times the phrase "let freedom ring."

   Find one other example of repetition in the speech. Why do you think King chooses to repeat these phrases? What effect does the repetition have?

4. **Appreciating Metaphors.** King uses metaphors that draw striking mental pictures for his listeners. Explain the following comparisons. What image does each create? Why is each appropriate and powerful?

   a. . . . the life of the Negro is still sadly crippled by the manacles of segregation and the chains of discrimination.

b. . . . the Negro lives on a lonely island of poverty in the midst of a vast ocean of material prosperity.

c. This momentous decree came as a great beacon light of hope . . .

Find one other metaphor in King's speech. Explain how it gives additional meaning to the speech.

5. **Understanding Purpose.** Why do you think King wrote this speech? Do you think his purpose was to persuade, to inform, or to inspire? Explain your answer.

Developing Vocabulary Skills

Recognizing Homographs. Words that are spelled alike but are different both in meaning and origin are called **homographs**. These words are listed as separate entries in a dictionary. Here is an example of homograph entries for *arm*:

> **arm**[1] (ärm) *n.* [ME. < OE *earm;* akin to Goth. *arms,* OHG. *arm:* for IE. base see ART[1]] **1.** an upper limb of the human body; part between shoulder and hand **2.** anything resembling this in structure or function . . .
>
> **arm**[2] (ärm) *n.* [ME. & OFr. *armes,* pl. < L. *arma,* implements, weapons, akin to *armus,* shoulder, upper arm < IE. base **ar-,* to join, fit, whence ARM[1], ART[1]; for semantic development cf. ARM[1], sense 3] **1.** any instrument used in fighting; weapon: *usually used in pl* . . .

The underlined words in the following passages are homographs. Use an unabridged dictionary to locate the homograph entries. Explain how the homographs differ in meaning and origin. Then write the definitions of the words as they are used in the passages.

1. . . . slaves who had been <u>seared</u> in the flames of withering injustice.

2. . . . they will not be judged by the color of their skin but by the <u>content</u> of their character.

3. . . . every hill and mountain shall be made <u>low</u>, . . .

4. Let freedom <u>ring</u> . . .

5. Free at <u>last</u>!

6. . . . crooked places will be made <u>straight</u>.

7. . . . I <u>still</u> have a dream.

8. With this faith we will be able to transform the jangling <u>discords</u> of our nation into a beautiful symphony of brotherhood.

9. <u>Land</u> where my Fathers died . . . .

10. . . . the same revolutionary beliefs for which our forebears fought are still at <u>issue</u> around the globe.

Developing Writing Skills

1. **Writing a Report.** Martin Luther King, Jr. was one of the chief leaders of the civil rights movement of the 1960's. Write a report on some aspect of the civil rights movement. You may choose to write about an event or a leader, for example.

   Pre-Writing. Decide on your topic. To get ideas, you may wish to do some general reading in encyclopedias or in history books about the American civil rights movement. You could also ask someone who may have been active in the movement. After you have completed your research, limit your topic to a subject you can deal with in a short report.

   As you gather information in books, magazines, encyclopedias, and reference works, take notes carefully. Follow the guidelines explained on pages 48–51. In addition, keep a record of your sources on bibliography cards. See the guidelines on page 705 for help with this step.

Once you have gathered all your information, organize your notes. Group your notes under major headings. Drop unrelated or unnecessary information. Plan the order in which you will present information, and make an outline for your report. See page 705 for information on how to make an outline.

Writing. Begin your report with an introduction. This introduction should capture the reader's attention while presenting the subject of your report. Then, follow the outline you have made as you continue to write the body of your report. Each group of ideas in your outline will probably be a paragraph in your report. Try to make your facts and ideas flow smoothly between and within paragraphs. End your report with a brief conclusion. It should summarize the role of your subject in the civil rights movement.

Revising. Check the facts in your report for accuracy. Make sure that you have used quotation marks around any words that are taken directly from a source. Does each paragraph focus on one main idea? Are there any unrelated facts or ideas that need to be taken out? Have you provided complete information on your topic? Make needed changes and proofread your report before you make a final copy. Finally, use your bibliography cards to make a bibliography of the sources you used for your report. Follow the form on page 705 in making your bibliography. Position the bibliography at the end of your report, on a separate sheet of paper.

2. **Writing a Speech.** Martin Luther King, Jr. eloquently expresses his hopes for the future in "I Have a Dream." Write a speech of your own expressing your dream for the future. Remember to choose words that will appeal to the ear as well as the mind.

Developing Skills in Critical Thinking

Evaluating Speeches. What makes a speech successful and memorable? Why do some speeches achieve the speaker's purpose while others fail? Set up criteria, or standards for evaluating speeches. One, for example, might be, "Does the speech achieve the writer's purpose?" Other criteria might deal with the clear explanation of ideas, a clear organization, or the use of language that is easy to understand and remember. Compare your list with those of your classmates. Do you want to add any of their ideas?

Developing Skills in Speaking and Listening

Presenting a Speech. Present the speech that you prepared for Developing Writing Skills on this page. Be sure to rehearse your speech aloud several times. You may improve your delivery if you practice in front of a mirror or record your speech on tape. You may also want to practice it in front of a friend or family member. When you deliver the speech, follow these guidelines:

Stand erect, but comfortably.
Maintain eye contact with your audience.
Use natural gestures and facial expressions to emphasize key points.
Speak loudly enough to be heard.
Say words clearly.
Speak at a pace that is slightly slower than you normally use in conversation.
Pause for dramatic effect.

Richard Armour's explanation of American history is not what you would find in your history book. What makes his version of early history so entertaining?

It All Started with Columbus

RICHARD ARMOUR

The Discovery of America

America was founded by Columbus in 1492. This is an easy date for you to remember because it rhymes with "ocean blue," which was the color of the Atlantic in those days. If he had sailed a year later the date would still be easy to remember because it would rhyme with "boundless sea."

Columbus fled to this country because of persecution by Ferdinand and Isabella, who refused to believe the world was round, even when Columbus showed them an egg. Ferdinand later became famous because he objected to bullfights and said he preferred to smell flowers if he had to smell anything. He was stung in the end by a bee.

Before Columbus reached America, which he named after a man called American Vesuvius, he cried "Ceylon! Ceylon!" because he wanted to see India, which was engraved on his heart, before he died. When he arrived, he cried again. This time he cried "Excelsior!" meaning "I have founded it." Excelsior has been widely used ever since by persons returning with chinaware from China, with indiaware from India, and with underware from Down Under.

Columbus was mistaken in thinking he had reached India when actually he had not got even as far as Indiana. There is still a great deal of confusion about the East and the West. As Columbus discovered, if you go west long enough you find yourself in the east, and vice versa. The East and the West are kept apart by the Date Line, just as the North and South are kept apart by the Masons' Dixon Line. In the New World most of the eastern half of the country is called the Middle West, although it is known as the East by those who live in the Far West.

Columbus, who was as confused as anybody who has been at sea for a long time, called the first people he saw "Indians." It is not known what they called Columbus. His unfortunate error has been perpetuated through the centuries. The original Americans are still known as "Indians," while all manner of immigrants from England, Ireland, Angora, and Lichtenstein are referred to as "Americans."

Accompanied by his devoted followers, the Knights of Columbus, Columbus made several other voyages in search of India. Try as he might, however, he kept discovering America,

First Landing of Christopher Columbus, 1800–05, FREDERICK KEMMELMEYER. National Gallery of Art, gift of Edgar William and Bernice Chrysler Garbisch. Washington, D.C.

and finally returned to Spain to die. He lived for a time in Madrid, but spent his last days in Disgrace.

Further Explorations

After Columbus proved the world was round, a great many people went around it. Marco Polo, who was one of the earlier explorers, had the misfortune to live several centuries before Columbus. Therefore, although he got around a good deal, he did not get completely around. He went far to the north, however, and is remembered for his discovery of the Polo regions.

The chief rivals in exploration were England and Spain. England had men like Cabot, who spoke only to a man named Lowell, and Sir Francis Drake, who had a singed beard and a ship called the *Golden Behind*.

Nor should we forget Sir Martin Four-flusher.

The struggle between England and Spain came to a climax in an epic sea battle off the Azores known as the Last Fight of the Revenge. In this decisive conflict, Sir Richard Grenville and Alfred Lord Tennyson proved conclusively that the lighter English warships could get more miles to the galleon.

England has ruled the waves ever since and has kept the sun from setting anywhere on her empire, thus providing a longer working day than in other countries.

Still Further Explorations

Other explorers included Bilbo, Cabbage de Vaca, Cortez (known as The Stout, who traveled much in realms looking for gold), and Pantsy de Lion, a thirsty old man who was looking for a drinking fountain. He never found it, but he founded Florida, to which a great many thirsty old men have gone ever since.

The Indians

The early colonists found the Indians living in toupees, or wigwams, and sending up smoke signals, or wigwags, with piece pipes. Apparently because of a shortage of pipes, they sat in a circle and passed one pipe around, each biting off a piece as it passed. The chief Indian was named Hiawatha, and his squaw, whose name was Evangeline, did all the work. This was later to become an Old American Custom.

The Chiefs, it must be said in all fairness, were too busy to work. They were engaged in making wampum, or whoopee, when they were not mixing war paint or scattering arrowheads about, to be found centuries later.

In order to have their hands free to work, the squaws carried their babies, or cabooses, on their back, very much as kangaroos carry their babies on their front, only different.

The Indians were stern, silent people who never showed their feelings, even while being scalped. They crept up on their enemies without breaking a twig and were familiar with all the warpaths. Despite their savage ways, they sincerely loved peace, and were called Nobel Savages.

Their favorite word was "How," which the colonists soon learned was not a question.

The whites feared the redskins and considered them the forest's prime evil. Some went so far as to say that "The only good Indian is a wooden Indian." The redskins resented the whiteskins because they thought they had come to take their lands away from them, and their fears were well grounded.

Captain John Smith was the first of a long line of Smiths who came to this country to keep up with the Joneses.

He was captured by the great Indian Chief, Powhatan, and was about to be killed when Popocatepetl, the fiery young daughter of the Chief, stepped in. We are not told what she stepped in, but she saved Captain John Smith's life, for which he thanked her. Later she married an Englishman, which improved relations.

The Pilgrims

The Pilgrims were a branch of the Puritans, and were proud of their family tree. They wore tall hats, which they had to take off when they went inside because they attended a low church. This displeased King James, who raised the roof. He demanded that they attend the same church as he did. At least this is his side of the story, which became known as the King James Version.

Although the King insisted, the Puritans, who were very stiff-necked from years of wearing truffles on their collars, stubbornly declined. They would probably still be declining if they had not left England and gone to

Leyden, a city in Holland noted for the discovery of electricity in a jar. (Electricity was subsequently lost for a while, but was rediscovered, by accident, when Benjamin Franklin was told to go fly a kite, and did.)

While in Holland, the Pilgrims suffered from pangs of sin, and sent their children to Dutch Reform Schools when they misbehaved. These children, naturally enough, became Protestants, but their protests were ignored.

After several years in Holland, the Pilgrims decided to set out for the New World. This decision to move is known as Pilgrims' Progress.

The ship on which they sailed was the *Mayflower*. In stormy weather the women and children descended below the heaving decks, thus becoming the *Mayflower* descendants. There they huddled with the Colonial Dames and other early settlers and passed the weary hours comparing genealogies.

It was a long and perilous voyage across the Atlantic. Several times they were blown off their course. But finally, in 1620, which was a doubly Memorable Year because it was also the year in which they set sail, they sighted the rocky coast. The rock on which they landed they called Plymouth Rock because it reminded them of another rock of the same name in England. They built a small picket fence around it and made it a national shrine.

The first four men ashore became our fourfathers.

The First Winter

After a short stay on Plymouth Rock, which was windy and damp, the Pilgrims sought a more sheltered place to build a town. One party went in one direction and one went in another. This was the beginning of the two-party system. When the two parties met, they held the first town meeting.

The first winter was cold, which was a distinct surprise to the Pilgrims. Indeed, they might not have survived but for the corn that was given them by friendly Indians. By a curious quirk of history, it has since become illegal for white men to give Indians either corn or rye.

The next spring the crops were good, and in the fall the Pilgrims celebrated their first Thanksgiving, which fell, that fall, on a Thursday. The friendly Indians were invited, and the unfriendly Indians stayed in the background, muttering.

One of the leaders of the little band at Plymouth was Captain Miles Standish. He was known throughout the township for his courtship.

He was an exceptional man. Except for him, almost all the Pilgrims were named William or John. One of the latter was Miles Standish's friend, quiet John Alden, a man who did not speak for himself until spoken to. He was spoken to, and sharply, by the fair Priscilla, whom he married, much to the annoyance of Miles Standish, who thought he was stood up by his stand-in.

Life in Old New England

Most of the Puritans were ministers. Each week they could hardly wait until Sunday, when they preached for several hours on such subjects as "Hellfire" and "Damnation." In those days, church attendance was as good every Sunday as it is today on Easter.

The homes of the Puritans were simple and

austere, but their furniture was antique and therefore frightfully expensive. The chairs were as straight and stiff as the Puritans themselves, and had hard bottoms. They became known as period pieces because they went to pieces after a short period of sitting on them.

Stores were known as Shoppes, or Ye Olde Shoppes. Prices were somewhat higher at the latter.

The Puritans believed in justice. A woman who was a witch, or a man who was a son of a witch, was punished by being stuck in the stocks. These were wooden devices that had holes to put the arms and legs through, and were considered disgraceful. They were also considered uncomfortable.

Every day the men went out into the fields in their blunderbusses and sowed corn. The women, meanwhile, were busy at home embroidering the alphabet and the date on a piece of cloth.

Other amusements were pillories, whipping posts, and Indian massacres.

Test

1. Why do you think Columbus was so interested in traveling to distant places? What else do you know about his home life?

2. Are you really convinced that the world is round? Do you worry much about it?

3. To what extent would the course of American history have been altered if America had never been discovered?

4. What would you say about the Puritans? Would you say the same if they were listening?

5. Can the passengers on the *Mayflower* be considered immigrants? With their strong sense of duty, do you suppose they tried to conceal anything from the customs officials?

6. Have you ever thought how much of a Pilgrim was wasted when an Indian kept only his scalp?

Developing Comprehension Skills

1. What are some of the interesting facts about Columbus, as told by Armour?

2. Armour's "history" often trades accuracy for humor. Find an example of a statement that is false. What makes the statement humorous?

3. Although humorous, some of Armour's statements also contain some truth. Find an example of a statement that is accurate.

4. How does Armour describe the relationship between Native Americans and the early set-tlers? Point out the irony in what the Native Americans are called.

5. How does Armour poke fun at the Pilgrims? the Puritans?

6. Do you think Armour's humor could be offensive to any group of people? Explain.

Reading Literature

1. **Recognizing a Parody.** A **parody** is an imitation of a piece of writing or music. It is often written to poke fun at the original. What does Armour parody in this selection?

2. **Identifying Puns.** A **pun** is the humorous use of words that have nearly the same sound or spelling, but different meanings. A pun is also called "a play on words." Richard Armour makes a pun on the word *gallon* when he describes ships that "get more miles to the galleon." His use of the words *underware* and *four-fathers* are also puns. Find two more examples of puns in "It All Started with Columbus." How do they add to the humor of the essay?

3. **Recognizing Malapropisms.** Besides puns, Armour uses another humorous device, the malapropism, to play on words. A **malapropism** is a word or expression that sounds something like the word the speaker intends. Unless it is used for humor, a malapropism shows a misunderstanding of the meaning and use of words.

   Armour often substitutes words with similar sounds. For example, he uses *toupees* in place of *teepees* and *cabooses* instead of *papooses*. Find two other examples of malapropisms in "It All Started with Columbus." What makes each one humorous?

4. **Explaining Allusions.** The allusions that Armour makes often are ridiculously inaccurate or inappropriate. For example, Armour refers to Vasco de Gama as "Cabbage de Vaca," and Ponce de Leon as "Pantsy de Lion." Find the inaccurate allusions to the following. Explain what makes each one humorous:

   a. the famous book *Pilgrim's Progress*
   b. the cartoon character Ferdinand
   c. the famous quotation, "The sun never sets on the British empire."
   d. the famous story of Miles Standish and John Alden
   e. the poem "Hiawatha" and the characters in it.

5. **Recognizing Idioms.** An **idiom** is a common expression that has a meaning different from the actual meaning of the words. Examples of idioms are "hanging around" and "time is running out."

   In "It All Started with Columbus," Armour has fun with the actual and the idiomatic meanings of phrases. For example, explain the humor in Armour's use of this idiom: "Columbus, who was as confused as anybody who has been at sea for a long time . . . ." Find passages in the selection where Armour plays with the idioms "raise the roof" and "go fly a kite." Explain how Armour's use of idioms adds to the humor of the essay.

Developing Vocabulary Skills

Defining Idioms. An idiom, as you recall, is a phrase or expression that has a meaning different from the meaning of the individual words. Examples of idioms are *head and shoulders above*, *give in*, and *set one's heart on*. Idioms are defined in a dictionary. These phrases are found under the key word in the idiom. The idioms above, for example, appear in the entries for *head*, *give*, and *heart*. Here are the idiom listings under the word *heart*:

> —**after one's own heart** that suits or pleases one perfectly —**at heart** in one's innermost or hidden nature; secretly or fundamentally —**break one's heart** to cause one to be overcome with grief or disappointment —**by heart** by or from memorization —☆**change of heart** a change of mind, affections, loyalties, etc. —**do one's heart good** to make one happy; please one —**eat one's heart out** to brood or feel keenly unhappy over some frustration or in regret

The following sentences are from Armour's essay. Look up the underlined idioms in a dictionary. On your paper, write each idiom and its key word, then write its meaning.

1. Captain John Smith was the first of a long line of Smiths who came to this country to keep up with the Joneses.

2. . . . Popocatepetl, the fiery young daughter of the Chief, stepped in.

3. This displeased King James, who raised the roof.

4. After several years in Holland, the Pilgrims decided to set out for the New World.

5. But finally, in 1620, which was a doubly Memorable Year because it was also the year in which they set sail, they sighted the rocky coast.

6. He was spoken to, and sharply, by the fair Priscilla, whom he married, much to the annoyance of Miles Standish, who thought he was stood up by his stand-in.

Developing Writing Skills

1. **Analyzing Humor.** As you have seen, Richard Armour uses many different humorous devices in "It All Started with Columbus." Choose one humorous device that you enjoyed most. In one paragraph, explain how Armour uses this device in his essay.

2. **Writing a Parody.** Write your own parody of a historical event. Choose an actual event or well known figure as your subject. Use Armour's writing as a model for your own humorous parody.

   Pre-Writing. Choose a topic for your parody. Become familiar with your topic by reading history textbooks and encyclopedia articles. Make notes on the actual historical facts. Think about how you could insert humor or poke fun through your "creative history." Make notes. Include ideas for puns, exaggeration, and other kinds of humor. Organize your notes in chronological order.

   Writing. Use the ideas from your notes as you write a humorous history. Include jokes, puns, malapropisms, and other devices you have thought of. Keep your tone light, and the mood humorous.

   Revising. Have you provided enough factual information to give the feeling of a historical account? Have you included enough fiction and foolishness to make the account funny?

Developing Skills in Critical Thinking

Separating Facts and Fiction. Armour mixes fact with foolishness in "It All Started with Columbus." You can determine if statements by Armour are factual by checking them with a reference source, such as an encyclopedia or history textbook. Use such sources to check these facts from Armour's essay. Revise the incorrect facts, if necessary.

1. Columbus was mistaken in thinking he had reached India. . . .

2. The East and the West are kept apart by the Date Line. . . .

3. The struggle between England and Spain came to a climax in an epic sea battle off the Azores known as the Last Fight of the Revenge.

4. The rock on which they landed they called Plymouth Rock because it reminded them of another rock of the same name in England.

How much of the world do you truly see each day? As you read this essay, pay attention to how the small details in nature can give you the most pleasure.

Seeing

ANNIE DILLARD

When I was six or seven years old, growing up in Pittsburgh, I used to take a precious penny of my own and hide it for someone else to find. It was a curious compulsion; sadly, I've never been seized by it since. For some reason I always "hid" the penny along the same stretch of sidewalk up the street. I would cradle it at the roots of a sycamore, say, or in a hole left by a chipped-off piece of sidewalk. Then I would take a piece of chalk, and, starting at either end of the block, draw huge arrows leading up to the penny from both directions. After I learned to write I labeled the arrows: SURPRISE AHEAD OR MONEY THIS WAY. I was greatly excited, during all this arrow-drawing, at the thought of the first lucky passer-by who would receive in this way, regardless of merit, a free gift from the universe. But I never lurked about. I would go straight home and not give the matter another thought, until, some months later, I would be gripped again by the impulse to hide another penny.

It is still the first week in January, and I've got great plans. I've been thinking about seeing. There are lots of things to see, unwrapped gifts and free surprises. The world is fairly studded and strewn with pennies cast broadside from a generous hand. But—and this is the point—who gets excited by a mere penny? If you follow one arrow, if you crouch motionless on a bank to watch a tremulous ripple thrill on the water and are rewarded by the sight of a muskrat kit paddling from its den, will you count that sight a chip of copper only, and go your rueful way? It is dire poverty indeed when a man is so malnourished and fatigued that he won't stoop to pick up a penny. But if you cultivate a healthy poverty and simplicity, so that finding a penny will literally make your day, then, since the world is in fact planted in pennies, you have with your poverty bought a lifetime of days. It is that simple. What you see is what you get.

I used to be able to see flying insects in the air. I'd look ahead and see, not the row of hemlocks across the road, but the air in front of it. My eyes would focus along that column of air, picking out flying insects. But I lost interest, I guess, for I dropped the habit. Now I can see birds. Probably some people can look at the grass at their feet and discover all the crawling creatures. I would like to know grasses and sedges—and care. Then my least journey into the world would be a field trip, a series of happy recognitions. Thoreau, in an expansive mood, exulted, "What a rich book might be made about buds, including, perhaps, sprouts!" It would be nice to think so. I cherish mental images I have of three perfectly happy people. One collects stones. Another—an Englishman, say—watches clouds. The third lives on a coast and collects drops of seawater which he examines microscopically and mounts. But I don't see what the specialist sees, and so I cut myself off, not only from the total picture, but from the various forms of happiness.

Unfortunately, nature is very much a now-you-see-it, now-you-don't affair. A fish flashes, then dissolves in the water before my eyes like so much salt. Deer apparently ascend bodily into heaven; the brightest oriole fades into leaves. These disappearances stun me into stillness and concentration; they say of nature that it conceals with a grand nonchalance; and they say of vision that it is a deliberate gift, the revelation of a dancer who for my eyes only flings away her seven veils. For nature does reveal as well as conceal: now-you-don't-see-it, now-you-do. For a week last September migrating red-winged blackbirds were feeding heavily down by the creek at the back of the house. One day I went out to investigate the racket; I walked up to a tree, an Osage orange, and a hundred birds flew away. They simply materialized out of the tree. I saw a tree, then a whisk of color, then a tree again. I walked closer and another hundred blackbirds took flight. Not a branch, not a twig budged: the birds were apparently weightless as well as invisible. Or, it was as if the leaves of the Osage orange had been freed from a spell in the form of red-winged blackbirds; they flew from the tree, caught my eye in the sky, and vanished. When I looked again at the tree the leaves had reassembled as if nothing had happened. Finally I walked directly to the trunk of the tree and a final hundred, the real diehards, appeared, spread, and vanished. How could so many hide in the tree without my seeing them? The Osage orange, unruffled, looked just as it had looked from the house, when three hundred red-winged blackbirds cried from its crown. I looked downstream where they flew, and they were gone. Searching, I couldn't spot one. I wandered downstream to force them to play their hand, but they'd crossed the creek and scattered. One show to a customer. These appearances catch at my throat; they are the free gifts, the bright coppers at the roots of trees.

It's all a matter of keeping my eyes open. Nature is like one of those line drawings of a tree that are puzzles for children: Can you find hidden in the leaves a duck, a house, a boy, a bucket, a zebra, and a boot? Specialists can find the most incredibly well-hidden things. A book I read when I was young recommended an easy way to find caterpillars to rear: you simply find some fresh caterpillar droppings, look up, and there's your caterpillar. More recently an author advised me to set my mind at ease about those piles of cut stems on the ground in grassy fields. Field mice make them; they cut the grass down by degrees to reach the seeds at the head. It seems that when the grass is tightly packed, as in a field of ripe grain, the blade won't topple at a single cut through the stem; instead, the cut stem simply drops vertically, held in the crush of grain. The mouse severs the bottom again and again, the stem keeps dropping an inch at a time, and finally the head is low enough for the mouse to reach the seeds. Meanwhile, the mouse is positively littering the field with its little piles of cut stems into which, presumably, the author of the book is constantly stumbling.

If I can't see these minutiae, I still try to keep my eyes open. I'm always on the lookout for antlion traps in sandy soil, monarch pupae near milkweed, skipper larvae in locust leaves. These things are utterly common, and I've not seen one. I bang on hollow trees near water, but so far no flying squirrels have appeared. In flat country I watch every sunset in hopes of seeing the green ray. The green ray is a seldom-seen streak of light that rises from the sun like a spurting fountain at the moment of sunset; it throbs into the sky for two seconds and disappears. One more reason to keep my eyes open.

Peacock in the Woods, 1907, ABBOTT HENDERSON THAYER and RICHARD SUMNER MERYMAN. National Museum of American Art, Smithsonian Institution, gift of the heirs of Abbott H. Thayer. Washington, D.C.

Developing Comprehension Skills

1. What satisfaction did Annie Dillard get from hiding pennies along the sidewalk?

2. What does Dillard mean by this statement: "There are lots of things to see, unwrapped gifts and free surprises"?

3. Who appreciates the "small gifts" in nature, according to Dillard?

4. Based on this essay, do you think Dillard really becomes less aware of life's little things as she grows older? Do you think most people become more or less aware as they grow older? Explain your answer.

5. Why does Dillard vow to keep her eyes open?

Reading Literature

1. **Understanding Theme.** Dillard's essay has a strong message. What main point about seeing does she wish to get across? Why do you think she feels so strongly about this?

2. **Appreciating Description.** Writers create word pictures with descriptive writing. In order to make those pictures meaningful, the writer must observe closely and then write carefully. The writer must use words that appeal to the reader's sense of touch, taste, smell, and hearing as well as sight.

   Which passages in "Seeing" show Annie Dillard's ability to observe closely? Find a passage that has specific details dealing with the senses. Explain the mental picture each one suggests.

3. **Understanding Metaphor.** A metaphor, as you recall, is a comparison between two unlike things. In "Seeing," Dillard compares nature's small sights and wonders to the pennies she planted as a child.

What makes the penny an especially good metaphor? Think about the value of a penny. Is it valued by society? Who values it most? Think of several similarities between pennies and nature's hidden gifts.

4. **Inferring Character.** Many of Dillard's actions and comments reveal things about the kind of person she is. What do you think "Seeing" shows the reader about Annie Dillard? What specific passages in the essay are especially revealing?

Developing Vocabulary Skills

Using Field Labels. Some words have general meanings and also specialized meanings. For example, a word might have a special meaning in the field of medicine, baseball, grammar, music, law, printing, or philosophy, among others. A specialized meaning is listed in the word entry and labeled with a field label. Here is an example of a field label for the word *linkage*:

> **link·age** (lin′kij) *n.* **1.** a linking or being linked **2.** a series or system of links; esp., a series of connecting rods for transmitting power or motion **3.** *Biol.* the tendency of some genes to remain together and act as a unit (**linkage group**) in inheritance, generally in the same chromosome, without segregation throughout maturation.

Field labels help you to find the special meanings you seek.

The following words are from "Seeing." Use a dictionary to find specialized meanings for each word. Write down any field labels you find in each word's dictionary entry. Also write the definitions of the words in those specialized fields. Then find each word in "Seeing," and determine if it is used in a specialized sense or a general one.

1. crown   3. blade   5. ray
2. line   4. head

Developing Writing Skills

1. **Using Comparison.** Annie Dillard writes about the wonders of nature and the simple life. She also refers to Thoreau's experience leading a simple life. How are her ideas similar to those of Henry David Thoreau? Write a brief composition comparing the ideas in "Seeing" with those in *Walden*.

    Pre-Writing. Reread the selection from Thoreau's *Walden* in Chapter 6. Make notes on the ideas it has in common with "Seeing." Think about the writers' views of nature and of the simple things. List examples and quotations that you can use to develop your comparison. Finally, organize your notes in a logical order, grouping together related ideas.

    Writing. Write an introduction that will capture the reader's attention. Your introduction should also state the main idea of your composition, which is that Thoreau and Dillard share similar ideas. In each paragraph of your composition, discuss one point of similarity between Thoreau's and Dillard's ideas. Develop each comparison with specific examples and quotations from the selections. End your composition with a strong conclusion that summarizes your main ideas.

    Revising. Read your composition aloud. As you revise, check for the following:

    Is the introduction interesting?
    Is the main idea clearly stated in the introduction?
    Does each paragraph focus on one point of similarity?
    Does the conclusion summarize the main points?

2. **Keeping a Journal.** For one week, follow Dillard's advice about trying to see the small details in nature. Keep a journal in which you record your observations and descriptions each day. Pay careful attention to small things that you normally take for granted. Be sure to use specific sensory details to make your description come alive.

Developing Skills in Study and Research

Locating Photographs. Find pictures of "small" things in nature that you would like to see in person. Look in nature books, magazines, or in the vertical file in your library. Some magazines that have high-quality nature photography include *National Geographic, Arizona Highways, GEO, Sports Afield, Field and Stream, Audubon,* and *The Naturalist.*

Recent magazines in your library will be stored on shelves. Back issues may be stored on microfilm. Check with your librarian. Share several of your favorite pictures with the class. Note a few key sensory words that you associate with each picture.

Developing Skills in Speaking and Listening

Developing Listening Abilities. You can learn to listen for, as well as see, fascinating details in the world around you. Close your eyes and concentrate on the sounds that usually go unnoticed. Describe each sound. Do this exercise in different places and at different times of the day. In your daily journal note any unusual sounds you hear.

SETTING A PURPOSE *In this fable, Rachel Carson describes how a town mysteriously changes. What causes the "strange blight" in this charming town?*

From
Silent Spring

RACHEL CARSON

A Fable for Tomorrow

There was once a town in the heart of America where all life seemed to live in harmony with its surroundings. The town lay in the midst of a checkerboard of prosperous farms, with fields of grain and hillsides of orchards where, in spring, white clouds of bloom drifted above the green fields. In autumn, oak and maple and birch set up a blaze of color that flamed and flickered across a backdrop of pines. Then foxes barked in the hills and deer silently crossed the fields, half hidden in the mists of the fall mornings.

Along the roads, laurel, viburnum, and alder, great ferns and wildflowers delighted the traveler's eye through much of the year.

Dawn, 1926, CHARLES BURCHFIELD. Watercolor on paper, 11¾" × 17¼". Whitney Museum of American Art, gift of Charles Simon. New York.

Even in winter the roadsides were places of beauty, where countless birds came to feed on the berries and on the seed heads of the dried weeds rising above the snow. The countryside was, in fact, famous for the abundance and variety of its bird life, and when the flood of migrants was pouring through in spring and fall people traveled from great distances to observe them. Others came to fish the streams, which flowed clear and cold out of the hills and contained shady pools where trout lay. So it had been from the days many years ago when the first settlers raised their houses, sank their wells, and built their barns.

Then a strange blight crept over the area and everything began to change. Some evil spell had settled on the community: mysterious maladies swept the flocks of chickens; the cattle and sheep sickened and died. Everywhere was a shadow of death. The farmers spoke of much illness among their families. In the town the doctors had become more and more puzzled by new kinds of sickness appearing among their patients. There had been several sudden and unexplained deaths, not only among adults but even among children, who would be stricken suddenly while at play and die within a few hours.

There was a strange stillness. The birds, for example—where had they gone? Many people spoke of them, puzzled and disturbed.

The feeding stations in the backyards were deserted. The few birds seen anywhere were moribund; they trembled violently and could not fly. It was a spring without voices. On the morning that had once throbbed with the dawn chorus of robins, catbirds, doves, jays, wrens, and scores of other bird voices there was now no sound; only silence lay over the fields and woods and marsh.

On the farms the hens brooded, but no chicks hatched. The farmers complained that they were unable to raise any pigs—the litters were small and the young survived only a few days. The apple trees were coming into bloom but no bees droned among the blossoms, so there was no pollination and there would be no fruit.

The roadsides, once so attractive, were now lined with browned and withered vegetation as though swept by fire. These, too, were silent, deserted by all living things. Even the streams were now lifeless. Anglers no longer visited them, for all the fish had died.

In the gutters under the eaves and between the shingles of the roofs, a white granular powder still showed a few patches; some weeks before it had fallen like snow upon the roofs and lawns, the fields and streams.

No witchcraft, no enemy action had silenced the rebirth of new life in this stricken world. The people had done it themselves.

Developing Comprehension Skills

1. Describe the setting for Rachel Carson's "A Fable for Tomorrow." Why do you think Carson places the town "in the heart of America"?

2. "It was a spring without voices," Carson writes. Explain what she means by this.

3. What mysterious effect was being felt by people, animals, farms, and plants?

4. What might the white powdery substance have to do with the problems described?

5. What do you think is the purpose of the last paragraph?

6. Do you think writers can help to solve problems facing society, such as the one described in "A Fable for Tomorrow"? Explain your answer.

Reading Literature

1. **Understanding Fables.** A **fable** is a fictional story meant to teach a moral, or lesson. How does Carson's "A Fable for Tomorrow" fit this definition? In your opinion, what is its moral?

2. **Identifying Author's Purpose.** Do you think Carson's purpose in writing "A Fable for Tomorrow" is to instruct, to persuade, or to move people to action? Might it be all of these? Support your answer with specific passages from the selection.

3. **Identifying Irony.** In irony, as you recall, the opposite of what is expected occurs. What is ironic about the situation described in the final sentence of "A Fable for Tomorrow": "The people had done it themselves"? Up to that point, what kinds of things might a reader think had caused the blight?

4. **Analyzing Style.** In some ways, Carson's story resembles a fairy tale. For example, she begins with the phrase "there once was a town." This opening is similar to the familiar fairy tale opening, "Once upon a time." In what other ways is Carson's style similar to that of a fairy tale? Why do you think Carson chose to create a fairy-tale quality?

5. **Appreciating the Significance of a Title.** "A Fable for Tomorrow" appears at the beginning of Rachel Carson's book about the dangers of pollution, *Silent Spring*. How does the title *Silent Spring* reflect an important idea in "A Fable for Tomorrow"?

Developing Vocabulary Skills

Using Synonymies. The dictionary contains explanations of synonyms and how they differ. Although synonyms are nearly the same in meaning, there are always slight differences between them. If you want to use language precisely, you should understand the differences between synonyms. By using synonymies in the dictionary, you can learn about these shades of meaning.

Synonymies can be found after the definitions of certain words. Sometimes the dictionary will refer you to a synonymy listed under a synonym. Here is the synonymy listed under habit:

SYN.—**habit** refers to an act repeated so often by an individual that it has become automatic with him [his *habit* of tugging at his ear in perplexity]; **practice** also implies the regular repetition of an act but does not suggest that it is automatic [the *practice* of reading in bed]; **custom** applies to any act or procedure carried on by tradition and often enforced by social disapproval of any violation [the *custom* of dressing for dinner]; **usage** refers to custom or practice that has become sanctioned through being long established *[usage* is the only authority in language]; **wont** is a literary or somewhat archaic equivalent for **practice** [it was his *wont* to rise early]

It explains the differences among the synonyms *habit, practice, custom, usage,* and *wont.*

The following sentences are from this chapter. Find synonymies for the underlined words. Then explain how the underlined word and its synonym in parentheses differ in meaning.

1. These, too, were <u>silent</u> (reticent), deserted by all living things.

2. . . . I used to take a precious penny of my own and hide it for someone else to find. It was a <u>curious</u> (inquisitive) compulsion. . . .

3. . . . Whether you are citizens of America or citizens of the world, ask of us here the same high <u>standards</u> (gauge) of strength and sacrifice. . . .

4. . . . I was too young and too small to <u>perform</u> (execute) the duties. . . .

5. Although I was upset, neither of the women was in the least <u>shaken</u> (trembled) by what I thought an unceremonious greeting.

Developing Writing Skills

1. **Supporting an Opinion.** *Silent Spring* was written in 1962. At this time, DDT was widely used as a pesticide. People were largely unaware of its possible dangers. Do you think "A Fable for Tomorrow" still has meaning for people today? Write a composition in which you tell one way that people today may be harming themselves and their environment.

   Pre-Writing. Discuss this issue with your classmates. Then decide on a topic for your composition. Do research to gather facts on your topic. You will probably want to use

The Readers' Guide to Periodical Literature to help you with your research. For information on using *The Readers' Guide,* see Developing Skills in Study and Research.

Take notes on facts that show the harmful nature of the situation you are explaining. Organize your facts and ideas by grouping related subjects together. Make an outline for your composition.

   Writing. Begin with an introduction that relates Rachel Carson's "A Fable for Tomorrow" to your topic. Then follow your outline as you write your first draft. Be sure to develop one main idea in each paragraph. Specific facts, examples, and reasons are effective ways of developing ideas. In a concluding paragraph, summarize your important points and make a recommendation for the future.

   Revising. Does your composition show that you have carefully researched your topic? Have you checked your facts for accuracy? Have you achieved your purpose? Is your writing clear and well organized? Make necessary changes before making a final copy of your composition.

2. **Writing a Fable.** "A Fable for Tomorrow" is a story with a lesson. Write a similar kind of fable by exaggerating the result of a modern-day problem. Set your fable in the future, but make sure it has a moral for people today.

Developing Skills in Study and Research

1. **Using *The Readers' Guide.*** The *Readers' Guide to Periodical Literature* lists the titles of various newspaper and magazine articles. The *Readers' Guide* is issued twice a month

from September through June and once a month in July and August.

In each volume, articles are listed alphabetically under subject, author, and title headings. The following are sample entries from a *Readers' Guide:*

> **ARMSTRONG, Dave**
> Falling in love with four-wheel drive. J.A. Latham. il pors
> > *Esquire* 91: 23-30 Je 5 '79
> **ARMSTRONG, Joe**
> Between the lines. pors *NY* 12:5 My 14 '79

At the beginning of each volume is an explanation of the abbreviations used in the entries. Refer to them when looking for an article.

Rachel Carson's *Silent Spring* attacks the use of pesticides because they pollute the environment. Use the *The Readers' Guide to Periodical Literature* to find out ways that pollution is currently being controlled. Look in recent *Readers' Guide* indexes under the headings "pollution" or "ecology." After you read a few of the articles that are indexed, make a list of the ways that pollution is being controlled.

2. **Interpreting Data in a Table.** A **table** is a graphic aid that lists information. This information, or data, often consists of numbers. A table allows a reader to compare data and draw conclusions.

Study the following table from the *Pocket Data Book*, a publication of the United States Department of Commerce. What is the subject of the table? What sort of data is listed?

Air Pollutant Emissions

Source	Carbon monoxide	Hydro-carbons	Nitrogen oxides
In millions of tons. Total includes sources not shown separately.			
Transportation	88.7	13.4	8.2
Fuel combustion	1.4	1.7	12.2
Industrial processes	8.8	9.5	.7
Solid waste disposal	6.8	1.9	.3
1970, total	112.7	32.5	21.6
Transportation	94.5	12.7	10.1
Fuel combustion	1.3	1.7	14.3
Industrial processes	9.1	11.1	.8
Solid waste disposal	2.9	.8	.1
1977, total	113.2	31.2	25.5

According to the chart, where does the worst pollution come from? In the years between 1970 and 1977, how much did carbon monoxide pollution increase in transportation? in industrial processes? In which categories did pollution decrease during the seven years compared? From the information in this table, what conclusion can you draw about pollution in the United States from 1970 to 1977?

What do you think has happened to the quality of our air since 1977? Has pollution decreased or increased? Find information on this topic by using reference materials in your library. Compare the air pollution today with that of 1977. Discuss your findings with your classmates.

Chapter 8 Review

Using Your Skills in Reading Literature

The following is from an essay by Ruth McKenney about lifesaving. Read it and answer the questions that follow.

> After what I suffered from amateur lifesaving, I should have known enough to avoid even the merest contact with the professional variety of water mercy. I learned too late that being socked with an oar is as nothing compared to what the Red Cross can think up.
>
> From the very beginning of that awful lifesaving course I took the last season I went to a girls' camp, I was a marked woman . . . .

1. Is the piece written from the first-person or from the third-person point of view?

2. Is the purpose to entertain, persuade, inform, or express feelings? Is it a combination of these purposes? Explain.

3. Is the piece organized by time order or logical order?

4. What tone does the writer use?

Using Your Comprehension Skills

Here is part of a poem by Paul Laurence Dunbar that you will read in Chapter Nine. Read these lines and decide on the poet's purpose and audience. Look beyond the literal meaning of the words.

> I know what the caged bird feels, alas!
> When the sun is bright on the upland slopes;
> When the wind stirs soft through the springing grass
> And the river flows like a stream of glass;

Using Your Vocabulary Skills

The underlined words in the following sentences are used in Chapter Nine. Look up each underlined word in a dictionary. Tell the definition. In addition, tell if the word 1) has a meaning in a specialized field, 2) is a homograph, or 3) has irregular inflected forms.

1. People's reactions to TV are sometimes an <u>enigma</u>.
2. Poets should be able to <u>commune</u> with nature.
3. There is a difference between parallel movement and <u>lateral</u> movement.
4. They felt a <u>twinge</u> of regret as they looked at the past.
5. Old scars have a <u>keen</u> sting.
6. Life without meaning is <u>torture</u>.

Using Your Writing Skills

Choose one of the following writing assignments.

1. Select one biography, one autobiography, and one speech from this chapter. Compare and contrast each writer's vision of the dream that America offers. First, define each writer's idea of the American dream. Then explain each writer's tone in discussing that dream. Also give reasons why you chose the selections that you did.

2. Write a personal essay that attempts to persuade your audience about a deeply felt belief. Use facts that you have researched, along with personal experiences, to support your stand.

Using Your Skills in Study and Research

Write down eight facts that you learned from the nonfiction in this chapter. Recall the sources you have learned from checking information. List them on a piece of paper. If you had to check the eight facts, which of the sources would be best to use for each one?

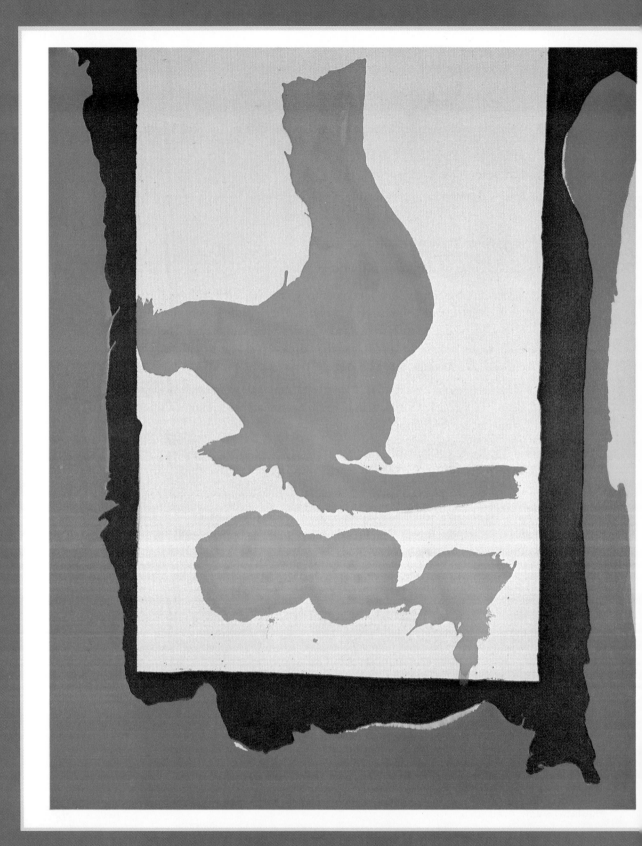

CHAPTER NINE

Twentieth Century Poetry

OPTIONS FOR RESPONDING

Activity Ideas

As you read:
- Decide whether each poem would best be read by one person or by a group, with or without sound effects, and later record your favorites.
- Jot down in a journal favorite phrases and lines, along with your response.
- Read the selected poems aloud, accompanied by a rhythm-producing instrument.
- Choose four colors that represent different moods, and then match each poem to a color.

After you read:
- Play charades, using the titles of the poems in this chapter.
- Illustrate with original art or photography a booklet of poems by the poets represented in this chapter.
- Examine a greeting card display and identify quotations from poems used on the cards.
- Write the titles of the poems on index cards (one title per card) and then group and regroup the cards according to different categories: for example, contemporary poems and poems written long ago; poems about humans, about animals, about things, and about ideas.
- Locate in your library recordings of poems by Edgar Lee Masters, Carl Sandburg, and Robert Frost, and bring the recordings to class.

Orange Shapes in Frame, 1964, HELEN
FRANKENTHALER. Collection of Mrs. Robert B. Mayer, Chicago.

Reading Literature

Poetry

Poetry is a form of literature that uses language in a special way. Poets choose words carefully in order to express ideas and emotions. They also use such techniques as rhyme, rhythm, and figures of speech.

The Purpose of Poetry

Poetry has existed for thousands of years. The first poems were passed orally from one generation to another. These poems told stories of exciting events or were used as songs, prayers, or chants.

Through the centuries, people from many cultures used poetry for these purposes. The ancient Greeks and Romans wrote **epic poems,** long poems that told about fantastic adventures and brave heroes. William Shakespeare, the English playwright, wrote plays in poetic form that told about historical events. In this text, poems of Native Americans, early colonists, and other writers also illustrate the many purposes of poetry.

Today, poetry continues to be an important form of literature. However, modern writers use poetry mainly to express their ideas and feelings about the world around them. Many poets share their inner lives and concerns with the reader. Because of this, modern poetry can be an especially private and personal form of writing.

The Elements of Poetry

Form. The words in a poem are arranged in lines that are grouped together in stanzas. Poets sometimes arrange lines so that the poem has a recognizable shape which can add to the poem's meaning.

Rhyme. Poets often use rhyming words—words that end with the same sound. When these words appear at the ends of lines, the rhyme is called **end rhyme.** The rhyme scheme of a poem is its pattern of end rhyme. Refer to Chapter Four for an example of how to determine a rhyme scheme.

Poets also use **internal rhyme**—rhyme within a single line in a poem. This kind of rhyme can add to the rhythm and musical quality of a poem.

Rhythm. The pattern of stressed and unstressed syllables in poetry is called **rhythm.** In some poems, the rhythm, or beat, is steady and regular. Poetry without a regular pattern of beats is called **free verse.** In free verse, every line of a poem may have a different pattern of accented and unaccented syllables. In **blank verse,** however, each line includes five pairs of syllables. The first syllable in each pair is unaccented, while the second syllable is accented. Poems written in blank verse do not contain rhyme.

Sounds. In poetry, the sounds of words can be as important as their meanings. Chapter Four discussed how poets use alliteration, assonance, consonance, and onomatopoeia in their work. Look for these sounds of language as you read poetry.

Figurative Language. Poets often use figurative language to force the reader to look at familiar things in a fresh, new way. They also use such language to describe ideas or feelings that may be unfamiliar to the reader. In Chapter Four, you learned about various types of figurative language, including similes, metaphors, personification, and hyperbole. Be aware of them as you read the poems in this chapter.

How to Read a Poem

1. Read each poem aloud, listening carefully to the sounds the words make. Think about how the meanings of the words and the sounds of the poem work together.
2. Reread the poem several times. Try to imagine the objects or feelings that the poet is describing. Think about your reaction to the words.
3. Look at the form of the poem. Does it have a special shape? Does the poet use capitalization, punctuation, or spelling in special ways? How do these add to the poem's meaning?
4. Think about the message the poet is trying to communicate. Poets sometimes express their deepest thoughts and feelings in their work. At other times, they write poems that are meant to inform, to teach, or simply to entertain.

Comprehension Skills

Poetic Language

You have learned that poets use language in special ways. They take great care to choose words that express their ideas and feelings exactly. Poets also carefully arrange the words they choose, sometimes departing from the usual or expected order. Therefore, most poets use punctuation to help the reader identify and understand the idea groups in a poem.

Understanding Word Order

In poetry, words are sometimes arranged in unusual ways. In non-poetic writing, or prose, the subject of a sentence usually is given first. The verb generally follows the subject, as in this example:

subject verb

Joyce works in the school library.

This order often is reversed in poetry.

verb   subject

Brightly shines the morning sun.

To understand unusual word order, first find the verb. Then find the word the verb tells about. If necessary, rearrange the words in the usual order.

subject verb

The morning sun shines brightly.

Using Punctuation Clues

Poems usually are written in lines rather than sentences. When you read poetry, remember that the end of a line does not necessarily signal the end of a complete thought. As you read a poem, look for periods, question marks, and exclamation points. These punctuation marks tell you that you have come to the end of a complete thought. Commas and semicolons help you separate the different parts of a complete idea.

Read these lines from "Mending Wall," a poem by Robert Frost. Notice that the poet expresses one complete thought, which extends over three lines. The comma indicates a break in ideas.

> Before I built a wall I'd ask to know
> What I was walling in or walling out,
> And to whom I was like to give offense.

In "Choices" Nikki Giovanni uses little or no punctuation.

> if i can't do
> what i want to do
> then my job is to not
> do what i don't want
> to do

Read poems like this one several times in order to identify each complete thought. Remember that the end of a line may or may not signal the end of a complete thought. Why did the poet use no punctuation? How does this affect the pace or rhythm of the poem? What meaning does it add?

Exercises: Understanding Poetic Language

A. Rearrange the words in these lines from "The Debt," by Paul Laurence Dunbar. Begin each rewritten sentence with the underlined word.

> Slight was the thing I bought,
> Small was the debt I thought,
> Poor was the loan at best—

B. Read "Fire and Ice" by Robert Frost, pausing only at punctuation marks. What complete thoughts are expressed? How do commas break up ideas?

> Some say the world will end in fire,
> Some say in ice.
> From what I've tasted of desire
> I hold with those who favor fire.
> But if it had to perish twice,
> I think I know enough of hate
> To say that for destruction ice
> Is also great
> And would suffice.

$\mathcal{V}$ocabulary Skills

Application

By now you are familiar with many aspects of words. In this chapter, you will review and strengthen the vocabulary skills you have learned.

Word Origins

As you remember, words come into our language in many ways. These include borrowing, compounding, blending, and clipping. Words can also originate from names of people or places, specialized fields, or imitations of sounds. Pages 8 and 9 review these word origins.

In poetry, you may find that writers sometimes coin, or make up, words. An example of a coined word in this chapter is *chipware.*

Levels of Language

There are two levels of standard English, formal and informal. **Formal English** is the serious, dignified language of public speeches, official documents, and other formal writing. **Informal English** is the less formal language of conversation, letters, and other informal writing.

Occasionally, a writer may use **nonstandard English** to achieve a certain effect. Nonstandard English, you will recall, is language that does not conform to acceptable standards. It includes slang, jargon, and errors in grammar, usage, and mechanics.

Context Clues and Inferring Word Meaning

When you find an unfamiliar word, **context clues** can help you to understand that word's meaning. The main types of context clues are synonyms, antonyms, examples, comparison/contrast clues, and restatement/definition clues. Pages 138 and 139 review context clues.

Sometimes there are no direct context clues. Still, you can often infer the meaning of the new word from specific information in the context.

Word Parts

A solid knowledge of word parts can help you to determine the meaning of an unfamiliar word. You need to know the meanings of common prefixes or suffixes. **Prefixes** are word parts added in front of a base word or a root. **Suffixes** are added at the end. To review prefixes and suffixes, refer to pages 232, 233, 241, 262, 271, 272, and 277.

Another helpful tool for unlocking word meaning is knowing Greek and Latin roots. You can review the roots you learned on pages 233, 296, 302, 306, 317, and 324.

Dictionary

In Chapter Eight, you learned that the dictionary can tell you more about words than just their meanings. Each entry may provide the following:

respelling	definition	field labels
origin	inflected forms	synonomy
part of speech	usage labels	idioms

Exercises: Applying Vocabulary Skills

A. The following words are used in poems from this chapter. Make the words into their own antonyms by adding a prefix from the list on page 232.

violent	understanding	restrained	constant
sensible	advantages	parallel	satisfied
content	human	hero	afraid

B. Use your knowledge of word origins to decide the origins of the following words from this chapter. Then check your answers with a dictionary.

rainbow	parka	sideline	typewriter	tobacco
snicker	lulled	bang	banjo	June

C. Read the following lines and determine the level of language.

> To him who in the love of Nature holds
> Communion with her visible forms, she speaks
> A various language;
>
> —William Cullen Bryant, "Thanatopsis"

Lucinda Matlock

EDGAR LEE MASTERS

SETTING A PURPOSE

In the collection of poems called The Spoon River Anthology, *all the characters speak from their graves. As you read this poem, think about the kind of life Lucinda Matlock lived.*

I went to the dances at Chandlerville,
And played snap-out[1] at Winchester.
One time we changed partners,
Driving home in the moonlight of middle June,
And then I found Davis.
We were married and lived together for
    seventy years,
Enjoying, working, raising the twelve children,
Eight of whom we lost
Ere I had reached the age of sixty.
I spun, I wove, I kept the house, I
    nursed the sick,
I made the garden, and for holiday
Rambled over the fields where sang the larks,
And by Spoon River gathering many a shell,
And many a flower and medicinal weed—
Shouting to the wooded hills, singing to
    the green valleys.
At ninety-six I had lived enough, that is all,
And passed to a sweet repose.
What is this I hear of sorrow and weariness,
Anger, discontent, and drooping hopes?
Degenerate sons and daughters,
Life is too strong for you—
It takes life to love Life.

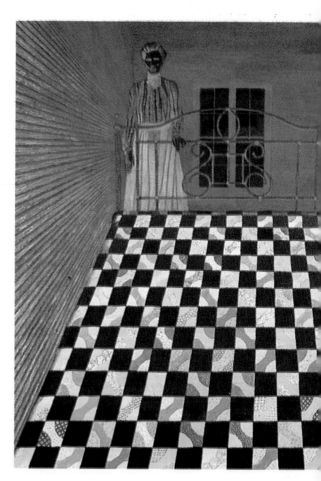

---

1. **snap-out**, a game in which everyone joins hands, forming a long line. When the leader whips quickly to one side, those at the end of the line are snapped away.

Developing Comprehension Skills

1. How did Lucinda Matlock meet her husband?

2. How many children did Lucinda have? What happened to most of them? What does this tell you about her life?

3. Lucinda's life involved a great deal of hard work and many disappointments. How did she deal with the joys and sorrows in her life?

4. What does the speaker mean by the last line?

5. To whom is Lucinda speaking? Is she being fair in her judgment of them?

Reading Literature

1. **Appreciating the Differences Between Prose and Poetry.** **Prose**, or nonpoetic writing, is written to imitate people's speech. Prose is usually divided into paragraphs. Each paragraph has a main idea with several sentences that support and explain that idea.

   Poetry is language that is rich in sound and meaning. It often appeals to a reader's emotions. Poetry expresses ideas in a compact form. A poem can sometimes say in one line what a work of prose might say in a paragraph.

   Do you think the story of "Lucinda Matlock" is more effective as a poem than it would be as an essay? If her story were told as an essay, what might the reader miss? Explain your answer.

2. **Recognizing Character Traits.** A **character trait** is a quality that a character shows by his or her actions, statements, or thoughts. Character traits can include such qualities as honesty, courage, laziness, or cowardice.

   From what Lucinda said in this poem, list a few of her outstanding character traits. Support your choices with specific lines from the poem.

3. **Understanding Tone.** The **tone** of a poem is the writer or speaker's attitude toward the subject of the poem. For example, the tone might be humorous or sorrowful. It might be lighthearted or serious. How would you describe the tone of this poem? Use specific words and phrases from the poem to support your answer.

4. **Understanding Mood.** The feeling the reader gets while reading a poem is the **mood**. Poets are very careful to choose words that create a specific mood. The mood of a poem can be sad, funny, hopeless, hopeful, or a combination of these and other feelings. What is the mood of this poem? What words and phrases does the poet use to create this mood?

The Ghost, 1955, CARROLL CLOAR. Collection of Marjorie T. Rome.

George Gray

EDGAR LEE MASTERS

SETTING A PURPOSE

Some people take advantage of all that life has to offer. Others choose not to experience the joys and sorrows of a full, meaningful life. How did George Gray choose to live his life? Do you agree with his conclusions?

I have studied many times
The marble which was chiseled for me—
A boat with a furled sail at rest in a harbor.
In truth it pictures not my destination
But my life.
For love was offered me and I shrank from its dis-
    illusionment;
Sorrow knocked at my door, but I was afraid;
Ambition called to me, but I dreaded the chances.
Yet all the while I hungered for meaning in my life.
And now I know that we must lift the sail
And catch the winds of destiny
Wherever they drive the boat.
To put meaning in one's life may end in madness,
But life without meaning is the torture
Of restlessness and vague desire—
It is a boat longing for the sea and yet afraid.

Seascape, 1967, ELMER BISCHOFF.
Private collection. Photograph by White
Line Photography, San Francisco.

Developing Comprehension Skills

1. In the first three lines of the poem, George Gray compares his life to something. What is it? Where is it?

2. What opportunities did George Gray have while alive? Did he take advantage of these opportunities? In each situation, why does he say that he did what he did?

3. What did Gray secretly desire during his lifetime?

4. How does Gray now feel about the way he lived his life? Do you think he judges himself too harshly?

5. Explain the last three lines. Do you agree with Gray's ideas of a meaningful life? Explain your answer.

Reading Literature

1. **Understanding Theme.** How would George Gray now explain the value of life? Think about the way Lucinda Matlock lived her life. Do you think she would agree with his new attitude?

2. **Recognizing Metaphor.** Twice in this poem, George Gray compares his life to a boat at rest in a harbor. What similarities does he see? Do you think this is a good comparison?

3. **Identifying Opposites.** A poet may emphasize an idea by placing it next to an opposite idea. Throughout this poem, the speaker tells of chances he had to experience life. What were some of these opportunities? What did the speaker do with these opportunities?

Sympathy

PAUL LAURENCE DUNBAR

SETTING A PURPOSE

Paul Laurence Dunbar was a black American poet who inspired many other black writers. As you read this poem, see if you can understand how he knew what the caged bird feels.

I know what the caged bird feels, alas!
When the sun is bright on the upland slopes;
When the wind stirs soft through the springing grass
And the river flows like a stream of glass;
When the first bird sings and the first bud opes,
And the faint perfume from its chalice steals—
I know what the caged bird feels!

I know why the caged bird beats his wing
Till its blood is red on the cruel bars;
For he must fly back to his perch and cling
When he fain would be on the bough a-swing;
And a pain still throbs in the old, old scars
And they pulse again with a keener sting—
I know why he beats his wing!

I know why the caged bird sings, ah me,
When his wing is bruised and his bosom sore,
When he beats his bars and would be free;
It is not a carol of joy or glee,
But a prayer that he sends from his heart's deep core,
But a plea, that upward to Heaven he flings—
I know why the caged bird sings!

Developing Comprehension Skills

1. What tells you the season is spring?

2. Where would the caged bird rather be perched?

3. The speaker says when the caged bird sings, "It is not a carol of joy or glee. . . ." What kind of song is it?

4. What does this poem tell you about the speaker's inner longings?

5. Why do you think the title of this poem is "Sympathy"?

6. Do you think most people have something in common with the caged bird? Explain your answer.

Reading Literature

1. **Recognizing the Stanza.** A group of lines that form a unit is a **stanza.** A stanza, like a paragraph in prose, shows the organization of ideas in a poem.

    In "Sympathy," there are three stanzas. Each contains seven lines. Explain what you think is the main idea of each stanza.

2. **Understanding Rhyme.** The repetition of sounds at the ends of words is called **rhyme.** Rhyme often occurs at the ends of lines of poetry. Look at the last word in each line of the first stanza of this poem. Which of these final words rhyme? How does rhyme help you to enjoy this poem?

3. **Charting the Rhyme Scheme.** A **rhyme scheme** is the pattern of end rhyme in a poem. To chart a rhyme scheme, assign letters of the alphabet to stand for different rhyming sounds. Assign letters in alpha-betical order. The first rhyme would be labeled "a." The second set of rhyming sounds would be labeled "b" and so on. Look at the chart of the rhyme scheme for the first three lines of "Sympathy."

> I know what the caged bird feels,
>   alas!   *a*
> When the sun is bright on the upland
>   slopes;   *b*
> When the wind stirs soft through the
>   springing grass   *a*

Chart the rhyme scheme for the entire first stanza of "Sympathy."

4. **Recognizing Alliteration.** The repetition of consonant sounds at the beginning of words is called **alliteration.** Alliteration often gives a music-like quality to poetry and prose. It can also help to create a certain feeling, or mood. Find an example of alliteration in the second and third lines of this poem. What feeling does the alliteration of this sound help create?

5. **Appreciating Symbols.** A **symbol** is something that stands for, or represents, something other than itself. For example, the American flag represents the United States.

    When Dunbar wrote his poetry during the late 1800's, blacks were not truly free. At that time, so-called "Jim Crow" laws separated blacks and whites. Blacks were often not allowed to use the same restaurants, restrooms, hotels, or streetcars used by whites.

    Why do you think the poet used the caged bird as a symbol of the black person in America at the turn of the century? What words, or ideas, do you think the symbol represents?

The Debt

PAUL LAURENCE DUNBAR

SETTING A PURPOSE | *A moment of irresponsible behavior can cost much more than a person might expect. What is the speaker of this poem paying for? Was it worth the price?*

This is the debt I pay
Just for one riotous day,
Years of regret and grief,
Sorrow without relief.

Pay it I will to the end—
Until the grave, my friend,
Gives me a true release—
Gives me the clasp of peace.

Slight was the thing I bought,
Small was the debt I thought,
Poor was the loan at best—
God! but the interest!

Developing Comprehension Skills

1. In what ways is the speaker paying for "one riotous day"?

2. What is the only thing that will free the speaker of his debt?

3. Interest is the additional cost a person must pay on a loan. What do you think is the meaning of the last line, "God! but the interest!"?

4. What kind of choice do you think someone could make today that he or she could spend a lifetime paying for?

Reading Literature

1. **Understanding Rhyme Scheme.** Chart the rhyme scheme in each stanza of "The Debt." Remember to assign the letters for rhyming sounds in alphabetical order.

2. **Recognizing Form.** How many stanzas are there in "The Debt"? Explain what you think is the main idea of each stanza.

3. **Appreciating Theme.** With what important idea is the speaker of this poem concerned? Can what he learned be applied to the lives of most people?

Developing Vocabulary Skills

Reviewing Word Parts. As you learned in Chapter 6, you can use word parts to help unlock the meaning of a word. Study the prefixes and suffixes listed on pages 232, 233, 241, 262, 271, 272, and 277.

The lines that follow are from the poems you have read in this chapter. Label the word parts in each of the underlined words: prefix, base word or root, and suffix. Write the meaning of each word part and then the meaning of the word as a whole.

1. And many a flower and <u>medicinal</u> weed—

2. What is this I hear of sorrow and <u>weariness</u>,

3. Anger, <u>discontent</u>, and drooping hopes?

4. <u>Degenerate</u> sons and daughters,

5. In truth it pictures not my <u>destination</u>

6. For love was offered me and I shrank from its <u>disillusionment</u>;

7. Just for one <u>riotous</u> day,

Developing Writing Skills

1. **Analyzing Poems.** The four poems you have read express different attitudes about life. The writers' tone in "Lucinda Matlock" and "George Gray" differs greatly from the tone in Dunbar's poems. Write a paragraph that explains the difference in the writers' attitudes.

Pre-Writing. Reread each poem. For each one, write a clear statement of the tone as you see it. Then, examine how the words and phrases, images, and ideas reflect the writers' tone or attitude. Make a chart similar to the one below. Under each heading, list words or groups of words that help create this tone. This chart will help you to organize your ideas into groups.

	Poem 1	Poem 2	Poem 3	Poem 4
tone				
phrases				
images				
ideas				

Writing. Begin your paragraph with a topic sentence explaining the differences in the tones of the four poems. Refer to your list to write several sentences that support your topic sentence. Make sure your ideas are stated clearly. Use words such as *like, same, however,* and *unlike* to signal comparisons and contrasts.

Revising. Look over what you have written. Then, read your paragraph aloud. Revise sentences that do not clearly state your ideas. Check your grammar, punctuation, and spelling. Make a clean final copy if necessary.

2. **Describing a Person.** As you recall, a character trait is a quality a character shows by action, statement, or thought. Together, all of a person's traits make up his or her whole character.

Choose a person you know well. You may even write about yourself. First, identify the person's traits. Make a list of specific things that the person may have said or done that show his or her character traits. Then, in the form of a poem, or in paragraph form, write a character sketch similar to the one in "Lucinda Matlock."

Developing Skills in Speaking and Listening

Orally Interpreting a Poem. A poem should be read aloud if you want to fully appreciate its meaning. The following suggestions will help you prepare and read a poem aloud. They will also help you to be a good listener.

1. **Preparing the Poem.** Choose a poem from the four you have read so far. Or, choose a different poem from Edgar Lee Masters's *Spoon River Anthology*. Read the poem silently several times. Look for key words and phrases that you think should be emphasized. Next, read your poem aloud several times. Use your voice to create a mood. Lower it and raise it when it is appropriate. Pause where punctuation marks indicate a break in thought.

   When you feel comfortable with your reading of the poem, have a friend listen to you. Is your voice creating a mood? Are you reading at an appropriate speed? Are you pronouncing the words correctly? Are you speaking too softly or too loudly?

2. **Presenting the Poem.** Concentrate on all the things you practiced. Read loudly enough for everyone to hear, but do not shout. Remember to lower and raise your voice and to pause when necessary. Make a special effort to appear relaxed. Show your audience that you are confident and enjoying yourself.

Chicago

CARL SANDBURG

SETTING A PURPOSE | *During the early 1900's, a number of American cities grew rapidly. Chicago, in particular, was bursting with new industry and excitement. What opinion did Carl Sandburg have of this bustling, sprawling city?*

Hog Butcher for the World,
Tool Maker, Stacker of Wheat,
Player with Railroads and the Nation's Freight Handler;
Stormy, husky, brawling,
City of the Big Shoulders: 5

They tell me you are wicked and I believe them, for I have seen your
    painted women under the gas lamps luring the farm boys.
And they tell me you are crooked and I answer:
    Yes, it is true I have seen the gunman kill and go free to kill again.
And they tell me you are brutal and my reply is: On the faces of   10
    women and children I have seen the marks of wanton hunger.
And having answered so I turn once more to those who sneer at this
    my city, and I give them back the sneer and say to them:
Come and show me another city with lifted head singing so proud to be
    alive and coarse and strong and cunning.   15
Flinging magnetic curses amid the toil of piling job on job, here is a tall
    bold slugger set vivid against the little soft cities;
Fierce as a dog with tongue lapping for action, cunning as a savage
    pitted against the wilderness,
        Bareheaded,   20
        Shoveling,
        Wrecking,
        Planning,
        Building, breaking, rebuilding,
Under the smoke, dust all over his mouth, laughing with white teeth,   25
Under the terrible burden of destiny laughing as a young man laughs,

Laughing even as an ignorant fighter laughs who has never lost a battle,
Bragging and laughing that under his wrist is the pulse, and under his
    ribs the heart of the people,
                Laughing!   30
Laughing the stormy, husky, brawling laughter of Youth, half-naked,
    sweating, proud to be Hog Butcher, Tool Maker, Stacker of
    Wheat, Player with Railroads and Freight Handler to the Nation.

Developing Comprehension Skills

1. Referring to lines from the poem, list some of the industries Chicago was famous for.

2. As Chicago grew, more and more people moved into the city from the country seeking steady work in factories. According to the speaker, what "wicked" influences did they face when first arriving in the city?

3. What positive qualities does Chicago have?

4. Despite the "wickedness" of the city, how does the speaker feel about Chicago? What lines in the poem prove this?

5. From what the poet has written, would you have wanted to live in Chicago during this time? Why or why not?

Reading Literature

1. **Recognizing Free Verse.** Sandburg's poems are written in **free verse**. This form does not have a rhyme scheme or regular rhythm. Free verse often features repetition of key words and phrases.

   Why do you think Sandburg chose to write the poem "Chicago" in free verse? What kinds of things was he able to do that would not have been possible with a form of poetry that allowed less freedom?

2. **Understanding Parallelism.** Sometimes a poet will emphasize ideas of equal importance by presenting the ideas in similar phrases or sentences. This is called **parallelism**. Consider this example of parallelism.

   > Let me pry loose old walls.
   > Let me lift and loosen old foundations.

   Find two other examples of parallelism in "Chicago." What ideas is the poet trying to emphasize?

3. **Recognizing Figures of Speech.** This poem contains several similes and metaphors. Explain how each comparison adds additional meaning in the following examples.

   > Fierce as a dog with tongue lapping for action, . . .
   > here is a tall, bold slugger set vivid against the little soft cities;
   > Laughing even as an ignorant fighter laughs who has never lost a battle.

4. **Recognizing Personification.** Sandburg uses personification in this poem. What kind of person does Chicago look like? What character traits does "he" have?

   Why do you think Sandburg chose this image? If you met this person, what would you think of him? Explain your answer.

Buffalo Dusk

CARL SANDBURG

SETTING A PURPOSE *In 1850, twenty million buffaloes roamed the plains. By 1889, hunting had reduced their number to 551. As you read this poem, ask yourself who, besides the buffaloes, the speaker sorrows for.*

The buffaloes are gone
And those who saw the buffaloes are gone.
Those who saw the buffaloes by thousands and how they
    pawed the prairie sod into dust with their hoofs, their
    great heads down pawing on in a great pageant of dusk,
Those who saw the buffaloes are gone.
And the buffaloes are gone.

A Herd of Buffaloes on the Bed of the River Missouri (detail), about 1860, WILLIAM JACOB HAYS.
The Thomas Gilcrease Institute of American History and Art, Tulsa, Oklahoma.

Developing Comprehension Skills

1. In what numbers was one once able to see the buffaloes?

2. Who are "those who saw the buffaloes"? Where have they gone?

3. What lesson do you think can be learned from what happened to the buffaloes and "those who saw the buffaloes"?

Reading Literature

1. **Understanding Repetition.** The repetition of certain words or phrases adds to the mood of this poem. What words or phrases are repeated in "Buffalo Dusk"? Why did the poet emphasize these words? What feelings do these words suggest?

2. **Recognizing Imagery.** Very often a single image, or mental picture, can make the purpose or meaning of a poem clear. What image do you get when you read lines 3–5? How does it contrast with the situation today?

3. **Appreciating a Title.** The title of a poem can sometimes provide a key to its meaning. Poems that use dawn as their title, often deal with new beginnings. What do you think the poet wanted the reader to understand by using the word "Dusk" in the title of this poem?

4. **Recognizing Unusual Word Order.** Lines 3–7 are written in the form of a run-on sentence. A run-on sentence is two or more sentences written as one. Why do you think the poet linked his ideas in this way? How does this affect your mood as you read the poem? What does it add to the meaning of the poem?

5. **Understanding Tone.** How would you describe the poet's feeling about what happened to the buffalo and Native Americans? Do you think he is blaming anyone or simply reporting the situation? Explain your answer.

Jazz Fantasia

SETTING A PURPOSE | *Jazz music originated in the United States near the end of the 1800's. As you read, see if you can hear the music in the words.*

CARL SANDBURG

At the Savoy, 1975,
ROMARE BEARDEN.
Mr. and Mrs. Oscar Kolin,
New York.

Drum on your drums, batter on your banjoes,
sob on the long cool winding saxophones.
Go to it, O jazzmen.

Sling your knuckles on the bottoms of the happy
tin pans, let your trombones ooze, and go husha-
husha-hush with the slippery sand-paper.

Moan like an autumn wind high in the lonesome treetops, moan soft like you wanted somebody terrible, cry like a racing car slipping away from a motorcycle cop, bang-bang! you jazzmen, bang altogether drums, traps, banjoes, horns, tin cans—make two people fight on the top of a stairway and scratch each other's eyes in a clinch tumbling down the stairs.

Can the rough stuff . . . now a Mississippi steamboat pushes up the night river with a hoo-hoo-hoo-oo . . . and the green lanterns calling to the high soft stars . . . a red moon rides on the humps of the low river hills . . . go to it, O jazzmen.

Developing Comprehension Skills

1. What three instruments are mentioned in the first stanza? What other unusual items are used as instruments in this poem?

2. Jazz can create several different moods, sometimes all at once. How many different "sides" of jazz do you see in this poem?

3. What do you think is the meaning of the line that begins "make two people fight"? What is the speaker asking the musicians to do?

4. How well do you think Sandburg re-created the emotions and excitement of jazz?

Reading Literature

1. **Understanding Onomatopoeia.** The use of words that sound like what they describe is called **onomatopoeia.** An example of this in the poem is the words "husha-husha-hush." These words imitate the sound of sandpaper scraping wood. Find two other examples of onomatopoeia in this poem. Explain how these sounds add to your enjoyment of the poem.

2. **Recognizing Assonance.** The repetition of vowel sounds within words is called **assonance.** Assonance helps produce a musical quality in poems. It can also add to the meaning. An example of assonance in this poem is the repetition of the "o" sound in the line, "sob on the long cool winding saxophones." It helps re-create the moan of a saxophone. Find another example of assonance. What mood is created by the sound?

3. **Recognizing Alliteration.** Poets often use alliteration to get readers to pay special attention to words. They may also use it to re-create a sound or add to the rhythm of a piece. Find two examples of alliteration in this poem. Why do you think Sandburg chose to repeat these sounds?

4. **Appreciating a Title.** Look up the word "fantasia" in a dictionary. Why do you think the poet calls this poem "Jazz Fantasia"?

Grass

CARL SANDBURG

SETTING A PURPOSE *Carl Sandburg wrote this poem shortly after World War I. As you read, try to decide if his message is still important today.*

Pile the bodies high at Austerlitz and Waterloo.[1]
Shovel them under and let me work—
        I am the grass; I cover all.

And pile them high at Gettysburg[2]
And pile them high at Ypres and Verdun.[3]
Shovel them under and let me work.
Two years, ten years, and passengers ask the conductor:
        What place is this?
        Where are we now?

        I am the grass.
        Let me work.

---

1. **Austerlitz and Waterloo**, sites of battles of the Napoleonic Wars.
2. **Gettysburg**, U.S. Civil War battlefield.
3. **Ypres and Verdun**, sites of World War I battles.

Gravestone at the National Cemetery, Gettysburg, Pennsylvania. Photo Researchers, New York.
Copyright © Farrell Grehan.

Developing Comprehension Skills

1. Who or what is the speaker in this poem? What work does the speaker do?

2. List the places named in this poem. What do they have in common?

3. What idea is brought out by the two questions in this poem?

4. War is often described in glorious terms. Do you think Sandburg would think of war as glorious? Explain your answer.

Reading Literature

1. **Understanding Theme.** Look at lines 7–9. What do you think the speaker is saying about people and their ability to learn from the past? Do you agree with the speaker? Why or why not?

2. **Recognizing Repetition.** A poet repeats an idea to give it special emphasis. What phrases are repeated in "Grass"? What point is the poet trying to make by repeating these phrases?

3. **Identifying Purpose.** Poets write poems with a purpose in mind. Poems can teach a lesson, give an opinion, or simply entertain the reader. In your opinion, what was the poet trying to accomplish by writing "Grass"?

Developing Vocabulary Skills

Reviewing Word Origins. In Chapter One, you learned about some of the ways words come into our language. These include borrowing, compounding, blending, clipping, making words from names, and creating echoic words. Often, if you understand the origin of a word, you will remember its meaning.

The following lines are from Sandburg's poems. Look up each underlined word in a dictionary. Identify it as a borrowed word, a word from a name, a compound, or an echoic word. Explain how the meaning of each word relates to its origin.

1. Hog <u>Butcher</u> for the World,

2. <u>cunning</u> as a savage pitted against the wilderness, <u>Bareheaded</u>,

3. sob on the long cool winding <u>saxophones</u>.

4. <u>husha-hush</u> with the slippery <u>sand-paper</u>.

5. Drum on your drums, batter on your <u>banjoes</u>.

6. Go to it, O <u>jazzmen</u>.

Developing Writing Skills

1. **Analyzing Style.** You can appreciate a poet's **style**, or personal method of writing, only after reading several of his or her poems. You have seen several interesting techniques in Sandburg's poems. Write a five paragraph composition about Sandburg's writing style. Choose three techniques he uses in the poems and explain the effect each has on the reader.

   Pre-Writing. Read the poems carefully. Look for techniques dealing with the sound of language. Also look for figurative language. Can you find other techniques? Choose the three techniques you enjoyed the most. Find passages from the poems to illustrate each one.

   Writing. Write a paragraph that introduces your topic and states your purpose. Next, write your three body paragraphs. Write a topic sentences for each one. Each topic sentence should present the technique to be discussed in that paragraph. Then, develop each topic sentence. Use specific lines from the poems to illustrate each idea. Finally, write a concluding paragraph that summarizes your main ideas.

Revising. Check your work carefully. Make sure each paragraph has a clear topic sentence. Make sure your words and ideas flow together smoothly. It may help to read your essay aloud. Finally, check for proper grammar, capitalization, punctuation, and spelling. Make a clean final copy if necessary.

2. **Creating Poetry.** Choose one of the three techniques you wrote about in the preceding exercise. Create a poem of your own, using that technique. When you have finished, be sure to read your poem aloud.

Developing Skills in Study and Research

Using the Vertical File. Most libraries have a valuable reference called the **vertical file**. The vertical file is a cabinet that contains current brochures, pamphlets, and catalogs on a variety of subjects. These are arranged in alphabetical order. It is the most up-to-date source of information available to you.

Use an encyclopedia and the vertical file to find information about a city you are interested in. Use the encyclopedia for general information. Find one thing the city was famous for in the early 1900's. Using the vertical file, check to see if the city is still famous for that particular thing. For example, Chicago was once famous for its meat-packing industry and railroads. If you chose Chicago, you would see that only the second fact is still true.

Write a short paragraph reporting on what you find.

Developing Skills in Speaking and Listening

Appreciating Jazz Music. Locate a recording of jazz music in your library. Listen carefully to a few selections. Listen for sounds that seem to express emotions. As you listen, jot down any words and feelings that come to mind. Then, compare your list with those of your classmates. What does this experience tell you about jazz music? Do you think Sandburg captured the music well in "Jazz Fantasia"?

Mending Wall

ROBERT FROST

SETTING A PURPOSE

Benjamin Franklin wrote, "Love your neighbor; yet don't pull down your hedge." Does the neighbor in this poem share this attitude? Does Frost?

Something there is that doesn't love a wall,
That sends the frozen-ground-swell under it
And spills the upper boulders in the sun,
And makes gaps even two can pass abreast.
The work of hunters is another thing: 5
I have come after them and made repair
Where they have left not one stone on a stone,
But they would have the rabbit out of hiding,
To please the yelping dogs. The gaps I mean,
No one has seen them made or heard them made,   10
But at spring mending-time we find them there.
I let my neighbor know beyond the hill;
And on a day we meet to walk the line
And set the wall between us once again.
We keep the wall between us as we go.   15
To each the boulders that have fallen to each.
And some are loaves and some so nearly balls
We have to use a spell to make them balance:
"Stay where you are until our backs are turned!"
We wear our fingers rough with handling them.   20
Oh, just another kind of outdoor game,
One on a side. It comes to little more:
There where it is we do not need the wall:
He is all pine and I am apple orchard.
My apple trees will never get across   25
And eat the cones under his pines, I tell him.
He only says, "Good fences make good neighbors."
Spring is the mischief in me, and I wonder
If I could put a notion in his head:

An Abandoned Farm, about 1908, ERNEST LAWSON. National Museum of American Art, Smithsonian Institution, gift of William T. Evans. Washington, D.C.

"*Why* do they make good neighbors? Isn't it   30
Where there are cows? But here there are no cows.
Before I built a wall I'd ask to know
What I was walling in or walling out,
And to whom I was like to give offense.
Something there is that doesn't love a wall,   35
That wants it down." I could say "Elves" to him,
But it's not elves exactly, and I'd rather
He said it for himself. I see him there,
Bringing a stone grasped firmly by the top
In each hand, like an old-stone savage armed.   40
He moves in darkness as it seems to me,
Not of woods only and the shade of trees.
He will not go behind his father's saying,
And he likes having thought of it so well
He says again, "Good fences make good neighbors."   45

Developing Comprehension Skills

1. At what time of year do the speaker and his neighbor mend the wall?

2. What effect does the winter have on the wall? What do the hunters do to the wall?

3. What purpose does the wall serve? Does the speaker think it is really necessary?

4. Is there more than one kind of wall between the speaker and his neighbor? Why is this the case?

5. The neighbor tells the speaker that the reason for repairing the wall every year is simply, "Good fences make good neighbors." What do you think he means by this statement? Do you agree with him?

Reading Literature

1. **Identifying Theme.** What might the poet be suggesting about human nature in "Mending Wall"? Do you agree with the poet? Why or why not?

2. **Understanding Form.** The basic unit of rhythm in poetry is called a **foot.** A foot is a combination of stressed (´) and unstressed (˘) syllables. When you read poetry aloud, a stressed syllable receives greater emphasis.

One type of two syllable foot has the following pattern: ˘ ´. This foot is called the **iamb.**

Read these lines from "Mending Wall" aloud. The stressed and unstressed syllables are marked. How many feet in each line are iambs? Which lines of the poem vary the pattern?

Something / there is / that does / n't
    love / a wall,
That sends / the fro / zen ground /
    swell un / der it . . . /

3. **Recognizing Character Traits.** The speaker and the neighbor meet to mend the fence each year. Each has a different reason for doing so. What character trait, or personal quality, makes each take part in this yearly ritual? Find lines in the poem to support your conclusions.

4. **Appreciating Symbols.** You remember that a symbol is something that stands for, or represents, something other than itself. In your opinion, what does the wall in this poem represent? Why do you think the poet chose the wall as a symbol?

A Time To Talk

ROBERT FROST

SETTING A PURPOSE | *Is working more important than speaking with a friend? Read to see what the speaker of this poem knows about the "right" time to talk.*

When a friend calls to me from the road
And slows his horse to a meaning walk,
I don't stand still and look around
On all the hills I haven't hoed,
And shout from where I am, "What is it?"
No, not as there is a time to talk.
I thrust my hoe in the mellow ground,
Blade-end up and five feet tall,
And plod: I go up to the stone wall
For a friendly visit.

Developing Comprehension Skills

1. What is the speaker doing when his friend arrives? How does the speaker know his friend wants to talk?

2. What does the speaker decide *not* to do? What does the choice he made say about the speaker's character?

3. Do you think the speaker made the correct choice? Explain your answer.

Reading Literature

1. **Understanding Setting.** What is the setting of this poem? How is the setting similar to the one in "Mending Wall"? Do you think the setting is important to the subject of the poem? Could the same idea be expressed if the two friends lived and worked in a city? Why or why not?

2. **Identifying Theme.** What might the theme of this poem be? Do you think this theme is still important today? Explain your answer.

3. **Recognizing Rhyme Scheme.** This poem has a very unusual rhyme scheme. Chart the rhyme scheme. You will have to use five different letters to record the various rhyme patterns. How does this irregular rhyme scheme fit the subject of the poem?

The Road Not Taken

ROBERT FROST

SETTING A PURPOSE | *Making choices is often difficult. Sometimes, it is not clear whether the decision has been the right one. How does the speaker of this poem feel about his or her decision?*

Two roads diverged in a yellow wood,
And sorry I could not travel both
And be one traveler, long I stood
And looked down one as far as I could
To where it bent in the undergrowth;   5

Then took the other, as just as fair,
And having perhaps the better claim,
Because it was grassy and wanted wear;
Though as for that, the passing there
Had worn them really about the same,   10

And both that morning equally lay
In leaves no step had trodden black.
Oh, I kept the first for another day!
Yet knowing how way leads on to way,
I doubted if I should ever come back.   15

I shall be telling this with a sigh
Somewhere ages and ages hence:
Two roads diverged in a wood, and I—
I took the one less traveled by,
And that has made all the difference.   20

Developing Comprehension Skills

1. Where is the speaker standing at the beginning of the poem?

2. How are the roads different?

3. What choice does the speaker have to make? What does he decide?

4. Look at the last three lines of the poem. How does the speaker seem to feel about the decision? Support your answer with words and phrases from the poem.

5. What does the speaker think is hardest about the decision?

6. What advice might the speaker give about looking back?

Reading Literature

1. **Appreciating Symbols.** There are two roads in this poem. Each represents a different way of life. What idea does each road symbolize?

2. **Recognizing Theme.** What do you think is the theme of this poem? How well does it apply to choices you have made in your life?

3. **Using Punctuation To Aid Understanding.** Readers of poetry often pause at the end of each line. However, this is not the way most poems are meant to be read. As you read poetry, use punctuation to help you to decide when to pause. What does a colon or a dash tell you to do?

| *Poets often use symbols to suggest meaning. Read this poem to see how Frost looks at fire and ice.*

Fire and Ice

ROBERT FROST

Some say the world will end in fire,
Some say in ice.
From what I've tasted of desire
I hold with those who favor fire.
But if it had to perish twice,
I think I know enough of hate
To say that for destruction ice
Is also great
And would suffice.

Frozen Sounds II, 1952, ADOLPH GOTTLIEB. Oil on canvas, 36" × 48". Albright-Knox Art Gallery, gift of Seymour H. Knox, 1956. Buffalo, New York.

Developing Comprehension Skills

1. What emotion does the speaker link to fire? What emotion is linked to ice?

2. How could the two emotions linked to fire and ice destroy the world?

3. The poet says he has "tasted" desire. What might he mean?

4. Which do you think is the most frightening way for the world to end?

Reading Literature

1. **Understanding Theme.** The speaker in this poem seems to be simply stating an opinion. Might there be a message or warning in the poem as well? Explain your answer.

2. **Appreciating Understatement.** To use **understatement** is to say something with less emphasis, or force, than the truth would allow. For example, the statement, "Nuclear weapons could cause a few problems," is an understatement. Poets and writers use understatement to emphasize important ideas. What ideas in this poem are presented as understatements? Why is understatement an effective way for the poet to get the reader to think about these ideas?

3. **Understanding Tone.** How would you describe the poet's attitude in this poem? Is there anything about it that you find disturbing or frightening? Explain your answer.

Developing Vocabulary Skills

Reviewing Context Clues and Inferring Meaning. As you learned in Chapter 5, you can sometimes find context clues that will help you to determine the meaning of a word. Context clues include synonyms, antonyms, comparisons, contrasts, examples, and definitions or restatements. If there is no definite context clue, you can often infer the meaning of a word from the main idea of the passage in which it is found.

The following passages are from Frost's poems. Use context clues and inference to determine the meaning of each underlined word. Write the meaning of the word as you understand it.

1. If I could put a notion in his head: "*Why* do they make good neighbors? Isn't it Where there are cows? But here there are no cows.

2. I thrust my hoe in the mellow ground . . . And plod: I go up to the stone wall

3. Two roads diverged in a yellow wood, And sorry I could not travel both

4. In leaves no step had trodden black.

5. I shall be telling this with a sigh Somewhere ages and ages hence:

6. Some say the world will end in fire, . . . But if it had to perish twice, I think I know enough of hate To say that for destruction ice Is also great And would suffice.

Developing Writing Skills

1. **Comparing Poems.** The speakers in the poems "Mending Wall" and "A Time To Talk" express different attitudes about human relationships. Compare these attitudes in one well organized paragraph.

Pre-Writing. Read the two poems aloud. List words and lines in the poems that clearly indicate an attitude or feeling that one person has about another.

Writing. Write a topic sentence telling the purpose of your paragraph. Then write a sentence summarizing the attitude of the speaker in "Mending Wall." Follow this with supporting sentences using specific words and phrases from the poem. Next, write a sentence that summarizes the speaker's attitude in "A Time To Talk." Again, support your statement with specific words from the poem.

Revising. Read your paragraph aloud. Is your topic sentence clear? Have you used good supporting quotations? Remember to enclose quotations within quotation marks. Finally, check for correct spelling, grammar, and punctuation. Make a clean final copy.

2. **Explaining a Choice.** Each of us makes important choices in life. Making such choices is often difficult.

Write a paragraph explaining an especially difficult choice you had to make at one time. Explain why you had to make the decision. Tell what different courses of action you could have taken. Then, explain why you made the decision that you did. What were the consequences?

Developing Skills in Study and Research

Using Biographical Resources. When looking for information about a famous writer or poet, such as Robert Frost, you might refer to a number of references. You could begin with an encyclopedia. It would provide you with general information about Frost's life and poetry.

If you need more information about Frost, you could refer to a number of **biographical resources.** These books can provide detailed information not found in encyclopedias and other general references. Check to see which of the following biographical references can be found in your library. Check the reference shelves or ask your librarian.

> *Oxford Companion to American Literature,* 5th ed. New York: Oxford University Press, 1983.
> *Dictionary of American Biography,* New York: Scribner, 1928–1958, 20 vols.
> *Twentieth Century Authors,* ed. by S.J. Kunitz and H. Haycraft. New York: Wilson, 1942, 1955.
> *Webster's New Biographical Dictionary,* Springfield: Merriam, 1983.

Locate information about Robert Frost in one of these references. Read the articles and write down a few facts that you did not find in an encyclopedia. What did you conclude about the kind of information you can find in specialized biographical references that you might not find in a general encyclopedia? Write a short report on your findings.

Reading Literature

More About Poetry

You have learned how poets use the elements of form, sound, and figurative language to express ideas and feelings. Other elements of poetry include speaker, tone, imagery, and mood.

Speaker

The **speaker** in a poem is like the narrator in a work of fiction. It is the voice that "talks" to the reader. The speaker and the poet are not necessarily the same. Some poems even have more than one speaker.

The following is part of "Lucinda Matlock" by Edgar Lee Masters. What can you infer about the speaker?

We were married and lived together for
    seventy years,
Enjoying, working, raising the twelve children,
Eight of whom we lost
Ere I had reached the age of sixty.
I spun, I wove, I kept the house, I
    nursed the sick,

What clues tell you that the speaker is not the poet, but rather a woman looking back over her life?

Tone

Tone is the writer's attitude toward a subject. The tone of a poem may be lighthearted, respectful, or sorrowful, for example. Can you identify the writer's tone in this excerpt from Paul Dunbar's "The Debt"?

This is the debt I pay
Just for one riotous day,
Years of regret and grief,
Sorrow without relief.

Imagery

Imagery is any words or phrases that create vivid mental pictures. Poets use images that appeal to the senses of sight, hearing, touch, taste, and smell. In William Carlos Williams' "The Red Wheelbarrow" uses sight images that help the reader "see":

so much depends
upon

a red wheel
barrow

glazed with rain
water

beside the white
chickens.

Which senses does the poet appeal to in this excerpt from "The New Direction" by Emerson Blackhorse Mitchell?

This vanishing old road,
    Through hail-like dust storm,
It stings and scratches,
    Stuffy, I cannot breathe.

Mood

Mood is the feeling a writer creates in the reader. Poets consider not only the **denotations,** or dictionary definitions, of words but also their **connations**—the thoughts and emotions the words bring to mind. Look at these lines from "Sympathy" by Paul Laurence Dunbar:

I know why the caged bird beats his wing
Till its blood is red on the cruel bars;

The words *caged, beats, blood, cruel,* and *bars* all carry strong *violent* or *sorrowful* connotations. Together they help to create a disturbed mood.

The level of language used in a poem also can affect its mood. Informal language can create a relaxed, friendly mood. Formal language can create a mood that is serious or respectful.

Is there any easy way to end a relationship? How does the speaker in this poem hope to lessen the pain of parting?

If You Should Go

COUNTEE CULLEN

Love, leave me like the light,
  The gently passing day;
We would not know, but for the night,
  When it has slipped away.

Go quietly; a dream,
  When done, should leave no trace
That it has lived, except a gleam
  Across the dreamer's face.

Yellow Over Purple, 1956, MARK ROTHKO. The Morton Neumann Family Collection.
Copyright © Estate of Mark Rothko.

Developing Comprehension Skills

1. Who or what is the speaker addressing?

2. How do you think the speaker feels about the person who is leaving? Which words and phrases tell you this?

3. How would the speaker prefer that dreams end? Why?

4. How do you think the speaker will remember the person who is leaving? Will the memory be pleasant or painful? How do you know?

5. Do you agree with the speaker's feelings about how a relationship should end? Why or why not?

Reading Literature

1. **Understanding Mood.** What mood do you feel as you read this poem? What specific words and phrases bring about these feelings? Explain your answer.

2. **Understanding Meter. Meter** is the arrangement of accented syllables in a line of poetry. As you remember, the basic unit of meter in poetry is called a **foot**. A foot is made up of accented (′) and one or two unaccented (‿) syllables. When the number and pattern of feet repeat without any changes, the rhythm is said to be regular. If there are differences in the pattern, the rhythm is said to be irregular.

    Look at these two lines from the poem "Old Ironsides":

    The har / pies of / the shore / shall pluck

    The ea / gle of / the sea!

    The foot that follows the pattern ‿ ′ is called the *iamb*. How many iambic feet are there in each of these lines? How does the number of feet effect the rhythm of the excerpt?

3. **Identifying Figures of Speech.** This poem contains both a simile and a metaphor. Remember that a simile uses *like* or *as* to make a comparison, while a metaphor suggests a comparison without using those words. Look at both stanzas. Identify the figure of speech used in each comparison. What image, or mental picture, is created by each figure of speech? How do these comparisons add to the poem?

4. **Appreciating Alliteration and Consonance.** The repetition of beginning consonant sounds is called **alliteration. Consonance** is the repetition of consonant sounds in the middle or at the ends of words. These techniques are sometimes used to emphasize words. They can also create a musical feeling or reinforce the meaning of the words.

    What consonant sounds are repeated throughout the poem? Look not only at the beginnings of words for the sounds, but also within words. What does the alliteration add to the poem?

5. **Recognizing Rhyme Scheme.** Chart the rhyme scheme of this poem. Use a different letter to identify each new line. Why do you think the poet rhymed particular words? For example, what is the significance of rhyming "day" with "away"?

Our five senses often awaken thoughts and feelings. Why might the sight of a red wheelbarrow be important to this speaker?

The Red Wheelbarrow

WILLIAM CARLOS WILLIAMS

so much depends
upon

a red wheel
barrow

glazed with rain
water

beside the white
chickens.

Developing Comprehension Skills

1. What is being described in this poem?

2. Why does the speaker say "so much depends" on the scene that is described?

3. Why might it be important for a poet to be aware of small bits of beauty?

4. Do you think it is important for us always to notice the beauty in the world? Why or why not?

Reading Literature

1. **Recognizing Imagery.** **Imagery** is language that makes an object or idea so real that a reader can almost experience it. Which sense does the imagery in this poem appeal to? List details, or specific descriptive words or phrases that help make this image so real.

2. **Using Punctuation To Aid Understanding.** The poet uses no capitalization or punctuation in this poem. Why do you think he does this? What important quality do you think he might be trying to remind us of?

3. **Appreciating Form.** Why do you think the poet broke up the lines as he did? What is important about each set of two lines? How does the first set of lines differ from the other three sets? Would the effect of the poem be changed if all the lines ran together? Explain your answers.

in Just-

e. e. cummings

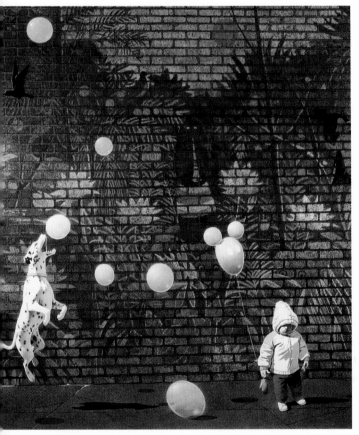

Midwinter Dreams (detail), 1984, ROBERT VICKREY.
Courtesy of ACA Galleries, New York.

in Just-
spring   when the world is mud-
luscious the little
lame balloonman

whistles   far   and wee

and eddieandbill come
running from marbles and
piracies and it's
spring

when the world is puddle-wonderful

the queer
old balloonman whistles
far   and   wee
and bettyandisbel come dancing

from hop-scotch and jump-rope and

it's
spring
and
      the
           goat-footed

balloonMan   whistles
far
and
wee

Developing Comprehension Skills

1. What do you think is the meaning of the phrase "in Just-/spring"?

2. Who might see the world as "mud-luscious" and "puddle-wonderful"?

3. Who are the people mentioned in this poem? What kinds of things are they doing?

4. How well do you think the poet captured the excitement and happiness of spring?

Reading Literature

1. **Appreciating Form.** The words in this poem are spaced in an unusual manner. Consider this line for example:

    whistles   far   and wee

    Why do you think the poet put extra space between the words? How does this help the words to match their meaning?

    What additional meaning does the poet add by using no space between the words in the phrases "eddieandbill" and "bettyand-isbel"?

2. **Using Punctuation To Aid Understanding.** This poem uses few punctuation marks and only two capitalized words. Read the first few lines aloud. What is the effect of the hyphen in the first line? Is the poet signaling an important idea? Now read the rest of the poem. How does the lack of punctuation and capitalization add to the meaning of the poem? Why do you think that Cummings capitalized the two words that he did?

3. **Recognizing Allusion.** An **allusion** is a reference to a well known person, event, or work of literature. Poets use allusions to provide additional meaning for the reader. In his poem, Cummings alludes to both the Pied Piper and to Pan.

    According to an old folk tale, the Pied Piper rid a German town of rats by playing on his pipe. When the mayor of the town refused to pay him for his work, the Piper played his pipe again and led all the children out of town. They were never seen again.

    In Greek mythology, Pan was the god of forests and meadows. He had the haunches and feet of a goat. He was worshipped by shepherds because he protected their flocks and herds. He wandered the woods, dancing and playing the pipes.

    In what ways does the poet allude to these mythical characters? What ideas does he communicate through these allusions?

Developing Vocabulary Skills

Understanding Word Origins: Coined Words. Sometimes new words are created by joining existing words into compounds. In poetry, poets often coin, or make up, new words to suit their needs. Coined words can be fresh and exciting. They can also carry special meaning.

The following compound words are from "in Just-." Identify the ones that are coined, and explain their meaning. Tell why you think cummings coined each word rather than use an existing word.

1. Just-spring   4. puddle-wonderful
2. mud-luscious   5. hop-scotch
3. balloonman   6. goat-footed

Developing Writing Skills

1. **Evaluating Imagery.** Reread the three poems in this section. Think about the images you enjoyed. Choose your favorite one. In a para-

graph, explain why you find this image particularly appealing.

Pre-Writing. Study the image you chose. List the sensory details that help create the image. Decide which sense these details appeal to. Then jot down several words that describe the feelings this image creates in you as you read it.

Writing. Begin your paragraph with a sentence that introduces the poem and makes a general statement about it.

Next focus on the topic of the paragraph. Describe the image you liked best. Tell why it appealed to you. Point out specific words and sensory details that helped make the image so lifelike. Then discuss how the image affected you, as a reader.

Revising. Work with an editing partner. Read each other's paragraph. Is the description of the image clear? Is it clear why this image is the writer's favorite? Is the explanation of the effect of the image easy to understand?

2. **Imitating a Poem.** Write a poem imitating "in Just-." Your poem may be serious or humorous. Use a different time of year as the subject of the poem. You might use fall, for instance, and express your feelings about returning to school. Think of sensory details that would help the reader appreciate your feelings. Do not use punctuation and try to use the same general form of "in Just-."

Developing Skills in Study and Research

Classifying Poems. When you classify, you arrange people, things, or ideas according to categories. A category is a group of items having something in common. Look at the poems in this section. In what other ways might they be grouped? Think of ways in which the poems are similar. Consider such categories as theme, subject, and mood. What other categories might you use in classifying these poems?

Report your ideas to the class and explain your choice of classification.

Focus on

LANGSTON HUGHES
1902–1967

To Langston Hughes, a poet is a "dream keeper." Throughout his long, productive career, Hughes tried to keep dreams alive for black people.

Most black poets voice social protest. Langston Hughes's poetry voices social protest too—with a difference. His poems call attention to the problems of black Americans, including their struggles against poverty, prejudice, and despair. However, he does not give in to bitterness. Underlying the social protest is a deep faith in the American ideal of equality and justice.

Hughes discovered his talent and interest in poetry early in his life. At the age of thirteen, he was voted class poet in his Lincoln, Illinois, grade school. His poems were published in his high-school newspaper. In his earliest poems, such as "The Negro Speaks of Rivers" (page 541), Hughes wrote romantically of Africa and the beauty of blackness. Later, he began to identify himself with Harlem which to him symbolized the heart of black America.

In 1923, drawn by his zest for travel, he worked at a series of jobs in Africa, Holland, France, and other places. His many experiences provided raw material for his poems.

Langston Hughes (detail), about 1925, WINOLD REISS. National Portrait Gallery, Smithsonian Institution, gift of W. Tjark Reiss in memory of his father, Winold Reiss. Washington, D.C.

While he was working as a busboy in Washington, he was "discovered" by a mass audience. The poet Vachel Lindsay was giving a poetry reading at the hotel where Hughes worked. Hughes put three of his poems next to Lindsay's plate, and the next day he was in the headlines. Hughes published his first volume of poetry, *The Weary Blues,* when he was twenty-four years old. A New York patroness paid for his college education as a Christmas present, and he graduated from Lincoln University, Pennsylvania, in 1926.

Hughes was a very productive writer. He wrote books of poetry, short stories, a novel, two autobiographies, and plays.

Langston Hughes once wrote, "No great poet has ever been afraid to be himself." For Hughes, being himself meant using his great talent to express his vision for black America.

Aunt Sue's Stories

LANGSTON HUGHES

SETTING A PURPOSE | *Much of black history and culture was passed on through songs and stories. As you read this poem, decide why Aunt Sue has so much to offer those who listen to her stories.*

Aunt Sue has a head full of stories.
Aunt Sue has a whole heart full of stories.
Summer nights on the front porch
Aunt Sue cuddles a brown-faced child to her bosom
And tells him stories.

Black slaves
Working in the hot sun,
And black slaves
Walking in the dewy night,
And black slaves
Singing sorrow songs on the banks of a mighty river
Mingle themselves softly
In the flow of old Aunt Sue's voice,
Mingle themselves softly
In the dark shadows that cross and recross
Aunt Sue's stories.

And the dark-faced child, listening,
Knows that Aunt Sue's stories are real stories.
He knows that Aunt Sue never got her stories
Out of any book at all,
But that they came
Right out of her own life.

The dark-faced child is quiet
Of a summer night
Listening to Aunt Sue's stories.

The Cotton Pickers, 1876, WINSLOW HOMER. Los Angeles County Museum of Art, acquisition made possible through the Museum Trustees. (See page 748.)

Developing Comprehension Skills

1. When does Aunt Sue tell her stories? Whom does she tell them to?

2. What is the difference between a "head full of stories" and a "heart full of stories"?

3. What are Aunt Sue's stories about? Where did she get the ideas for her stories?

4. Why is the child quiet as he listens to Aunt Sue's stories? Why do you think Aunt Sue tells the child these stories?

5. Do you think stories told from personal experience have greater impact than fictional stories? Explain what makes stories based on personal experience universal.

Reading Literature

1. **Appreciating Mood.** What mood is created in this poem? What repeated words and phrases help create the mood?

2. **Recognizing Alliteration.** Read the four lines in the poem that begin with "Singing sorrow songs . . . ." What sound is repeated several times? How does this add a "sound-effect" to the scene being described?

3. **Identifying Tone.** Aunt Sue's stories describe the experiences of slaves. What does the speaker's attitude toward this subject seem to be? How do you think the speaker feels about Aunt Sue?

The Negro Speaks of Rivers

LANGSTON HUGHES

I've known rivers:
I've known rivers ancient as the world and older than the flow
    of human blood in human veins.

My soul has grown deep like the rivers.

I bathed in the Euphrates[1] when dawns were young.
I built my hut near the Congo[2] and it lulled me to sleep.
I looked upon the Nile[3] and raised the pyramids above it.
I heard the singing of the Mississippi when Abe Lincoln went
    down to New Orleans, and I've seen its muddy bosom turn
    all golden in the sunset.

I've known rivers:
Ancient, dusky rivers.

My soul has grown deep like the rivers.

---

1. **Euphrates**, a river in the Middle East. With the Tigris River, it defines the area
  known as "the cradle of civilization."
2. **Congo**, a river in central Africa.
3. **Nile**, a river in Africa, generally associated with Egypt.

Developing Comprehension Skills

1. What rivers are mentioned in this poem?

2. What is the significance of each of these rivers?

3. Is the speaker referring only to one person's experience? If not, who is it that has "known rivers"?

4. The line, "My soul has grown deep like the rivers" is stated twice in the poem. What do you think the speaker is saying about how their past has affected black people?

5. Do you think most people feel that their past is part of them? Is it important for people to feel this way? Explain your answer.

Reading Literature

1. **Understanding the Importance of a Title.** What is important about the word "Negro" in the title of this poem? Why didn't the poet simply use the title "I Speak of Rivers"? Explain your answer.

2. **Appreciating Symbols.** Rivers are the key symbols in this poem. They represent something other than themselves. What period of black history do you think each river symbolizes? Why is the river an especially good symbol for the main ideas of this poem?

3. **Understanding Tone.** What do you think is the poet's attitude toward the past he refers to? Find specific words and phrases from the poem to support your answer.

Developing Vocabulary Skills

Using Formal and Informal Language. Langston Hughes uses simple, informal language in some of the lines in "Aunt Sue's Stories" and "The Negro Speaks of Rivers." Rewrite the following lines from the poems. Substitute more formal synonyms for the informal words that are underlined. You may use a dictionary or a thesaurus to help you.

1. . . . Working in the hot sun,

2. Singing sorrow songs on the banks of a mighty river.

3. . . . Knows that Aunt Sue's stories are real stories.

4. I built my hut near the Congo . . . .

5. My soul has grown deep like the rivers.

How does the more formal language affect the mood and meaning of the poem? Why do you think Hughes chose the language that he did?

Developing Writing Skills

1. **Analyzing Poems.** You have now read two poems by Langston Hughes. Both explore the heritage of black Americans. Write a short composition analyzing the black heritage as it is treated in "Aunt Sue's Stories" and "The Negro Speaks of Rivers."

   Pre-Writing. Reread the poems. Make a list of the experiences from black history that are referred to in each poem. Also take notes on how the past seems to have affected each speaker or character. Finally, write down the feelings, or mood, that the poem created in you. You may want to use these three groups of notes as the basis for the paragraphs of your composition.

   Writing. Write an introduction that will capture your readers' interest and introduce the topic of your composition. This introduction should also include the titles of the poems.

Using your notes, write several sentences that point out the specific elements of black heritage that are covered in the poem. Then write a paragraph about the mood or tone, and how this reflects the attitude of the speaker toward the subject.

Finally, write about the effect the poem had on your own feelings about black history. Remember that it is natural to think of new ideas as you write. Include these if they suit your purpose and audience.

Revising. Look over your writing carefully. Do your sentences flow smoothly? Are the explanations clear? Check your punctuation. Have you put quotation marks around quoted lines? Finally, check for correct grammar, capitalization, and spelling.

2. **Exploring Your Past.** Think about the elements of your own personal history. For example, consider your religion, your ethnic or racial background, or the history of your own family. Which of these are most important to you? Write a composition that describes some part of your background. Explain why it is important to you, and what effect it has had on your life.

Developing Skills in Study and Research

Using Specialized Reference Works. Aunt Sue passed down information about her heritage by telling stories. In this way, new generations could learn about their past.

Many libraries contain special reference sections for genealogy, which is the study of family history. These sections contain books on the history of names, public records, documents, and other reference works that allow a person to trace his or her family back through several decades. Check to see if your library has such a genealogy reference center. If so, see what facts you can trace about your own "roots."

Harlem

LANGSTON HUGHES

SETTING A PURPOSE *Everyone has dreams. Some are within reach, and some are not. What happens to a dream that never becomes real?*

What happens to a dream deferred?

Does it dry up
like a raisin in the sun?
Or fester like a sore—
And then run?
Does it stink like rotten meat?
Or crust and sugar over—
like a syrupy sweet?

Maybe it just sags
like a heavy load.

Or does it explode?

Harlem Nocturne, 1952, ALICE NEEL. Courtesy of Robert Miller Gallery, New York.

Developing Comprehension Skills

1. To "defer" is to put something off or delay it. What is a "dream deferred"?

2. The speaker compares a dream to a raisin. How can a dream "dry up"? Why is the comparison a good one?

3. The speaker describes several other things that can happen to a dream. What are these possibilities?

4. What might the last line of the poem mean? Do you think it is the dream or something else that explodes?

5. What dreams do you think the poet refers to in this poem? Do you think these dreams stand a better chance of coming true today? Explain your answer.

Reading Literature

1. **Appreciating a Title.** Harlem is a district in the city of New York. For the most part, living conditions there are very bad. There is a great deal of poverty and crime. Yet without certain advantages or opportunities, many of the people who live there have trouble escaping to another kind of life.

Why do you think the poet chose "Harlem" as the title of his poem? What does the poem say about the lives of people in Harlem? What does it say about their hopes and dreams? Finally, what warning about this and similar areas is implied in the last line?

2. **Understanding the Arrangement of Ideas.** In line 1 of this poem, the speaker asks a question: "What happens to a dream deferred?" The last idea in the poem stands alone. Why do you think the poet separated this idea from the rest?

3. **Recognizing Similes.** This poem is developed almost entirely around similes. Identify the similes in this poem. What images or mental pictures do they create? Are any of these images pleasant? What kind of dream is implied by each one? What kind of mood? Why do you think each one is particularly appropriate for the subject of this poem?

4. **Identifying Purpose.** Hughes wrote "Harlem" during a time of great frustration for blacks. What audience do you think he had in mind as he wrote this poem? Look at the last line of the poem. Might this poem be a plea or a warning? If so, to whom?

Blues at Dawn

LANGSTON HUGHES

SETTING A PURPOSE

Have you ever forced yourself not to think about something that bothers you? As you read this poem, ask yourself whether this approach is a wise one.

I don't dare start thinking in the morning
I don't dare start thinking in the morning.
    If I thought thoughts in bed,
      Them thoughts would bust my head—
So I don't dare start thinking in the morning.

I don't dare remember in the morning.
Don't dare remember in the morning.
    If I recall the day before,
      I wouldn't get up no more—
So I don't dare remember in the morning.

Developing Comprehension Skills

1. Why doesn't the poet "dare start thinking in the morning"?

2. What does the speaker say will happen if he dares to "remember in the morning"?

3. What kinds of things do you think the speaker doesn't dare think about or remember?

4. What two meanings might the word "blues" have in the title of this poem?

5. Do you think it is wise not to think about things that could disturb you? On the other hand, might it be dangerous to avoid dealing with these things?

Reading Literature

1. **Appreciating Form.** Traditional blues music is made up of several three-line stanzas. The first two lines of each stanza are identical. The third line is a response to or comment on the first two. In some types of blues, the first idea is then repeated once again. A blues song usually reflects loneliness or sorrow. In what ways is this poem similar to a blues song?

2. **Appreciating Dialect.** Dialects contain differences in pronunciation, vocabulary, and grammar. What examples of dialect can you find in this poem? Why do you think the poet used dialect in this poem?

Subway Rush Hour

LANGSTON HUGHES

SETTING A PURPOSE

Sometimes good things happen in unusual places. As you read this poem, look for the good thing that happens on a crowded subway.

Mingled
breath and smell
so close
mingled
black and white
so near
no room for fear.

Sly's Eye, 1977, COLLEEN BROWNING. Private collection. Courtesy of Kennedy Galleries, New York.

Developing Comprehension Skills

1. What two pairs of things are "mingled" in this poem?

2. What could make the ride on the subway during rush hour seem unpleasant?

3. What makes the subway ride a positive experience?

4. Do you think that, in a different situation or location, the same people might find "room for fear"? Why or why not?

5. Do you think this is a hopeful or depressing poem? Explain your answer.

Reading Literature

1. **Appreciating Imagery.** As you recall, imagery refers to words or groups of words that create strong sense experiences for the reader. Images may appeal to sight, sound, smell, touch, or taste. What image is created in this poem? What senses does this image appeal to?

2. **Recognizing Tone.** How would you describe the poet's attitude toward what is taking place in this poem? Is it positive or negative? Use specific words from the poem to support your answer.

3. **Noticing Unusual Grammar and Mechanics.** This poem is made up of a series of idea fragments. It also has only one punctuation mark, a period at the end of the final line. What effect does this style have on the poem? What might the poet be trying to imitate?

Developing Vocabulary Skills

Reviewing Levels of Language. In Chapter 3, you learned about the levels of language.

Formal English, as you know, is dignified and serious. Informal English is everyday conversational language. It is appropriate in informal and social situations. Nonstandard English is language that is not considered acceptable in most situations. It includes slang, jargon, and usage errors.

Read over Langston Hughes's poems. Notice the levels of language that he uses. Then answer the following questions:

1. What level of language is used in "The Negro Speaks of Rivers"? How does it compare to the language in "Aunt Sue's Stories"? What are the different effects of these two types of language?

2. In "Blues at Dawn," which line in each stanza is written in nonstandard English? What makes each line nonstandard? Why do you think Hughes intentionally uses nonstandard English in these lines?

3. In "Harlem," is the first line written using the same level of language as the others? Why do you think this is so?

Developing Writing Skills

1. **Inferring a Poet's Character.** A reader often forms an impression of a writer after reading several poems or stories by that person. Write a four or five paragraph composition describing your impression of Langston Hughes. Explain how the poems you have studied helped to create this impression.

Pre-Writing. Reread the five poems by Langston Hughes. For each poem, take notes on your ideas about the poet's beliefs, attitudes, hopes, and experiences as they are shown in that poem. Organize your ideas into groups. For example, you might put all the ideas you have about the experiences of the poet in one group, and all the ideas you have about the attitudes of the poet in another.

Writing. Write an introductory paragraph that briefly explains what you will be discussing in your composition. Include a sentence that gives your general impression of Langston Hughes. Next, write body paragraphs using your pre-writing notes. Make sure each paragraph has a topic sentence. When it would be helpful, use specific lines from the poems to support your statements. Present your paragraphs in a logical order. For example, you might present the most obvious or strongest impression first, and then cover others that are less strong.

Revising. Reread your composition. Make sure the purpose, or main idea, of each paragraph is clear. Check to see if your supporting ideas are easy to understand. Rewrite your paragraphs until you are confident that your ideas are well stated. Check for proper grammar, spelling, and punctuation. Make a clean final copy.

2. **Creating Poetry.** How do you get to school every day? Do you take the subway or bus? Do you walk or ride with friends? Write a short poem about it. First, make notes about your impressions while on your way to school. Note things you see, people you talk to. Then write your poem. You could write it in one sentence as Langston Hughes did in "Subway Rush Hour" or you could make several stanzas.

Developing Skills in Critical Thinking

Appreciating Connotation and Denotation. The **denotation** of a word is its dictionary definition. The feeling a person gets in response to a word is its **connotation**. It is the connotation of words that produces the most pleasing and interesting effects in poetry.

Look carefully at the following list of lines from Hughes's poems. Look up the dictionary meaning of each underlined word. Then describe the feeling you get from the word as it is used in the poem.

1. Black slaves / Working in the hot sun, / And black slaves / Walking in the dewy night, ...

2. I've known rivers:/ Ancient, dusky rivers.

3. Does it stink like rotten meat?

4. Maybe it just sags / like a heavy load.

5. so close / mingled / black and white . . .

Developing Skills in Speaking and Listening

Appreciating Music. Use the audio-visual index of your library to find several examples of classic blues songs. You might, for example, look for songs by Bessie Smith, Robert Johnson, and Ma Rainey. Listen carefully to several songs. How well does each song fit the definition of blues presented on page 546? Do you think the poem "Blues at Dawn" would make a good blues song?

Ancient History

ARTHUR GUITERMAN

I hope the old Romans
Had painful abdomens.

I hope that the Greeks
Had toothache for weeks.

I hope the Egyptians
Had chronic conniptions.

I hope that the Arabs
Were bitten by scarabs.[1]

I hope that the Vandals[2]
Had thorns in their sandals.

I hope that the Persians
Had gout in all versions.

I hope that the Medes[3]
Were kicked by their steeds.

They started the fuss
And left it to us!

---

1. **scarab**, a beetle or a stone carved like a beetle.
2. **Vandal**, a member of an East Germanic tribe that overran Europe and sacked Rome in 455 A.D.
3. **Mede**, a native of the ancient kingdom of Media, now northern Iran.

Developing Comprehension Skills

1. What kind of luck does the speaker wish for the groups mentioned in this poem?

2. Why do you think the speaker wishes this?

3. What is the "fuss" created by the various groups? What people are affected by it?

4. Is this poem funny to you? Why or why not?

Reading Literature

1. **Identifying Couplets.** How many couplets are there in this poem? Why do you suppose the poet chose to use this form?

2. **Appreciating Purpose.** Poets write poems with a specific purpose in mind. Some mean to teach us something, while others wish to entertain. What do you think the poet's purpose was when he wrote "Ancient History"? Do you think he might have had more than one purpose in mind? Explain.

3. **Noticing Unusual Uses of Language.** Language can be used in unusual ways to create humorous effects. What is amusing about the rhyming words in the first couplet? What other unusual rhymes add to the humorous mood of the poem?

Money

RICHARD ARMOUR

SETTING A PURPOSE *There are many ways of getting and losing money. Which of the following ways are you familiar with?*

Workers earn it,
Spendthrifts burn it,
Bankers lend it,
Women spend it,
Forgers fake it,
Taxes take it,
Dying leave it,
Heirs receive it,
Thrifty save it,
Misers crave it,
Robbers seize it,
Rich increase it,
Gamblers lose it,
I could use it.

Dollar Signs, 1981, ANDY WARHOL.
Courtesy of Leo Castelli Gallery, New York.

Developing Comprehension Skills

1. How many ways does the speaker list for getting or losing money?

2. How is the last line of the poem different from the others? How does it affect everything that comes before it?

3. If you had written a poem about what people do with money, would your list be like the speaker's? What would you keep in the poem? What additions or omissions would you make?

Reading Literature

1. **Understanding Hyperbole.** You know that hyperbole is a figure of speech that exaggerates the truth. It is used to make a point or to create a humorous effect. What is being exaggerated in line two? Is the purpose to make a point or to create humor? Explain.

2. **Recognizing Rhyme.** The end rhyme in this particular poem is unusual. In order to determine the rhyme scheme it is necessary to look at the last *two* words in each line. What is the rhyme scheme of "Money"?

3. **Understanding the Importance of the Title.** The title of a work often provides a clue as to what the piece is about. Why is the title of Armour's poem important? Is it possible to determine what the poem is about without the title? Explain.

Developing Vocabulary Skills

Making Inferences About Word Meaning. Even when there are no direct context clues, sometimes you can infer the meaning of an unfamiliar word. Specific information in the context can help you figure out word meaning.

Find the following words in "Ancient History" and "Money." Try to infer each word's meaning from specific information. Write down a definition for each word. Check that definition by looking up the word in a dictionary.

Ancient History	Money
1. chronic	1. spendthrifts
2. scarabs	2. forgers
3. steeds	3. Heirs

Developing Writing Skills

1. **Analyzing Humor in Poetry.** Both "Ancient History" and "Money" use humor to entertain the reader. Write a composition explaining how each poet achieves a humorous effect.

    Pre-Writing. Reread both poems. What details and techniques does each writer use to create a humorous effect? Take notes on such things as tone, rhyme, and mood. Group your ideas according to these categories.

    Writing. Write an introduction that presents the main ideas of your composition. It should also include the names of the two poems. Using your notes, explain how the humor is created in the poems. You may want to write one paragraph telling how humor is created in "Ancient History" and another paragraph related to "Money." Or, you may want to organize your paragraphs around the idea groups in your pre-writing notes. Where there are similarities or differences use transitional words and phrases such as *similarly, also, on the other hand,* and *contrary to.*

    Revising. Look over your writing carefully. Is your topic sentence clear? Do your ideas flow smoothly? Are they easy to understand? Check your paper for errors in grammar, capitalization, punctuation, and spelling. Make corrections if necessary.

2. **Writing a Poem.** The poems you have just read present a humorous view of two different subjects. Create a short poem in which you humorously describe a particular topic. Your topic might be schools, teenagers, sports, or government. You may want to use couplets.

Developing Skills in Critical Thinking

Recognizing Generalizations and Stereotypes. As you know, a generalization is a statement that refers to several people, places, things, or events. The following statement is a generalization: "Many people work best in the morning."

If the generalization is so broad that it includes places, things, or events that should not be included, it is an **overgeneralization**. An example of an overgeneralization would be, "All people work best in the morning."

A **stereotype** is a type of overgeneralization. It gives an entire group the characteristics of a few members of the group. For example, to say "Women go to college to find a husband," stereotypes women.

Read the poem "Money" again. Do you find examples of generalization, overgeneralization, or stereotype? Explain.

What makes a person a model citizen? As you read this poem, decide whether or not you agree that the man being described was a "saint."

The Unknown Citizen

W. H. AUDEN

(To JS/07/M/378
This Marble Monument
Is Erected by the State)

He was found by the Bureau of Statistics to be
One against whom there was no official complaint,
And all the reports on his conduct agree
That, in the modern sense of an old-fashioned word, he was a saint,
For in everything he did he served the Greater Community.
Except for the War till the day he retired
He worked in a factory and never got fired,
But satisfied his employers, Fudge Motors Inc.
Yet he wasn't a scab[1] or odd in his views,
For his Union reports that he paid his dues,
(Our report on his Union shows it was sound)
And our Social Psychology workers found
That he was popular with his mates and liked a drink.
The Press are convinced that he bought a paper every day
And that his reactions to advertisements were normal in every way.
Policies taken out in his name prove that he was fully insured,
And his Health-card shows he was once in hospital but left it cured.
Both Producers Research and High-Grade Living declare
He was fully sensible to the advantages of the Installment Plan
And had everything necessary to the Modern Man,
A phonograph, a radio, a car and a frigidaire.
Our researchers into Public Opinion are content
That he held the proper opinions for the time of year;

---

1. **scab**, a worker who refuses to strike or replaces a striking worker.

When there was peace, he was for peace; when there was war, he
    went.
He was married and added five children to the population,
Which our Eugenist[2] says was the right number for a parent of his
    generation,
And our teachers report that he never interfered with their
    education.
Was he free? Was he happy? The question is absurd:
Had anything been wrong, we should certainly have heard.

---

2. **Eugenist**, one who works to improve the human species by improving inherited
traits.

Developing Comprehension Skills

1. What did the Bureau of Statistics find to be true about the man in the poem?

2. What do you think "the modern sense" of the word "saint" is? What is most valued by this society?

3. What kind of society did the unknown citizen live in? How does it judge its people?

4. The man "held the proper opinions for the time of year." Who believed them to be proper? Why do you suppose they were considered proper?

5. Why does the speaker say it is "absurd" to ask if this man was happy? Is the speaker correct?

6. How does this society learn about its people? Do you think our own society is similar to this? Why or why not?

Reading Literature

1. **Appreciating Titles.** After World War I, the governments of Belgium, France, Great Britain, Italy, and the United States decided to honor the memory of soldiers who had died but who could not be identified. Each government chose a symbolic "unknown soldier" and buried him at the national capital.

   Why do you think "The Unknown Citizen" is an appropriate title for Auden's poem? What is ironic about the honor given to the man in the poem?

2. **Understanding Theme.** "The Unknown Citizen" deals with society and the role of each person in society. In the society to which the unknown citizen belonged, how is everyone expected to act? How do you suppose such a lifestyle would affect an individual? What do you think Auden was saying about our society when he wrote this poem?

The Death of the Ball Turret Gunner

The ball turret was a small glass bubble in the belly of a World War II bomber. It could hold a man and two machine guns. What happens to the ball turret gunner in this poem?

RANDALL JARRELL

From my mother's sleep I fell into the State,
And I hunched in its belly till my wet fur froze.
Six miles from earth, loosed from its dream of life,
I woke to black flak[1] and the nightmare fighters.
When I died they washed me out of the turret with a hose.

---

1. **flak**, fire from antiaircraft guns.

Developing Comprehension Skills

1. Several pronouns are used in this poem. Who is the "I"? What two different things does "its" refer to?

2. What is a "mother's sleep"? How could the speaker fall out of it?

3. What do you think the speaker means when he says he "fell into the State"?

4. How high up in the air was the plane?

5. Reread the last two lines of the poem. What kind of death did the speaker meet?

6. What do you suppose the poet's attitude is toward war? Do you agree? Explain.

Reading Literature

1. **Understanding Theme.** "The Death of the Ball Turret Gunner" deals with war and death. What details suggest that humans become like animals in war? How does the phrase "loosed from its dream of life" tell what happened to the ball turret gunner? How does it relate to all victims of war?

2. **Appreciating Imagery.** The themes of this poem depend a great deal on the imagery that is used. For example, the speaker describes himself hunched in the turret like a baby in the womb, or like a small frightened animal.

   What image is created by each of the following:
   a. my wet fur froze
   b. black flak and nightmare fighters
   c. they washed me out of the turret with a hose

   How do these images help develop the theme? Explain.

3. **Identifying Mood.** "The Death of the Ball Turret Gunner" is meant to create a specific mood in the reader. What feelings do you have after reading the poem? What words or phrases helped to create that mood?

Bombardment, 1937–38, PHILIP GUSTON. Estate of Philip Guston. Courtesy of David McKee Gallery, New York.

Night Practice

MAY SWENSON

SETTING A PURPOSE

Sometimes it is only through intense will that a person achieves his or her goal. What is the speaker in the following poem desperately hoping to accomplish?

NIGHT PRACTICE

I
will
remember
with my breath
to make a mountain,
with my sucked-in breath
a valley, with my pushed-out
breath a mountain. I will make
a valley wider than the whisper, I
will make a higher mountain than the cry;
will with my will breathe a mountain, I will
with my will breathe a valley. I will push out
a mountain, suck in a valley, deeper than the shout
YOU MUST DIE, harder, heavier, sharper a mountain than
the truth YOU MUST DIE. I will remember. My breath will
make a mountain. My will will remember to will. I, sucking, pushing, I will breathe a valley, I will breathe a mountain.

Developing Comprehension Skills

1. What will the speaker remember to make with "sucked-in breath"? What will the speaker make with "pushed-out breath"?

2. What exercise is the speaker practicing?

3. The speaker has a reason for this practice. What reality is the speaker trying to avoid?

4. What is meant by the line, "My will will remember to will"? Why does the speaker think her "will" is so important?

5. Do you think a person's will, or determination, can make a difference in the outcome of events? Why or why not?

Reading Literature

1. **Recognizing Concrete Poems.** When the arrangement of words in a poem suggests a picture it is called a **concrete poem.** The shape often suggests something about the meaning. For example, a poem about clouds might resemble the shape of a cloud.

   Look at the poem "Night Practice" again. What does its shape remind you of? How does the shape of the poem relate to what is said in the poem?

2. **Appreciating the Title.** Often a title will provide clues about the meaning of the poem. What kinds of things do you think the night reminds the speaker of? Why would these things cause the speaker to "practice"?

3. **Understanding Mood.** In this poem, the poet creates a feeling of desperation and concentration. What techniques does the poet use to create these particular feelings?

4. **Using Capitalization To Aid Understanding.** The phrase "YOU MUST DIE" is used twice in the poem. Why do you suppose it is capitalized? What does it tell you about the feelings of the speaker?

5. **Identifying a Dramatic Monologue.** A conversation or speech that is delivered by one person is called a **monologue.** A **dramatic monologue** is a poem in which a speaker addresses a silent listener in a moment of deep emotion. Why is the dramatic monologue effective for "Night Practice"?

Developing Vocabulary Skills

1. **Using Word Parts To Find Meaning.** In Chapter 6, you studied several Greek and Latin roots. Review these roots and their meanings on pages 233, 296, 302, 306, 317, and 324. If you recognize a Greek or Latin word root, you can often unlock the meaning of the new word.

   In the following lines from "The Unknown Citizen," the underlined words have Greek or Latin roots. Use your knowledge of root words to analyze each underlined word. Write the root, its meaning, and the meaning of the entire word. Then write another word that uses the same root.

   a. He worked in a factory and never got fired,

   b. And our Social Psychology workers . . .

   c. Both Producers Research and High-Grade living declare . . .

   d. A phonograph, a radio, a car and a frigidaire.

   e. He was married and added five children to the population,

   f. Which our Eugenist says was the right number for a parent of his generation,

   g. He was found by the Bureau of Statistics to be . . .

   h. And all the reports on his conduct . . .

2. **Using the Dictionary.** Use the dictionary to find a synonym for each of the following words from "The Death of the Ball Turret Gunner." Then explain what makes each word in the poem more precise and vivid than its synonym.

a. State   d. flak
b. hunched   e. nightmare
c. loosed   f. washed

Developing Writing Skills

1. **Analyzing the Mood of a Poem.** The three poems you have just read create a definite feeling for the reader. Write a composition in which you analyze the mood in one of the poems.

   Pre-Writing. Skim the poems "The Death of the Ball Turret Gunner," "The Unknown Citizen," and "Night Practice." What is the mood of each? Decide which one appealed to you or affected you most strongly. Then, take notes on how the poet creates mood. What techniques does he or she use? What words and phrases are effective in creating the mood?

   Writing. Write an introduction that tells the reader what poem you are discussing and what it is about. Describe the mood of the poem. In the body of the composition, tell how the mood is created. Try to cover a different technique in each paragraph. When possible, refer to a particular phrase or passage from the poem to support your ideas.

   Conclude your composition with a paragraph that summarizes your topic.

   Revising. Read your rough draft to someone who has read the poem. Ask if your ideas are clear. Have you clearly stated what the mood of the poem is? Do you use specific examples to support your ideas? If the person does not understand one or more things in your composition, rewrite it so it is clear. Then, check your grammar, capitalization, punctuation, and spelling.

2. **Imitating a Poem.** Write a poem in the style of "The Unknown Citizen." You can take a serious or humorous approach to this assignment. For example, you could call your poem "The Unknown Student." Other choices might be the unknown teenager, parent, or teacher.

Developing Skills in Critical Thinking

Recognizing Vague and Undefined Terms. Weak statements often result from using words that have no clear definition. Such words are called **vague terms** or **undefined terms.**

The word *best*, for example, must be used carefully. If you say, "Schools should teach only the *best* literature," you are being vague. Who is to say what the "best" literature is? Such a term must be clearly defined if it is to be used to state an opinion or support an argument.

The poem "The Unknown Citizen" has many vague and undefined terms. Look at the phrases below and identify the vague or undefined terms in each one. Why is each unclear?

1. He wasn't . . . odd in his views . . .
2. . . . his reactions to advertisements were normal . . .
3. . . . the right number for a parent of his generation . . .
4. . . . he held the proper opinions . . .

Breaking and Entering

JOYCE CAROL OATES

One of us touched the door and it swung open.

Slowly, we went inside,
Knowing better, we went inside.

The kitchen was darkened,
the light we'd left on in the hallway was out.   5
Downstairs, no sign of disorder.
Knowing better, we went upstairs.
If I had tried to caution you, you would have pulled away,
eager, anxious, needing to see—
and there in the bedroom   10
the acted-out drama, there
bureau drawers yanked out, overturned, thrown,
a skid mark on one wall—
our clothes tumbled together—
twisted, kicked, someone's fury run to earth.   15
On the doorframe there is a smear of blood.

Later we will discover the smashed window in the basement;
the drops of a stranger's blood.
He must have been very small, the police said,
to crawl through there.   20
Later, slowly, as if shy of knowledge,
we discover things missing:
my wristwatch, a small typewriter,
a tarnished silver vase.
We are slowed-down, stupefied.   25

We want none of our possessions back,
we don't care what else has been stolen,
yet we talk about it constantly:
the mess! the surprise!

Later, we will transform it into an anecdote.   30
We will say, *One of us touched the door and it swung open. . . .*
knowing no way to explain the stupor, the despair,
the premonition of theft to come.

Developing Comprehension Skills

1. The characters in the poem say that "Slowly, we went inside, Knowing better, we went inside." Why should they have known better than to enter? What clue did they have that something was wrong?

2. In what room is "the acted-out drama" discovered? Briefly describe what the characters see.

3. What do the characters discover in the basement?

4. The speaker says, "We want none of our possessions back. . . ." Why do you suppose they feel this way?

5. When telling others about the burglary, what is it they can't explain? Why is it unexplainable?

6. Do you think the couple in this poem reacted in a typical manner? Why or why not? How would you have reacted?

Reading Literature

1. **Recognizing Narrative Poems.** A poem that tells a story is called a **narrative poem**. Like a short story, it contains such elements as characters, setting, and plot.

   In what ways does this poem remind you of a short story? How is it different? Be specific.

2. **Understanding Foreshadowing.** The first line of "Breaking and Entering" provides a hint to events that will occur later in the poem. How does the first line foreshadow the events that follow? What other clues indicate that something is wrong?

3. **Appreciating Figurative Language.** As you know, figurative language creates fresh and vivid impressions. What do you think is meant by the line, "someone's fury run to earth"? How would you describe the image created in this line? How does this image affect the mood of the poem?

| *Football is a game of reflexes and fast decisions. How does the player in this poem react to pressure?*

In the Pocket

JAMES DICKEY

NFL

Going backward
All of me and some
Of my friends are forming a shell   my arm is looking
Everywhere and some are breaking
In   breaking down
And out   breaking
Across, and one is going deep   deeper
Than my arm. Where is Number One hooking
Into the violent green alive
With linebackers? I cannot find him he cannot beat
His man   I fall back more
Into the pocket   it is raging and breaking
Number Two has disappeared into the chalk
Of the sideline   Number Three is cutting with half
A step of grace   my friends are crumbling
Around me the wrong color
Is looming   hands are coming
Up and over between
My arm and Number Three: throw it hit him in the middle
Of his enemies   hit move scramble
Before death and the ground
Come up   LEAP STAND KILL DIE STRIKE

Now.

Developing Comprehension Skills

1. What is the speaker in this poem trying to do?

2. What is the "shell" that is being formed? What gradually happens to it?

3. In what direction is the speaker moving? What is "the wrong color" that is around him?

4. Who are Number One, Number Two, and Number Three? Why are they important to the speaker? What happens to each one?

5. What action is implied in the poem's last word, "Now"?

6. Do you think this poem presents a good description of the experiences of a football player? Why or why not?

Reading Literature

1. **Understanding Concrete Poetry.** As you remember, the shape of a poem may suggest something about its meaning. Does the shape of the poem suggest anything about players on a football field? Does the location of "NFL" and "Now" have any significance? Explain.

2. **Appreciating Rhythm and Repetition.** The rhythm in this poem is fast and jerky. What causes this particular rhythm? How does the repetition of the word "breaking" add to the rhythm? Explain how the rhythm and repetition help to create a feeling of confusion.

3. **Using Capitalization To Aid Understanding.** Why do you think the words "LEAP STAND KILL DIE STRIKE" are capitalized. What do these capitalized words add to the meaning of the phrase?

4. **Appreciating Point of View.** The events in "In the Pocket" are told from the quarterback's point of view. Why is this point of view important to this particular poem? How would the poem have been different if told from another player's point of view?

Developing Vocabulary Skills

Reviewing Context Clues and Inferences About Word Meaning. The following words are from the two poems you have just read. Some have meanings that are different from their usual ones. Use context clues to infer the meaning of each word. Then write down the dictionary definition for each.

"Breaking and Entering"

1. stupefied   3. stupor
2. anecdote   4. premonition

"In the Pocket"

1. looming   3. linebackers
2. pocket   4. cutting

Developing Writing Skills

1. **Analyzing Poems.** Each of the poems you have just read deals with a different topic. One deals with burglary and one with football. How do these poems, taken together, present a view of modern life? Write a composition in which you answer this question.

    Pre-Writing. Reread the poems. Take notes on what each poem describes. What is the mood and tone of each? Then, jot down notes about how each poem represents part of modern life. Find specific phrases and details to support your ideas. Also, make notes that reflect your own opinions. Is the view of life positive or negative? Is it realistic?

Writing. Write an introduction that expresses the view that the poems deal with modern society. Cover one main idea in each paragraph. For example, one paragraph might deal with violence in society, and one might cover entertainment. Use details from the poems, as well as from your own experiences, to make your points clear. Finish with a concluding sentence that summarizes your main idea.

Revising. Read over your first draft. Have you stated your ideas clearly? Do your sentences flow smoothly from one to the other? If not, try adding transitional words and phrases. Be sure to check your grammar, capitalization, punctuation, and spelling. Make a clean final copy.

2. **Writing a Newspaper Report.** The events in "Breaking and Entering" could be the basis of a newspaper article. The article could tell about the burglary that took place.

Using the information contained in the poem, and your imagination, write a newspaper account of the burglary. Your first sentence should contain all the important facts and information. It should answer the questions "Who?" "What?" "Where?" "When?" and "Why?" Remember to report facts only, not your feelings or opinions.

Developing Skills in Speaking and Listening

Giving a Sportscast. "In the Pocket" describes a play in a football game. Imagine that you are a sportscaster. Using the information provided in the poem, describe the play as you might hear it on radio or television. Be sure to include all the important details, and use colorful words to bring the action alive. Also, use your voice to create the excitement.

Practice giving the play-by-play on your own. When you are comfortable doing so, present it to the class. You might, also, try describing a play from another sporting event.

The Bean Eaters

GWENDOLYN BROOKS

They eat beans mostly, this old yellow pair.
Dinner is a casual affair.
Plain chipware on a plain and creaking wood,
Tin flatware.

Two who are Mostly Good.
Two who have lived their day,
But keep on putting on their clothes
And putting things away.

And remembering . . .
Remembering, with twinklings and twinges,
As they lean over the beans in their rented back room
    that is full of beads and receipts and dolls and cloths,
    tobacco crumbs, vases and fringes.

Developing Comprehension Skills

1. Briefly describe the life style of the two people in the poem.

2. The two people in this poem are old and have "lived their day." What does the fact that they "keep on putting on their clothes/And putting things away" tell us about them?

3. What is important about the beads, dolls, cloths, vases, and fringes in the last line?

What do these things suggest about their lives?

4. What kinds of things do you think these people are "remembering, with twinklings and twinges"?

5. How could the people in this poem be rich, even though they have few material things? Explain your answer. Do you think they consider themselves rich?

The Lord Is My Shepherd, about 1926, THOMAS HART BENTON. Tempera on Canvas, 33¼″ x 27¼″. Whitney Museum of American Art, New York.

Reading Literature

1. **Understanding Theme.** The people in the poem have very little in the way of material goods, but they seem content and happy. What do you think the main idea is that the poet wants to get across?

2. **Understanding Titles.** Why do you think the poet chose the title "The Bean Eaters"? What does the fact that the two old people "eat beans mostly" tell about them? Why was this fact so important to the poet that she made it the title? Explain.

3. **Appreciating Word Choice.** A poet's choice of words depends on many factors. Mood and setting are two of the factors to be considered. What words in "The Bean Eaters" help create a mood and a vivid setting?

Expect Nothing

ALICE WALKER

SETTING A PURPOSE | *Do you think we set ourselves up for disappointment when our dreams are too big? Read this poem to see what advice the speaker gives about life and expectations.*

Expect nothing. Live frugally
On surprise.
Become a stranger
To need of pity
Or, if compassion be freely
Given out
Take only enough
Stop short of urge to plead
Then purge away the need.

Wish for nothing larger
Than your own small heart
Or greater than a star;

Tame wild disappointment
With caress unmoved and cold
Make of it a parka
For your soul.

Discover the reason why
So tiny human midget
Exists at all
So scared unwise
But expect nothing. Live frugally
On surprise.

Developing Comprehension Skills

1. What do you suppose is meant by the lines "Become a stranger/To need of pity"?

2. Explain the meaning of the lines, "Wish for nothing larger/Than your own small heart/Or greater than a star." Do the two lines contradict each other?

3. How do you think the speaker feels we should deal with dreams and hope? How can we turn disappointment to our advantage?

4. What do you consider the best piece of advice in this poem? Explain.

Reading Literature

1. **Understanding Stanzas.** This poem is divided into three stanzas. Explain the main idea of each stanza.

2. **Appreciating Form.** The form of this poem is almost circular. It ends as it begins. Why do you think the poet did this? How does this affect the meaning of the poem?

3. **Identifying Tone.** "Expect Nothing" presents one approach toward life. What attitude does the speaker have? Is it a positive or negative attitude?

SETTING A PURPOSE

We all regret things that we have done in the past. According to this poem, however, what is the real cause for sorrow?

If There Be Sorrow

MARI EVANS

If there be sorrow
let it be
for things undone . . .
undreamed
   unrealized
     unattained
to these add one:
Love withheld . . .
. . . restrained

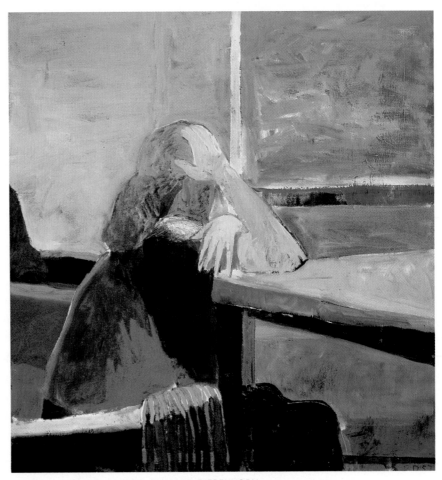

Woman in a Window, 1957, RICHARD DIEBENKORN. Oil on canvas, 59″ × 56″.
Albright-Knox Art Gallery, gift of Seymour H. Knox, 1958. Buffalo, New York.

Developing Comprehension Skills

1. What are the things the speaker says we should feel sorrow for?

2. The speaker also suggests that some things are not worth sorrow. What are they?

3. Do you agree that things left undone are sadder than things we have done? Why or why not?

Reading Literature

1. **Understanding Organization.** List the causes for sorrow according to when they appear in the poem. What do you think the speaker feels is the greatest cause for sorrow? How does the placement of this idea in the poem emphasize it?

2. **Recognizing Mood.** How would you describe the mood of this poem? What feeling, or feelings, do you get as you read it?

3. **Appreciating Repetition.** One meaning of the prefix *un-* is "not." Why do you suppose the poet chose to use words that have this prefix? Why did she use them in a row?

Developing Vocabulary Skills

Reviewing Prefixes and Suffixes. Review the meanings of prefixes and suffixes on pages 232, 233, 241, 262, 271, 272, and 277. Then use your understanding of word parts to define each of the following underlined words. Write the meaning of the prefix and/or suffix, as well as the meaning of the whole word.

1. for things undone . . .
   undreamed
   unrealized
   unattained

2. Just for one riotous day

3. Building, breaking, rebuilding

4. Two years, ten years, and passengers ask the conductor:

5. Forgers fake it

6. He was fairly sensible to the advantages of the Installment Plan

7. Later we will transform it into an anecdote

8. Downstairs, no sign of disorder.

Developing Writing Skills

1. **Evaluating Ideas.** The poems you have just read present people and their ways of living and approaching life. Examine the three poems closely. Is there one main idea, or theme, that is contained in all of them? Is there one piece of advice that is present? Write a composition in which you explain how the ideas in all three poems are related. Use specific details to show why they are related.

2. **Imitating a Poem.** The poem "The Bean Eaters" deals with people who have worked hard during their lives and have little to show for it. Yet they are happy. Write a poem imitating the style of "The Bean Eaters." Describe such an individual. You can choose someone you know as your subject, or create an imaginary individual.

   Pre-Writing. Before you begin writing your first draft, do some brainstorming. This simply means starting with one idea and then building on it or branching out from it. Your goal is to describe a person similar to the individuals in "The Bean Eaters." Try to choose details that reveal the inner characteristics of your subjects as well as their appearance. Also choose details that will create a mood. Then decide whether to use structured or unstructured form in your poem to present your ideas.

Writing. The first line or two of your poem should provide a clue as to whom your poem is about. Then give specific details that describe the individual and his or her surroundings. Use your notes from the prewriting activity. As you write, you may wish to try some of the techniques used by poets such as figurative language, rhyme, or repetition to emphasize ideas. Always, however, keep the main idea of your poem in mind.

Revising. Read your poem aloud. Is the rhythm, or tempo, right for your topic? Does it move too slowly or too fast? Use punctuation, if necessary, to change the rhythm. Add or delete words to alter the tempo. Are your main points clear? Have you achieved a mood? Make corrections as needed.

Developing Skills in Critical Thinking

Completing Analogies. One way of seeing the relationship between two things is through an **analogy.** An analogy consists of two pairs of words that are related in some way to each other. Here is an example:

Finger is to *hand* as *toe* is to *foot.*

The relationship between *finger* and *hand* is that a *finger* is part of a *hand*. In the same way, a *toe* is part of a *foot.*

In an analogy question, one of the four words is missing. You must figure out how the two words in the first pair are related. Then you can supply the missing word to create the same relationship in the other pair.

Complete the following analogies.

1. *In* is to *out* as *hot* is to ____.
2. *Hand* is to *glove* as *foot* is to ____.
3. *Plane* is to *air* as *boat* is to ____.
4. *Artist* is to *brush* as *carpenter* is to ____.
5. *Day* is to *week* as *minute* is to ____.
6. *State* is to *country* as *country* is to ____.
7. *Fire* is to *burn* as *ice* is to ____.

Developing Skills in Speaking and Listening

Interpreting the Mood of a Poem. Choose one of the three poems you have just read to present orally to the class. Before making your presentation, practice reading the poem aloud.

First, decide what the mood of the poem is. What words and phrases help create this mood? As you practice, use your voice to emphasize these particular words and phrases. By raising and lowering your voice, or by using pauses, you can create emphasis.

When you feel comfortable reading the poem aloud, make your presentation.

Celebration

ALONZO LOPEZ

I shall dance tonight.
When the dusk comes crawling,
There will be dancing
    and feasting.
I shall dance with the others
    in circles,
      in leaps,
        in stomps.
Laughter and talk
    will weave into the night,
Among the fires
    of my people.
Games will be played
and I shall be
    a part of it.

Developing Comprehension Skills

1. What kinds of things does the speaker say will happen "When the dusk comes crawling"?

2. What kind of dancing is described?

3. The speaker refers to "the fires of my people." Is the speaker talking about something larger than his immediate group? Explain.

4. How does the speaker feel about the situation? How can you tell?

5. Can you understand the speaker's feelings on being part of the group? Explain.

Reading Literature

1. **Identifying the Speaker.** Why is the speaker's Native American identity so important to understanding the meaning of this poem?

2. **Analyzing Mood.** The title of this poem helps set the mood for the rest of the poem. The mood is joyous and festive. What words in the poem create this mood?

3. **Appreciating Imagery.** What images of sight and sound do you find in this poem? How does each add to the mood?

The New Direction

EMERSON BLACKHORSE MITCHELL

SETTING A PURPOSE

Very often, we are swept along by changes in the world. Sometimes we must stop and decide whether we really want to be a part of these changes. What choice does the speaker in this poem make?

Yesterday They Rode, 1967, JEROME TIGER. Museum of the American Indian, Heye Foundation. New York.

This vanishing old road,
    Through hail-like dust storm,
It stings and scratches,
    Stuffy, I cannot breathe.

Here once walked my ancestors,
    I was told by the old ones,
One can dig at the very spot,
    And find forgotten implements.

Wasting no time I urged on,
　　　Where I'd stop I knew not,
Startled I listened to the wind,
　　　It whistled, screamed, cried,
"You! Go back, not this path!"

Then I recalled this trail
　　　Swept away by the north wind,
It wasn't for me to follow,
　　　The trail of the Long Walk.[1]

Deciding between two cultures,
　　　I gave a second thought,
Reluctantly I took the new one,
　　　The paved rainbow highway.
I had found a new direction.

---

1. **Long Walk**. After their defeat in 1863, 8,500 Nava-
   hos were forced to march 300 miles from Fort
   Defiance, Arizona, to Fort Sumner, New Mexico.

Developing Comprehension Skills

1. What is the "vanishing old road"? What is the "paved rainbow highway"?

2. Who does the poet say had walked on the old road before? How did the speaker find this out?

3. What choice is the speaker faced with? What decision does he make? Why do you suppose the speaker makes his decision "reluctantly"?

4. What is the "new direction" that the speaker finds?

5. Do you think the speaker made the right choice? Why or why not?

Reading Literature

1. **Identifying the Theme.** Do the events in the poem relate only to the person telling the story? How might the poem relate to all people? Explain.

2. **Recognizing Symbols.** You have seen that the "vanishing old road" and the "paved rainbow highway" are symbols for different ways of life. Why do you think the poet chose the symbol of the roads?

3. **Recognizing Personification.** As you know from your readings, the Native Americans were close to Nature. What object in Nature is given human qualities in "The New Direction"? Why do you suppose it is personified?

Choices

NIKKI GIOVANNI

SETTING A PURPOSE | *Many of Nikki Giovanni's poems express the frustration of being black, and a woman, in America. According to the following poem, what choices does one have for dealing with frustration?*

if i can't do
what i want to do
then my job is to not
do what i don't want
to do

it's not the same thing
but it's the best i can
do

if i can't have
what i want   then
my job is to want
what i've got
and be satisfied
that at least there
is something more
to want

since i can't go
where i need
to go   then i must go
where the signs point
though always understanding
parallel movement
isn't lateral

when i can't express
what i really feel
i practice feeling
what i can express
and none of it is equal
i know
but that's why mankind
alone among the mammals
learns to cry

Developing Comprehension Skills

1. What does the speaker say is her "job" if she can't do what she wants?

2. What do you think the speaker means when she says "it's not the same thing but it's the best i can do"?

3. In the third stanza, the speaker must adjust to a situation. What other situations are described by the speaker that call for making a compromise?

4. In the fourth stanza, where does the speaker say she must go? What does she mean when she says "parallel movement isn't lateral?"

5. Why does the speaker think "mankind alone . . . learns to cry"?

6. Do you think the speaker has come up with good ways to deal with the limitations placed on her? Do you think the choices she makes are the best ones? Why or why not?

Reading Literature

1. **Recognizing Contrasts.** Giovanni uses contrasts to make a point. What the speaker wants in this poem contrasts with what she can have or do. Why do you think the speaker chose to use contrasts to express her theme? Why didn't she just explain her way of dealing with life?

2. **Using Capitalization and Punctuation To Aid Understanding.** "Choices" contains no capitalization or punctuation. In addition, ideas are often run on. Why do you suppose the poet decided to write the poem in this way? How does this help to show the mood of the speaker?

3. **Inferring Motivation.** Reread the introduction to "Choices." Considering the poet's background, what experiences do you think might have led Giovanni to write this poem?

For Poets

AL YOUNG

SETTING A PURPOSE

One poet has said, "An actual poem is the succession of experiences." According to the following poem, what experiences must a poet have?

Stay beautiful
but don't stay down underground too long
Dont turn into a mole
or a worm
or a root
or a stone

Come on out into the sunlight
Breathe in trees
Knock out mountains
Commune with snakes
& be the very hero of birds

Dont forget to poke your head up
& blink
Think
Walk all around
Swim upstream

Dont forget to fly

Source, 1980, JOSEPH RAFFAEL.
Courtesy of Nancy Hoffman Gallery, New York.

Developing Comprehension Skills

1. What do you think is the meaning of the line, "...don't stay down underground too long"? What kind of attitude or outlook might this suggest? Why do you think this is especially good advice for poets?

2. What could a poet turn into if he or she stays underground too long?

3. What do you suppose the experiences are that the poet refers to in the lines that begin "Knock out ..."?

4. What do you think the speaker means when he tells poets, "Dont forget to fly"?

5. This poem is entitled "For Poets." Do you think the advice in this poem is useful for people other than poets? Explain your answer.

Reading Literature

1. **Appreciating Mood.** The first and second stanzas have different moods. Contrast the feeling you get when reading the first stanza with the feeling you get when reading the second. How does this change in mood relate to the meaning of the poem?

2. **Understanding Imagery.** What images are used in the first stanza? In what ways are they appropriate to the speaker's advice, "don't stay down underground too long"? What images are used in the second stanza? In what ways are they appropriate to the speaker's advice?

Developing Vocabulary Skills

Recognizing Slang and Colloquialism. As you know, colloquialisms are found in informal English. They are words and phrases that are not incorrect, but that are not suitable in formal situations. Slang is a type of nonstandard English. **Slang** is popular language that usually disappears quickly from the language. Find the colloquialism and slang in the following lines from poems that are in this unit. Identify and define each one.

1. Flinging magnetic curses amid the toil of piling job on job, here is a tall bold slugger set vivid against the little soft cities;

2. Can the rough stuff

3. Go to it, O jazzmen.

4. "Blues at Dawn"

5. That he was popular with his mates and liked a drink.

Developing Writing Skills

1. **Evaluating the Speaker.** The poems "Choices" and "New Directions," deal with choices. Write a composition in which you discuss the choices made by one of the speakers. Which speaker seems happier with the results? What do you admire about or disapprove of in the speaker's choice? Explain your answer.

   Pre-Writing. Review each of these poems. Decide which speaker you will discuss. Then, take notes about the speaker. What is he or she like? What situation does he or she face? Why do you admire or disapprove of the speaker's choice? Jot down your answers.

   Writing. Use your pre-writing notes to write a rough draft. Your introduction should include a sentence that explains the main idea of your composition. Then describe in detail the speaker and his or her situation. Use words and phrases from the poem to help you. Next write a paragraph telling the speaker's choice. Finally write a paragraph explaining your opinion of this choice.

Revising. Have a friend read your composition. Can he or she understand your ideas? Are your opinions clear and well supported? If your ideas and opinions are not clear to your friend, rewrite them until they are. Do not forget to check your grammar, capitalization, punctuation, and spelling. Make a clean final copy.

2. **Evaluating Poets.** In the poem "For Poets," Al Young advises "don't stay underground too long" and "Dont forget to fly." In this chapter, you have read several different poems by several different poets. Which poets would you consider to be "underground"? Which ones are "flying"?

Choose one of the poets and tell why you consider him or her to be "underground" or "flying." In a well-developed composition, give details about the poet and specific examples from his or her poetry to support your opinion.

3. **Comparing Poems.** Reread "The Road Not Taken" by Robert Frost, on page 526. It is very similar in theme and imagery to "The New Direction." Write a paragraph comparing these two poems. If you notice differences, discuss these as well.

Developing Skills In Study and Research

1. **Using the *Readers' Guide to Periodical Literature*.** As you know, the *Readers' Guide* lists articles, stories, and poems published in over one hundred leading magazines. Go to your library and find the *Readers' Guide*. Using volumes from the past three years, look under the subject "Native Americans." Try to find one article that discusses the current situation of the Native Americans, then read it.

For example, where do the majority of Native Americans now live? Are they experiencing any special problems? Briefly report your findings to the class.

2. **Locating Additional Poetry.** As you know, books are classified in the library according to the Dewey Decimal System. The major category for literature is 800–899. This category is then subdivided. Poetry is in the 811 category.

In this chapter you read poems by several different poets. Choose your favorite poet. Look in the 811 section of the library for a collection of poems by this poet. Find another poem by him or her to read and present to the class. If collections by an individual poet are not available, look in an anthology. Skim the table of contents and the index for the name of your poet.

Chapter 9 *Review*

Using Your Skills in Reading Literature

Read the following part of a poem called "Old Florist," by Theodore Roethke. Then answer the questions that follow it.

> That hump of a man bunching chrysanthemums
> Or pinching-back asters, or planting azaleas,
> Tamping and stamping dirt into pots,—
> How he could flick and pick
> Rotten leaves or yellowy petals,
> Or scoop out a weed close to flourishing roots,
> Or make the dust buzz with a light spray,

1. What type of rhyme is used—end rhyme or internal rhyme?

2. Identify which of these sound techniques are used:

   rhythm   alliteration   assonance   consonance   onomatopoeia

3. What is the tone of the poem?

4. Identify one example of figurative language. Explain it.

Using Your Skills in Comprehension

The following passages are from the play you will read in Chapter Ten.

1. Read these sentences aloud. Use the punctuation marks to tell you where to pause. Then explain how punctuation marks break up ideas. Also explain how they help the reader to read the lines as the playwright intended.

   Annie *mutters each word as she writes her letter, slowly, her eyes close to and almost touching the page, to follow with difficulty her pen-work.*

   Annie. . . . and, nobody, here, has, attempted, to, control, her. . . .

2. Put the words in these sentences into a more usual order, with the subject before the verb.

   Smallest Child. Don't go, Annie, where the sun is fierce.

   Keller. Is there no key on your side?

Using Your Vocabulary Skills

The sentences below are from Chapter Ten. Use context clues and word parts to help you define each underlined word. In addition, tell the level of language of each sentence.

1. *Now the distant belfry chimes commence to toll the hour, also very slowly, almost—it is twelve—interminably; . . .*

   Viney *(Presently).* What am I gone do, Miss Kate? It's noontime; dinner's comin'; I didn't get them breakfast dishes out of there yet.

2. **Man's Voice.** Can nothing be done to disinter this human soul? The whole neighborhood would rush to save this woman if she were buried alive by the caving in of a pit, and labor with zeal until she were dug out. Now, if there were one who had as much patience as zeal, he might awaken her to a consciousness of her immortal—

Using Your Writing Skills

Choose one of the writing assignments below.

1. Choose one poem from this chapter. Analyze its use of figurative language and sound techniques. Also explain how figurative language, sound, form, and imagery help develop its theme.

2. Several of the poems in this chapter deal with the idea of choices. Write a poem or essay of your own about a choice you have made or will have to make. Describe your feelings precisely by using similes, metaphors, or personification. Include alliteration in your writing.

Using Your Skills in Study and Research/Speaking and Listening

Research the life of one of the poets represented in this chapter. Also read at least four poems by that poet. Then prepare an oral report on the poet's life, including an oral reading of your favorite poem.

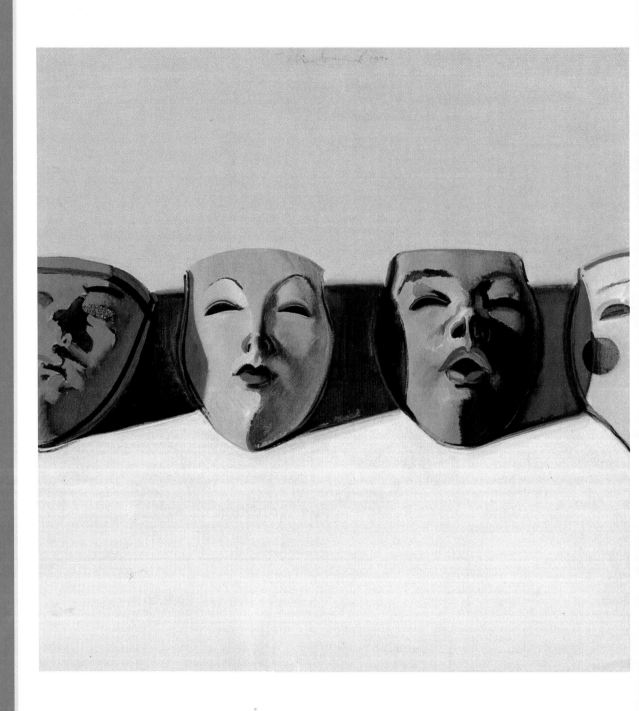

CHAPTER TEN

Twentieth Century Drama

Masks, 1970, WAYNE THIEBAUD. Private collection.
Courtesy of Allan Stone Gallery, New York.

Reading Literature

Drama

Drama is a form of literature that tells a story through the words and actions of the characters. A drama, also called a play, usually is meant to be performed by actors and actresses in front of an audience.

Types of Drama

Dramas were first put into writing by the ancient Greeks. They staged plays before large audiences and held annual playwriting contests.

During the Middle Ages, plays based on Bible stories became popular. **Morality plays** also were staged toward the end of this period. In these plays, characters were forced to choose between good and evil.

The late 1500's were an important time for drama in England. This is due primarily to William Shakespeare, who is considered by many to be the best playwright of all time. He wrote comedies, tragedies, and historical dramas. A **comedy** is a light, humorous play. A **tragedy** is a play that ends in disaster. **Historical dramas** deal with the lives of famous people.

The Elements of Drama

You must understand the elements of drama to imagine how the actors look, speak, and move and how scenery, lighting, and music affect the play.

Acts and Scenes. Long plays are divided into **acts.** In some plays, acts are divided into smaller parts called **scenes.** A scene generally takes place in a single location, at a specific point in time.

Dialogue. The conversation among characters in a play is called **dialogue.** The dialogue advances the action, provides background information, and reveals the characters' personalities.

Stage Directions. These are instructions for the director, actors, and actresses. Stage directions tell how characters should speak or move. They also may describe the setting, sound effects, music, and props.

Sound and Lighting Effects. Often, sounds must be created as part of the play. These sound effects are especially important in helping listeners picture offstage action.

Lighting effects are also important in a play. They can help set a mood. They can focus attention on a character. They can even help divide the stage, creating the illusion of different settings.

Modern Plays

In this chapter, you will read a stage play. Other types of drama are the radio play and the television play.

Television Play. A television play opens up a range of possibilities. For example, the camera can focus attention on a specific character or location. Scenes in a play can change quickly and dramatically. Special effects can be used to create fantastic illusions.

Stage Play. A stage play is performed in front of an audience. Most stage plays have only a few simple settings. Stage directions give specific information about the costumes, scenery, sound effects, and lighting.

Radio Play. Radio plays depend on dialogue, narration, sound effects, and music to present the action of the story. The listeners must picture the characters and events in their minds.

How To Read a Play

1. Picture the play as if it were being performed by actors and actresses. Read the stage directions carefully in order to understand how the lines should be read and picture the settings, actions, and costumes.
2. Read the dialogue carefully. Keep in mind that most of the story is told through the characters' conversations.
3. Be an active observer. Evaluate the words and actions of the characters. Try to guess the outcome of situations and events.

Comprehension Skills

Inferences and Outcomes

For all forms of literature, you must look for relationships as you read. Understanding these relationships will help you to make inferences about what is happening and to predict what will happen next.

Making Inferences in Drama

You have learned that an **inference** is a logical guess based on specific facts. As you read a play or watch one being performed, you can make inferences. That is, you can use reasoning to discover ideas or facts that the writer did not specifically state. These inferences might concern background, character traits, and actions that the characters are performing.

Read the following selections from *The Miracle Worker.* Use the dialogue and the stage directions to guess, or infer, what has happened before this specific event. How would this situation affect the characters? What expressions do you think cross the parents' faces as the doctor speaks?

> **Doctor.** She'll live.
>
> **Kate.** Thank God.
>
> *(The doctor leaves them together over the crib, packs his bag.)*
>
> **Doctor.** You're a pair of lucky parents. I can tell you now, I thought she wouldn't.

Predicting Outcomes in Drama

As you read a play, you often can **predict outcomes.** That is, you can use the information already given to make an intelligent guess about what will happen next. Examine the speech and actions of the characters carefully. Look for recognizable patterns. For example, in *The Miracle Worker,* young Helen Keller throws tantrums whenever she can't get her own way. What will happen when a new, no-nonsense teacher comes to take charge? The pattern of Helen's behavior tells you that a violent conflict is likely.

You can also use your understanding of cause and effect or logical sequence to predict future action. Remember, predicting outcomes as you read can make literature more exciting. This is because you become involved in what you are reading. Also, the characters become more real to you. You care about what happens to them.

Exercises: Making Inferences and Predicting Outcomes

A. Read the following lines from *The Miracle Worker.* Based on this dialogue, what can you infer about the relationship between Keller and his son, James? What does James think about the arrival of Miss Sullivan? about his stepmother, Mrs. Keller?

Keller. Jimmie?

James *(unmoving).* Sir?

Keller *(eyes him).* You don't look dressed for anything useful, boy.

James. I'm not. It's for Miss Sullivan.

Keller. Needn't keep holding up that porch; we have wooden posts for that. I asked you to see that those strawberry plants were moved this evening.

James. I'm moving your——Mrs. Keller, instead. To the station.

Keller *(heavily).* Mrs. Keller. Must you always speak of her as though you haven't met the lady?

B. Read the following lines from the same play. Young Helen has just jabbed her teacher Annie's hand with a needle and then received a sweet from her mother. Use the information given to predict how future meetings between Annie and Helen might develop. Will the encounters be friendly or hostile? What kind of teacher will Annie be? How will Helen react to her teacher? Do you anticipate any problems between Annie and Kate, Helen's mother?

Annie *(indignantly).* Why does she get a reward? For stabbing me?

Kate. Well—We catch our flies with honey, I'm afraid. We haven't the heart for much else, and so many times she simply cannot be compelled.

Annie *(ominous).* Yes. I'm the same way myself. [*As* Kate *and* Helen *leave,* Annie *begins to write.*] "The more I think, the more certain I am that obedience is the gateway through which knowledge enters the mind of the child—"

Vocabulary Skills

Multiple Meanings

Read the following sentences:

1. Her *fair* hair contrasts with her dark eyes.
2. The employment practices were judged to be *fair*.
3. The weather will be *fair* and cool.
4. The patient is in *fair* condition.
5. Do you think of Mona Lisa as *fair* or unattractive?

In each sentence, *fair* has a different meaning. See if you can tell which of the following meanings fits each sentence.

a. clear and sunny
b. just and honest
c. attractive, beautiful, lovely
d. light in color; blond
e. average; neither very good nor very bad

If a word has multiple meanings, use context clues and specific information in the sentence to determine which definition is correct.

Multiple Parts of Speech

Sometimes a word not only has multiple meanings, but it can also be used as more than one part of speech. The word *single,* for example, can be used as an adjective, a verb, and a noun.

If you are looking up the definition of a word in the dictionary, it helps to know how the word is being used in the sentence. If the word is used as a noun, for example, then you need consider only noun definitions.

Here is an example of a sentence from *The Miracle Worker.* It uses the word *blunder,* which can be either a verb or a noun.

The second she is free, Helen *blunders* away, collides violently with a chair, falls, and sits weeping.

You can see that *blunder* is used as a verb in the sentence. Therefore, you would have to check only the verb definitions of *blunder.* These are some of the verb definitions for *blunder:*

    a. to move clumsily; stumble
    b. to make a foolish mistake
    c. to say stupidly

Clearly, definition *a* fits the context best.

Exercise: Identifying the Correct Meaning

Which meaning of each underlined word best fits each sentence?

1. A <u>benign</u> visitor in a hat, Aunt Ev, is sharing the sewing basket . . . .
    a. not cancerous
    b. kindly, good-natured
    c. favorable

2. It takes her a <u>racked</u> moment to find herself. . . .
    a. arranged on a rack
    b. troubled, tormented
    c. oppressed by unfair demands

3. Helen <u>recoils</u>, gropes, and touches her cheek instantly.
    a. to start or shrink back, as in fear or disgust
    b. to fly back when released, as a spring
    c. to return to the starting point

4. James considers a moment, glances across at Annie . . . and <u>obliges</u>.
    a. to compel by force
    b. to make indebted
    c. to do a favor

5. James, now you're pulling my—lower <u>extremity</u>.
    a. the outermost point; end
    b. the greatest degree
    c. a body limb

The Miracle Worker

WILLIAM GIBSON

SETTING A PURPOSE | *Annie Sullivan is brought to the Keller household to teach a child who has been blind, mute, and deaf almost since birth. Does Annie have the necessary traits to be a good teacher?*

(Above) Helen Keller and her teacher, Anne Sullivan. American Foundation for the Blind, New York.

Actress Patty Duke in her role as Anne Sullivan with Melissa Gilbert as Helen Keller in a filmed version of *The Miracle Worker*, October 1979. NBC Photos, Burbank, California.

CHARACTERS

A Doctor	Percy	Viney
Kate	Aunt Ev	Blind Girls
Keller	James	A Servant
Helen	Anagnos	Offstage Voices
Martha	Annie Sullivan	

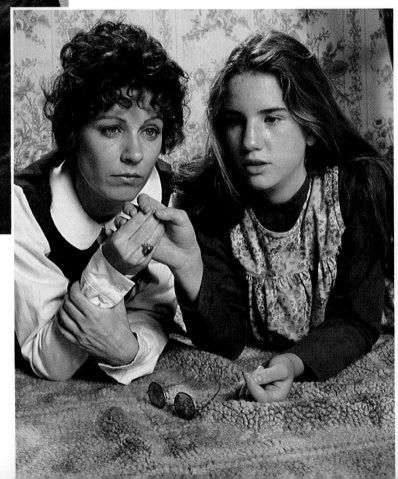

TIME. *The 1880's.*

PLACE. *In and around the Keller homestead in Tuscumbia, Alabama; also, briefly, the Perkins Institution for the Blind, in Boston.*

The playing space is divided into two areas by a more or less diagonal line, which runs from downstage right to upstage left.

The area behind this diagonal is on platforms, and represents the Keller house. Inside we see, down right, a family room; and up center, elevated, a bedroom. On stage level near center, outside a porch, there is a water pump.

The other area, in front of the diagonal, is neutral ground. It accommodates various places as designated at various times—the yard before the Keller home, the Perkins Institution for the Blind, the garden house, and so forth.

The convention of the staging is one of cutting through time and place, and its essential qualities are fluidity and spatial counterpoint. To this end, the less set there is, the better; in a literal set, the fluidity will seem merely episodic. The stage therefore should be free, airy, unencumbered by walls. Apart from certain practical items—such as the pump, a window to climb out of, doors to be locked— locales should be only skeletal suggestions, and the movement from one to another should be accomplishable by little more than lights.

ACT ONE

It is night over the Keller homestead.

Inside, three adults in the bedroom are grouped around a crib, in lamplight. They have been through a long vigil, and it shows in their tired bearing and disarranged clothing. One is a young gentlewoman with a sweet girlish face, Kate Keller; the second is an elderly Doctor, *stethoscope at neck, thermometer in fingers; the third is a hearty gentleman in his forties with chin whiskers,* Captain Arthur Keller.

Doctor. She'll live.

Kate. Thank God.

(The Doctor *leaves them together over the crib, packs his bag.)*

Doctor. You're a pair of lucky parents. I can tell you now, I thought she wouldn't.

Keller. Nonsense, the child's a Keller; she has the constitution of a goat. She'll outlive us all.

Doctor *(amiably).* Yes, especially if some of you Kellers don't get a night's sleep. I mean you, Mrs. Keller.

Keller. You hear, Katie?

Kate. I hear.

Keller *(indulgent).* I've brought up two of them, but this is my wife's first; she isn't battle-scarred yet.

Kate. Doctor, don't be merely considerate. Will my girl be all right?

Doctor. Oh, by morning she'll be knocking down Captain Keller's fences again.

Kate. And isn't there anything we should do?

Keller (*jovial*). Put up stronger fencing, ha?

Doctor. Just let her get well; she knows how to do it better than we do.

(*He is packed, ready to leave.*)

Main thing is the fever's gone. These things come and go in infants; never know why. Call it acute congestion of the stomach and brain.

Keller. I'll see you to your buggy, Doctor.

Doctor. I've never seen a baby with more vitality, that's the truth.

(*He beams a good night at the baby and Kate, and Keller leads him downstairs with a lamp. They go down the porch steps, and across the yard, where the Doctor goes off left; Keller stands with the lamp aloft. Kate, meanwhile, is bent lovingly over the crib, which emits a bleat; her finger is playful with the baby's face.*)

Kate. Hush. Don't you cry now; you've been trouble enough. Call it acute congestion, indeed. I don't see what's so cute about a congestion, just because it's yours. We'll have your father run an editorial in his paper, the wonders of modern medicine. They don't know what they're curing even when they cure it. Men, men and their battle scars; we women will have to—

(*But she breaks off, puzzled, moves her finger before the baby's eyes.*)

Will have to—Helen?

(*Now she moves her hand, quickly.*)

Helen.

(*She snaps her fingers at the baby's eyes twice, and her hand falters; after a moment she calls out, loudly.*)

Captain. Captain, will you come—

(*But she stares at the baby, and her next call is directly at her ears.*)

Captain!

(*And now, still staring, Kate screams. Keller in the yard hears it, and runs with the lamp back to the house. Kate screams again, her look intent on the baby and terrible. Keller hurries in and up.*)

Keller. Katie? What's wrong?

Kate. Look.

(*She makes a pass with her hand in the crib, at the baby's eyes.*)

Keller. What, Katie? She's well; she needs only time to—

Kate. She can't see. Look at her eyes.

(*She takes the lamp from him, moves it before the child's face.*)

She can't *see!*

Keller (*hoarsely*). Helen.

Kate. Or hear. When I screamed, she didn't blink. Not an eyelash—

Keller. Helen. Helen!

Kate. She can't *hear* you!

Keller. *Helen!*

(*His face has something like fury in it, crying the child's name. Kate, almost fainting, presses her knuckles to her mouth, to stop her own cry.*

The room dims out quickly.

Time, in the form of a slow tune of distant belfry chimes that approaches in a crescendo and then fades, passes; the light comes up again on a day five years later, on three kneeling children and an old dog outside around the pump.

The dog is a setter named Belle, *and she is sleeping. Two of the children are blacks,* Martha *and* Percy. *The third child is* Helen, *six and a half years old, quite unkempt, in body a vivacious little person with a fine head; attractive, but noticeably blind, one eye larger and protruding. Her gestures are abrupt, insistent, lacking in human restraint, and her face never smiles. She is flanked by the other two, in a litter of paper-doll cutouts; and while they speak,* Helen's *hands thrust at their faces in turn, feeling baffledly at the movement of their lips.)*

Martha *(snipping)*. First I'm gonna cut off this doctor's legs, one, two, now then—

Percy. Why you cuttin' off that doctor's legs?

Martha. I'm gonna give him a operation. Now I'm gonna cut off his arms, one, two. Now I'm gonna fix up—

(She pushes Helen's *hand away from her mouth.)*

You stop that.

Percy. Cut off his stomach; that's a good operation.

Martha. No, I'm gonna cut off his head first; he got a bad cold.

Percy. Ain't gonna be much of that doctor left to fix up, time you finish all them opera—

(But Helen *is poking her fingers inside his mouth, to feel his tongue; he bites at them, annoyed, and she jerks them away.* Helen *now fingers her own lips, moving them in imitation, but soundlessly.)*

Martha. What you do, bite her hand?

Percy. That's how I do. She keep pokin' her fingers in my mouth; I just bite 'em off.

Martha. What she tryin' do now?

Percy. She tryin' *talk*. She gonna get mad. Looka her tryin' talk.

(Helen is scowling, the lips under her fingertips moving in ghostly silence, growing more and more frantic; until in a bizarre rage, she bites at her own fingers. This sends* Percy *off into laughter, but alarms* Martha.*)*

Martha. Hey, you stop now.

(She pulls Helen's *hand down.)*

You just sit quiet and—

(But at once Helen *topples* Martha *on her back, knees pinning her shoulders down, and grabs the scissors.* Martha *screams.* Percy *darts to the bell string on the porch, yanks it, and the bell rings.*

Inside, the lights have been gradually coming up on the main room, where we see the family informally gathered, talking, but in pantomime: Kate *sits darning socks near a cradle, occasionally rocking it.* Captain Keller *in spectacles is working over newspaper pages at a table. A benign visitor in a hat,* Aunt Ev, *is sharing the sewing basket, putting the finishing touches on a big, shapeless doll made out of towels. An indolent young man,* James Keller, *is at the window watching the children.*

With the ring of the bell, Kate *is instantly on her feet and out the door onto the porch, to take in the scene. Now we see what these five years have done to her. The girlish playfulness is gone; she is a woman steeled in grief.)*

Kate *(for the thousandth time).* Helen.

(She is down the steps at once to them, seizing Helen's *wrists and lifting her off* Martha. Martha *runs off in tears and screams for momma, with* Percy *after her.)*

Let me have those scissors.

(Meanwhile the family inside is alerted, Aunt Ev *joining* James *at the window;* Captain Keller *resumes work.)*

James *(blandly).* She only dug Martha's eyes out. Almost dug. It's always almost. No point worrying till it happens, is there?

(They gaze out, while Kate *reaches for the scissors in* Helen's *hand. But* Helen *pulls the scissors back. They struggle for them a moment; then* Kate *gives up, lets* Helen *keep them. She tries to draw* Helen *into the house.* Helen *jerks away.* Kate *next goes down on her knees, takes* Helen's *hands gently, and using the scissors like a doll, makes* Helen *caress and cradle them; she points* Helen's *finger housewards.* Helen's *whole body now becomes eager; she surrenders the scissors.* Kate *turns her toward the door and gives her a little push.* Helen *scrambles up and toward the house, and* Kate, *rising, follows her.)*

Aunt Ev. How does she stand it? Why haven't you seen this Baltimore man? It's not a thing you can let go on and on, like the weather.

James. The weather here doesn't ask permission of me, Aunt Ev. Speak to my father.

Aunt Ev. Arthur. Something ought to be done for that child.

Keller. A refreshing suggestion. What?

*(Kate *entering turns* Helen *to* Aunt Ev, *who gives her the towel doll.)*

Aunt Ev. Why, this very famous oculist in Baltimore I wrote you about. What was his name?

Kate. Dr. Chisholm.

Aunt Ev. Yes, I heard lots of cases of blindness that people thought couldn't be cured, he's cured. He just does wonders. Why don't you write to him?

Keller. I've stopped believing in wonders.

Kate *(rocks the cradle).* I think the Captain will write to him soon. Won't you Captain?

Keller. No.

James *(lightly).* Good money after bad, or bad after good. Or bad after bad—

Aunt Ev. Well, if it's just a question of money, Arthur, now you're marshal you have this Yankee money. Might as well—

Keller. Not money. The child's been to specialists all over Alabama and Tennessee. If I thought it would do good, I'd have her to every fool doctor in the country.

Kate. I think the Captain will write to him soon.

Keller. Katie, how many times can you let them break your heart?

Kate. Any number of times.

(Helen, *meanwhile, sits on the floor to explore the doll with her fingers, and her hand pauses over the face. This is no face, a blank area of towel, and it troubles her. Her hand searches for features, and taps questioningly for eyes, but no one notices. She then yanks at her Aunt's* dress, *and taps again vigorously for eyes.*)

Aunt Ev. What, child?

(*Obviously not hearing,* Helen *commences to go around, from person to person, tapping for eyes, but no one attends or understands.*)

Kate (no break). As long as there's the least chance. For her to see. Or hear, or—

Keller. There isn't. Now I must finish here.

Kate. I think, with your permission, Captain, I'd like to write.

Keller. I said no, Katie.

Aunt Ev. Why, writing does no harm, Arthur, only a little bitty letter. To see if he can help her.

Keller. He can't.

Kate. We won't know that to be a fact, Captain, until after you write.

Keller (rising, emphatic). Katie, he can't.

(*He collects his papers.*)

James (facetiously). Father stands up; that makes it a fact.

Keller. You be quiet! I'm badgered enough here by females without your impudence.

(James *shuts up, makes himself scarce.* Helen *now is groping among things on* Keller's *desk, and paws his papers to the floor.* Keller *is exasperated.*)

Katie.

(Kate *quickly turns* Helen *away, and retrieves the papers.*)

I might as well try to work in a henyard as in this house—

James (placating). You really ought to put her away, Father.

Kate (staring up). What?

James. Some asylum. It's the kindest thing.

Aunt Ev. Why, she's your sister, James, not a nobody—

James. Half sister, and half-mentally defective; she can't even keep herself clean. It's not pleasant to see her about all the time.

Kate. Do you dare? Complain of what you *can* see?

Keller (very annoyed). This discussion is at an end! I'll thank you not to broach it again, Ev.

(*Silence descends at once.* Helen *gropes her way with the doll, and* Keller *turns back for a final word, explosive.*)

I've done as much as I can bear; I can't give my whole life to it! The houses is at sixes and sevens from morning till night over the child. It's time some attention was paid to Mildred here instead!

Kate (gently dry). You'll wake her up, Captain.

Keller. I want some peace in the house. I don't care how, but one way we won't have it is by rushing up and down the country every time someone hears of a new quack. I'm as sensible to this affliction as anyone else; it hurts me to look at the girl.

Kate. It was not our affliction I meant you to write about, Captain.

(Helen *is back at* Aunt Ev, *fingering her dress, and yanks two buttons from it.*)

Aunt Ev. Helen! My buttons.

(Helen *pushes the buttons into the doll's face.* Kate *now sees, comes swiftly to kneel, lifts* Helen's *hand to her own eyes in question.*)

Kate. Eyes?

(Helen *nods energetically.*)

She wants the doll to have eyes.

(*Another kind of silence now, while* Kate *takes pins and buttons from the sewing basket and attaches them to the doll as eyes.* Keller *stands, caught, and watches morosely.* Aunt Ev *blinks, and conceals her emotions by inspecting her dress.*)

Aunt Ev. My goodness me, I'm not decent.

Kate. She doesn't know better, Aunt Ev. I'll sew them on again.

James. Never learn with everyone letting her do anything she takes it into her mind to—

Keller. You be quiet!

James. What did I say now?

Keller. You talk too much.

James. I was agreeing with you!

Keller. Whatever it was. Deprived child, the least she can have are the little things she wants.

(James, *very wounded, stalks out of the room onto the porch; he remains here, sulking.*)

Aunt Ev (*indulgently*). It's worth a couple of buttons, Kate, look.

(Helen *now has the doll with eyes, and cannot contain herself for joy; she rocks the doll, pats it vigorously, kisses it.*)

This child has more sense than all these men Kellers, if there's ever any way to reach that mind of hers.

(*But* Helen *suddenly has come upon the cradle, and unhesitatingly overturns it; the swaddled baby tumbles out, and* Captain Keller *barely manages to dive and catch it in time.*)

Keller. *Helen!*

(*All are in commotion. The baby screams, but* Helen, *unperturbed, is laying her doll in its place.* Kate, *on her knees, pulls her hands off the cradle, wringing them;* Helen *is bewildered.*)

Kate. Helen, Helen, you're not to do such things; how can I make you understand—

Keller (*hoarsely*). Katie.

Kate. How can I get it into your head, my darling, my poor—

Keller. Katie, some way of teaching her an iota of discipline has to be—

Kate (*flaring*). How can you discipline an afflicted child? Is it her fault?

(Helen's *fingers have fluttered to her* Mother's *lips, vainly trying to comprehend their movements.*)

Keller. I didn't say it was her fault.

Kate. Then whose? I don't know what to do! How can I teach her, beat her—until she's black and blue?

Keller. It's not safe to let her run around loose. Now there must be a way of confining her, somehow, so she can't—

Kate. Where, in a cage? She's a growing child; she has to use her limbs!

Keller. Answer me one thing. Is it fair to Mildred here?

Kate (*inexorably*). Are you willing to put her away?

(*Now* Helen's *face darkens in the same rage as at herself earlier, and her hand strikes at* Kate's *lips.* Kate *catches her hand again, and* Helen *begins to kick, struggle, twist.*)

Keller. Now what?

Kate. She wants to talk, like—*be* like you and me.

(*She holds* Helen, *struggling, until we hear from the child her first sound so far, an inarticulate, weird noise in her throat such as an animal in a trap might make; and* Kate *releases her. The second she is free,* Helen *blunders away, collides violently with a chair, falls, and sits weeping.* Kate *comes to her, embraces, caresses,* soothes her, and buries her own face in her hair, until she can control her voice.*)

Every day she slips further away. And I don't know how to call her back.

Aunt Ev. Oh, I've a mind to take her up to Baltimore myself. If that doctor can't help her, maybe he'll know who can.

Keller (*presently, heavily*). I'll write the man, Katie.

(*He stands with the baby in his clasp, staring at* Helen's *head, hanging down on* Kate's *arm. The lights dim out, except the one on* Kate *and* Helen. *In the twilight,* James, Aunt Ev, *and* Keller *move off slowly, formally, in separate directions;* Kate, *with* Helen *in her arms, remains, motionless, in an image that overlaps into the next scene and fades only when it is well under way.*

Without pause, from the dark down left we hear a man's voice with a Greek accent speaking.)

Anagnos. —who could do nothing for the girl, of course. It was Dr. Bell who thought she might somehow be taught. I have written the family only that a suitable governess, Miss Annie Sullivan, has been found here in Boston—

(*The lights begin to come up, down left, on a long table and chair. The table contains equipment for teaching the blind by touch—a small replica of the human skeleton, stuffed animals, models of flowers and plants, piles of books. The chair contains a girl of twenty,* Annie Sullivan, *with a face that in repose is grave and rather obstinate; and when active is impudent, combative, twinkling with all the life that is lacking in* Helen's, *and handsome. There is a crude vitality to her. Her suitcase is at her knee.* Anagnos, *a stocky, bearded man, comes into the light only towards the end of his speech.*)

Anagnos. —and will come. It will no doubt be difficult for you there, Annie. But it has been difficult for you at our school too, hm? Gratifying, yes, when you came to us and could not spell your name, to accomplish so much here in a few years, but always an Irish battle. For independence.

(*He studies* Annie, *humorously; she does not open her eyes.*)

This is my last time to counsel you, Annie, and you do lack some—by some I mean *all*—what, tact or talent to bend. To others. And what has saved you on more than one occasion here at Perkins is that there was nowhere to expel you to. Your eyes hurt?

Annie. My ears, Mr. Anagnos.

(*And now she has opened her eyes. They are inflamed, vague, slightly crossed, clouded by the granular growth of trachoma;[1] and she often keeps them closed to shut out the pain of light.*)

Anagnos (*severely*). Nowhere but back to Tewksbury, where children learn to be saucy. Annie, I know how dreadful it was there, but that battle is dead and done with. Why not let it stay buried?

Annie (*cheerily*). I think God must owe me a resurrection.

---

1. **trachoma**, a contagious eye infection.

Anagnos (*a bit shocked*). What?

Annie (*taps her brow*). Well, He keeps digging up that battle!

Anagnos. That is not a proper thing to say, Annie. It is what I mean.

Annie (*meekly*). Yes. I know what I'm like. What's this child like?

Anagnos. Like?

Annie. Well—bright or dull, to start off.

Anagnos. No one knows. And if she is dull, you have no patience with this?

Annie. Oh, in grownups you have to, Mr. Anagnos. I mean in children it just seems a little—precocious. Can I use that word?

Anagnos. Only if you can spell it.

Annie. Premature. So I hope at least she's a bright one.

Anagnos. Deaf, blind, mute—who knows? She is like a little safe, locked, that no one can open. Perhaps there is a treasure inside.

Annie. Maybe it's empty, too?

Anagnos. Possible. I should warn you; she is much given to tantrums.

Annie. Means something is inside. Well, so am I, if I believe all I hear. Maybe you should warn *them.*

Anagnos (*frowns*). Annie, I wrote them no word of your history. You will find yourself among strangers now, who know nothing of it.

Annie. Well, we'll keep them in a state of blessed ignorance.

Anagnos. Perhaps *you* should tell it?

Annie (*bristling*). Why? I have enough trouble with people who don't know.

Anagnos. So they will understand. When you have trouble.

Annie. The only time I have trouble is when I'm right.

(*But she is amused at herself, as is* Anagnos.)

Is it my fault it's so often? I won't give them trouble, Mr. Anagnos. I'll be so ladylike they won't notice I've come.

Anagnos. Annie, be—humble. It is not as if you have so many offers to pick and choose. You will need their affection, working with this child.

Annie (*humorously*). I hope I won't need their pity.

Anagnos. Oh, we can all use some pity.

(*Crisply.*)

So. You are no longer our pupil; we throw you into the world, a teacher. *If* the child can be taught. No one expects you to work miracles, even for twenty-five dollars a month. Now, in this envelope a loan, for the railroad, which you will repay me when you have a bank account. But in this box, a gift. With our love.

(Annie *opens the small box he extends, and sees a garnet ring. She looks up, blinking, and down.*)

I think other friends are ready to say goodbye.

(*He moves as though to open doors.*)

Annie. Mr. Anagnos.

(*Her voice is trembling.*)

Dear Mr. Anagnos, I—

(*But she swallows while getting the ring on her finger, and cannot continue until she finds a woebegone joke.*)

Well, what should I say? I'm an ignorant, opinionated girl, and everything I am I owe to you?

Anagnos (*smiles*). That is only half true, Annie.

Annie. Which half? I crawled in here like a drowned rat. I thought I died when Jimmie died, that I'd never again—come alive. Well, you say with love so easy, and I haven't *loved* a soul since, and I never will, I suppose; but this place gave me more than my eyes back. Or taught me how to spell, which I'll never learn anyway; but with all the fights and the trouble I've been here, it taught me what help is, and how to live again; and I don't want to say goodbye. Don't open the door; I'm crying.

Anagnos (*gently*). They will not see.

(*He moves again as though opening doors, and in comes a group of girls, eight-year-olds to seventeen-year-olds; as they walk, we see they are blind. Anagnos shepherds them in with a hand.*)

A Child. Annie?

Annie (*her voice cheerful*). Here, Beatrice.

(*As soon as they locate her voice, they throng joyfully to her, speaking all at once. Annie is down on her knees to the smallest, and the following are the more intelligible fragments in the general hubbub.*)

Children. There's a present. We brought you a going-away present, Annie!

Annie. Oh, now, you shouldn't have—

Children. We did, we did. Where's the present?

Smallest Child (*mournfully*). Don't go, Annie, away.

Children. Alice has it. Alice! Where's Alice? Here I am! Where? Here!

(*An arm is aloft of the group, waving a present; Annie reaches for it.*)

Annie. I have it. I have it, everybody. Should I open it?

Children. Open it! Everyone be quiet! Do, Annie! She's opening it. Ssh!

(*A setting of silence while Annie unwraps it. The present is a pair of smoked glasses, and she stands still.*)

Is it open, Annie?

Annie. It's open.

Children. It's for your eyes, Annie. Put them on, Annie! 'Cause Mrs. Hopkins said your eyes hurt since the operation. And she said you're going where the sun is *fierce*.

Annie. I'm putting them on now.

Smallest Child (*mournfully*). Don't go, Annie, where the sun is fierce.

Children. Do they fit all right?

Annie. Oh, they fit just fine.

Children. Did you put them on? Are they pretty, Annie?

Annie. Oh, my eyes feel hundreds of percent better already, and pretty. Why, do you know how I look in them? Splendiloquent. Like a race horse!

Children (*delighted*). There's another present! Beatrice! We have a present for Helen, too! Give it to her, Beatrice. Here, Annie!

(*This present is an elegant doll, with movable eyelids and a momma sound.*)

It's for Helen. And we took up a collection to buy it. And Laura dressed it.

Annie. It's beautiful!

Children. So don't forget; you be sure to give it to Helen from us, Annie!

Annie. I promise it will be the first thing I give her. If I don't keep it for myself, that is; you know I can't be trusted with dolls!

Smallest Child (*mournfully*). Don't go, Annie, to her.

Annie (*her arm around her*). Sarah, dear. I don't *want* to go.

Smallest Child. Then why are you going?

Annie (*gently*). Because I'm a big girl now, and big girls have to earn a living. It's the only way I can. But if you don't smile for me first, what I'll just have to do is—

(She pauses, inviting it.)

Smallest Child. What?

Annie. Put *you* in my suitcase, instead of this doll. And take *you* to Helen in Alabama!

(This strikes the children as very funny, and they begin to laugh and tease the smallest child, who after a moment does smile for Annie.)

Anagnos *(then).* Come, children. We must get the trunk into the carriage and Annie into her train, or no one will go to Alabama. Come, come.

(He shepherds them out, and Annie is left alone on her knees with the doll in her lap. She reaches for her suitcase, and by a subtle change in the color of the light, we go with her thoughts into another time. We hear a boy's voice whispering; perhaps we see shadowy intimations of these speakers in the background.)

Boy's Voice. Where we goin', Annie?

Annie *(in dread).* Jimmie.

Boy's Voice. Where we goin'?

Annie. I said—I'm takin' care of you—

Boy's Voice. Forever and ever?

Man's Voice *(impersonal).* Annie Sullivan, aged nine, virtually blind. James Sullivan, aged seven—What's the matter with your leg, Sonny?

Annie. Forever and ever.

Man's Voice. Can't he walk without that crutch?

(Annie shakes her head, and does not stop shaking it.)

Girl goes to the women's ward. Boy to the men's.

Boy's Voice *(in terror).* Annie! Annie, don't let them take me—Annie!

Anagnos *(offstage).* Annie! Annie?

(But this voice is real, in the present, and Annie comes up out of her horror, clearing her head with a final shake. The lights begin to pick out Kate in the Keller house, as Annie in a bright tone calls back.)

Annie. Coming!

(This word catches Kate, who stands half turned and attentive to it, almost as though hearing it. Meanwhile Annie turns and hurries out, lugging the suitcase.

The room dims out; the sound of railroad wheels begins from off left, and maintains itself in a constant rhythm underneath the following scene; the remaining lights have come up on the Keller homestead. James is lounging on the porch, waiting. In the upper bedroom which is to be Annie's, Helen is alone, puzzledly exploring, fingering and smelling things, the curtains, empty drawers in the bureau, water in the pitcher by the washbasin, fresh towels on the bedstead. Downstairs in the family room, Kate, turning to a mirror, hastily adjusts her bonnet, watched by a black servant in an apron, Viney.)

Viney. Let Mr. Jimmy go by hisself. You been pokin' that garden all day; you ought to rest your feet.

Kate. I can't wait to see her, Viney.

Viney. Maybe she ain't gone be on this train neither.

Kate. Maybe she is.

Viney. And maybe she ain't.

Kate. And maybe she is. Where's Helen?

Viney. She upstairs, smellin' around. She know somethin' funny's going' on.

Kate. Let her have her supper as soon as Mildred's in bed, and tell Captain Keller when he comes that we'll be delayed tonight.

Viney. Again?

Kate. I don't think we need say *again*. Simply delayed will do.

(*She runs upstairs to* Annie's *room,* Viney *speaking after her.*)

Viney. I mean that's what he gone say. "What, again?"

(Viney *works at setting the table. Upstairs* Kate *stands in the doorway, watching* Helen's *groping explorations.*)

Kate. Yes, we're expecting someone. Someone for my Helen.

(Helen *happens upon her skirt, clutches her leg.* Kate *in a tired dismay, kneels to tidy her hair and soiled pinafore.*)

Oh, dear, this was clean not an hour ago.

(Helen *feels her bonnet, shakes her head darkly, and tugs to get it off.* Kate *retains it with one hand, diverts* Helen *by opening her other hand under her nose.*)

Here. For while I'm gone.

(Helen *sniffs, reaches, and pops something into her mouth, while* Kate *speaks a bit guiltily.*)

I don't think one peppermint drop will spoil your supper.

(*She gives* Helen *a quick kiss, evades her hands, and hurries downstairs again. Meanwhile* Captain Keller *has entered the yard from around the rear of the house, newspaper under arm, cleaning off and munching on some radishes. He sees* James *lounging at the porch post.*)

Keller. Jimmie?

James (*unmoving*). Sir?

Keller (*eyes him*). You don't look dressed for anything useful, boy.

James. I'm not. It's for Miss Sullivan.

Keller. Needn't keep holding up that porch; we have wooden posts for that. I asked you to see that those strawberry plants were moved this evening.

James. I'm moving your—Mrs. Keller, instead. To the station.

Keller (*heavily*). Mrs. Keller. Must you always speak of her as though you haven't met the lady?

(Kate *comes out on the porch, and* James *inclines his head.*)

James (*ironic*). Mother.

(*He starts off the porch, but sidesteps* Keller's *glare like a blow.*)

Helen Keller's childhood home "Ivy Green" in Tuscumbria, Alabama. American Foundation for the Blind, New York.

I said mother!

Kate. Captain.

Keller. Evening, my dear.

Kate. We're off to meet the train, Captain. Supper will be a trifle delayed tonight.

Keller. What, again?

Kate (*backing out*). With your permission, Captain?

(*And they are gone,* Keller *watches them offstage, morosely.*

Upstairs, Helen *meanwhile has groped for her mother, touched her cheek in a meaningful gesture, waited, touched her cheek, waited, then found the open door, and made her way down. Now she comes into the family room, touches her cheek again;* Viney *regards her.*)

Viney. What you want, honey, your momma?

(Helen *touches her cheek again.* Viney *goes to the sideboard, gets a tea-cake, gives it into* Helen's *hand;* Helen *pops it into her mouth.*)

Guess one little tea-cake ain't gone ruin your appetite.

(*She turns* Helen *toward the door.* Helen *wanders out onto the porch, as* Keller *comes up the steps. Her hands encounter him, and she touches her cheek again, waits.*)

Keller. She's gone.

(*He is awkward with her. When he puts his hand on her head, she pulls away.* Keller *stands regarding her, heavily.*)

She's gone; my son and I don't get along; you don't know I'm your father; no one likes me; and supper's delayed.

(Helen *touches her cheek, waits.* Keller *fishes in his pocket.*)

Here. I brought you some stick candy; one nibble of sweets can't do any harm.

(*He gives her a large stick candy;* Helen *falls to it.* Viney *peers out the window.*)

Viney (*reproachfully*). Cap'n Keller, now how'm I gone get her to eat her supper you fill her up with that trash?

Keller (*roars*). Tend to your work!

(Viney *beats a rapid retreat.* Keller *thinks better of it, and tries to get the candy away from* Helen, *but* Helen *hangs on to it; and when* Keller *pulls, she gives his leg a kick.* Keller *hops about.* Helen *takes refuge with the candy down behind the pump, and* Keller *then irately flings his newspaper on the porch floor, stamps into the house past* Viney, *and disappears.*

The lights half dim on the homestead, where Viney *and* Helen, *going about their business, soon find their way off. Meanwhile, the railroad sounds off left have mounted in a crescendo to a climax typical of a depot at arrival*

time. The lights come up on stage left, and we see a suggestion of a station. Here Annie *in her smoked glasses and disarrayed by travel is waiting with her suitcase, while* James *walks to meet her. She has a battered paper-bound book, which is a Perkins report, under her arm.*)

James (*coolly*). Miss Sullivan?

Annie (*cheerily*). Here! At last. I've been on trains so many days I thought they must be backing up every time I dozed off—

James. I'm James Keller.

Annie. James?

(*The name stops her.*)

I had a brother Jimmie. Are you Helen's?

James. I'm only half a brother. You're to be her governess?

Annie (*lightly*). Well. Try!

James (*eyeing her*). You look like half a governess.

(Kate *enters.* Annie *stands moveless, while* James *takes her suitcase.* Kate's *gaze on her is doubtful, troubled.*)

Mrs. Keller, Miss Sullivan.

(Kate *takes her hand.*)

Kate (*simply*). We've met every train for two days.

(Annie *looks at* Kate's *face, and her good humor comes back.*)

Annie. I changed trains every time they stopped. The man who sold me that ticket ought to be tied to the tracks—

James. You have a trunk, Miss Sullivan?

Annie. Yes.

(*She passes* James *a claim check, and he bears the suitcase out behind them.* Annie *holds the battered book.* Kate *is studying her face, and* Annie *returns the gaze. This is a mutual appraisal, southern gentlewoman and working-class Irish girl, and* Annie *is not quite comfortable under it.*)

You didn't bring Helen, I was hoping you would.

Kate. No, she's home.

(*A pause.* Annie *tries to make ladylike small talk, though her energy now and then erupts. She catches herself up whenever she hears it.*)

Annie. You—live far from town, Mrs. Keller?

Kate. Only a mile.

Annie. Well. I suppose I can wait one more mile. But don't be surprised if I get out to push the horse!

Kate. Helen's waiting for you, too. There's been such a bustle in the house; she expects something, heaven knows what.

(*Now she voices part of her doubt, not as such, but* Annie *understands it.*)

I expected—a desiccated spinster. You're very young.

Annie (*resolutely*). Oh, you should have seen me when I left Boston. I got much older on this trip.

Kate. I mean, to teach anyone as difficult as Helen.

Annie. *I* mean to try. They can't put you in jail for trying!

Kate. Is it possible, even? To teach a deaf-blind child *half* of what an ordinary child learns—has that ever been done?

Annie. Half?

Kate. A tenth.

Annie (*reluctantly*). No.

(Kate's *face loses its remaining hope, still appraising her youth.*)

Dr. Howe did wonders, but—an ordinary child? No, never. But then I thought when I was going over his reports—

(*She indicates the one in her hand.*)

—he never treated them like ordinary children. More like—eggs everyone was afraid would break.

Kate (*a pause*). May I ask how old you are?

Annie. Well, I'm not in my teens, you know! I'm twenty.

Kate. All of twenty.

(Annie *takes the bull by the horns, valiantly.*)

Annie. Mrs. Keller, don't lose heart just because I'm not on my last legs. I have three big advantages over Dr. Howe that money couldn't buy for you. One is his work behind me. I've read every word he wrote about it, and he wasn't exactly what you'd call a man of few words. Another is *be* young; why, I've got energy to do anything. The third is, I've been blind.

(But it costs her something to say this.)

Kate *(quietly)*. Advantages.

Annie *(wry)*. Well, some have the luck of the Irish; some do not.

(Kate smiles; she likes her.)

Kate. What will you try to teach her first?

Annie. First, last, and—in between, language.

Kate. Language.

Annie. Language is to the mind more than light is to the eye. Dr. Howe said that.

Kate. Language.

(She shakes her head.)

We can't get through to teach her to sit still. You *are* young, despite your years, to have such—confidence. Do you, inside?

(Annie studies her face; she likes her, too.)

Annie. No, to tell you the truth, I'm as shaky inside as a baby's rattle!

(They smile at each other, and Kate pats her hand.)

Kate. Don't be.

(James returns to usher them off.)

We'll do all we can to help, and to make you feel at home. Don't think of us as strangers, Miss Annie.

Annie *(cheerily)*. Oh, strangers aren't so strange to me. I've known them all my life!

(Kate smiles again, Annie smiles back, and they precede James offstage.

The lights dim on them, having simultaneously risen full on the house. Viney has already entered the family room, taken a water pitcher, and come out and down to the pump. She pumps real water. As she looks offstage, we hear the clop of hoofs, a carriage stopping, and voices.)

Viney. Cap'n Keller! Cap'n Keller, they comin'!

(She goes back into the house, as Keller comes out on the porch to gaze.)

She sure 'nuff came, Cap'n.

(Keller descends, and crosses toward the carriage; this conversation begins offstage and moves on.)

Keller *(very courtly)*. Welcome to Ivy Green, Miss Sullivan. I take it you are Miss Sullivan—

Kate. My husband, Miss Annie, Captain Keller.

Annie *(her best behavior)*. Captain, how do you do.

Keller. A pleasure to see you, at last. I trust you had an agreeable journey?

Annie. Oh, I had several! When did this country get so big?

James. Where would you like the trunk, father?

Keller. Where Miss Sullivan can get at it, I imagine.

Annie. Yes, please. Where's Helen?

Keller. In the hall, Jimmie—

Kate. We've put you in the upstairs corner room, Miss Annie. If there's any breeze at all this summer, you'll feel it—

(*In the house, the setter* Belle *flees into the family room, pursued by* Helen *with groping hands. The dog doubles back out the same door, and* Helen, *still groping for her, makes her way out to the porch. She is messy; her hair tumbled, her pinafore now ripped, her shoelaces untied.* Keller *acquires the suitcase, and* Annie *gets her hands on it too, though still endeavoring to live up to the general air of propertied manners.*)

Keller. *And* the suitcase—

Annie (*pleasantly*). I'll take the suitcase, thanks.

Keller. Not at all, I have it, Miss Sullivan.

Annie. I'd like it.

Keller (*gallantly*). I couldn't think of it, Miss Sullivan. You'll find in the South we—

Annie. Let me.

Keller. —view women as the flowers of civiliza—

Annie (*impatiently*). I've got something in it for Helen!

(*She tugs it free;* Keller *stares.*)

Thank you. When do I see her?

Kate. There. There is Helen.

(Annie *turns, and sees* Helen *on the porch. A moment of silence. Then* Annie *begins across the yard to her, lugging her suitcase.*)

Keller (*sotto voce*[2]). Katie—

(Kate *silences him with a hand on his arm. When* Annie *finally reaches the porch steps, she stops, contemplating* Helen *for a last moment before entering her world. Then she drops the suitcase on the porch with intentional heaviness.* Helen *starts with the jar, and comes to grope over it.* Annie *puts forth her hand, and touches* Helen's. Helen *at once grasps it, and commences to explore it, like reading a face. She moves her hand on to* Annie's *forearm, and dress; and* Annie *brings her face within reach of* Helen's *fingers, which travel over it, quite without timidity, until they encounter and push aside the smoked glasses.* Annie's *gaze is grave, unpitying, very attentive. She puts her hands on* Helen's *arms, but* Helen *at once pulls away, and they confront each other with a distance between. Then* Helen *returns to the suitcase, tries to open it, cannot.* Annie *points* Helen's *hand overhead.* Helen *pulls away, tries to open the suitcase again;* Annie *points her hand overhead again.* Helen *points overhead, a question; and* Annie, *drawing* Helen's *hand to her own face, nods.* Helen *now begins tugging the suitcase toward the door. When* Annie *tries to take it from her, she fights her off and backs through the doorway with it.* Annie *stands a moment, then follows her in, and together they get the suitcase up the steps into* Annie's *room.*)

Kate. Well?

Keller. She's very rough, Katie.

Kate. I like her, Captain.

Keller. Certainly rear a peculiar kind of young woman in the North. How old is she?

---

2. **sotto voce**, (Italian) in a low tone of voice, so as not to be overheard.

Kate (*vaguely*). Ohh— Well, she's not in her teens, you know.

Keller. She's only a child. What's her family like, shipping her off alone this far?

Kate. I couldn't learn. She's very close-mouthed about some things.

Keller. Why does she wear those glasses? I like to see a person's eyes when I talk to—

Kate. For the sun. She was blind.

Keller. Blind.

Kate. She's had nine operations on her eyes. One just before she left.

Keller. Blind, good heavens, do they expect one blind child to teach another? Has she experience at least? How long did she teach there?

Kate. She was a pupil.

Keller (*heavily*). Katie, Katie. This is her first position?

Kate (*bright voice*). She was valedictorian—

Keller. Here's a houseful of grownups can't cope with the child. How can an inexperienced, half-blind Yankee schoolgirl manage her?

(James *moves in with the trunk on his shoulder.*)

James (*easily*). Great improvement. Now we have two of them to look after.

Keller. You look after those strawberry plants!

(James *stops with the trunk.* Keller *turns from him without another word, and marches off.*)

James. Nothing I say is right.

Kate. Why say anything?

(*She calls.*)

Don't be long, Captain. We'll have supper right away—

(*She goes into the house, and through the rear door of the family room.* James *trudges in with the trunk, takes it up the steps to* Annie's *room, and sets it down outside the door. The lights elsewhere dim somewhat.*

Meanwhile, inside, Annie *has given* Helen *a key. While* Annie *removes her bonnet,* Helen *unlocks and opens the suitcase. The first thing she pulls out is a voluminous shawl. She fingers it until she perceives what it is; then she wraps it around her, and acquiring* Annie's *bonnet and smoked glasses as well, dons the lot. The shawl swamps her, and the bonnet settles down upon the glasses, but she stands before a mirror cocking her head to one side, then to the other, in a mockery of adult action.* Annie *is amused, and talks to her as one might to a kitten, with no trace of company manners.*)

Annie. All the trouble I went to, and that's how I look?

(Helen *then comes back to the suitcase, gropes for more, lifts out a pair of female drawers.*)

Oh, no. Not the drawers!

(*But* Helen, *discarding them, comes to the elegant doll. Her fingers explore its features,* and when she raises it and finds its eyes open and close, she is at first startled, then delighted. She picks it up, taps its head vigorously, taps her own chest, and nods questioningly. Annie *takes her finger, points it to the doll, points it to* Helen, *and touching it to her own face, also nods.* Helen *sits back on her heels, clasps the doll to herself and rocks it.* Annie *studies her, still in bonnet and smoked glasses like a caricature of herself, and addresses her humorously.*)

All right, Miss O'Sullivan. Let's begin with doll.

(*She takes* Helen's *hand. In her palm,* Annie's *forefinger points, thumb holding her other fingers clenched.*)

D.

(*Her thumb next holds all her fingers clenched, touching* Helen's *palm.*)

O.

(*Her thumb and forefinger extend.*)

L.

(*Same contact repeated.*)

L.

(*She puts* Helen's *hand to the doll.*)

Doll.

James. You spell pretty well.

(Annie, *in one hurried move, gets the drawers swiftly back into the suitcase, the lid banged shut, and her head turned, to see* James *leaning in the doorway.*)

Finding out if she's ticklish? She is.

(Annie *regards him stonily, but* Helen, *after a scowling moment, tugs at her hand again, imperious.* Annie *repeats the letters, and* Helen *interrupts her fingers in the middle, feeling each of them, puzzled.* Annie *touches* Helen's *hand to the doll, and begins spelling into it again.*)

James. What is it, a game?

Annie (*curtly*). An alphabet.

James. Alphabet?

Annie. For the deaf.

(Helen *now repeats the finger movements in air, exactly, her head cocked to her own hand, and* Annie's *eyes suddenly gleam.*)

Ho. How *bright* she is!

James. You think she knows what she's doing?

(*He takes* Helen's *hand, to throw a meaningless gesture into it; she repeats this one too.*)

She imitates everything; she's a monkey.

Annie (*very pleased*). Yes, she's a bright little monkey, all right.

(*She takes the doll from* Helen, *and reaches for her hand;* Helen *instantly grabs the doll back.* Annie *takes it again, and* Helen's *hand next, but* Helen *is incensed now. When* Annie *draws her hand to her face to shake her head no, then tries to spell to her,* Helen *slaps at* Annie's *face.* Annie *grasps* Helen *by both arms, and swings her into a chair, holding her pinned there, kicking, while glasses, doll, bonnet fly in various directions.* James *laughs.*)

James. She wants her doll back.

Annie. When she spells it.

James. Spell, she doesn't know the thing has a name, even.

Annie. Of course not. Who expects her to, now? All I want is her fingers to learn the letters.

James. Won't mean anything to her.

(Annie *gives him a look. She then tries to form* Helen's *fingers into the letters, but* Helen *swings a haymaker instead, which* Annie *barely ducks, at once pinning her down again.*)

Doesn't like that alphabet, Miss Sullivan. You invent it yourself?

(Helen *is now in a rage, fighting tooth and nail to get out of the chair, and* Annie *answers while struggling and dodging her kicks.*)

Annie. Spanish monks under a—vow of silence. Which I wish *you'd* take!

(And *suddenly releasing* Helen's *hands, she comes and shuts the door in* James's *face.* Helen *drops to the floor, groping around for the doll.* Annie *looks around desperately, sees her purse on the bed, rummages in it, and comes up with a battered piece of cake wrapped in newspaper. With her foot she moves the doll deftly out of the way of* Helen's *groping; and going on her knee, she lets* Helen *smell the cake. When* Helen *grabs for it,* Annie *removes the cake and spells quickly into the reaching hand.*)

Cake. From Washington, up north; it's the best I can do.

(Helen's *hand waits, baffled.* Annie *repeats it.*)

C, a, k, e. Do what my fingers do; never mind what it means.

(She *touches the cake briefly to* Helen's *nose, pats her hand, presents her own hand.* Helen *spells the letters rapidly back.* Annie *pats her hand enthusiastically, and gives her the cake.* Helen *crams it into her mouth with both hands.* Annie *watches her, with humor.*)

Get it down fast; maybe I'll steal that back, too. Now.

(She *takes the doll, touches it to* Helen's *nose, and spells again into her hand.*)

D, o, l, l. Think it over.

(Helen *thinks it over, while* Annie *presents her own hand. Then* Helen *spells three letters.* Annie *waits a second, then completes the word for* Helen *in her palm.*)

L.

(She *hands over the doll, and* Helen *gets a good grip on its leg.*)

Imitate now, understand later. End of the first les—

(She *never finishes, because* Helen *swings the doll with a furious energy. It hits* Annie *squarely in the face, and she falls back with a cry of pain, her knuckles up to her mouth.* Helen *waits, tensed for further combat. When* Annie *lowers her knuckles, she looks at blood on them. She works her lips, gets to her feet, finds the mirror, and bares her teeth at herself. Now she is furious herself.*)

You little wretch, no one's taught you *any* manners? I'll—

NBC Photos, Burbank, California.

(But rounding from the mirror, she sees the door slam. Helen *and the doll are on the outside, and* Helen *is turning the key in the lock.* Annie *darts over, to pull the knob; the door is locked fast. She yanks it again.*)

Helen! Helen, let me out of—

(*She bats her brow at the folly of speaking but* James, *now downstairs, hears her and turns to see* Helen *with the key and doll groping her way down the steps.* James *takes in the whole situation, makes a move to intercept* Helen, *but then changes his mind, lets her pass, and amus-* edly follows her out onto the porch. Upstairs, Annie *meanwhile rattles the knob, kneels, peers through the keyhole, gets up. She goes to the window, looks down, frowns.* James *from the yard sings gaily up to her.*)

James. Buffalo girl, are you coming out tonight,

Coming out tonight,
Coming out—

(*He drifts back into the house.* Annie *takes a handkerchief, nurses her mouth, stands in the middle of the room, staring at door and window in turn; and so catches sight of herself in the mirror, her cheek scratched, her hair dishevelled, her handkerchief bloody, her face disgusted with herself. She addresses the mirror, with some irony.)*

Annie. Don't worry. They'll find you; you're not lost. Only out of place.

(But she coughs, spits something into her palm, and stares at it, outraged.)

And toothless.

(She winces.)

Oo! It hurts.

(She pours some water into the basin, dips the handkerchief, and presses it to her mouth. Standing there, bent over the basin in pain—with the rest of the set dim and unreal, and the lights upon her taking on the subtle color of the past—she hears again, as do we, the faraway voices; and slowly she lifts her head to them. The boy's voice is the same; the others are cracked old crones in a nightmare, and perhaps we see their shadows.)

Boy's Voice. It hurts, Annie, it hurts.

First Crone's Voice. Keep that brat shut up, can't you, girlie. How's a body to get any sleep in this darn ward?

Boy's Voice. It hurts. It hurts.

Second Crone's Voice. Shut up, you!

Boy's Voice. Annie, when we goin' home? You promised!

Annie. Jimmie—

Boy's Voice. Forever and ever, you said forever—

(Annie drops the handkerchief, averts to the window, and is arrested there by the next cry.)

Annie? Annie, you there? Annie! It *hurts!*

Third Crone's Voice. Grab him; he's fallin'!

Boy's Voice. *Annie!*

Doctor's Voice *(a pause, slowly)*. Little girl. Little girl, I must tell you your brother will be going on a—

(But Annie claps her hands to her ears, to shut this out; there is instant silence.
As the lights bring the other areas in again, James goes to the steps to listen for any sound from upstairs. Keller, re-entering from left, crosses toward the house; he passes Helen en route to her retreat under the pump. Kate re-enters the rear door of the family room, with flowers for the table.)

Kate. Supper is ready, Jimmie. Will you call your father?

James. Certainly.

(But he calls up the stairs, for Annie's benefit,)

Father! Supper!

Keller *(at the door)*. No need to shout; I've been cooling my heels for an hour. Sit down.

James. Certainly.

Keller. Viney!

(Viney *backs in with a roast, while they get settled around the table.*)

Viney. Yes, Cap'n, right here.

Kate. Mildred went directly to sleep, Viney?

Viney. Oh, yes, that babe's an angel.

Kate. And Helen had a good supper?

Viney *(vaguely)*. I dunno, Miss Kate, somehow she didn't have much of a appetite tonight—

Kate *(a bit guilty)*. Oh, dear.

Keller *(hastily)*. Well, now. Couldn't say the same for my part. I'm famished. Katie, your plate.

Kate *(looking)*. But where is Miss Annie?

(A silence.)

James *(pleasantly)*. In her room.

Keller. In her room? Doesn't she know hot food must be eaten hot? Go bring her down at once, Jimmie.

James *(rises)*. Certainly. I'll get a ladder.

Keller *(stares)*. What?

James. I'll need a ladder. Shouldn't take me long.

Kate *(stares)*. What shouldn't take you—

Keller. Jimmie, do as I say! Go upstairs at once and tell Miss Sullivan supper is getting cold—

James. She's locked in her room.

Keller. Locked in her—

Kate. What on earth are you—

James. Helen locked her in and made off with the key.

Kate *(rising)*. And you sit here and say nothing?

James. Well, everyone's been telling me not to say anything.

(He goes serenely out and across the yard, whistling. Keller thrusting up from his chair, makes for the stairs.)

Kate. Viney, look out in back for Helen. See if she has that key.

Viney. Yes, Miss Kate.

(Viney goes out the rear door.)

Keller *(calling down)*. She's out by the pump!

(Kate goes out on the porch after Helen, while Keller knocks on Annie's door, then rattles the knob, imperiously,)

Miss Sullivan! Are you in there?

Annie. Oh, I'm here, all right.

Keller. Is there no key on your side?

Annie *(with some asperity)*. Well, if there was a key in here, I wouldn't be in here. Helen took it; the only thing on my side is me.

Keller. Miss Sullivan. I—

(He tries, but cannot hold it back.)

Not in the house ten minutes, I don't see *how* you managed it!

(He stomps downstairs again, while Annie mutters to herself.)

Annie. And even I'm not on my side.

Keller (*roaring*). Viney!

Viney (*reappearing*). Yes, Cap'n?

Keller. Put that meat back in the oven!

(Viney *bears the roast off again, while* Keller *strides out onto the porch.* Kate *is with* Helen *at the pump, opening her hands.*)

Kate. She has no key.

Keller. Nonsense, she must have the key. Have you searched in her pockets?

Kate. Yes. She doesn't have it.

Keller. Katie, she must have the key.

Kate. Would you prefer to search her yourself, Captain?

Keller. No, I would not prefer to search her! She almost took my kneecap off this evening, when I tried merely to—

(James *reappears carrying a long ladder, with* Percy *running after him.*)

Take that ladder back!

James. Certainly.

(*He turns around with it.* Martha *comes skipping around the upstage corner of the house to be in on things, accompanied by the setter* Belle.)

Kate. She could have hidden the key.

Keller. Where?

Kate. Anywhere. Under a stone. In the flower beds. In the grass—

Keller. Well, I can't plow up the entire grounds to find a missing key! Jimmie!

James. Sir?

Keller. Bring me a ladder!

James. Certainly.

(Viney *comes around the downstage side of the house to be in on things; she has* Mildred *over her shoulder, bleating.* Keller *places the ladder against* Annie's *window and mounts.* Annie, *meanwhile, is running about making herself presentable, washing the blood off her mouth, straightening her clothes, tidying her hair. Another black servant enters to gaze in wonder, increasing the gathering ring of spectators.*)

Kate (*sharply*). What is Mildred doing up?

Viney. Cap'n woke her, ma'am, all that hollerin'.

Keller. Miss Sullivan!

(Annie *comes to the window, with as much air of gracious normality as she can manage;* Keller *is at the window.*)

Annie (*brightly*). Yes, Captain Keller?

Keller. Come out!

Annie. I don't see how I can. There isn't room.

Keller. I intend to carry you. Climb onto my shoulder and hold tight.

Annie. Oh, no. It's—very chivalrous of you, but I'd really prefer to—

Keller. Miss Sullivan, follow instructions! I will not have you also tumbling out of our windows.

(Annie *obeys, with some misgivings.*)

I hope this is not a sample of what we may expect from you. In the way of simplifying the work of looking after Helen.

Annie. Captain Keller, I'm perfectly able to go down a ladder under my own—

Keller. I doubt it, Miss Sullivan. Simply hold onto my neck

(He *begins down with her, while the spectators stand in a wide and somewhat awe-stricken circle, watching.* Keller *half-misses a rung, and* Annie *grabs at his whiskers.*)

My *neck,* Miss Sullivan!

Annie. I'm sorry to inconvenience you this way—

Keller. No inconvenience, other than having that door taken down and the lock replaced, if we fail to find that key.

Annie. Oh, I'll look everywhere for it.

Keller. Thank you. Do not look in any rooms that can be locked. There.

(He *stands her on the ground.* James *applauds.*)

Annie. Thank you very much.

(She *smooths her skirt, looking as composed and ladylike as possible.* Keller *stares around at the spectators.*)

Keller. Go, go, back to your work. What are you looking at here? There's nothing here to look at.

(They *break up, move off.*)

Now would it be possible for us to have supper, like other people?

(He *marches into the house.*)

Kate. Viney, serve supper. I'll put Mildred to sleep.

(They *all go in.* James *is the last to leave, murmuring to* Annie *with a gesture.*)

James. Might as well leave the l, a, d, d, e, r, hm?

(Annie *ignores him, looking at* Helen; James *goes in too. Imperceptibly the lights commence to narrow down.* Annie *and* Helen *are now alone in the yard,* Helen *seated at the pump, where she has been oblivious to it all, a battered little savage, playing with the doll in a picture of innocent contentment.* Annie *comes near, leans against the house, and taking off her smoked glasses, studies her, not without awe. Presently* Helen *rises, gropes around to see if anyone is present;* Annie *evades her hand, and when* Helen *is satisfied she is alone, the key suddenly protrudes out of her mouth. She takes it in her fingers, stands thinking, gropes to the pump, lifts a loose board, drops the key into the well, and hugs herself gleefully.* Annie *stares. But after a moment she shakes her head; she cannot keep the smile from her lips.*)

Annie. You *devil.*

(Her *tone is one of great respect, humor, and acceptance of challenge.*)

You think I'm so easily gotten rid of? You have a thing or two to learn first. I have nothing else to do.

(*She goes up the steps to the porch, but turns for a final word, almost of warning.*)

And nowhere to go.

(*And presently she moves into the house to the others, as the lights dim down and out, except for the small circle upon* Helen *solitary at the pump, which ends the act.*)

Developing Comprehension Skills

1. What causes Helen's loss of sight and hearing? What is the first clue her parents have that Helen is blind and deaf?

2. What is James's relationship with his father? What relationship does the Captain have with his wife? Find passages that support your answer.

3. How has Helen been treated by the family? What has been the result of this treatment?

4. Are there any indications, or clues, that Helen understands what is wrong with her? How might this add to her problems?

5. What does the family finally decide to do to help Helen? What incident leads to this decision?

6. What was Annie Sullivan's early childhood like? Given her background, are there any aspects of her character that are surprising? Explain.

7. How do the different members of the family first react to Annie? Does each one have reason to feel as he or she does?

8. Why do you think the Kellers have failed to discipline Helen? Based on what you know of Annie so far, do you think she will spoil Helen the way Helen's parents have?

Reading Literature

1. **Understanding a Three-Act Drama.** A dramatic play contains the same five parts of a plot that a short story does:

   Introduction—the characters and setting are introduced; the characters become involved in a conflict.

   Rising Action—the characters struggle with the conflict; tension grows.

   Climax—the action reaches a turning point; often, the main character makes an important discovery or reaches a new understanding.

Falling Action—the conflict is resolved, and events head toward a conclusion.

Resolution, or Dénouement—the story is brought to a close.

In a three-act play, the first act usually serves as an introduction. The second act continues the rising action. The climax, falling action, and resolution are covered in the third act.

How does the first act of *The Miracle Worker* act as an introduction? What information does it provide the reader with? What hints does it give about how the conflict will develop in the second act?

2. **Identifying Conflict.** As you remember, **conflict** is the struggle between the main character and another person or situation. Conflict can also exist between the main character and his or her own thoughts and feelings. What is the major conflict that is introduced in Act One? What other conflicts do Annie Sullivan and the other characters experience? Find examples to support your answers.

3. **Understanding Character.** When Annie Sullivan is first introduced in the play, she is described as "obstinate, impudent, combative," and lacking "the tact or talent to bend to others." Find examples of Annie's behavior that support this statement. What other character traits does Annie display? Are any of them positive? Do you think that Annie's personality will help her deal with Helen's problems, or will it make Annie's work even more difficult?

4. **Analyzing Stage Directions.** Throughout a play the author gives many directions to the performers to help direct their actions on stage. These stage directions are found in parentheses and are usually printed in italic type. Reread some of the stage directions for *The Miracle Worker*. In particular, look at the stage directions in the scenes between Helen and Annie. Why are stage directions especially important in this play? Why would they be most important for the character of Helen Keller?

5. **Appreciating Lighting Effects and Staging.** The author of a play cannot easily reveal a character's thoughts. He or she also cannot easily change settings. However, the author of *The Miracle Worker* used special techniques to do both of these things.

Look at the scene where Annie says goodbye to Mr. Anagnos and her friends at the Perkins School for the Blind. How does the author quickly change settings from the Kellers's house to the school? What happens to the color of the light when Annie begins thinking about her past with her brother Jimmie? How does the author bring Annie back into the present? What happens to the lights then? When does the author use this technique again in Act One?

6. **Understanding the Flashback.** You have seen how the author interrupts the main story to present scenes from Annie's past. This device is called a **flashback**. Why do you suppose the author uses flashbacks in this play? What important information do they provide?

Developing Vocabulary Skills

Using Multiple Meanings. The underlined words in the following sentences from Act One have more than one meaning. In a dictionary, find possible definitions for each word. Use the context to determine which meaning suits the sentence. Write that definition. Then write a sentence that reflects a different meaning of the word.

1. The convention of the staging is one of cutting through time and place, and its essential qualities are fluidity and spatial counterpoint.

2. Call it acute congestion, indeed.

3. The third child is Helen, six and a half years old, quite unkempt, . . .

4. The child's been to specialists all over Alabama and Tennessee.

5. James, very wounded, stalks out of the room onto the porch; he remains here, sulking.

6. Nonsense, the child's a Keller; she has the constitution of a goat. She'll outlive us all.

7. She [Annie] addresses the mirror with the same irony.

8. Annie drops the handkerchief, averts to the window, and is arrested there by the next cry.

9. She's very rough, Katie.

10. The boy's voice is the same; the others are cracked old crones . . .

11. He beams a good night at the baby and Kate, and Keller leads him downstairs with a lamp.

12. (Crisply.) So. You are no longer our pupil;

Developing Writing Skills

1. **Writing an Interior Monologue.** A **monologue** is a speech made by one person. An **interior monologue** is a speech that occurs inside someone's mind.

We learn a great deal about Annie Sullivan from her words, actions, and thoughts in this play. We do not learn as much about the other characters. Imagine that you are a character from the play. You might, for example, choose to be the Captain, James, Mrs. Keller, or Helen herself. Write a paragraph in which you explore your thoughts on the day that Annie Sullivan arrives. You might think about the past, your feelings, about the present situation, or your impressions of the new teacher. Remember that if you choose Helen, her experiences are limited to sensations of touch, taste, and smell.

2. **Preparing To Write a Report.** In the second-act section, you will write a report on Annie Sullivan. Prepare yourself by reading a few general articles on your subject. You may, for example, refer to an encyclopedia or use the *Readers' Guide to Periodical Literature* to find an article about Annie Sullivan's life and accomplishments. Use the information from your general reading to narrow your topic so that it can be covered in a short report. For example, you might choose to report on Annie's years before she met Helen, or on Annie's later career as an author, teacher, and lecturer.

Once you have decided on your topic, write down at least ten questions that you think you or your reader would want answered about the topic. At this point, you are ready to begin your in-depth research. Use the card catalog, the *Readers' Guide*, and reference works to locate books and other material on your subject. Be sure to keep a record of the sources that you use. Take notes on ideas that are related to your narrowed topic. However, don't be afraid to change your topic somewhat if you find something more interesting. As you take notes, follow the guidelines for notetaking presented on page 704. Look at the Critical Thinking activity that follows for help with your next step.

Developing Skills in Critical Thinking

Organizing Your Information. Once you have taken notes for your report, you must organize them. First, make sure that all of your notes are related to your topic. If they are not, delete them.

You should find that most of the remaining information relates to a few main ideas. Identify these main ideas. Now put your note cards into groups, with each group representing one of the main ideas of the report. Then put the groups and the notes within each group in some sort of logical order. Often, chronological order, or time sequence, works well for a report on the life of a person. However, choose an arrangement that works best with your material.

The Miracle Worker

ACT TWO

It is evening.

The only room visible in the Keller *house is* Annie's, *where by lamplight,* Annie *is at a desk writing a letter. At her bureau,* Helen *in her customary unkempt state is tucking her doll in the bottom drawer as a cradle, the contents of which she has dumped out, creating as usual a fine disorder.*

Annie *mutters each word as she writes her letter, slowly, her eyes close to and almost touching the page, to follow with difficulty her penwork.*

Annie. " . . . and, nobody, here, has, attempted, to, control, her. The, greatest, problem, I, have, is, how, to, discipline, her, without, breaking, her, spirit."

(Resolute voice.)

"But, I, shall, insist, on, reasonable, obedience, from, the, start—"

(At which point Helen, *groping about on the desk, knocks over the inkwell.* Annie *jumps up, rescues her letter, rights the inkwell, grabs a towel to stem the spillage, and then wipes at* Helen's *hands;* Helen *as always pulls free, but not until* Annie *first gets three letters into her palm.)*

Ink.

*(Helen *is enough interested in and puzzled by this spelling that she proffers her hand again; so* Annie *spells, and impassively dunks it back in the spillage.)*

Ink. It has a name.

(She wipes the hand clean, and leads Helen *to her bureau, where she looks for something to engage her. She finds a sewing card, with needle and thread, and going to her knees, shows* Helen's *hand how to connect one row of holes.)*

Down. Under. Up. And be careful of the needle—

*(Helen *gets it, and* Annie *rises.)*

Fine. You keep out of the ink, and perhaps I can keep out of—the soup.

(She returns to the desk, tidies it, and resumes writing her letter, bent close to the page.)

"These, blots, are, her, handiwork. I—"

(She is interrupted by a gasp; Helen has stuck her finger, and sits sucking at it, darkly. Then with vengeful resolve she seizes her doll, and is about to dash its brains out on the floor when Annie, diving, catches it in one hand, which she at once shakes with hopping pain but otherwise ignores, patiently.)

All right, let's try temperance.

(Taking the doll, she kneels, goes through the motion of knocking its head on the floor, spells into Helen's hand,)

Bad, girl.

(She lets Helen feel the grieved expression on her face. Helen imitates it. Next she makes Helen caress the doll and kiss the hurt spot and hold it gently in her arms, then spells into her hands,)

Good, girl.

(She lets Helen feel the smile on her face. Helen sits with a scowl, which suddenly clears. She pats the doll, kisses it, wreathes her face in a large, artificial smile, and bears the doll to the washstand, where she carefully sits it. Annie watches, pleased.)

Very good girl—

(Whereupon Helen elevates the pitcher and dashes it on the floor instead. Annie leaps to her feet, and stands inarticulate; Helen calmly gropes back to sit by the sewing card and needle.

Annie manages to achieve self-control. She picks up a fragment or two of the pitcher, sees Helen is puzzling over the card, and resolutely kneels to demonstrate it again. She spells into Helen's hand.

Kate, meanwhile, coming around the corner with folded sheets on her arm, halts at the doorway and watches them for a moment in silence; she is moved, but level.)

Kate (presently). What are you saying to her?

(Annie, glancing up, is a bit embarrassed, and rises from the spelling, to find her company manners.)

Annie. Oh, I was just making conversation. Saying it was a sewing card.

Kate. But does that—

(She imitates with her fingers.)

—mean that to her?

Annie. No. No, she won't know what spelling is till she knows what a word is.

Kate. Yet you keep spelling to her. Why?

Annie (cheerily). I like to hear myself talk!

Kate. The Captain says it's like spelling to the fence post.

Annie (a pause). Does he, now.

Kate. Is it?

Annie. No, it's how I watch you talk to Mildred.

Kate. Mildred.

Annie. Any baby. Gibberish, grown-up gibberish, baby-talk gibberish, do they understand one word of it to start? Somehow they begin to. If they hear it. I'm letting Helen hear it.

Kate. Other children are not—impaired.

Annie. Ho, there's nothing impaired in that head; it works like a mousetrap!

Kate (*smiles*). But after a child hears how many words, Miss Annie, a million?

Annie. I guess no mother's ever minded enough to count.

(*She drops her eyes to spell into* Helen's *hand, again indicating the card;* Helen *spells back, and* Annie *is amused.*)

Kate (*too quickly*). What did she spell?

Annie. I spelt card. She spelt cake!

(*She takes in* Kate's *quickness, and shakes her head, gently.*)

No, it's only a finger-game to her, Mrs. Keller. What she has to learn first is that things have names.

Kate. And when will she learn?

Annie. Maybe after a million and one words.

(*They hold each other's gaze;* Kate *then speaks quietly.*)

Kate. I should like to learn those letters, Miss Annie.

Annie (*pleased*). I'll teach you tomorrow morning. That makes only half a million each!

Kate (*then*). It's her bedtime.

(Annie *reaches for the sewing card.* Helen *objects;* Annie *insists, and* Helen *gets rid of* Annie's *hand by jabbing it with the needle.* Annie *gasps, and moves to grip* Helen's *wrist; but* Kate *intervenes with a proffered sweet, and* Helen *drops the card, crams the sweet into her mouth, and scrambles up to search her mother's hands for more.* Annie *nurses her wound, staring after the sweet.*)

I'm sorry, Miss Annie.

Annie (*Indignantly*). Why does she get a reward? For stabbing me?

Kate. Well—

(*Then tiredly.*)

We catch our flies with honey, I'm afraid. We haven't the heart for much else, and so many times she simply cannot be compelled.

Annie (*ominous*). Yes. I'm the same way myself.

(Kate *smiles, and leads* Helen *off around the corner.* Annie, *alone in her room, picks up things; and in the act of removing* Helen's *doll, gives way to unmannerly temptation. She throttles it. She drops it on her bed, and stands pondering. Then she turns back, sits decisively, and writes again, as the lights dim on her.*) (*Grimly*).

"The, more, I, think, the, more, certain, I, am, that, obedience, is, the, gateway, through, which, knowledge, enters, the, mind, of, the, child—"

(*On the word "obedience" a shaft of sunlight hits the water pump outside, while* Annie's *voice ends in the dark, followed by a distant cockcrow. Daylight comes up over another corner of the sky, with* Viney's *voice heard at once.*)

Viney. Breakfast ready!

(Viney *comes down into the sunlight beam, and pumps a pitcherful of water. While the pitcher is brimming, we hear conversation from the dark. The light grows to the family room of the house, where all are either entering or already seated at breakfast, with* Keller *and* James *arguing the war.* Helen *is wandering around the table to explore the contents of the other plates. When* Annie *is in her chair, she watches* Helen. Viney *re-enters, sets the pitcher on the table;* Kate *lifts the almost empty biscuit plate with an inquiring look;* Viney *nods and bears it off back, neither of them interrupting the men.* Annie, *meanwhile, sits with fork quiet, watching* Helen, *who at her mother's plate, pokes her hand among some scrambled eggs.* Kate *catches* Annie's *eyes on her, smiles with wry gesture.* Helen *moves on to* James's *plate, the male talk continuing,* James *deferential and* Keller *overriding.*)

James. —no, but shouldn't we give the devil his due, Father? The fact is we lost the

South two years earlier when he out-thought us behind Vicksburg.

Keller. Out-thought is a peculiar word for a butcher.

James. Harness maker, wasn't he?

Keller. I said butcher; his only virtue as a soldier was numbers, and he led them to slaughter with no more regard than for so many sheep.

James. But even if in that sense he was a butcher, the fact is he—

Keller. And a drunken one, half the war.

James. Agreed, Father. If his own people said he was, I can't argue he—

Keller. Well, what is it you find to admire in such a man, Jimmie, the butchery or the drunkenness?

James. Neither, Father, only the fact that he beat us.

Keller. He didn't.

James. Is it your contention we won the war, sir?

Keller. He didn't beat us at Vicksburg. We lost Vicksburg because Pemberton gave Bragg five thousand of his cavalry; and Loring, whom I knew personally for a nincompoop before you were born, marched away from Champion's Hill with enough men to have held them. We lost Vicksburg by stupidity verging on treason.

James. I would have said we lost Vicksburg because Grant was one thing no Yankee general was before him—

Keller. Drunk? I doubt it.

James. Obstinate.

Keller. Obstinate. Could any of them compare even in that with old Stonewall? If he'd been there, we would still have Vicksburg.

James. Well, the butcher simply wouldn't give up; he tried four ways of getting around Vicksburg, and on the fifth try he got around. Anyone else would have pulled north and—

Keller. He wouldn't have got around if we'd had a Southerner in command, instead of a half-breed Yankee traitor like Pemberton—

(While this background talk is in progress, Helen *is working around the table, ultimately toward* Annie's *plate. She messes with her hands in* James's *plate, then in* Keller's, *both men taking it so for granted they hardly notice. Then* Helen *comes groping with soiled hands past her own plate, to* Annie's; *her hand goes to it, and* Annie, *who has been waiting, deliberately lifts and removes her hand.* Helen *gropes again.* Annie *firmly pins her by the wrist, and removes her hand from the table.* Helen *thrusts her hands again;* Annie *catches them; and* Helen *begins to flail and make noises. The interruption brings* Keller's *gaze upon them.)*

What's the matter there?

Kate. Miss Annie. You see, she's accustomed to helping herself from our plates to anything she—

Annie *(evenly).* Yes, but *I'm* not accustomed to it.

Keller. No, of course not. Viney!

Kate. Give her something, Jimmie, to quiet her.

James (*blandly*). But her table manners are the best she has. Well.

(*He pokes across with a chunk of bacon at Helen's hand, which Annie releases; but Helen knocks the bacon away and stubbornly thrusts at Annie's plate. Annie grips her wrists again; the struggle mounts.*)

Keller. Let her this time, Miss Sullivan; it's the only way we get any adult conversation. If my son's half merits that description.

(*He rises.*)

I'll get you another plate.

Annie (*gripping Helen*). I have a plate, thank you.

Keller (*at the door*). Viney, bring Miss Sullivan another plate—

Kate (*calling*). Viney! I'm afraid what Captain Keller says is only too true; she'll persist in this until she gets her own way.

Annie (*stonily*). I have a plate; nothing's wrong with the *plate.* I intend to keep it.

(*Silence for a moment, except for Helen's noises as she struggles to get loose. The Kellers are a bit nonplussed, and Annie is too darkly intent on Helen's manners to have any thoughts now of her own.*)

James. Ha. You see why they took Vicksburg?

Keller (*uncertainly*). Miss Sullivan. One plate or another is hardly a matter to struggle with a deprived child about.

Annie. Oh, I'd sooner have a more—

(*Helen begins to kick, Annie moves her ankles to the opposite side of the chair.*)

—heroic issue myself, I—

Keller. No, I really must insist you—

(*Helen bangs her toe on the chair and sinks to the floor, crying with rage and feigned injury. Annie keeps hold of her wrists, gazing down, while Kate rises.*)

Now she's hurt herself.

Annie (*grimly*). No, she hasn't.

Keller. Will you please let her hands go?

Kate. Miss Annie, you don't know the child well enough yet, she'll keep—

Annie. I know an ordinary tantrum well enough, when I see one, and a badly spoiled child—

James. Hear, hear.

Keller (*very annoyed*). Miss Sullivan! You would have more understanding of your pupil if you had some pity in you. Now kindly do as I—

Annie. Pity?

(*She releases Helen to turn equally annoyed on Keller across the table. Instantly Helen scrambles up and dives at Annie's plate. This time Annie intercepts her by pouncing on her wrists like a hawk, and her temper boils.*)

For this *tyrant*? The whole house turns on her whims. Is there anything she wants she doesn't get? I'll tell you what I pity, that the sun won't rise and set for her all her life, and every day you're telling her it will. What good will your pity do her when you're under the strawberries, Captain Keller?

Keller (*outraged*). Kate, for the love of heaven will you—

Kate. Miss Annie, please, I don't think it serves to lose our—

Annie. It does you good, that's all. It's less trouble to feel sorry for her than to teach her anything better, isn't it?

Keller. I fail to see where you have taught her anything yet, Miss Sullivan!

Annie. I'll begin this minute, if you'll leave the room, Captain Keller!

Keller (*astonished*). Leave the—

Annie. Everyone, please.

(*She struggles with* Helen, *while* Keller *endeavors to control his voice.*)

Keller. Miss Sullivan, you are here only as a paid teacher. Nothing more, and not to lecture—

Annie. I can't *unteach* her six years of pity if you can't stand up to one tantrum! Old Stonewall, indeed. Mrs. Keller, you promised me help.

Kate. Indeed I did, we truly want to—

Annie. Then leave me alone with her. Now!

Keller (*in a wrath*). Katie, will you come outside with me? At once, please.

(*He marches to the front door.* Kate *and* James *follow him. Simultaneously* Annie *releases* Helen's *wrists, and the child again sinks to the floor, kicking and crying her weird noises.* Annie *steps over her to meet* Viney *coming in the rear doorway with biscuits and a clean plate, surprised at the general commotion.*)

Viney. Heaven sakes—

Annie. Out, please.

(*She backs* Viney *out with one hand, closes the door on her astonished mouth, locks it, and removes the key.* Keller, *meanwhile, snatches his hat from a rack, and* Kate *follows him down the porch steps.* James *lingers in the doorway to address* Annie *across the room with a bow.*)

James. If it takes all summer, general.

(Annie *comes over to his door in turn, removing her glasses grimly. As* Keller *outside begins speaking,* Annie *closes the door on* James, *locks it, removes the key, and turns with her back against the door to stare ominously at* Helen, *kicking on the floor.*

James *takes his hat from the rack, and going down the porch steps, joins* Kate *and* Keller *talking in the yard,* Keller *in a sputter of ire.*)

Keller. This girl, this—cub of a girl— presumes! I tell you, I'm half a mind to ship her back to Boston before the week is out. You can inform her so from me!

Kate (*eyebrows up*). I, Captain?

Keller. She's a *hireling!* Now I want it clear, unless there's an apology and complete change of manner, she goes back on the next train! Will you make that quite clear?

Kate. Where will you be, Captain, while I am making it quite—

Keller. At the office!

(*He begins off left, finds his napkin still in his irate hand, is uncertain with it, dabs his lips with dignity, gets rid of it in a toss to* James, *and marches off.* James *turns to eye* Kate.)

James. Will you?

(Kate's *mouth is set, and* James *studies it lightly.*)

I thought what she said was exceptionally intelligent. I've been saying it for years.

Kate (*not without scorn*). To his face?

(*She comes to relieve him of the white napkin, but reverts again with it.*)

Or will you take it, Jimmie? As a flag?

(James *stalks out, much offended; and* Kate, *turning, stares across the yard at the house. The lights narrowing down to the following pantomime in the family room, leave her motionless in the dark.*

Annie, *meanwhile, has begun by slapping both keys down on a shelf out of* Helen's *reach. She returns to the table, upstage.* Helen's *kicking has subsided, and when from the floor her hand finds* Annie's *chair empty, she pauses.* Annie *clears the table of* Kate's, James's, *and* Keller's *plates. She gets back to her own across the table just in time to slide it deftly away from* Helen's *pouncing hand. She lifts the hand and moves it to* Helen's *plate, and after an instant's exploration,* Helen *sits again on the floor and drums her heels.* Annie *comes around the table and resumes her chair. When* Helen *feels her*

skirt again, she ceases kicking, waits for whatever is to come, renews some kicking, waits again.* Annie, *retrieving her plate, takes up a forkful of food, stops it halfway to her mouth, gazes at it devoid of appetite, and half-lowers it; but after a look at* Helen *she sighs, dips the forkful toward* Helen *in a for-your-sake toast, and puts it in her own mouth to chew, not without an effort.*

Helen *now gets hold of the chair leg, and half-succeeds in pulling the chair out from under her.* Annie *bangs it down with her rear, heavily, and sits with all her weight.* Helen's *next attempt to topple it is unavailing, so her fingers dive in a pinch at* Annie's *flank.* Annie, *in the middle of her mouthful, almost loses it with startle, and she slaps down her fork to round on* Helen. *The child comes up with curiosity to feel what* Annie *is doing, so* Annie *resumes eating, letting* Helen's *hand follow the movement of her fork to her mouth; whereupon* Helen *at once reaches into* Annie's *plate.* Annie *firmly removes her hand to her own plate.* Helen *in reply pinches* Annie's *thigh, a good, mean pinchful that makes* Annie *jump.* Annie *sets the fork down, and sits with her mouth tight.* Helen *digs another pinch into her thigh, and this time* Annie *slaps her hand smartly away.* Helen *retaliates with a roundhouse fist that catches* Annie *on the ear, and* Annie's *hand leaps at once in a forceful slap across* Helen's *cheek.* Helen *is the startled one now.* Annie's *hand in compunction falters to her own face, but when* Helen *hits at her again,* Annie *deliberately slaps her again.* Helen *lifts her fist irresolute for another roundhouse;* Annie *lifts her hand resolute for another slap; and they freeze in this posture, while* Helen *mulls it over. She thinks better of it, drops her fist, and giving* Annie *a wide berth, gropes around to her* Mother's *chair, to find it empty. She blunders her way along the table upstage, and encountering the empty chairs and missing plates, she looks bewildered. She gropes back to her* Mother's *chair, again touches her cheek and indicates the chair, and waits for the world to answer.*

Annie *now reaches over to spell into her hand, but* Helen *yanks it away. She gropes to the front door, tries the knob, and finds the door locked, with no key. She gropes to the rear door, and finds it locked, with no key. She commences to bang on it.* Annie *rises, crosses, takes her wrists, draws her resisting back to the table, seats her, and releases her hands upon her plate. As* Annie *herself begins to sit,* Helen *writhes out of her chair, runs to the front door, and tugs and kicks at it.* Annie *rises again, crosses, draws her by one wrist back to the table, seats her, and sits.* Helen *escapes back to the door, knocking over her* Mother's *chair en route.* Annie *rises again in pursuit, and this time lifts* Helen *bodily from behind and bears her kicking to her chair. She deposits her, and once more turns to sit.* Helen *scrambles out, but as she passes,* Annie *catches her up again from behind and deposits her in the chair.* Helen *scrambles out on the other side, for the rear door, but* Annie *at her heels catches her up and deposits her again in the chair. She stands behind it.* Helen *scrambles out to her right, and the instant her feet hit the floor,* Annie *lifts and deposits her back. She scrambles out to her left, and is at once lifted and deposited back. She tries right again and is deposited back, and tries left again and is deposited back; and now feints* Annie *to the right but is off to her left, and is promptly deposited back. She sits a moment,*

and then starts straight over the tabletop, dishware notwithstanding. Annie *hauls her in and deposits her back, with her plate spilling in her lap, and she melts to the floor and crawls under the table, laborious among its legs and chairs; but* Annie *is swift around the table and waiting on the other side when she surfaces, immediately bearing her aloft.* Helen *clutches at* James's *chair for anchorage, but it comes with her, and halfway back she abandons it to the floor.* Annie *deposits her in her chair and waits.* Helen *sits tensed motionless. Then she tentatively puts out her left foot and hand,* Annie *interposes her own hand, and at the contact* Helen *jerks hers in. She tries her right foot;* Annie *blocks it with her own, and* Helen *jerks hers in. Finally, leaning back, she slumps down in her chair, in a sullen biding.*

Annie *backs off a step, and watches;* Helen *offers no move.* Annie *takes a deep breath. Both of them and the room are in considerable disorder, two chairs down and the table a mess, but* Annie *makes no effort to tidy it; she only sits on her own chair, and lets her energy refill. Then she takes up knife and fork, and resolutely addresses her food.* Helen's *hand comes out to explore, and seeing it,* Annie *sits without moving. The child's hand goes over her hand and fork, pauses—*Annie *still does not move—and withdraws. Presently it moves for her own plate, slaps about for it, and stops, thwarted. At this,* Annie *again rises, recovers* Helen's *plate from the floor and a handful of scattered food from the deranged tablecloth, drops it on the plate, and pushes the plate into contact with* Helen's *fist. Neither of them now moves for a pregnant moment—until* Helen *suddenly takes a grab of food and wolfs it down.* Annie *permits herself the humor of a minor bow and* *warming her hands together; she wanders off a step or two, watching.* Helen *cleans up the plate.*

After a glower of indecision, she holds the empty plate out for more. Annie *accepts it, and crossing to the removed plates, spoons food from them onto it. She stands debating the spoon, tapping it a few times on* Helen's *plate; and when she returns with the plate, she brings the spoon, too. She puts the spoon first into* Helen's *hand, then sets the plate down.* Helen, *discarding the spoon, reaches with her hand, and* Annie *stops it by the wrist; she replaces the spoon in it.* Helen *impatiently discards it again, and again* Annie *stops her hand, to replace the spoon in it. This time* Helen *throws the spoon on the floor.* Annie, *after considering it, lifts* Helen *bodily out of the chair; and in a wrestling match on the floor, closes her fingers upon the spoon, and returns her with it to the chair.* Helen *again throws the spoon on the floor.* Annie *lifts her out of the chair again; but in the struggle over the spoon* Helen, *with* Annie *on her back, sends her sliding over her head.* Helen *flees back to her chair and scrambles into it. When* Annie *comes after her, she clutches it for dear life.* Annie *pries one hand loose, then the other, then the first again, then the other again, and then lifts* Helen *by the waist, chair and all, and shakes the chair loose.* Helen *wrestles to get free, but* Annie *pins her to the floor, closes her fingers upon the spoon, and lifts her kicking under one arm. With her other hand, she gets the chair in place again, and plunks* Helen *back on it. When she releases her hand,* Helen *throws the spoon at her.*

Annie *now removes the plate of food.* Helen, *grabbing, finds it missing, and commences to bang with her fists on the table.* Annie *collects a fistful of spoons and descends with them and the plate on* Helen; *she lets her smell the plate, at which* Helen *ceases banging, and* Annie *puts the plate down and a spoon in* Helen's *hand.* Helen *throws it on the floor.* Annie *puts another spoon in her hand.* Helen *throws it on the floor.* Annie *puts another spoon in her hand.* Helen *throws it on the floor. When* Annie *comes to her last spoon she sits next to* Helen, *and gripping the spoon in* Helen's *hand compels her to take food in it up to her mouth.* Helen *sits with lips shut.* Annie *waits a stolid moment, then lowers* Helen's *hand. She tries again;* Helen's *lips remain shut.* Annie *waits, lowers* Helen's *hand. She tries again; this time* Helen *suddenly opens her mouth and accepts the food.* Annie *lowers the spoon with a sigh of relief, and* Helen *spews the mouthful out at her face.* Annie *sits a moment with eyes closed, then takes the pitcher and dashes its water into* Helen's *face, who gasps astonished.* Annie, *with* Helen's *hand, takes up another spoonful, and shoves it into her open mouth.* Helen *swallows involuntarily, and while she is catching her breath,* Annie *forces her palm open, throws four swift letters into it, then another*

four, and bows toward her with devastating pleasantness.)

Annie. Good girl.

(Annie *lifts* Helen's *hand to feel her face, nodding;* Helen *grabs a fistful of her hair, and yanks. The pain brings* Annie *to her knees, and* Helen *pummels her. They roll under the table, and the lights commence to dim out on them.*

Simultaneously the light at left has been rising, slowly, so slowly that it seems at first we only imagine what is intimated in the yard: a few ghostlike figures, in silence, motionless, waiting. Now the distant belfry chimes commence to toll the hour, also very slowly, almost—it is twelve—interminably; the sense is that of a long time passing. We can identify the figures before the twelfth stroke, all facing the house in a kind of watch: Kate *is standing exactly as before, but now with the baby* Mildred *sleeping in her arms; and placed here and there, unmoving, are* Aunt Ev *in her hat with a hanky to her nose, and the two black children,* Percy *and* Martha *with necks outstretched eagerly, and* Viney *with a knotted kerchief on her head and a feather duster in her hand.*

The chimes cease, and there is silence. For a long moment, none of the group moves.)

Viney *(presently).* What am I gone do, Miss Kate? It's noontime; dinner's comin'; I didn't get them breakfast dishes out of there yet.

(Kate *says nothing, stares at the house,* Martha *shifts* Helen's *doll in her clutch, and it plaintively says* momma.)

Kate *(presently).* You run along, Martha.

(Aunt Ev *blows her nose.)*

Aunt Ev (*wretchedly*). I can't wait out here a minute longer, Kate. Why, this could go on all afternoon, too.

Kate. I'll tell the Captain you called.

Viney (*to the children*). You hear what Miss Kate say? Never you mind what's going on here.

(*Still no one moves.*)

You run along, tend your own bizness.

(*Finally* Viney *turns on the children with the feather duster.*)

Shoo!

(*The two children divide before her. She chases them off.* Aunt Ev *comes to* Kate, *in her dignity.*)

Aunt Ev. Say what you like, Kate, but that child is a *Keller*.

(*She opens her parasol, preparatory to leaving.*)

I needn't remind you that all the Kellers are cousins to General Robert E. Lee. I don't know *who* that girl is.

(*She waits; but* Kate, *staring at the house, is without response*).

The only Sullivan I've heard of—from Boston too, and I'd think twice before locking her up with that kind—is that man John L.[1]

(*And* Aunt Ev *departs, with head high. Presently* Viney *comes to* Kate, *her arms out for the baby.*)

---

1. **John L.**, a reference to John L. Sullivan, world heavyweight boxing champion during the 1880's.

Viney. You give me her, Miss Kate; I'll sneak her in back, to her crib.

(*But* Kate *is moveless, until* Viney *starts to take the baby;* Kate *looks down at her before relinquishing her.*)

Kate (*slowly*). This child never gives me a minute's worry.

Viney. Oh yes, this one's the angel of the family, no question bout *that*.

(*She begins off rear with the baby, heading around the house; and* Kate *now turns her back on it, her hand to her eyes. At this moment there is the slamming of a door, and when* Kate *wheels,* Helen *is blundering down the porch steps into the light, like a ruined bat.* Viney *halts, and* Kate *runs in.* Helen *collides with her mother's knees, and reels off and back to clutch them as her savior.* Annie, *with smoked glasses in hand, stands on the porch, also much undone, looking as though she had indeed just taken Vicksburg.* Kate, *taking in* Helen's *ravaged state, becomes steely in her gaze up at* Annie.)

Kate. What happened?

(Annie *meets* Kate's *gaze, and gives a factual report, too exhausted for anything but a flat voice.*)

Annie. She ate from her own plate.

(*She thinks a moment.*)

She ate with a spoon. Herself.

(Kate *frowns, uncertain with thought, and glances down at* Helen.)

And she folded her napkin.

(Kate's *gaze now wavers, from* Helen *to* Annie, *and back.*)

Kate (*softly*). Folded—her napkin?

Annie. The room's a wreck, but her napkin is folded.

(*She pauses, then,*)

I'll be in my room, Mrs. Keller.

(*She moves to re-enter the house; but she stops at* Viney's *voice.*)

Viney (*cheery*). Don't be long, Miss Annie. Dinner be ready right away!

(Viney *carries* Mildred *around the back of the house.* Annie *stands unmoving, takes a deep breath, stares over her shoulder at* Kate *and* Helen; *then inclines her head graciously, and goes with a slight stagger into the house. The lights in her room above steal up in readiness for her.*
Kate *remains alone with* Helen *in the yard, standing protectively over her, in a kind of wonder.*)

Kate (*slowly*). Folded her napkin.

(*She contemplates the wild head in her thighs, and moves her fingertips over it, with such a tenderness, and something like a fear of its strangeness, that her own eyes close. She whispers, bending to it,*)

My Helen—folded her napkin—

(*And still erect, with only her head in surrender,* Kate *for the first time that we see, loses her protracted war with grief; but she will not let a sound escape her, only the grimace of tears comes, and sobs that shake her in a grip of*

silence. But Helen *feels them, and her hand comes up in its own wondering, to interrogate her mother's face, until* Kate *buries her lips in the child's palm.*

Upstairs, Annie *enters her room, closes the door, and stands back against it. The lights, growing on her with their special color, commence to fade on* Kate *and* Helen. *Then* Annie *goes wearily to her suitcase, and lifts it to take it toward the bed. But it knocks an object to the floor, and she turns back to regard it. A new voice comes in a cultured murmur, hesitant as with the effort of remembering a text,*)

Man's Voice. This—soul—

(Annie *puts the suitcase down, and kneels to the object. It is the battered Perkins report, and she stands with it in her hand, letting memory try to speak,*)

This—blind, deaf, mute—woman—

(Annie *sits on her bed, opens the book, and finding the passage, brings it up an inch from her eyes to read, her face and lips following the overheard words, the voice quite factual now.*)

Can nothing be done to disinter this human soul? The whole neighborhood would rush to save this woman if she were buried alive by the caving in of a pit, and labor with zeal until she were dug out. Now, if there were one who had as much patience as zeal, he might awaken her to a consciousness of her immortal—

(*When the boy's voice comes,* Annie *closes her eyes, in pain.*)

Boy's Voice. Annie? Annie, you there?

Annie. Hush.

Boy's Voice. Annie, what's that noise?

(Annie *tries not to answer; her own voice is drawn out of her, unwilling.*)

Annie. Just a cot, Jimmie.

Boy's Voice. Where they pushin' it?

Annie. To the deadhouse.

Boy's Voice. Annie. Does it hurt, to be dead?

(Annie *escapes by opening her eyes; her hand works restlessly over her cheek. She retreats into the book again, but the cracked old crones interrupt, whispering. Annie slowly lowers the book.*)

First Crone's Voice. There is schools.

Second Crone's Voice. There is schools outside—

Third Crone's Voice. —schools where they teach blind ones, worse'n you—

First Crone's Voice. To read—

Second Crone's Voice. To read and write—

Third Crone's Voice. There is schools outside where they—

First Crone's Voice. There is schools—

(*Silence.* Annie *sits with her eyes shining, her hand almost in a caress over the book. Then,*)

Boy's Voice. You ain't goin' to school, are you, Annie?

Annie (*whispering*). When I grow up.

Boy's Voice. You ain't either, Annie. You're goin' to stay here take care of me.

Annie. I'm goin' to school when I grow up.

Boy's Voice. You said we'll be together, forever and ever and ever—

Annie (*fierce*). I'm goin' to school when I grow up!

Doctor's Voice (*slowly*). Little girl. Little girl, I must tell you. Your brother will be going on a journey, soon.

(Annie *sits rigid, in silence. Then the boy's voice pierces it, a shriek of terror.*)

Boy's Voice. *Annie!*

(*It goes into* Annie *like a sword; she doubles onto it. The book falls to the floor. It takes her a racked moment to find herself and what she was engaged in here. When she sees the suitcase she remembers, and lifts it once again toward the bed. But the voices are with her, as she halts with suitcase in hand.*)

First Crone's Voice. Goodbye, Annie.

Doctor's Voice. Write me when you learn how.

Second Crone's Voice. Don't tell anyone you came from here. Don't tell anyone—

Third Crone's Voice. Yeah, don't tell anyone you come from—

First Crone's Voice. Yeah, don't tell anyone—

Second Crone's voice. Don't tell any—

(*The echoing voices fade. After a moment,* Annie *lays the suitcase on the bed; and the last voice comes faintly, from far away.*)

Boy's Voice. Annie. It hurts, to be dead. Forever.

(Annie *falls to her knees by the bed, stifling her mouth in it. When at last she rolls blindly away from it, her palm comes down on the open report. She opens her eyes, regards it dully, and then, still on her knees, takes in the print.*)

Man's Voice (*factual*). —might awaken her to a consciousness of her immortal nature. The chance is small indeed; but with a smaller chance they would have dug desperately for her in the pit; and is the life of the soul of less importance than that of the body?

(Annie *gets to her feet. She drops the book on the bed, and pauses over her suitcase; after a moment, she unclasps and opens it. Standing before it, she comes to her decision. She at once turns to the bureau, and taking her things out of its drawers, commences to throw them into the open suitcase.*

In the darkness down left, a hand strikes a match, and lights a hanging oil lamp. It is Keller's *hand, and his voice accompanies it, very angry. The lights rising here before they fade on* Annie, *show* Keller *and* Kate *inside a suggestion of a garden house, with a bay-window seat towards center and a door at back.*)

Keller. Katie, I will not *have* it! Now you did not see when that girl after supper tonight went to look for Helen in her room—

Kate. No.

Keller. The child practically climbed out of her window to escape from her! What kind of teacher *is* she? I thought I had seen her at her worst this morning, shouting at me, but I come home to find the entire house disorganized by her—Helen won't stay one sec-

ond in the same room, won't come to the table with her, won't let herself be bathed or undressed or put to bed by her, or even by Viney now; and the end result is that you have to do more for the child than before we hired this girl's services! From the moment she stepped off the train, she's been nothing but a burden, incompetent, impertinent, ineffectual, immodest—

Kate. She folded her napkin, Captain.

Keller. What?

Kate. Not ineffectual. Helen did fold her napkin.

Keller. What in heaven's name is so extraordinary about folding a napkin?

Kate (*with some humor*). Well. It's more than you did, Captain.

Keller. Katie, I did not bring you all the way out here to the garden house to be frivolous. Now, how does Miss Sullivan propose to teach a deaf-blind pupil who won't let her even touch her?

Kate (*a pause*). I don't know.

Keller. The fact is, today she scuttled any chance she ever had of getting along with the child. If you can see any point or purpose to her staying on here longer, it's more than—

Kate. What do you wish me to do?

Keller. I want you to give her notice.

Kate. I can't.

Keller. Then if you won't, I must. I simply will not—

(He is interrupted by a knock at the back door. Keller, *after a glance at* Kate, *moves to open the door.* Annie, *in her smoked glasses, is standing outside.* Keller *contemplates her heavily.)*

Miss Sullivan.

Annie. Captain Keller.

(She is nervous, keyed up to seizing the bull by the horns again, and she assumes a cheeriness which is not unshaky.)

Viney said I'd find you both over here in the garden house. I thought we should—have a talk?

Keller *(reluctantly).* Yes, I— Well, come in.

(Annie enters, and is interested in this room; she rounds on her heel, anxiously, studying it. Keller *turns the matter over to* Kate, *sotto voce.)*

Katie.

Kate *(turning it back, courteously).* Captain.

(Keller clears his throat, makes ready.)

Keller. I, ah—wanted first to make my position clear to Mrs. Keller, in private. I have decided I—am not satisfied—in fact, am deeply dissatisfied—with the manner in which—

Annie *(intent).* Excuse me, is this little house ever in use?

Keller *(with patience).* In the hunting season. If you will give me your attention, Miss Sullivan.

(Annie turns her smoked glasses upon him; they hold his unwilling stare.)

I have tried to make allowances for you because you come from a part of the country where people are—women, I should say—come from who—well, for whom—

(It begins to elude him.)

allowances must—be made. I have decided, nevertheless, to—that is, decided I—

(Vexedly.)

Miss Sullivan, I find it difficult to talk through those glasses.

Annie *(eagerly, removing them).* Oh, of course.

Keller *(dourly).* Why do you wear them, the sun has been down for an hour.

Annie *(pleasantly, at the lamp).* Any kind of light hurts my eyes.

(A silence; Keller *ponders her, heavily.)*

Keller. Put them on. Miss Sullivan, I have decided to—give you another chance.

Annie *(cheerfully).* To do what?

Keller. To—remain in our employ.

(Annie's eyes widen.)

But on two conditions. I am not accustomed to rudeness in servants or women, and that is the first. If you are to stay, there must be a radical change of manner.

Annie *(a pause).* Whose?

Keller *(exploding).* Yours, young lady, isn't it obvious? And the second is that you persuade me there's the slightest hope of your teaching a child who flees from you now like the plague, to anyone else she can find in this house.

Annie (*a pause*). There isn't.

(Kate *stops sewing, and fixes her eyes upon* Annie.)

Kate. What, Miss Annie?

Annie. It's hopeless here. I can't teach a child who runs away.

Keller (*nonplussed*). Then—do I understand you—propose—

Annie. Well, if we all agree it's hopeless, the next question is what—

Kate. Miss Annie.

(*She is leaning toward* Annie, *in deadly earnest; it commands both* Annie *and* Keller.)

I am not agreed. I think perhaps you—underestimate Helen.

Annie. I think everybody else here does.

Kate. She did fold her napkin. She learns, she learns. Do you know she began talking when she was six months old? She could say "water." Not really—"wahwah." "Wahwah," but she meant water. She knew what it meant, and only six months old; I never saw a child so—bright, or outgoing—

(*Her voice is unsteady, but she gets it level.*)

It's still in her, somewhere, isn't it? You should have seen her before her illness, such a good-tempered child—

Annie (*agreeably*). She's changed.

(*A pause,* Kate *not letting her eyes go; her appeal at last is unconditional, and very quiet.*)

Kate. Miss Annie, put up with it. And with us.

Keller. Us!

Kate. Please? Like the lost lamb in the parable, I love her all the more.

Annie. Mrs. Keller, I don't think Helen's worst handicap is deafness or blindness. I think it's your love. And pity.

Keller. Now what does that mean?

Annie. All of you here are so sorry for her you've kept her—like a pet, why, even a dog you housebreak. No wonder she won't let me come near her. It's useless for me to try to teach her language or anything else here. I might as well—

Kate (*cuts in*). Miss Annie, before you came we spoke of putting her in an asylum.

(Annie *turns back to regard her. A pause.*)

Annie. What kind of asylum?

Keller. For mental defectives.

Kate. I visited there, I can't tell you what I saw, people like—animals, with—*rats* in the halls, and—

(*She shakes her head on her vision.*)

What else are we to do, if you give up?

Annie. Give up?

Kate. You said it was hopeless.

Annie. Here. Give up, why, I only today saw what has to be done, to begin!

(She glances from Kate *to* Keller, *who stare, waiting; and she makes it as plain and simple as her nervousness permits.)*

I—want complete charge of her.

Keller. You already have that. It has resulted in—

Annie. No, I mean day and night. She has to be dependent on me.

Kate. For what?

Annie. Everything. The food she eats, the clothes she wears, fresh—

(She is amused at herself, though very serious.)

—air, yes, the air she breathes, whatever her body needs is a—primer, to teach her out of. It's the only way; the one who lets her have it should be her teacher.

(She considers them in turn; they digest it, Keller *frowning,* Kate *perplexed.)*

Not anyone who *loves* her. You have so many feelings they fall over each other like feet. You won't use your chances and you won't let me.

Kate. But if she runs from you—*to* us—

Annie. Yes, that's the point. I'll have to live with her somewhere else.

Keller. What!

Annie. Till she learns to depend on and listen to me.

Kate *(not without alarm).* For how long?

Annie. As long as it takes.

(A pause. She takes a breath.)

I packed half my things already.

Keller. Miss—Sullivan!

(But when Annie *attends upon him, he is speechless, and she is merely earnest.)*

Annie. Captain Keller, it meets both your conditions. It's the one way I can get back in touch with Helen, and I don't see how I can be rude to you again if you're not around to interfere with me.

Keller *(red-faced).* And what is your intention if I say no? Pack the other half, for home, and abandon your charge to—to—

Annie. The asylum?

(She waits, appraises Keller's *glare and* Kate's *uncertainty, and decides to use her weapons.)*

I grew up in such an asylum. The state almshouse.

*(*Kate's *head comes up on this, and* Keller *stares hard;* Annie's *tone is cheerful enough, albeit level as gunfire.)*

Rats—why, my brother Jimmie and I used to play with the rats because we didn't have toys. Maybe you'd like to know what Helen will find there, not on visiting days? One ward was full of the—old women, crippled, blind, most of them dying; but even if what they had was catching, there was nowhere else to move them; and that's where they put us. There were younger ones across the hall, with T.B., and epileptic fits, and some insane. The youngest were in another ward to have babies they didn't want; they started at thirteen, fourteen. They'd leave afterwards, but the babies stayed, and we played with them, too, but not many of them lived. The first year we had eighty; seventy died. The room Jimmie and I played in was the deadhouse, where they kept the bodies till they could dig—

Kate (*closes her eyes*). Oh, my dear—

Annie. —the graves.

(*She is immune to* Kate's *compassion.*)

No, it made me strong. But I don't think you need send Helen there. She's strong enough.

(*She waits again; but when neither offers her a word, she simply concludes.*)

No, I have no conditions, Captain Keller.

Kate (*not looking up*). Miss Annie.

Annie. Yes.

Kate (*a pause*). Where would you—take Helen?

Annie. Ohh—

(*Brightly*)

Italy?

Keller (*wheeling*). What?

Annie. Can't have everything. How would this garden house do? Furnish it, bring Helen here after a long ride so she won't recognize it, and you can see her every day. If she doesn't know. Well?

Kate (*a sigh of relief*). Is that all?

Annie. That's all.

Kate. Captain.

(Keller *turns his head; and* Kate's *request is quiet but firm.*)

With your permission?

Keller (*teeth in cigar*). Why must she depend on you for the food she eats?

Annie (*a pause*). I want control of it.

Keller. Why?

Annie. It's a way to reach her.

Keller (*stares*). You intend to *starve* her into letting you touch her?

Annie. She won't starve; she'll learn. All's fair in love and war. Captain Keller, you never cut supplies?

Keller. This is hardly a war!

Annie. Well, it's not love. A siege is a siege.

Keller (*heavily*). Miss Sullivan. Do you *like* the child?

Annie (*straight in his eyes*). Do you?

(*A long pause.*)

Kate. You could have a servant here—

Annie (*amused*). I'll have enough work without looking after a servant! But the boy Percy could sleep here, run errands—

Kate (*also amused*). We can let Percy sleep here, I think, Captain?

Annie (*eagerly*). And some old furniture, all our own—

Kate (*also eager*). Captain? Do you think that walnut bedstead in the barn would be too—

Keller. I have not yet consented to Percy! Or to the house, or to the proposal! Or to Miss Sullivan's—staying on when I—

(*But he erupts in an irate surrender.*)

Very well, I consent to everything!

(*He shakes his cigar at* Annie.)

For two weeks. I'll give you two weeks in this place, and it will be a miracle if you get the child to tolerate you.

Kate. Two weeks? Miss Annie, can you accomplish anything in two weeks?

Keller. Anything or not, two weeks; then the child comes back to us. Make up your mind, Miss Sullivan, yes or no?

Annie. Two weeks. For only one miracle?

(*She nods at him, nervously.*)

I'll get her to tolerate me.

(Keller *marches out, and slams the door.* Kate *on her feet regards* Annie, *who is facing the door.*)

Kate (*then*). You can't think as little of love as you said.

(Annie *glances questioning.*)

Or you wouldn't stay.

Annie (*a pause*). I didn't come here for love. I came for money!

(Kate *shakes her head to this, with a smile; after a moment, she extends her open hand.* Annie *looks at it, but when she puts hers out it is not to shake hands, it is to set her fist in* Kate's *palm.*)

Kate (*puzzled*). Hm?

Annie. A. It's the first of many. Twenty-six!

(Kate *squeezes her fist, squeezes it hard, and hastens out after* Keller. Annie *stands as the door closes behind her, her manner so apprehensive that finally she slaps her brow, holds it, sighs, and, with her eyes closed, crosses herself for luck.*

The lights dim into a cool silhouette scene around her, the lamp paling out, and now, in formal entrances, persons appear around Annie *with furniture for the room.* Percy *crosses the stage with a rocking chair and waits.* Martha, *from another direction, bears in a stool.* Viney *bears in a small table, and the other black servant rolls in a bed partway from left; and* Annie, *opening her eyes to put her glasses back on, sees them. She turns around in the room once, and goes into action, pointing out locations for each article. The servants place them and leave, and* Annie *then darts around, interchanging them. In the midst of this—while* Percy *and* Martha *reappear with a tray of food and a chair, respectively—*James *comes down from the house with* Annie's *suitcase, and stands viewing the room and her quizzically;* Annie *halts abruptly under his eyes, embarrassed, then seizes the suitcase from his hand, explaining herself brightly.*)

Annie. I always wanted to live in a doll's house!

(*She sets the suitcase out of the way, and continues.* Viney *at left appears to position a rod with drapes for a doorway, and the other servant at center pushes in a wheelbarrow loaded with a couple of boxes of* Helen's *toys and clothes.* Annie *helps lift them into the*

The garden house where Annie and Helen spent two weeks. American Foundation for the Blind, New York.

room, and the servant pushes the wheelbarrow off. In none of this is any heed taken of the imaginary walls of the garden house. The furniture is moved in from every side, and itself defines the walls.

Annie *now drags the box of toys into center, props up the doll conspicuously on top. With the people melted away, except for* James, *all is again still. The lights turn again without pause, rising warmer.)*

James. You don't let go of things easily, do you? How will you—win her hand now, in this place?

Annie *(curtly).* Do I know? I lost my temper, and here we are!

James *(lightly).* No touching, no teaching. Of course, you *are* bigger—

Annie. I'm not counting on force; I'm counting on her. That little imp is dying to know.

James. Know what?

Annie. Anything. Any and every crumb in God's creation. I'll have to use that appetite too.

(She gives the room a final survey, straightens the bed, arranges the curtain.)

James *(a pause)*. Maybe she'll teach you.

Annie. Of course.

James. That she isn't. That there's such a thing as—dullness of heart. Acceptance. And letting go. Sooner or later we all give up, don't we?

Annie. Maybe you all do. It's my idea of the original sin.

James. What is?

Annie *(witheringly)*. Giving up.

James *(nettled)*. You won't open her. Why can't you let her be? Have some—pity on her, for being what she is—

Annie. If I'd ever once thought like that, I'd be dead!

James *(pleasantly)*. You will be. Why trouble?

(Annie turns to glare at him; he is mocking.)

Or will you teach me?

(And with a bow, he drifts off.
Now in the distance there comes the clopping of hoofs, drawing near, and nearer, up to the door; and they halt. Annie wheels to face the door. When it opens this time, the Kellers—Kate in traveling bonnet, Keller also hatted—are standing there with Helen between them; she is in a cloak. Kate gently cues her into the room. Helen comes in groping, baffled, but interested in the new surroundings; Annie evades her exploring hand, her gaze not leaving the child.)

Annie. Does she know where she is?

Kate *(shakes her head)*. We rode her out in the country for two hours.

Keller. For all she knows, she could be in another town—

(Helen stumbles over the box on the floor, and in it discovers her doll and other battered toys, is pleased, sits by them, then becomes puzzled and suddenly very wary. She scrambles up and back to her mother's thighs; but Annie steps in, and it is hers that Helen embraces. Helen recoils, gropes, and touches her cheek instantly.)

Kate. That's her sign for me.

Annie. I know.

(Helen waits, then recommences her groping, more urgently. Kate stands indecisive, and takes an abrupt step toward her, but Annie's hand is a barrier.)

In two weeks.

Kate. Miss Annie, I—Please be good to her. These two weeks, try to be very good to her—

Annie. I will.

(Kate, turning then, hurries out. The Kellers cross back to the main house.
Annie closes the door. Helen starts toward the door jamb, and rushes it. Annie holds her off. Helen kicks her, breaks free, and careens around the room like an imprisoned bird, colliding with furniture, groping wildly repeatedly touching her cheek in a growing panic. When she has covered the room, she commences her weird screaming. Annie moves

to comfort her, but her touch sends Helen *into a paroxysm of rage. She tears away, falls over her box of toys, flings its contents in handfuls in* Annie's *direction, flings the box too, reels to her feet, rips curtains from the window, bangs and kicks at the door, sweeps objects off the mantelpiece and shelf, a little tornado incarnate, all destruction, until she comes upon her doll and, in the act of hurling it, freezes. Then she clutches it to herself, and in exhaustion sinks sobbing to the floor.* Annie *stands contemplating her, in some awe.)*

Two weeks.

(She shakes her head, not without a touch of disgusted bewilderment.)

What did I get into now?

(The lights have been dimming throughout, and the garden house is lit only by moonlight now, with Annie *lost in the patches of dark.* Kate, *now hatless and coatless, enters the family room by the rear door, carrying a lamp.* Keller, *also hatless, wanders simultaneously around the back of the main house to where* James *has been waiting, in the rising moonlight, on the porch.)*

Keller. I can't understand it. I had every intention of dismissing that girl, not setting her up like an empress.

James. Yes, what's her secret, sir?

Keller. Secret?

James. That enables her to get anything she wants out of you? When I can't.

(James turns to go into the house, but Keller *grasps his wrist, twisting him half to his knees.* Kate *comes from the porch.)*

Keller *(angrily).* She does not get anything she—

James *(in pain).* Don't—don't—

Kate. Captain.

Keller. He's afraid.

(He throws James *away from him, with contempt.)*

What does he want out of me?

James *(an outcry).* My God, don't you know?

(He gazes from Keller *to* Kate.*)*

Everything you forgot, when you forgot my mother.

Keller. What!

(James wheels into the house. Keller *takes a stride to the porch, to roar after him.)*

One thing that girl's secret is not; she doesn't fire one shot and disappear!

(Kate stands rigid, and Keller *comes back to her.)*

Katie. Don't mind what he—

Kate. Captain, *I* am proud of you.

Keller. For what?

Kate. For letting this girl have what she needs.

Keller. Why can't my son be? He can't bear me; you'd think I treat him as hard as this girl does Helen—

(He breaks off, as it dawns on him.)

Kate *(gently).* Perhaps you do.

Keller. But he has to learn some respect!

Kate (*a pause wryly*). Do you like the child?

(*She turns again to the porch, but pauses reluctant.*)

How empty the house is, tonight.

(*After a moment she continues on in. Keller stands moveless, as the moonlight dies on him. The distant belfry chimes toll, two o'clock, and with them, a moment later, comes the boy's voice on the wind, in a whisper.*)

Boy's Voice. Annie. Annie.

(*In her patch of dark Annie, now in her nightgown, hurls a cup into a corner as though it were her grief, getting rid of its taste through her teeth.*)

Annie. No! No pity, I won't have it.

(*She comes to Helen, prone on the floor.*)

On either of us.

(*She goes to her knees, but when she touches Helen's hand, the child starts up awake, recoils, and scrambles away from her under the bed. Annie stares after her. She strikes her palm on the floor, with passion.*)

I *will* touch you!

(*She gets to her feet, and paces in a kind of anger around the bed, her hand in her hair, and confronting Helen at each turn.*)

How, how? How do I—

(*Annie stops. Then she calls out urgently, loudly.*)

Percy! Percy!

(*She moves swiftly to the drapes, at left.*)

Percy, wake up!

(*Percy's voice comes in a thick sleepy mumble, unintelligible.*)

Get out of bed and come in here. I need you.

(*Annie darts away, finds and strikes a match, and touches it to the hanging lamp. The lights come up dimly in the room, and Percy stands bare to the waist in torn overalls, between the drapes, with eyes closed, swaying. Annie goes to him, pats his cheeks vigorously.*)

Percy. You awake?

Percy. No'm.

Annie. How would you like to play a nice game?

Percy. Whah?

Annie. With Helen. She's under the bed. Touch her hand.

(*She kneels Percy down at the bed, thrusting his hand under it to contact Helen's. Helen emits an animal sound and crawls to the opposite side, but commences sniffing. Annie rounds the bed with Percy and thrusts his hand again at Helen. This time Helen clutches it, sniffs in recognition, and comes scrambling out after Percy, to hug him with delight. Percy, alarmed, struggles, and Helen's fingers go to his mouth.*)

Percy. Lemme go. Lemme go—

(*Helen fingers her own lips, as before, moving them in dumb imitation.*)

She tryin' talk. She gonna hit me—

Annie (*grimly*). She *can* talk. If she only knew. I'll show you how. She makes letters.

(*She opens* Percy's *other hand, and spells into it.*)

This one is C.C.

(*She hits his palm with it a couple of times, her eyes upon* Helen *across him.* Helen *gropes to feel what* Percy's *hand is doing, and when she encounters* Annie's, *she falls back from them.*)

She's mad at me now, though, she won't play. But she knows lots of letters. Here's another, A. C, a. C, a.

(*But she is watching* Helen, *who comes groping, consumed with curiosity.* Annie *makes the letters in* Percy's *hand, and* Helen *pokes to question what they are up to. Then* Helen *snatches* Percy's *other hand, and quickly spells four letters into it.* Annie *follows them aloud.*)

C, a, k, e! She spells cake; she gets cake.

(*She is swiftly over to the tray of food, to fetch cake and a jug of milk.*)

She doesn't know yet it means this. Isn't it funny. She knows how to spell it and doesn't *know* she knows?

(*She breaks the cake into two pieces, and extends one to each;* Helen *rolls away from her offer.*)

Well, if she won't play it with me, I'll play it with you. Would you like to learn one she doesn't know?

Percy. No'm.

(*But* Annie *seizes his wrist, and spells to him.*)

Annie. M, i, l, k. M is this. I, that's an easy one, just the little finger. L is this—

(*And* Helen *comes back with her hand, to feel the new word.* Annie *brushes her away, and continues spelling aloud to* Percy. Helen's *hand comes back again, and tries to get in.* Annie *brushes it away again.* Helen's *hand insists, and* Annie *puts it away rudely.*)

No, why should I talk to you? I'm teaching Percy a new word. L. K is this—

(Helen *now yanks their hands apart. She butts* Percy *away, and thrusts her palm insistently.* Annie's *eyes are bright, with glee.*)

Ho, you're *jealous*, are you!

(Helen's *hand waits, intractably waits.*)

All *right*.

(Annie *spells into it, milk; and* Helen *after a moment spells it back to* Annie. Annie *takes her hand, with her whole face shining. She gives a great sigh.*)

Good! So I'm finally back to where I can touch you, hm? Touch and go! No love lost, but here we go.

(*She puts the jug of milk into* Helen's *hand and squeezes* Percy's *shoulder.*)

You can go to bed now; you've earned your sleep. Thank you.

(Percy, *stumbling up, weaves his way out through the drapes.* Helen *finishes drinking, and holds the jug out, for* Annie. *When* Annie takes it, Helen *crawls onto the bed, and makes for sleep.* Annie *stands, looks down at her.*)

Now all I have to teach you is—one word. Everything.

(*She sets the jug down. On the floor, now* Annie *spies the doll, stoops to pick it up, and with it dangling in her hand, turns off the lamp. A shaft of moonlight is left on* Helen *in the bed, and a second shaft on the rocking chair; and* Annie, *after putting off her smoked glasses, sits in the rocker with the doll. She is rather happy, and dangles the doll on her knee, and it makes its momma sound.* Annie *whispers to it in mock solicitude.*)

Hush, little baby. Don't—say a word—

(*She lays it against her shoulder, and begins rocking with it, patting its diminutive behind; she talks the lullaby to it, humorously at first.*)

Momma's gonna buy you—a mockingbird:
If that—mockingbird don't sing—

(*The rhythm of the rocking takes her into the tune, softly, and more tenderly.*)

Momma's gonna buy you a diamond ring:
If that diamond ring turns to brass—

(*A third shaft of moonlight outside now rises to pick out* James *at the main house, with one foot on the porch step; he turns his body, as if hearing the song.*)

Momma's gonna buy you a looking-glass:
If that looking-glass gets broke—

(*In the family room, a fourth shaft picks out* Keller *seated at the table, in thought; and he, too, lifts his head, as if hearing.*)

Momma's gonna buy you a billy goat:
If that billy goat won't pull—

(*The fifth shaft is upstairs in* Annie's *room, and picks out* Kate, *pacing there; and she halts, turning her head, too, as if hearing.*)

Momma's gonna buy you a cart and bull:
If that cart and bull turns over,
Momma's gonna buy you a dog named Rover;
If that dog named Rover won't bark—

(*With the shafts of moonlight on* Helen, *and* James, *and* Keller, *and* Kate, *all moveless, and* Annie *rocking the doll, the curtain ends the act.*)

Developing Comprehension Skills

1. What is Annie's greatest problem in dealing with Helen? What did she feel that Helen needed above all else?

2. Why does Annie keep spelling words into Helen's hand, even though Helen does not understand them?

3. After several hours of struggling with Helen, Annie comes out of the locked room to tell Kate, "She ate from her own plate. . . And she folded her napkin." Why is this minor victory so important?

4. After the battle with Helen, Annie remembers a scene from her past. What is the scene? Who are the characters involved in this scene? What do you think triggered this memory?

5. What is Annie's plan to gain complete control over Helen? Why does she feel this is necessary?

6. During this discussion, why does Annie reveal her past life to the Kellers?

7. At one point, Captain Keller wants to fire Annie. Instead, he gives her another chance. Why do you think Annie has been successful in dealing with Captain Keller? How would the story have been different if Annie had given in to Captain Keller's wishes?

8. At the end of Act Two, Annie says to Helen, "Now all I have to teach you is—one word. Everything." What does she mean?

Reading Literature

1. **Identifying Rising Action.** The conflict between Annie and Helen grows in Act Two when Annie refuses to accept Helen's behavior. What kind of tension does this create?

Before she can deal with Helen, however, Annie must also deal with another conflict that has developed. What is that conflict? How does Annie respond to it? Explain your answer.

2. **Understanding Character.** Captain Keller's attitude toward women, especially Yankee women, is revealed as Act Two continues. What is this attitude? What behavior does he expect of Annie? Find examples to support your answer.

Now examine the Captain's attitude toward his wife. Why do you think she calls him "Captain" instead of "Arthur"? Does he seem to respect her opinions and intelligence? From these examples, what can you conclude about Captain Keller's attitude toward women in general? How does this attitude reflect the period, or time, in which he lives?

3. **Appreciating Special Lighting Effects.** As you learned in Act One, the author uses special lighting effects to help the audience understand Annie's thoughts about her past life. In Act Two, when does the author again use this special lighting? What thoughts of Annie's past life once again trouble her? How does the author make the change from present to past and from past to present again?

Developing Vocabulary Skills

Identifying the Correct Meaning. Read the following sentences from Act Two. Several meanings for the underlined word follow each sentence. Use context clues to infer which definition fits the sentence. On your paper write the letter of the correct definition.

1. Annie leaps to her feet, and stands inarticulate:
   a. produced without the normal pronunciation of understandable speech
   b. not able to speak
   c. not able to be expressed

2. In the act of removing Helen's doll . . . she throttles it.
   a. the valve that regulates the amount of fuel entering an engine
   b. to choke, strangle
   c. to stop the action of

3. Is it your contention we won the war, sir?
   a. a dispute, struggle
   b. a contest or controversy
   c. a point that one argues for

4. Helen digs another pinch into her thigh, and this time Annie slaps her hand smartly away.
   a. vigorously, sharply
   b. cleverly
   c. stylishly

5. Annie again rises, recovers Helen's plate from the floor and a handful of scattered food from the deranged tablecloth . . . .
   a. upset in arrangement
   b. disturbed in actions
   c. made insane

6. From the moment she stepped off the train, she's been nothing but a burden, incompetent, impertinent, ineffectual, immodest—
   a. having no connection with a given matter
   b. not showing proper respect or manners
   c. inappropriate

7. The fact is, today she scuttled any chance she ever had of getting along with the child.
   a. to run or move quickly
   b. to throw away or abandon
   c. to make or open holes in the hull of a boat

8. Helen kicks her, breaks free, and careens around the room like an imprisoned bird, colliding with furniture, groping wildly . . . .
   a. to lean sideways
   b. to lurch from side to side, especially while moving rapidly
   c. to caulk, clean, or repair

Developing Writing Skills

1. **Analyzing a Character.** The character of Annie Sullivan is a complex and fascinating one. In several paragraphs, examine her most outstanding character traits. Use details and incidents from the play to illustrate each one.

2. **Writing the Report.** If you have planned your report well, writing it is not a difficult task. Using your organized note cards, write a rough draft of your report. At this point, do not try to create a perfect paper. Just concentrate on getting your ideas on paper.

   When your first draft is complete, read it several times to see where it could be improved. First, read for content. Have you covered your topic thoroughly? Should any information be added or deleted? Have you used the most exact words to express your ideas? Now read your paper a second time. Is the information presented in a logical order? Could you add any transitional words to make the ideas flow more smoothly?

   On your third reading, check for errors in grammar and mechanics. After any of these readings, you may want to make a new draft so that you don't try to correct too many things at once.

When you are satisfied with your report, ask someone else to read it. Have this person check for the same things that you did. Use any suggestions that you think will improve your report. Then read your draft over one more time and make a clean final copy. Finally, make a bibliography for your report. Follow the guidelines on page 705.

Developing Skills in Speaking and Listening

Presenting a Demonstration Speech. Annie Sullivan worked with a special type of finger-spelling, or manual alphabet, to communicate with Helen Keller. Look at the chart below. Prepare a demonstration speech in which you teach some of this alphabet to others in your class. First, provide some background on the alphabet. You may find this information in the encyclopedia under **Deafness** or **Sign Language.** Then use visual aids, such as diagrams or charts, to help you show your classmates how to make the different letters. Be sure to describe each hand position as you display it. You may want to conclude your speech by "signing" a short sentence to them.

The American Manual Alphabet of the deaf-blind. Some finger spellers use the alphabet to communicate with each other by touch. Each word must be spelled out into the hand of the person receiving the message. The American Foundation for the Blind, New York.

The Miracle Worker

ACT THREE

The stage is totally dark, until we see Annie *and* Helen *silhouetted on the bed in the garden house.* Annie's *voice is audible, very patient, and worn; it has been saying this for a long time.*

Annie. Water, Helen. This is water. W, a, t, e, r. It has a *name.*

(A silence. Then,)

Egg, e, g, g. It has a *name,* the name stands for the thing. Oh, it's so simple, simple as birth, to explain.

(The lights have commenced to rise, not on the garden house but on the homestead. Then,)

Helen, Helen, the chick *has* to come out of its shell, sometime. You come out, too.

(In the bedroom upstairs, we see Viney *unhurriedly washing the window, dusting, turning the mattress, readying the room for use again; then in the family room a diminished group at one end of the table—*Kate, Keller, James*—finishing up a quiet breakfast; then outside, down right, the other black servant on his knees, assisted by* Martha, *working with a trowel around a new trellis and wheelbarrow.*

The scene is one of everyday calm, and all are oblivious to Annie's *voice.)*

There's only one way out, for you, and it's language. To learn that your fingers can talk. And say anything, anything you can name. This is a mug. Mug, m, u, g. Helen, it has a *name.* It—has—a—*name—*

(Kate rises from the table.)

Keller *(gently).* You haven't eaten, Katie.

Kate *(smiles, shakes her head).* I haven't the appetite. I'm too—restless, I can't sit to it.

Keller. You should eat, my dear. It will be a long day, waiting.

James *(lightly).* But it's been a short two weeks. I never thought life could be so—noiseless, went much too quickly for me.

*(Kate *and* Keller *gaze at him, in silence.* James *becomes uncomfortable.)*

Annie. C, a, r, d. Card. C, a—

James. Well, the house has been practically normal, hasn't it?

Keller *(harshly).* Jimmie.

James. Is it wrong to enjoy a quiet breakfast, after five years? And you two even seem to enjoy each other—

Keller. It could be even more noiseless, Jimmie, without your tongue running every minute. Haven't you enough feeling to imagine what Katie has been undergoing, ever since—

(Kate *stops him, with her hand on his arm.*)

Kate. Captain.

(*To* James.)

It's true. The two weeks have been normal, quiet, all you say. But not short. Interminable.

(*She rises, and wanders out; she pauses on the porch steps, gazing toward the garden house.*)

Annie (*fading*). W, a, t, e, r. But it means *this.* W, a, t, e, r. *This.* W, a, t—

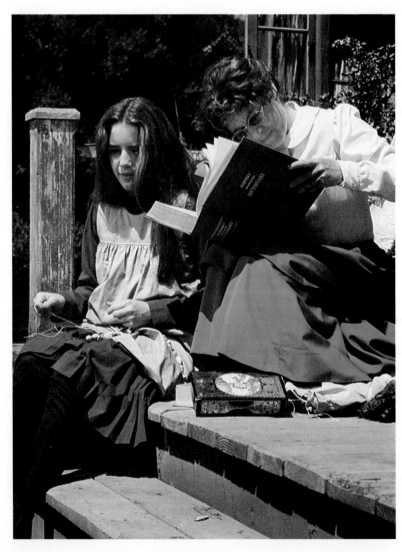

James. I only meant that Miss Sullivan is a boon. Of contention, though, it seems.

Keller (*heavily*). If and when you're a parent, Jimmie, you will understand what separation means. A mother loses a—protector.

James (*baffled*). Hm?

Keller. You'll learn; we don't just keep our children safe. They keep us safe.

(*He rises, with his empty coffee cup and saucer.*)

There are, of course, all kinds of separation. Katie has lived with one kind for five years. And another is disappointment. In a child.

(*He goes with the cup out the rear door. James sits for a long moment of stillness. In the garden house, the lights commence to come up. Annie, haggard at the table, is writing a letter, her face again almost in contact with the stationery. Helen, apart on the stool, and for the first time as clean and neat as a button, is quietly crocheting an endless chain of wool, which snakes all around the room.*)

Annie. "I, feel, every, day, more, and, more, in—"

(*She pauses, and turns the pages of a dictionary open before her; her finger descends the words to a full stop. She elevates her eyebrows, then copies the word.*)

"—adequate."

(*In the main house James pushes up, and goes to the front doorway, after Kate.*)

James. Kate?

(*Kate turns her glance. James is rather weary.*)

I'm sorry. Open my mouth, like that fairy tale, frogs jump out.

Kate. No. It has been better. For everyone.

(*She starts away, up center.*)

Annie (*writing*). "If, only, there, were, someone, to, help, me, I, need, a, teacher, as, much, as, Helen—"

James. Kate.

(*Kate halts, waits.*)

What does he want from me?

Kate. That's not the question. Stand up to the world, Jimmie; that comes first.

James (*a pause, wryly*). But the world is him.

Kate. Yes. And no one can do it for you.

James. Kate.

(*His voice is humble.*)

At least we— Could you—be my friend?

Kate. I am.

(*Kate turns to wander, up back of the garden house. Annie's murmur comes at once; the lights begin to die on the main house.*)

Annie. "—my, mind, is, undisiplined, full, of, skips, and, jumps, and—"

(*She halts, rereads, frowns.*)

Hm.

(*Annie puts her nose again in the dictionary, flips back to an earlier page, and fingers down the words; Kate presently comes down toward the bay window with a trayful of food.*)

Disinter—disinterested—disjoin—dis—

(She backtracks, indignant.)

Disinterested, disjoin— Where's disipline?

(She goes a page or two back, searching with her finger, muttering.)

What a dictionary; have to know how to spell it before you can look up how to spell it; disciple, *discipline!* Diskipline.

(She corrects the word in her letter.)

(But her eyes are bothering her; she closes them in exhaustion and gently fingers the eyelids. Kate watches her through the window.)

Kate. What are you doing to your eyes?

(Annie glances around; she puts her smoked glasses on, and gets up to come over, assuming a cheerful energy.)

Annie. It's worse on my vanity! I'm learning to spell. It's like a surprise party; the most unexpected characters turn up.

Kate. You're not to overwork your eyes, Miss Annie.

Annie. Well.

(She takes the tray, sets it on her chair, and carries chair and tray to Helen.)

Whatever I spell to Helen I'd better spell right.

Kate *(almost wistful).* How—serene she is.

Annie. She learned this stitch yesterday. Now I can't get her to stop!

(She disentangles one foot from the wool chain, and sets the chair before Helen. Helen, at its contact with her knee, feels the plate, promptly sets her crocheting down, and tucks the napkin in at her neck; but Annie *withholds the spoon. When Helen* finds it missing, *she folds her hands in her lap, and quietly waits. Annie* twinkles at Kate *with mock devoutness.)*

Such a little lady; she'd sooner starve than eat with her fingers.

(She gives Helen *the spoon, and Helen begins to eat, neatly.)*

Kate. You've taught her so much, these two weeks. I would never have—

Annie. Not enough.

(She is suddenly gloomy; shakes her head.)

Obedience isn't enough. Well, she learned two nouns this morning, *key* and *water*, brings her up to eighteen nouns and three verbs.

Kate *(hesitant).* But—not—

Annie. No. Not that they mean things. It's still a finger-game, no meaning.

(She turns to Kate, *abruptly.)*

Mrs. Keller—

(But she defers it; she comes back, to sit in the bay and lift her hand.)

Shall we play our finger-game?

Kate. How will she learn it?

Annie. It will come.

(She spells a word; Kate *does not respond.)*

Kate. How?

Annie *(a pause).* How does a bird learn to fly?

(She spells again.)

We're born to use words, like wings; it has to come.

Kate. How?

Annie *(another pause, wearily).* All right. I don't know how.

(She pushes up her glasses, to rub her eyes.)

I've done everything I could think of. Whatever she's learned here—keeping herself clean, knitting, stringing beads, meals, setting-up exercises each morning; we climb trees; hunt eggs; yesterday a chick was born in her hands—all of it I spell; everything we do, we never stop spelling. I go to bed with—writer's cramp from talking so much!

Kate. I worry about you, Miss Annie. You must rest.

Annie. Now? She spells back in her *sleep;* her fingers make letters when she doesn't know! In her bones, those five fingers know; that hand aches to—speak out, and something in her mind is asleep. How do I—nudge that awake? That's the one question.

Kate. With no answer.

Annie *(long pause).* Except keep at it. Like this.

(She again begins spelling—I, need—and Kate's *brows gather, following the words.)*

Kate. More—time?

(She glances at Annie, *who looks her in the eyes, silent.)*

Here?

Annie. Spell it.

*(Kate *spells a word—no—shaking her head;* Annie *spells two words—why, not—back, with an impatient question in her eyes; and* Kate *moves her head in pain to answer it.)*

Kate. Because I can't—

Annie. Spell it! If she ever learns, you'll have a lot to tell each other. Start now.

*(Kate *painstakingly spells in air. In the midst of this the rear door opens, and* Keller *enters with the setter* Belle *in tow.)*

Keller. Miss Sullivan? On my way to the office, I brought Helen a playmate—

Annie. Outside please, Captain Keller.

Keller. My dear child, the two weeks are up today; surely you don't object to—

Annie *(rising).* They're not up till six o'clock.

Keller *(indulgent).* Oh, now. What difference can a fraction of one day—

Annie. An agreement is an agreement. Now you've been very good, I'm sure you can keep it up for a few more hours.

(She escorts Keller *by the arm over the threshold; he obeys, leaving* Belle.*)*

Keller. Miss Sullivan, you are a tyrant.

Annie. Likewise, I'm sure. You can stand there, and close the door if she comes.

Kate. I don't think you know how eager we are to have her back in our arms—

Annie. I do know; it's my main worry.

Keller. It's like expecting a new child in the house. Well, she *is*, so—composed, so—

(Gently)

Attractive. You've done wonders for her, Miss Sullivan.

Annie *(not a question).* Have I.

Keller. If there's anything you want from us in repayment, tell us; it will be a privilege to—

Annie. I just told Mrs. Keller. I want more time.

Kate. Miss Annie—

Annie. Another week.

(Helen lifts her head, and begins to sniff.)

Keller. We miss the child. *I* miss her, I'm glad to say, that's a different debt I owe you—

Annie. Pay it to Helen. Give *her* another week.

Kate *(gently).* Doesn't she miss us?

Keller. Of course she does. What a wrench this unexplainable—exile must be to her. Can you say it's not?

Annie. No. But I—

(Helen is off the stool, to grope about the room; when she encounters Belle, she throws her arms around the dog's neck in delight.)

Kate. Doesn't she need affection too, Miss Annie?

Annie *(wavering).* She—never shows me she needs it, she won't have any—caressing or—

Kate. But you're not her mother.

Keller. And what would another week accomplish? We are more than satisfied. You've done more than we ever thought possible, taught her constructive—

Annie. I can't promise anything. All I can—

Keller *(no break).* —things to do, to behave like—even look like—a human child, so manageable, contented, cleaner, more—

Annie *(withering).* Cleaner.

Keller. Well. We say cleanliness is next to godliness, Miss—

Annie. Cleanliness is next to nothing. She has to learn that everything has its name! That words can be her *eyes*, to everything in the world outside her, and inside too. What is she without words? With them, she can think, have ideas, be reached; there's not a thought or fact in the world that can't be hers. You publish a newspaper, Captain Keller. Do I have to tell you what words are? And she has them already—

Keller. Miss Sullivan.

Annie. —eighteen nouns and three verbs. They're in her fingers now. I need only time to push *one* of them into her mind! One, and everything under the sun will follow. Don't you see what she's learned here is only clearing the way for that? I can't risk her unlearning it. Give me more time alone with her, another week to—

Keller. Look.

(He points, and Annie turns. Helen is playing with Belle's claws; she makes letters with

her fingers, *shows them to* Belle, *waits with her palm, then manipulates the dog's claws.*)

What is she spelling?

(*A silence.*)

Kate. Water?

(Annie *nods.*)

Keller. Teaching a dog to spell.

(*A pause.*)

The dog doesn't know what she means, any more than she knows what you mean, Miss Sullivan. I think you ask too much, of her and yourself. God may not have meant Helen to have the—eyes you speak of.

Annie (*toneless*). I mean her to.

Keller (*curiously*). What is it to you?

(Annie's *head comes slowly up.*)

You make us see how we indulge her for our sake. Is the opposite true, for you?

Annie (*then*). Half a week?

Keller. An agreement *is* an agreement.

Annie. Mrs. Keller?

Kate (*simply*). I want her back.

(*A wait;* Annie *then lets her hands drop in surrender, and nods.*)

Keller. I'll send Viney over to help you pack.

Annie. Not until six o'clock. I have her till six o'clock.

Keller (*consenting*). Six o'clock. Come, Katie.

(Kate, *leaving the window, joins him around back, while* Keller *closes the door; they are shut out.*

Only the garden house is daylit now, and the light on it is narrowing down. Annie *stands watching* Helen *work* Belle's *claws. Then she settles beside them on her knees, and stops* Helen's *hand.*)

Annie (*gently*). No.

(*She shakes her head, with* Helen's *hand to her face, then spells.*)

Dog. D, o, g. Dog.

(*She touches* Helen's *hand to* Belle. Helen *dutifully pats the dog's head, and resumes spelling to its paw.*)

Not water.

(Annie *rolls to her feet, brings a tumbler of water back from the tray, and kneels with it, to seize* Helen's *hand and spell.*)

Here, Water. *Water.*

(*She thrust* Helen's *hand into the tumbler.* Helen *lifts her hand out dripping, wipes it daintly on* Belle's *hide; and taking the tumbler from* Annie, *endeavors to thrust* Belle's *paw into it.* Annie *sits watching, wearily.*)

I don't know how to tell you. Not a soul in the world knows how to tell you. Helen, Helen.

(*She bends in compassion to touch her lips to* Helen's *temple, and instantly* Helen *pauses, her hands off the dog, her head slightly averted. The lights are still narrowing, and* Belle *slinks off. After a moment,* Annie *sits back.*)

Yes, what's it to me? They're satisfied. Give them back their child and dog, both house-broken; everyone's satisfied. But me, and you.

(Helen's *hand comes out into the light, groping.*)

Reach. *Reach!*

(Annie, *extending her own hand, grips* Helen's; *the two hands are clasped, tense in the light, the rest of the room changing in shadow.*)

I wanted to teach you—oh, everything the earth is full of, Helen, everything on it that's ours for a wink, and it's gone; and what we are on it, the—light we bring to it and leave behind in—words. Why, you can see five thousand years back in a light of words, everything we feel, think, know—and share, in words, so not a soul is in darkness, or done with, even in the grave. And I know, I *know*, one word and I can—put the world in your hand—and whatever it is to me, I won't take less! How, how, how do I tell you that *this*—

(She spells.)

—means a *word*, and the word means this *thing*, wool?

(She thrusts the wool at *Helen's hand;* Helen *sits, puzzled.* Annie *puts the crocheting aside.*)

Or this—s, t, o, o, l—means this *thing*, stool?

(She claps *Helen's palm to the stool.* Helen *waits, uncomprehending.* Annie *snatches up her napkin, spells,*)

Napkin!

(She forces it in *Helen's hand, waits, discards it, lifts a fold of the child's dress, spells,*)

Dress!

(She lets it drop, spells,)

F, a, c, e, face!

(She draws *Helen's hand to her cheek, and pressing it there, staring into the child's responseless eyes, hears the distant belfry begin to toll, slowly: one, two, three, four, five, six.*

On the third stroke, the lights stealing in around the garden house show us figures waiting: Viney, *the other servant,* Martha, Percy *at the drapes, and* James *on the dim porch.* Annie *and* Helen *remain, frozen. The chimes die away. Silently* Percy *moves the drape-rod back out of sight;* Viney *steps into the room—not using the door—and unmakes the bed; the other servant brings the wheelbarrow over, leaves it handy, rolls the bed off;* Viney *puts the bed linens on top of a waiting boxful of* Helen's *toys, and loads the box on the wheelbarrow;* Martha *and* Percy *take out the chairs, with the trayful, then the table; and* James *coming down and into the room, lifts Annie's suitcase from its corner.* Viney *and the other servant load the remaining odds and ends on the wheelbarrow, and the servant wheels it off.* Viney *and the children departing leave only* James *in the room with* Annie *and* Helen. James *studies the two of them, without mockery, and then, quietly going to the door and opening it, bears the suitcase out, and housewards. He leaves the door open.*

Kate *steps into the doorway, and stands.* Annie, *lifting her gaze from* Helen, *sees her;*

she takes Helen's *hand from her cheek, and returns it to the child's own, stroking it there twice, in her mother-sign, before spelling slowly into it,)*

M, o, t, h, e, r. Mother.

(Helen, *with her hand free, strokes her cheek, suddenly forlorn.* Annie *takes her hand again.)*

M, o, t, h—

(*But* Kate *is trembling with such impatience that her voice breaks from her, harsh.)*

Kate. Let her *come!*

(Annie *lifts* Helen *to her feet, with a turn, and gives her a little push. Now* Helen *begins groping, sensing something, trembling herself; and* Kate, *falling one step in onto her knees, clasps her, kissing her.* Helen *clutches her, tight as she can.* Kate *is inarticulate, choked, repeating* Helen's *name again and again. She wheels with her in her arms, to stumble away out the doorway.* Annie *stands unmoving, while* Kate *in a blind walk carries* Helen *like a baby behind the main house, out of view.*

Annie *is now alone on the stage. She turns, gazing around at the stripped room, bidding it silently farewell, impassively, like a defeated general on the deserted battlefield. All that remains is a stand with a basin of water; and here* Annie *takes up an eyecup, bathes each of her eyes, empties the eyecup, drops it in her purse, and tiredly locates her smoked glasses on the floor. The lights alter subtly; in the act of putting on her glasses,* Annie *hears something that stops her, with head lifted. We hear it too, the voices out of the past, including her own now, in a whisper,)*

Boy's Voice. You said we'd be together, forever— You promised, forever and— Annie!

Anagnos' Voice. But that battle is dead and done with. Why not let it stay buried?

Annie's Voice (*whispering*). I think God must owe me a resurrection.

Anagnos' Voice. What?

(*A pause, and* Annie *answers it herself, heavily.)*

Annie. And I owe God one.

Boy's Voice. Forever and ever—

(Annie *shakes her head.)*

—forever, and ever, and—

(Annie *covers her ears.)*

—forever, and ever, and ever—

(*It pursues* Annie; *she flees to snatch up her purse, wheels to the doorway, and* Keller *is standing in it. The lights have lost their special color.)*

Keller. Miss—Annie.

(*He has an envelope in his fingers.)*

I've been waiting to give you this.

Annie (*after a breath*). What?

Keller. Your first month's salary.

(*He puts it in her hand.)*

With many more to come, I trust. It doesn't express what we feel; it doesn't pay our debt. For what you've done.

Annie. What have I done?

Keller. Taken a wild thing, and given us back a child.

Annie (*presently*). I taught her one thing, no. Don't do this, don't do that—

Keller. It's more than all of us could, in all the years we—

Annie. I wanted to teach her what language is. I wanted to teach her yes.

Keller. You will have time.

Annie. I don't know how. I know without it to do nothing but obey is—no gift. Obedience without understanding is a—blindness, too. Is that all I've wished on her?

Keller (*gently*). No, no—

Annie. Maybe. I don't know what else to do. Simply go on, keep doing what I've done, and have—faith that inside she's— That inside it's waiting. Like water, underground. All I can do is keep on.

Keller. It's enough. For us.

Annie. You can help, Captain Keller.

Keller. How?

Annie. Even learning no has been at a cost. Of much trouble and pain. Don't undo it.

Keller. Why should we wish to—

Annie (*abruptly*). The world isn't an easy place for anyone. I don't want her just to obey, but to let her have her way in everything is a lie, to *her*. I can't—

(*Her eyes fill; it takes her by surprise, and she laughs through it.*)

And I don't even love her. She's not my child! Well. You've got to stand between that lie and her.

Keller. We'll try.

Annie. Because *I* will. As long as you let me stay, that's one promise I'll keep.

Keller. Agreed. We've learned something too, I hope.

(*A pause*)

Won't you come now, to supper?

Annie. Yes.

(*She wags the envelope, ruefully.*)

Why doesn't God pay His debts each month?

Keller. I beg your pardon?

Annie. Nothing. I used to wonder how I could—

(*The lights are fading on them, simultaneously rising on the family room of the main house, where Viney is polishing glassware at the table set for dinner.*)

—earn a living.

Keller. Oh, you do.

Annie. I really do. Now the question is, can I survive it!

(Keller *smiles, offers his arm.*)

Keller. May I?

(Annie *takes it, and the lights lose them as he escorts her out.*)

Now in the family room the rear door opens, and Helen *steps in. She stands a moment, then sniffs in one deep, grateful breath; and her hands go out vigorously to familiar things, over the door panels, and to the chairs around the table, and over the silverware on the table, until she meets* Viney; *she pats her flank approvingly.)*

Viney. Oh, we glad to have you back too, prob'ly.

(Helen hurries groping to the front door, opens and closes it, removes its key, opens and closes it again to be sure it is unlocked, gropes back to the rear door and repeats the procedure, removing its key and hugging herself gleefully.

Aunt Ev *is next in by the rear door, with a relish tray; she bends to kiss* Helen's *cheek.* Helen *finds* Kate *behind her, and thrusts the keys at her.)*

Kate. What? Oh.

(To Ev).

Keys.

(She pockets them; lets Helen *feel them.)*

Yes, *I'll* keep the keys. I think we've had enough of locked doors, too.

(James, having earlier put Annie's *suitcase inside her door upstairs and taken himself out of view around the corner, now reappears and comes down the stairs as* Annie *and* Keller *mount the porch steps. Following them into the family room, he pats* Annie's *hair in passing, rather to her surprise.)*

James. Evening, General.

(He takes his own chair opposite.

Viney *bears the empty water pitcher out to the porch. The remaining suggestion of garden house is gone now, and the water pump is unobstructed.* Viney *pumps water into the pitcher.*

Kate, *surveying the table, breaks the silence.)*

Kate. Will you say grace, Jimmie?

(They bow their heads, except for Helen, *who palms her empty plate and then reaches to be sure her mother is there.* James *considers a moment, glances across at* Annie, *lowers his head again, and obliges.)*

James *(lightly).* And Jacob was left alone, and wrestled with an angel until the breaking of the day; and the hollow of Jacob's thigh was out of joint, as he wrestled with him; and the angel said, Let me go, for the day breaketh. And Jacob said, I will not let thee go, except thou bless me. Amen.

(Annie has lifted her eyes suspiciously at James, *who winks expressionlessly and inclines his head to* Helen.)*

Oh, you angel.

(The others lift their faces; Viney *returns with the pitcher, setting it down near* Kate; *then goes out the rear door; and* Annie *puts a napkin around* Helen.)*

Aunt Ev. That's a very strange grace, James.

Keller. Will you start the muffins, Ev?

James. It's from the Good Book, isn't it?

Aunt Ev *(passing a plate).* Well, of course it is. Didn't you know?

James. Yes, I knew.

Keller (*serving*). Ham, Miss Annie?

Annie. Please.

Aunt Ev. Then why ask?

James. I meant it *is* from the Good Book, and therefore a fitting grace.

Aunt Ev. Well. I don't know about *that*.

Kate (*with the pitcher*). Miss Annie?

Annie. Thank you.

Aunt Ev. There's an awful *lot* of things in the Good Book that I wouldn't care to hear just before eating.

(*When* Annie *reaches for the pitcher,* Helen *removes her napkin and drops it to the floor.* Annie *is filling* Helen's *glass when she notices it. She considers* Helen's *bland expression a moment, then bends, retrieves it, and tucks it around* Helen's *neck again.*)

James. Well, fitting in the sense that Jacob's thigh was out of joint, and so is this piggie's.

Aunt Ev. I declare, James—

Kate. Pickles, Aunt Ev?

Aunt Ev. Oh, I should say so; you know my opinion of your pickles—

Kate. This is the end of them, I'm afraid. I didn't put up nearly enough last summer; this year I intend to—

(*She interrupts herself, seeing* Helen *deliberately lift off her napkin and drop it again to the floor. She bends to retrieve it, but* Annie *stops her arm.*)

Keller (*not noticing*). Reverend looked in at the office today to complain his hens have stopped laying. Poor fellow, *he* was out of joint; all he could—

(*He stops too, to frown down the table at* Kate, Helen, *and* Annie *in turn, all suspended in mid-motion.*)

James (*not noticing*). I've always suspected those hens.

Aunt Ev. Of what?

James. I think they're Papist.[1] Has he tried—

(*He stops, too, following* Keller's *eyes.* Annie *now stoops to pick the napkin up.*)

Aunt Ev. James, now you're pulling my— lower extremity, the first thing you know we'll be—

(*She stops, too, hearing herself in the silence.* Annie, *with everyone now watching, for the third time puts the napkin on* Helen. Helen *yanks it off, and throws it down.* Annie *rises, lifts* Helen's *plate, and bears it away.* Helen, *feeling it gone, slides down and commences to kick up under the table; the dishes jump.* Annie *contemplates this for a moment; then, coming back, takes* Helen's *wrists firmly and swings her off the chair.* Helen, *struggling, gets one hand free, and catches at her mother's skirt. When* Kate *takes her by the shoulders,* Helen *hangs quiet.*)

Kate. Miss Annie.

Annie. No.

Kate (*a pause*). It's a very special day.

---

1. **Papist**, Roman Catholic.

Annie (*grimly*). It will be, when I give in to that.

(*She tries to disengage* Helen's *hand;* Kate *lays hers on* Annie's.)

Kate. Please. I've hardly had a chance to welcome her home—

Annie. Captain Keller.

Keller (*embarrassed*). Oh. Katie, we—had a little talk, Miss Annie feels that if we indulge Helen in these—

Aunt Ev. But what's the child done?

Annie. She's learned not to throw things on the floor and kick. It took us the best part of two weeks and—

Aunt Ev. But only a napkin; it's not as if it were breakable!

Annie. And everything she's learned *is*? Mrs. Keller, I don't think we should—play tug-of-war for her. Either give her to me or you keep her from kicking.

Kate. What do you wish to do?

Annie. Let me take her from the table.

Aunt Ev. Oh, let her stay. My goodness, she's only a child; she doesn't have to wear a napkin if she doesn't want to to her first evening—

Annie (*level*). And ask outsiders not to interfere.

Aunt Ev (*astonished*). Out—outsi— I'm the child's *aunt!*

Kate (*distressed*). Will once hurt so much, Miss Annie? I've—made all Helen's favorite foods, tonight.

(*A pause.*)

Keller (*gently*). It's a homecoming party, Miss Annie.

(Annie *after a moment releases* Helen. *But she cannot accept it. At her own chair, she shakes her head and turns back, intent on* Kate.)

Annie. She's testing you. You realize?

James (*to Annie*). She's testing you.

Keller. Jimmie, be quiet.

(James *sits, tense.*)

Now she's home, naturally she—

Annie. And wants to see what will happen. At your hands. I said it was my main worry. Is this what you promised me not half an hour ago?

Keller (*reasonably*). But she's *not* kicking, now—

Annie. And not learning not to. Mrs. Keller, teaching her is bound to be painful, to everyone. I know it hurts to watch, but she'll live up to just what you demand of her, and no more.

James (*palely*). She's testing *you.*

Keller (*testily*). Jimmie.

James. I have an opinion. I think I should—

Keller. No one's interested in hearing your opinion.

Annie. *I'm* interested. Of course she's testing me. Let me keep her to what she's learned, and she'll go on learning from me. Take her out of my hands, and it all comes apart.

The Miracle Worker 661

(Kate *closes her eyes, digesting it;* Annie *sits again, with a brief comment for her.*)

Be bountiful; it's at her expense.

(*She turns to* James, *flatly.*)

Please pass me more of—her favorite foods.

(*Then* Kate *lifts* Helen's *hand, and turning her toward* Annie, *surrenders her;* Helen *makes for her own chair.*)

Kate (*low*). Take her, Miss Annie.

Annie (*then*). Thank you.

(*But the moment* Annie, *rising, reaches for her hand,* Helen *begins to fight and kick, clutching to the tablecloth, and uttering laments.* Annie *again tries to loosen her hand, and* Keller *rises.*)

Keller (*tolerant*). I'm afraid you're the difficulty, Miss Annie. Now I'll keep her to what she's learned; you're quite right there—

(*He takes* Helen's *hands from* Annie, *pats them;* Helen *quiets down.*)

—but I don't see that we need send her from the table; after all, she's the guest of honor. Bring her plate back.

Annie. If she was a seeing child, none of you would tolerate one—

Keller. Well, she's not, I think some compromise is called for. Bring her plate, please.

(Annie's *jaw sets, but she restores the plate, while* Keller *fastens the napkin around* Helen's *neck; she permits it.*)

There. It's not unnatural. Most of us take some aversion to our teachers, and occasionally another hand can smooth things out.

(*He puts a fork in* Helen's *hand;* Helen *takes it. Genially,*)

Now. Shall we start all over?

(*He goes back around the table, and sits.* Annie *stands watching.* Helen *is motionless, thinking things through, until with a wicked glee she deliberately flings the fork on the floor. After another moment, she plunges her hand into her food, and crams a fistful into her mouth.*)

James (*wearily*). I think we've started all over—

(Keller *shoots a glare at him, as* Helen *plunges her other hand into* Annie's *plate.* Annie *at once moves in, to grasp her wrist; and* Helen, *flinging out a hand, encounters the pitcher. She swings with it at* Annie. Annie, *falling back, blocks it with an elbow, but the water flies over her dress.* Annie *gets her breath, then snatches the pitcher away in one hand, hoists* Helen *up bodily under the other arm, and starts to carry her out, kicking.* Keller *stands.*)

Annie (*savagely polite*). Don't get up!

Keller. Where are you going?

Annie. Don't smooth anything else out for me; don't interfere in any way! I treat her like a seeing child because I *ask* her to see. I *expect* her to see. Don't undo what I do!

Keller. Where are you taking her?

Annie. To make her fill this pitcher again!

(*She thrusts out with* Helen *under her arm, but* Helen *escapes up the stairs and* Annie *runs after her.* Keller *stands rigid.* Aunt Ev *is astounded.*)

Aunt Ev. You let her speak to you like that, Arthur? A creature who *works* for you?

Keller (*angrily*). No. I don't.

(*He is starting after* Annie *when* James, *on his feet with shaky resolve, interposes his chair between them in* Keller's *path.*)

James. Let her go.

Keller. What!

James (*a swallow*). I said—let her go. She's right.

(Keller *glares at the chair and him.* James *takes a deep breath, then headlong,*)

She's right, Kate's right, I'm right, and you're wrong. If you drive her away from here, it will be over my dead—chair. Has it never occurred to you that on one occasion you might be consummately wrong?

(Keller's *stare is unbelieving, even a little fascinated.* Kate *rises in trepidation, to mediate.*)

Kate. Captain.

(Keller *stops her with his raised hand; his eyes stay on* James's *pale face, for a long hold. When he finally finds his voice, it is gruff.*)

Keller. Sit down, everyone.

(*He sits.* Kate *sits.* James *holds onto his chair.* Keller *speaks mildly.*)

Please sit down, Jimmie.

(James *sits, and a moveless silence prevails;* Keller's *eyes do not leave him.*

Annie *has pulled* Helen *downstairs again by one hand, the pitcher in her other hand, down the porch steps, and across the yard to the pump. She puts* Helen's *hand on the pump handle, grimly.*)

Annie. All right. Pump.

(Helen *touches her cheek, waits uncertainly.*)

No, she's not here. Pump!

(*She forces* Helen's *hand to work the handle, then lets go. And* Helen *obeys. She pumps till the water comes. Then* Annie *puts the pitcher in her other hand and guides it under the spout, and the water tumbling half into and half around the pitcher douses* Helen's *hand.* Annie *takes over the handle to keep water coming, and does automatically what she has done so many times before, spells into* Helen's *free palm,*)

Water. W, a, t, e, r. *Water.* It has a— *name*—

(*And now the miracle happens.* Helen *drops the pitcher on the slab under the spout. It shatters. She stands transfixed.* Annie *freezes on the pump handle. There is a change in the sundown light, and with it a change in* Helen's *face, some light coming into it we have never seen there, some struggle in the depths behind it; and her lips tremble, trying to remember something the muscles around them once knew, till at last it finds its way out, painfully, a baby sound buried under the debris of years of dumbness.*)

Helen. Wah. Wah.

(*And again, with great effort,*)

Wah. Wah.

(Helen *plunges her hand into the dwindling water, spells into her own palm. Then she gropes frantically.* Annie *reaches for her hand, and* Helen *spells into* Annie's *hand.*)

Annie (*whispering*). Yes.

(Helen *spells into it again.*)

Yes!

(Helen *grabs at the handle, pumps for more water, plunges her hand into its spurt, and grabs* Annie's *to spell it again.*)

Yes! Oh, my dear—

(She falls to her knees to clasp Helen's hand, but Helen pulls it free, stands almost bewildered, then drops to the ground, pats it swiftly, holds up her palm, imperious. Annie spells into it,)

Ground.

(Helen spells it back.)

Yes!

(Helen whirls to the pump, pats it, holds up her palm, and Annie spells into it.)

Pump.

(Helen spells it back.)

Yes! Yes!

(Now Helen is in such an excitement she is possessed, wild, trembling, cannot be still, turns, runs, falls on the porch steps, claps it, reaches out her palm, and Annie is at it instantly to spell,)

Step.

(Helen has no time to spell back now. She whirls, groping, to touch anything, encounters the trellis, shakes it, thrusts out her palm, and Annie, while spelling to her, cries wildly at the house.)

Trellis. Mrs. Keller! Mrs. Keller!

(Inside, Kate starts to her feet. Helen scrambles back onto the porch, groping, and finds the bell string, tugs it. The bell rings; the distant chimes begin tolling the hour; all the bells in town seem to break into speech, while Helen reaches out and Annie spells feverishly into her hand. Kate hurries out, with Keller after her. Aunt Ev is on her feet, to peer out the window.

Only James remains at the table, and with a napkin wipes his damp brow. From up right and left the servants—Viney, the two black children, the other servant—run in, and stand watching from a distance as Helen, ringing the bell, with her other hand encounters her mother's skirt. When she throws a hand out, Annie spells into it,)

Mother.

(Keller now seizes Helen's hand. She touches him, gestures a hand, and Annie again spells,)

Papa—She knows!

(Kate and Keller go to their knees, stammering, clutching Helen to them; and Annie steps unsteadily back to watch the threesome, Helen spelling wildly into Kate's hand, then into Keller's, Kate spelling back into Helen's. They cannot keep their hands off her, and rock her in their clasp.

Then Helen gropes, feels nothing, turns all around, pulls free, and comes with both hands groping to find Annie. She encounters Annie's thighs. Annie kneels to her, Helen's hand pats Annie's cheek impatiently, points a finger, and waits; and Annie spells into it,)

Teacher.

(Helen spells it back, slowly; Annie nods.)

Teacher.

(She holds Helen's hand to her cheek. Presently Helen withdraws it, not jerkily, only with reserve, and retreats a step. She stands thinking it over, then turns again and stumbles back to her parents. They try to embrace her, but she has something else in mind. It is to get the keys, *and she hits* Kate's *pocket until* Kate *digs them out for her.*

Annie, *with her own load of emotion, has retreated, her back turned, toward the pump, to sit.* Kate *moves to* Helen, *touches her hand questioningly, and* Helen *spells a word to her.* Kate *comprehends it, their first act of verbal communication, and she can hardly utter the word aloud, in wonder, gratitude, and deprivation. It is a moment in which she simultaneously finds and loses a child.)*

Kate. Teacher?

*(*Annie *turns; and* Kate, *facing* Helen *in her direction by the shoulders, holds her back, holds her back, and then relinquishes her.* Helen *feels her way across the yard, rather shyly, and when her moving hands touch* Annie's *skirt, she stops. Then she holds out the keys and places them in* Annie's *hand. For a moment neither of them moves. Then* Helen *slides into* Annie's *arms, and lifting away her smoked glasses, kisses her on the cheek.* Annie *gathers her in.*

Kate, *torn both ways, turns from this, gestures the servants off, and makes her way into the house, on* Keller's *arm. The servants go, in separate directions.*

The lights are half down now, except over the pump. Annie *and* Helen *are here, alone in the yard.* Annie *has found* Helen's *hand, almost without knowing it, and she spells slowly into it, her voice unsteady, whispering,)*

Annie. I, love, Helen.

(She clutches the child to her, tight this time, not spelling, whispering into her hair.)

Forever, and—

(She stops. The lights over the pump are taking on the color of the past, and it brings Annie's *head up, her eyes opening, in fear; and as slowly as though drawn she rises, to listen, with her hand on* Helen's *shoulder. She waits, waits, listening with ears and eyes both, slowly here, slowly there; and hears only silence. There are no voices. The color passes on, and when her eyes come back to* Helen, *she can breathe the end of her phrase without fear,)*

—ever.

(In the family room, Kate *has stood over the table, staring at* Helen's *plate, with* Keller *at her shoulder. Now* James *takes a step to move her chair in, and* Kate *sits, with head erect, and* Keller *inclines his head to* James; *so it is Aunt Ev, hesitant, and rather humble, who moves to the door.*

Outside, Helen *tugs at* Annie's *hand, and* Annie *comes with it.* Helen *pulls her toward the house; and hand in hand, they cross the yard, and ascend the porch steps, in the rising lights, to where Aunt Ev is holding the door open for them.*

The curtain ends the play.)

Developing Comprehension Skills

1. At the beginning of Act Three, what signs do we get that Annie may not be as confident as she appears?

2. What is the Kellers' opinion of Annie's accomplishments with Helen? Does Annie agree with them? Why is she so dissatisfied with what she has taught Helen?

3. What does Annie want from the Kellers? What breakthrough is she hoping for? Why do the Kellers refuse her request?

4. Why does Helen behave so badly at her first dinner with the family? How do Annie and the various members of the family respond to her actions?

5. When does Jimmie finally stand up to the Captain? Were you surprised at the Captain's response? Why or why not?

6. When Helen knocks over the pitcher of water, what is Annie's plan of action? When she drags Helen to the pump, what does Annie hope to accomplish? What far greater accomplishment occurs instead?

7. At the end of the play, Annie spells into Helen's hand, "I love Helen," and then whispers "forever and. . . . " Then, Annie stops and waits for the voices, but there are none. Who used to say "forever and ever" to Annie? Why do you think Annie no longer hears the voices from the past?

8. How appropriate is the title for this play? Do you agree that Annie was, indeed, a "miracle worker"? Was it luck, a miracle, or Annie's stubbornness and hard work that eventually helped her to reach Helen? Explain your answer.

Reading Literature

1. **Understanding Character Development.** Characters can be either static or dynamic. A **static character** stays the same throughout a story. A **dynamic character** changes, usually growing in understanding.

   Jimmie and the Captain both change a great deal as the play continues. How does each one grow and develop? How do these changes affect their relationship?

2. **Recognizing the Climax.** You remember that the first act introduced two conflicts in the play. In Act Two, the tension increased as Annie struggled to convince the Kellers to give her a free hand in disciplining Helen. A second struggle involved Annie's attempt to teach Helen. The **climax**, or turning point, of the play as a whole occurs in Act Three. What is the climax of the play? How does the author use lighting to show this breakthrough with Helen?

3. **Identifying the Theme.** You remember that the **theme** is the point that the author is trying to get across to the reader or audience. Plays, like novels and short stories, can have more than one theme. What do you think the main theme of this play is? How does the author communicate this theme to the audience? Can you find at least one minor theme in the play? Find examples to support your answer.

4. **Recognizing Symbols.** A symbol, as you remember, is an object that stands for something other than itself. In Act One, Annie gives Helen a doll when she first meets her. The doll's eyes open and close. This doll is a symbol for something even more important

that Annie gives Helen at the end of the play. What is that special gift that the doll represents?

Developing Vocabulary Skills

Understanding Multiple Meanings. Read the following sentences from Act Three. The underlined words have multiple meanings. Some can be used as different parts of speech. Write down the part of speech of each underlined word as it is used in the sentence. Then write the dictionary definition of the word that fits the context of the sentence.

1. This table contains equipment for teaching the blind, by touch.
2. And if she is dull, have you no patience with that?
3. Annie's gaze is grave, unpitying, very attentive.
4. She stands transfixed. Annie freezes on the pump handle.
5. I'm sorry to inconvenience you in this way.
6. Kate, facing Helen in her direction by the shoulders, holds her back, holds her back, and then relinquishes her.

Developing Writing Skills

1. **Comparing Fact and Fiction.** You have now completed a report on Annie Sullivan. How do the facts you learned compare with the character as she is presented in the play? Did the author of the play present the facts accurately, or did he exaggerate or invent details to make good drama? Present your opinion in a well-planned composition.

   Pre-Writing. Make two columns on a piece of paper. In the first column, write notes about Sullivan's actions and background as presented in the play. In the second column, write information about how each detail compares to the facts in her real life. When you are done with your list, make a judgment as to whether you think the author did or did not present a realistic version of the story.

   Writing. Write an introduction that presents your opinion of the story in *The Miracle Worker*. In the rest of your composition, support your opinion with details from your notes. You may wish to cover the material point by point. On the other hand, you may want to group them so that you discuss the people in one paragraph, the events in another, and historical facts in a third.

   Revising. Reread your rough draft. Have you supported your opinion well? Have you presented your ideas in a logical order? Have you used transitional words and phrases to show how the ideas are related?

2. **Writing an Essay.** Helen Keller wrote an essay called "Three Days To See." In it she imagined what she would do if she were given the gifts of sight and hearing for three days.

   Imagine that you had spent the first years of your life deaf and blind. Then imagine that you had been given the gift that Helen Keller describes. Where would you go? What would you do? Write a composition describing what those three days would be like.

Developing Skills in Study and Research

Using the *Readers' Guide to Periodical Literature*. Use the *Readers' Guide to Periodical Literature* to find articles describing the attempts by disabled people to be treated more fairly. Explore areas such as job opportunities, public transportation, and access to buildings. Prepare a short report on your findings.

Developing Skills in Speaking and Listening

Presenting a Scene from a Play. With several of your classmates, present a key scene from *The Miracle Worker*. First, practice reading the lines until you feel that you are interpreting them correctly. Then, plan the blocking, or movements, for the scene. Use the stage directions to help you with this part. With the others in the group, walk through the blocking several times, reading your lines as you move. Finally, memorize your lines and movements and work on polishing the scene. When your acting group feels confident, present the scene to the class.

Chapter 10 Review

Using Your Skills in Reading Literature

The following is from a play *The Crucible,* by Arthur Miller. This play is about the Puritan witch trials in 1692. In this scene, Deputy-Governor Danforth is investigating charges of witchcraft. These charges have been brought against John Proctor by Abigail Williams and other disturbed girls. Just before this scene, one of the girls, Mary Warren, confessed that the girls' bewitched behavior was a hoax. Read the passage and answer the questions that follow.

> **Abigail.** Why—? *(She gulps.)* Why do you come, yellow bird?
>
> **Proctor.** Where's a bird? I see no bird! . . .
>
> **Abigail** *(unperturbed, continuing to the "bird").* Oh, Mary, this is a black art to change your shape. No, I cannot, I cannot stop my mouth; it's God's work I do.
>
> **Mary Warren.** Abby, I'm *here!*
>
> **Proctor** *(Frantically).* They're pretending, Mr. Danforth!
>
> **Abigail** *(now she takes a backward step, as though in fear the bird will swoop down momentarily).* Oh, please, Mary! Don't come down.
>
> **Susanna Walcott.** Her claws, she's stretching her claws!
>
> **Proctor.** Lies, lies.
>
> **Abigail** *(backing further, eyes still fixed above).* Mary, please don't hurt me!
>
> **Mary Warren** *(to Danforth).* I'm not hurting her!
>
> **Danforth** *(to Mary Warren).* Why does she see this vision?
>
> **Mary Warren.** She sees nothin'!

1. Point out several examples of stage directions. Identify the stage directions that are very simple and those that describe action in some detail.

2. What is the mood of this passage?

3. What does this dialogue reveal about Abigail's character?

4. What conflict has developed in this scene?

Using Your Comprehension Skills

Answer the following questions concerning the passage from *The Crucible* on the preceding page. They ask you to make inferences and to predict outcomes.

1. What inferences can you draw about Puritan beliefs?
2. Why do you think the girls are trying to show that Mary is a witch?
3. Do you predict that Mary will continue to stick up for herself or give in to the girls?

Using Your Vocabulary Skills

The following words from *The Crucible* excerpt have multiple meanings: *art, shape, step, lies, fixed,* and *vision.* Use a dictionary to find all the definitions for these words. Then determine which definition of each word is intended in the play.

Using Your Writing Skills

Choose one of the writing assignments below.

1. Choose a character from *The Miracle Worker.* Analyze that character's traits, as revealed by the character's words, actions, and reactions.
2. Select one of the short stories from Chapter Seven. Imagine that you are writing a television version of that story. Write the script for one scene. Use your awareness of stage directions, lighting, and sound effects as you portray characters and action through dialogue.

Using Your Skills in Critical Thinking/Study and Research

Imagine that you are writing a report on space travel between planets. Determine the main categories of information you would research. Then, decide on the best sources for your report. Finally, decide how you would organize your information for a report.

Handbook for Reading and Writing

Adage. An adage is an old and supposedly wise saying. Adages are brief and generally expressed in a clever, easy-to-remember style. Examples of adages are: "Easy come, easy go," "A stitch in time saves nine," and "One good turn deserves another." Another name for adages is proverbs.

For more about adages and proverbs, see pages 75 and 79. See also *Epigram.*

Alliteration. Repetition of consonant sounds at the beginning of words is called alliteration. Alliteration is used in prose and poetry, as well as in everyday speech. It gives a musical quality and rhythm to writing. It also adds to the mood and emphasizes important words.

> *L*ove, *l*eave me *l*ike the *l*ight,
>   The gentle passing day;
> *W*e *w*ould *n*ot *k*now, but for the *n*ights,
>   When it has slipped away.
> ("If You Should Go," page 532)

For more about alliteration, see page 109.

Allusion. A reference to a well known work of literature, a famous person, or an historical event is called an allusion. Recognizing allusions can add to a reader's understanding of a piece of writing. The allusions to Achilles and Zeus in "Stelmark," (page 439) refer to characters from Greek mythology. These allusions and others in the story are used to support the author's ideas on the importance of cultural heritage.

For more about allusion, see page 235.

Analogy. In literature, an analogy is an extended comparison of two different things that have certain similar characteristics. Writers can use analogies to explain something unfamiliar by comparing it to something familiar.

For more about analogy, see page 331.

Assonance. The repetition of the same vowel sound within words is called assonance. Assonance can help to create a mood and stress certain words or ideas in prose and poetry. Note how the repetition of the long *O* sound in this example creates the feeling of sadness.

> The buffal*o*es are gone
> And th*o*se who saw the buffal*o*es are gone.
> Th*o*se who saw the buffal*o*es by thousands
> ("Buffalo Dusk," page 551)

For more about assonance, see page 111.

Autobiography. A story a person writes about his or her own life is an autobiography. It is written from the first-person point of view and generally focuses on significant experiences in the person's life. An example is "My Bondage and My Freedom" (page 247).

For more about autobiography, see page 75.

Biography. Nonfiction writing that tells the story of a person's life is called a biography. Biographies often include important events as well as less important yet interesting facts about a person's life. While biographies focus on the subject's personality, they may also provide details about the times when the person lived. "The Legend of Amelia Earhart" on page 454 is an example of a biography.

For more about biography, see page 424.

Blank Verse. See *Rhythm.*

Character. Each person or animal who takes part in the action of a story, poem, or play is a character. The more important characters are called major characters. Everyone else in the selection is a minor character. In "A Visit of Charity" (page 367), Marian is a major character, while the nurse is a minor character.

A dynamic character is one that develops and grows during the course of a story. A static character does not.

For more about characters, see page 354. See also *Character Trait* and *Characterization.*

Characterization. The method a writer uses to define a character is called characterization. The character may be revealed through a physical description, through dialogue, through the character's thoughts and actions, or through the reactions of other characters.

When direct characterization is used, the author makes specific statements about the character.

> He had known all the grief, the joy, the peril and the labor such a man could know; he had grown seamed and weathered . . . he had grown old, and had the grandeur and the wisdom these men have.
> ("The Far and the Near," page 375)

When indirect characterization is used, a character is revealed by the way he or she speaks, thinks, or acts.

For more about characterization, see page 157. See also *Character, Character Trait,* and *Description.*

Character Trait. A quality exhibited by a character through his or her actions, statements, or thoughts is a character trait. In "The Tell-Tale Heart" (page 174), for example, the main character displays the traits of patience, cunning, and insanity.

For more about character traits, see page 261. See also *Character* and *Characterization.*

Chronological Order. See *Time Order.*

Climax. The climax of a story generally involves an important event, decision, or discovery. It is the turning point in the action of the story and affects the final outcome. In "The Far and the Near" (page 374), for example, the climax occurs when the engineer faces the woman who had waved to him for years.

For more about climax, see page 354. See also *Plot.*

Comparison. A comparison is used in prose or poetry to show how two different things may have something in common. Writers often use comparisons to make things clearer for the reader. For example, in "A Visit of Charity" (page 367), the author uses figurative language and description to compare the old women to sheep. This comparison allows the reader to form a vivid image of how the old women look, sound, and move.

For more about comparison, see page 245. See also *Contrast, Metaphor,* and *Simile.*

Concrete Poem. A poem that is placed on the page so that the arrangement of the words in the poem suggests a picture is called a concrete poem. The shape often expands on the meaning of the poem. "Night Practice" (page 558) is an example of a concrete poem.

For more about concrete poems, see page 559. See also *Poetry.*

Conflict. The struggle between opposing forces creates the conflict in a story. Conflict is a necessary ingredient in any story or play. It is the basic framework for the development of the plot. There are two types of conflict, external and internal.

A struggle between two characters, or between a character and a force such as nature or society is called external conflict. In "The Tell-Tale Heart" (page 174), the confrontation between the narrator and the police officers is an external conflict.

The struggle within a character is called internal conflict. This battle often involves a decision the character must make. In "The Tell-Tale Heart," the narrator's mental turmoil leading to the decision to murder the old man is an example of internal conflict.

For more about conflict, see page 179. See also *Plot*.

Consonance. The repetition of consonant sounds within and at the end of words is called consonance. This repetition can add rhythm and emphasis to prose as well as poetry. In the following lines from "The Raven" (page 181), the consonance of the *p* and *d* sounds create a feeling of insistent, rhythmic knocking.

While I no*dd*ed, nearly na*pp*ing, su*dd*enly
    there came a ta*pp*ing,
As of someone gently ra*pp*ing, ra*pp*ing at
    my chamber door.

For more about consonance, see pages 113 and 114.

Contrast. Contrast is often used by writers to show the differences between two things or ideas. In "The Far and the Near" (page 374), the powerful impact of the story is based on the contrast that is seen in the title. The image of the cottage and woman as viewed from the train is contrasted with the image seen by the engineer when he visits the house.

For more about contrast, see page 19. See also *Comparison*.

Couplet. See *Rhyme*.

Description. In a description, the writer creates word pictures of a character, setting, or action. There are two types of description, direct and indirect.

In direct description the writer directly states an idea that tells about a character, setting, or event. An example can be seen in the description of Daniel Webster in "The Devil and Daniel Webster" (page 159).

. . . he was the biggest man in the country. He never got to be President, but he was the biggest man. There were thousands that trusted in him right next to God Almighty, . . .

In indirect description the reader learns about characters, setting, and events by inferring information from what others say and do.

For more about description, see page 7. See also *Characterization* and *Imagery*.

Dialect. The language that is characteristic of a specific geographical area is called a regional dialect. Dialects may vary in vocabulary, pronunciation, and grammar. Stephen Crane uses dialect in "A Mystery of Heroism" (page 264) to make the soldiers' conversations sound realistic.

For more about dialect, see page 271.

Dialogue. Conversation among characters in a story or play is called dialogue. In stories, the exact words are set off by quotation marks.

"Where do you come from?" I asked him.
"From San Carlos," he said and smiled. . . .

"I was taking care of animals," he explained.

"Oh," I said, not quite understanding. ("Old Man at the Bridge," page 379)

In a play, no quotation marks are used. The words spoken by each character follow that character's name.

For more about dialogue, see page 584.

Dialogue Tag. See *Dialogue*.

Direct Description. See *Characterization* and *Description*.

Drama. A form of literature that is meant to be performed on stage before an audience is a drama or play. A drama is told through dialogue and the actions of the characters. Like other forms of fiction, drama uses characters, setting, plot, dialogue, and sometimes a narrator. Written drama may also include suggestions for the set, costumes, sound, and lighting, as well as instructions for the actors. Most plays are divided into parts called acts. An act may be divided into smaller parts called scenes.

A stage play usually has only a few simple settings. *The Miracle Worker* (page 590) is an example of a stage play.

For more about drama, see pages 584 and 585. See also *Stage Directions*.

Dynamic Character. See *Character*.

Epigram. A brief, witty saying that expresses a truth about life is called an epigram. For examples of epigrams, see pages 77, 205, and 331.

For more about epigrams, see page 205.

Epitaph. A statement written on a tombstone is called an epitaph. Most epitaphs tell something memorable about the person buried there. See Benjamin Franklin's epitaph on page 83.

For more about epitaphs, see page 84.

Essay. A type of nonfiction in which the writer expresses an opinion or provides information on a given topic is called an essay. An essay may inform, entertain, or persuade. An informal essay is often humorous. It reflects the writer's feelings in a light and casual way. It may be looser in structure than a formal essay.

A formal essay examines a topic in a logical, thorough way. It usually has a serious tone, a formal structure, and careful organization. "Seeing" (page 484) is an example of a formal essay.

For more about the essay, see pages 67 and 203. See also *Nonfiction*.

External Conflict. See *Conflict*.

Fable. A story that is meant to teach a lesson about human nature is called a fable. The lesson that it teaches is called a moral. "Silent Spring" (page 489) is an example of a fable.

For more about fables, see page 491.

Falling Action. Falling action is the part of the plot that follows the climax. After the intensity and action have peaked, the events follow their logical course to the end of the story. For example, in "One-Shot Finch" on page 392, the climax occurs when Atticus shoots the rabid dog. The falling action follows, with the children discussing their new feelings about their father.

For more on falling action, see page 354. See also *Climax* and *Plot*.

Fiction. Fiction is imaginative writing, although it may be inspired by actual events or real people. Some types of fiction are short stories, novels, and fables.

For more about fiction, see pages 354 and 355. See also *Short Story* and *Science Fiction*.

Figurative Language. Speaking or writing about familiar things in unusual ways is called figurative language. This type of writing gives new meaning to ordinary words.

Figurative language is used to encourage readers to think about things in a fresh new way. It includes several specific methods of putting words together known as figures of speech. The most common figures of speech are: simile, metaphor, personification, and hyperbole.

For more about figurative language, see page 199. See also *Hyperbole, Metaphor, Personification*, and *Simile*.

Flashback. Flashback is a technique used to tell about something that happened before the beginning of a story, or at an earlier point in the story. An example is in "An Occurrence at Owl Creek Bridge," (page 253).

For more about flashback, see pages 261–262.

Folklore. A body of traditional beliefs, legends, stories, and sayings that is passed on orally from generation to generation is called folklore. The original author of a particular piece is generally unknown. For example, the plot of "Rip Van Winkle" (page 145) is based on folklore.

For more about folklore, see page 157. See also *Oral Literature*.

Foot. See *Rhythm*.

Foreshadowing. A clue or hint of what will take place later in a story is called foreshadowing. The writer uses this technique to prepare the reader for an important event or to create suspense. In "To Build a Fire" (page 333) the author gives several hints that the man will eventually meet his death.

For more about foreshadowing, see page 346.

Free Verse. When there is no regular rhyme scheme, rhythm, or line length in a poem, it is called free verse. Much twentieth-century poetry falls in this category. "Cavalry Crossing a Ford" (page 273) and "Chicago" (page 513) are examples of free verse.

For more about free verse, see page 273. See also *Poetry* and *Rhythm*.

Hyperbole. A figure of speech that uses great exaggeration is called hyperbole. It often gives the reader a humorous image of what the writer is describing. The exaggeration also may be used to make a point or to create a certain effect. The following example of hyperbole is from "The Devil and Daniel Webster" on page 159.

They said when he stood up to speak, stars and stripes came right out in the sky, and once he spoke against a river and made it sink into the ground.

For more about hyperbole, see pages 39, 127, and 128. See also *Figurative Language*.

Idiom. A common phrase or expression that has a different meaning from the actual meaning of the individual words is called an idiom. For example, in the sentence, "I ran across my music teacher in the parking lot," the phrase "ran across" is an idiom. It means "to come upon by chance" not, literally, "to run over."

For more about idioms, see page 429.

Imagery. Descriptive writing that creates vivid mental pictures is called imagery. Sensory details are used to help the reader see, feel, smell, hear, or taste the things described.

He noted the prismatic colors in all the dewdrops upon a million blades of grass. The humming of the gnats that danced above the eddies of the stream, the beating of the dragon-flies' wings, the strokes of the water-spiders' legs, like oars which had lifted their boat—all these made audible music. ("An Occurrence at Owl Creek Bridge," page 257)

For more about imagery, see page 13. See also *Figurative Language*.

Indirect Description. See *Characterization* and *Description*.

Internal Conflict. See *Conflict*.

Internal Rhyme. See *Rhyme*.

Introduction. The first part of a plot is called the introduction. In it, the reader is introduced to the characters, the setting, and the conflict.

> It was mid-morning—a very cold, bright day. Holding a potted plant before her, a girl of fourteen jumped off the bus in front of the Old Ladies' Home, in the outskirts of town. . . .
> "I'm a Campfire Girl. . . . I have to pay a visit to some old lady," she told the nurse at the desk.
> ("A Visit of Charity," page 367)

For more about the introduction, see page 354. See also *Plot*.

Irony. The contrast between what appears to be true and what is actually true is called irony. For example, in "The Possibility of Evil" (page 402), it is ironic that Mrs. Strangeworth is not the sweet old lady she appears to be.

Another type of irony occurs when the reader understands something that a character does not. In "The Gift of the Magi" (page 360), the reader understands the irony of the two Christmas gift purchases long before the characters are aware of it.

Verbal irony occurs when a writer says one thing but means something completely different. The title of "A Visit of Charity" (page 367) is an example. The girl's visit to the nursing home has nothing to do with charitable feelings.

For more about irony, see page 179.

Journal. A record of a writer's personal experiences is called a journal. A journal may be written in a formal or an informal style. Some journals record historical events. An example is "Of Plymouth Plantation" (page 25).

For more about journals, see page 28.

Local Color. See *Realism*.

Lyric Poem. In a lyric poem, a single speaker expresses his or her thoughts and feelings. "Faith Is a Fine Invention" (page 283) is a short, lyric poem by Emily Dickinson.

For more about lyric poems, see page 283.

Malapropism. The mistake made when a speaker uses the wrong word is called a malapropism. The confusion usually occurs because the misused word sounds similar to the actual word intended by the speaker. Malapropisms are often intentionally used to create humor in a piece of writing.

In "It All Started with Columbus" (page 477), for example, Richard Armour uses the word *toupees* instead of *teepees*.

For more about malapropisms, see page 482. See also *Pun*.

Metaphor. A metaphor is a figure of speech that finds similarities between two things that are basically dissimilar. Unlike the simile, the comparison in a metaphor is made without the use of the words *like* or *as*.

A metaphor usually states that one thing is another.

> Fame is a bee.
>   It has a song—
> It has a sting—
>   Ah, too, it has a wing.
> ("Fame Is a Bee," page 282)

In an implied metaphor, a comparison is implied or suggested. The reader must examine the selection more closely to see the comparison being made.

When a metaphor is developed throughout an entire verse, poem, or paragraph, the metaphor is called an extended metaphor.

For more about metaphors, see pages 13, 79, 123, and 124. See also *Comparison, Figurative Language,* and *Simile.*

Monologue. A long speech by one person is called a monologue. This speech may be part of a story; it may be a poem; or it may be delivered by a character in a play.

A dramatic monologue is addressed to a silent or imaginary listener. It is spoken during a moment of deep emotion and usually expresses the character's innermost thoughts and fears.

For more about monologues, see page 618.

Mood. The feeling or atmosphere that the writer creates for the reader is called the mood. There are several ways mood can be established. The description of the setting, what characters say, the use of imagery and figurative language—all can be used to develop mood.

For more about mood, see page 11.

Narrative Poem. A poem that tells a story is a narrative poem. Like a short story, it has characters, setting, and plot. "I Went To Kill the Deer" (page 14) is an example of a narrative poem.

For more about narrative poems, see page 14.

Narrator. The narrator is the person from whose point of view a story is told. There are different types of narrators. The first-person narrator is usually a character in the story. "The Tell-Tale Heart" (page 174) is an example of first-person narration.

The third-person narrator tells the story from outside the action. There are two types of third-

person narrators. A narrator who knows how all the characters think and feel is omniscient, as in "The Gift of the Magi" (page 360). The limited third-person narrator knows the thoughts and feelings of only one character.

For more about the narrator, see page 75. See also *Point of View.*

Naturalism. Naturalism is an extreme form of realism that was developed in the second half of the 1800's. This writing style portrays people and events precisely and objectively without idealizing them. The characters in such writing have little control over what happens to them. They are generally helpless victims of their own emotions and the world around them.

For more about naturalism, see page 229. See also *Realism.*

Nonfiction. Writing that presents factual information is called nonfiction. It deals with real people, places, and events. Autobiographies and biographies are examples of nonfiction. Other types are articles, journals, essays, speeches, and letters.

For more about nonfiction, see page 323. See also *Autobiography, Biography, Essay,* and *Journal.*

Off Rhyme. See *Rhyme.*

Onomatopoeia. The use of words that imitate sounds is called onomatopoeia.

Sling your knuckles on the bottoms of
the happy tin pans, let
your trombones ooze, and go husha-
husha-hush with the slippery sand-paper.
("Jazz Fantasia," page 517)

For more about onomatopoeia, see page 119.

Oral Literature. Literature that has been passed to new generations by word of mouth is called oral literature. Oral literature is the product of many storytellers; the texts change as details are added or left out. Its purpose is to entertain, teach, or reinforce customs and values. Myths, folk tales, and poems are examples of oral literature.

For more about oral literature, see pages 4 and 10. See also *Folklore*.

Parallelism. A technique used to emphasize ideas that are of equal importance by presenting them in similar phrases or sentences is called parallelism. This powerful literary tool can be used to persuade, build emotion, and reinforce the writer or speaker's ideas. Martin Luther King, Jr.'s "I Have a Dream" speech on page 472, uses this technique. Several groups of sentences throughout the address use identical beginning phrases. For example, "One hundred years later. . . ," "I have a dream. . . ," and "Let freedom ring. . . ."

For more about parallelism, see page 235.

Parody. A parody is an imitation of another work of literature. Parody can be used to criticize or praise, but it is most often used to point out the humor in something that is ordinarily taken seriously. In *The Adventures of Huckleberry Finn*, the poem "Ode to Stephen Dowling Bots, Dec'd." is a parody on the romantic verse popular in Mark Twain's time.

For more about parody, see page 220.

Personification. A figure of speech that gives human qualities to an object, a place, or an idea is called personification. Poet Carl Sandburg personifies a city in his poem "Chicago" (page 513). Giving the city human qualities emphasizes the mood of vitality and strength in the poem.

For more about personification, see pages 11 and 125. See also *Figurative Language*.

Play. See *Drama*.

Plot. The sequence of events in a story is called the plot. One event logically follows the next. Usually, each thing that happens is caused by what precedes it. The elements, or parts of the plot include the introduction, the rising action, the climax, the falling action, and the resolution.

For more about plot, see page 178. See also *Climax, Falling Action, Introduction, Resolution,* and *Rising Action*.

Poetry. Poetry is a form of literature arranged in lines. It condenses ideas and feelings into a few words. The sounds of the words and their arrangement are often as important as the meaning of the words themselves.

Some poetry follows definite rules for form, rhythm, and rhyme. The lines of verse are regular and divided into groups called stanzas. Poetry that has no regular pattern of beats is called free verse. Poetry with lines or words arranged in a recognizable shape or picture is called concrete poetry.

For more about poetry, see page 39. See also *Concrete Poem, Free Verse, Rhyme, Rhyme Scheme, Rhythm,* and *Stanza*.

Point of View. The narrative method in a piece of writing is called the point of view. The writer may use a first-person point of view, as in "The Algonquian Confederacy Speech" (page 18), or a third-person point of view, as in "Migrant People" (page 384).

For more about point of view, see page 355. See also *Narrator*.

Proverb. See *Adage*.

Pun. The humorous use of words that have almost the same sound or spelling but different meanings is a pun. Notice, for example, how the author plays with the word *disgrace* in the following line from "It All Started with Columbus" (page 478).

> He lived for a time in Madrid, but spent his last days in Disgrace.

For more about puns, see page 482. See also *Malapropism*.

Purpose. The purpose is the writer's reason for writing. It may be to entertain, to inform, to persuade, or to express feelings about a certain subject. The writer must decide on his or her purpose before beginning to write.

For more about purpose, see pages 36 and 40. See also *Theme*.

Realism. A type of writing that presents people and things as they really are is called realism. Nothing is added or deleted that would idealize a character or situation. Realism began in the second half of the 1800's when writers began taking a close look at their growing country. The realists believed that people controlled their own fates.

Regionalism is a type of realism that focuses attention on the unique character of the different regions of the country.

Local color is added to the writing to give interest to the story, as well as to portray the characters, their speech, customs, and attitudes in an accurate manner.

For more about realism, see pages 228–229.

Refrain. See *Repetition*.

Regionalism. See *Realism*.

Repetition. A literary technique in which words or lines are repeated at regular intervals throughout a selection is called repetition. Poets use repetition for emphasis or to create a particular sound pattern or rhythm. The repetition of the line or phrase is often called a refrain.

In "Beat! Beat! Drums!" (page 274), the phrase "Beat! beat! drums!—blow! bugles! blow!" is used as a refrain.

For more about repetition, see page 13.

Resolution. The fifth and final element of a plot is the resolution. Any remaining questions about the events in the story are usually answered in the resolution, and the action is completed.

For more about resolution, see page 354. See also *Plot*.

Rhyme. The repetition of sounds at the ends of words is called rhyme. When words rhyme at the end of lines of poetry it is called end rhyme. An example of end rhyme can be found in "The Debt" (page 510). The rhyming words are *pay/day* and *grief/relief*.

> This is the debt I pay
> Just for one riotous day,
> Years of regret and grief,
> Sorrow without relief.

When two consecutive lines of poetry rhyme, they are called a couplet. The four lines of poetry above consist of two rhyming couplets.

Some poems have internal rhyme, or rhyming words within a single line. "The Raven" (page 181) offers many examples of internal rhyme.

> Once upon a midnight *dreary,* while I pondered, weak and *weary,*

Poetry with end rhymes that are not exact have off rhyme. An example is "The Bustle in a House" (page 287).

For more about rhyme, see pages 115–116. See also *Rhyme Scheme*.

Rhyme Scheme. Rhyme schemes are the different patterns in which end rhyme is used in poetry. A rhyme scheme is written using a different letter of the alphabet to stand for each different rhyming sound.

> Love, leave me like the light,   *a*
>   The gently passing day;   *b*
> We would not know, but for the night,   *a*
>   When it has slipped away.   *b*
> ("If You Should Go," page 532)

For more about rhyme scheme, see pages 115–116. See also *Rhyme* and *Rhythm*.

Rhythm. The pattern of stressed and unstressed syllables in poetry is called rhythm. The stressed or accented syllables are marked with ´ while the unstressed or unaccented syllables are marked with ˘. The pattern these syllables make in a line of poetry may be divided into units. Each unit is called a foot, which is a combination of stressed and unstressed syllables. One type of foot is the iamb. It is made up of an unstressed syllable followed by a stressed syllable. (˘ ´)

"Because I Could Not Stop for Death" (page 285) is an example of a poem with a regular rhythm. It is divided into iambic feet.

> Because I could not stop for Death—
>
> He kindly stopped for me—
>
> The Carriage held but just Ourselves—
>
> And Immortality.

Free verse has no regular pattern of beats. Blank verse has five pairs of syllables. The first syllable is unaccented; the second syllable is accented. Blank verse, however, does not rhyme.

For more about rhythm, see pages 117 and 118.

Rising Action. The second element of a plot diagram is the rising action. In this part of the story, it becomes apparent that the characters face problems or conflicts. Complications usually arise as a struggle develops. The events in the rising action build to the climax, the third part of the plot. In "The Possibility of Evil" (page 402), the rising action occurs as the reader learns more and more about the character of Mrs. Strangeworth and her relationships with the other people in the town.

For more about rising action, see page 354. See also *Plot*.

Romanticism. Romanticism was a movement that began in Europe in the early 1800's. It was adopted by many American writers of the time. Romantic writing emphasizes emotions and feelings instead of reason and logic. It also focuses on the life of common people and encourages an appreciation of nature instead of society.

Transcendentalism grew out of the Romantic movement. Transcendentalist writers believed that true spiritual goodness and knowledge could be found within each individual. They therefore urged people to rely on their intuition and conscience in all matters.

For more about romanticism and transcendentalism, see pages 134 and 135.

Satire. Writing that ridicules a subject by combining humor and criticism is called satire. It generally makes fun of ideas or customs that are taken seriously by many, but are considered foolish by the writer. In *The Adventures of Huckleberry Finn* (page 309), Mark Twain satirizes the lifestyle of the Grangerfords.

For more about satire, see page 317.

Science Fiction. Fantasy writing that focuses on the possibilities of the future is called science fiction. It uses a base of scientific facts, theories, and technology to create fantasy. It frequently gives the reader an imaginary view into the future. "Time in Thy Flight" (page 413) is an example of science fiction.

For more about science fiction, see page 417.

Sensory Image. See *Imagery*.

Sequence. The arrangement of a series of events or ideas is called its sequence, or order. A writer can arrange, or order, his or her ideas in many different ways. The arrangement usually depends on the content and purpose of the writing. The writer of a story often uses chronological, or time, order. The author of a persuasive essay might use a logical sequence by stating an opinion and then following it with supporting statements in order of their importance. Other sequences include spatial order, order of familiarity, comparison or contrast, or a combination of orders.

For more about sequence, see *Time Order*.

Setting. The time and place where the action of a story occurs are called the setting. All stories have a setting, but some are described in greater detail than others depending on the importance of the setting to the story.

For example, the setting in "The Gift of the Magi" (page 360) is less important than the development of the plot; therefore it is not described in great detail.

On the other hand, much time is devoted to the description of the Yukon wilderness in "To Build a Fire," because of the setting's importance to the story.

For more about setting, see page 354.

Short Story. A piece of fiction that is short enough to be read at one sitting is a short story. It usually tells about one major character and one major conflict. The four main elements of a short story are setting, character, plot, and theme. Examples of twentieth-century short stories can be found in Chapter 7.

For more about the short story, see page 178. See also *Character, Plot, Setting,* and *Theme*.

Simile. A simile is a figure of speech that makes a comparison between two things that are unlike. Similes use the words *like* or *as*.

> What happens to a dream deferred?
> Does it dry up
> like a raisin in the sun?
> ("Harlem," page 544)

For more about simile, see pages 34, 121, and 122. See also *Comparison, Figurative Language,* and *Metaphor*.

Speaker. The speaker in a poem may be compared to the narrator in fiction. The speaker and the poet are not necessarily the same. The speaker may be a character created by the poet to express a certain kind of idea.

For more about the speaker, see page 16.

Stage Directions. In drama, stage directions are often provided for the actors and the director of a play. These directions may suggest how to read certain lines, how to move, or what sound effects are needed. Stage directions may also help a reader understand the characters and "see" the action of the play. The author of *The Miracle Worker* (page 590) makes extensive use of stage directions. In Act Two, for example, the entire dining room scene between Helen and Annie is explained through directions to the actors. There is no spoken dialogue.

For more about stage directions, see pages 585 and 617.

Stanza. A group of lines that form a unit in poetry is called a stanza. Like a paragraph, a stanza develops a single main idea. When the stanzas are put together, they show the organization of ideas in a poem.

For more about stanzas, see page 189.

Static Character. See *Character*.

Style. The unique way in which a writer expresses his or her ideas is called the writer's style. Style refers to *how* something is said, not to *what* is said. The length and order of sentences, choice of words, and use of figurative language all contribute to a writer's style.

For more about style, see page 16.

Surprise Ending. An unexpected turn of events at the conclusion of a story is called a surprise ending. O. Henry is well known for using this technique. An example can be found in his story "The Gift of the Magi" (page 360).

For more about the surprise ending, see page 261.

Suspense. The tension that is created when the reader is unsure about the outcome of a situation is called suspense. In "The Tell-Tale Heart" (page 174), Poe builds suspense by carefully detailing the narrator's painstaking plans for murdering the old man. The suspense continues as the narrator imagines he hears the beating of the dead man's heart becoming louder and louder.

For more about suspense, see page 179.

Symbol. A symbol is something that stands for or represents something else. A light bulb is a symbol for an idea in a cartoon. In "The Road Not Taken" (page 526), the roads are symbols for the choices one might make in life.

For more about symbols, see page 186.

Theme. The theme of a piece of literature is the main idea or message that the author wishes to share with the reader. A writer rarely states the theme directly. The reader must infer what the theme is after a careful examination of the selection. One of the themes of "The Devil and Daniel Webster" (page 159), for example, might be that good triumphs over evil.

For more about theme, see page 158.

Time Order. The progression of events in the order in which they occurred in time is called time order, or chronological order. Time order is a common method of organizing the details in a piece of writing.

For more about time order, see page 50.

Tone. The writer's attitude toward a subject is the tone of the selection. It tells how the writer feels about the subject or a character. The tone can be determined by carefully examining the writer's choice of words, the style of writing, and the content. The tone of "Annabel Lee" (page 187) is one of sadness and loneliness.

For more about tone, see pages 36 and 98.

Transcendentalism. See *Romanticism*.

Understatement. The opposite of exaggeration is understatement. The writer makes a statement with less emphasis or force than the situation would seem to call for. "Fire and Ice" (page 527) uses understatement. The poem deals very casually with the end of the world and the destructive emotions of human beings.

For more about understatement, see page 528.

Summary of Comprehension Skills

Cause and Effect. Sometimes events are related by cause and effect. One event causes another event. The second event is the effect of the first event.

Certain key words can alert a reader to look for a cause and effect relationship. These key words include: *because, so that, since, in order that,* and *if—then.*

Sometimes, when one event happens after another, a reader or writer mistakenly assumes that the first event caused the second, when, in fact, the two events have no relationship to each other. This is called *false cause and effect reasoning.*

For more about cause and effect, see pages 136–137. See also *False Cause and Effect Reasoning* in the Summary of Critical Thinking Terms, page 707.

Chronological Order. See *Paragraph Organization.*

Comparison and Contrast. Looking for similarities between two works of literature is called making a comparison. Finding the differences between selections is called making a contrast. Some of the elements that can be compared and contrasted are character, setting, plot, mood, tone, and theme.

For more about comparison and contrast, see pages 19, 67, 245, and 276.

Connotation. Connotation refers to the emotional meaning a word carries with it. This meaning can go far beyond the **denotation**, or straight dictionary meaning of the word. The denotation of *peace,* for example, is simply "freedom from war." The connotation, however, may create strong feelings. Some people may hear the word "peace" and feel hopeful, serene, or secure. Others may feel sad or frustrated because they see "peace" as an unattainable goal.

For more about connotations, see pages 62–63.

Errors in Reasoning. See the Summary of Critical Thinking Terms, page 706.

Evaluation. After reading a selection, one should be able to make a judgment, or evaluation, of it. A fair evaluation is objective and unbiased. It is based on established standards of good writing. When evaluating a piece of writing, each element should be considered individually. Elements to examine include characterization, setting, plot, mood, tone, theme, and the writer's style.

For more about evaluation, see the Summary of Critical Thinking Terms, pages 706 and 707.

Fact and Opinion. Facts are statements that can be proved to be true. Opinions express only the beliefs of the writer. They cannot be proved. Facts and opinions are sometimes combined in writing. A careful reader should be able to distinguish between facts and opinions. In the example at the top of the next page, the writer begins with a statement of opinion. The opinion is underlined. The writer then provides two statements of fact which serve to back up this opinion.

> Soccer is the best sport for young children. All ages can play. Above average strength and size are not required and no special equipment is necessary except shin guards and a ball.

For more about separating fact and opinion, see page 62. See also the Summary of Critical Thinking Terms, page 707.

Figurative Language. Figurative language is a way of speaking or writing that uses ordinary words in unusual ways. It requires the reader to look beyond the usual meanings of words.

For example, if someone is "only a hop, skip, and a jump away from home," it does not really mean that the person can reach home with one hop, one skip, and one jump. It only means that the person's home is nearby.

The opposite of figurative language is literal language. Literal language means exactly what it says.

For more about figurative language, see pages 199 and 230–231.

Inferences. Making a logical guess by using given evidence is called making an inference. A reader is often expected to make inferences. One must infer what the writer has not stated directly by examining clues or hints. For example, you might read a sentence such as the following:

> As Sharon lifted the bag from her car, several cans tore through the bottom and scattered on the pavement of the driveway.

From this information, you might infer, or conclude, that Sharon has probably been grocery shopping. The bag was overpacked with heavy items, causing it to tear when lifted. Sharon is not a child because she is old enough to drive and own a car. She is probably returning home, since the bag broke as she was removing it from the car, not putting it in the car.

Literal Language. See *Figurative Language.*

Main Idea. A paragraph is a group of sentences that work together to tell about one idea. This idea is the main idea of the paragraph. It is often stated in one sentence, called the topic sentence. All the other sentences in the paragraph should relate to or support the idea in the topic sentence.

Outcome. Making a reasonable guess about what will happen next in a story is called predicting an outcome. Some outcomes are easy to predict; others are more difficult.

When predicting outcomes, use the clues provided by the writer. Consider information about the characters, the plot, and the setting. Use your own knowledge and experience to judge what people do in similar situations.

For more about predicting outcomes, see pages 586 and 587.

Overgeneralization. See the Summary of Critical Thinking Terms, page 708.

Paragraph Organization. There are four basic kinds of paragraphs. Each has a different purpose and a different order, or sequence in which the information is presented.

A *narrative paragraph* tells about a series of events. The sentences are usually arranged in the order in which the events happen. Therefore, the sequence they follow is in time order, or chronological order. Here is an example from "The Gift of the Magi."

> Della finished her cry and attended to her cheeks with a powder rag. She stood by the

window and looked out dully at a gray cat walking a gray fence in a gray backyard (page 360).

For more about recognizing time order, see page 50.

A *descriptive paragraph* describes a person, an object, or a scene. Details are generally arranged in the order or sequence in which you would notice them. This is called spatial order. In "A Visit of Charity" the writer describes the following scene in spatial order.

> Holding a potted plant before her, a girl of fourteen jumped off the bus in front of the Old Ladies' Home, in the outskirts of town. She wore a red coat, and her straight yellow hair was hanging down loose from the pointed white cap all the little girls were wearing that year (page 367).

A *persuasive paragraph* tries to convince the reader to accept a certain idea. Sentences are arranged in a logical sequence. The writer's argument must make sense to the reader. Usually a persuasive paragraph is arranged with reasons presented in the order of importance to the writer. The reasons explain why the reader should think or behave in a certain way. "A Letter from Thomas Jefferson to His Daughter" (page 96) is an example of persuasive writing.

An *explanatory paragraph* explains something. After the topic sentence, the other sentences give details, usually in chronological order or order of importance.

> He motioned at the row of jars filled with varied spices. "There is origanon there and basilikon and daphne and sesame and miantanos, all the flavorings that we have used in our food for thousands of years. The men of Marathon carried small packets of these spices into battle, and the scents reminded

them of their homes, their families, and their children." ("Stelmark", page 439)

Punctuation Clues. Punctuation marks are like road signs. They tell a reader where to pause, when to break a thought, and how to interpret a sentence. Punctuation is especially important in poetry. In poems, words are arranged in lines. A reader could logically assume that each line contains a complete thought. This is rarely the case, however, and the careful reader will look for periods, question marks, and exclamation marks to signal the actual end of a thought.

Sometimes, a poem will be only one or two long sentences. When this is the case, the reader will have to divide the long sentence into meaningful phrases or shorter sentences.

For more about punctuation clues, see pages 16, 93, 141, 239, and 298.

Purpose. Before putting pen to paper, a writer must decide what he or she wants to accomplish with the writing. This is called the writer's purpose. The purpose of a piece of writing can be to inform, to entertain, to persuade, or to express feelings or thoughts. The writer often chooses a topic or organization after considering the purpose for the writing. The handling of elements such as plot, character, and setting also depends on the author's purpose.

For more about an author's purpose, see pages 36, 40–41, 87, 93, 102, 171, 192, 220, 245, and 323.

Sequence. See *Paragraph Organization.*

Slanted Writing. See the Summary of Critical Thinking Terms, page 708.

Spatial Order. See *Paragraph Organization.*

Subjective/Objective Language. Objective language conveys information in a factual and impartial way without giving a personal opinion. Subjective language uses words that have an emotional appeal.

For more about subjective language, see pages 28 and 62–63.

Time Order. See *Paragraph Organization*.

Transitional Words. Words or phrases that suggest the relationship of ideas within or between paragraphs are called transitional words. These words help a writer to move smoothly and logically from idea to idea and paragraph to paragraph. Examples of transitional words are: *tomorrow, then, for a long time, however, meanwhile, soon, next, later,* and *finally*.

Word Choice. A writer considers all of the following when he or she chooses a word: the mood of the selection, the tone, his or her personal style, the setting, and the audience to whom the writing is aimed.

For more about word choice, see pages 235 and 237.

Word Order. For variety or emphasis, a writer might occasionally arrange the words in a sentence in an order that is different than normal. In most sentences the subject is followed by a verb. Sometimes, however, the sentence will be reversed. The verb will come before the subject. Poets, especially, like to use this reverse word order. To understand a poem with reverse word order it may be necessary to put the sentences back in the usual order by finding out who or what the sentence is about (the subject) and then asking what the subject does or what happens to the subject (the verb).

For more about word order, see page 500.

Summary of Vocabulary Skills

1. Word Parts

Words are sometimes made by combining word parts. When you know the meanings of each of the word parts, you may be able to discover the meaning of the entire word. Three kinds of word parts are base words, prefixes, and suffixes.

Base Word. A word to which other word parts are added is called a base word. For example, the base word in *recover* is *cover*. The base word in *successful* is *success*.

Prefix. A prefix is a word part added to the beginning of a base word. When you add a prefix to a base word, you change the meaning of the word.

Prefix	+	Base Word	=	New Word
dis-	+	satisfy	=	dissatisfy

For a list of frequently used prefixes, see page 232.

Suffix. A suffix is a word part that is added to the end of a base word. The new word that is created has a different meaning from the base word alone.

Base Word	+	Suffix	=	New Word
sleep	+	-less	=	sleepless

For a list of frequently used suffixes, see page 233.

You must make spelling changes before you can add suffixes to some words.

1. When a suffix beginning with a vowel is added to a word ending in silent *e*, the *e* is usually dropped.

$$\text{move} + \text{-ing} = \text{moving}$$

The *e* is not dropped when a suffix beginning with a consonant is added.

$$\text{hope} + \text{-ful} = \text{hopeful}$$

2. When a suffix is added to a word ending in *y* preceded by a consonant, the *y* is usually changed to an *i*.

$$\text{healthy} + \text{-est} = \text{healthiest}$$

When *y* is preceded by a vowel, the base word does not change.

$$\text{stay} + \text{-ing} = \text{staying}$$

3. Double the final consonant when adding *-ing*, *-ed*, or *-er* to a one-syllable word that ends in one consonant preceded by one vowel.

$$\text{run} + \text{-ing} = \text{running}$$

When two vowels precede the final consonant in a one-syllable word, the final consonant is not doubled.

$$\text{steer} + \text{-ing} = \text{steering}$$

2. Context Clues

Clues to the meaning of a new word can often be found in context. Context refers to the sentences and paragraphs that surround the word.

Antonyms. An antonym, or opposite, may be used as a clue to the meaning of a word. The antonym may be in the same sentence or in a nearby sentence. It often appears in the same position in the sentence as the new word.

> My grandfather is infirm, but my grandmother is strong and healthy.

Infirm is the opposite of "strong and healthy." Therefore, you can infer that *infirm* means "weak or sick."

For more about antonyms, see pages 138–139.

Comparison and Contrast Clues. Writers often compare one idea with another. Sometimes an unfamiliar word may be used in one part of the comparison. Then the other part of the comparison may give you a clue to the meaning of the word. Key words such as *also, as, similar to, both, than*, and *in addition* indicate a comparison.

> Jill sometimes feigns illness. Her sister also pretends to be sick once in a while.

The comparison tells you that *feign* means "pretend."

Writers also show how certain things are opposites by using contrast. A contrast clue tells what the new word is not. Some key words in contrast clues are *although, however, yet, on the other hand*, and *different from*.

> The group held a clandestine meeting. Usually, however, they met openly.

From this example, *clandestine* must mean the opposite of "openly."

For more about comparison and contrast clues, see page 139.

Definition and Restatement. The most direct clues to the meaning of a word are definition and restatement.

When definition is used, the meaning of a word is stated directly.

> A numismatist is a person who collects coins.

When restatement is used, the unfamiliar word is restated in a different way.

> Alex is a numismatist. That is, he collects coins.

The following key words and punctuation tell you to look for a definition or restatement: *is, who is, which is, that is, in other words, or,* dashes, commas, and parentheses.

For more about definition and restatement clues, see page 138.

Example Clues. In an example clue, a new word is related to a group of familiar words. The new word may be an example of a familiar term. Sometimes, familiar terms are examples of the new word.

The following key words signal an example clue: *for example, an example, one kind, some types, for instance*, and *such as*.

> The botany class studied succulents, such as cactus plants.

For more information about example clues, see page 139.

Inference Clues. Writers sometimes leave clues about the meaning of unfamiliar words in different parts of the sentence. For example, clues to a new word in the subject can often be found in the predicate.

>Malachite is mined in the Ural Mountains of Russia.

From this sentence, you can guess that *malachite* is a type of mineral ore.

Sometimes the sentence in which a new word appears has no clues to its meaning. However, it may be possible to find clues to the meaning somewhere else in the same paragraph.

>The Mexican craftsman spent several days making new huaraches. First, he cut thin strips of leather and softened them until they were flexible. Next, he wove the strips into an intricate pattern and fastened them to a pair of thick leather soles. Finally, to get a perfect fit, he soaked the huaraches in water, put them on his feet, and wore them until they were dry.

Context clues tell you that *huaraches* must be shoes or sandals made of woven leather strips.

Sometimes the main idea of a paragraph will give you a clue about the meaning of a new word. In this example there are several clues to the meaning of the underlined word.

>Information on the President's decision was disseminated as soon as the cabinet meeting ended. Radio and TV stations interrupted their regular programming to make the announcement, and newspapers rearranged their front pages to give more coverage to the story.

The main idea of the paragraph tells you that *disseminated* means "to spread" or "send out."

For more about inferring meanings from context, see pages 358 and 359.

Synonyms. A word that means the same or nearly the same as another word is called a synonym. Sometimes a word is used in the same sentence or paragraph as its synonym. The writer counts on you to understand either the word or its synonym. In the following example you can infer that *nebulous* means "vague."

>Eileen's answer was nebulous. She was being intentionally vague because her plans for Saturday were not definite.

For more on synonyms, see page 138.

3. Word Origins

Words in the English language come from many different sources. One ancient source is thought to be a prehistoric language called Indo-European. The first settlers of the island now called Great Britain spoke a form of Indo-European. However, in the centuries since that time, the English language has changed. Words have become part of the language in the following ways:

Acronyms. Words that are made from the first letters of other words are called acronyms. For example:

ASCAP	American Society of Composers, Authors, and Publishers
CORE	Congress of Racial Equality
UNICEF	United Nations International Children's Emergency Fund

Blended Words. Blended words are similar to compound words. Two words are joined together to make a new word. In this case, however, some letters from one or both of the words are dropped. *Smog* is a blended word made from *smoke* and *fog*. *Brunch* is a blended word made from *breakfast* and *lunch*.

Borrowed Words. Throughout its history, the English language has taken words from other languages. Many words came from the French, Spanish, Italian, Latin, and Greek languages, as well as others. Early American settlers borrowed words from Native American tribes.

Clipped Words. New words are often made by shortening existing words. For example, *quote* was clipped from *quotation*. *Telephone* was shortened to make the word *phone*.

Coined Words. Sometimes writers, especially poets, coin or invent words to suit their needs. Coined words can give freshness and sparkle to a line of poetry. *Mud-luscious* from "in Just-" (page 535) is an example of a coined word.

Compound Words. Two words may be combined to form one new word. An example is *handcuff*.

Root Words. Many Greek and Latin words form roots, or those parts of words that contain the basic meaning. If you know the meaning of the Greek or Latin root, you can figure out the meaning of the whole word. For example, the Greek root *geo-* means "earth." The root *logy* means "the study of." Together, these word parts make the word *geology*, which is another word for the study of the earth.

Words from Names and Places. Some words are based on the name of a person or a place. For example, the sandwich was named for the fourth Earl of Sandwich. He is said to have thought of putting meat between slices of bread so that he could eat without interrupting his card game.

Words from Sounds. Some words imitate sounds. These words are called echoic words. Some examples are *chirp* and *coo*.

Words from Specialized Areas. Sometimes members of a professional or technical field have a special vocabulary of words pertaining to their work. Such words are called jargon. Occasionally, jargon words become part of our everyday vocabulary.

For more about word origins, see pages 8 and 9.

4. Multiple Meanings

A given word can have many different meanings and serve as more than one part of speech. The noun *grace*, for example, can mean "charm," "good will," "mercy," "a certain time period," "a prayer," "a title of respect," "a musical note," or "God's favor." The word can also be used as a verb: "She graced us with her presence."

Use context clues and inference to help you decide which use or definition of the word is intended by the writer.

5. Reference Books: The Dictionary, Glossary, and Thesaurus

A **dictionary** is an alphabetical listing of words and their meanings. If context clues and word parts do not provide enough information for you to understand an unfamiliar word, you can use a dictionary.

A **glossary** can be found in the back of some nonfiction books. Like the dictionary, it is an alphabetical listing of words and their meanings.

However, the words a glossary defines are limited to the new or unfamiliar words in the book.

A **thesaurus** lists words with other words of similar meanings, and sometimes with opposites. You use a thesaurus when you need to find the exact word for your meaning.

For more about reference books, see the Guidelines for Study and Research.

6. Levels of Language

Standard English is English that is accepted and understood everywhere English is spoken. Standard English may be formal or informal. Formal standard English is used in serious or formal situations, such as in business letters, classroom assignments, and speeches. Informal standard English is used in everyday conversation. It follows all the rules of grammar, just as formal English does, but it sounds more natural. It also uses some words or meanings called colloquialisms, words not used in formal English but acceptable in informal speech.

Colloquialisms are common, informal expressions. One type of colloquialism is the idiom. This is a word or phrase that has a meaning that differs from what the actual words suggest. Saying "skip it" to someone means "forget it" and has nothing to do with the physical act of skipping.

Nonstandard English includes language that does not follow the traditional rules of grammar. Words such as *ain't* and local dialects are considered nonstandard.

Slang is a type of nonstandard English. It includes new words or words with new meanings. Most slang words are used for only a short time and may have meaning for only a small group of people.

"Gobbledygook" is another form of nonstandard English. It refers to jargon from specialized fields that is overused and confusing to the reader.

For more about recognizing the levels of language, see pages 64 and 65.

There are many different types of writing that you will do both in and out of school. Whatever you write, however, requires you to complete the same steps.

These steps or stages are called the process of writing:

Pre-writing, writing, and **revising**

Stage 1. Pre-Writing

The pre-writing stage is the planning stage. In this stage, you think of ideas, do research, and organize. Below are the five pre-writing steps.

1. Choose and limit a topic. If you have not been assigned a specific topic, you may choose one of your own. Make a list of ideas or topics that you might like to write about. Choose the one that is most interesting to you. Next, list the things you might write about that topic. List only the ideas that will match the length of the piece you plan to write.

For example, a student was asked to write a short composition on understanding history through the literature of the time. First she thought of the selections she had read. Then she chose a few that offered historical viewpoints. She scanned these selections looking for one that could be covered well in a short composition. She found several possibilities:

Of Plymouth Plantation
Rain-in-the-Face
The Declaration of Women's Rights
My Bondage and My Freedom

Finally, she chose "My Bondage and My Freedom." She decided to explain how a reader could learn about the history of slavery by examining Douglass's writing.

2. Decide on your purpose. Decide how you want to handle your topic. Do you want to explain it, describe it, or criticize it? Do you intend to teach, persuade, or simply amuse your readers? Your purpose will determine how you write about your subject.

The student writing about understanding history through literature decided to explain how looking at one person's experience could increase understanding of history in general.

3. Decide on your audience. Determine who will read your writing. You will then be able to choose the level of language you will use and the details you will include.

4. Gather supporting information. List all the facts that you know about the topic. Then decide whether or not you need to find additional information. If so, you may need to refer to various reference sources such as encyclopedias.

The student writing about history and literature did some background reading and note-taking on both slavery and Frederick Douglass. Then she carefully reread the selection "My Bondage and My Freedom," jotting down ideas as she read. Here are some of her notes.

Historical background
—pre-Civil War period
—unrest in country was building because of feelings against slavery
—treatment of slaves
—slaves necessary to economy of South

Frederick Douglass
—b. 1817 d. 1895
—changed name and escaped north in 1838
—wrote autobiography in 1845
—British friends bought his freedom in 1846
—held government posts (1881–1891)

"My Bondage and My Freedom"
—unstoppable desire for learning
—mistress taught Douglass, until husband stopped her
—white playmates helped him
—children generally condemned slavery
—Douglass afraid to mention names of those who helped him

Ideas for organization of paper
—State main idea in introduction
—Also in introduction, mention general ideas to be discussed in following paragraphs

5. Organize your ideas. Reread the list of details that you have written. Cross out whatever does not fit the main idea or purpose.

Select a logical order for your details. Descriptive paragraphs might use spatial order. A story might use time order. Explanatory paragraphs may have points organized in the order of importance. Make an outline showing the order of your ideas.

Here is the student's outline for the introductory paragraph of her composition. She has written out the main idea and underlined it. This will help her keep to her subject as she continues the process of writing.

Insight into History

Main Idea: Frederick Douglass's autobiography offers a special insight into the history of slavery.

Important Details:
I. Douglass's autobiography a good way to learn about pre-Civil War history
II. Important factor at the time was slavery
III. Douglass's first hand account of slavery offers different perspective than history book

Stage 2: Writing a First Draft

Now you are ready to put your ideas on paper. Following your outline as you write, keep your purpose and your audience in mind. Do not be concerned with spelling and punctuation at this time. Errors can be corrected later during the revision stage. The important thing at this point is to get your ideas down in written form. If new or better ideas come to you while you are writing, do not hesitate to include them in your draft.

The first draft of the student's introductory paragraph on understanding history through literature is at the top of the next page.

First Draft

> The biography of Frederick Douglas provides an interesting view of history during the early and mid 1800s. One of the most important issues of that time was slavery and Douglass's first hand story offers lots of information not found in your average History leson. A history book gives us real information on the economical and politics of slavery and douglass gives us his very own account of what it was like to be a slave and how slavery corrupted others. Who were not slaves. Although my Bondage and my Freedom are one man's story, it's insights help us gain a deeper understanding of slavery as a whole.

Stage 3: Revising

In the revision stage you are given a chance to refine and correct your work. Reread what you have written and ask yourself these questions.

1. Is my writing interesting? Will others want to read it?
2. Did I stick to my topic? Are there any unnecessary details? Should any other details be added?
3. Is my organization easy to follow? Do my ideas flow together smoothly?
4. Is every group of words a sentence? Is every word the best word?

Mark any corrections on your first draft. You may even want to write a new draft.

Proofreading. After you have revised the content of your writing, you will need to proofread it carefully. Look for errors in capitalization, punctuation, grammar, and spelling. Make your corrections by using the proofreading symbols in the box at the right.

Notice how the first draft has been revised. The writer has improved the piece by deleting unnecessary words, and making the vocabulary more formal. She has revised sentence structure and has also corrected several errors in capitalization, punctuation, grammar, and spelling. Study this draft and compare it to the final draft at the bottom of page 698.

Proofreading Symbols

Symbol	Meaning	Example
∧	insert	lesᵒn
≡	capitalize	douglass
/	lower case	History
∼	transpose	veiw
ℓ	take out	lots of
¶	paragraph	¶ The
⊙	add a period	slavery⊙
⌃	add a comma	Finally,

Revised Draft

¶The ~~auto~~biography of Frederick Douglas[s] provides an ~~interesting~~ enriching view of ~~history~~ United States history during the early and mid 1800's. One of the ~~most important~~ critical issues of that time was ~~slavery~~ the institution of slavery. and Douglass's first-hand ~~story~~ account offers ~~lots~~ a wealth of information not found in ~~your average~~ a ~~History leson.~~ history lesson. ~~A~~ While a history book ~~gives us real~~ provides factual information on the economic[s] and politics of slavery, ~~and~~ douglass gives us ~~his very own~~ a deeply personal account of what it was like to be a slave and how slavery corrupted others. ~~Who were not slaves.~~ Although "my Bondage and my Freedom," ~~are~~ is one man's story, it's insights help us all gain a deeper understanding of slavery as a whole.

Writing the final copy. When you are completely satisfied with your work, make a clean, neat final copy. Proofread your paper once more, looking for any errors.

Notice that in making her final copy, the student found and corrected an error in punctuation. She also changed one phrase into a quotation from the selection.

Final Copy

The autobiography of Frederick Douglass provides an enriching view of United States history during the early and mid 1800's. One of the critical issues of that time was the institution of slavery. Douglass's first-hand account offers a wealth of information not found in a history lesson. While a history book provides factual information on the economics and politics of slavery, Douglass gives us a deeply personal account of what it was like to be a slave and how "slavery destroys man's better inclinations." Although "My Bondage and My Freedom" is one man's story, its insights help us all gain a deeper understanding of slavery as a whole.

Checklist for the Process of Writing

Pre-Writing

1. Choose and limit a topic.
2. Decide on your purpose.
3. Decide on your audience.
4. Gather supporting information.
5. Organize your ideas.

Writing Your First Draft

1. Begin writing. Keep your topic, purpose, and audience in mind at all times.
2. As you write, you may add new details.
3. Concentrate on ideas. Do not be concerned with grammar and mechanics at this time.

Revising

1. Read your first draft. Ask yourself these questions:
   a. Do you like what you have written? Is it interesting? Will others want to read it?
   b. Did you accomplish your purpose?
   c. Is your writing organized well? Do the ideas flow smoothly from one paragraph to the next? Are the ideas arranged logically?
   d. Do paragraphs have topic sentences? Does every sentence stick to the topic? Should any sentence be moved?
   e. Should any details be left out? Should any be added?
   f. Does every sentence express a complete thought? Are your sentences easy to understand?
   g. Is every word the best possible word?
2. Mark any changes on your paper.

Proofreading

1. **Grammar and Usage**
   a. Is each word group a complete sentence?
   b. Does every verb agree with its subject?
   c. Are pronoun forms correct?
   d. Is the form of each adjective correct?
   e. Is the form of each adverb correct?

2. **Capitalization**
   a. Is the first word in every sentence capitalized?
   b. Are all proper nouns and adjectives capitalized?
   c. Are titles capitalized correctly?

3. **Punctuation**
   a. Does each sentence have the correct end mark?
   b. Have you used punctuation marks correctly?

4. **Spelling**
   a. Did you check unfamiliar words in a dictionary?
   b. Did you spell plural and possessive forms correctly?

Preparing the Final Copy

1. Make a clean copy of your writing. Make all changes and correct all errors. Then ask yourself these questions:
   a. Is your handwriting easy to read?
   b. Are your margins wide enough?
   c. Is every paragraph indented?
2. Proofread your writing again. Read it aloud. Correct any mistakes neatly.

Guidelines for Study and Research

1. Using Reference Materials

The Dictionary

A dictionary is an alphabetical listing of words and their definitions. The **glossary** in a nonfiction book is like a dictionary. However, its entries are limited to words from that book.

How To Find a Word. The two words printed in heavy black type at the top of each page are called guide words. They show the first and last words on the page. If the word you are looking for is between the two guide words, then you know your word is on that page.

What the Entry Tells You. A word entry may provide any or all of the following:

Syllabification. The entry word is printed in bold type and divided into syllables. This division shows you where to break a word at the end of a line of writing or typing.

Homographs. Words that are spelled alike but are different in meaning are called homographs. They are listed as separate entries.

Pronunciation. The respelling that appears in parentheses following the entry word gives the pronunciation of the word. The pronunciation key at the bottom of the page indicates the system used for pronunciation.

Part of Speech. Following the pronunciation of the word, the part of speech is indicated.

Inflected Forms. After the part of speech, the dictionary lists inflected forms that are irregular. Inflected forms are the changes that occur when a word is changed to another form. Plural forms

of nouns, principal parts of verbs, and comparative and superlative forms of modifiers are inflected forms.

Word Origin. The word origin, or *etymology*, traces a word back to its origins. This information is enclosed in brackets.

Definition. Some words have more than one definition. Each new definition is preceded by a number. Definitions for each part of speech are grouped together.

Synonymy. The fine shades of meaning among the synonyms for a word are explained in the synonymy. The synonymy is indicated by the abbreviation SYN after the definition.

Usage Labels. The level of usage of a word or idiom is usually indicated in brackets. The various usage labels include *obsolete, archaic, poetic, dialect, British, colloquial*, and *slang*.

Field Labels. A field label indicates that the word has a special meaning in a specialized field of knowledge.

Symbols. Americanisms, words or phrases that began in the United States, are indicated with an open star ☆. Foreign words and phrases are marked with a double dagger ‡.

For more on using the dictionary, see pages 428–429.

The Thesaurus

A thesaurus is a listing of words and related words such as synonyms. It is an invaluable aid when you are looking for just the right word to express your meaning. The thesaurus also lists antonyms, words that have the opposite meaning from the entry word.

Each thesaurus is organized a little differently. To use a thesaurus, you need to read the directions in that book.

The Encyclopedia

An encyclopedia is a collection of factual articles on almost all subjects. The articles are arranged alphabetically in volumes. Guide letters on the spine of each volume help you to locate the proper book. An index telling what topics are included in the encyclopedia appears in the final volume. The index will list the volume and page number where you can find each article.

Readers' Guide to Periodical Literature

Magazines are a good source of information for anyone writing a report. They give current information on a wide variety of topics. To find a listing of current articles, use the *Readers' Guide to Periodical Literature*.

The *Readers' Guide* is an alphabetical listing of topics that have been discussed in magazine articles during a specific period of time. Under the topic, the guide lists the titles of articles on that subject and the magazines in which they were printed.

For more on using the *Readers' Guide*, see pages 492–493.

Specialized Reference Works

Almanacs and yearbooks are useful sources of the latest facts and statistics. They are published annually and provide information on current events, government, sports, population, and other fields. The *Guinness Book of World Records* and the *Information Please Almanac* are examples.

Atlases such as the *National Geographic Atlas of the World*, contain maps as well as information on subjects related to specific geographic areas.

Literary reference books are helpful in locating quotations and finding specific poems and stories. *Bartlett's Familiar Quotations* and *Granger's Index to Poetry* are examples.

Biographical references can help you locate information on well known people. Examples are *Twentieth Century Authors, The Dictionary of American Biography*, and *The Oxford Companion to American Literature*.

For more on specialized reference works, see page 43.

2. Finding the Right Resource Material

The Classification of Books

The library contains many different sources of information. Among them are magazines, newspapers, records, filmstrips, movies, and microfilm, as well as books.

The books in a library are divided into two major categories: fiction and nonfiction.

Fiction books are arranged alphabetically according to the author's last name. The name appears on the spine of the book.

Nonfiction books are usually arranged according to the Dewey Decimal System. Each book is assigned a number in one of ten categories. That number is referred to as a call number and is printed on the spine of the book. The books are then arranged on the shelves in numerical order. Biographies are usually shelved in a separate section of the library. They may have a B on the spine.

THE DEWEY DECIMAL SYSTEM

000–099	General Works	encyclopedias, almanacs, handbooks
100–199	Philosophy	conduct, ethics, psychology
200–299	Religion	the Bible, mythology, theology
300–399	Social Science	economics, law, education, commerce, government, folklore
400–499	Language	languages, grammar, dictionaries
500–599	Science	mathematics, chemistry, physics
600–699	Useful Arts	farming, cooking, sewing, radio, nursing, engineering, television, business, gardening, cars
700–799	Fine Arts	music, painting, drawing, acting, photography, sports
800–899	Literature	poetry, plays, essays
900–999	History	biography, travel, geography

The Card Catalog

The card catalog lists all the books in the library. The cards are arranged in alphabetical order according to the words on the top line of each card.

Each book has three cards. The author card lists the author's name on the first line. The title card lists the title of the book on the first line. The subject card lists the subject or topic of the book on the first line. On the top left corner of each card you will find the call number.

Your library may also have a computerized catalog, and a card catalog for audio-visual materials such as films or video cassettes.

Author Card

B
DOUGLASS
G742T

Graham, Shirley

There was once a slave; the heroic story of Frederick Douglass. New York: Messner, © 1947.

Title Card

B
DOUGLASS
G742T

There was once a slave;

Graham, Shirley

There was once a slave; the heroic story of Frederick Douglass. New York: Messner, © 1947.

Subject Card

B
DOUGLASS
G742T

Douglass, Frederick, 1817?–
1895

Graham, Shirley

There was once a slave; the heroic story of Frederick Douglass. New York: Messner, © 1947.

The Vertical File

The vertical file is a cabinet containing brochures, pamphlets, catalogs, and other current information on a variety of subjects. The material is arranged alphabetically and is often the most up-to-date information available.

The Parts of a Nonfiction Book

After locating the books for your research, you must decide whether they contain the information you need. Knowing what is contained in the various parts of a book will help you decide.

The title page gives the complete title of the book, the names of the authors or editors, the name of the publisher, and the place of publication.

The copyright page gives the copyright dates, the copyright holder, and the dates of editions or printings. If your topic requires up-to-date information, it is important to know when the book was written.

The table of contents is an outline of the contents of the book, arranged in order of appearance. Skimming the chapter and part heads can tell you whether the book might be useful in your research.

The bibliography is a list of sources that have been used in preparing the book. These sources can provide further information on a subject.

The index is an alphabetical list of subjects covered in the book and their page numbers.

For more about the parts of a book, see page 29.

3. Preparing to Study

Preparations in Class

The first step to effective studying is listening carefully to assignment directions.

1. Concentrate on only the directions about to be given.
2. Note how many steps there are.
3. Relate a key word to each step, such as *Read, Answer,* or *Write.*
4. If you do not understand a step, ask questions.
5. Repeat the directions to yourself and write them down.

An assignment notebook will be helpful in organizing your studying. For each assignment, write the following:

1. The subject
2. The assignment and any details
3. The date the assignment is given
4. The date the assignment is due

Your Schedule for Study Time

Some assignments can be completed quickly. These are short-term goals. Set aside time each day to work on these assignments.

Assignments that cannot be completed overnight are called long-term goals. They become more manageable when you break them down into smaller tasks and do each part separately.

A study plan will help you complete your work. On your plan, show when you will work and what you will accomplish each day.

4. Study and Research

Three Types of Reading

There are three types of reading that you will find useful as you study. Each type has a particular purpose.

Scanning is one kind of fast reading. It lets you find a specific piece of information quickly. Scanning means moving your eyes rapidly over the page. Look for key words that point out the information you need. Then, slow down and read the information carefully.

Skimming is another type of fast reading. It gives you an overview of the material you are about to read. Skimming means moving your eyes quickly over the material looking for titles, subtitles, and illustrations that will give you clues about the content of the material.

The third kind of reading is **in-depth reading**. Take your time for this type of reading. Identify the order in which the information is arranged and look for connections between ideas. The SQ3R study method is an effective way to plan in-depth reading.

The SQ3R Study Method

SQ3R stands for five steps: Survey, Question, Read, Recite, and Review.

Survey. Get a general idea of what the material is about. Look at graphic aids, such as pictures, maps, graphs, or tables. Read the titles and subtitles. Read the introduction and the summary.

Question. Read any study questions provided. If there are none, make your own by turning titles and headings into questions.

Read. Read the material. Keep the study questions and main ideas in mind.

Recite. After reading, recite the answers to the study questions. Write a few notes to help you remember any important ideas.

Review. Look back at the study questions and try to answer them without using your notes. Finally, study your notes.

Note-Taking

There are two uses for taking notes when you study: 1) it helps you concentrate on the material and 2) it helps you study for a review or test.

Notes should be written clearly so you will be able to understand them later. They do not have to be written in sentences. You may want to write a **summary**, or a short version, of the original material. Or you may want to **paraphrase** the information. When you paraphrase what someone has written, you put the main ideas of the selection in your own words.

When you are researching a subject for a writing project, use note cards. Be sure to write down where your information came from. You may need to refer to that source again. Include the following source information in your notes.

Books. Give the title, the author, the copyright date, and the page number.

Magazine or Newspaper Articles. Give the name and date of the periodical, the title of the article, the name of the author, and the page numbers of the article.

Encyclopedias. Give the name of the set, the title of the entry, the volume number where the entry appears, and the page numbers of the entry.

Direct Interviews. Write the name of the person you interviewed and the date.

Sample Note Card

Title of book	Copyright date
<u>There Was Once a Slave</u>;	1947
Author	Page number
Shirley Graham	page 170

Frederick Douglass became secretary of the "Free Democracy" party in 1849.

Outlining

An **outline** is a way of organizing ideas and facts. It helps you see which ideas are main ideas and which ones are supporting details. When you outline something, you begin to see the connections between ideas.

To make an outline follow the form below.

    I. Main Idea
        A. Subtopic
            1. Detail
            2. Detail
        B. Subtopic

    II. Main Idea
        A. Subtopic
        B. Subtopic
            1. Detail
            2. Detail

Preparing a Bibliography

A **bibliography** lists the sources you used in gathering information for a report. The bibliography comes at the end of your paper and should be arranged alphabetically according to the author's last name. If no author is indicated, use the title of the source. Sample bibliography entries follow:

Bibliography

Encyclopedia   "Frederick Douglass." The World Book Encyclopedia. 1985 ed.

Magazine   Wojahn, David. "The Man Who Knew Too Much." New Yorker, 8 Feb. 1982, p. 42.

Newspaper   Werner, Leslie. "Busing and Quotas Assailed by Meese," New York Times, 16 March 1985, p. 8.

Book   Graham, Shirley. There Was Once a Slave. New York: Julian Messner, Inc., 1947.

Interview   Francis, Donald E. Professor, Department of Music, University of Michigan. Personal Interview. 26 Feb. 1985.

Summary of Critical Thinking Terms

Absolute Words. See *Generalization.*

Analogy. Word analogies, such as those on standardized tests, present two pairs of words that are related in some way. Such a comparison can show a relationship between two things. For example:

calf is to *cow* as *cub* is to _____

The missing word is *bear,* since it has the same relationship to *cub* as *cow* does to *calf.* Writers sometimes make literary analogies to show a comparison between a familiar thing and one that is more difficult to understand. They hope that this will help their readers understand the more unfamiliar idea. A reader, however, must watch for *false analogies.* A false analogy leads someone into making a comparison when none exists. For example, some people in favor of heavy spending on the space exploration program have compared it to the exploration of the American frontier. A thoughtful reader could see this is really an unfair comparison. Differences between the two concepts are far greater than any similarities.

Analysis. When you analyze something, you break it up into smaller units and study each part individually. For example, to analyze a short story, you could look at its characters, its setting, its dialogue, or any other element found in a short story.

When you study each part of a selection separately, you can understand the entire selection more thoroughly. Analysis can also help you see the similarities and differences that exist between selections.

Categorizing and Classifying. Categorizing and classifying mean making groups according to common elements. If, for example, you wanted to write a paper on the structure of poetry, you would first review some of the poems that you have read. Then you might group together poems with a regular pattern of end rhyme. Next, you might group the poems written in free verse. You might also make groups of the poems that have regular stanzas, irregular stanza lengths, and no stanzas at all.

Cause and Effect. See *Summary of Comprehension Skills,* page 686.

Connotation/Denotation. See *Summary of Comprehension Skills* page 686.

Emotional Appeals. When a writer or speaker tries to create strong feelings in others, he or she might use an emotional appeal.

See *Flag Waving, Loaded Language,* and *Transfer.*

Errors in Reasoning. Errors in reasoning can confuse readers and listeners. These errors can also lead to false conclusions.

See *Analogy, False Cause and Effect Reasoning, Generalization, Stacking,* and *Stereotype.*

Evaluation. In evaluating a piece of writing, you study it carefully and decide on its merit.

Writing can be evaluated in several different ways. First, you can judge the abilities of the writer. Has the writer's purpose been achieved? Are the important elements in this type of writing developed well? Has the writer presented his or her ideas effectively? Is the writing organized in a logical fashion?

The second type of evaluation involves what the writer says, not simply how it is said. Is the writing truthful and accurate? Have opinions been backed by facts?

Finally, is the writer qualified to write about this subject? Do you think that the writer is biased in any way?

When evaluating a piece of literature, watch for evidence of loaded language, emotional appeals, and errors in reasoning.

Fact and Opinion. Facts are statements that can be proved to be true. Opinions are statements of a person's beliefs. They may or may not be supported by facts.

Fact: Collies are dogs.
Opinion: Collies are the most beautiful of all dog breeds.

When you write or speak, you should always make sure that your opinions are backed by facts.

For more about separating fact from opinion, see pages 686–687.

False Analogy. See *Analogy.*

False Cause and Effect Reasoning. When one event happens shortly after another in time, a person might mistakenly assume that the first event was the cause of the second. Many superstitions are based on this error in reasoning. If, for example, you walk under a ladder and then have bad luck, you might incorrectly assume that the two events are related.

Flag Waving. Making an emotional appeal by using patriotism is a technique called flag wav-

ing. Patriotic slogans and images are unfairly used to persuade readers or listeners to accept a certain point of view.

Generalization. A generalization is a statement about a group of things or people that is supposedly true of all members of the group. When generalizations are based on fact and logic they are a useful and necessary part of the thought process. "Water is wet," is a generalization. It states that whenever or wherever we find water, we can assume it will be wet. We do not have to experiment each time to see if the statement is still true.

An *overgeneralization* is based on an inadequate number of facts. The statement it makes is too broad to be accurate or fair. For example:

All fair-skinned blondes burn easily in the sun.

If just one fair-skinned blonde does not burn easily, then the statement is false. Part of the problem with this statement is the word *all,* which is called an *absolute word.* These words, such as *everyone, never, no one, always,* either include or exclude every member or thing in the group.

One way to change the example stated above into a fair statement is to change the absolute word to a *qualifier.* Qualifiers, such as *most, some, many,* and *few* make a statement acceptable. For example:

Most fair-skinned blondes burn easily in the sun.

For more about generalizations, see page 553.

Inference. See the *Summary of Comprehension Skills,* page 687.

Judgment Words. These are words used to strongly label something as good or bad. They express the opinion of the writer. When a writer uses such terms as *pleasant, horrible, brilliant,* he or she is making a judgment that can influence the opinion of others. To be effective, a judgment must be supported by facts.

Loaded Language. Language that carries strong emotional connotations is called loaded language. It can be used to sway an audience by appealing to their emotions rather than their reason. The words a writer or speaker chooses can create powerful positive or negative feelings. For example, *snarl words* such as *ugly, stupid,* or *disgusting* can be used to arouse negative feelings. *Purr words* such as *intelligent, desirable,* or *wonderful,* could be used to create positive feelings.

For more about loaded language, see page 62. See also *Judgment Words* and *Slanted Writing.*

Overgeneralization. See *Generalization.*

Qualifiers. See *Generalization.*

Slanted Writing. When loaded language or subjective language is used to lead a reader to a particular point of view, it is called slanted writing.

For more about slanted writing, see pages 62–63.

Stacking. When a writer presents only one side of a question in order to make a point, he or she is using stacking. The writer purposely leaves out important facts or does not mention things that might show another side of the issue.

Subjective/Objective Language. See the *Summary of Comprehension Skills,* pages 688–689.

Transfer. Transfer is an emotional appeal that tries to carry the authority, expertise, or prestige of one thing over to another thing. For example, a commercial that shows young, energetic, attractive people with a particular product is trying to convince the reader or viewer that he or she can have the same qualities by buying the product.

The **glossary** is an alphabetical listing of words from the selections, with meanings. The glossary gives the following information:

1. **The entry word broken into syllables.**

2. **The pronunciation of each word.** The **respelling** is shown in parentheses. The most common way to pronounce a word is listed first. The Pronunciation Key below shows the symbols for the sounds of letters and key words that contain those sounds.

   A **primary accent** ' is placed after the syllable that is stressed the most when the word is spoken. A **secondary accent** ' is placed after a syllable that has a lighter stress.

3. **The part of speech of the word.** These abbreviations are used:

   n. noun   *v.* verb   *adj.* adjective   *adv.* adverb

4. **The meaning of the word.** The definitions listed in the glossary apply to selected ways a word is used in these selections.

5. **Related forms.** Words with suffixes such as *-ing, -ed, -ness,* and *-ly* are listed under the base word.

1. entry word ⎯⎯⎯ **re·cal·ci·trant** (ri kal′ si trənt) ⎯⎯ 2. respelling
   adj. refusing to obey authority
3. part of speech ⎯⎯ or rules. ⎯⎯⎯⎯⎯⎯⎯ 4. meaning

Pronunciation Key

a	fat	**i**	hit	**o͝o**	look		**a** *in* ago	**ch**	chin
ā	ape	**ī**	bite, fire	**o͞o**	tool		**e** *in* agent	**sh**	she
ä	car	**ō**	go	**ou**	out	ə	**i** *in* sanity	**th**	thin
e	ten	**ô**	law, horn	**u**	up		**o** *in* comply	***th***	then
ē	even	**oi**	oil	**ur**	fur		**u** *in* focus	**zh**	leisure
				'l	able	ər	perhaps	**ng**	ring

This pronunciation key used with permission, from *Webster's New World Dictionary, Students Edition;* Copyright © 1981 by Simon & Schuster, Inc.

A

ab·bot (ab′ ət) *n.* a man who heads a monastery of monks.

ab·hor (ab hôr′ or ab hôr′) *v.* deep hatred.

ab·ject (ab′ jekt or ab jekt′) *adj.* miserable; lacking self respect.

a·bys·mal (ə biz′ m'l) *adj.* **1.** Like a bottomless gulf. **2.** bad or hateful beyond measure.

ac·cliv·i·ty (ə kliv′ ə tē) *n.* an upward sloping of the ground.

ac·me (ak′ mē) *n.* the highest point or peak.

ac·qui·si·tion (ak′wə zish′ ən) *n.* something that is gotten by one's own efforts.

ad·duce (ə dōōs′ or ə dyōōs′) *v.* to give as reason or proof.

ad·her·ent (əd hir′ ənt) *n.* a supporter.

ad·ver·sar·y (ad′ vər ser′ ē) *n.* an opponent or enemy.

ae·o·li·an harp (ē ō′ lē ən härp) *n.* a boxlike stringed instrument that produces musical sounds when air blows on it.

a·gue (ā′ gyōō) *n.* a chill.

a·kim·bo (ə kim′ bō) *adj.* with hands on one's hips and elbows bent outward.

a·lac·ri·ty (ə lak′ rə tē) *n.* eagerness or willingness.

a·list (ə list′) *v.* to tilt to one side.

alms·house (ämz′ hous′) *n.* poorhouse.

al·tim·e·ter (al tim′ ə tər) *n.* an instrument used to measure altitude.

a·mi·a·ble (ā′ mē ə b'l) *adj.* pleasant or friendly in nature.

am·ply (am′ plē) *adv.* fully; more than enough.

an·nex (ə neks′) *v.* to add on.

a·noint (ə noint′) *v.* to put oil on in a ceremony to make holy.

an·thra·cite (an′ thrə sīt) *n.* a hard coal that gives much heat yet little smoke.

ap·a·thet·ic (ap′ ə thət′ ik) *adj.* uninterested. —**apathetically** *adv.*

ap·os·tol·ic (ap′ əs täl ik) *adj.* of the Pope.

ap·pall (ə pôl′) *v.* to fill with horror or shock.

ap·pend·age (ə pen′ dij) *n.* anything attached.

ap·pre·hend (ap′ rə hend′) *v.* to dread.

ap·pre·hen·sive (ap′ rə hen′ siv) *adj.* fearful or uneasy about the future.

ap·pren·tice (ə pren′ tis) *n.* a person under a legal agreement to work for a specified length of time for a master craftsman in a trade or craft in return for instruction.

ap·prise (ə prīz′) *v.* to notify or to inform.

ap·pro·ba·tion (ap′ rə bā′ shən) *n.* official approval or praise.

ar·dent (är′ d'nt) *adj.* having intense feelings; very enthusiastic. —**ardently** *adv.*

ar·du·ous (är′ jōō wəs) *adj.* difficult.

ar·id (ar′ id or er′ id) *adj.* dull.

ar·ray (ə rā′) *n.* an orderly group.

ar·tic·u·late (är tik′ yə lit) *adj.* able to speak or express oneself clearly.

a·skance (ə skans′) *adv.* **1.** with a side way glance. **2.** with suspicion.

as·per·i·ty (as per′ ə tē) *n.* a roughness or harshness.

as·pi·rate (as′ pər it) *adj.* the type of sound made by following a consonant with a puff of suddenly released breath.

as·ser·tion (ə sur′ shən) *n.* a statement made positively.

as·si·du·i·ty (as′ ə dyōō′ə tē or as′ ə dōō′ə tē) *n.* the quality of working with constant, careful attention.

as·sign (ə sīn′) *n.* a person appointed to act for another person.

as·suage (ə swāj′) *v.* to lessen the pain or distress.

a·sun·der (ə sun′ dər) *adv.* apart.

au·dac·i·ty (ô das′ ə tē) *n.* boldness.

aught (ôt) *n.* anything.

au·gust (ô gust′) *adj.* worthy of great respect.

au·ra (ôr′ ə) *n.* the atmosphere or quality that seems to surround a thing.

aus·tere (ô stir′) *adj.* **1.** plain; not luxurious. **2.** stern or harsh.

a·vert (ə vurt′) *v.* to turn away from.

a·wry (ə rī′) *adv.* with a twist to one side.

az·ure (azh′ ər) *adj.* clear blue, the color of the sky.

B

bade (bad) *v.* to express a greeting or departure.

bale·ful (bāl′ fəl) *adj.* evil; harmful.

ban·ish (ban′ ish) *v.* to get rid of; to send away.

bat·ter·y (bat′ ər ē or bat′ rē) *n.* the men who operate a set of heavy guns.

be·dev·il (bi dev′ ′l) *v.* to torment.

be·guile (bi gīl′) *v.* to charm or delight; to deceive.

be·la·bor (bi lā′ bər) *v.* to verbally attack.

bel·low (bel′ ō) *n.* anything that produces a stream of air. —**bellowing** *adj.*

be·nign (bi nīn′) *adj.* kindly; good-natured.

be·reave (bi rēv′) *v.* to leave in a lonely or sad state, as by death. —**bereavement** *n.*

be·seech·ing (bi sēch′ ing) *adj.* begging.

be·set (bi set′) *v.* to attack from all sides.

be·twixt (bi twikst′) *adv.* between.

bil·ious (bil′ yəs) *adj.* cross or bad-tempered.

blanch (blanch) *v.* to make pale.

blight (blīt) *n.* anything that destroys or prevents growth.

blithe (blī*th* or blīth) *adj.* cheerful; carefree.

bond·age (bän′ dij) *n.* slavery; controlled by some force.

boon (bo͞on) *n.* a blessing.

bor·er (bôr′ ər) *n.* an insect or worm that bores holes in vegetables or fruits.

bow·er (bou′ ər) *n.* a place enclosed by overhanging branches or vines.

breast·work (brest′ wʉrk) *n.* a low wall erected quickly as a defense.

breech·es (brich′ iz) *n.* trousers that reach to the knees.

brim·stone (brim′ stōn′) *n.* sulfur.

brook (brook) *v.* to put up with.

brute (bro͞ot) *adj.* not having the ability to reason.

bull·doze (bo͝ol′ dōz′) *v.* to frighten or force by threatening.

C

cais·son (kā′ sän or kas′ ′n) *n.* **1.** a chest used for holding ammunition. **2.** a two-wheeled wagon for transporting ammunition.

ca·lam·i·ty (kə lam′ ə tē) *n.* a great misfortune that brings suffering and loss.

ca·reen (kə rēn′) *v.* to lurch from side to side usually while moving rapidly.

cas·cade (kas kād′) *n.* a small, usually steep waterfall. —**cascading** *v.*

cat·a·mount (kat′ ə mount) *n.* a wild animal of the cat family; a leopard; a cougar.

ce·les·tial (sə les′ chəl) *adj.* of the heavens.

cen·ser (sen′ sər) *n.* a container used to burn incense.

cen·sure (sen′ shər) *v.* to blame or to find fault with; to express strong disapproval.

chafe (chāf) *v.* to wear away by rubbing; to irritate.

chal·ice (chal′ is) *n.* a cup or goblet.

charg·er (chär′ jər) *n.* a horse that is ridden in battle.

chasm (kaz′ ′m) *n.* **1.** a deep crack in the surface of the earth. **2.** a wide difference in interests or feelings.

chaste (chāst) *adj.* simple; pure.

chid·den (chid′ ′n) *v.* to scold, usually in a mild way.

chif·fo·robe (shif′ ə rōb) *n.* a high, narrow chest of drawers, often with a mirror.

chink (chingk) *n.* narrow opening or crack.

chron·ic (krän′ ik) *adj.* lasting a long period of time or coming back again and again.

chron·i·cle (krän′ i k′l) *n.* an historical record.

ci·pher (sī′ fər) *v.* to use a secret system based on a key.

cleft (kleft) *n.* a crack.

come·ly (kum′ lē) *adj.* attractive.

com·mune (kə myo͞on′) *v.* to talk with in deep understanding.

com·pul·sion (kəm pul′ shən) *n.* **1.** a driving force. **2.** in psychology, a senseless, repeated impulse to do a specific thing that a person is not able to resist.

com·punc·tion (kəm pungk′ shən) *n.* a feeling of regret for something done.

con·cil·i·at·ting (kən sil′ ē āt ing) *v.* trying to win over or make friendly.

con·fla·gra·tion (kän′ fla grā′ shən) *n.* a large fire that does much damage.

con·found·ed (kən foun′ did) *adj.* confused.

---

at, āte, fär, pen, ēqual; sit, mīne; sō, côrn, join, too͝k, fo͞ol, our; us, tʉrn; chill, shop, thick, *th*ey, sing; zh *in* measure; ′l *in* idle; ə *in* alive, cover, family, robot, circus.

con·nu·bi·al (kə noo′ bē əl) *adj.* of marriage.

con·se·crate (kän′ sə krāt′) *v.* to make or set apart as sacred or holy.

con·so·la·tion (kän sə lā′ shən) *n.* comfort.

con·ster·na·tion (kän stər nā′ shən) *n.* a fear that makes one feel helpless or bewildered.

con·strain (kən strān′) *v.* to hold back by force.

con·sum·mate (kən sum′ it) *adj.* complete.

con·ten·tion (kən ten′ shən) *n.* struggle or quarrel.

con·tort (kən tôrt′) *v.* to twist out of its usual shape.

con·tre·temps (kōn trə tän′ or kän trə tanz′) *n.* awkward mishaps.

con·trive (kən trīv′) *v.* to cleverly plan.

con·ven·ti·cle (kən ven′ ti k'l) *n.* a secret or illegal religious assembly.

corn·crib (kôrn′ krib′) *n.* a small, ventilated structure for the storage of ears of corn.

cor·nice (kôr′ nis) *n.* a horizontal molding projecting along the top of a house or building.

cor·rob·o·rate (kə räb′ ə rāt) *v.* to support or confirm.

coun·te·nance (koun′ tə nəns) *n.* appearance; the expression of one's face.

coun·ter·pane (koun′ tər pān′) *n.* a bedspread.

coun·ter·point (koun′ tər point′) *n.* the art of adding related yet independent melodies to a basic melody.

cove (kōv) *n.* a small, sheltered spot.

cov·e·nant (kuv′ ə nənt) *n.* a binding agreement.

cov·et (kuv′ it) *v.* to long for in an envious way. — **coveted** *adj.*

cra·ven (krā′ vən) *n.* a complete coward.

creed (krēd) *n.* a statement of belief.

crest (krest) *n.* a comb or tuft on the heads of some animals.

crev·ice (krev′ is) *n.* a narrow opening usually caused by a crack.

crone (krōn) *n.* an ugly, withered-looking old lady.

crony (krō′ nē) *n.* a friend or companion.

crum·pet (krum′ pit) *n.* a batter cake baked on a griddle.

crypt (kript) *n.* a chamber underground.

cum·brous (kum′ brəs) *adj.* difficult to handle because of size or weight.

cur·lew (kur′ loo or kur′ lyoo) *n.* a large wading bird with long legs.

cyn·i·cal (sin′ i k'l) *adj.* doubting the sincerity of others' motives or actions.

D

dap·per (dap′ ər) *adj.* neatly and carefully dressed.

daunt (dônt or dänt) *v.* to make fearful or discouraged.

de·co·rum (di kôr′ əm) *n.* dignified and proper behavior. —**decorous** *adj.*

de·crep·it (di krep′ it) *adj.* broken down or worn out due to old age or long use.

de·cry (di krī′) *v.* to condemn openly.

de·fer (di fur′) *v.* to put off until another time.

def·er·ence (def′ ər əns) *n.* regard or respect for.

def·er·en·tial (def′ ə ren′ shəl) *adj.* showing respect.

deft (deft) *adj.* skillful in a quick, easy manner. — **deftly** *adv.*

de·funct (di fungkt′) *adj.* no longer living.

de·mean·or (di mēn′ ər) *n.* conduct.

de·nun·ci·a·tion (di nun sē ā′ shən) *n.* a public accusation.

de·prav·i·ty (di prav′ ə tē) *n.* a corrupt or wicked condition.

de·pre·ci·ate (di prē′ shē āt) *v.* to cause to appear unimportant.

de·ride (di rīd′) *v.* to laugh at in scorn or ridicule.

de·ri·sion (di rizh′ ən) *n.* ridicule or contempt. —**deride** *v.*

de·scry (di skrī′) *v.* to look for and catch sight of.

des·ic·cate (des′ i kāt′) *v.* to completely dry.

des·o·late (des′ ə lit) *adj.* deserted; destroyed.

des·pot·ism (des′ pə tiz'm) *n.* a government by an absolute ruler.

di·a·bol·i·cal (di ə bäl′ ik əl) *adj.* cruel or wicked.

dil·i·gent (dil′ ə jənt) *adj.* working hard. —**diligently** *adv.*

dim·i·nu·tion (dim′ ə nyoo′ shən or dim′ ə noo′ shən) *n.* a lessening or decrease.

di·min·u·tive (də min′ yoo tiv) *adj.* very small.

din (din) *n.* loud, continuous noise.

dire (dīr) *adj.* terrible.

dirge (durj) *n.* a slow, sad song, showing grief for the dead.

dis·con·so·late (dis kän′ sə lit) *adj.* so unhappy that nothing can be of comfort.

dis·cord (dis′ kôrd) *n.* disagreement.

dis·crep·an·cy (dis krep′ ən sē) *n.* a lack of agreement.

dis·fran·chise (dis fran′ chīz) *v.* to deprive of rights or privileges. —**disfranchisement** *n.*

dis·heart·en (dis här′ t'n) *v.* to discourage or depress.

dis·in·ter (dis′ in tʉr′) *v.* to bring to light.

dis·pose (dis pōz′) *v.* to make willing or inclined.

dis·pu·ta·tious (dis′ pyo͞o tā′ shəs) *adj.* controversial or argumentative.

dis·sem·ble (di sem′ b'l) *v.* to conceal the truth or one's true motives.

dis·sev·er (di sev′ ər) *v.* to separate.

dis·sim·u·late (di sim′ yə lāt′) *v.* to hide by deception. —**dissimulation** *n.*

dis·suade (di swād′) *v.* to turn aside from a course of action by persuasion.

di·verge (də vʉrj′ or dī vʉrj′) *v.* to branch off in different directions.

di·vest (də vest′ or dī vest′) *v.* to deprive or take away from.

di·vine prov·i·dence (də vīn′ präv′ ə dəns) *n.* God.

di·vin·ing rod (də vīn′ ing röd) *n.* a forked stick that is supposed to reveal hidden water or minerals by dipping downward.

do·min·ion (də min′ yən) *n.* the power to rule.

dou·blet (dub′ lit) *n.* a man's close-fitting jacket worn in the 16th or 17th century.

draught (draft or dräft) *n.* a drink.

dray (drā) *n.* a low, sturdy cart having detachable sides, used for carrying heavy loads.

drone (drōn) *v.* to make a constant humming sound.

drudg·er·y (druj′ ər ē) *n.* work that is tiresome and difficult.

druth·ers (dru*th*′ ərz) *n.* choice.

duck (duk) *n.* a cotton or linen cloth-like canvas that is finer and lighter in weight than canvas.

E

ebb (eb) *v.* **1.** to flow back. **2.** to weaken or lessen.

ef·face (i fās′ or e fās′) *v.* to erase or wipe out.

e·lic·it (i lis′ it) *v.* to evoke or draw forth.

em·bra·sure (im brā′ zhər) *n.* an opening with the sides slanting outward to increase the angle of fire of a gun.

em·i·nence (em′ ə nəns) *n.* superiority in position or rank.

en·sign (en′ sīn or en′ s'n) *n.* a flag.

en·sue (in so͞o′ or in syo͞o′) *v.* to follow.

en·treat (in trēt′) *v.* to beg or plead.

ep·i·taph (ep′ ə taf′) *n.* the written message on a tomb in memory of the person buried there.

ep·i·thet (ep′ ə thet′ or ep′ ə thət) *n.* a word or phrase used to suggest some quality of a person or thing in a mocking way.

e·rad·i·cate (i rad′ ə kāt′) *v.* to wipe out.

er·rat·ic (i rat′ ik) *adj.* having an irregular course. —**erratically** *adv.*

es·sence (es′ 'ns) *n.* the most important quality of something.

es·teem (ə stēm′) *v.* to value highly.

e·vince (i vins′) *v.* to show plainly or make clear.

ex·alt (ig zôlt′) *v.* to intensify or heighten the effect of.

ex·panse (ik spans′) *n.* a large, open area.

ex·pan·sive (ik span′ siv) *adj.* having a generous or sympathetic nature.

ex·pe·di·ent (ik spē′ dē ənt) *n.* something that is useful for bringing about a desired result.

ex·tem·po·ra·ne·ous (ik stem′ pə rā′ nē əs) *adj.* done without any preparation.

ex·trem·i·ty (ik strem′ ə tē) *n.* a body limb.

ex·ude (ig zo͞od′ or ig zyo͞od′) *v.* to ooze.

ex·ult (ig zult′) *v.* to greatly rejoice.

F

fa·cil·i·tate (fə sil′ ə tāt′) *v.* to make easier.

fain (fān) *adj.* glad or willing.

fal·set·to (fôl set′ ō) *adj.* of singing or speaking in an unnatural way that is much higher than one's usual voice.

fal·ter (fôl′ tər) *v.* to act uncertainly or hesitantly.

fan·tod (fan′ täd) *n.* a nervous condition.

feign (fān) *v.* to pretend.

fer·vent (fʉr′ vənt) *adj.* showing intense, earnest feelings.

---

at, āte, fär, pen, ēqual; sit, mīne; sō, côrn, join, too͝k, fo͞ol, our; us, tʉrn; chill, shop, thick, *th*ey, sing; zh *in* measure; 'l *in* idle; ə *in* alive, cover, family, robot, circus.

fes·ter (fes′ tər) *v.* to form pus.

fet·a (fet′ ə) *n.* a soft, white cheese made in Greece from goat's milk.

fi·at (fī′ at or fī′ ət) *n.* authorization.

fil·i·al (fil′ ē əl or fil′ yəl) *adj.* suitable from a son or daughter.

fire·lock (fīr läk′) *n.* an early type of firearm used before the invention of the rifle.

flag·on (flag′ ən) *n.* a container for liquids, usually having a handle and spout.

flak (flak) *n.* the fire from antiaircraft guns.

flank (flaŋk) *v.* to be located or placed at the side.

flay (flā) *v.* to scold or criticize without mercy.

flot·sam (flät′ səm) *n.* the wreckage of a ship floating at sea.

floun·der (floun′ dər) *v.* to struggle awkwardly.

foal (fōl) *v.* to give birth to.

for·ay (fôr′ ā) *n.* a sudden raid or attack.

for·bear (fôr ber′ or fər ber′) *v.* to avoid.

ford (fôrd) *n.* a shallow place in a river that can be crossed by wading or by riding on horseback.

forge (fôrj) *n.* a furnace for heating metal.

for·mi·da·ble (fôr′ mə də b'l) *adj.* causing dread or fear.

for·ti·fy (for′ tə fī′) *v.* to strengthen against an attack.

fo·rum (fôr′ əm) *n.* **1.** a court of law. **2.** an assembly for public discussion.

fow·ling piece (fou′ liŋ pēs′) *n.* a type of shotgun for fowl.

fran·chise (fran′ chīz) *n.* the right to vote.

fren·zied (fren′ zēd) *adj.* showing a wild outburst of feeling.

fru·gal·i·ty (frōō gal′ ə tē) *n.* the act of being thrifty or not wasteful.

fume (fyōōm) *v.* to show that one is annoyed or angry.

fur·row (fʉr′ ō) *n.* a narrow groove formed in the ground.

fur·tive (fʉr′ tiv) *adj.* done in a sneaky way.

G

ga·ble (gā′ b'l) *n.* the triangular part of a wall in between the sloping ends of a ridged roof.

gait (gāt) *n.* a manner of walking.

gale (gāl) *n.* a very strong wind.

gal·li·gas·kins (gal′ i gas′ kinz) *n.* loosely fitting pants.

gal·lows (gal′ ōz) *n.* a structure used for hanging condemned persons.

gam·bol (gam′ bəl) *n.* **1.** merriment. **2.** a trick.

gar·ret (gar′ it) *n.* the attic.

gar·ri·son (gar′ ə s'n) *n.* troops in a fort for its defense.

gaud·y (gôd′ ē) *adj.* bright and showy, yet in bad taste.

gaunt (gônt) *adj.* thin or bony.

ge·ne·al·o·gy (jē′ nē äl′ ə jē or jē nē al′ ə jē) *n.* the study of the descent or ancestry of a family.

ge·ne·va gown (je nē′ və goun) *n.* a long, loose black gown with wide sleeves first worn by the clergy of Geneva.

ge·nial (jēn′ yəl or jē′ nē əl) *adj.* cheerful and friendly.

gen·tile (jen′ tīl) *n.* any person not of the Jewish religion.

ges·tic·u·late (jes tik′ yə lāt′) *v.* to use gestures, usually with the hands or arms. —**gesticulation** *n.*

gim·let (gim′ lit) *n.* a small tool used for making holes.

gin·ger·ly (jin′ jər lē) *adv.* extremely carefully or cautiously.

glen (glen) *n.* a narrow valley.

glow·er (glou′ ər) *n.* an angry stare.

goad (gōd) *v.* to drive or urge on.

gout (gout) *n.* a disease marked by pain and swelling of the hands and feet.

grap·ple (grap′ 'l) *n.* a struggle or hand to hand fight.

gui·don (gīd′ 'n or gī′ dän) *n.* the identifying flag of a military unit.

gul·ly (gul′ ē) *n.* a small, narrow hollow in the earth's surface worn by water.

gy·rate (jī′ rāt) *v.* to move in a circular or spiral direction. —**gyration** *n.*

H

hal·cy·on (hal′ sē ən) *adj.* happy or peaceful.

hal·low (hal′ ō) *v.* to make or regard as holy.

hang·er (haŋ′ ər) *n.* a short sword hung from the belt.

hank·er·ing (hang′ kər ing) *n.* a strong longing. —**hanker** *v.*

ha·rangue (hə rang′) *n.* a long noisy speech. —**haranguing** *v.*

har·py (här′ pē) *n.* in Greek mythology, a hideous, filthy monster.

hash (hash) *v.* to make a mess out of. —**hashed** *adj.*

haunch (hônch or hänch) *n.* the hind quarter of an animal.

hay·mak·er (hā′ mā kər) *n.* a powerful blow with one's fist.

heath (hēth) *n.* a tract of open wasteland covered with heather and low shrubs.

heft (heft) *v.* to estimate the weight of something by lifting.

hem·lock (hem′ lök) *n.* an evergreen tree of the pine family.

hemp (hemp) *n.* the tough fiber of an Asiatic plant used to make rope.

herb·al·ist (hʉr′ b'l ist or ʉr′ b'l ist) *n.* a person who grows, collects, or deals in medicinal herbs.

hew (hyo͞o) *v.* to shape or make as by cutting or chopping.

ho·gan (hō′ gôn or hō′ gän) *n.* a dwelling of the Navaho Indians made of earth and timber.

hos·tler (häs′ lər or äs′ lər) *n.* one who cares for horses at a stable or inn.

hulk (hulk) *n.* **1.** the body of a ship that is old and taken apart. **2.** a large ship that is difficult to handle.

hyp·o·crit·i·cal (hip ə krit′ i k'l) *adj.* pretending to be better than one really is; appearing virtuous without really being so.

I

im·pel (im pel′) *v.* to urge or force.

im·pend (im pend′) *v.* to threaten. —**impending** *adj.*

im·pen·e·tra·ble (im pen′ i trə b'l) *adj.* that cannot be passed through.

im·pe·ri·al (im pir′ ē əl) *adj.* having great authority.

im·pe·ri·ous (im pir′ ē əs) *adj.* urgent or necessary.

im·pi·ous (im′ pē əs) *adj.* having no religious devotion.

im·por·tune (im′ pôr to͞on′ or im′ pôr tyo͞on′ or im-pôr′ chən) *v.* to urge repeatedly.

im·pre·cate (im′ prə kāt′) *v.* to pray for a curse or an evil. —**imprecation** *n.*

im·pu·ni·ty (im pū′ nə tē) *n.* free from punishment or harm.

in·ar·tic·u·late (in är tik′ yə lit) *adj.* unable to speak clearly.

in·car·na·tion (in′ kär nā′ shən) *n.* a person who is a living example or symbol.

in·cense (in sens′) *v.* to make extremely angry.

in·ces·sant (in ses′ 'nt) *adj.* constant, never ending.

in·clu·sive (in klo͞o′ siv) *adj.* taking everything into account. —**inclusively** *adv.*

in·do·lent (in′ də lənt) *adj.* lazy.

in·duce (in do͞os′ or in dyo͞os′) *v.* to persuade. —**inducement** *n.*

in·ef·fa·ble (in ef′ ə b'l) *adj.* not expressible.

in·es·ti·ma·ble (in es′ tə mə b'l) *adj.* too valuable or great to be accurately measured.

in·fat·u·at·ed (in fach′ o͞o wāt id) *adj.* totally carried away by foolish love.

in·fi·del (in′ fə d'l) *n.* an unbelieving person; one who holds no religious belief.

in·flux (in′ fluks′) *n.* a continuous flowing in.

in·gen·ious (in jen′ yo͞o wəs) *adj.* clever or inventive. —**ingenuity** *n.*

in·so·lent (in′ sə lənt) *adj.* boldly disrespectful.

in·sti·gate (in′ stə gāt′) *v.* to urge on to an action.

in·tan·gi·ble (in tan′ jə b'l) *adj.* that cannot be touched.

in·ter (in tʉr′) *v.* to bury or put into a grave.

in·ter·mi·na·ble (in tʉr′ mi nə b'l) *adj.* seeming to last forever.

in·to·na·tion (in′ tə nā′ shən) *n.* the way the voice rises and falls in pitch when a person speaks.

in·trac·ta·ble (in trak′ tə b'l) *adj.* stubborn or unruly. —**intractably** *adv.*

in·vec·tive (in vek′ tiv) *n.* harsh criticism.

ir·res·o·lute (i rez′ ə lo͞ot) *adj.* not able to make up one's mind.

---

at, āte, fär, pen, ēqual; sit, mīne; sō, côrn, join, to͞ok, fo͞ol, our; us, tʉrn; chill, shop, thick, *th*ey, sing; zh *in* measure; 'l *in* idle;
ə *in* alive, cover, family, robot, circus.

J

ja·pan (jə pan') *n.* a varnish or lacquer giving a glossy, hard finish. —**japanned** *adj.*

jeer (jir) *n.* a mocking remark; a comment made in a rude, sarcastic way.

jer·kin (jur' kin) *n.* a sleeveless, closefitting jacket worn in the 16th or 17th century.

ju·bi·lant (jōō' b'l ənt) *adj.* joyful.

jun·to (jun' tō) *n.* a group of people who are political plotters.

K

knoll (nōl) *n.* a small, rounded hill.

L

lag·gard (lag' ərd) *n.* a slow person who always seems to fall behind.

lance (lans) *n.* a long, wooden weapon having a sharp metal head.

lan·guish (lang' gwish) *v.* to live under distressing or unfortunate conditions.

lat·i·tude (lat' ə tōōd' or lat' ə tyōōd') *n.* freedom of opinion or action.

leg·a·cy (leg' ə sē) *n.* money or property left to one by a will.

lev·ee (lev' ē) *n.* a landing place for ships along a river bank.

loom (lōōm) *v.* to come into sight indistinctly.

loth (lōth) *adj.* unwilling.

lurk (lurk) *v.* to stay hidden as if to attack.

M

ma·cho (mä' chō) *adj.* masculine.

mag·got (mag' ət) *n.* an insect larva, worm-like in nature.

mag·na·nim·i·ty (mag' nə nim' ə tē) *n.* a quality that rises above meanness or pettiness.

mal·a·dy (mal' ə dē) *n.* a disease or illness.

ma·lign (mə līn') **1.** *v.* to say unfair things about. **2.** *adj.* evil.

mal·le·a·ble (mal' ē ə b'l) *adj.* that can be pounded or pressed into different shapes without breaking.

man·a·cle (man' ə k'l) *n.* a handcuff or restraint.

man·i·fes·ta·tion (man' ə fes tā' shən or man' ə fəs tā' shen) —*n.* a formal demonstration of.

man·i·fold (man' ə fōld) *adj.* having many sorts.

man·tle (man' t'l) *n.* a covering.

mar·tial (mär' shəl) *adj.* connected with the military; war-like.

mar·ti·net (mär' t'n et') *n.* a strict disciplinarian.

mast (mast) *n.* the tall structure rising upward from the deck of a ship used to support the sails or flags.

mas·tiff (mas' tif) *n.* a large, powerful dog with hanging lips and drooping ears.

mau·so·le·um (mô' sə lē' əm or mô' zə lē' əm) *n.* a large, impressive looking tomb.

mean (mēn) *adj.* low in value or importance. —**meanly** *adv.*

me·di·oc·ri·ty (mē' dē äk' rə tē) *n.* the state of being neither very good nor very bad; ordinary.

mel·an·chol·y (mel' ən käl ē) *adj.* sad or depressed.

mel·low (mel' ō) *adj.* moist and rich.

mer·e·tri·cious (mer' ə trish' əs) *adj.* attractive in a showy, false way.

met·a·mor·phose (met' ə môr' fōz or met' ə môr' fōs) *v.* to change or alter in form or nature.

met·tle (met' 'l) *n.* courage or spirit.

mien (mēn) *n.* manner.

mi·grant (mī' grənt) *n.* a person who moves from one place to another, especially to another country.

mi·li·tia (mə lish' ə) *n.* a military force.

minc·ing (min' sing) *adj.* dainty or elegant in an unnatural way. —**mincingly** *adv.*

mine (mīn) *n.* a tunnel dug under an enemy's fort in which an explosive is placed to destroy the enemy.

mi·nu·ti·ae (mi nōō' shi ē' or mi nyōō' shi e') *n.* small, unimportant details.

mire (mīr) *n.* wet, soggy ground.

mirth·ful (murth' fəl) *adj.* showing joyfulness, usually shown by laughter.

moor (moor) *n.* open wasteland, usually covered with heather, a low-growing plant common in the British Isles.

mor·i·bund (môr' ə bund') *adj.* **1.** dying. **2.** having no vitality left.

mo·roc·co (mə rä' kō) *n.* a soft, fine leather originally made in Morocco from the skins of goats. —**Moroccan** *adj.*

mo·rose (mə rōs' or mô rōs') *adj.* gloomy.

mot·ley (mät' lē) *adj.* consisting of many different or clashing elements.

mu·lat·to (mə lat′ ō or myo͞o lat′ ō) *n.* a person with mixed Negro and Caucasian ancestry.

muse (myo͞oz) *v.* to think about a variety of things in a quiet, unhurried manner.

N

ne·pen·the (ni pen′ thē) *n.* a drug believed by the ancient Greeks to cause forgetfulness of sorrow.

net·tle (net′ ′l) *v.* to annoy or irritate.

non·con·form·ist (nän kən fôr′ mist) *n.* one who does not follow the customs or beliefs that most people accept.

non·plus (nän plus′ or nän′ plus′) *n.* the condition of being so confused that one is not able to speak or act.

nu·cle·us (no͞o′ klē əs or nyo͞o′ klē əs) *n.* a central part around which other things are grouped.

O

o·bei·sance (ō bā′ s′ns or ō bē′ s′ns) *n.* a showing of deep respect.

ob·lit·er·ate (ə blit′ ə rāt′ or ō blit′ ə rāt) *v.* to destroy or do away with.

ob·se·qui·ous (əb sē′ kwē əs or äb sē′ kwē əs) *adj.* showing too much willingness to obey or serve.

om·i·nous (äm′ ə nəs) *adj.* threatening.

orb (orb) *n.* a small globe.

os·cil·late (äs′ ə lāt′) *v.* to move or swing back and forth.

os·tra·cism (äs′ trə siz′m) *n.* the action of a group in deciding to have nothing to do with someone.

P

pac·i·fism (pas′ ə fiz′m) *n.* opposition to the use of force in any situation. —**pacifist** *n.*

pack·et (pak′ it) *n.* a boat that travels a regular route carrying freight, mail or passengers.

pall (pôl) *n.* a dark, gloomy covering.

pal·lid (pal′ id) *adj.* pale.

par·ox·ysm (par′ ək siz′m) *n.* a sudden outburst.

pa·tri·arch (pā′ trē ärk) *n.* the father and ruler of a family or a tribe.

pat·ri·mony (pat′ rə mō′ nē) *n.* property that is inherited from one's father.

pen·sive (pen′ siv) *adj.* thinking deeply of sad things.

per·emp·to·ry (pə remp′ tər ē) *adj.* forcing one's wishes on another in a bullying manner. —**peremptorily** *adv.*

per·en·ni·al (pə ren′ ē əl) *adj.* having a life cycle lasting two or more years.

per·il (per′ əl) *n.* danger.

per·ish (per′ ish) *v.* to be destroyed; to die.

per·plex (pər pleks′) *v.* to confuse. —**perplexity** *n.*

per·se·vere (pur′ sə vir′) *v.* to continue a course of action in spite of difficulty.

pe·ruse (pə ro͞oz′) *v.* to read thoroughly and carefully.

per·vade (per vād′) *v.* to spread throughout.

pes·ky (pes′ kē) *adj.* annoying or troublesome.

pes·ti·lent (pes′ t′l ənt) *adj.* annoying or troublesome.

phlegm (flem) *n.* calmness or sluggishness.

pier glass (pir′ glas) *n.* a tall mirror set in a wall section between windows.

pi·e·ty (pī′ ə tē) *n.* a devotion to religious practices.

pil·lo·ry (pil′ ər ē) *n.* a wooden board with holes for the head and hands, in which petty offenders were locked to cause them public shame.

pin·na·cle (pin′ ə k′l) *n.* the highest point.

piv·ot·al (piv′ ə t′l) *adj.* on which something turns.

pla·cate (plā′ kāt or plak′ āt) *v.* to stop from being angry.

plac·id (plas′ id) *adj.* calm.

plain·tive (plān′ tiv) *adj.* sad or mournful.

plow·share (plou′ sher′) *n.* the cutting blade of an early plow.

poign·ant (poin′ yənt) *adj.* painful to one's feelings.

pre·cept (prē′ sept) *n.* a rule of moral conduct.

prec·i·pice (pres′ ə pis) *n.* a steep cliff.

pre·cip·i·ta·tion (pri sip′ ə tā′ shən) *n.* a sudden throwing or falling headlong.

---

at, āte, fär, pen, ēqual; sit, mīne; sō, côrn, join, to͝ok, fo͞ol, our; us, turn; chill, shop, thick, *th*ey, sing; zh *in* measure; ′l *in* idle;
ə *in* **a**live, cov**e**r, fam**i**ly, rob**o**t, circ**u**s.

pre·mo·ni·tion (prē′ mə nish′ ən or prem′ ə nish′ ən) *n.* an advance warning.

pre·rog·a·tive (pri räg′ ə tiv) *n.* a special privilege of rank.

pres·age (pri sāj′) *v.* a sign or warning of something that is going to happen.

pre·ter·nat·u·ral (prē′ tər nach′ ər əl) *adj.* beyond what is natural. —**preternaturally** *adv.*

pris·mat·ic (priz mat′ ik) *adj.* like the colors visible when white light is passed through a prism; red, orange, yellow, green, blue, indigo, and violet.

pro·di·gious (prə dij′ əs) *adj.* **1.** impressive. **2.** enormous.

prof·fer (präf′ ər) *v.* to offer.

pro·found (prə found′) *adj.* deeply intellectual.

prom·is·so·ry note (pröm′ i sôr′ ē nōt) *n.* a written promise to pay a specific sum of money on a specified date.

pro·trude (prō trōōd′) *v.* to project or jut out.

Prov·i·dence (pröv′ ə dens) *n.* God.

pru·dence (prōōd′ ′ns) *n.* the quality of using sound judgment. —**prudent** *adj.*

pum·mel (pum′ ′l) *v.* to hit with repeated blows.

Q

quad·ru·ped (kwäd′ rōō ped′) *n.* an animal with four feet.

quaff (kwäf or kwaf) *v.* to drink deeply in a thirsty manner.

quag·mire (kwag′ mīr′) *n.* wet, swamp-like ground that gives way under the feet.

quest (kwest) *n.* search.

quick (kwik) *n.* the living.

quill (kwil) *n.* a pen made from the stem of a feather.

quirk (kwʉrk) *n.* a sudden twist.

quiv·er (kwiv′ ər) *n.* a case used for holding arrows.

R

rapt (rapt) *adj.* carried away with love or joy.

rav·age (rav′ ij) *n.* result of violent destruction.

ra·ven (rā′ vən) *n.* a large bird with shiny black feathers and a sharp beak, belonging to the crow family.

raze (rāz) *v.* to demolish or tear down.

re·coil (ri koil′) *v.* to draw back or shrink as in fear.

rec·om·pense (rek′ əm pens′) *n.* something given in return for something else.

red·o·lent (red′ ′l ənt) *adj.* smelling sweetly.

re·it·er·ate (rē it′ ə rāt′) *v.* to say again.

ren·der (ren′ dər) *v.* to make or cause to be.

ren·e·gade (ren′ ə gād′) *n.* a traitor; one who abandons his party, principles, or group to join the other side.

re·past (ri past′) *n.* a meal.

rep·re·hen·si·ble (rep ri hen′ sə b′l) *adj.* deserving to be blamed.

res·ig·na·tion (rez′ ig nā′ shən) *n.* the act of surrendering.

re·solve (ri zölv′ or ri zôlv′) *v.* to reach a decision to change.

res·pite (res′ pit) *n.* a postponement or delay.

ret·i·cule (ret′ ə kyōōl′) *n.* a woman's handbag with a drawstring.

re·trac·tion (ri trak′ shən) *n.* a withdrawal of a statement, charge, or promise.

rev·er·ence (rev′ ər əns) *v.* to treat with respect as for something sacred. —**reverently** *adv.*

re·vile (ri vīl′) *v.* to call bad names.

rheu·ma·tism (rōō′ mə tiz′m) *n.* a painful condition of the muscles and joints.

rift (rift) *v.* to burst or split open.

rig·ma·role (rig′ mə rōl′) *n.* nonsense or rambling talk.

ro·bust (rō bust′ or rō′ bust) *adj.* healthy and strong.

rop·y (rō′ pē) *adj.* forming rope-like or sticky threads.

round·a·bout (round′ ə bout′) *n.* **1.** a short, tight-fitting jacket. **2.** not direct.

round·house (round′ hous′) *n.* **1.** a building with a turntable in the center for repairing or storing locomotives. **2.** in boxing, a wide swing or hook to the head.

rouse (rouz) *v.* to wake.

rout (rout) *v.* to defeat in an overwhelming way; to force out.

roy·ster (rois′ tər) *v.* **1.** to boast. **2.** to be lively or noisy.

ru·bi·cund (rōō′ bi kund′) *adj.* reddish or rosy.

ruck (ruk) *n.* a mass of ordinary people or things.

ru·di·ment (r$\overline{oo}$′ də mənt) *n.* something that is to be learned first.

rue·ful (r$\overline{oo}$′ fəl) *adj.* showing sorrow or regret.

S

sac·ri·le·gious (sak′ rə lij′ əs or sak′ rə lē′ jəs) *adj.* guilty of giving disrespectful treatment to anything thought of as sacred or holy.

sa·gac·i·ty (sə gas′ ə tē) *n.* the quality of being wise or shrewd.

sage (sāj) *n.* a very wise, usually old man respected for his wisdom.

sa·lient (sāl′ yənt or sā′ lē ənt) *adj.* noticeable or standing out.

sal·low (sal′ ō) *adj.* having an unhealthy yellowish look.

sal·vage (sal′ vij) *n.* the saving of anything from waste or destruction.

sas·sa·fras (sas′ ə fras′) *n.* a tree with yellow flowers and bluish fruit.

sau·cy (sô′ sē) *adj.* bold and lively.

saun·ter (sôn′ tər) *v.* a slow or leisurely manner of walking.

sa·vor (sā′ vər) *n.* the taste or flavor.

scab (skab) *n.* a worker who refuses to join a union or a worker who refuses to go on strike.

scaf·fold (skaf′ ′ld or skaf′ ōld) *n.* a platform used for executing criminals.

scant·ling (skant′ liŋ) *n.* a long, thin piece of wood.

scar·ab (skar′ əb) *n.* a type of beetle.

scone (skōn) *n.* a small, flat cake baked on a griddle.

score (skôr) *n.* twenty things.

scour (skour) *v.* 1. to go through quickly yet thoroughly as in hunting. 2. to clean or polish by rubbing hard with something rough or gritty.

scourge (skʉrj) *n.* a cause of severe suffering.

scut·tle (skut′ ′l) *v.* to abandon.

sear (sir) *v.* to burn or scorch the surface.

se·ces·sion·ist (si sesh′ ən ist) *n.* a person who favored the withdrawal of the southern states from the union at the beginning of the Civil War.

sedge (sej) *n.* a coarse grasslike plant often found on wet ground or in water.

sep·ul·cher (sep′ ′l kər) *n.* a tomb.

ser·a·phim (ser′ ə fim) *n.* in the Bible, one of the heavenly beings surrounding the throne of God.

ser·pen·tine (sʉr′ pən tēn′ or sʉr′ pən tīn′) *adj.* twisted or winding.

shaft (shaft) *n.* a flagpole.

sham (sham) *n.* an imitation that is meant to deliberately mislead.

sheath (shēth) *n.* a case used for the blade of a knife.

shied (shīd) *v.* moved back suddenly when startled.

siege (sēj) *n.* a stubborn and continued effort to win or control something.

sim·per (sim′ pər) *v.* to smile in a silly way.

sin·ew·y (sin′ yoo wē) *adj.* possessing good muscular development.

singe (sinj) *v.* to hold in or near a flame to burn off bristles. —**singed** *adj.*

sire (sīr) *n.* a forefather.

skid (skid) *n.* a plank or log used for a support or a track to roll a heavy object on.

skir·mish·er (skʉr′ mish ər) *n.* one involved in a fight between small groups, usually part of a battle.

skulk (skulk) *v.* to move about in a cowardly or threatening way.

slack (slak) *n.* the part that hangs loose.

sleep·er (slē′ pər) *n.* a tie supporting a railroad track.

smite (smīt) *v.* 1. to strike very hard. 2. to affect strongly and suddenly.

sniv·el (sniv′ ′l) *v.* to cry or complain in a whining manner.

sol·ace (säl′ is) *v.* to give comfort.

sop (säp) *v.* to soak in or with a liquid.

sov·er·eign (säv′ rən or säv′ ər in) *adj.* independent of all others.

spav·in (spav′ in) *n.* a disease of horses that usually cripples.

squall (skwôl) *n.* a brief violent windstorm usually accompanied by rain or snow.

---

at, āte, fär, pen, ēqual; sit, mīne; sō, côrn, join, took, f$\overline{oo}$l, our; us, tʉrn; chill, shop, thick, *th*ey, siŋg; zh *in* measure; ′l *in* idle;
ə *in* alive, cover, family, robot, circus.

squal·or (skwäl′ ər or skwôl ər) *n.* a condition of misery or filth.

squee·gee (skwē′ jē) *n.* a T-shaped tool, usually with a blade of rubber, used for wiping liquid from a surface, such as in washing windows.

stag·ger (stag′ ər) *n.* a nervous disease of horses that causes them to stagger or fall when walking.

stat·ure (stach′ ər) *n.* **1.** the height of one's body in a natural standing position. **2.** a level of achievement considered worthy of respect.

stealth·y (stel′ thē) *adj.* quiet; sneaky. —**stealthily** *adv.*

stock (stok) *n.* a piece of rifle or similar firearm that holds the barrel.

stol·id (stäl′ id) *adj.* showing little or no emotion. —**stolidity** *n.*

strin·gent (strin′ jənt) *adj.* severe or strict. —**stringency** *n.*

suav·i·ty (swä′ və tē) *n.* polite in a smooth manner.

sub·ver·sion (səb vʉr′ zhən or səb vʉr′ shən) *n.* overthrow or ruin.

sue (so͞o) *v.* to make an appeal.

suf·fer·ance (suf′ ər əns or suf′ rəns) *n.* **1.** the ability to bear up under pain. **2.** permission.

suf·fice (sə fīs′ or sə fīz′) *v.* to be enough.

suf·frage (suf′ rij) *n.* a short, humble prayer.

sur·cease (sʉr sēs′) *v.* to stop or end.

surge (sʉrj) *n.* a strong increase.

sur·mise (sər mīz′) *v.* to form an opinion without much evidence.

sur·mount (sər mount′) *v.* **1.** to be at the top of. **2.** to overcome.

swath (swäth or swôth) *n.* the space covered with one cut of a scythe or other mowing device.

swoon (swo͞on) *n.* a fit of fainting.

T

tal·on (tal′ ən) *n.* a bird of prey's claw.

tarn (tärn) *n.* a small mountain lake.

tar·ry (tar′ ē) *v.* to be slow.

tat·too (ta to͞o′) *n.* a loud drumming or rapping.

taunt (tônt or tänt) *v.* to make fun of by using scornful or sarcastic language. —**taunter** *n.*

taut (tôt) *adj.* **1.** stretched tightly. **2.** strained.

tem·per·ance (tem′ pər əns or tem′ prəns) *n.* the drinking of little or no alcoholic beverages.

tem·pest (tem′ pist) *n.* a violent storm accompanied by high winds, often bringing rain.

te·nac·i·ty (tə nas′ ə tē) *n.* the quality of being persistent.

ten·der (ten′ dər) *v.* to offer.

ten·dril (ten′ dril) *n.* the threadlike part of a climbing plant.

ter·ma·gant (tʉr′ mə gənt) *n.* a quarrelsome or scolding woman.

there·at (*t*here at′) *adv.* at that place or time.

throt·tle (thrät′ ′l) *v.* to strangle or choke.

toil (toil) *n.* hard, tiring work or effort.

tor·por (tôr′ pər) *n.* a state of being asleep.

tor·rent (tôr′ ənt or tär′ ənt) *n.* a flood or a rush, as of water.

tor·so (tôr′ sō) *n.* the trunk of a human body.

To·ry (tôr′ ē) *n.* formerly a member of one of the two major political parties in England.

tra·cho·ma (trə kō′ mə) *n.* a contagious infection of the eye caused by a virus.

tract (trakt) *n.* pamphlet on a religious or political subject.

tran·scend (tran send′) *v.* to be superior to. —**transcendent** *n.*

tran·sient (tran′ shənt) *adj.* temporary; passing quickly.

trav·erse (tra vʉrs′ or trə vʉrs′) *v.* to cross over or through.

tree (trē) *v.* to corner or put in an inescapable situation.

trem·u·lous (trem′ yoo ləs) *adj.* trembling or quivering.

trep·i·da·tion (trep′ ə dā′shən) *n.* worry or fearful uncertainty.

tres·tle (tres′ ′l) *n.* a type of frame.

trib·u·la·tion (trib′ yə lā′ shən) *n.* great sorrow or distress.

tri·fle (trī′ f′l) *n.* something of little importance. —**trifling** *adj.*

trow·el (trou′ əl) *n.* a tool with a pointed scoop used for digging.

tulle (to͞ol) *n.* a thin, fine netting made of silk, rayon, or nylon that is used for veils.

tur·bu·lent (tʉr′ byə lənt) *adj.* violently stirred up; turmoil.

tur·ret (tʉr′ it) *n.* a low, revolving structure for guns.

U

un·al·ien·a·ble (un āl′ yən ə b'l or un al′ ē ən ə b'l) *adj.* not transferable to anyone else.

un·a·ton·a·ble (un ə tōn′ ə b'l) *adj.* that cannot be amended.

un·daunt·ed (un dôn′ tid or un dän′ tid) *adj.* not discouraged or afraid.

un·du·la·tion (un′ joo lā′ shən or un′ dyoo lā′ shən or un′ doo lā′ shən) *n.* a wavy movement.

un·en·cum·ber (un in kum′ ber) *v.* not burdening or hindering.

un·gain·ly (un gān′ lē) *adj.* awkward.

un·wont·ed (un wun′ tid or un wôn′ tid) *adj.* not usual or common.

ur·chin (ʉr′ chin) *n.* a small, mischievous boy.

u·surp (yoo sʉrp′ or yoo zʉrp′) *v.* to take and hold without right. —**usurpation** *n.*

u·til·i·ty (yoo til′ ə tē) *n.* usefulness.

V

val·or (val′ ər) *n.* courage or bravery.

van·quish (vaŋ′ kwish or van′ kwish) *v.* to conquer or defeat.

vas·sal (vas′ 'l) *n.* a servant.

ve·he·ment (vē′ ə mənt) *adj.* showing very strong feeling.

ven·er·y (ven′ ər ē) *n.* the satisfying of a sexual need.

ver·i·ly (ver′ ə lē) *adv.* truly.

vex (veks) *v.* to make trouble.

vex·a·tion (vek sā′ shən) *n.* cause of distress or annoyance.

vig·il (vij′ əl) *n.* a watch kept during normal hours of sleep.

vi·ra·go (vi rā′ gō or vī rā′ gō) *n.* a loud, ill-tempered, quarrelsome woman.

vis·age (viz′ ij) *n.* a person's facial expression; the face.

vis·ta (vis′ tə) *n.* a view, usually as seen through a long passage.

voile (voil) *n.* a sheer, thin fabric.

vol·ley (väl′ ē) *n.* a burst of words suggestive of the shooting of a number of guns at the same time.

vor·tex (vôr teks) *n.* a whirling mass of water with a vacuum at the center, catching anything caught in its motion; a whirlpool.

vo·tive (vōt′ iv) *adj.* done in fulfillment of a vow.

W

wane (wān) *v.* to approach an end.

wan·ton (wän′ t'n or wôn′ t'n) *adj.* without reason or sense.

ward (wôrd) *v.* to turn aside.

warp (wôrp) *n.* in weaving, the threads running lengthwise in the loom.

weft (weft) *n.* in weaving, the horizontal threads that cross the warp in a woven fabric.

whit·low (hwit′ lō or wit′ lō) *n.* a painful, pus-producing inflammation.

witch (wich) *v.* to charm or put a magic spell on.

witch ha·zel (wich′ hā z'l) *n.* a shrub with yellow flowers and woody fruit.

with·al (with ôl′ or with ôl′) *adv.* besides.

wont (wōnt or wônt or wunt or wänt) *adj.* accustomed.

wran·gle (raŋ′ g'l) *v.* to argue or quarrel angrily and noisily.

wrath (rath) *n.* rage or intense anger.

writ (rit) *n.* a formal legal document that orders or prohibits an action.

wrought (rôt) *v.* to use effort or energy to do something; to do work.

Y

yoke (yōk) *n.* something that unites or connects.

Z

zeph·yr (zef′ ər) *n.* the west wind.

---

at, āte, fär, pen, ēqual; sit, mīne; sō, côrn, join, took, fool, our; us, turn; chill, shop, thick, they, sing; zh *in* measure; 'l *in* idle; ə *in* alive, cover, family, robot, circus.

Biographies of Authors

Maya Angelou

Photograph © 1985 by Jill Krementz

W.H. Auden

Stephen Vincent
Benét

Abigail Smith Adams *(1744–1818)* was the only woman in American history to be both wife and mother to Presidents. Although she had little formal education, she was an avid reader. At twenty she married John Adams. Because of political necessity, the Adamses were often separated. During those times Abigail became a great letter writer and successfully managed the Adams's farm. One of her greatest concerns was the lack of education for women.

John Adams *(1735–1826)*, the husband of Abigail Adams, was the second President of the United States. Adams graduated from Harvard, was admitted to the bar, and shortly thereafter, entered public life. He was a delegate to the First Continental Congress and helped draft the Declaration of Independence. The letters to his wife are among the most widely read of his writings.

Maya Angelou *(born 1928)* has experienced success in many different fields. Her careers include playwright, poet, editor, stage and screen performer, composer, singer, and teacher. Angelou is best known for her autobiographical books, *I Know Why the Caged Bird Sings* and *Gather Together in My Name.*

Richard Armour *(born 1906)* began composing light verse while still a student at Harvard University. He enjoys writing about life's minor frustrations, such as non-flowing ketchup bottles or people who hum. Armour has been a scholar, teacher, critic, and poet. His most widely read books are his collections of parodies which satirize everyone from Adam and Eve to Columbus to Shakespeare.

W.H. Auden *(1907–1973)* was born in England and came to the United States in 1939. He became a citizen in 1946. Although Auden worked as a playwright, critic, editor, and translator, he achieved the most prominence for his poetry. One collection, *The Age of Anxiety*, received the 1948 Pulitzer Prize in poetry.

Stephen Vincent Benét *(1898–1943)* was born in the city of Bethlehem, Pennsylvania. The son of an army officer, Benét attended schools all over the country. He received his undergraduate and graduate degrees from Yale University. As a writer, Benét achieved popular acceptance for both his short

Ambrose Bierce

Ray Bradbury

William Bradford

Gwendolyn Brooks

stories and poems. In 1928, he issued *John Brown's Body,* which earned him the Pulitzer Prize. He had planned to write a five-volume epic that traced the history of American immigration and the migration west. However, after completing the first volume, *Western Star,* he died suddenly. The work was readied for publication by his brother and received the 1944 Pulitzer Prize.

Ambrose Bierce *(1842–1914?)* was born in Ohio and spent his childhood on a poor Indiana farm. Although he had little education, he was a successful career officer in the Union Army during the Civil War. Bierce's writing reflected his shame for his poor background, as well as his eventual disillusionment with war and the military. He became known as "Bitter Bierce." His use of satire and cruel wit are seen in his short stories, journalistic pieces, and essays. "An Occurrence at Owl Creek Bridge" is considered one of his finest works.

Ray Bradbury *(born 1920)* grew up in Waukegan, Illinois, and says that he has lived in a fantasy world for most of his life. It is, therefore, not surprising that his writing reflects this bent toward the strange and fantastic. He has written hundreds of stories, as well as novels, plays, and movie and television scripts. *The Martian Chronicles* and *Fahrenheit 451* are among his best-known works. Bradbury's science fiction writing is finely crafted and rich in description and figurative language. His futuristic tales often provide thoughtful viewpoints on today's problems.

William Bradford *(1590–1657)* was one of the first great political leaders in America. Born in Yorkshire, England, Bradford emigrated to the New World on the *Mayflower,* to find religious freedom. His journal, *Of Plymouth Plantation,* describes the difficulties and hardships that the Pilgrims faced after their landing at Plymouth.

Anne Bradstreet *(1612–1672)* has been called the first noteworthy American poet. She was born in 1612 in England. As she grew up, her father saw to it that she was well-educated. In 1630, she emigrated to the Massachusetts Bay Colony with her husband and parents. Although the writing of poetry was not considered acceptable for a Puritan woman of her position, her brother-in-law secretly had her first book of poetry published in 1650. Her writing reflects her idea that spiritual wealth is of far greater importance than material wealth.

Gwendolyn Brooks *(born 1917)* has spent nearly all of her life in Chicago, Illinois. At age thirteen, she published her first poem. A collection of her work, *Annie Allen,* won the Pulitzer Prize in 1950. A fine novelist as well as a poet, Brooks's works are characterized by her sympathy for the poor who seem doomed to squalor yet still dream of a better life. Poet Laureate of Illinois, Brooks teaches and sponsors poetry competitions for young writers.

Rachel Carson

Stephen Crane

Countee Cullen

e.e. cummings

Rachel Carson *(1907–1964)* combined her interests in science and writing into a notable career. She taught at Johns Hopkins University and the University of Maryland and later accepted a job with the United States Bureau of Fisheries. Her writing, such as *Silent Spring* and *The Sea Around Us,* reflected her grave concern with the effects of pesticides on animal and human life. It has had a profound effect on the American public's awareness of environmental concerns.

Stephen Crane *(1871–1900)* distinguished himself in baseball during his school years, but while at Syracuse University, he decided on a writing career. His work reflects his belief that individuals are products of their environment and heredity. Crane also felt that a responsible writer should record events as they happen without interpreting or moralizing. *The Red Badge of Courage,* which is a brutally realistic description of the Civil War battle of Chancellorsville, is considered a classic of American literature.

Jean de Crèvecoeur *(1735–1813)* was born in Normandy, France, and educated in French religious schools. He emigrated to Canada as a young man, wandered, and eventually settled in the state of New York. During a stay in England, de Crèvecoeur published a group of essays entitled *Letters from an American Farmer,* which made him instantly famous. The warm and optimistic essays grew in number, eventually filling three volumes. De Crèvecoeur's work offers a first-hand account of the American immigrant's progress and the religious, political, and economic struggles of the New World.

Countee Cullen *(1903–1946),* the adopted son of a fundamentalist minister, was part of the explosion of black creativity during the 1920's known as the Harlem Renaissance. Cullen, and other writers in this literary movement, expressed the reality of what it meant to be black in America. Although he wrote drama and one novel, Cullen's career is most noted for poetry. Two of his collections are *Color* and *Copper Sun.*

e.e. cummings *(1894–1962),* born Edward Estlin Cummings, created a unique form of poetry by flouting the conventional rules of punctuation, capitalization, and verse form. After receiving two degrees from Harvard University, Cummings became a volunteer ambulance driver in France during World War I. After the war, he stayed in France working as a writer and an artist. He exhibited exceptional talent in both areas, but it was his controversial poetry that made him most famous. He often ran words together to suggest speed or separated them, one to a line, to indicate a slower pace. As an extension of his unusual use of grammar, Cummings chose to eliminate capital letters in his name and signed his work "e.e. cummings."

Photograph © 1985 by Jill Krementz

James Dickey

Frederick Douglass

Paul Laurence
Dunbar

Charles Eastman

James Dickey (*born 1923*) is a writer of poetry, novels, screenplays, and criticism. He was born in Atlanta and educated at Clemson and Vanderbilt University. Dickey has been an English professor and Writer-in-Residence at the University of South Carolina. His novel *Deliverance* exhibits two contrasting themes commonly found in his work: a love of nature and the possibility of violence. His poems are strongly autobiographical.

Emily Dickinson. For biographical information, see page 279.

Annie Dillard (*born 1945*) is one of the few writers to receive critical acclaim and a Pulitzer Prize for her first published book. This book, *Pilgrim at Tinker Creek,* which has been compared to Thoreau's *Walden,* gives a detailed account of the time she spent observing nature at Tinker Creek in Virginia.

Frederick Douglass (*1817–1895*) was born a slave in Maryland. He escaped to New York in 1838 and became a famous lecturer against slavery. His autobiography, *Narrative of the Life of Frederick Douglass, An American Slave,* 1845, brought him worldwide fame and, later, official appointments.

Paul Laurence Dunbar (*1872–1906*) was the son of former slaves. Poverty forced him to abandon plans for college. He accepted a job as an elevator operator, instead, and began writing poetry in his off hours. His first book of poems, *Oak and Ivory,* was published in 1893. Dunbar's varied career also included a position with the Library of Congress.

Charles Eastman (*1858–1939*) was a South Dakota physician and author who wrote of his Sioux heritage in such works as *Rain-in-the-Face: Biography of a Sioux Warrior.* He was one of the first Native Americans to assume the life style of the white man. Eastman, a Santee Sioux, spent much of his life trying to create a greater understanding between white and Indian cultures.

Jonathan Edwards (*1703–1758*) was born in Connecticut, the son of a Puritan minister. Entering Yale University at thirteen, Edwards studied the ideas of the new Age of Reason. He became an assistant pastor and later principal minister at his grandfather's church in Massachusetts. His sermons were aimed at awakening his listeners' sense of sinfulness and need for God.

Ralph Waldo Emerson (*1803—1882*) entered Harvard University at the age of fourteen. He served as junior pastor of the Second Church of Boston but soon left the church because of his disbelief in the orthodox religious views of the day. Emerson and a group of friends founded their own journal, *The Dial,* which published their essays and criticism. Their philosophy became known as Transcendentalism, and was based on their belief that there is God in all of us and a unity between human life and nature.

Robert Frost

Nikki Giovanni

Pete Hamill

Ernest Hemingway

Mari Evans has written poetry, television programs, a play, and various children's works. Her poetry has been choreographed and used in television specials and off-Broadway productions. In 1970 Evans was awarded the first annual poetry award from the Black Academy of Arts and Letters and Indiana University's Writers' Conference award, both for *I Am a Black Woman.*

Benjamin Franklin. For biographical information, see page 69.

Robert Frost *(1874–1963)* was born in San Francisco, although his poetry is often set in rural New England, where he spent most of his life. The only American poet to be awarded four Pulitzer Prizes and a congressional medal, Frost also had the distinction of reading one of his poems at the inauguration of John F. Kennedy in 1960. On the surface, Frost's work appears simple and straightforward. Its simplicity, however, masks many serious themes.

William Gibson *(born 1914)* began his career as a novelist and poet, and then switched to playwriting. *Two for the Seesaw* was a Broadway success. It brought fame to Gibson as well as to his leading lady, Anne Bancroft, who later played Anne Sullivan in Gibson's *The Miracle Worker.* Gibson originally wrote the story of Helen Keller and her teacher as a TV script. He adapted it for the stage in 1959 and again for film in 1962.

Nikki Giovanni *(born 1943)* was active in the civil rights movement as a college student and still plays a role in the affairs of the national black community. In 1968, her first collection of poems, *Black Feeling, Black Talk,* was published. Giovanni later established her own publishing firm. She has written poetry, autobiographical essays, articles, and reviews as well as collaborating with James Baldwin on a collection of verse.

Arthur Guiterman *(1871–1943)* was a New York journalist who became well known for his humorous verse. His poems deal with ancient and American history and legends, especially about the West. Among his books are *I Sing the Pioneer* and *Brave Laughter.*

Pete Hamill *(born 1935)* attended Pratt Institute and Mexico City College (now called the University of the Americas). He has lived in many countries including North Africa, Malaysia, Puerto Rico, Italy, and Spain. Hamill has written novels, such as *A Killing for Christ,* as well as articles and screenplays.

Ernest Hemingway *(1899–1961),* recipient of the 1954 Nobel Prize for Literature, began writing while in high school. He then went to Europe where he served in World War I with the Red Cross. Later he worked in Paris as a foreign correspondent and published his first novels, *The Sun Also Rises* and *A Farewell to Arms.* These books, and the novels and short stories that followed, established Hemingway as one of the most influential writers of the twentieth cen-

O. Henry

Oliver Wendell
Holmes

Washington Irving

tury. His stark, simple style contrasts with the subject matter and settings of his work, which are filled with potential violence or danger. One's courage, honor, and dignity in these situations are major themes of Hemingway's work.

O. Henry *(1862–1910)* was the pen name of William Sydney Porter. After leaving school, he went to Texas, and while working there as a bank teller, he was charged with embezzlement. Although there was serious doubt about his guilt, Porter fled to Central America. He eventually returned and surrendered because of his wife's serious illness. He was convicted and spent three years in prison, during which time he began to write short stories under his pen name. *Cabbages and Kings* was his first collection. O. Henry was a master of irony and wit and known for the "surprise endings" of his stories.

Oliver Wendell Holmes *(1809–1894)* was the son of a minister, born in Cambridge, Massachusetts. Holmes was a doctor and professor at Harvard University for many years, during which time he wrote many significant scientific papers. He is most remembered, however, for his essays and poems, such as "The Chambered Nautilus." He also helped found the *Atlantic Monthly*, a popular magazine in the United States.

Langston Hughes. For biographical information, see page 538.

Washington Irving *(1783–1859)* was born into a wealthy New York family where he was encouraged in the appreciation of literature, art, theater, and opera. *The Sketch Book of Geoffrey Crayon, Gent.*, published in 1819, is Irving's most famous book. It contains the folktales "Rip Van Winkle" and "The Legend of Sleepy Hollow." One of the first successful American literary figures, Irving is noted for his vivid characterizations and use of supernatural occurrences.

Shirley Jackson *(1916–1965)* was born in San Francisco and grew up on the West Coast. Her work is unusual in that it can be divided into two distinct categories. Some of her writing is lighthearted description of family life. These humorous, semi-autobiographical pieces include *Life Among the Savages* and the short story "Charles." Jackson's other body of work delves deeply into evil and the supernatural. These tales include the famous story "The Lottery" and the novel *The Haunting of Hill House.*

Randall Jarrell *(1914–1965)* used his World War II experiences as a basis for many of his war poems, such as "The Death of the Ball Turret Gunner." Before his service in the Army Air Corps, he taught at several colleges. In his later works, Jarrell looked at old age and loneliness as preliminary forms of death. This theme can be found in *Woman at the Washington Zoo,* for which he received the 1962 National Book Award.

Thomas Jefferson

Martin Luther King, Jr.

Abraham Lincoln

Jack London

Thomas Jefferson *(1743–1826)* was a wealthy young lawyer who was elected to the Virginia House of Burgesses at the age of twenty-five. He became an outspoken supporter of American rights, and in 1776, as a delegate to the Second Continental Congress, he was chosen to draft the Declaration of Independence. In 1801, Jefferson became President of the United States. After serving two terms, he retired to his estate in Monticello, Virginia. There he read, studied, conducted experiments, invented, and worked for free public education.

John F. Kennedy *(1917–1963)* was born in Massachusetts and educated at Harvard University. During World War II, Kennedy distinguished himself by rescuing the survivors of a stricken PT boat under his command. After serving in the House of Representatives and the Senate, Kennedy became the thirty-fifth President of the United States. He was killed by an assassin's bullet in 1963 before the completion of his term in office.

Martin Luther King, Jr. *(1929–1968)* was a Baptist pastor in Montgomery, Alabama. As president of the Southern Christian Leadership Conference, King was a leading spokesman of American blacks in the civil rights movement. King's insistence on non-violence eventually led to his receiving the 1964 Nobel Peace Prize. In 1968, King was assassinated in Memphis, Tennessee, while planning a peaceful march.

Harper Lee *(born 1926)* was raised in Alabama and educated at the state university. She won a Pulitzer Prize in 1961 for her first novel, *To Kill a Mockingbird*. The book has been translated into many languages and was made into a popular movie starring Gregory Peck.

Abraham Lincoln *(1809–1865),* sixteenth President of the United States, was brought up in Kentucky and later moved to New Salem, Illinois, where he studied law and became a skilled lawyer. In 1858 he was nominated to oppose Stephen Douglas in the Illinois senatorial race. It was during this campaign that Lincoln made his anti-states' rights and anti-slavery views apparent. He was elected President in 1860 and guided the United States through the Civil War. On Good Friday, April 14, 1865, Lincoln was assassinated by John Wilkes Booth in Ford's Theater in Washington. Lincoln's letters and speeches reveal his simple but eloquent style, and his deep sense of compassion.

Jack London *(1876–1916)* was raised in poverty along the California coast. To earn a living, he raided oyster beds, went on a seal hunt, and prospected for gold in the Yukon. Though generally unprofitable, these adventures provided background material for what was to become a successful and lucrative career—that of a writer. His action novels such as *The Call of the Wild* and *The Sea Wolf* won instant popularity and are still widely read.

Henry Wadsworth
Longfellow

Edgar Lee Masters

Photograph © 1985 by Jill Krementz

Joyce Carol Oates

Photograph © 1985 by Jill Krementz

Harry Mark Petrakis

Henry Wadsworth Longfellow *(1807–1882)* was the most popular and widely read American poet of the 1800's. It is said that more than a million copies of "The Song of Hiawatha" were sold before he died. Longfellow's poetry, which focuses on uplifting and romantic themes, appealed to a wide variety of tastes. He was foremost of a group known as the Fireside Poets, because their verse was popular for family fireside reading.

Alonzo Lopez writes poetry in English as well as his native Navajo. Born in Pina County, Arizona, Lopez attended the Institute of American Indian Arts. He then did postgraduate work at Yale University and Wesleyan University, where he pursued his American Indian studies and the Navajo language. In his poetry, Lopez portrays the character of his people and their land.

Edgar Lee Masters *(1869–1950)* grew up in Lewistown, Illinois, which was the rural model for the imaginary Spoon River setting made famous in his *Spoon River Anthology.* A series of free verse monologues, *Spoon River* brought Masters his greatest success.

Emerson Blackhorse Mitchell *(born 1945)* was raised in New Mexico and spoke only the Navajo language until he was six. Mitchell attended the Institute of American Indian Arts and Fort Lewis College, which prepared him as a teacher. He has worked with Navajo children, helping them cope with two different worlds while still respecting their own culture and identity.

Joyce Carol Oates *(born 1938)* was born in Lockport, New York. Educated at Syracuse University and the University of Wisconsin, Oates has been an instructor in English at the University of Detroit. *By the North Gate* is a collection of her stories. Oates claims that before she could write, she drew pictures to tell her stories.

Thomas Paine *(1737–1809)* was born and raised in Thetford, England. A self-educated man, he came to the United States in his thirties when America was on the brink of revolution. Paine, who enthusiastically supported the American Revolution, became a political pamphleteer. His pamphlet "Common Sense" was published in 1776. It urged the colonists to break with England. During the war, he printed a number of "crisis" papers to keep up the morale of the troops. Paine devoted his life to the fight for human equality, civil liberties, and natural rights.

Harry Mark Petrakis *(born 1923)* attended the University of Illinois and worked at such varied jobs as laborer, real estate salesman, speechwriter, free-lance writer, teacher, and lecturer before becoming a novelist. In much of his work, Petrakis interprets the immigrant experience in America, often describing the Greek-American community in which he was raised.

Carl Sandburg

John Smith

Elizabeth Cady
Stanton

Edgar Allan Poe. For biographical information, see page 173.

Powhatan *(died 1618)* was the chief of the Powhatan Indian federation which extended throughout the colony of Virginia. His father was from a southern tribe, which was said to have been driven north by the Spaniards. He conquered five of the local tribes, and Powhatan conquered many more. After the marriage of his daughter, Pocahontas, to John Rolfe, Powhatan made a peace treaty with the English.

Norman H. Russell *(born 1921)* is a Cherokee Indian who was born in Big Stone Gap, Virginia. He holds a doctorate in botany and is a respected science professor. Russell is an author of botany textbooks as well as several books of poetry. *At the Zoo* and *Open the Flower* are two of his verse collections.

Carl Sandburg *(1878–1967)* was born in Galesburg, Illinois, the son of Swedish immigrants. In addition to serving in the army during the Spanish-American War, Sandburg worked as a barbershop porter and brickyard hand. In 1913 he moved to Chicago, where he began working on the *Chicago Daily News*. He won overnight acclaim as a poet with the publishing of "Chicago" in 1914. Sandburg intended his work to be for and about the common man. His style is characterized by roughness and boldness using free verse, dialect, and street talk. He won a Pulitzer Prize in history in 1940 for his multi-volume biography of Lincoln and another in poetry in 1951 for his *Complete Poems*.

Mari Sandoz *(1896–1966)* was a Nebraska author, the daughter of a Swiss emigrant. Her writing records history as well as her personal feelings. *The Sioux Woman* and *The Beaver Men* are among her works.

Chief Seattle *(?1786–1866)* was the chief of several Indian tribes in the Pacific Northwest. He befriended the first white settlers and subsequently signed a treaty ceding land to them in 1855. The city of Seattle, Washington, was developed near the area of his birth.

John Smith *(1580–1631)* was born in Lincolnshire, England, in 1580. He came to the New World with the Jamestown settlers at the age of twenty-seven. Although he spent less than five years in America, his leadership played an important role in the establishment and survival of the Jamestown colony. He is responsible for some remarkably accurate maps as well as some of the first writing to be produced in colonial America.

Elizabeth Cady Stanton *(1815–1902)* was an abolitionist and a woman's suffrage leader. After being denied attendance at an anti-slavery convention because she was female, Stanton organized the first women's rights convention in 1848. She was editor of the *Revolution*, a militant feminist magazine and one of the authors of *History of Woman Suffrage*.

May Swenson

Henry David
Thoreau

Alice Walker

Eudora Welty

John Steinbeck *(1902–1968)* is most noted for his moving descriptions of life during the Great Depression of the 1930's. Born and raised in California, Steinbeck studied marine biology at Stanford University while supporting himself with such varied jobs as bricklayer, caretaker, and migrant fruit picker. The variety of jobs he held may explain his sympathetic portrayals of the common, working people. He received the Pulitzer Prize for *The Grapes of Wrath* in 1940 and the Nobel Prize for Literature in 1962.

May Swenson *(born 1919)* likes to create new forms for her poetry, often making shaped poems whose physical appearance on the page suggests their subject. She enjoys expressing ordinary ideas in new and unusual ways and is inventive with sounds as well. To accomplish her desired results, she encourages her readers to use all five senses in experiencing a poem. Swenson graduated from Utah State University and has taught at several universities. She has also worked as an editor at New Directions, an innovative New York publishing house.

Henry David Thoreau *(1817–1862)* was born and spent most of his life in Concord, Massachusetts. He studied classics at Harvard and taught for many years. Just before his twenty-eighth birthday, Thoreau began his famous experiment in "essential" living. He built a small cabin on the shores of Walden Pond, land near Concord owned by Ralph Waldo Emerson. There he lived for two years, writing and communing with nature. He worked about six weeks each year performing physical labor so that he could support himself simply for the remainder of the year. A true Transcendentalist, Thoreau devoted his time to mental and spiritual activity.

Mark Twain. For biographical information, see page 308.

Alice Walker *(born 1944)* was born in Georgia. She worked her way through college and pursued a career in teaching and writing. A poet, novelist, and the author of a biography on Langston Hughes, Walker's writing reflects the social injustice experienced by some blacks. Her novel *The Color Purple* received the Pulitzer Prize for literature in 1983.

Eudora Welty *(born 1909)* was born in Mississippi. While attending Mississippi State College for Women, she helped found a literary magazine. Later she decided upon writing as a career. *The Optimist's Daughter* won her the 1973 Pulitzer Prize for fiction. The recipient of many awards, Welty has written many stories, essays, and children's books.

Walt Whitman *(1819–1892)* was the son of a farmer and a carpenter. Born in rural Long Island, New York, Whitman spent his time between his quiet home there and bustling Manhattan. Primarily self-educated, he worked as

Walt Whitman

William Carlos
Williams

Thomas Wolfe

Richard Wright

office boy, printer, editor, and teacher as he continued to write poetry for his book *Leaves of Grass*. This collection, first published in 1855, was rewritten and expanded throughout Whitman's lifetime. The first edition contained twelve of his poems; the final edition contains more than four hundred. *Leaves of Grass* has been called the greatest single book of poetry in American literature. Its intense and joyous subject matter and innovative verse form had a profound influence on decades of poets that followed.

Roger Williams *(1603–1683)* was born in England and studied law at Cambridge. After receiving his degree, he became an Anglican minister. Later he became a Baptist, then a Seeker. Williams emigrated to America in 1630. His outspoken insistence on religious freedom and justice for Native Americans caused him difficulty with the colonial establishment. He eventually purchased wilderness land from the Indians and founded the colony of Rhode Island.

William Carlos Williams *(1883–1963)*, the son of an English father and a Puerto Rican mother, produced poetry, drama, novels, and essays while maintaining a successful medical career. His poetry is especially noted for its insights into urban America. Although Williams did not receive acclaim for his writing until late in his career, he received many honors, including the 1963 Pulitzer Prize in poetry for *Pictures from Brueghel, and Other Poems*.

Thomas Wolfe *(1900–1938)* was the son of a stonecutter who liked to recite Shakespeare to his son. Born in Asheville, North Carolina, Wolfe used this setting in his fiction. He began writing while at the University of North Carolina, which he entered at the age of fifteen. His first novel, *Look Homeward, Angel*, is typical of Wolfe's writing which is highly autobiographical in content.

Richard Wright *(1908–1960)* overcame a childhood of hunger and prejudice to become a powerful writer. Wright grew up with no formal education past the ninth grade, yet he read "mountains" of books in his pursuit of knowledge. *Native Son* and *Black Boy* convey Wright's feelings on oppression and the hardships suffered by his generation. His spirit and determination are reflected in his novels, short stories, and essays.

Al Young *(born 1939)* worked as a disc jockey before attending Stanford University on a creative writing fellowship. He now teaches and writes and also enjoys lecturing and reading his work throughout the country. His first collection of poems, *Dancing*, was published in 1969, followed in 1970 by his first novel, *Snakes*. His works have been published in such magazines as *Rolling Stone* and *The Journal of Black Poetry*. Young is also a gifted musician and singer.

Guidelines for Capitalization, Punctuation, and Spelling

Capitalization

Punctuation

Spelling

Guidelines for Capitalization

1 Proper Nouns and Adjectives

> **Capitalize proper nouns and proper adjectives.**

A **common noun** is a general name of a person, place, thing, or idea. A **proper noun** is the name of a particular person, place, thing, or idea. A **proper adjective** is an adjective formed from a proper noun.

Common Noun	Proper Noun	Proper Adjective
person	Elizabeth	Elizabethan
country	Spain	Spanish
city	Paris	Parisian

There are many different proper nouns. The following rules and examples will help you solve the capitalization problems that proper nouns present.

> **Capitalize the names of persons and also the initials or abbreviations that stand for those names.**

J. R. R. Tolkien   John Ronald Revel Tolkien
Elizabeth M. Grant   Elizabeth Mason Grant

> **Capitalize titles used with names of persons and also the initials or abbreviations that stand for those titles.**

The titles *Mr., Mrs., Ms.,* and *Miss* are always capitalized.

Rev. M. R. Eaton   Judge Esther Falks
Lt. Patricia Smith   Dr. John J. DeBender
Mr. Edward Scott   Professor White

Do not capitalize titles used as common nouns:

Have you seen your doctor?
She is the company president.
The judge entered the courtroom.

Capitalize titles of very high importance, even when these titles are used without proper names.

the Pope   the President of the United States
a United States Senator   the Prime Minister of England

Capitalize such words as *mother, father, aunt,* and *uncle* when these words are used as names.

When the noun is modified by a possessive word, *a,* or *the,* it is not capitalized.

Hello, Mother. Is Dad home yet?
My aunt is going to visit my grandmother next week.

Capitalize the pronoun *I*.

Is he taller than I?   I am sure that he is.

Capitalize all words referring to God, the Holy Family, and religious scriptures.

the Gospel   Buddha   the Torah
God   the Lord   the Bible
Allah   the Virgin Mary   the Book of Exodus

Capitalize personal pronouns referring to God.

God spoke to His prophets.

> **In a geographical name, capitalize the first letter of each word except articles and prepositions.**

The article *the* appearing before a geographical name is not part of the geographical name and is therefore not capitalized.

Continents: Europe, Asia, Africa, Australia

Bodies of Water: the Pacific Ocean, Puget Sound, the Columbia River, Hudson Bay

Landforms: the Cape of Good Hope, the Mojave Desert, the Atlas Mountains

Political Units: Los Angeles, Commonwealth of Puerto Rico, Utah, Great Britain

Public Areas: Badlands National Monument, Grant Park, Shawnee National Forest

Roads and Highways: Lincoln Highway, Broad Street, 34th Avenue, Tri-State Tollway

> **Capitalize names of sections of the country.**

Industrial production was high in the North.
The first English settlements were along the East Coast.
The Southwest is our fastest-growing region.

> **Capitalize proper adjectives derived from names of sections of the country.**

Western dress   a New England town
Southern-style cooking   Midwestern twang

Do not capitalize directions of the compass.

We headed south for our vacation.
The pioneers moved west over the Oregon Trail.
The school is southwest of our home.

Do not capitalize adjectives derived from words indicating direction.

a north wind   the east side of the building

> **Capitalize the names of organizations and institutions, including political parties, governmental bodies or agencies, schools, colleges, churches, hospitals, clubs, businesses, and abbreviations of these names.**

Gillette Company   Children's Hospital
Oakwood High School   St. Mark's Church
University of Southern California   U.S.C.

Do not capitalize such words as *school, college, church,* and *hospital* when they are not used as parts of names:

This fund drive benefits the hospital.

> **Capitalize the names of historical events, documents, and periods of time.**

Battle of Hastings   Treaty of Paris   Age of Discovery
World War II   Bill of Rights   Middle Ages

> **Capitalize names of months, days, holidays, but not the names of seasons.**

March   Labor Day   summer
Friday   Feast of the Passover   spring

> **Capitalize the names of races, languages, nationalities, and religions and adjectives derived from them.**

Caucasian   African   Lutheranism
French   Buddhism   Catholic

> **Do not capitalize the names of school subjects, except course names followed by a number.**

physical education   History of Civilization II
social studies   Algebra I

> **Remember that the names of languages are always capitalized.**

English   Spanish   Hebrew   German

> **Capitalize the names of ships, trains, airplanes, and automobiles.**

U.S.S. Constitution   Santa Fe Chief
Cutlass   *Spirit of St. Louis*

> **Capitalize the abbreviations B.C. and A.D.**

The first Olympic Games were held in 776 B.C.
The Norman Conquest took place in A.D. 1066.

2 First Words and Titles

> **Capitalize the first word of every sentence and the first word in most lines of poetry.**

My sister likes tennis. She is the captain of her team.

Listen my children, and you shall hear
Of the midnight ride of Paul Revere . . . .
      —*from* "Paul Revere's Ride" by Henry Wadsworth Longfellow

Sometimes, especially in modern poetry, the lines of a poem do not begin with capital letters.

> **Capitalize the first word of a direct quotation.**

When you write the exact words of a speaker or writer, you are giving a **direct quotation.**

Ralph Waldo Emerson said, "Hitch your wagon to a star."

Sometimes a direct quotation is interrupted by explaining words like *she said.* This is called a **divided quotation.** Do not capitalize the first word of the second part of a divided quotation unless it starts a new sentence.

"Well," he said, "what you say is quite true."
"I agree," he said. "What you say is quite true."

Capitalize the first word, words like *Sir* and *Madam*, and the name of the person addressed in the greeting of a letter.

Dear Mrs. Gomez   Dear Ms. Perkins   Dear Mr. Castillo

In the complimentary close, capitalize the first word only.

Yours very truly   Sincerely yours

Capitalize the letters and the first word of each line of an outline.

  I. Improve your handwriting.
    A. Form letters carefully.
      1. Watch *a, e, r, l,* and *t.*
      2. Watch *u, v,* and *o.*
    B. Proofread your work.

Capitalize the first word and all important words in chapter titles; titles of magazine articles; titles of short stories, essays, or single poems; and titles of songs or short pieces of music.

Chapter: Chapter 5, "The Undersea World"
Magazine article: "Sleep and Dreams"
Short story: "The Last Leaf"
Essay: "Nature"
Poem: "O Captain! My Captain!"
Song: "America the Beautiful"

> **Capitalize the first word and all important words in titles of books, newspapers, magazines, plays, movies, television programs, works of art, and long musical compositions.**

Underline these titles. (When these titles are printed, they are *italicized*.)

Book Title: *The Call of the Wild*
Newspaper: *Miami Herald*
Magazine: *People*
Play: *The Glass Menagerie*
Movie: *The Last Emperor*
Television Program: *The Evening News*
Work of art: Gainsborough's *Blue Boy*
Long musical composition: *Peter and the Wolf*

Guidelines for Punctuation

1 The Period

Use a period at the end of a declarative sentence.

A **declarative sentence** is a sentence that makes a statement. It is the kind of sentence you use when you want to tell something.

My brother plays the guitar.

Use a period at the end of most imperative sentences.

An **imperative sentence** is a sentence that requests or orders someone to do something.

Please close the door.

If the imperative sentence also expresses excitement or emotion, an exclamation point is used after it.

Watch out!

Use a period at the end of an indirect question.

An **indirect question** tells what someone asked. However, it does not give the exact words of the person who asked the question.

She asked us whether we liked strawberries.

Use a period after an abbreviation or after an initial.

An **abbreviation** is a shortened form of a word. An **initial** is a single letter that stands for a word.

Dr. Marla E. Corona   Trenton, N. J.
Rev. John L. Haeger, Jr.   2:30 P.M.

Periods are omitted in some abbreviations. If you are not sure whether or not to use periods, look up the abbreviation in your dictionary.

FM (*frequency modulation*)
UN (*United Nations*)
FBI (*Federal Bureau of Investigation*)

> **Use a period after each number or letter that shows a division of an outline or that precedes an item in a list.**

An Outline
I. Poets
   A. American
      1. Robert Frost

A List
1. eggs
2. milk
3. butter

> **Use a period in numerals between dollars and cents and before a decimal.**

$18.98   2.853

2 The Question Mark and the Exclamation Point

> **Use a question mark at the end of an interrogative sentence.**

An **interrogative sentence** is a sentence that asks a question.

Has anyone brought a flashlight?

The above sentence gives the exact words of the person who asked the question. It is called a **direct question.** A question mark is used only with a direct question.

> **Do not use a question mark with an indirect question. Instead use a period.**

Kelly asked whether anyone had brought a flashlight.

> **Use an exclamation point at the end of an exclamatory sentence.**

How great that looks!

> **Use an exclamation point after an interjection or after any other exclamatory expression.**

An **interjection** is a word or group of words used to express strong feeling. It may be a real word or simply a group of letters used to represent a sound. It is one of the eight parts of speech.

Hurrah!   Wow!   Ugh!

3 The Comma

Commas are used to separate words that do not belong together. In speaking, you can keep words apart by pausing. In writing, you must use commas.

> **Use a comma after every item in a series except the last.**

The items in a series may be single words, phrases, or clauses.

Words: The flag is red, white, and blue.

Phrases: The dog ran out the door, down the steps, and across the lawn.

Clauses: How kangaroos run, what jumps they can take, and how they live are explained in this book.

> **Use commas after the adverbs *first, second, third*, and so on, when these adverbs introduce a series of parallel items.**

There are three ways to get good marks: first, pay attention; second, take notes; third, study.

> **When two or more adjectives come before a noun, use a comma after each adjective except the last one.**

They drove away in a bright, shiny, expensive car.

Sometimes two adjectives are used together to express a single idea made up of two closely related thoughts. Adjectives so used are not usually separated by a comma.

Kim's dog is the small brown one.
Many young children go to that large elementary school.

> **Use a comma to separate an introductory word, phrase, or clause from the rest of the sentence.**

Yes, I will go.
After circling twice, the airplane landed.
Although Dick needed help, he said nothing.

The comma may be omitted if there would be little pause in speaking or if the phrase is very short.

At first I didn't know what to do.

> **Use commas to set off words or groups of words that interrupt the flow of thought in a sentence.**

Anne, to tell the truth, was quite happy.
The report, moreover, is altogether wrong.

Other examples of interrupters are *however, I think,* and *nevertheless.*

The name of someone directly spoken to is a **noun of direct address.**

If you look, Peggy, you will see the book I mean.

Sarah, you won the election!

I'll be right back, Cathy.

An **appositive** is a word or group of words used directly after another word to explain it.

The speaker, a famous explorer, told about New Guinea.

An appositive phrase may have a prepositional phrase within it.

The leader, the person on horseback, moved away.

Nouns used as appositives are called **nouns in apposition.** When the noun in apposition is a short name, it is not usually set off by commas.

This is my friend Rhoda.

The explaining words used in giving a direct quotation are such brief statements as *Tina said, Christie answered,* or *Bill asked.*

The pilot said, "We will land in a few minutes."

In the sentence above, the explaining words come before the quotation. A comma is then placed after the last explaining word.

Now look at this quotation:

"We will land in a few minutes," the pilot said.

If the explaining words come *after* the quotation, as in the example above, place a comma within the quotation marks after the last word of the quotation.

Sometimes a quotation is separated into two parts by the explaining words. This is often done to add variety to the sentence construction. Here is an example:

"We will land," the pilot said, "in a few minutes."

The sentence above is an example of a divided quotation. A comma is used after the last word of the first part. Another comma is used after the last explaining word.

Do not confuse direct and indirect quotations. Indirect quotations are not set off from the rest of the sentence by commas.

The pilot said that the plane would land in a few minutes.

Use a comma before the conjunction that joins the two main clauses in a compound sentence.

Kimberly seemed to agree, and no one else objected.

Sometimes very short compound sentences have clauses joined by *and*. It is not necessary to use a comma if there is no change in the thought. Always use a comma before *or* or *but*. These words do change the direction of the thought.

Pete finally arrived *and* we started off.

Pete finally arrived, *but* it was too late to go anywhere.

Do not use a comma before the *and* that joins a compound subject or a compound predicate.

Sally turned on the radio *and* sat down to read a magazine.

In dates, use a comma between the day of the month and the year.

July 4, 1776   December 7, 1787

In a sentence, a comma follows the year.

The postmark read September 10, 1985, Chicago, Illinois.

> **Use a comma between the name of a city or town and the name of its state or country.**

    Tucson, Arizona   Munich, Germany

In writing an address as part of a sentence, use a comma after each item.

    Forward our mail to 651 Sentinel Drive, Milwaukee, Wisconsin 53203, where we will be moving next month.

Note that you do not place a comma between the state and the ZIP code.

> **Use a comma after the salutation of a friendly letter and after the complimentary close of a friendly letter or a business letter.**

    Dear Tim,   Yours sincerely,

> **When no specific rule applies, but there is danger of misreading, use a comma.**

    Who she is, is a mystery.   Inside, it was warm and cozy.

4 The Colon and the Semicolon

> **Use a colon after the greeting in a business letter.**

    Dear Sir or Madam: Ladies and Gentlemen:

> **Use a colon between numbers indicating hours and minutes.**

    10:00 P.M.   6:30 A.M.

> **Use a colon to introduce a list of items.**

If you are trying out for the team, bring the following things: a pair of gym shoes, your P.E. uniform, and your consent form.

Do not use a colon if the list immediately follows a verb or a preposition.

If you are trying out for the team, bring a pair of gym shoes, your P.E. uniform, and your consent form.

> **Use a semicolon to join the parts of a compound sentence when no coordinating conjunction is used.**

Dan has finished his homework; Darcy has not begun hers.

> **When there are commas in the first part of a compound sentence, use a semicolon to separate the main clauses.**

McCurdy of Illinois made the most spectacular shot of the game, a toss from mid-court; and Indiana, which had been favored to win, went down to defeat.

> **When there are commas within items in a series, use semicolons to separate the items.**

Hartford, New Haven, and Norwich, Connecticut; Springfield, Lowell, and Worcester, Massachusetts; and Pine Bridge, Mt. Kisco, and Chappaqua, New York, have all tried this experiment.

> **Use a semicolon before a word that joins the main clauses of a compound sentence.**

Such joining words are *therefore, however, hence, so, then, moreover, besides, nevertheless, yet,* and *consequently.*

It was a sunny day; however, it was quite cool.

5 The Hyphen and the Apostrophe

> **Use a hyphen if a syllable of a word must be carried over from one line to the next.**

In the library you will find several authorita-
tive books on solar energy.

Only words of two or more syllables can be divided at the end of a line. Never divide words of one syllable, such as *worse*.

A single letter must not be left at the end of a line. For example, this division would be wrong: *a-waken*. A single letter must not appear at the beginning of a line, either. This division would be incorrect: *dictionar-y*.

> **Use a hyphen in compound numbers from twenty-one through ninety-nine.**

twenty-three cents   forty-two students

> **Use a hyphen in fractions.**

We won a two-thirds majority.

> **Use a hyphen or hyphens in such compound nouns as *great-aunt* and *commander-in-chief*.**

A Portuguese man-of-war stung the swimmer.

> **Use a hyphen or hyphens between words that make up a compound adjective used before a noun.**

It was a school-sponsored dance.
But: The dance was school sponsored.

When compound adjectives are used after the noun, they usually are not hyphenated. If you are unsure, look in a dictionary.

> **To form the possessive of a singular noun, add an apostrophe and an *s* after the apostrophe.**

girl + 's = girl's   man + 's = man's
boy + 's = boy's   Ross + 's = Ross's

> **To form the possessive of a plural noun that does not end in *s*, add an apostrophe and an *s* after the apostrophe.**

men + 's = men's   children + 's = children's

> **To form the possessive of a plural noun that ends in *s*, add only an apostrophe.**

drivers + ' = drivers'   pilots + ' = pilots'

> **Use an apostrophe and an *s* to form the possessive of indefinite pronouns.**

someone + 's = someone's   anybody + 's = anybody's

Never use an apostrophe in a possessive personal pronoun.

ours   yours   its   hers   theirs

The game reached *its* high point in the second quarter.

> **Use an apostrophe in a contraction.**

In a contraction, the apostrophe simply replaces one or more omitted letters.

he's = he is   aren't = are not   I'm = I am
it's = it is   isn't = is not   I've = I have
won't = will not   don't = do not   we've = we have

> **Use an apostrophe to show the omission of numbers in a date.**

the class of '84 (*the class of 1984*)

> **Use an apostrophe and s to form the plurals of letters, figures, and words used as words.**

two *m*'s   four *6*'s   *and*'s and *but*'s

6 Quotation Marks

> **Quotation marks tell your reader that you are quoting directly the exact spoken or written words of another person.**

Use quotation marks before and after the words of a direct quotation.

Sarah said, "My feelings were hurt."

Quotation marks are not used with indirect quotations:

Sarah said that her feelings were hurt.

Explaining words at the beginning of a sentence are followed by a comma before the quotation marks. At the end of a sentence a period is placed inside the quotation marks.

My sister announced, "There is someone to see you."

A quotation that begins the sentence is followed by a comma inside the quotation marks. A period follows the explaining words at the end of a sentence.

"There is someone to see you," my sister announced.

Sometimes the explaining words break into the middle of a direct quotation creating a **divided quotation.** Each part of the quotation is enclosed in quotation marks.

"Do you think," Don asked, "that you will like alfalfa sprouts?"

The second part of a divided quotation starts with a small letter, as in the last example. The only exceptions are the beginning of a new sentence and proper nouns or adjectives.

"We got drenched," said Sheila. "Our car roof leaks."

The first part of a divided quotation is followed by a comma inside the quotation marks.

"I want to see you," said Ms. Lazar, "before you leave."

The punctuation after the explanatory words in a divided quotation depends on the second part of the quotation. If the second part does not start a new sentence, a comma is used. If the second part does start a new sentence, a period is used.

"When you arrive," said Ben, "beep your horn."

"I can't go," said Janet. "I have to study."

> **Place question marks and exclamation points inside quotation marks if they belong to the quotation itself.**

Dad asked, "Is Cindy working in the garage?"

"Look out!" Terry shouted.

Place question marks and exclamation points outside quotation marks if they do not belong to the quotation.

Did she say, "I'll be home at midnight"?

The man said, "You've won the contest"!

Occasionally, two or more sentences of a single speaker are quoted. Notice the punctuation of such a quotation:

"Is the council going to meet tomorrow?" asked Carly. "I wasn't sure whether we had decided to meet tomorrow or the next day. We have important things to discuss."

Dialogue is conversation between two or more people. Begin a new paragraph every time the speaker changes.

"Do you like horror movies?" asked Clyde.

"I don't," said Ted. "Real life can be horrifying enough. I don't understand why anyone needs any more fright."

"Well," said JoAnn, "maybe a few fake scares can help prepare you for real ones."

7 Punctuating Titles

> **Use quotation marks to enclose the titles of magazine articles, chapters, titles of short stories, essays, or single poems, songs, and short pieces of music.**

Chapter: Chapter 3, "Americans in London"
Magazine article: "Images of Youth Past"
Short story: "The Lottery"
Essay: "My First Article"
Poem: "The Raven"
Song: "The Star-Spangled Banner"

> **Underline the titles of books, newspapers, magazines, plays, television programs, movies, works of art, and long musical compositions.**

In writing or typewriting, these titles are underlined, like this: <u>The Right Stuff.</u>

In print, these titles appear in italics instead of being underlined.

Book: *Native Son*
Newspaper: *Des Moines Register*
Magazine: *Time*
Play: *You Can't Take It With You*
Television program: *Good Morning America*
Movie: *Casablanca*
Work of art: Rembrandt's *The Night Watch*
Long musical composition: *Nutcracker Suite*

Guidelines for Spelling

How to Become a Better Speller

1. **Find out what your personal spelling enemies are and conquer them.**

Go over your written assignments and make a list of the words you misspelled. Keep this list and master the words on it.

2. **Pronounce words carefully.**

Maybe you misspell words because you don't pronounce them carefully. For example, if you write *probly* for *probably,* you are no doubt mispronouncing the word.

3. **Get into the habit of seeing the letters in a word.**

Many people have never really looked at everyday words. As a result, they misspell even simple words.

Take a good look at unfamiliar words or difficult words. Copy their spellings several times.

4. **Proofread everything you write.**

Learn to examine carefully everything you write. To proofread a piece of writing, read it slowly, word for word. Otherwise, your eyes may play tricks on you and you may skip over misspelled words.

5. **Use a dictionary to check troublesome words.**

6. **Study the rules for spelling.**

Mastering Particular Words

1. Look at the word and say it to yourself.

Be sure you pronounce it correctly. If it has more than one syllable, say it again, one syllable at a time. Look at each syllable as you say it.

2. Look at the letters and say each one.

If the word has more than one syllable, divide the word into syllables when you say the letters.

3. Write the word without looking at it.

4. Now look at your book or list and see whether you have spelled the word correctly.

If you have, write it again and compare it with the correct form again. Do this once more.

5. If you made a mistake, note exactly what it was.

Then repeat steps 3 and 4 until you have written the word correctly three times.

Rules for Spelling

Adding Prefixes and Suffixes

> **Prefixes**

When a prefix is added to a word, the spelling of the word remains the same.

re- + elect = reelect   mis- + direct = misdirect
mis- + spell = misspell   re- + enter = reenter
im- + moderate = immoderate   dis- + satisfy = dissatisfy
il- + legible = illegible   ir- + regular = irregular

The Final Silent e

When a suffix beginning with a vowel is added to a word ending in a silent e, the e is usually dropped.

create + -ion = creation   grieve + -ing = grieving
graze + -ing = grazing   relate + ive = relative
fame + -ous = famous   continue + -ing = continuing

When a suffix beginning with a consonant is added to a word ending in a silent e, the e is usually retained.

spite + -ful = spiteful   taste + -ful = tasteful
state + -ment = statement   move + -ment = movement
voice + -less = voiceless   wide + -ly = widely

The following words are exceptions:

truly   argument   ninth   wholly

Words Ending in y

When a suffix is added to a word ending in y preceded by consonant, the y is usually changed to i.

crazy + -ly = crazily   puppy + -es = puppies
seventy + -eth = seventieth   silly + -ness = silliness
hilly + -est = hilliest   marry + -age = marriage

Note the following exception: When *-ing* is added, the *y* does not change:

scurry + -ing = scurrying   carry + -ing = carrying
ready + -ing = readying   worry + -ing = worrying

When a suffix is added to a word ending in *y* preceded by a vowel, the *y* usually does not change.

employ + -ed = employed   stay + -ing = staying
play + -er = player   relay + -ing = relaying

The Suffixes *-ness* and *-ly*

When the suffix *-ly* is added to a word ending in *l*, both *l*'s are kept. When *-ness* is added to a word ending in *n*, both *n*'s are kept.

normal + -ly = normally   open + -ness = openness

Doubling the Final Consonant

In words of one syllable that end in one consonant preceded by one vowel, double the final consonant before adding *-ing*, *-ed*, or *-er*.

hit + -ing = hitting   spot + -ed = spotted
nod + -ed = nodded   rob + -er = robber

The following words do not double the final consonant because *two* vowels precede final consonant:

near + -ing = nearing   cool + -er = cooler
look + -ed = looked   meet + -ing = meeting

Words with the "Seed" Sound

Only one English word ends in *sede: supersede.*
Three words end in *ceed: exceed, proceed, succeed.*
All other words ending in the sound of *seed* are spelled *cede:*

concede   precede   recede   secede

Words with *ie* and *ei*

When the sound is long *e* (*ē*), the word is spelled *ie* except after *c*.

I before E

relieve   grieve   field   pierce
belief   piece   pier   reprieve

Except after C

conceit   conceive   perceive   deceive   receive

Or when sounded like A

weigh   eight   neighbor

The following words are exceptions:

either   weird   species   neither   seize   leisure

Words Often Confused

accept means to agree to something or to receive something willingly.
except means to keep out or leave out. As a preposition, *except* means "but" or "leaving out."

▶ My brother will *accept* the job the grocer offered him.
▶ Michelle likes every flavor of ice cream *except* pistachio.

capital means chief, most serious, or most important. It is also the official seat of government.
capitol is a building in which a state legislature meets.
the Capitol is the building in Washington, D.C., where the United States Congress meets.

▶ Murder is a *capital* crime.
▶ The state *capitol* building is in Springfield.
▶ The nation's laws are made in the *Capitol*.

des'·ert means a barren, dry region.
de·sert' means to leave or to abandon.

dessert (note the two *s*'s) is a sweet food, the last course of a meal.

▶ Lizards thrive in the *desert*.
▶ One soldier *deserted* his company.
▶ Order the cheesecake for *dessert*.

hear means to listen to or to take notice of.
here means in this place.

▶ Did you *hear* the news on the radio?
▶ The fire hose is kept *here*.

its is a word that shows possession by *it*.
it's is a contraction for *it is* or *it has*.

▶ The violin has *its* own case.
▶ *It's* time for a break.

loose means free, not fastened, not tight.
lose means to mislay or suffer the loss of something.

▶ Runners wear *loose* clothing.
▶ Did you *lose* track of time?

peace is calm or stillness or the absence of disagreement.
piece means a portion or part.

▶ After two years of war, *peace* was finally achieved.
▶ This statue was carved from a *piece* of jade.

principal refers to something which is chief or of highest importance. It is also the name for the head of an elementary or high school.
principle is a basic truth, rule, or policy.

▶ The *principal* speaker is the mayor.
▶ The Bill of Rights states basic *principles*.

quiet means free from noise or disturbance.
quite means truly or almost completely.

▶ The only time our classroom is *quiet* is when it's empty.
▶ The aquarium tank is *quite* full.

stationary means fixed or unmoving.
stationery refers to paper and envelopes used for writing letters.

▶ The boat in the distance looks *stationary.*
▶ Cindy has *stationery* with her name on it.

their is a possessive word meaning belonging to *them.*
there means in that place.
they're is the contraction for *they are.*

▶ The children rode *their* bicycles.
▶ The trail begins *there.*
▶ Plants turn yellow when *they're* watered too often.

to means toward or in the direction of.
too means also or extremely.
two is the number.

▶ This bus goes *to* the civic center.
▶ Marla wears glasses, and Dave does *too.*
▶ We reserved *two* tickets.

weather refers to the state of the atmosphere, including temperature, wind, and moisture.
whether introduces choices or alternatives.

▶ Bad *weather* spoiled the picnic.
▶ The player must decide *whether* to pass or kick the ball.

who's is a contraction for *who is* or *who has.*
whose is the possessive form of *who.*

▶ *Who's* going to Sue's party?
▶ *Whose* locker is that?

your means belonging to *you.*
you're is the contraction for *you are.*

▶ Do *your* new boots feel comfortable?
▶ *You're* taking the bus, aren't you?

Index of Titles and Authors

Index of Fine Art

Skills in Comprehending Literature

Vocabulary Skills

Study and Research Skills

Speaking and Listening Skills

Skills in Critical Thinking

Acknowledgments

(continued from copyright page)

Brandt & Brandt Literary Agents, Inc.: For "Robert E. Lee" by Stephen Vincent Benét, from *Selected Works of Stephen Vincent Benét*, Holt, Rinehart & Winston, Inc.; copyright renewed 1955, 1956 by Rosemary Carr Benét. For "The Devil and Daniel Webster" by Stephen Vincent Benét, from *The Selected Works of Stephen Vincent Benét*; copyright 1936 by The Curtis Publishing Company; copyright renewed © 1964 by Thomas C. Benét, Stephanie B. Mahin and Rachel Benét Lewis. For "The Possibility of Evil" by Shirley Jackson; copyright © 1965 by Stanley Edgar Hyman, first published in *The Saturday Evening Post*. Don Congdon Associates, Inc.: For "Time In Thy Flight" by Ray Bradbury; copyright © 1953 by Ray Bradbury, renewed 1981. Joan Daves: For "I Have a Dream" by Martin Luther King, Jr.; copyright © 1963 by Martin Luther King, Jr. Dodd, Mead & Company: For "Sympathy" and "The Debt" by Paul Laurence Dunbar, from *The Complete Poems of Paul Laurence Dunbar*. Doubleday & Company, Inc.: For "The New Direction" by Emerson Blackhorse Mitchell and "Celebration" by Alonzo Lopez, from *Whispering Wind* by Terry Allen; copyright © 1972 by The Institute of American Indian Arts. For "In the Pocket" by James Dickey, from *The Eye-Beaters, Blood, Victory, Madness, Buckhead and Mercy* by James Dickey; copyright © 1970 by James Dickey. Mari Evans: For "If There Be Sorrow" by Mari Evans, from *I Am a Black Woman*. Farrar, Straus & Giroux, Inc.: For "The Death of the Ball Turret Gunner" by Randall Jarrell, from *The Complete Poems*; copyright 1945, 1969 by Mrs. Randall Jarrell; copyright renewed © 1973 by Mrs. Randall Jarrell. Blanche C. Gregory, Inc.: For "Breaking and Entering," from *The Fabulous Beasts* by Joyce Carol Oates; copyright © 1975 by Louisiana State University Press. Harcourt Brace Jovanovich, Inc.: For "Buffalo Dusk" and "Jazz Fantasia," from *Smoke and Steel* by Carl Sandburg; copyright 1920 by Harcourt Brace Jovanovich, Inc.; renewed 1948 by Carl Sandburg, reprinted by permission of the publisher. For "Expect Nothing," from *Revolutionary Petunias & Other Poems* by Alice Walker; copyright © 1973 by Alice Walker. For "Grass," from *Cornhuskers* by Carl Sandburg; copyright 1918 by Holt, Rinehart and Winston, Inc.; renewed 1946 by Carl Sandburg. For "Chicago," from *Chicago Poems* by Carl Sandburg; copyright 1916 by Holt, Rinehart & Winston, Inc.; renewed 1944 by Carl Sandburg. For "A Visit of Charity," from *A Curtain of Green and Other Stories* by Eudora Welty; copyright 1941, 1969 by Eudora Welty. Harper & Row, Publishers, Inc.: For "The Bean Eaters," from *The World of Gwendolyn Brooks*; copyright © 1959 by Gwendolyn Brooks. For pp. 14–17 from *Pilgrim at Tinker Creek* by Annie Dillard; copyright © 1974 by Annie Dillard. For "The Boy's Ambition," from *Life on the Mississippi* and "The Grangerfords Take Me In," from *The Adventures of Huckleberry Finn* by Samuel L. Clemens (Mark Twain). For "If You Should Go," from *On These I Stand:* An Anthology of the Best Poems of Countee Cullen; copyright 1925 by Harper & Row, Publishers, Inc.; renewed 1953 by Ida M. Cullen. For Chapter 10 ("Ol' One Shot"), from *To Kill a Mockingbird* by Harper Lee (J. B. Lippincott Co.); copyright © 1960 by Harper Lee. For specified excerpts (pp. 73–80), slightly abridged, from *Black Boy: A Record of Childhood and Youth* by Richard Wright; copyright 1937, 1942, 1944, 1945 by Richard Wright. Harvard University Press: For "To My Dear and Loving Husband" by Anne Bradstreet, from *The Works of Anne Bradstreet*; copyright © 1967 by the President and Fellows of Harvard College. For six poems by Emily Dickinson, from *The Poems of Emily Dickinson*, edited by Thomas H. Johnson, Cambridge, Mass.: The Belknap Press of Harvard University Press, copyright 1951, © 1955, 1979, 1983 by the President and Fellows of Harvard College, reprinted by permission of the publishers and the Trustees of Amherst College. Holt, Rinehart and Winston, Publishers: For "Mending Wall," "Fire and Ice," "A Time to Talk," "The Road Not Taken," from *The Poetry of Robert Frost*, edited by Edward Connery Lathem, copyright 1916, 1923, 1939, © 1969 by Holt, Rinehart and Winston, copyright 1944, 1951, © 1958 by Robert Frost. Houghton Mifflin Company: For "The Declaration of Women's Rights," from *Women in American Life*, by Anne Firor Scott; copyright © 1970 by Houghton Mifflin Company. For "A Fable for Tomorrow," from *Silent Spring* by Rachel Carson; copyright © 1962 by Rachel L. Carson. Little, Brown and Company: For "Night Practice," from *New and Selected Things Taking Place* by May Swenson; copyright © 1963 by May Swenson, first published in the *Hudson Review*. Liveright Publishing Corporation: For "in Just-," from *Tulips & Chimneys* by E. E. Cummings; copyright 1923, 1925 and renewed 1951, 1953 by E. E. Cummings, copyright © 1973, 1976 by the Trustees for the E. E. Cummings Trust, copyright © 1973, 1976 by George James Firmage. Macmillan Publishing Co.: For "Pocahontas," from *The Generall Historie of Virginia* by John Smith. Ellen C. Masters: For "Lucinda Matlock" and "George Gray," from *Spoon River Anthology* by Edgar Lee Masters; copyright 1915, 1916, 1942, 1949 by Edgar Lee Masters. McGraw-Hill Book Company: For "The Discovery of America," from *It All Started with Columbus* by Richard Armour; copyright © 1961, McGraw-Hill. McIntosh and Otis, Inc.: For "The Sioux Woman," from *These Were the Sioux* by Mari Sandoz; copyright © 1961 by Mari Sandoz. Mrs. Ernst E. Mensel: For "Rain in the Face," from *Indian Heroes and Great Chieftains* by Charles A. Eastman; original edition published by Little, Brown & Co., Boston, permission granted by Eleanor Eastman Mensel and Virginia Eastman Whitbeck. William Morrow and Company, Inc.: For "Choices," from *Cotton Candy on a Rainy Day* by Nikki Giovanni; copyright © 1978 by Nikki Giovanni. Ms. Magazine Corp.: For "The Legend of Amelia Earhart" by Pete Hamill; *MS* September 1976; copyright © 1976 MS Magazine Corp. New Directions Publishing Corp.: For "The Red Wheelbarrow," from *Collected Earlier Poems* by William Carlos Williams; copyright 1938 by New Directions Publishing Corporation. Harold Ober Associates, Inc.: For "Subway Rush Hour" and "Blues at Dawn," from *Montage of a Dream Deferred* by Langston Hughes; copyright 1951 by Langston Hughes, copyright renewed 1979 by George Houston Bass. Harry Mark Petrakis: For an excerpt from *Stelmark*, published by David McKay; copyright © 1970. Princeton University Press: For "A Letter from Thomas Jefferson to His Daughter," from *The Papers of*

Art Credits

Cover

Canoe in Rapids, 1897, Winslow Homer. Fogg Art Museum, Harvard University, Cambridge, Massachusetts; Louise E. Bettens Fund.

Illustrations

William Cigliano, 183; Chris F. Payne, 279; Candace Haught, 648.

Continued credit for *The Cotton Pickers,* page 540: Los Angeles County Museum Trustees—Robert O. Anderson, R. Stanton Avery, B. Gerald Cantor, Edward W. Carter, Justin Dart, Charles E. Ducommon, Mrs. Daniel Frost, Julian Ganz, Jr., Dr. Armand Hammer, Harry Lenart, Dr. Franklin D. Murphy, Mrs. Joan Palevsky, Richard E. Sherwood, Maynard J. Toll, and Hal B. Wallis.

Photographs of Authors

The Bettmann Archive: W.H. Auden, William Bradford, Robert Frost, O. Henry, Jack London, Carl Sandburg, Walt Whitman, William Carlos Williams. Bettmann UPI: Frederick Douglass, Martin Luther King, Jr. Brown Bros.: Ambrose Bierce, Stephen Crane. Culver Pictures: Stephen Vincent Benét, Countee Cullen, e.e. cummings, Charles Eastman, Ernest Hemingway, Oliver Wendell Holmes, Thomas Jefferson, Henry Wadsworth Longfellow, Edgar Lee Masters, John Smith, Thomas Wolfe, Richard Wright. Historical Pictures Service: Rachel Carson, Elizabeth Cady Stanton. Library of Congress: Abraham Lincoln. Wm. Morrow & Co.: Nikki Giovanni. National Portrait Gallery: Washington Irving, Henry David Thoreau. Moorland Spingarn Research Center, Howard University: Paul Lawrence Dunbar. James Wilson; Courtesy of *Newsweek:* Alice Walker. Wide World Photos: Pete Hamill.